Collins

The Shanghai Maths Project

For the English National Curriculum

Teacher's Guide 5B

Teacher's Guide Series Editor: Amanda Simpson
Practice Books Series Editor: Professor Lianghuo Fan
Authors: Sarah Eaton, Linda Glithro, Paul Hodge, Richard Perring, Paul Wrangles

Collins

William Collins' dream of knowledge for all began with the publication of his first book in 1819.

A self-educated mill worker, he not only enriched millions of lives, but also founded a flourishing publishing house. Today, staying true to this spirit, Collins books are packed with inspiration, innovation and practical expertise. They place you at the centre of a world of possibility and give you exactly what you need to explore it.

Collins. Freedom to teach.

MIX
Paper from responsible sources
www.fsc.org FSC™ C007454

This book is produced from independently certified FSC paper to ensure responsible forest management.

For more information visit:
www.harpercollins.co.uk/green

Published by Collins
An imprint of HarperCollins*Publishers*
The News Building
1 London Bridge Street
London
SE1 9GF

Browse the complete Collins catalogue at
www.collins.co.uk

© HarperCollins*Publishers* Limited 2018

10 9 8 7 6 5 4 3 2 1

978-0-00-822605-3

The authors assert their moral rights to be identified as the authors of this work.

Teacher's Guide Series Editor: Amanda Simpson

Practice Books Series Editor: Professor Lianghuo Fan

Authors: Sarah Eaton, Linda Glithro, Paul Hodge, Richard Perring, Paul Wrangles

All rights reserved. No part of this publication may be reproduced, stored in a retrieval system, or transmitted in any form by any means, electronic, mechanical, photocopying, recording or otherwise, without the prior written permission of the Publisher or a licence permitting restricted copying in the United Kingdom issued by the Copyright Licensing Agency Ltd, Barnard's Inn, 86 Fetter Lane, London, EC4A 1EN.

British Library Cataloguing in Publication Data

A catalogue record for this publication is available from the British Library.

Publishing Manager: Fiona McGlade and Lizzie Catford
In-house Editor: Mike Appleton
In-house Editorial Assistant: August Stevens
Project Manager: Karen Williams
Copy Editors: Tanya Solomons and Karen Williams
Proofreader: Gerard Delaney
Cover design: Kevin Robbins and East China Normal University Press Ltd.
Internal design: 2Hoots Publishing Services Ltd
Typesetting: Ken Vail Graphic Design Ltd
Illustrations: QBS
Production: Sarah Burke

Printed and bound by CPI Group (UK) Ltd, Croydon, CR0 4YY

Photo acknowledgements

The publishers wish to thank the following for permission to reproduce photographs. Every effort has been made to trace copyright holders and to obtain their permission for the use of copyright materials. The publishers will gladly receive any information enabling them to rectify any error or omission at the first opportunity.

(t = top, c = centre, b = bottom, r = right, l = left)

p81 br A-R-T/Shutterstock; p94 and p279 tl Susan Law Cain/Shutterstock, p94 and p279 tr alexmisu/Shutterstock, p94 and p279 bl Santiago Cornejo/Shutterstock, br p94 and p279 Alaettin YILDIRIM/Shutterstock; p181 tl Nisa Paobunthorn/Shutterstock, p181 tc Customdesigner/Shutterstock, p181 tr Sashkin/Shutterstock, p181 bl valdis torms/Shutterstock, p181 bc WilleeCole Photography/Shutterstock, p181 br FabrikaSimf/Shutterstock

Contents

The Shanghai Maths Project: an overview		**iv**
Chapter 6 Addition and subtraction of decimal numbers		**1**
Unit 6.1	Multiplying and dividing decimals by 10, 100 and 1000 (1)	3
Unit 6.2	Multiplying and dividing decimals by 10, 100 and 1000 (2)	10
Unit 6.3	Addition of decimals	17
Unit 6.4	Subtraction of decimals	24
Unit 6.5	Addition and subtraction of decimals (1)	31
Unit 6.6	Addition and subtraction of decimals (2)	37
Unit 6.7	Practice and exercise (2)	42
Chapter 7 Introduction to positive and negative numbers		**49**
Unit 7.1	Positive and negative numbers (1)	50
Unit 7.2	Positive and negative numbers (2)	58
Unit 7.3	Number lines (1)	63
Unit 7.4	Number lines (2)	68
Chapter 8 Geometry and measurement (1)		**75**
Unit 8.1	Knowing circles (1)	76
Unit 8.2	Knowing circles (2)	82
Unit 8.3	Knowing circles (3)	87
Unit 8.4	Angle concept and notation	92
Unit 8.5	Measurement of angles (1)	98
Unit 8.6	Measurement of angles (2)	104
Unit 8.7	Measurement of angles (3)	110
Unit 8.8	Calculation of angles	117
Unit 8.9	Angles and sides in polygons	123
Chapter 9 Geometry and measurement (2)		**131**
Unit 9.1	Volume	132
Unit 9.2	Cubic centimetres and cubic metres (1)	138
Unit 9.3	Cubic centimetres and cubic metres (2)	145
Unit 9.4	Metric units and imperial units for measurement	153
Unit 9.5	Introduction to cubes and cuboids	159
Unit 9.6	Volumes of cubes and cuboids (1)	167
Unit 9.7	Volumes of cubes and cuboids (2)	174
Unit 9.8	Volume and capacity (1)	180
Unit 9.9	Volume and capacity (2)	186
Chapter 10 Factors, multiples and prime numbers		**192**
Unit 10.1	Meaning of integers and divisibility	193
Unit 10.2	Factors and multiples	201
Unit 10.3	Square numbers and cube numbers	206
Unit 10.4	Numbers divisible by 2 and 5	212
Unit 10.5	Prime numbers, composite numbers and prime factorisation (1)	217
Unit 10.6	Prime numbers, composite numbers and prime factorisation (2)	223
Resources		**228**
Answers		**330**

The Shanghai Maths Project: an overview

The Shanghai Maths Project is a collaboration between Collins and East China Normal University Press Ltd. adapting their bestselling maths programme, *One Lesson, One Exercise*, for England, using an expert team of authors and reviewers. This carefully crafted programme has been continually reviewed in China over the last 24 years, meaning that the materials have been tried and tested by teachers and children alike. Some new material has been written for The Shanghai Maths Project, but the structure of the original resource has been preserved and as much original material as possible has been retained.

The Shanghai Maths Project is a programme from Shanghai for Years 1–11. Teaching for mastery is at the heart of the entire programme, which, through the guidance and support found in the Teacher's Guides and Practice Books, provides complete coverage of the curriculum objectives for England. Teachers are well supported to deliver a high-quality curriculum using the best teaching methods; pupils are enabled to learn mathematics with understanding and the ability to apply knowledge fluently and flexibly in order to solve problems.

The programme consists of five components: Teacher's Guides (two per year), Practice Books (two per year), Shanghai Learning Book, Homework Guide and Collins Connect digital package.

In this guide, information and support for all teachers of primary maths is set out, unit by unit, so they are able to teach The Shanghai Maths Project coherently and confidently, and with appropriate progression through the whole mathematics curriculum.

The Shanghai Maths Project: an overview

Practice Books

The Practice Books are designed to serve as both teaching and learning resources. With graded arithmetic exercises, plus varied practice of key concepts and summative assessments for each year, each Practice Book offers intelligent practice and consolidation to promote deep learning and develop higher-order thinking.

There are two Practice Books for each year group: A and B. Pupils should have ownership of their copies of the Practice Books so they can engage with relevant exercises every day, integrated with preparatory whole-class and small-group teaching, recording their answers in the books.

The Practice Books contain:
- chapters made up of units, containing small steps of progression, with practice at each stage
- a test at the end of each chapter
- an end-of-year test in Practice Book B.

Each unit in the Practice Books consists of two sections: 'Basic questions' and 'Challenge and extension questions'.

We suggest that the 'Basic questions' be used for all pupils. Many of them, directly or sometimes with a little modification, can be used as starting questions, for motivation or introduction or as examples for clear explanation. They can also be used as in-class exercise questions – most likely for reinforcement and formative assessment, but also for pupils' further exploration. Almost all questions can be given for individual or peer work, especially when used as in-class exercise questions. Some are also suitable for group work or whole-class discussion.

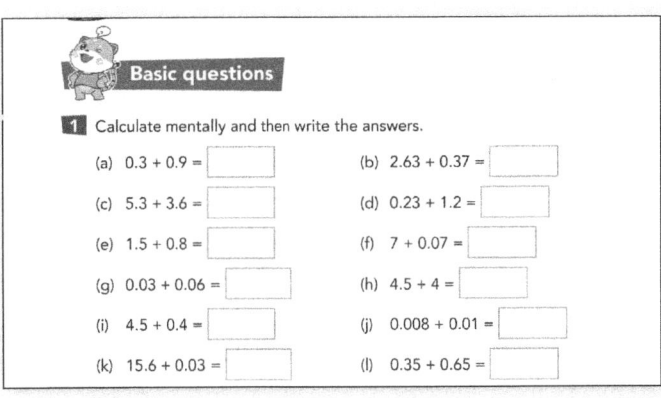

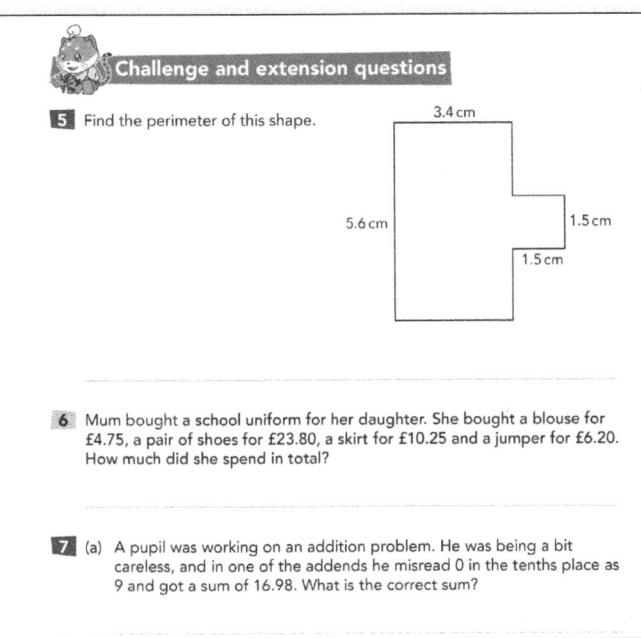

All pupils should be given the opportunity to solve some of the 'Challenge and extension questions', which are good for building confidence, but they should not always be required to solve all of them. A general suggestion is that most pupils try about 40–60 per cent of the 'Challenge and extension questions'.

Unit tests sometimes include questions that relate to content in the 'Challenge and extension questions'. This is clearly shown in the diagnostic assessment grids provided in the Teacher's Guides. Teachers should make their own judgments about how to use this information since not all pupils will have attempted the 'Challenge and extension questions'.

The Shanghai Maths Project: an overview

Teacher's Guides

Theory underpinning the Teacher's Guides

The Teacher's Guides contain everything teachers need in order to provide the highest quality teaching in all areas of mathematics, in line with the English National Curriculum. Core mathematics topics are developed with deep understanding in every year group. Some areas are not visited every year, though curriculum coverage is in line with Key Stage statutory requirements, as set out in the National curriculum in England: mathematics programmes of study (updated 2014).

There are two Teacher's Guides for each year group: one for the first part of the year (Teacher's Guide 5A) and the other for the second (Teacher's Guide 5B).

The Shanghai Maths Project is different from other maths schemes that are available, in that there is no book called a 'textbook'. Lessons are a mixture of teacher-led, peer and independent work. The Teacher's Guides set out subject knowledge that teachers might need, as well as guidance on pedagogical issues – the best ways to organise activities, to ask questions and to increase difficulty in small steps. Most importantly, the Teacher's Guides contain, threaded throughout the whole book, a strong element of professional development for teachers, focusing on the way mathematics concepts can be enabled to develop and connect with each other.

The Shanghai Maths Project Teacher's Guides are a complete reference for teachers working with the Practice Books. Each unit in the Practice Book for each year group is set out in the corresponding Teacher's Guide over a number of pages.

Most units will need to be taught over more than one lesson – some might need three lessons. In the Practice Books, units contain a great deal of learning, densely packed into a few questions. If pupils are to be able to tackle and succeed with the Practice Book questions, they need to have been guided to learn new mathematics and to connect it to their existing knowledge.

This can only be achieved when teachers are able to break down the conceptual learning that is needed and to provide relevant and high-quality teaching. The Teacher's Guides show teachers how to build up pupils' knowledge and experience so they learn with understanding in small steps. This way, learning is secure, robust and not reliant on memorisation.

The small steps that are necessary must be in line with what international research tells us about conceptual growth and development. The Shanghai Maths Project embodies that knowledge about conceptual development and about teaching for mastery of mathematics concepts and skills. The way that difficulty is varied, and the same ideas are presented in different contexts, is based on the notion of 'teaching with variation'. 'Variation' in Chinese mathematics carries particular meaning as it has emerged from a great deal of research in the area of 'variation theory'. Variation theory is based on the view that, 'When a particular aspect varies whilst all other aspects of the phenomenon are kept invariant, the learner will experience variation in the varying aspect and will discern that aspect. For example, when a child is shown three balls of the same size, shape, and material, but each of a different color: red, green and yellow, then it is very likely that the child's attention will be drawn to the color of the balls because it is the only aspect that varies.' (Bowden and Marton 1998, cited in Pang and Ling 2012)

In summary, two types of variation are necessary, each with a different function; both are necessary for the development of conceptual understanding.

Variation

Conceptual
Function – this variation provides pupils with multiple experiences from different perspectives.

'multi-dimensional variation'

Procedural
Function – this variation helps learners:
- acquire knowledge step by step
- develop pupils' experience in problem solving progressively
- form well-structured knowledge.

'developmental variation'

Teachers who are aiming to provide conceptual variation should vary the way the problem is presented without varying the structure of the problem itself.

The problem itself doesn't change, but the way it is presented (or represented) does. Incorporation of a Concrete–Pictorial–Abstract (CPA) approach to teaching activities provides conceptual variation since pupils experience the same mathematical situations in parallel concrete, pictorial and abstract ways.

The Shanghai Maths Project: an overview

CPA is integrated in the Teacher's Guides so teachers are providing questions and experiences that incorporate appropriate conceptual variation.

Procedural variation is the process of:
- forming concepts logically and/or chronologically (i.e. scaffolding, transforming)
- arriving at solutions to problems
- forming knowledge structures (generalising across contexts).

In the Practice Book, there are numerous examples of procedural variation in which pupils gradually build up knowledge, step by step; often they are exposed to patterns that teachers should guide them to perceive and explore.

It is this embedded variation that means that when The Shanghai Maths Project is at the heart of mathematics teaching throughout the school, teachers can be confident that the curriculum is of the highest order and it will be delivered by teachers who are informed and confident about how to support pupils to develop strong, connected concepts.

Teaching for mastery

There is no single definition of mathematics mastery. The term 'mastery' is used in conjunction with various aspects of education – to describe goals, attainment levels or a type of teaching. In teaching in Shanghai, mastery of concepts is characterised as 'thorough understanding' and is one of the aims of maths teaching in Shanghai.

Thorough understanding is evident in what pupils do and say. A concept can be seen to have been mastered when a pupil:
- is able to interpret and construct multiple representations of aspects of that concept
- can communicate relevant ideas and reason clearly about that concept using appropriate mathematical language
- can solve problems using the knowledge learned in familiar and new situations, collaboratively and independently.

Within The Shanghai Maths Project, mastery is a goal, achievable through high-quality teaching and learning experiences that include opportunities to explore, articulate thinking, conjecture, practise, clarify, apply and integrate new understandings piece by piece. Learning is carefully structured throughout and across the programme, with Teacher's Guides and Practice Books interwoven – chapter by chapter, unit by unit, question by question.

Since so much conceptual learning is to be achieved with each of the questions in any Practice Book unit, teachers are provided with guidance for each question, breaking down the development that will occur and how they should facilitate this – suggestions for teachers' questions, problems for pupils, activities and resources are clearly set out in an appropriate sequence.

In this way, teaching and learning are unified and consolidated. Coherence within and across components of the programme is an important aspect of The Shanghai Maths Project, in which Practice Books and Teacher's Guides, when used together, form a strong, effective teaching programme.

Promoting pupil engagement

The digital package on Collins Connect contains a variety of resources for concept development, problem solving and practice, provided in different ways. Images can be projected and shared with the class from the Image Bank. Other resources, for pupils to work with directly, are provided as photocopiable resource sheets at the back of the Teacher's Guides, and on Collins Connect. These might be practical activities, games, puzzles or investigations, or are sometimes more straightforward practice exercises. Teachers are signposted to these as 'Resources' in the Unit guidance.

Coverage of the curriculum is comprehensive, coherent and consolidated. Ideas are developed meaningfully, through intelligent practice, incorporating skilful questioning that exposes mathematical structures and connections.

Shanghai Year 5 Learning Book

Shanghai Year 5 Learning Books are for pupils to use. They are concise, colourful references that set out all the key ideas taught in the year, using images and explanations pupils will be familiar with from their lessons. Ideally, the books will be available to pupils during their maths lessons and at other times during the school day so they can access them easily if they need support for thinking about maths. The books are set out to correspond to each chapter* as it is taught and provide all the key images and vocabulary pupils will need in order to think things through independently or with a partner, resolving issues for themselves as much as possible. The Year 5 Learning Book might sometimes be taken home and shared with parents: this enables pupils, parents and teachers to form positive relationships around maths teaching that is of great benefit to children's learning.

---

* Note that because Chapter 5 in Year 5 is a Consolidation and Enhancement Chapter, there is no Chapter 5 in the Year 5 Learning Book.

The Shanghai Maths Project: an overview

How to use the Teacher's Guides

Teaching

Units taught in the second half of Year 5:

Contents

Chapter 6 Addition and subtraction of decimal numbers
- 6.1 Multiplying and dividing decimals by 10, 100 and 1000 (1) .. 1
- 6.2 Multiplying and dividing decimals by 10, 100 and 1000 (2) .. 5
- 6.3 Addition of decimals 9
- 6.4 Subtraction of decimals 12
- 6.5 Addition and subtraction of decimals (1) 15
- 6.6 Addition and subtraction of decimals (2) 18
- 6.7 Practice and exercise (2) 21
- Chapter 6 test 24

Chapter 7 Introduction to positive and negative numbers
- 7.1 Positive and negative numbers (1) 29
- 7.2 Positive and negative numbers (2) 32
- 7.3 Number lines (1) 36
- 7.4 Number lines (2) 41
- Chapter 7 test 45

Chapter 8 Geometry and measurement (1)
- 8.1 Knowing circles (1) 51
- 8.2 Knowing circles (2) 54
- 8.3 Knowing circles (3) 57
- 8.4 Angle concept and notation 60
- 8.5 Measurement of angles (1) 63
- 8.6 Measurement of angles (2) 67
- 8.7 Measurement of angles (3) 70
- 8.8 Calculation of angles 74
- 8.9 Angles and sides in polygons 77
- Chapter 8 test 82

Chapter 9 Geometry and measurement (2)
- 9.1 Volume 87
- 9.2 Cubic centimetres and cubic metres (1) 89
- 9.3 Cubic centimetres and cubic metres (2) 92
- 9.4 Metric units and imperial units for measurement ... 95
- 9.5 Introduction to cubes and cuboids 98
- 9.6 Volumes of cubes and cuboids (1) 102
- 9.7 Volumes of cubes and cuboids (2) 105
- 9.8 Volume and capacity (1) 109
- 9.9 Volume and capacity (2) 113
- Chapter 9 test 117

Chapter 10 Factors, multiples and prime numbers
- 10.1 Meaning of integers and divisibility 121
- 10.2 Factors and multiples 124
- 10.3 Square numbers and cube numbers 126
- 10.4 Numbers divisible by 2 and 5 128
- 10.5 Prime numbers, composite numbers and prime factorisation (1) 131
- 10.6 Prime numbers, composite numbers and prime factorisation (2) 134
- Chapter 10 test 137

Teacher's Guide 5B sets out, for each chapter and unit in Practice Book 5B, a number of things that teachers will need to know if their teaching is to be effective and their pupils are to achieve mastery of the mathematics contained in the Practice Book.

Each chapter begins with a chapter overview that summarises, in a table, how Practice Book questions and classroom activities suggested in the Teacher's Guide relate to National Curriculum statutory requirements.

Chapter overview

Area of mathematics	National Curriculum statutory requirements for Key Stage 2	Shanghai Maths Project reference
Number – addition and subtraction	Year 5 Programme of study: Pupils should be taught to: ■ add and subtract numbers mentally with increasingly large numbers.	Year 5, Units 6.3, 6.4, 6.5, 6.6, 6.7
Number – multiplication and division	Year 5 Programme of study: Pupils should be taught to: ■ multiply and divide whole numbers and those involving decimals by 10, 100 and 1000.	Year 5, Units 6.1, 6.2, 6.3
Number – fractions (including decimals and percentages)	Year 5 Programme of study: Pupils should be taught to: ■ read, write, order and compare numbers with up to three decimal places	Year 5, Units 6.1, 6.2
	■ solve problems involving number up to three decimal places.	Year 5, Units 6.1, 6.2, 6.3, 6.4, 6.5, 6.6, 6.7
	Year 6 Programme of study: Pupils should be taught to: ■ identify the value of each digit in numbers given to three decimal places and multiply and divide numbers by 10, 100 and 1000 giving answers up to three decimal places.	Year 5, Units 6.1, 6.2

The Shanghai Maths Project: an overview

It is important to note that the National Curriculum requirements are statutory at the end of each Key Stage and that The Shanghai Maths Project does fulfil (at least) those end of Key Stage requirements. However, some aspects are not covered in the same year group as they are in the National Curriculum Programme of Study – for example, end of Key Stage 1 requirements for 'Money' are achieved in Year 2 and 'Money' is not taught again in Year 2.

All units will need to be taught over 1–3 lessons. Teachers must use their judgment as to when pupils are ready to move on to new learning within each unit – it is a principle of teaching for mastery that pupils are given opportunities to grasp the learning that is intended before moving to the next variation of the concept or to the next unit.

All units begin with a unit overview, which has four sections:

Conceptual context – a short section summarising the conceptual learning that will be brought about through Practice Book questions and related activities. Links with previous learning and future learning will be noted in this section.

Conceptual context

This unit introduces multiplication and division of decimals by 10, 100 and 1000 and builds towards an efficient strategy for these calculations.

It is important for pupils to understand that, although it may look as if the decimal point is moving, what is happening is that all of the digits around that point are moving and the decimal point remains static. (The use of a place value slider reinforces this.) Pupils are likely to abstract the movement of the digits to a movement of the decimal point, but it is important that this is an end point, and is the condensing of deep understanding, rather than a starting point in which pupils learn a method without the conceptual structure that supports it.

Learning pupils will have achieved at the end of the unit

- Pupils' understanding about place value including decimal numbers will have become more secure (Q1)
- Pupils will have exploited place value to multiply and divide decimals by 10, 100 and 1000 (Q1, Q2, Q3, Q4)
- Pupils will understand digits move across the place value grid, that the decimal point is static and that any gaps created by moving the digits should be filled with zeros (Q1, Q2, Q4)
- Pupils will have identified opportunities for multiplying and dividing by 10, 100 and 1000 to develop efficient strategies when tackling problems (Q5)

This list indicates how skills and concepts will have formed and developed during work on particular questions within this unit.

These are resources useful for the lesson, including photocopiable resources supplied in the Teacher's Guide. (Those listed are the ones needed for 'Basic questions' – not for 'Challenge and extension questions'.)

This is a list of vocabulary necessary for teachers and pupils to use in the lesson.

Resources

place value charts; sticky notes; mini whiteboards; paper/card; scissors; **Resource 5.6.1a** Place value slider; **Resource 5.6.1b** Make the calculation; **Resource 5.6.1c** × and ÷ trail; **Resource 5.6.1d** Find a number that when …

Vocabulary

multiply, divide, hundredth, thousandth, decimal, decimal place

The Shanghai Maths Project: an overview

After the unit overview, the Teacher's Guide goes on to describe how teachers might introduce and develop necessary, relevant ideas and how to integrate them with questions in the Practice Book unit. For each question in the Practice Book, teaching is set out under the following headings:

What learning will pupils have achieved at the conclusion of Question X?

This list responds to the following questions: Why is this question here? How does this question help pupils' existing concepts to grow? What is happening in this unit to help pupils prepare for a new concept about …? This list of bullet points will give teachers insight into the rationale for the activities and exercises and will help them to hone their pedagogy and questioning.

> **What learning will pupils have achieved at the conclusion of Questions 2 and 3?**
> - Pupils will have exploited place value to multiply and divide decimals by 10, 100 and 1000.
> - Pupils will understand digits move across the place value grid, that the decimal point is static and that any gaps created by moving the digits should be filled with zeros.

> **Activities for whole-class instruction**
> - Show pupils some calculations where symbols have replaced digits (you might like to use letters, or different coloured sticky notes rather than these symbols, to represent the digits). For example:
>   ❖✢◐■¤★◆ ×10 =
>   ❖✢◐■¤★◆ ×100 =
>   ❖✢◐■¤★◆ ×1000 =
>   ❖✢◐■¤★◆ ÷10 =
>   ❖✢◐■¤★◆ ÷100 =

Activities for whole-class instruction

This is the largest section within each unit. For each question in the Practice Book, suggestions are set out for questions and activities that support pupils to form and develop concepts and deepen understanding. Suggestions are described in some detail and activities are carefully sequenced to enable coherent progression. Procedural fluency and conceptual learning are both valued and developed in tandem and in line with the Practice Book questions. Teachers are prompted to draw pupils' attention to connections and to guide them to perceive links for themselves so mathematical relationships and richly connected concepts are understood and can be applied.

The Concrete–Pictorial–Abstract (CPA) approach underpins suggestions for activities, particularly those intended to provide conceptual variation (varying the way the problem is presented without varying the structure of the problem itself). This contributes to conceptual variation by giving pupils opportunities to experience concepts in multiple representations – the concrete, the pictorial and the abstract. Pupils learn well when they are able to engage with ideas in a practical, concrete way and then go on to represent those ideas as pictures or diagrams, and ultimately as symbols. It is important, however, that a CPA approach is not understood as a one-way journey from concrete to abstract and that pupils do not need to work with concrete materials in practical ways if they can cope with abstract representations – this is a fallacy. Pupils of all ages do need to work with all kinds of representations since it is 'translating' between the concrete, pictorial and abstract that will deepen understanding, by rehearsing the links between them and strengthening conceptual connections. It is these connections that provide pupils with the capacity to solve problems, even in unfamiliar contexts.

In this section, the reasons underlying certain questions and activities are explained, so teachers learn the ways in which pupils' concepts need to develop and how to improve and refine their questioning and provision.

Usually, for each question, the focus will at first be on whole-class and partner work to introduce and develop ideas and understanding relevant to the question. Once the necessary learning has been achieved and practised, pupils will complete the Practice Book question, when it will be further reinforced and developed.

The Shanghai Maths Project: an overview

Same-day intervention

Pupils who have not been able to achieve the learning that was intended must be identified straight away so teachers can try to identify the barriers to their learning and help pupils to build their understanding in another way. (This is a principle of teaching for mastery.) In the Teacher's Guide, suggestions for teaching this group are included for each unit. Ideally, this intervention will take place on the same day as the original teaching. The intervention activity always provides a different experience from that of the main lesson – often the activity itself is different; sometimes the changes are to the approach and the explanations that enable pupils to access a similar activity.

Same-day intervention
- Use a place value slider and draw the symbols from the task in the appropriate place on slider.
- By substituting the digits, pupils' attention will focus on the movement of the symbols that is required by the different operations, and repeating the task as above will support pupils in making sense of this.

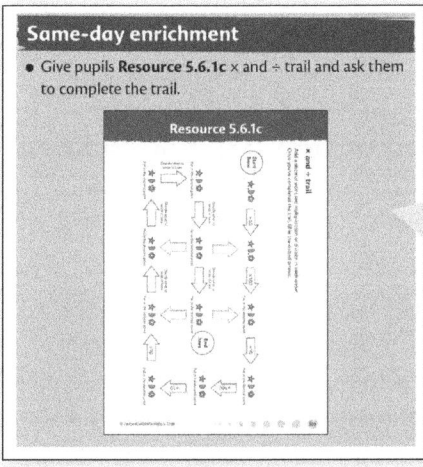

Same-day enrichment

For pupils who do manage to achieve all the planned learning, additional activities are described. These are intended to enrich and extend the learning of the unit. This activity is often carried out by most of the class, while others are engaged with the intervention activity.

Lessons might also have some of the following elements:

Information point

Inserted at points where it feels important to point something out along the way.

Zero is neither positive nor negative. An integer can either be greater than zero, called positive, or less than zero, called negative.

All say …

Phrases and sentences to be spoken aloud by pupils in unison and repeated on multiple occasions whenever opportunities present themselves during, within and outside of the maths lesson.

Twelve and positive twelve (or 'plus twelve') have the same meaning and value.

 *… pupils who think that the diagonals of a rectangle (oblong) are lines of symmetry. The two right-angled triangles that result from the fold look similar visually and will in fact rotate around the centre of the rectangle to match perfectly. Provide pupils with mirrors and ask them to align a mirror along the diagonal of a rectangle. Confirm that the shape after reflection is a kite and not a square thus proving that the diagonal is not a line of symmetry.*

Look out for …

Common errors that pupils make and misconceptions that are often evident in a particular aspect of maths. Do not try to prevent these, but recognise them where they occur and take opportunities to raise them in discussion in sensitive ways so pupils can align their conceptual understanding in more appropriate ways.

Within the guidance there are many prompts for teachers to ask pupils to explain their thinking or their answers. The language that pupils use when responding to questions in class is an important aspect of teaching with The Shanghai Maths Project. Pupils should be expected to use full sentences, including correct mathematical terms and language, to clarify the reasoning underpinning their solutions. This articulation of pupils' thinking is a valuable step in developing concepts, and opportunities should be taken wherever possible to encourage pupils to use full sentences when talking about their maths.

Ideas for resources and activities are for guidance; teachers might have better ideas and resources available. The principle guiding elements for each question should be 'What learning will pupils have achieved at the conclusion of Question X?' and the 'Information points'. If teachers can substitute their own questions and tasks and still achieve these learning objectives, they should not feel concerned about diverging from the suggestions here.

The Shanghai Maths Project: an overview

Planning

The Teacher's Guides and Practice Books for Year 5 are split into two volumes, 5A and 5B, one for each part of the year.
- Teacher's Guide 5A and Practice Book 5A cover Chapters 1–5.
- Teacher's Guide 5B and Practice Book 5B cover Chapters 6–10.

Each unit in the Practice Book will need 1–3 lessons for effective teaching and learning of the conceptual content in that unit. Teachers will judge precisely how to plan the teaching year, but, as a general guide, they should aim to complete Chapters 1–3 in the autumn term, Chapters 4–7 in the spring term and Chapters 8–10 in the summer term.

The recommended teaching sequence is as set out in the Practice Books.

Statutory requirements of the National Curriculum in England 2013 (updated 2014) are fully met, and often exceeded, by the programme contained in The Shanghai Maths Project. It should be noted that some curriculum objectives are not covered in the same year group as they are in the National Curriculum Programme of Study – however, since it is end of Key Stage requirements that are statutory, schools following The Shanghai Maths Project are meeting legal curriculum requirements.

A chapter overview at the beginning of each chapter shows, in a table, how Practice Book questions and classroom activities suggested in the Teacher's Guide relate to National Curriculum statutory requirements.

Level of detail

Within each unit, a series of whole-class activities is listed, linked to each question. Within these are questions for pupils that will:
- structure and support pupils' learning,
- aid teachers' assessments during the lesson.

Questions and questioning

Within the guidance for each question are sequences of questions that teachers should ask pupils. Embedded within these is the procedural variation that will help pupils to make connections across their knowledge and experience and support them to 'bridge' to the next level of complexity in the concept being learned.

In preparing for each lesson, teachers will find that, by reading the guidance thoroughly, they will learn for themselves how these sequences of questions very gradually expose more of the maths to be learned, how small those steps of progression need to be, and how carefully crafted the sequence must be. With experience, teachers will find they need to refer to the pupils' questions in the guidance less, as they learn more about how maths concepts need to be nurtured and as they become skilled at 'designing' their own series of questions.

Is it necessary to do everything suggested in the Teacher's Guide?

Activities are described in some detail so teachers understand how to build up the level of challenge and how to vary the contexts and representations used appropriately. These two aspects of teaching mathematics are often called 'intelligent practice'. If pupils are to learn concepts so they are long-lasting and provide learners with the capacity to apply their learning fluently and flexibly in order to solve problems, it is these two aspects of maths teaching that must be achieved to a high standard. The guidance contained in this Teacher's Guide is sufficiently detailed to support teachers to do this.

Teachers who are already expert practitioners in teaching for mastery might use the Teacher's Guide in a different way from those who feel they need more support. The unit overview provides a summary of the concepts and skills learned when pupils work through the activities set out in the guidance and integrated with the Practice Book. Expert mastery teachers might, therefore, select from the activities described and supplement with others from their own resources, confident in their own 'intelligent practice'.

There is more material in the Teachers' Guide than most teachers will need. This is because there are enrichment and intervention activities designed to match each question in the Practice Book. Teachers might find that they are able to deliver the programme, keeping their whole class focused on the same content at all times. This means that all pupils receive teaching input, then complete particular Practice Book questions, before returning for teaching related to the next part of the lesson together. This would look like this:

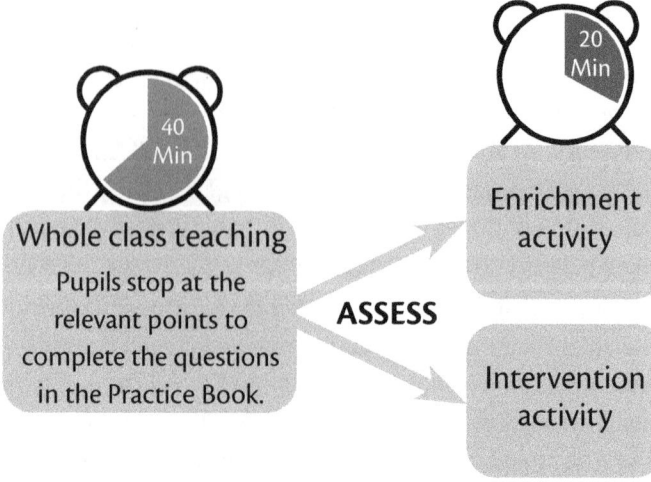

Following this model, at the end of the first session of the day, teachers will use pupils' attainment, evident in class interactions and Practice Book exercises to assess which pupils require intervention. Teachers then select which of the enrichment and intervention activities, linked to the content taught, are most relevant for their class that day. Usually, more than one question will have been covered during the lesson so some activities will not be used.

There is also scope for teachers to be more flexible if they find it difficult to keep the whole class working at the same pace. If there is a disparity among pupils in the time taken to complete Practice Book questions, teachers can select one enrichment activity for all early finishers to move on to if they complete the Practice Book questions quickly. The enrichment activity might be something that pupils work on in two or three 'bites' following completion of successive Practice Book questions at different stages in the lesson.

All pupils should come together for the second and consecutive teaching inputs. Following the next input, all pupils should complete the relevant practice questions and, if appropriate, return to their enrichment activity.

The enrichment activity selected to be used would be the same for all pupils and would not then be available for use in the second part of the maths input later in the day (or next day).

As with the previous, simpler, model, at the end of the first session of the day, teachers will use pupils' attainment, evident in class interactions and Practice Book exercises to assess which pupils require intervention and which should go on to complete other enrichment activities.

Assessing

Ongoing assessment, during lessons, will need to inform judgments about which pupils need further support. Of course, prompt marking will also inform these decisions, but this should not be the only basis for daily assessments – teachers will learn a lot about what pupils understand through skilful questioning and observation during lessons.

At the end of each chapter, a chapter test will revisit the content of the units within that chapter. Attainment in the text can be mapped to particular questions and units so teachers can diagnose particular needs for individuals and groups. Analysis of results from chapter tests will also reveal questions or units that caused difficulties for a large proportion of the class, indicating that more time is needed on that question/unit when it is next taught.

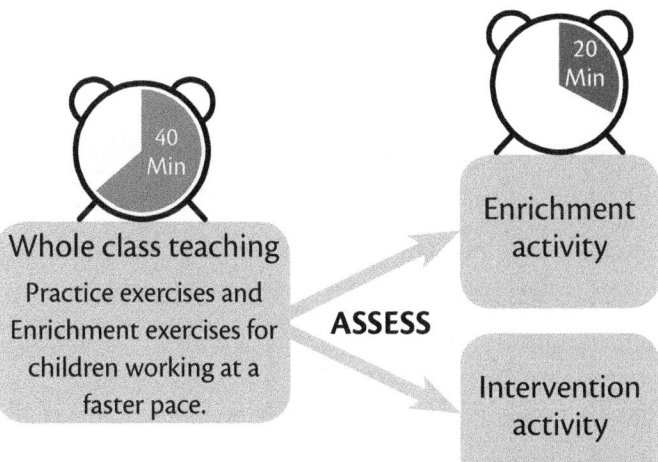

The Shanghai Maths Project: an overview

Shanghai Year 5 Learning Book

As referenced on page vii, The Shanghai Maths Project Year 5 Learning Book is a pupil textbook containing the Year 5 maths facts and full pictorial glossary to enable children to master the Year 5 maths programmes of study for England. It sits alongside the Practice Books to be used as a reference book in class or at home.

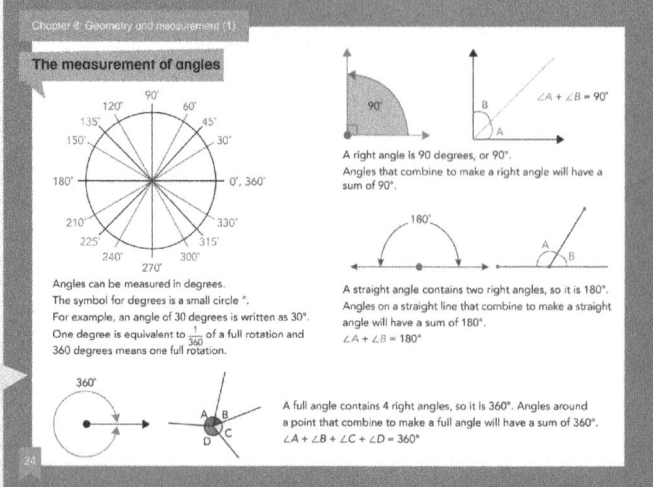

Maths facts correspond to the chapters in the Practice Books for ease of use.

Key models and images are provided for each mathematical concept.

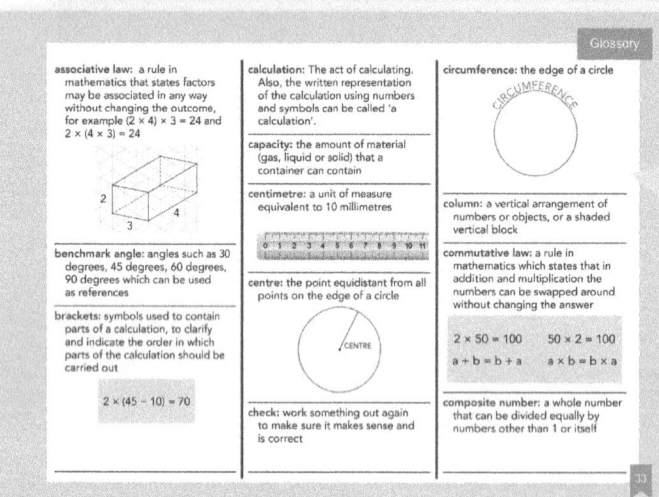

A visual glossary defines the key mathematical vocabulary pupils need to master.

Homework Guides

The Shanghai Maths Project Homework Guide 5 is a photocopiable master book for the teacher. There is one book per year, containing a homework sheet for every unit, directly related to the maths being covered in the Practice Book unit. There is a 'Learning Together' activity on each page that includes an idea for practical maths the parent or guardian can do with the child.

Homework is directly related to the maths being covered in class.

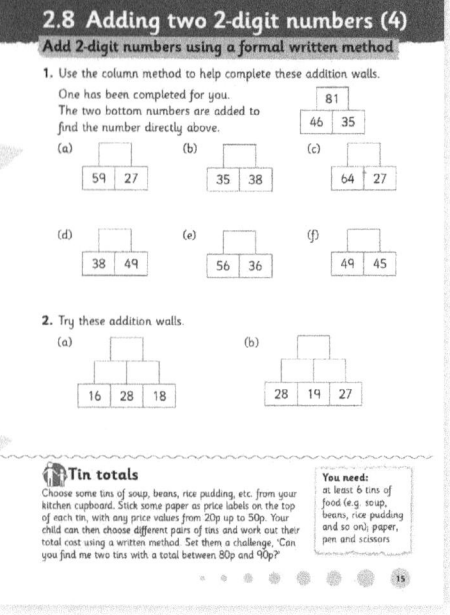

An idea for practical maths the parent or guardian can do with the child.

The Shanghai Maths Project: an overview

Collins Connect

Collins Connect is the home for all the digital teaching resources provided by The Shanghai Maths Project.

The Collins Connect pack for The Shanghai Maths Project consists of four sections: Teach, Resources, Record, Support.

Teach

The Teach section contains all the content from the Teacher's Guides and Homework Guides, organised by chapter and unit.
- The entire book can be accessed at the top level so teachers can search and find objectives or key words easily.
- Chapters and units can be re-ordered and customised to match individual teachers' planning.
- Chapters and units can be marked as complete by the teacher.
- All the teaching resources for a chapter are grouped together and easy to locate.
- Each unit has its own page from which the contents of the Teacher's Guide, Homework Guide and any accompanying resources can be accessed.
- Teachers can record teacher judgments against National Curriculum attainment targets for individual pupils or the whole class with the record-keeping tool.
- Units from the Teacher's Guide and Homework Guide are provided in PDF and Microsoft Word versions so teachers can edit and customise the contents.
- Any accompanying resources can be displayed or downloaded from the same page.

Resources

The Resources section contains 35 interactive whiteboard tools and an image bank for front-of-class display.
- The 35 maths tools cover all topics, and can be customised and used flexibly by teachers as part of their lessons.
- The image bank contains the images from the Teacher's Guide, which can support pupils' learning. They can be enlarged and shown on the whiteboard.

Record

The Record section is the home of the record-keeping tool for The Shanghai Maths Project. Each unit is linked to attainment targets in the National Curriculum for England, and teachers can easily make records and judgments for individual pupils, groups of pupils or whole classes using the tool from the 'Teach' section. Records and comments can also be added from the 'Record' section, and reports generated by class, by pupil, by domain or by National Curriculum attainment target.
- View and print reports in different formats for sharing with teachers, senior leaders and parents.
- Delve deeper into the records to check on the progress of individual pupils.
- Instantly check on the progress of the class in each domain.

Support

The Support section contains the Teacher's Guide introduction in PDF and Word formats, along with CPD advice and guidance.

Chapter 6
Addition and subtraction of decimal numbers

Chapter overview

Area of mathematics	National Curriculum statutory requirements for Key Stage 2	Shanghai Maths Project reference
Number – addition and subtraction	Year 5 Programme of study: Pupils should be taught to: ■ add and subtract numbers mentally with increasingly large numbers.	Year 5, Units 6.3, 6.4, 6.5, 6.6, 6.7
Number – multiplication and division	Year 5 Programme of study: Pupils should be taught to: ■ multiply and divide whole numbers and those involving decimals by 10, 100 and 1000.	Year 5, Units 6.1, 6.2, 6.3
Number – fractions (including decimals and percentages)	Year 5 Programme of study: Pupils should be taught to: ■ read, write, order and compare numbers with up to three decimal places ■ solve problems involving number up to three decimal places.	Year 5, Units 6.1, 6.2 Year 5, Units 6.1, 6.2, 6.3, 6.4, 6.5, 6.6, 6.7
	Year 6 Programme of study: Pupils should be taught to: ■ identify the value of each digit in numbers given to three decimal places and multiply and divide numbers by 10, 100 and 1000 giving answers up to three decimal places.	Year 5, Units 6.1, 6.2

Measurement	Year 5 Programme of study: Pupils should be taught to:	
	■ convert between different units of metric measure (for example, kilometre and metre; centimetre and metre; centimetre and millimetre; gram and kilogram; litre and millilitre)	Year 5, Units 6.2, 6.3, 6.4
	■ use all four operations to solve problems involving measure [for example, length, mass, volume, money] using decimal notation, including scaling.	Year 5, Unit 6.2
	Year 6 Programme of study: Pupils should be taught to:	
	■ use, read, write and convert between standard units, converting measurements of length, mass, volume and time from a smaller unit of measure to a larger unit, and vice versa, using decimal notation to up to three decimal places.	Year 5, Unit 6.2
General Upper Key Stage 2 Programme of study requirement	By the end of Year 6, pupils should be fluent in written methods for all four operations, including long multiplication and division, and in working with fractions, decimals and percentages.	Year 5, Units 6.3, 6.4, 6.5, 6.6, 6.7

Chapter 6 Addition and subtraction of decimal numbers

Unit 6.1
Multiplying and dividing decimals by 10, 100 and 1000 (1)

Conceptual context

This unit introduces multiplication and division of decimals by 10, 100 and 1000 and builds towards an efficient strategy for these calculations.

It is important for pupils to understand that, although it may look as if the decimal point is moving, what is happening is that all of the digits around that point are moving and the decimal point remains static. (The use of a place value slider reinforces this.) Pupils are likely to abstract the movement of the digits to a movement of the decimal point, but it is important that this is an end point, and is the condensing of deep understanding, rather than a starting point in which pupils learn a method without the conceptual structure that supports it.

Learning pupils will have achieved at the end of the unit

- Pupils' understanding about place value including decimal numbers will have become more secure (Q1)
- Pupils will have exploited place value to multiply and divide decimals by 10, 100 and 1000 (Q1, Q2, Q3, Q4)
- Pupils will understand digits move across the place value grid, that the decimal point is static and that any gaps created by moving the digits should be filled with zeros (Q1, Q2, Q4)
- Pupils will have identified opportunities for multiplying and dividing by 10, 100 and 1000 to develop efficient strategies when tackling problems (Q5)

Resources

place value charts; sticky notes; mini whiteboards; paper/card; scissors; **Resource 5.6.1a** Place value slider; **Resource 5.6.1b** Make the calculation; **Resource 5.6.1c** × and ÷ trail; **Resource 5.6.1d** Find a number that when …

Vocabulary

multiply, divide, hundredth, thousandth, decimal, decimal place

Chapter 6 Addition and subtraction of decimal numbers　　　Unit 6.1 Practice Book 5B, pages 1–4

Question 1

1 Calculate mentally and then write the answers.

(a) 0.12 × 10 =
(b) 0.12 × 100 =
(c) 0.12 × 1000 =
(d) 3.12 × 10 =
(e) 3.12 × 100 =
(f) 3.12 × 1000 =
(g) 40.9 ÷ 10 =
(h) 40.9 ÷ 100 =
(i) 40.9 ÷ 1000 =
(j) 1.35 × 10 =
(k) 1.35 ÷ 100 =
(l) 1.35 ÷ 1000 =

2 Fill in the spaces to make each statement correct.

What learning will pupils have achieved at the conclusion of Question 1?

- Pupils' understanding about place value including decimal numbers will have become more secure.
- Pupils will have exploited place value to multiply and divide decimals by 10, 100 and 1000.
- Pupils will understand digits move across the place value grid, that the decimal point is static and that any gaps created by moving the digits should be filled with zeros.

Activities for whole-class instruction

- Draw a place value chart on the board and enter a decimal number such as 3.14. Work though one digit at a time from left to right, asking pupils to multiply each digit by 10 and to write the answer on their mini whiteboards.
- First, point to the 3 and ask: *What's 3 multiplied by 10?* Gather the answers and write 3 in the tens column below the original number.
- Now repeat this with the 0.1 and the 0.04, writing the number 31.4 below the original decimal.

1000	100	10	1	0.1	0.01
			3	1	4
		3	1	4	

- Ensure pupils understand that this process is the same as calculating 3.14 × 10.
- Show pupils **Resource 5.6.1a** Place value slider and use it to show 3.14 × 10, drawing attention to the way the digits are sliding past the decimal point.

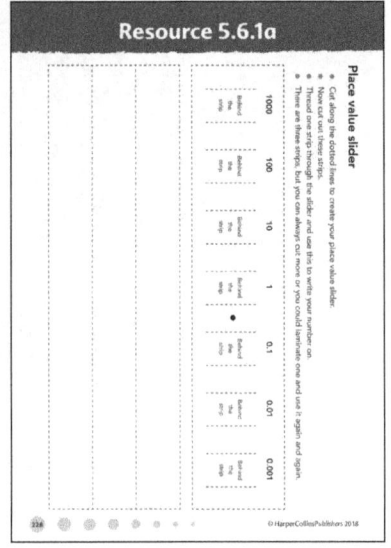
Resource 5.6.1a

- Point to each digit in turn, asking what it will be when multiplied by 10, and recording its new value on the line below. Your board will now look like this.

1000	100	10	1	0.1	0.01
			3	1	4
		3	1	4	
	3	1	4		

- Ask: *What will 314 multiplied by 10 be? How do you know?*
- Can pupils explain that, when multiplying by ten, all the digits move one place to the left because each digit is now 10 times bigger than it was before? Pupils should demonstrate, using the place value slider.
- Now use the place value slider to slide 314 one place to the right and ask pupils what mathematical operation would lead to this outcome. Give time for them to discuss and agree that this is dividing by 10.

 *Multiplying a number by 10 moves all the digits one place to the left and dividing by 10 moves all the digits one place to the right.*

- Next, ask pupils to write on their whiteboards the mathematical operations that would move the digits in a number two places left and two places right. Gather their answers and ask them to explain how they know. Ensure that you demonstrate this with a number such as 3.1 to show that the spaces are filled with zero.
- You might like to challenge pupils to think about what would happen when multiplying or dividing by 1000.
- Finally, ensure that pupils understand that:
  - the digits move, not the decimal point
  - any spaces that are created when the digits move are filled with zeros.
- Pupils should complete Question 1 in the Practice Book.

Chapter 6 Addition and subtraction of decimal numbers

Unit 6.1 Practice Book 5B, pages 1–4

Same-day intervention

- Use place value sliders (**Resource 5.6.1a** Place value slider is a template) to work with pupils. (Laminating the strips will allow pupils to change the digits on the moveable strip of paper using a dry wipe pen, but this is not essential.)

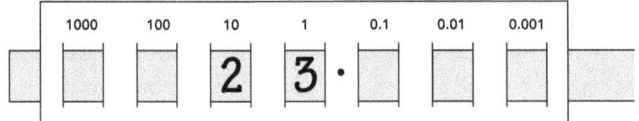

- Ask pupils to represent a decimal number on the slider, then to multiply it by 10. Ensure they notice that the digits have all moved the same distance to the left, that the order of the digits hasn't changed, and that the decimal point has not moved.

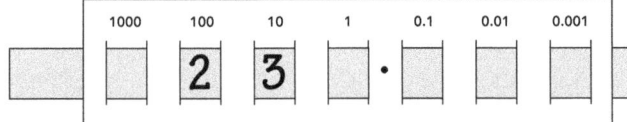

- Repeat and draw pupils' attention to the gap left in the 1s column. Explain that this space is filled with a zero to show that there are no 1s in this number, and write a zero in the gap.
- Now ask pupils to imagine a different number is on the strip, say 3.5, and ask them to imagine what will happen when it is multiplied by 10. Discuss and deal with any misconceptions, reverting back to the slider if necessary.
- Use the same structure to work with dividing by 10, ensuring that pupils include zeros as appropriate.
- By the end of the task, pupils should be able to use the sliders to extend their understanding of multiplying and dividing by 10 from whole numbers (where they already know that multiplying by 10 moves all the digits one space left and that dividing by 10 moves them all one space right, and that any gaps that are left should be filled with a zero) to decimals and know that the same rules apply to both.
- Draw pupils' attention to the way in which the rules are the same whether working with whole numbers or decimals.

ⓘ The place value slider is a scaffold to support pupils in building an image for multiplying and dividing by 10 and it is important that, once the key concepts have been understood, the sliders are put away and are not used as a calculation device.

Same-day enrichment

- Give pupils **Resource 5.6.1b** Make the calculation, in which they are asked to write increasingly complex calculations.

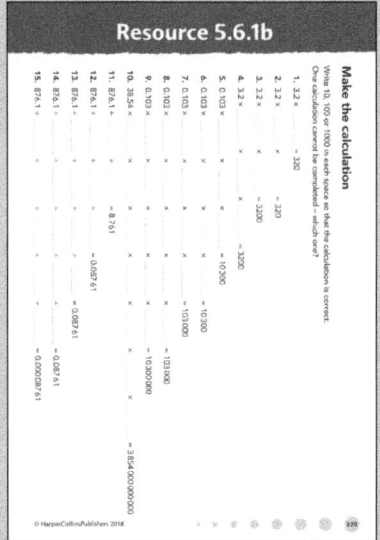

- If possible, discuss with pupils whether they worked out the answer at each stage of their calculation, or whether they used the relationship between multiplication and division to write calculations without needing to work out answers.

Answers: 1. 100; 2. 10, 10; 3. 10, 100; 4. 10, 10, 10; 5. 10, 10, 1000 or 10, 100, 100; 6. 10, 10, 10, 100; 7. 10, 10, 100, 100 or 10, 10, 10, 1000; 8. 10, 10, 10, 10, 100; 9. 10, 10, 100 100, 100 or 10, 10, 10, 100, 1000; 10. 10, 10, 10, 100 100 100, 100 or 10, 10, 10, 10, 10, 1000, 1000; 11. 10, 10; 12. 10, 10, 100; 13. 10, 10, 10, 10; 14. Cannot be completed; 15. 10, 10, 10, 100, 100 or 10, 10, 10, 10, 1000

Chapter 6 Addition and subtraction of decimal numbers

Unit 6.1 Practice Book 5B, pages 1–4

Questions 2 and 3

2 Fill in the spaces to make each statement correct.

(a) When a decimal number is multiplied by 10, 100, 1000 ... the decimal point stays still while all the digits in the number move one place, two places, three places, and so on, to the _____. When a decimal number is divided by 10, 100, 1000 all the digits in the number move _____ place, _____ places, _____ places to the _____ across the decimal point. If there are any gaps created then we add _____ accordingly.

(b) Missing out the decimal point from 2.3 gives the same result as multiplying it by ☐, or moving all the digits _____ place to the _____ across the decimal point.

(c) Moving the digits in 45.99 _____ place(s) to the _____ across the decimal point gives 0.4599.

(d) The unit of counting of 0.420 is _____, and there are ☐ such units. Multiplying this number by ☐, gives 42.

(e) 8.79 multiplied by 100 is ☐. If the result is further divided by 10 this gives ☐.

(f) Inserting a decimal point in 4009 to make a decimal number with two decimal places is the same as dividing the number by ☐.

(g) If the decimal point is removed from 1.03, the result is ☐, which is ☐ times the original number.

(h) If all the digits in the number 7.77 are moved two places to the right across the decimal point, the result is ☐ of the original number.

3 Fill in each ○ with × or ÷, and write a suitable number in each box.

(a) 101.2 ○ ☐ = 10120
(b) 36 ○ ☐ = 3.6
(c) 20.9 ○ 100 = 0.209
(d) 6.07 ÷ 10 ÷ ☐ = 0.0607
(e) ☐ × 1000 = 3256
(f) ☐ ÷ 10 ÷ 100 = 99.92

What learning will pupils have achieved at the conclusion of Questions 2 and 3?

- Pupils will have exploited place value to multiply and divide decimals by 10, 100 and 1000.
- Pupils will understand digits move across the place value grid, that the decimal point is static and that any gaps created by moving the digits should be filled with zeros.

Activities for whole-class instruction

- Show pupils some calculations where symbols have replaced digits (you might like to use letters, or different coloured sticky notes rather than these symbols, to represent the digits). For example:

❖✚☀.■¤★◆ × 10 =
❖✚☀.■¤★◆ × 100 =
❖✚☀.■¤★◆ × 1000 =
❖✚☀.■¤★◆ ÷ 10 =
❖✚☀.■¤★◆ ÷ 100 =

- Ask pupils to work in pairs to discuss and describe what these numbers will look like after the calculations. Gather their responses. The intention is to encourage pupils to further notice that the digits don't change and that the order of the digits stays the same; it is only the position of the digits relative to the decimal point that changes. Ensure that these two key points are discussed and emphasised.

- Now show pupils the outcome of some calculations using similar symbols. For example:

❖✚☀.■¤★◆ → ❖✚☀.■¤★◆
❖✚☀.■¤★◆ → ❖✚☀.■¤★◆
❖✚☀.■¤★◆ → ❖✚☀.■¤★◆

- Ask them to discuss what mathematical operation will result in the digits of the number making these movements. Draw pupils' attention to the connection between the power of 10 being used (whether it's 10, 100 or 1000) and the number of places that the digits shift around the decimal point.

- Pupils should complete Questions 2 and 3 in the Practice Book.

Same-day intervention

- Use a place value slider and draw the symbols from the task in the appropriate place on slider.
- By substituting the digits, pupils' attention will focus on the movement of the symbols that is required by the different operations, and repeating the task as above will support pupils in making sense of this.

Chapter 6 Addition and subtraction of decimal numbers

Unit 6.1 Practice Book 5B, pages 1–4

Same-day enrichment

- Give pupils **Resource 5.6.1c** × and ÷ trail and ask them to complete the trail.

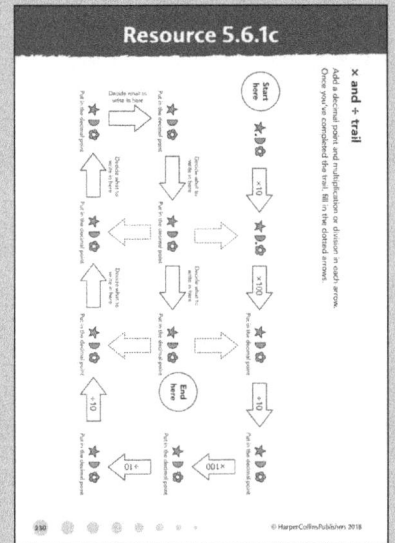

- For some answers, pupils need to include zeros to maintain the place value.
- As the trail progresses, pupils need to decide what operations to use. Encourage them to use 100 or 1000, and use this to discuss the importance of including zeros to show place value.

Answers: Various answers are possible, depending on pupils' choices.

What learning will pupils have achieved at the conclusion of Question 4?

- Pupils will have exploited place value to multiply and divide decimals by 10, 100 and 1000.
- Pupils will understand digits move across the place value grid, that the decimal point is static and that any gaps created by moving the digits should be filled with zeros.

Activities for whole-class instruction

- Show pupils these questions and answers:

  6.81 × 100 = 6.8100

  10.7 × 1000 = 107

  2.002 × 10 = 20.2

  31.7 ÷ 1000 = 0.317

- Ask them to discuss in pairs what is wrong with each answer and why the pupil may have made those mistakes.
- You might ask them to write a comment on a sticky note that the pupil could read to help them, or they could describe to you what they would say to the pupil to help them understand better. The intention of this task is to raise misconceptions and have other pupils address them.
- Ensure that all misconceptions raised through this task are addressed, but try to allow the other pupils to explain their understanding where possible.
- Pupils should complete Question 4 in the Practice Book.

Question 4

4 Multiple choice questions. (For each question, choose the correct answer and write the letter in the box.)

(a) Removing the decimal point in 0.022 is the same as multiplying the number by ☐.

A. 10   B. 100   C. 1000   D. 10000

(b) 1004.5 ☐ 10 000 is 0.100 45.

A. ×   B. ÷   C. +   D. −

(c) If we add two zeros after the decimal point in 6.7, it becomes 6.007. This number is ☐.

A. 0.693 less than the original number
B. 0.008 greater than the original number
C. the same as the original number
D. 0.792 less than the original number

(d) 0.0306 is ☐ 30.6.

A. one tenth of
B. one hundredth of
C. one thousandth of
D. 100 times

Chapter 6 Addition and subtraction of decimal numbers Unit 6.1 Practice Book 5B, pages 1–4

Same-day intervention

- Use place value sliders to work with pupils to complete this table.

	Can be written as ...	and moves all digits ...	by ...	For example:
× 10	× 10	←	1 place	3.14 × 10 = 31.4
× 10 × 10	× 100			
× 10 × 10 × 10				
÷ 10		→		
÷ 10 ÷ 10				
÷ 10 ÷ 10 ÷ 10				

- Ensure that pupils understand the equivalence of repeated multiplication by 10, and the single multiplication that can replace it.
- Pupils should create their own examples for the final column. Ask them to check and add to each other's examples.

Same-day enrichment

- Show pupils these calculations:

  17 × 10

  1.7 × 10

  0.17 × 10

- Tell pupils that two of the products consist of only the digits 1 and 7, but one of the answers has 1, 7 and an additional 0. Ask them to decide which one needs the extra zero. Draw pupils' attention to the fact that each calculation is × 10 and that sometimes an extra zero is needed when multiplying by 10 to fill the gap ('hold the place').
- Ask pupils if they can find an example where multiplying by 10 needs an extra two zeros, and agree that there is no situation where this is the case. Ask pupils to justify why.

- Now give pupils **Resource 5.6.1d** Find a number that when ... and ask them to place a number in as many cells as they can. Can they complete all of the cells? One row has been completed as an example.

Resource 5.6.1d

Find a number that when ...

Find a number to complete each row of the table.
One of the rows has been completed as an example.

Find a number that when ...	Needs one extra zero	Needs two extra zeros	Doesn't need an extra zero
× 10		It's impossible to get two zeros from multiplying by 10.	
× 100	3.2 (because 3.2 × 100 = 320)	3 (because 3 × 100 = 300)	3.21 (because 3.21 × 100 = 321)
× 1000			
÷ 10			
÷ 100			
÷ 1000			

Answers: 32, 3.2; 0.32, 0.3, 0.321; 3200, 3000, 3210; 32 000, 30 000, 32 100; 320 000, 300 000, 321 000

Question 5

> 5 One basketball costs £23.80. How much does it cost to buy 100 basketballs?

What learning will pupils have achieved at the conclusion of Question 5?

- Pupils will have identified opportunities for multiplying and dividing by 10, 100 and 1000 to develop efficient strategies when tackling problems.

Activities for whole-class instruction

- Tell pupils that they are going to imagine that they will run a doughnut stall to raise money for charity. They will buy 100 jam doughnuts from the bakery for £14.50.
- Ask them to discuss with a partner how much they should sell each doughnut for, and to work out how much profit they will make on each doughnut, as well as how much profit they will make in total if they sell all 100 doughnuts.
- Gather in their prices and their justification for those prices. Listen carefully for their strategies for calculation of

Chapter 6 Addition and subtraction of decimal numbers

Unit 6.1 Practice Book 5B, pages 1–4

the individual price of the doughnut, and for multiplying the profit on each doughnut by 100. Ask the class to come to an agreement about the best price to charge.
- The intention of this task is to place the idea of multiplying and dividing by 10, 100 and 1000 into a context in which pupils need to decide on a strategy, and to notice that they need not resort to written calculation methods.
- Pupils should complete Question 5 in the Practice Book.

Same-day intervention

- Give pupils a number sentence such as 32 × 10 = 320. Tell them that one story that this number sentence might describe is:
  – If thirty-two people each walk for ten steps, how many steps are taken in total?
- Ask them to write a different story for the same calculation.
- Listen to their stories and ensure they are correct multiplicative stories for the given calculation. Address any misconceptions that are exposed.
- Now change the calculation so the value being multiplied by 10 is a decimal, for example 5.4 × 10 = 54. Ask pupils to create a story that fits with this number sentence. Share stories. Challenge pupils to think of another story for the same number sentence.
- The purpose of this task is to ensure that pupils are able to identify a situation in which a multiplication is an appropriate calculation, and to recognise the same calculation in different contexts.

Same-day enrichment

- Tell pupils that the bakery from the original task also sells ring doughnuts. 100 ring doughnuts cost £10.45. Tell them the budget for the doughnut stall is £100.
- They should decide how many packs of jam doughnuts and how many packs of ring doughnuts they should buy, how much they should sell each type of doughnut for and what profit they would expect to make if they sell all the doughnuts.
- This task adds extra complexity to the original, and offers many opportunities for pupils to multiply and divide by 100 in a context, and to interpret their results and assumptions.

Challenge and extension questions

Question 6

> 6 Class 5B had a spelling and grammar test and the results were as follows: Alvin scored 9.87 marks, James scored 9.90 marks and Simon scored 9.96 marks.
> (a) Put the three students' scores in order, starting with the highest.
>
> (b) Lily's score was slightly lower than Simon's but higher than James's. Can you guess what Lily's score might have been?

This question gives pupils a context in which to practise interpreting and ordering decimals. Using a blank number line and positioning the scores on it may support pupils in accessing the question. Some pupils may find the freedom and range of possible answers offered by part (b) challenging. You might like to ask pupils to discuss their answers to part (b) to explore the possible range of solutions. You could challenge some to try to write down a correct answer that nobody else in the classroom will have written. (It is likely that this extension will lead them into increasing the number of decimal places in the number.)

Question 7

> 7 Mahu is sometimes a little absent-minded. Once, when he was doing his maths homework, he misread 12.1 as 1.21. But he didn't care, and said: 'It doesn't matter, as long as the value is close.'
> All the digits in 12.1 have moved one place to the right across the decimal point to become 1.21. Does it really not matter? If it does matter, what is the difference between 12.1 and 1.21?

This question provides an opportunity for pupils to explore and consider implications of being 'absentminded'. There is potentially a huge difference here, since one value is 10 times the other.

Question 8

> 8 A number is first multiplied by 100, then divided by 1000 and then divided by 10. The final result is 0.017. What was the original number?

In this question, pupils work with inverse operations to find an original quantity. The use of arrows, setting this up as a set of 'function machines', may support pupils in understanding the order in which to tackle the problem. Pupils with exceptional understanding may notice that the three calculations given are equivalent to dividing the original value by 100, and so simply multiplying 0.017 by 100 will efficiently give the correct solution.

Chapter 6 Addition and subtraction of decimal numbers

Unit 6.2
Multiplying and dividing decimals by 10, 100 and 1000 (2)

Conceptual context

Metric units provide a context to further explore multiplication and division by 10, 100 and 1000.

A focus on the vocabulary is also useful in this unit. It should be made explicit to pupils that the 'kilo' in both kilometre and kilogram represents the same multiplier, as does the 'milli' in millimetre, milligram and millilitre.

Learning pupils will have achieved at the end of the unit

- Pupils will be able to multiply and divide by 10, 100 and 1000 confidently and accurately (Q1, Q2, Q3, Q4, Q5)
- Pupils will be able to combine multiplications and divisions to build more efficient calculation strategies (Q1, Q3)
- Pupils will have begun to add decimal numbers by considering their integer and decimal parts (Q2)
- Pupils will have developed vocabulary and worked in complex situations with decimal numbers (Q3, Q4, Q5)
- Pupils will be able to work more flexibly with decimal numbers, identifying and viewing the integer and decimal parts in different ways (Q4, Q5)

Resources

place value charts; sticky notes; mini whiteboards; paper/card; scissors; **Resource 5.6.2a** Sorting calculations; **Resource 5.6.2b** Distance dominoes; **Resource 5.6.2c** Zero or not?

Vocabulary

multiply, divide, tenth, hundredth, thousandth, decimal, decimal place, inverse

Chapter 6 Addition and subtraction of decimal numbers

Unit 6.2 Practice Book 5B, pages 5–8

Question 1

1 Calculate mentally and then write the answers.

(a) $0.25 \times 100 =$ ☐
(b) $9.001 \times 10 =$ ☐
(c) $0.014 \times 100 =$ ☐
(d) $1.351 \times 1000 =$ ☐
(e) $256.6 \div 100 =$ ☐
(f) $100.1 \div 10 =$ ☐
(g) $29 \div 1000 \times 10 =$ ☐
(h) $55.5 \div 10 \div 10 =$ ☐
(i) $0.08 \times 100 \div 10 =$ ☐
(j) $0.06 \times 10 \times 100 =$ ☐
(k) $630 \div 10 \times 10 =$ ☐
(l) $2 \div 100 \times 1000 =$ ☐

What learning will pupils have achieved at the conclusion of Question 1?

- Pupils will be able to multiply and divide by 10, 100 and 1000 confidently and accurately.
- Pupils will be able to combine multiplications and divisions to build more efficient calculation strategies.

Activities for whole-class instruction

- Pupil pairs should use two mini whiteboards and write ×10, ×100 or ×1000 on one, and the inverse of that on the other. (You may need to explain the word 'inverse'.) For example:

| ×100 | ÷100 |

- Call one pair to the front of the class and line them up to make a living 'function machine', showing both of their calculations. Draw pupils' attention to the way that the same number comes out at the end of the machine as went in, and stress that this is because the two operations carried out are inverse operations. Swap the order of the calculations to demonstrate that the order does not change the result.

- Call a second pair to the front and combine the two pairs making a function machine with four component operations.

| ×10 | ÷100 | ×100 | ÷10 |

- Ask pupils to predict what might happen when a value is fed through the machine and then work through to show that the value doesn't change when this second pair of calculations is included.

- Rearrange the order of the four pupils and again feed a number through the 'machine', showing that the value doesn't change when the order is changed. (If appropriate, call up more pairs to create a complex 'machine'.)

- Call up one pupil from a different pair, but not their partner, and place them somewhere in the machine.

| ×10 | ÷10 | ×100 | ×10 | ÷10 |

- Ask pupils to predict what will happen to the input now, and then try this out by feeding a number in as an example. Choose a number to work through as an example, if necessary.

  Agree with pupils that this operation, without its inverse, changes the outcome of the calculation so the result is not the same as the starting number.

- Call out another pupil but not their partner and add them to the machine.

  Again, ask pupils to predict what the overall result will be and choose a number to work through as an example, if necessary.

- Ask pupils to discuss in pairs the easiest way to arrange pupils in the machine so the overall result can be found. Gather their thoughts. Different pupils will have different ideas, but key to this is to draw pupils' attention to the way in which they can calculate smartly by grouping calculations together.

- Pupils should complete Question 1 in the Practice Book.

Same-day intervention

- Use a place value slider and work with pupils to model some multi-stage calculations.
- Set a number on the slider, then multiply by 10, multiply by 10 again and then by 10 again, using the apparatus to show the way the digits of the number move at each stage.
- Draw pupils' attention to the way in which the overall result is the same as multiplying by 1000.
- Now divide the result by 10 and, again, show this on the place value slider.
- Draw pupils' attention to the way that multiplying by 1000, then dividing by 10 is equivalent to multiplying by 100.

Chapter 6 Addition and subtraction of decimal numbers   Unit 6.2 Practice Book 5B, pages 5–8

- Now use the slider to carry out the same operations in a different order (divide by, 10 then multiply by 1000) and show that the order of the calculation can be changed without affecting the outcome.
- Ask pupils to decide which of these calculations have the same result as multiplying by 100. They may use a place value slider to support them.

  7 × 1000 ÷ 10 × 100 ÷ 100

  7 × 100 ÷ 100 × 100

  7 × 1000 ÷ 100 × 100 ÷ 100

- Now ask pupils to write another calculation that also will multiply 7 by 100. See how complicated they can make their calculation!

What learning will pupils have achieved at the conclusion of Question 2?

- Pupils will be able to multiply and divide by 10, 100 and 1000 confidently and accurately.
- Pupils will have begun to add decimal numbers by considering their integer and decimal parts.

Activities for whole-class instruction

- Discuss how 'kilo' means thousand, so a kilometre is 1000 metres and a kilogram is 1000 grams. Record these on the board.
- Discuss how 'milli' means thousand, so there are 1000 millimetres in a metre, 1000 milligrams in a gram and 1000 millilitres in a litre. Record these values on the board.
- Pupils may not have have come across the word 'tonne' as a unit of measure or its abbreviation 't'. (See Question 2 part b.) Explain that there are 1000 kilograms in one tonne.
- Choose a quantity to work with, say 1.73 kg, and ask if this is more or less than 1000 g and why. Agree that 1.73 > 1.
- Draw a part/whole diagram to split 1.73 kg into an integer and decimal part. Agree that 1 kg is equivalent to 1000 g, and that the 0.73 kg is equivalent to 730 g so 1.73 kg can be thought of as 1730 g or as 1 kg and 730 g.

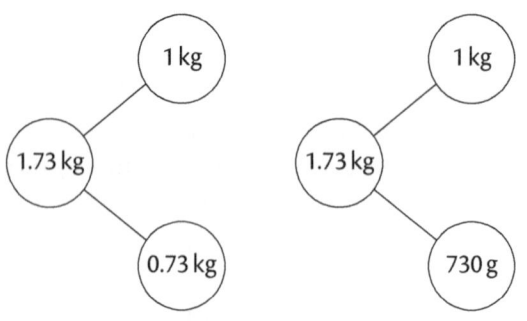

- Ask pupils to write on their mini whiteboards 2855 g as a decimal with kg, and as a combination of kg and g.
- Share pupils' responses and repeat as necessary.
- Pupils should complete Question 2 in the Practice Book.

Same-day enrichment

- Give pupils **Resource 5.6.2a** Sorting calculations in which they are asked to consider the outcome of a calculation without necessarily calculating each stage.

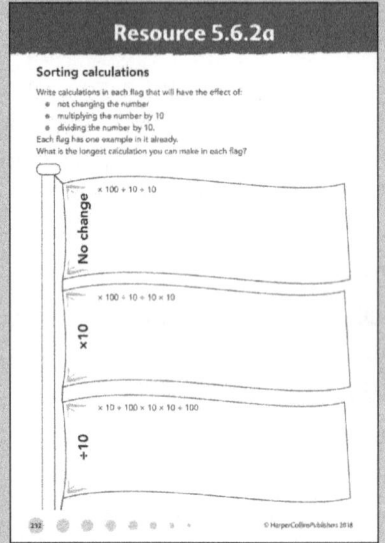

Answers: Various answers possible, depending on the choices pupils make.

Question 2

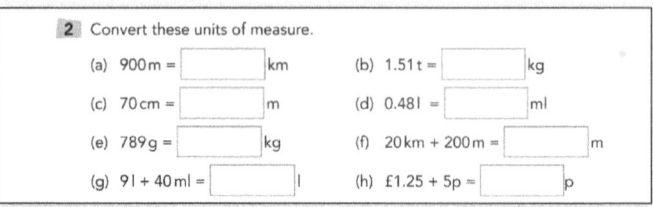

Same-day intervention

- Use a place value slider and mark the slider with two numbers, one 1000 times greater than the other.

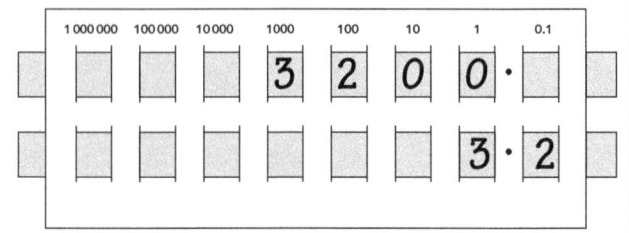

Chapter 6 Addition and subtraction of decimal numbers

Unit 6.2 Practice Book 5B, pages 5–8

- Use this slider to work with pupils to explore the relationships between units showing that, for example, if 32 kg = 32 000 g then it follows that 3.2 kg = 3200 g.
- Ensure that pupils understand the relationship between the two values and then ask them to imagine what the kg value will be if the grams show, for example, 320 000 g. The purpose of the place value slider is to help pupils see and explore the relationship between the units; it should not be used simply to work out an answer but as a tool to support understanding.

What learning will pupils have achieved at the conclusion of Question 3?

- Pupils will be able to multiply and divide by 10, 100 and 1000 confidently and accurately.
- Pupils will be able to combine multiplications and divisions to build more efficient calculation strategies.
- Pupils will have developed vocabulary and worked in complex situations with decimal numbers.

Same-day enrichment

- Show pupils the following image:

  - A yoctometre is 0.000 000 000 000 000 000 000 001 m
  - A zeptometre is 0.000 000 000 000 000 000 000 01 m

- Ask pupils to work out how many yoctometres make one zeptometre. (Ensure pupils understand that these are not real units but are made up.) Then ask them to measure some objects around the classroom and give the length of each object in the most sensible unit. They then convert that length to write it in metres, centimetres, millimetres, yoctometres and zeptometres.

Activities for whole-class instruction

- Write an equation such as 0.13 = 0.13 on the board and invite a pupil to the board to work with you.
- Each of you has a turn at adding a layer of complexity to your side of the equation by breaking down one value to make the number sentence more complex. You might find it easier to keep track of the changes by underlining the value that you're going to change. For example:

  $\underline{0.13} = 0.13$

  $0.1 + 0.03 = \underline{0.13}$

  $\underline{0.1} + 0.03 = 0.013 \times 10$

  $0.01 \times 10 + 0.03 = \underline{0.013} \times 10$

  $0.01 \times 10 + \underline{0.03} = 13 \div 1000 \times 10$

  $0.01 \times 10 + 0.01 + 0.02 = 13 \div 1000 \times 10$

First, 0.13 was changed to 0.1 + 0.03.
Next, 0.13 on the other side was changed to 0.013 × 10.
Then, back to the other side, 0.1 was changed to 0.01 × 10.
Then, on the right, 0.013 was changed to 13 divided by 1000, and so on.

- Tell pupils that for this game, any addition and subtraction are allowed but they are only allowed to multiply or divide by 10, 100, 1000, or 10 000.
- Model the game, again with another pupil if necessary, then pupils work in pairs to play the game. You might like to ask one pair of pupils to play their game on a mini whiteboard so you can refer to it during the whole-class discussion.

Question 3

3 Write the number sentences and then calculate.

(a) What is 1000 times 0.067?

Number sentence: _____

Answer: _____

(b) What is one hundredth of 4.6?

Number sentence: _____

Answer: _____

(c) How much greater is the sum of one hundred 1.5s than 10 times 7.5?

Number sentence: _____

Answer: _____

(d) All the digits in 0.74 were moved two places to the left across the decimal point, and then the number was divided by 10. How many times the original number was the final result?

Number sentence: _____

Answer: _____

(e) Marisa moved all the digits in a number two places to the right across the decimal point, and then multiplied the number by 10. Next, she moved all the digits in the result one place to the left across the decimal point and then divided by 10 again. Her final result was 9.45. What was the original number?

Number sentence: _____

Answer: _____

Chapter 6 Addition and subtraction of decimal numbers　　Unit 6.2 Practice Book 5B, pages 5–8

- Once pupils have finished playing the game, discuss how they decided which numbers to work with, and what strategies they used when multiplying and dividing by 10, 100, 1000 and 10 000.
- The intention of this task is to support pupils in feeling confident with greater complexity. By understanding the way in which complexity is increased, pupils are more likely to be able to approach calculations flexibly and be able to simplify fluently.
- Pupils should complete Question 3 in the Practice Book.

Same-day intervention

- Use a place value slider to carry out a calculation, for example: 1000 × 3.14. Ask pupils to describe the calculation in words.
- They should record the words, the calculation and the result on paper or a mini whiteboard.
- They should try to describe the calculation in at least two different ways, in this case it might be 'one thousand times 3.14', 'one thousand lots of 3.14', '3.14 multiplied by one thousand', '3 times 1000, 0.1 times 1000 and 0.04 times 10 000', or any other correct interpretation.
- The intention is to consider different ways of describing a calculation and so make a connection between the words, the symbols and the movement on the place value chart/slider.
- Repeat this for multiplication and division calculations as necessary.

Same-day enrichment

- Give pupils a calculation to work with, for example: 3.14 × 100 ÷ 10 × 1000. Ask them to write a word problem that describes the calculation but do not allow them to use particular words in their question. For example, you might ban the use of 'multiply', 'times', 'lots of', 'divide' and 'shared'.
- The intention of the task is to challenge pupils to consider the many different ways in which mathematical operations can be described.
- Once pupils have managed one such calculation, you might challenge them to reword again, 'banning' different words from their selection.

Question 4

> 4 Convert these units of measure.
> (a) 30.66 l = ☐ l ☐ ml　　(b) 50 kg 500 g = ☐ kg
> (c) 9 kg 9 g = ☐ kg　　(d) 8004 cm = ☐ m

What learning will pupils have achieved at the conclusion of Question 4?

- Pupils will be able to multiply and divide by 10, 100 and 1000 confidently and accurately.
- Pupils will have developed vocabulary and worked in complex situations with decimal numbers.
- Pupils will be able to work more flexibly with decimal numbers, identifying and viewing the integer and decimal parts in different ways.

Activities for whole-class instruction

- On the board, write: 3610 metres. Use a place value slider to convert this to km. Agree with pupils, and write on the board: 3610 m = 3.610 km.
- Now use a part/whole diagram to break this into a whole number and a decimal part.

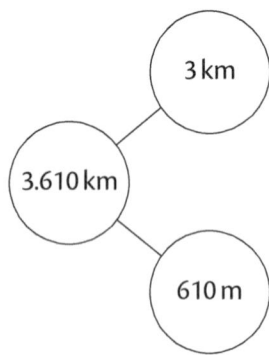

- Agree with pupils, and write on the board: 3610 metres = 3.610 km = 3 km 610 metres.
- Stress that the 3 in all versions represents the same distance, but is written in different ways – either as 3000 m or as 3 km. Stress too that the 610 also represents the same distance, but is written in two different ways – either as 610 m or as 0.61 km.
- Repeat with 13.061 kg. Be aware that the zero in the tenths position may cause some confusion for pupils when writing the quantity as 13 kg and 61 grams.
- Pupils should complete Question 4 in the Practice Book.

Chapter 6 Addition and subtraction of decimal numbers Unit 6.2 Practice Book 5B, pages 5–8

Same-day intervention

- Work with pupils on **Resource 5.6.2b** Distance dominoes, matching the different distances to make a loop of dominoes.

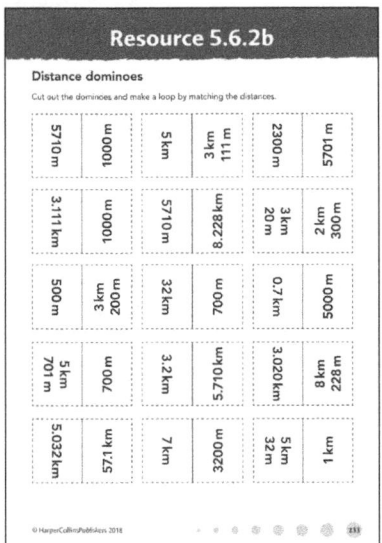

Same-day enrichment

- Give pupils **Resource 5.6.2c** Zero or not? in which they are asked to identify zeros in different representations of the same quantity.

Answers: ** km = *⊛*** m; ** km ⊛** m = **.* km; ***** g = ** kg *** g; *⊛**m = *.* km; * l = *⊛**ml; *** g = *.*** kg; *.*** kg = * kg ** g

Question 5

> 5. At the dog training school, four dogs had a race and their speeds are shown in the table.
>
> | Dog | Flippy | Ben | Pounder | Bobby |
> |---|---|---|---|---|
> | Speed | 0.9 km per minute | 400 m per minute | 1.67 km per minute | 1 km 200 m per minute |
>
> Based on the data above, put the dogs in the order they finished the race, starting with first place.

What learning will pupils have achieved at the conclusion of Question 5?

- Pupils will be able to multiply and divide by 10, 100 and 1000 confidently and accurately.
- Pupils will have developed vocabulary and worked in complex situations with decimal numbers.
- Pupils will be able to work more flexibly with decimal numbers, identifying and viewing the integer and decimal parts in different ways.

Activities for whole-class instruction

- Display the following table:

Name	Kilometres	Metres	Kilometres and metres
Alok	3.103 km	3103 m	3 km 103 m
Benny	2.719 km	2719 m	
Clare			4 km 817 m
Deepak	19.04 km		
Elinor			19 km 4 m
Frederik		19 400 m	

- Explain that the table shows the distance travelled by a group of people in one hour. Ask pupils to work in pairs to complete the table with equivalent distances. Share feedback, elicit misconceptions and discuss.
- Ask pupils to arrange these distances in order, from shortest to longest. Discuss strategies and agree that it is usually easier to compare distances if they are written in the same units.
- Pupils should identify who travelled fastest. Look out for any pupils who do not make the connection between greater distance travelled and greater speed.
- Pupils should complete Question 5 in the Practice Book.

Chapter 6 Addition and subtraction of decimal numbers

Unit 6.2 Practice Book 5B, pages 5–8

Same-day intervention

- Tell pupils that the world record for travelling 100 m on a space hopper is 30 seconds. (More precisely, the record is 30.2 seconds and was set in November 2004 by Ashrita Furman from New York.)
- Ask pupils how far they might expect Ashrita Furman to travel in one minute. How far would they expect him to travel in two minutes?
- Use their answers to reveal and address misconceptions and ensure that they understand that a constant speed that is given 'per minute' means that, in every minute of travel, the object will travel that distance. Agree that this means that Ashrita Furman was travelling at around 200 m per minute.
- Tell pupils that the runner who set the world record for running 100 m hurdles while wearing flippers travelled at approximately 400 metres per minute. (In fact, the world record for 100 m hurdles while wearing flippers is 14.82 seconds and was set by Christopher Irmscher in Cologne in September 2008.)
- Ask them which is faster, the space hopper world record or the flippers world record, and by how much.
- Work with pupils, using a place value slider if appropriate, to convert the speeds into km per minute.

Same-day enrichment

- Tell pupils that the fastest speed achieved by a monowheel motorcycle is 1 km 641 m per minute and that the fastest speed achieved on an electric skateboard is 95 830 metres per hour.
- Ask them to decide which is faster and by how much.
- (The monowheel record was set by Kevin Scott in the UK in September 2015 and the skateboard record was set by Mischo Erban in Slovenia in October 2015.)

Challenge and extension question

Question 6

6 Read the following number sentences and look for patterns.

We know that:
$\frac{1}{10} = 1 \div 10 = 0.1$
$\frac{1}{100} = 1 \div 100 = 0.01$
$\frac{1}{1000} = 1 \div 1000 = 0.001$

$34 \div 0.1$
$= 34 \div \frac{1}{10}$
$= 34 \div (1 \div 10)$
$= 34 \div 1 \times 10$
$= 34 \times 10$

Conclusion: $34 \div 0.1 = 34 \times 10$.

Follow the pattern above and calculate.

(a) $569.21 \div 0.001 =$

(b) $8.97 \div 0.1 =$

(c) $90.1 \div 0.01 =$

(d) $501.33 \div 0.001 =$

If you check the answers with a calculator, you will get the same results. So, we can draw the following conclusion:
A number divided by 0.1, 0.01, 0.001, and so on, is equal to the number multiplied by 10, 100, 1000, and so on.
The conversion from division to multiplication makes the calculation easier. Share the findings with your friends.

This question builds on pupils' existing understanding to show that dividing a number by 0.1 is equivalent to multiplying by 10, and that dividing by 0.01 is equivalent to multiplying by 100 and so on. Encouraging pupils to think of the division $3.4 \div 0.1$ as 'How many 0.1s are there in 3.4?' may support them in accessing the question and interpreting results.

Chapter 6 Addition and subtraction of decimal numbers

Unit 6.3
Addition of decimals

Conceptual context

This unit will bring together two aspects of pupils' conceptual knowledge – addition and decimals – so it is important to ensure that pupils' conceptual understanding of both of these is secure. It is common for pupils to over-generalise a rule they have noticed and to align the right-hand digits when setting out numbers for addition using the column method. They will have found that this 'works' with whole numbers but will, of course, come unstuck if they do the same thing when adding decimals that are not written to the same number of decimal places.

Pupils' understanding that zeros can be added or taken from the end of the decimal part of a number without affecting its value will be helpful to them.

Learning pupils will have achieved at the end of the unit

- Pupils will have related mental strategies for adding integers to adding decimal numbers (Q1, Q2, Q3, Q4)
- Pupils will be able to convert quantities to the same unit (Q3)
- Pupils will be able to use their understanding of addition of decimals to combine quantities appropriately (Q3, Q4)
- Pupils will be able to use number sentences including decimals to describe situations (Q4)

Resources

place value charts; counters; mini whiteboards; scissors; blank paper; **Resource 5.6.3a** Adding decimals; **Resource 5.6.3b** Matching pairs; **Resource 5.6.3c** Correct the mistake; **Resource 5.6.3d** Measuring rods – addition

Vocabulary

addition, sum, decimal point, column method

Chapter 6 Addition and subtraction of decimal numbers

Unit 6.3 Practice Book 5B, pages 9–11

Question 1

1 Calculate mentally and then write the answers.

(a) 0.3 + 0.9 = ☐
(b) 2.63 + 0.37 = ☐
(c) 5.3 + 3.6 = ☐
(d) 0.23 + 1.2 = ☐
(e) 1.5 + 0.8 = ☐
(f) 7 + 0.07 = ☐
(g) 0.03 + 0.06 = ☐
(h) 4.5 + 4 = ☐
(i) 4.5 + 0.4 = ☐
(j) 0.008 + 0.01 = ☐
(k) 15.6 + 0.03 = ☐
(l) 0.35 + 0.65 = ☐

What learning will pupils have achieved at the conclusion of Question 1?

- Pupils will have related mental strategies for adding integers to adding decimal numbers.

Activities for whole-class instruction

- Write a simple decimal addition on the board, for example 3.1 + 1.5 and ask pupils to discuss and describe in pairs how they calculated the answer mentally.
- Now write 31 + 15 on the board and again ask pupils to discuss and describe how they calculated the answer mentally.
- Gather pupils' responses and draw parallels between the strategies they used for addition of decimals and strategies used when adding integers. Agree with pupils that the same strategies can be used in both situations.
- Write 4.3 + 2.6 on the board and ask pupils what strategies they used to calculate the answer. Again, draw attention to the parallels between decimal and integer addition.
- Now write the following on the board:

  A: 11.3 + 5.4

  B: 1.13 + 5.4

- Ask pupils to calculate an answer to both of these calculations, and again to discuss their strategies. Draw attention to the possible pitfalls of using integer equivalents when calculating with decimals. The intention of this task is to encourage pupils to use familiar strategies and contexts (integers) and to connect these with contexts that they may be less comfortable with (decimal numbers).
- Draw pupils' attention to the way in which addition with decimals mirrors addition with integers, and that the strategies they already have for integers can also be used for decimals.
- Pupils should complete Question 1 in the Practice Book.

Same-day intervention

- Use **Resource 5.6.3a** Adding decimals to work with pupils to support them in connecting integer addition with decimal addition.

Resource 5.6.3a

Adding decimals

7 + 2 =	0.7 + 0.2 =
17 + 2 =	1.7 + 0.2 =
17 + 32 =	1.7 + 3.2 =
19 + 5 =	1.9 + 0.5 =
19 + 35 =	1.9 + 3.5 =
27 + 6 =	2.7 + 0.6 =
27 + 7 =	2.7 + 0.7 =
27 + 9 =	2.7 + 0.9 =
31 + 13 =	3.1 + 1.3 =

Answers: 9, 0.9; 19, 1.9; 49, 4.9; 24, 2.4; 54, 5.4; 33, 3.3; 34, 3.4; 36, 3.6; 44, 4.4

Same-day enrichment

- Give pupils **Resource 5.6.3b** Matching pairs in which they use place value to match integer and decimal calculation.

Resource 5.6.3b

Matching pairs

Look at this calculation:
283 + 112 = 395
If you divide each number in the calculation by 100 this gives another correct calculation:
2.83 + 1.12 = 3.95
Cut out and match more pairs of calculations like these.

317 + 28 =	19 + 15 =	731 + 280 =
0.02 + 0.11 =	731 + 28 =	2 + 110 =
73.1 + 2.8 =	3.17 + 2.8 =	7.31 + 2.8 =
317 + 280 =	190 + 15 =	0.2 + 11 =
31.7 + 2.8 =	0.19 + 0.15 =	2 + 11 =
19 + 1.5 =		

Answers: 317 + 28 = 345, 31.7 + 2.8 = 34.5; 19 + 15 = 34, 0.19 + 0.15 = 0.34; 731 + 280 = 1011, 7.31 + 2.8 = 1.011; 0.02 + 0.11 = 0.13, 2 + 11 = 13; 731 + 28 = 759, 73.1 + 2.8 = 75.9; 2 + 110 = 112, 0.2 + 11 = 11.2; 3.17 + 2.8 = 5.97, 317 + 280 = 597; 190 + 15 = 205, 19 + 1.5 = 20.5

Chapter 6 Addition and subtraction of decimal numbers

Unit 6.3 Practice Book 5B, pages 9–11

Question 2

> 2 Choose the most appropriate method, mental or written, to find the answer to each calculation. The first one has been done for you. (Note: When using the column method, the decimal points are placed directly under each other and the numbers in the columns are aligned by place value.)
>
> (a) 46.34 + 5.7 = 52.04
>
> ```
>   4 6 . 3 4
> +     5 . 7
>   5 2 . 0 4
> ```
>
> (b) 39.78 + 52.22 =
>
> (c) 92 + 28.97 =
>
> (d) 66.9 + 31 =
>
> (e) 8.1 + 9.089 =
>
> (f) 101.01 + 909.9 =

What learning will pupils have achieved at the conclusion of Question 2?

- Pupils will have related mental strategies for adding integers to adding decimal numbers.

Activities for whole-class instruction

- Write the following calculation on the board:

```
    3 7 1 8
  +   2 8 8
   5 15 9 8
```

- Tell pupils that there are at least two mistakes in the way that the calculation has been carried out. Ask pupils to work in pairs to spot the mistakes and to find the correct answer.
- Ask pupils to think of other mistakes that someone might make, or that they know they sometimes make when using the column method for addition. Record these on the board. Use the information offered to address mistakes and misconceptions and to ensure that all pupils can fluently use the column method for addition.
- Draw particular attention to the way in which the numbers are aligned. When working with integers, it is enough to line up the 'right-hand digit' but, when working with decimal numbers the decimal points must be aligned.
- Ask pupils to now show a correct method on their whiteboards for 3718 + 288 using column addition. Gather and discuss responses.

- Next, show pupils 371.8 + 28.8 and model this using column addition, drawing pupils' attention to the way in which the decimal points are aligned.
- Write on the board 37.18 + 2.88 and ask pupils to show how they would calculate this using column addition. Again, gather and discuss results as appropriate.
- Now ask pupils to calculate 37.18 + 28.8. Gather their responses and draw their attention to the way that the decimal points should be aligned. Explain that they might like to rewrite 28.8 as 28.80 to help with this alignment.
- Pupils should complete Question 2 in the Practice Book.

Same-day intervention

- Use a place value chart to model column addition with decimals. Ensure that, as you work with the counters, you also record those moves in the columns. Start with numbers that require no carrying – for example, 3.14 + 1.82 will build like this:

- Now repeat this with numbers where a digit needs to be 'carried'. A next step might be, for example, 3.14 + 1.93, and then moving to 3.14 + 7.96.
- When working with the counters and grids, ensure that you are making explicit the connection between the manipulative and the notation, adding counters to the 0.01s column first and working to the left.
- If appropriate, you might like to set up a number in the grid, and then to add to it, asking pupils to record what you are doing using the column method as you are moving the counters.

Chapter 6 Addition and subtraction of decimal numbers Unit 6.3 Practice Book 5B, pages 9–11

- You might, for example, make this sequence and ask pupils to record the calculation and the steps on their whiteboards using the column method:

10	1	0.1	0.01
●●	●●●	●●	
		●●●●	●

10	1	0.1	0.01
●●	●●●	●●	
		●●●●	●
		○○	
		○○	

10	1	0.1	0.01
●●	●●●	●●	
	●		●

10	1	0.1	0.01
●●	●●●	●●	
	●●●		●

- Pupils should record something like this:

```
  3 . 5 3      3 . 5 3      3 . 5 3
+     . 5 0  +   3 . 5 0  +   3 . 5 0
              ─────────    ─────────
                  . 0 3        7 . 0 3
                  1            1
```

- Ensure that pupils spend time working both with and without the place value charts to encourage them to move to efficient use of the column method.

Same-day enrichment

- Pupils work on **Resource 5.6.3c** Correct the mistake in which they are asked to identify and correct a mistake in an addition calculation.

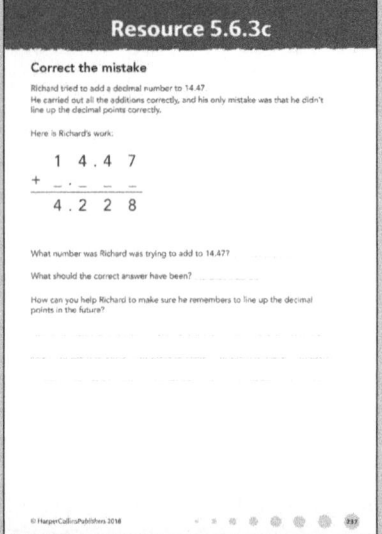

- Pupils should find that the number added is 2.781 (since 1447 + 2781 = 4228), meaning that the intended calculation is 14.47 + 2.781 which gives a correct answer of 17.251.

Question 3

3 Use decimals to calculate the answers.
(a) 6 pounds 93 pence + 57 pence =
(b) 340 cm + 1 m 15 cm =
(c) 20 ml + 9 l =
(d) 4 km 200 m + 900 m =
(e) $\frac{3}{10} + \frac{7}{10} =$
(f) $\frac{309}{1000} + \frac{276}{1000} =$

Chapter 6 Addition and subtraction of decimal numbers

Unit 6.3 Practice Book 5B, pages 9–11

What learning will pupils have achieved at the conclusion of Question 3?

- Pupils will have related mental strategies for adding integers to adding decimal numbers.
- Pupils will be able to convert quantities to the same unit.
- Pupils will be able to use their understanding of addition of decimals to combine quantities appropriately.

Activities for whole-class instruction

- Key to success in this task is pupils' understanding that converting quantities to the same unit is an essential part of the process when solving problems with units of measurement. Pupils should also be encouraged to choose the most convenient unit for them to work with and, on reaching a solution, to reflect on whether they made the correct choice.
- Show pupils the following table and explain that this shows the mass of some boxes in a delivery office.

	Kilograms	Grams	Kilograms and grams
Box A	4.817 kg	4817 g	4 kg and 817 g
Box B	3.992 kg	3992 g	
Box C			15 kg and 130 g
Box D	26.45 kg		
Box E			30 kg and 15 grams
Box F		31005 g	

- Together, complete the table, writing each mass in three different ways.
- Tell pupils that Box A and B are put on the scales together. Ask pairs of pupils to find the total mass of A and B and to write their answers on their mini whiteboards.
- Discuss with pupils who used different representations why they made that choice. For example, ask why pupils chose to add the masses given in kg or why they chose to add masses given in grams. Agree with pupils that, as long as the quantities are measured in the same units, it doesn't matter which units they use.
- Now tell pupils that Box C is added to the scales along with Boxes A and B. Ask: *What is the total mass?* Discuss solutions and address misconceptions and mistakes.
- Pupils should complete Question 3 in the Practice Book.

Same-day intervention

- Parts (a)–(d) in Question 3 require a conversion of units and then an addition calculation.
- Pupils should use place value sliders to support them in converting the units and place value charts to support them with the addition.
- Pupils should work in pairs – one working with a slider and one with a chart to answer the first question in **Resource 5.6.3d** Measuring rods – addition. They then swap for the second question.

Answers: The total length of the rods is either 270 cm + 225 cm or 2 m 70 cm + 2 m 25 cm. Adding these together gives 495 cm or 4 m 95 cm; The total length of the rods is either 165 cm + 90 cm or 1 m 65 cm + 0 m 90 cm. Adding these together gives 255 cm or 2 m 55 cm; The total length of the rods is either 310 cm + 150 cm or 3 m 10 cm + 1 m 50 cm. Adding these together gives 460 cm or 4 m 60 cm.

Same-day enrichment

- Show pupils a different and more unusual way to describe a quantity. For example, 4.817 kg could be described as '17 grams more than 4.8 kg'.
- Ask pupils to find as many different (and strange) ways to describe 18.994 kg.
- Discuss ideas and emphasise how different representations can show the same quantity but written in different ways.

Chapter 6 Addition and subtraction of decimal numbers Unit 6.3 Practice Book 5B, pages 9–11

Question 4

> 4 Write the number sentences and then calculate.
> (a) What number is 8.44 greater than 6?
>
>   Number sentence: _____
>
>   Answer: _____
>
> (b) What number is 100 more than the sum of one hundred 0.759s?
>
>   Number sentence: _____
>
>   Answer: _____
>
> (c) 0.03 is first multiplied by 1000 and then 69.33 is added. What is the result?
>
>   Number sentence: _____
>
>   Answer: _____

What learning will pupils have achieved at the conclusion of Question 4?

- Pupils will have related mental strategies for adding integers to adding decimal numbers.
- Pupils will be able to use their understanding of addition of decimals to combine quantities appropriately.
- Pupils will be able to use number sentences including decimals to describe situations.

Activities for whole-class instruction

- Write these calculations on the board:

    A: (3.7 + 2.3) × 10

    B: 3.7 + 2.3 × 10

- Ask: *What is the result when the sum of 3.7 and 2.3 is multiplied by 10?* Ask which of the number sentences fits the question. Give them time to discuss, then gather responses.

- Ask pupils to now work in pairs to write on their mini whiteboards a question (in words) that fits number sentence B. Gather responses and write some on the board. Draw pupils' attention to the way that there are different ways to describe the same calculation.

- Now ask pupils to write a different question that would be represented by number sentence A and, again, gather responses and compare the different words and phrases used to describe the same operations.

- Pupils should complete Question 4 in the Practice Book.

Same-day intervention

- Work with pupils to identify words that can represent the addition operation. Your list is likely to include:
    - plus
    - add
    - added to
    - (in) total
    - sum
    - more than
    - greater than
    - extra

- Now work with pupils to find as many different ways of writing the calculation 4.17 + 3.24 as possible. The intention here is to explore different 'stories' that can all be represented by one calculation rather than to build up a 'word bank' for addition.

- Ensure that all the different stories are correctly describing the addition operation, then give pupils a set of word problems and possible number sentences to go with them.

- Ask pupils to decide if the number sentence is the correct one and, if not, to write a correct version.

	Number sentence
What number is the sum of 3.7 and 2.6?	3.7 + 2.6
What number is 10 times greater than 0.7 added to 5.1?	0.7 + 5.1 × 10
0.15 is multiplied by 10 and the result is then added on to 4.3. What is the result?	0.15 × 10 + 4.3
2.8 is multiplied by 10 and 3.08 is multiplied by 100. What is the sum of the two answers?	2.8 × 10 + 3.08 × 100

Chapter 6 Addition and subtraction of decimal numbers Unit 6.3 Practice Book 5B, pages 9–11

Same-day enrichment

- Ask pupils to work in pairs. Give each pupil a sheet of A4 paper, which they should fold into eight equal pieces.

What is 3.8 more than 5.03?	4.41
What is the sum of 3.1 lots of 10 and 4.1 lots of 100?	1.12
One tenth of 4.2 is added to 10 lots of 0.07. What is the total?	8.11
10 lots of 0.8 are added to 0.11. What is the total?	8.83

- They should then write a word problem about adding decimals on four of the sections, and the answers to their questions on the other four sections (as above).
- Pupils should now tear or cut their paper into sections and give them to their partner to match the questions and solutions.

Challenge and extension questions

Question 5

> 5. A construction team is building a canal. In the first week, they build 1.3 km of the canal. In the second week, they build 0.15 km more than in the first week. There is still 1.05 km of the canal to complete. What will the total length of the canal be?

Although the calculation isn't any more challenging than others already tackled in this unit, this question adds complexity to addition of decimal numbers as pupils need to interpret the word problem. Encouraging pupils to sketch a diagram to support their route through the problem may help them in interpreting and accessing the question.

Question 6

> 6. Three identical paper strips are pasted together in a line. Each strip of paper is 80 cm long and the overlapping sections where the pairs of pieces are joined are 0.3 cm long. Find the total length of the paper formed by the three strips pasted together.

In this question, the calculation is also accessible, but picturing the way in which the overlap impacts on the total length adds complexity. Encouraging pupils to sketch and label a diagram will support them in finding a route through the question and structuring their solution.

Chapter 6 Addition and subtraction of decimal numbers

Unit 6.4
Subtraction of decimals

Conceptual context

This unit, about subtraction of decimals, echoes the structure and imagery used in the previous unit about addition of decimals.

Learning pupils will have achieved at the end of the unit

- Pupils will have related mental strategies for subtracting integers to subtracting decimal numbers (Q1, Q2)
- Pupils will be able to convert quantities to the same unit (Q3)
- Pupils will be able to use their understanding of subtraction of decimals to calculate correctly (Q3, Q4)
- Pupils will be able to use number sentences including decimals to describe situations (Q4)

Resources

place value charts; counters; mini whiteboards; **Resource 5.6.1a** Place value slider; **Resource 5.6.4a** Subtracting decimals; **Resource 5.6.4b** Make the subtraction …; **Resource 5.6.4c** Measuring rods – subtraction

Vocabulary

subtract, minuend, decimal point, column method, decomposition

Chapter 6 Addition and subtraction of decimal numbers　　Unit 6.4 Practice Book 5B, pages 12–14

Question 1

> **1** Calculate mentally and then write the answers.
>
> (a) 0.9 − 0.8 = ☐   (b) 0.09 − 0.05 = ☐
> (c) 0.007 − 0.003 = ☐   (d) 7.8 − 2.8 = ☐
> (e) 1 − 0.6 = ☐   (f) 3.6 − 1.8 = ☐
> (g) 5.4 − 0.6 = ☐   (h) 1 − 0.06 = ☐
> (i) 5.2 − 2.6 = ☐   (j) 8 − 2.5 = ☐
> (k) 1 − 0.01 = ☐   (l) 1.1 − 0.04 = ☐

What learning will pupils have achieved at the conclusion of Question 1?

- Pupils will have related mental strategies for subtracting integers to subtracting decimal numbers.

Activities for whole-class instruction

- Write a simple decimal subtraction on the board. The addition used in the previous unit was 3.1 + 1.5 = 4.6 and, if appropriate, you might like to use 4.6 − 3.1 = to stress the link between the two units. Ask pupils to discuss and describe, in pairs, how they calculated the answer mentally.

- Now write 46 − 31 on the board and again ask pupils to discuss and describe how they calculated the answer mentally. Gather pupils' responses and draw parallels between the strategies they used for subtraction of decimals and strategies used when subtracting integers. Agree with pupils that the same strategies can be used for both integer and decimal numbers.

- Write 4.8 − 1.9 on the board and ask pupils what strategies they used to calculate the answer. Again, draw attention to the parallels between decimal and integer subtraction.

- Now write the following on the board:

  A: 11.3 − 1.2

  B: 11.3 − 1.12

- Ask pupils to calculate an answer to both of these calculations, and again to discuss their strategies. Draw attention to the possible pitfalls of using integer equivalents when calculating with decimals – particularly look out for pupils calculating part B in the same way that they would 113 − 112, and so not using the correct integer equivalent calculation.

- The intention of this task is to encourage pupils to use familiar strategies and contexts (integers) and to connect these with contexts that they may be less comfortable with (decimal numbers).

- Draw pupils' attention to the way in which subtraction with decimals is similar to subtraction with integers, and that the strategies they already have for integers can also be used for decimals.

- Pupils should complete Question 1 in the Practice Book.

Same-day intervention

- Use **Resource 5.6.4a** Subtracting decimals to work with pupils to support them in connecting integer subtraction with subtraction of decimals.

  > **Resource 5.6.4a**
  > Subtracting decimals
  >
  > 7 − 2 = ___　　0.7 − 0.2 = ___
  > 17 − 2 = ___　　1.7 − 0.2 = ___
  > 17 − 32 = ___　　1.7 − 3.2 = ___
  > 19 − 5 = ___　　1.9 − 0.5 = ___
  > 19 − 35 = ___　　1.9 − 3.5 = ___
  > 27 − 6 = ___　　2.7 − 0.6 = ___
  > 27 − 7 = ___　　2.7 − 0.7 = ___
  > 27 − 9 = ___　　2.7 − 0.9 = ___
  > 31 − 13 = ___　　3.1 − 1.3 = ___

- Draw pupils' attention to the way in which strategies for integer subtraction can be used to subtract decimals. This task is not about identifying a formal process (for example, multiply the decimal by 10 to turn them into integers, subtract and then divide by 10) but is about noticing and using an informal method to support understanding of subtracting with decimal numbers.

  Answers: 5, 0.5; 15, 1.5; −15, −1.5; 14, 1.4; −16, −1.6; 21, 2.1; 20, 2.0; 18, 1.8; 18, 1.8

Chapter 6 Addition and subtraction of decimal numbers

Unit 6.4 Practice Book 5B, pages 12–14

Same-day enrichment

- Give pupils **Resource 5.6.4b** Make the subtraction ... in which they are asked to construct and calculate decimal subtractions.

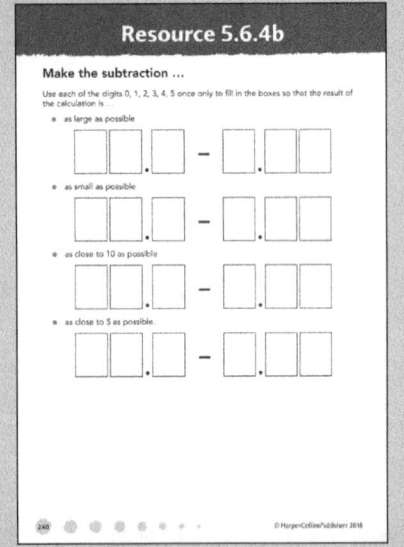

Answers: 54.3 – 0.12; 01.2 – 5.43; 13.0 – 2.54; 5.24 – 0.31 or 5.31 – 0.24

Question 2

2. Choose the most appropriate method, mental or written, to find the answer to each calculation. The first one has been done for you. (Check the answers to the questions marked with * using a different method.)

(a) 30.74 – 11.32 = 19.42

```
  3 0 . 7 4
- 1 1 . 3 2
  1 9 . 4 2
```

(b) *21.1 – 8.57 =

(c) 60 – 6.07 =

(d) 27.4 – 18.09 =

(e) 60.3 – 13.55 =

(f) *87.5 – 1.01 =

What learning will pupils have achieved at the conclusion of Question 2?

- Pupils will have related mental strategies for subtracting integers to subtracting decimal numbers.

Activities for whole-class instruction

- Write the following calculation on the board:

```
  3 8 2 1
-   3 1 4
  0 7 2 1
```

- Tell pupils that there are at least two mistakes in the way the calculation has been carried out. Ask pupils to work in pairs to spot the mistakes and to find the correct answer.
- Ask pupils to think of other mistakes that someone might make, or that they know that they sometimes make when using the column method for subtraction and record these on the board. Use the information offered to address mistakes and misconceptions and to ensure that all pupils can fluently use the column method for subtraction.
- Draw particular attention to the way in which the decimal points must be aligned. When using the column method with integers, this is achieved by lining up the 'right-hand digit' but, when working with decimals, the decimal points must be aligned.
- Ask pupils to now show a correct method on their whiteboards for 3821 – 314 using column subtraction. Gather and discuss responses
- Next, show pupils 338.21 – 3.14 and model this using column addition, drawing pupils' attention to the way in which the decimal points are aligned.
- Write on the board 3.821 – 0.314 and ask pupils to show how they would calculate this using column subtraction. Again, gather and discuss results as appropriate.
- Now ask pupils to calculate 38.21 – 31.4. Gather their responses and draw their attention to the way that the decimal points should be aligned. Explain that they might like to rewrite 31.4 as 31.40 to help with this alignment.
- Pupils should complete Question 2 in the Practice Book.

Same-day intervention

- Use a place value chart and counters to model column subtraction.
- Ensure that, as you move the counters, you also record those moves in the columns on the chart.
- Start with numbers that do not require regrouping – for example, 3.85 – 1.34 will build like this:

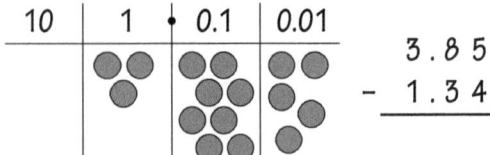

Chapter 6 Addition and subtraction of decimal numbers

Unit 6.4 Practice Book 5B, pages 12–14

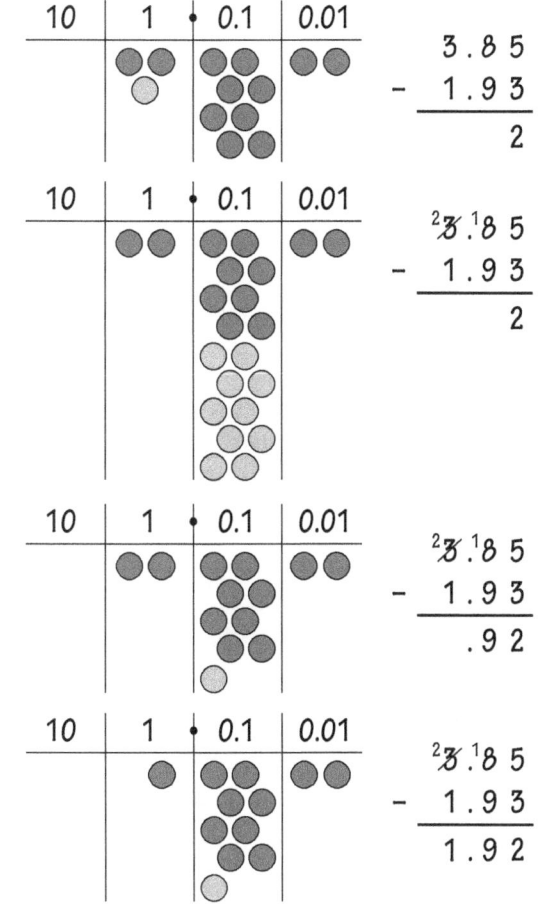

- Now repeat this with numbers that do need regrouping. A next step might be, for example, 3.85 − 1.93, and model the regrouping.

- If necessary, model a calculation with further regrouping, such as to 3.85 − 1.97.
- When working with the counters and the grids, ensure you are making explicit the connection between the materials you are using and the notation that you are recording.

Same-day enrichment

- Present pupils with the following statement:
  - When setting up a column subtraction, the last digit of each of the numbers must be in the same column.
- Ask them to decide whether the statement is always, sometimes or never true.
- If always or never, they should explain how they can be so sure. If sometimes, they should give at least one example of a case when it is true, and one when it is not.

Question 3

3 Use decimals to calculate the answers.
(a) 10 pounds 38 pence − 2 pounds 46 pence =
(b) 9 km − 4 km 140 m =
(c) $\frac{303}{1000} - \frac{28}{1000} =$
(d) 2 l 20 ml − 1 l 600 ml =
(e) $\frac{84}{100} - \frac{19}{100} - \frac{13}{100} =$

What learning will pupils have achieved at the conclusion of Question 3?

- Pupils will be able to convert quantities to the same unit.
- Pupils will be able to use their understanding of subtraction of decimals to calculate correctly.

Activities for whole-class instruction

- Write a distance on the board, for example 374 metres. Ask pupils to work on their mini whiteboards to write the distance in as many different ways as possible, then gather in their responses. You might need to prompt them to think of centimetres or kilometres, or to write the distance in words.

Chapter 6 Addition and subtraction of decimal numbers Unit 6.4 Practice Book 5B, pages 12–14

- Once you have a selection of responses, change the distance slightly by adding a decimal part to it, writing 374.75 m, and ask pupils what impact this makes on each of the representations you have gathered on the whiteboards.
- Ensure that pupils are aware that the way these distances are written might look different, but they have the same value.
- Write the calculation 3.3 m – 120 cm and ask pupil pairs to discuss how they would calculate an answer. Gather responses and agree with pupils that, when subtracting quantities, it is usually easier if the quantities are recorded in the same units. Remind them of the importance of correctly aligning the decimal points.
- On the board, write: 133 metres and 20 centimetres. Ask pupils how much longer 374.75 m is than 133 m 20 cm. Discuss with pupils which operation to use and which way of writing the two distances makes the calculation easier.
- Invite pupils to show their working using the column method on the board (or using a visualiser).
- Agree with pupils that, as long as both distances are measured in the same units, it doesn't matter which units they use.
- Pupils should complete Question 3 in the Practice Book.

Same-day intervention

- Each calculation in Question 3 requires a conversion then a subtraction.
- Pupils should use place value sliders (see **Resource 5.6.1a** Place value slider) to support them in converting the units and place value charts to support them in carrying out the subtraction.

- Pupils should work in pairs – one working with a slider and one with a chart to answer the first question on **Resource 5.6.4c** Measuring rods – subtraction. They then swap for the second question.

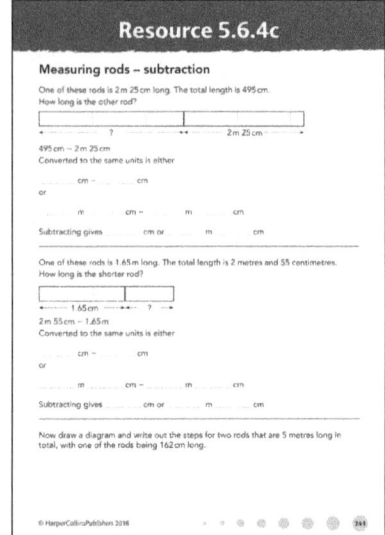

Answers: The length of the other rod is either 495 cm – 225 cm or 4 m 95 cm – 2 m 25 cm. Subtracting gives 270 cm or 2 m 70 cm; The length of the other rod is either 255 cm – 165 cm or 2 m 55 cm – 1 m 65 cm. Subtracting gives 90 cm or 0 m 90 cm; The length of the other rod is either 500 cm – 162 cm or 5 m 0 cm – 1 m 62 cm. Subtracting gives 338 cm or 3 m 38 cm.

Same-day enrichment

- Ask pupils to look at Question 3a in the Practice Book:
  10 pounds 38 pence – 2 pounds 46 pence
- Ask pupils to find a way to make £10.38 that uses the fewest coins or notes, but such that exactly £2.46 can be taken from it without having to change any of the coins.
- Also ask them to consider the way that uses the most coins or notes. This task is intended to encourage pupils to view the quantity in multiple ways, and to encourage efficiency and flexibility in calculation.

Chapter 6 Addition and subtraction of decimal numbers
Unit 6.4 Practice Book 5B, pages 12–14

Question 4

> 4 Write the number sentences and then calculate.
>
> (a) One tenth of 0.8 is subtracted from 0.8. What is the difference?
>
> Number sentence: _____
>
> Answer: _____
>
> (b) The quotient of 21.9 divided by 10 is added to the difference between 0.58 and 0.25. What is the sum?
>
> Number sentence: _____
>
> Answer: _____

What learning will pupils have achieved at the conclusion of Question 4?

- Pupils will be able to use their understanding of subtraction of decimals to calculate correctly.
- Pupils will be able to use number sentences including decimals to describe situations.

Activities for whole-class instruction

- Write the following number sentence on the board: $10 \times 2.08 - 1.7$.
- Display these questions:
    a. Which number is 1.7 less than 10 lots of 2.08?
    b. What is the result if 2.08 lots of 10 are calculated and then 1.7 is subtracted from the answer?
    c. What is the result if the difference between 2.08 and 1.7 is found, and the answer is then multiplied by 10?
    d. What is the difference between 1.7 and 10 multiplied by 2.08?
- Ask: *Which of these statements describes the number sentence?* Pupils should discuss in pairs. Share ideas, paying particular attention to the order of operations and to the different images the vocabulary implies (for example, the image of subtraction as a 'difference', and the image of subtraction as a 'take').
- The focus of this task is not the result of the calculation, but rather the different ways in which a number sentence can be described. Avoid asking pupils to evaluate the number sentence, at least until you have gathered in pupils' suggestions, as this numerical answer may become the focus rather than the intended objective.
- Pupils should complete Question 4 in the Practice Book.

Same-day intervention

- Work with pupils to identify words that can be used to represent subtraction. Your list is likely to include:
    - take
    - take away
    - less than
    - subtract
    - decrease
    - fewer
    - minus
    - difference
    - how many more is … than …
- Now work with pupils to find as many different ways of writing the calculation $10.81 - 1.26 = \square$ as possible. The intention here is to explore different 'stories' that can all be represented by one calculation rather than to build up a 'word bank'.
- Ensure that all the different stories are correctly describing the subtraction, then give pupils a set of word problems and possible number sentences to go with them. Ask pupils to decide if the number sentence is the correct one and, if not, to write a correct version.

	Number sentence
What number is 7.2 less than 9.15?	$9.15 - 7.2$
0.15 is subtracted from 8.19 ten times. What is the result?	$0.15 \times 10 - 8.19$
How much more is 10 lots of 3.16 than 100 lots of 0.17?	$10 \times 3.16 - 100 \times 0.17$
What number is 10 times the difference between 3.17 and 1.2?	$10 \times (3.17 - 1.2)$

Same-day enrichment

- Challenge pupils to rewrite Q4 parts (a) and (b) so the calculation and result are the same, but the question is worded differently. They should aim to make their version look as different from the original as they can.
- For example, part (a) might be: 0.8 is divided by 10. How much smaller is the result of this division than the original number?

Chapter 6 Addition and subtraction of decimal numbers

Unit 6.4 Practice Book 5B, pages 12–14

Challenge and extension questions

Question 5

5 When working on a subtraction sentence, Aiden misread 9 as 6 in the ones place in the minuend and 8 as 2 in the tenths place. He got a result of 3.6. What is the correct answer?

Although the calculation is relatively straightforward, requiring only the addition and subtraction of numbers with one decimal place, identifying the calculations that need to be carried out requires careful reading. Encourage pupils to sketch or to make rough notes as they make sense of the question and find their route through it.

Question 6

6 Bob planned to drive from Place A to Place B, which were 210.8 km apart. After he had travelled 66.8 km, he realised that he had left something important at Place A. He drove back to Place A to get the item and then continued his journey to Place B. How many more kilometres did he drive than he had originally planned?

Encouraging pupils to sketch a diagram may support them in working on this question, which can be carried out by working out the total distance that Bob travelled and then subtracting, but a more elegant and efficient strategy is to identify that the extra distance is the distance from 66.8 km home and back to that point, so the answer can be found by doubling this value. Encourage pupils to discuss their strategies for finding a solution and to consider the most efficient way to reach the correct answer.

Chapter 6 Addition and subtraction of decimal numbers

Unit 6.5
Addition and subtraction of decimals (1)

Conceptual context

Having been introduced to addition and subtraction of decimals in the previous two units, this and the following unit now focus on building fluency, working with both operations. Pupils should be supported with place value charts and other manipulatives where appropriate.

Learning pupils will have achieved at the end of the unit

- Pupils will be more fluent with mental calculation strategies when adding and subtracting decimals (Q1, Q2)
- Pupils will be able to use number bonds to calculate smartly with decimals (Q1, Q2)
- Pupils will be able to interpret and represent written problems using mathematical notation (Q3, Q4)

Resources

place value charts; counters; mini whiteboards; **Resource 5.6.5a** Decimal addogons; **Resource 5.6.5b** Makes 1 maze; **Resource 5.6.5c** Missing operations; **Resource 5.6.5d** Decimal addition and subtraction match (1); **Resource 5.6.5e** Decimal number boxes

Vocabulary

subtract, subtrahend, decimal point, difference, perimeter

Chapter 6 Addition and subtraction of decimal numbers

Unit 6.5 Practice Book 5B, pages 15–17

Question 1

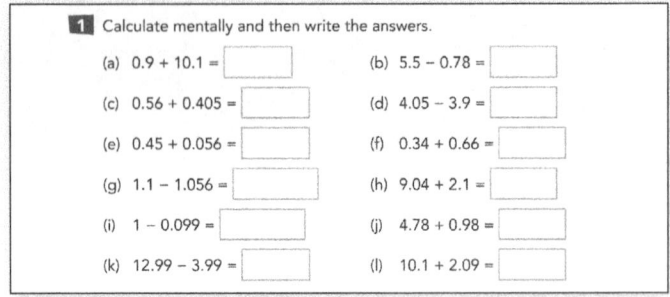

What learning will pupils have achieved at the conclusion of Question 1?

- Pupils will be more fluent with mental calculation strategies when adding and subtracting decimals.
- Pupils will be able to use number bonds to calculate smartly with decimals.

Activities for whole-class instruction

- Draw this bar model:

6.87	
2.31	4.56

- Ask pupils, working in pairs, to describe to each other where in the diagram they can see the following calculations:

2.31 + 4.56 = 6.87

4.56 + 2.31 = 6.87

6.87 − 4.56 = 2.31

6.87 − 2.31 = 4.56

- Now give pupils a second bar model:

17.71	
4.43	13.28

- Ask them to write down four calculations that this might help them with.
- Finally, draw this bar model and ask pupils to calculate the missing length, and to write down any other calculations they can see in the diagram.

10.2 m	
4.63 m	

- After each task, ask pupils to explain each image and how they carried out the calculation. Ensure that they see the relationship between addition and subtraction.
- The intention here is to support pupils in understanding that the relationships as explored when adding and subtracting integers are still true when decimals are used. This is a step towards pupils generalising additive relationships.
- You might like to keep these images on the board to use in preparation for Question 3.
- Pupils should complete Question 1 in the Practice Book.

Same-day intervention

- Use two place value charts simultaneously. Use counters to model two additions or subtractions on the place value charts. Start with 17 + 42 and 1.7 + 4.2 (since these calculations do not require any 'carrying') or, if subtracting, with 29 − 15 and 2.9 − 1.5. Then, when pupils are confident with this type of calculation, introduce carrying or regrouping in one digit, before moving on to a set of numbers that requires more manipulation.
- The intention of this modelling is not to focus on the addition or subtraction strategies (since these are mental strategies at this stage) but to focus on the parallels between integer addition and decimal addition – the generality of the process.

Same-day enrichment

- Give pupils **Resource 5.6.5a** Decimal addogons to work on.

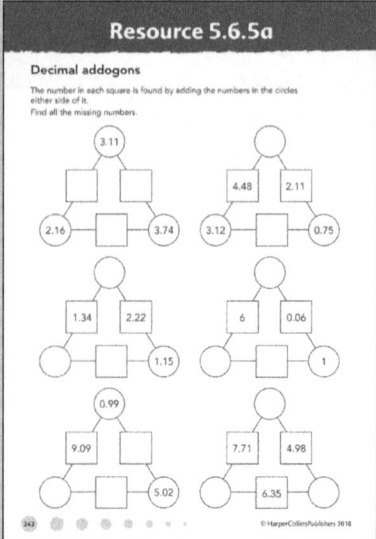

Answers: 5.27, 6.85, 5.90; 1.36 3.87; 1.07, 0.27, 1.42; −0.94, 6.94, 7.94; 6.01, 8.1 13.12; 3.17, 4.54 1.81

Chapter 6 Addition and subtraction of decimal numbers

Unit 6.5 Practice Book 5B, pages 15–17

Question 2

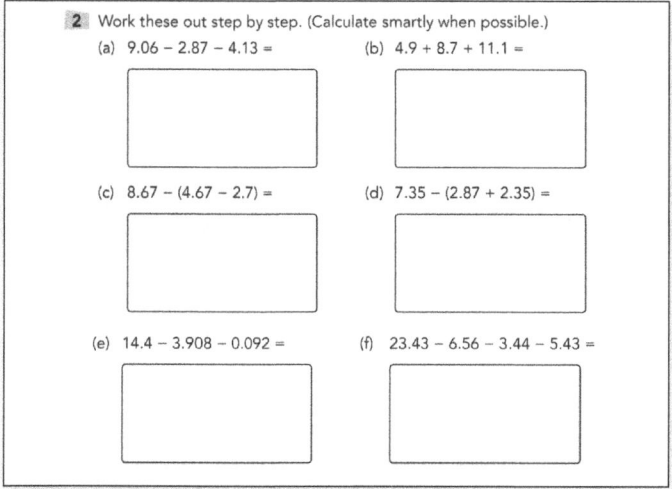

What learning will pupils have achieved at the conclusion of Question 2?

- Pupils will be more fluent with mental calculation strategies when adding and subtracting decimals.
- Pupils will be able to use number bonds to calculate smartly with decimals.

Activities for whole-class instruction

- Show pupils the following image:

0.01	0.02	0.03	0.04	0.05	0.06	0.07	0.08	0.09	0.1
0.11	0.12	0.13	0.14	0.15	0.16	0.17	0.18	0.19	0.2
0.21	0.22	0.23	0.24	0.25	0.26	0.27	0.28	0.29	0.3
0.31	0.32	0.33	0.34	0.35	0.36	0.37	0.38	0.39	0.4
0.41	0.42	0.43	0.44	0.45	0.46	0.47	0.48	0.49	0.5
0.51	0.52	0.53	0.54	0.55	0.56	0.57	0.58	0.59	0.6
0.61	0.62	0.63	0.64	0.65	0.66	0.67	0.68	0.69	0.7
0.71	0.72	0.73	0.74	0.75	0.76	0.77	0.78	0.79	0.8
0.81	0.82	0.83	0.84	0.85	0.86	0.87	0.88	0.89	0.9
0.91	0.92	0.93	0.94	0.95	0.96	0.97	0.98	0.99	1

- Tell pupils that you will tap on a number in the square and that they have to say how many they need to add to reach the end of the row. For example, if you tap on 0.47 they should say '0.03'; if you tap on 0.72 they should say '0.08', and so on.

- Make sure some of the numbers you choose lead to practice of number bonds and explicitly draw attention to these. For example, you might choose to tap 0.52, 0.62, 0.82 and 0.02 as a sequence, or tap pairs such as 0.57 and 0.53, 0.74 and 0.76 or 0.01 and 0.09, and make explicit the symmetries in the calculations.

- You might like to rehearse this (and the following) on a normal integer 100 square before moving on to the decimal 100 square to support pupils in making the links between decimal and integer addition and subtraction.

- Once you are confident that pupils understand the structure of the square and are able to identify the number to reach the end of the row, tell them that you will now tap one of the numbers in the right-hand column, and that they should tell you what needs to be added to reach the bottom right square.

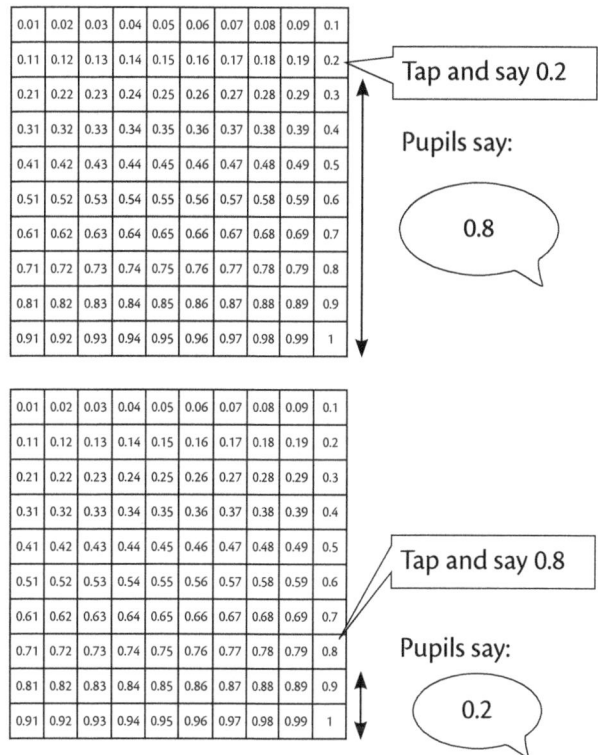

- Finally, tell pupils that you will now tap a number and they should say the number that needs to be added to reach the bottom right-hand square. You might like to support them in structuring this by thinking about getting from your number to the right-hand column, and then from the right-hand column to the bottom right-hand square.

Chapter 6 Addition and subtraction of decimal numbers

Unit 6.5 Practice Book 5B, pages 15–17

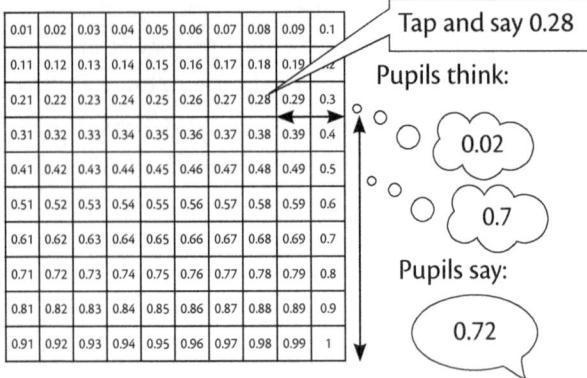

- The intention of the task is to support pupils in becoming fluent with decimal number bonds and so support them in 'calculating smartly'.
- Pupils should complete Question 2 in the Practice Book.

Same-day intervention

- Give pupils **Resource 5.6.5b** Makes 1 maze in which they are asked to find a route through a maze by spotting decimal number bonds to 1. (The answer is shown below.)

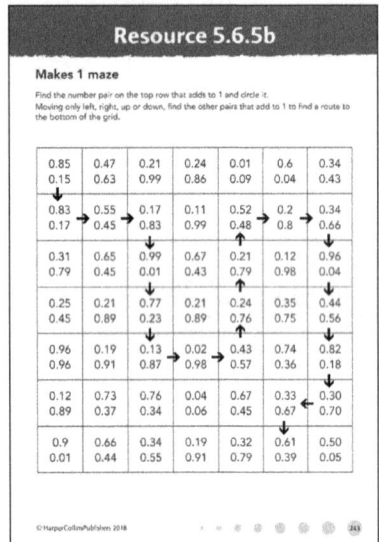

- To support pupils in making sense of the calculations in Question 2, use a bar model to represent each stage or the whole calculation as appropriate.
- For example, Questions 2(a) and (b) can be represented as:

9.06		
?	4.13	2.87

	?	
4.9	8.7	11.1

- Use the bar model to support pupils in calculating smartly, looking particularly for decimal parts of numbers that add to 1.
- Where a question has several parts, work with pupils to sequence the parts and use a bar model to solve them.

Same-day enrichment

- Give pupils **Resource 5.6.5c** Missing operations in which they are asked to identify the operations that have been used in addition and subtraction calculations.

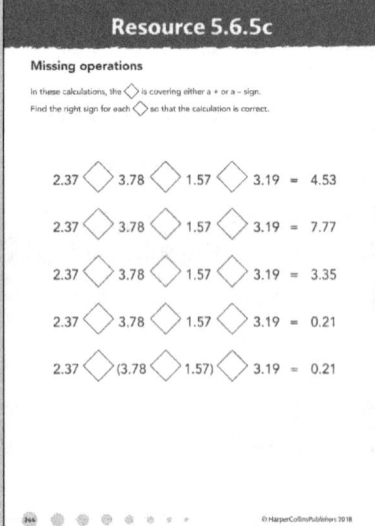

- Explain to pupils that the ◇ symbol represents either a + or a − sign, and that they should rewrite each calculation correctly to give the required answer.
- Challenge pupils to explain (maybe by representing in a diagram) why the last two calculations look different but give the same answer.

Answers: +, +, −; +, −, +; −, +, +; −, −, +; −, +, +

Chapter 6 Addition and subtraction of decimal numbers

Unit 6.5 Practice Book 5B, pages 15–17

Questions 3 and 4

> **3** Write the number sentences and then calculate.
>
> (a) The sum of Number A and Number B is 63.5. Number A is 24.5. What is Number B?
>
> Number sentence: _____
>
> Answer: _____
>
> (b) Number A is 30.52, which is 8.8 greater than Number B. What is the sum of Number A and Number B?
>
> Number sentence: _____
>
> Answer: _____
>
> (c) Number A is 42.62. Number B is half of Number A. Number C is 2.8 greater than Number B. What is Number C?
>
> Number sentence: _____
>
> Answer: _____
>
> **4** Sue wants to buy two antique vases from a second hand shop, one for £41.80 and the other for £38.20. She pays the shopkeeper £100. How much change should she get?

What learning will pupils have achieved at the conclusion of Questions 3 and 4?

- Pupils will be able to interpret and represent written problems using mathematical notation.

Activities for whole-class instruction

- Use bar models, and write the calculation being represented. For example, write 2.31 + 4.56 = 6.87 and draw:

6.87	
2.31	4.56

- Ask pupils to work in pairs to write a one or two sentence 'story' that the image and symbols could be describing. Gather some of the stories in and collect the different words and ways in which the calculation can be described.

- Next, use the same image but a different calculation that it might be describing, such as 6.87 − 4.56 = 2.31, and ask pupils to write a story to represent it. Again, gather the stories and discuss the different representations. Also, compare the two different ways of viewing the same image that the different sets of stories express.

- Present the following scenario:
  - Sarah and Matilda have some money. Matilda has £2.45 and Sarah has 17p more. How much do Sarah and Matilda have in total?

- Ask pupils to represent this story on mini whiteboards using a bar model. One pair should work on the main board at the front of the class.

- Use the diagrams on the main board as a discussion point to agree how the story described can be represented, and how this representation might help in 'calculating smartly'.

- Pupils should complete Questions 3 and 4 in the Practice Book.

Same-day intervention

- Work with pupils to use **Resource 5.6.5d** Decimal addition and subtraction match (1) to match the stories, the calculations and the bar image.

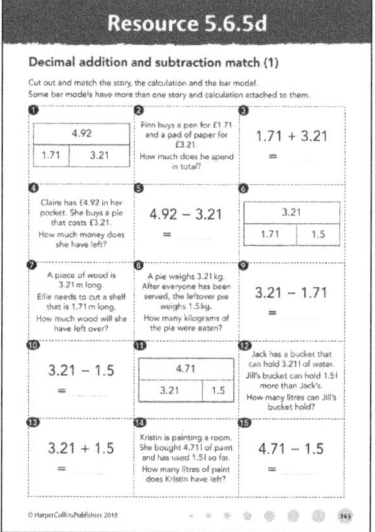

Answers: 2, 3, 1; 4, 5, 1; 7, 9, 6; 8, 10, 6; 12, 13, 11; 14, 15, 11

Chapter 6 Addition and subtraction of decimal numbers   Unit 6.5 Practice Book 5B, pages 15–17

Same-day enrichment

- Give pupils **Resource 5.6.5e** Decimal number boxes in which they need to use addition and subtraction of decimals, along with deductive reasoning, to solve a puzzle.

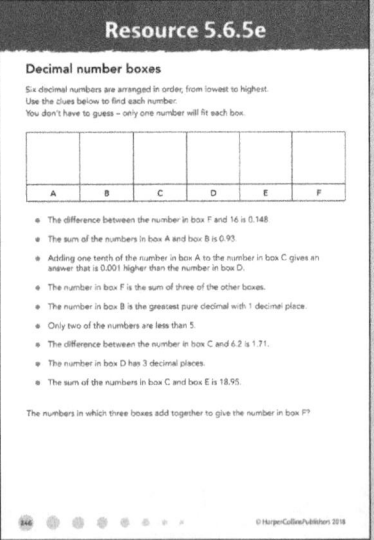

Answers: A is 0.03, B is 0.9, C is 7.91, D is 7.912, E is 11.04, F is 15.852. F is the sum of A, C and D.

- Pupils should find that the numbers are as shown below, and identify that the three numbers that add to give the value in box F are those in A, C and D.

  A: 0.03

  B: 0.9

  C: 7.91

  D: 7.912

  E: 11.04

  F: 15.852

Challenge and extension questions

Question 5

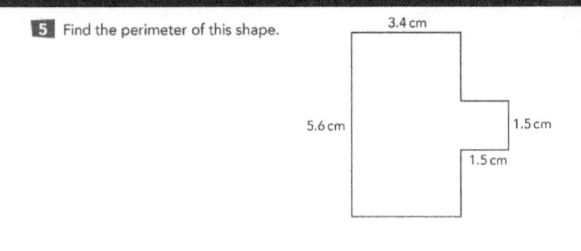

In finding the perimeter, pupils need to first identify lengths that have not been marked on the diagram. Suggest that pupils sketch a copy of the diagram. If asked, confirm that all angles in the diagram are 90°.

Question 6

6 Mum bought a school uniform for her daughter. She bought a blouse for £4.75, a pair of shoes for £23.80, a skirt for £10.25 and a jumper for £6.20. How much did she spend in total?

This question asks pupils to add decimals in the context of shopping. Pupils should spot that there are opportunities for them to calculate smartly.

Question 7

7 (a) A pupil was working on an addition problem. He was being a bit careless, and in one of the addends he misread 0 in the tenths place as 9 and got a sum of 16.98. What is the correct sum?

(b) When he was working on a subtraction problem, in the subtrahend he mistakenly wrote 5 in the hundredths place as 3. This gave a difference of 23.56. What is the correct difference?

Pupils may feel that there is not enough information available to answer this question. Key to accessing the question is to understand that the sum, in this case 16.98, is the result of the calculation and that this can be operated on without knowing the rest of the calculation. In the first instance, the misreading simply means that the given result is 0.9 too high (since the pupil misread 0 for 9 in the tenths column) and in the second calculation, the given result will be 0.02 too high. Give pupils time to work on the question – you might like to suggest that they write out what they can in the column method.

Chapter 6 Addition and subtraction of decimal numbers

Unit 6.6
Addition and subtraction of decimals (2)

Conceptual context

This unit continues from the previous unit, building fluency and working with both operations.

Learning pupils will have achieved at the end of the unit

- Pupils will be more fluent with mental calculation strategies when adding and subtracting decimals (Q1, Q2)
- Pupils will be able to use number bonds to calculate smartly with decimals (Q1, Q2)
- Pupils will be able to interpret and represent written problems using mathematical notation (Q3, Q4)

Resources

place value charts; counters; mini whiteboards; **Resource 5.6.6a** More decimal addogons; **Resource 5.6.6b** Makes 3 maze; **Resource 5.6.6c** Using bar models; **Resource 5.6.6d** More missing operations; **Resource 5.6.6e** Decimal addition and subtraction match (2); **Resource 5.6.6f** Missing digits

Vocabulary

subtract, product, decimal point, difference

Chapter 6 Addition and subtraction of decimal numbers   Unit 6.6 Practice Book 5B, pages 18–20

Question 1

1 Calculate mentally and then write the answers.

(a) 2.4 + 11.8 = ☐
(b) 2.5 + 0.57 = ☐
(c) 3.9 − 3 = ☐
(d) 2.8 − 0.28 = ☐
(e) 5.6 + 6.5 = ☐
(f) 13.3 − 0.8 = ☐
(g) 9 − 0.05 = ☐
(h) 1 − 0.999 = ☐
(i) 5.3 + 0.78 = ☐
(j) 10 − 0.42 = ☐
(k) 29 + 0.17 = ☐
(l) 0.06 − 0.023 = ☐

What learning will pupils have achieved at the conclusion of Question 1?

- Pupils will be more fluent with mental calculation strategies when adding and subtracting decimals.
- Pupils will be able to use number bonds to calculate smartly with decimals.

Activities for whole-class instruction

- Draw this bar model:

10.8	
3.28	7.52

- Ask pupils, working in pairs, to describe to each other where in the diagram they can see these calculations:

3.28 + 7.52 = 10.8
7.52 + 3.28 = 10.8
10.8 − 3.28 = 7.52
10.8 − 7.52 = 3.28

- Now give pupils a second bar model:

15	
4.87	10.13

- This time, ask pupils to write down four calculations that the bar model might help them with.
- Finally, draw this bar model and ask pupils to calculate the missing length, and to write down any other calculations they can see in the diagram.

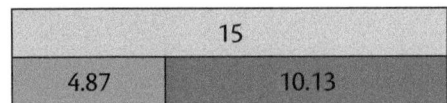

- After each task, ask pupils to explain each image and how they carried out the calculation. Ensure that they see the relationship between addition and subtraction.

- The intention here is to support pupils in understanding that the relationships as explored when adding and subtracting integers are still true when decimals are used. This is a step towards pupils generalising additive relationships.
- You might like to keep these images on the board to use in preparation for Question 3.
- Pupils should complete Question 1 in the Practice Book.

Same-day intervention

- Use two place value charts simultaneously. Use counters to model two additions or subtractions on the place value charts. Start with 32 + 41 and 3.2 + 4.1 (since these calculations do not require any 'carrying') or, if subtracting, with 98 − 31 and 9.8 − 3.1. Then, when pupils are confident with this type of calculation, introduce carrying or regrouping in one digit, before moving on to a set of numbers that require more manipulation.
- The intention of this modelling is not to focus on the addition or subtraction strategies (since these are mental strategies at this stage) but to focus on the parallels between integer addition and decimal addition – the generality of the process.

Same-day enrichment

- Give pupils **Resource 5.6.6a** More decimal addogons, which has a set of decimal addogons for pupils to work on.

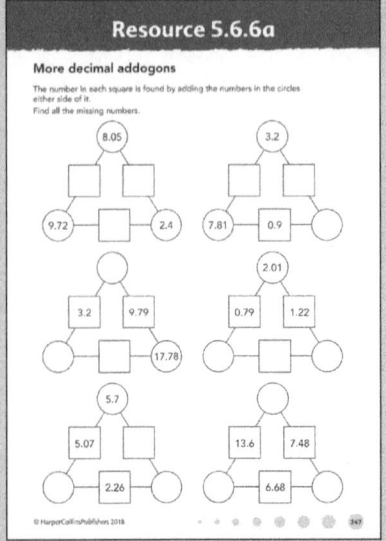

Answers: 17.77, 10.45, 12.12; 11.01, −3.71, −6.91; −7.99, 11.19, 28.97; −1.22, −2.01, −0.79; 8.59, −0.63, 2.89; 7.2, 6.4, 0.28

Chapter 6 Addition and subtraction of decimal numbers

Unit 6.6 Practice Book 5B, pages 18–20

Question 2

2 Work these out step by step. (Calculate smartly when possible.)

(a) 108.43 + 15.84 + 24.16 =

(b) 125.47 − 26.46 − 73.54 =

(c) 86.5 − (18.5 + 3.7) − 26.3 =

(d) 2.54 − 0.27 + (1.46 + 1.73) =

(e) 200 − [36.8 − (6.8 − 2.9)] =

(f) 985 ÷ 125 ÷ 8 =

(g) 6.4 × 7 + 6.4 × 3 =

(h) 2200 ÷ [436 ÷ (192 − 83)] =

What learning will pupils have achieved at the conclusion of Question 2?

- Pupils will be more fluent with mental calculation strategies when adding and subtracting decimals.
- Pupils will be able to use number bonds to calculate smartly with decimals.

Activities for whole-class instruction

- On the board, write: 3 × 8 + 7 × 8 = ☐. Ask pupils to shout out as soon as they have calculated the answer. In Chapter 5, pupils learned that when there are multiple operations, multiplication takes priority over addition; therefore, they should recognise that 3 × 8 + 7 × 8 = ☐ requires them to add together the products of 3 × 8 and 7 × 8. Can they see that, because both of the multiplications involve multiplying by 8, they can add the 3 and 7 together and multiply that sum by 8, so the answer is easily calculated as 10 × 8?

- Repeat with the following:

  2 × 9 + 3 × 9 + 5 × 9 = ☐. Pupils should see that 2 + 3 + 5 means they need to calculate 10 × 9.

  4 × 7 + 2 × 7 + 4 × 7 = ☐. Pupils should see that 4 + 2 + 4 means they need to calculate 10 × 7.

- When you are aware that one or two pupils have noticed the structure and are no longer calculating each step, introduce what will at first appear to be a difficult calculation such as:

  617 × 3 + 617 × 3 + 617 × 4

- Ask pupils to explain how they have been calculating the answers without having to work out each stage and draw their attention to the way that pausing and thinking before calculating help them to calculate smartly.

- Write 24 ÷ 4 ÷ 2 = ☐ on the board and ask pupils to calculate the answer. Gather solutions and assess pupils' interpretations of the calculation.

- Write 24 ÷ 4 ÷ 2 = 24 ÷ (4 ◯ 2) on the board and ask pupils what symbol should fill the circle. Pupils were introduced to the ideas being used here, that a ÷ b ÷ c = a ÷ bc, in Unit 5.5. Remind them that they have encountered this type of problem before.

- Use the rewritten number sentence to confirm the correct solution is 3. Reinforce this, first by writing these calculations:

  56 ÷ 4 ÷ 2 = 56 ÷ (4 ◯ 2)

  1800 ÷ 2 ÷ 3 = 1800 ÷ (2 ◯ 3)

  1000 ÷ 25 ÷ 4 = 1000 ÷ (25 ◯ 4)

- Then ask pupils to work in pairs on their mini whiteboards to write the calculation using the correct symbol in the circle and to calculate the result.

- Now write the calculation 24 ÷ 5 ÷ 2 and discuss pupils' methods again. Pupils should explain that the number sentence can be rewritten as 24 ÷ (5 ◯ 2) = 24 ÷ 10 and are then able to calculate this by sliding all the digits one place to the right over the decimal point.

- Pupils should complete Question 2 in the Practice Book.

Same-day intervention

- Give pupils who need support in identifying number bonds to 1 **Resource 5.6.6b** Makes 3 maze. (The answer is shown below.)

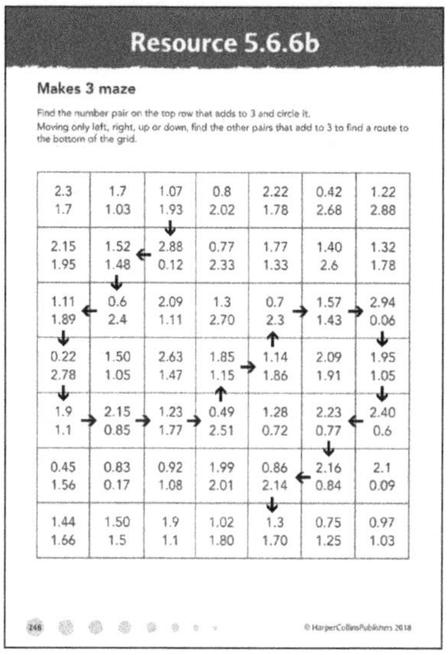

Resource 5.6.6b

Makes 3 maze

Find the number pair on the top row that adds to 3 and circle it. Moving only left, right, up or down, find the other pairs that add to 3 to find a route to the bottom of the grid.

2.3 1.7	1.7 1.03	1.07 1.93	0.8 2.02	2.22 1.78	0.42 2.68	1.22 2.88
2.15 1.95	1.52 1.48	2.88 0.12	0.77 2.33	1.77 1.33	1.40 2.6	1.32 1.78
1.11 1.89	0.6 2.4	2.09 1.11	1.3 2.70	0.7 2.3	1.57 1.43	2.94 0.06
0.22 2.78	1.50 1.05	2.63 1.47	1.85 1.15	1.14 1.86	2.09 1.91	1.95 1.05
1.9 1.1	2.15 0.85	1.23 1.77	0.49 2.51	1.28 0.72	2.23 0.77	2.40 0.6
0.45 1.56	0.83 0.17	0.92 1.08	1.99 2.01	0.86 2.14	2.16 0.84	2.1 0.09
1.44 1.66	1.50 1.5	1.9 1.1	1.02 1.80	1.3 1.70	0.75 1.25	0.97 1.03

Chapter 6 Addition and subtraction of decimal numbers

Unit 6.6 Practice Book 5B, pages 18–20

- Use **Resource 5.6.6c** Using bar models for pupils to work on multiplication and division.

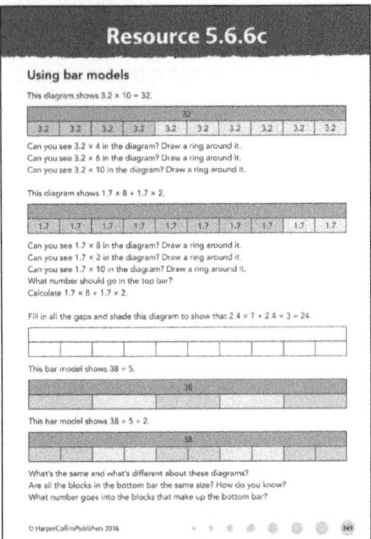

Answers: Draw a ring around the first four 3.2s. Draw a ring around the last six 3.2s. Draw a ring around all ten 3.2s; Draw a ring around the first eight 1.7s. Draw a ring around the last two 1.7s. Draw a ring around all ten 1.7s. 17 should go in the top bar. 1.7 × 8 + 1.7 × 2 = 13.6 + 3.4 = 17; Put 24 in the top bar. Put 2.4 in the first seven gaps and shade them in one colour. Put 2.4 in the last three gaps and shade them in another colour; Same – They each have 38 in the top bar. Different – The top bar has five gaps and the bottom bar has ten gaps. Yes, all the blocks in the bottom bar are the same size because 38 is divided evenly by 10. 3.8 goes into blocks in the bottom bar.

Same-day enrichment

- Give pupils **Resource 5.6.6d** More missing operations in which they are asked to identify the operations that have been used in addition and subtraction calculations.

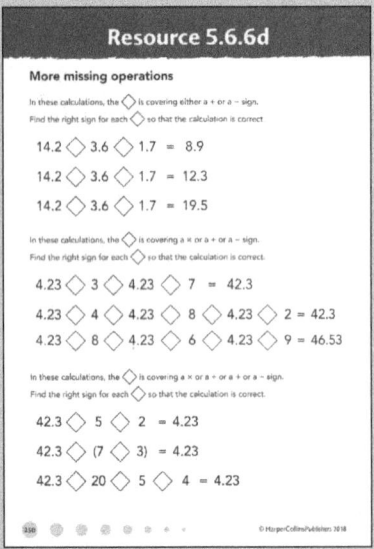

- Explain to pupils that the ◇ symbol can represent a combination of +, –, × or ÷ in the different calculations. They should rewrite each calculation correctly to give the required answer.
- Challenge pupils to explain (maybe by representing in a diagram) why the last three calculations look different but give the same answer.

Answers: –, –; –, +; +, +; ×, +, ×; ×, +, ×, –, ×; ×, –, ×, +, ×; ÷, ÷; ÷, +; –, +, ×

Questions 3 and 4

3 Write the number sentences and then calculate.
  (a) How much greater is 90.5 than the sum of 7.1 and 12.9?

  (b) How much greater is the sum of 56.04 and 0.99 than the difference between 14.6 and 0.26?

  (c) The difference between 6.1 and 0.61 is multiplied by 100. What is the product?

4 A science laboratory produced 8.92 kg of a new substance each day in the first 10 days. It produced a total of 21.45 kg of the same substance in the following 2 days. What was the total mass of the substance the laboratory produced in the 12 days?

What learning will pupils have achieved at the conclusion of Questions 3 and 4?

- Pupils will be able to interpret and represent written problems using mathematical notation.

Activities for whole-class instruction

- Use bar models, and write the calculation being represented. For example, write 3.28 + 7.52 = 10.8 and draw:

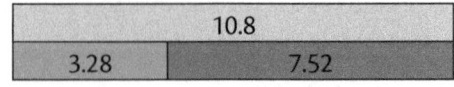

- Ask pupils to work in pairs to write a one or two sentence 'story' that the image and symbols could be describing. Gather some of the stories in and collect the different words and ways in which the calculation can be described.
- Next, use the same image but a different calculation that it might be describing, such as 10.8 – 3.28 = 7.52, and ask pupils to write a story to represent it. Again, gather the stories and discuss the different representations. Also, compare the two different ways of viewing the same image that the different sets of stories express.

Chapter 6 Addition and subtraction of decimal numbers

Unit 6.6 Practice Book 5B, pages 18–20

- Present the following scenario:
  - Sarah and Matilda have some wool. Matilda has 13.78 m of wool and Sarah has 25 cm less. How long is Sarah and Matilda's wool altogether?
- Ask pupils to represent this story using a bar model on mini whiteboards. One pair should work on the whiteboard at the front of the class.
- Use the diagrams on the main whiteboard as a discussion point to agree how the story described can be represented, and how this representation might help in 'calculating smartly'.
- Pupils should complete Questions 3 and 4 in the Practice Book.

Same-day intervention

- Work with pupils to use **Resource 5.6.6e** Decimal addition and subtraction match (2) to match the stories, the calculations and the bar image.

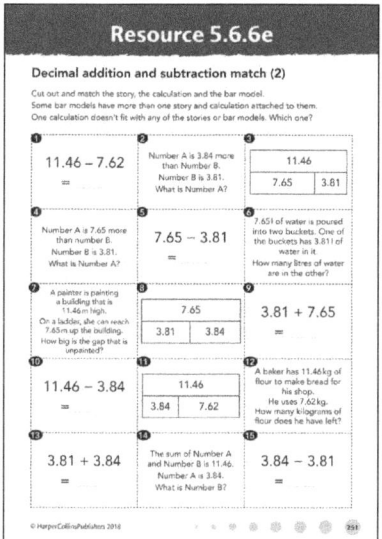

Answers: 2, 13, 8; 4, 9, 3; 6, 5, 8; 7, ?, 3; 12, 1, 11; 14, 10, 11; The calculation in the last section doesn't fit with any of the stories or bar models.

Same-day enrichment

- Give pupils **Resource 5.6.6f** Missing digits in which they need to use addition and subtraction of decimals, along with deductive reasoning, to find the missing digits.

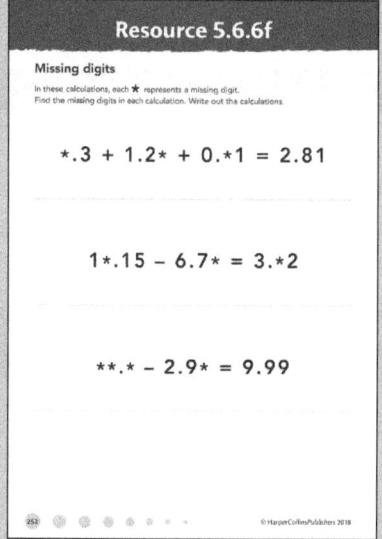

Answers: 1, 0, 3; 0, 3, 4; 1, 2, 9, 1

Challenge and extension questions

Question 5

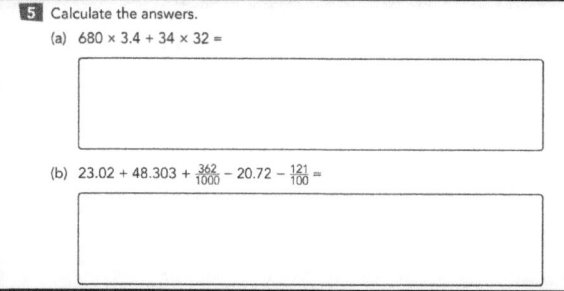

This question offers pupils a chance to manipulate the numbers within a calculation. Encourage pupils to calculate smartly, to look for what is the same in the different 'parts' of the calculation, and to think about how they could adjust the calculation to make it simpler.

Question 6

> 6 Three bags each contain the same quantity of sweets. Tina took one of the bags. Henry divided the sweets in the second bag into 10 equal parts and took 3 parts for himself. Alice divided the sweets in the third bag into 100 parts and took 7 parts for herself. How many bags of sweets did the three of them take in total? (Express your answer in decimals.)

This question challenges pupils to unpick a problem. Encourage them to work methodically and use diagrams to represent the stages in order to make the task more manageable.

Chapter 6 Addition and subtraction of decimal numbers

Unit 6.7
Practice and exercise (2)

Conceptual context

This unit revisits the content of this chapter, offering a chance for pupils to practise addition and subtraction of decimal numbers with up to three decimal places.

Learning pupils will have achieved at the end of the unit

- Pupils will be able to efficiently add and subtract decimal numbers mentally (Q1, Q3)
- Pupils will be able to use understanding of place value to multiply and divide decimal numbers by 10, 100 and 1000 fluently (Q1, Q4, Q5)
- Pupils will be able to add and subtract decimal numbers using the column method fluently (Q2)
- Pupils will be able to identify opportunities to use known facts, enabling them to calculate smartly (Q3)
- Pupils will be able to convert between metric units by multiplying and dividing by 10, 100 and 1000 (Q4, Q5)

Resources

place value counters; mini whiteboards; **Resource 5.6.1a** Place value slider; **Resource 5.6.7a** Multiplying and dividing by 10, 100 and 1000; **Resource 5.6.7b** Lining up the decimal points; **Resource 5.6.7c** Place the digits; **Resource 5.6.7d** Decimal cards; **Resource 5.6.7e** 10s, 100s, 1000s and 10 000s puzzles

Vocabulary

decimal point

Chapter 6 Addition and subtraction of decimal numbers

Unit 6.7 Practice Book 5B, pages 21–23

Question 1

1 Calculate mentally and then write the answers.

(a) 85.3 + 2.7 =   (b) 50 ÷ 100 =
(c) 9.1 × 100 =   (d) 4.65 + 2.45 =
(e) 765 ÷ 1000 =   (f) 12 − 9.3 =
(g) 0.231 × 1000 =   (h) 120 ÷ 24 =
(i) 20 − 18.06 =   (j) 5.5 + 5 =
(k) 3.5 × 100 =   (l) 7.66 ÷ 10 × 1000 =

What learning will pupils have achieved at the conclusion of Question 1?

- Pupils will be able to efficiently add and subtract decimal numbers mentally.
- Pupils will be able to use understanding of place value to multiply and divide decimal numbers by 10, 100 and 1000 fluently.

Activities for whole-class instruction

- Use a place value slider to remind pupils that, when a number is multiplied by 10, 100 or 1000, all the digits move to the left by 1, 2 or 3 places and, when divided, they move to the right.
- Model 3.52 × 10 followed by 3.52 × 100 and then 3.52 × 1000. Draw pupils' attention to the way that an additional zero is needed to fill the gap in the final calculation.
- Model 28.7 ÷ 10 followed by 28.7 ÷ 100 and 28.7 ÷ 1000. Again, draw pupils' attention to the use of zeros to fill the gaps.
- Show pupils the number 15.7 and ask them to write on mini whiteboards the result of:
  - multiplying it by 10
  - multiplying it by 100
  - dividing it by 10
  - dividing it by 100.
- Gather responses and address misconceptions and mistakes.
- Pupils should complete Question 1 in the Practice Book.

Same-day intervention

- Give pupils a place value slider (see **Resource 5.6.1a** Place value slider) and place value chart and work with them to multiply and divide numbers by 10, 100 and 1000 using both of these images.

- Ensure that you draw pupils' attention to the way in which the digits in the numbers move one place for each 'ten' in the 10, 100 or 1000 while also agreeing that the decimal point remains fixed.
- A sequence of calculations to work on can be found on **Resource 5.6.7a** Multiplying and dividing by 10, 100 and 1000. You might like to repeat the sequence of calculations, but use different digits to create the number.

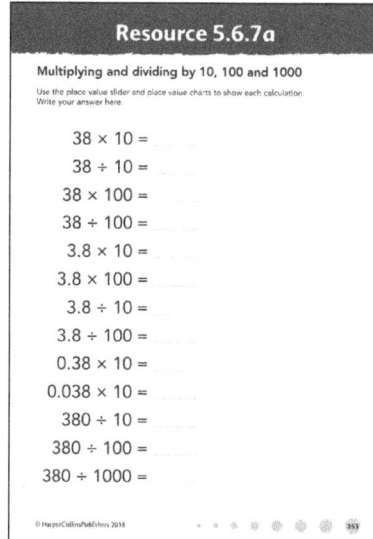

Answers: 380; 3.8; 3800; 0.38; 38; 380; 0.38; 0.038; 3.8; 0.38; 38; 3.8; 0.38

Same-day enrichment

- Show pupils this calculation:
  38.7 __ 10 __ 10 __ 10 __ 10 = 387
- Tell them that the gaps must be filled with a × or a ÷ and ask them to justify why the calculation is not possible.

Question 2

2 Choose the most appropriate method, mental or written, to find the answer to each calculation. (Check the answers to the questions marked with * using a different method.)

(a) 202.78 + 10.89 =   (b) *34.416 − 4.78 =

(c) 90.4 − 9.08 =   (d) *4.69 + 5.039 =

Chapter 6 Addition and subtraction of decimal numbers Unit 6.7 Practice Book 5B, pages 21–23

What learning will pupils have achieved at the conclusion of Question 2?

- Pupils will be able to add and subtract decimal numbers using the column method fluently.

Activities for whole-class instruction

- Show pupils the following image and ask them to discuss, in pairs, which are the correct and which are the incorrect calculations.

```
(3.72 – 1.5)              (13.9 – 1.32)
    6 1
   3.7̸2                      13.9
 –  1.5                    –  1.32
 ─────                     ──────
   3.56                     12.62

(17.8 + 1.29)             (125.7 + 14.83)
   17.8                     125.7
 + 1.29                   + 14.83
 ─────                    ───────
  19.09                    274.0
    1                       1 1
```

- Gather responses and address any misconceptions and mistakes. Ensure that pupils notice the importance of aligning the decimal points and filling any gaps with a zero.

- Pupils should complete Question 2 in the Practice Book.

Same-day intervention

- Give pupils **Resource 5.6.7b** Lining up the decimal points in which they first practise aligning the decimal points before carrying out calculations using the column method.

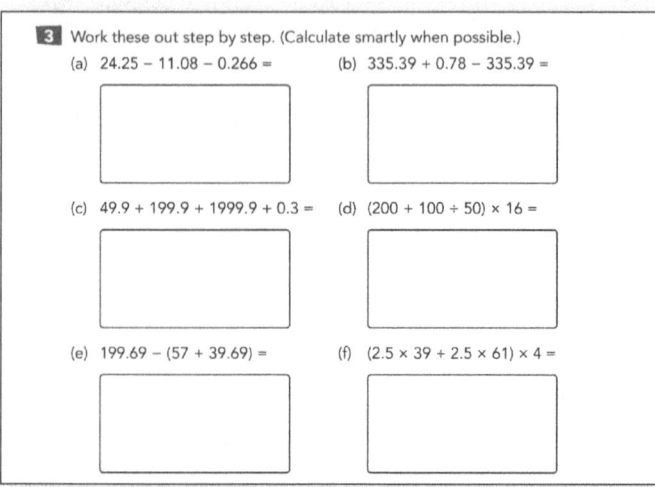

Answers: 39.63; 6.28; 10.2; 10.39; 11.02

Same-day enrichment

- Pupils work on **Resource 5.6.7c** Place the digits in which they arrange digits to complete an addition and subtraction calculation using decimal numbers.

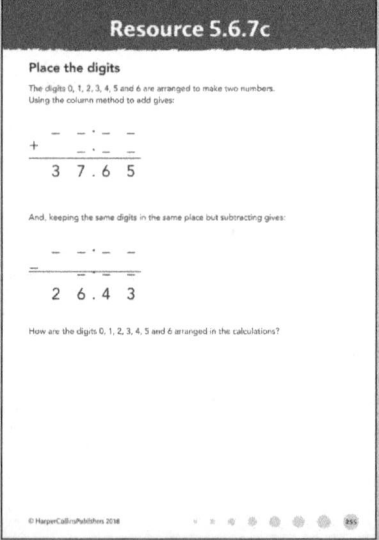

- Pupils might use a trial and improvement approach, using the magnitude of the numbers to estimate. Look out for pupils who are able to reason that, for example, the second place of decimal digits must be 4 and 1 since they add to 6 and have a difference of 3. The correct solutions are: 32.04 + 5.61 = 37.65 and 32.04 – 5.61 = 26.43.

Question 3

3 Work these out step by step. (Calculate smartly when possible.)
  (a) 24.25 – 11.08 – 0.266 =
  (b) 335.39 + 0.78 – 335.39 =
  (c) 49.9 + 199.9 + 1999.9 + 0.3 =
  (d) (200 + 100 ÷ 50) × 16 =
  (e) 199.69 – (57 + 39.69) =
  (f) (2.5 × 39 + 2.5 × 61) × 4 =

Chapter 6 Addition and subtraction of decimal numbers

Unit 6.7 Practice Book 5B, pages 21–23

What learning will pupils have achieved at the conclusion of Question 3?
- Pupils will be able to efficiently add and subtract decimal numbers mentally.
- Pupils will be able to identify opportunities to use known facts, enabling them to calculate smartly.

Activities for whole-class instruction

- This task revisits the whole-class activity for Question 2 in Unit 6.5.
- Show pupils the following image:

0.01	0.02	0.03	0.04	0.05	0.06	0.07	0.08	0.09	0.1
0.11	0.12	0.13	0.14	0.15	0.16	0.17	0.18	0.19	0.2
0.21	0.22	0.23	0.24	0.25	0.26	0.27	0.28	0.29	0.3
0.31	0.32	0.33	0.34	0.35	0.36	0.37	0.38	0.39	0.4
0.41	0.42	0.43	0.44	0.45	0.46	0.47	0.48	0.49	0.5
0.51	0.52	0.53	0.54	0.55	0.56	0.57	0.58	0.59	0.6
0.61	0.62	0.63	0.64	0.65	0.66	0.67	0.68	0.69	0.7
0.71	0.72	0.73	0.74	0.75	0.76	0.77	0.78	0.79	0.8
0.81	0.82	0.83	0.84	0.85	0.86	0.87	0.88	0.89	0.9
0.91	0.92	0.93	0.94	0.95	0.96	0.97	0.98	0.99	1

- Tell pupils that you will tap on a number in the square and that they have to say how many they need to add to reach the end of the row. For example, if you tap on 0.47 they should say 0.03; if you tap on 0.72 they should say 0.08, and so on.
- Make sure that some of the numbers you choose support pupils in identifying the number bonds and explicitly draw attention to these. For example, you might choose to tap 0.57, 0.67, 0.87 and 0.07 as a sequence, or tap pairs such as 0.47 and 0.43, 0.84 and 0.86 or 0.02 and 0.08 and make explicit the symmetries in the calculations.
- Once you are confident that pupils understand the structure of the square and are able to identify the number to reach the end of the row, say to them that you will now tap one of the numbers in the right-hand column, and that they should tell you what needs to be added to reach the bottom right square. For example, if you tap 0.3, they should say '0.7', and if you tap 0.7 they should say '0.3'. Again, choose pairs of numbers such as 0.1 and 0.9 to make the symmetry in the square explicit to pupils.
- Finally, tell pupils that you will now tap a number and they should say the number that needs to be added to reach the bottom right-hand square. You might like to support them in structuring this by thinking about getting from your number to the right-hand column, and then from the right-hand column to the bottom right-hand square. For example, if you tap on 0.15, they might think '0.05 and then 0.8' but they should say '0.85'.
- The intention of the task is to support pupils in becoming fluent with decimal number bonds and so support them in 'calculating smartly'.
- Pupils should complete Question 3 in the Practice Book.

Same-day intervention
- Use **Resource 5.6.7d** Decimal cards.

- Pupils work in pairs or small groups to play a game of 'pairs'. The cards should be cut out and spread face down across the table. Pupils then take turns to turn over two cards. If their pair sums to 1, they keep the cards and have another go. If they do not sum to 1, it is the next pupil's turn.
- Once all the cards have been gathered, the winner is the player with the most correct pairs.

Same-day enrichment
- Use **Resource 5.6.7d** Decimal cards.
- Pupils work in pairs or small groups to play a card game.
- Each player is dealt five cards and the rest of the cards are placed in a pile in the centre of the table.

Chapter 6 Addition and subtraction of decimal numbers

Unit 6.7 Practice Book 5B, pages 21–23

- Moving clockwise, players take turns to take a card from the top of the pile, and then either reject it and place it on the bottom of the pile, or accept it and put a card from their hand on the bottom of the pile.
- The winner is the first person to be able to make 1, using three or more of their cards by adding and subtracting (for example, a winning hand might include 0.25, 0.39 and 0.86 since 0.86 + 0.39 − 0.25 = 1).

Questions 4 and 5

4. Compare the quantities and put them in order, starting from the greatest.
   0.24 km, 2040 m, 2 km 400 m

5. Fill in the spaces to make each statement correct.
   (a) When 2.015 is multiplied by 100, the result is ☐. If the result is then divided by 10, the answer is ☐.
   (b) The result of 0.03 × 100 ÷ 1000 is to move all the digits in 0.03 _____ place(s) to the _____.
   (c) Adding ☐ 0.001s is the same as the sum of five 0.1s and one 0.001.
   (d) After moving all the digits in Number A two places to the left, it is equal to Number B. Number B is ☐ times Number A.
   (e) 0.112 kg + 20 g = ☐ g

What learning will pupils have achieved at the conclusion of Questions 4 and 5?
- Pupils will be able to use understanding of place value to multiply and divide decimal numbers by 10, 100 and 1000 fluently.
- Pupils will be able to convert between metric units by multiplying and dividing by 10, 100 and 1000.

Activities for whole-class instruction

- This task revisits the whole-class activity for Question 4 in Unit 6.2.
- On the board, write: 4750 metres. Use a place value slider to convert this to km.
- To draw attention to the mathematics that underpins the conversion, say: *Dividing 4750 by 1000 gives 4.750.*
- Agree with pupils, and write on the board:
  4750 m = 4.750 km

- Now use a part/whole diagram to break this into a whole number and a decimal part.

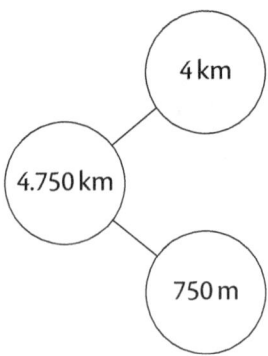

- Agree with pupils, and write on the board:
  4750 metres = 4.750 km = 4 km 750 metres.
- Stress that the 4 in all versions represents the same distance, but is written in different ways – either as 4000 m or as 4 km. Stress too that the 750 also represents the same distance, but is written in two different ways – either as 750 m or as 0.75 km. Discuss whether or not the zero should be used when written as 0.75 km.
- Stress that, when converting, you are multiplying or dividing by 1000, and illustrate this using the place value slider.
- Repeat with 12.002 kg. Be aware that the zeros in the tenths and hundredths positions may cause some confusion for pupils when writing the quantity as 12 kg and 2 grams.
- Pupils should complete Questions 4 and 5 in the Practice Book.

Same-day intervention
- This task revisits the Same-day intervention task for Question 4 Unit 6.1.
- Use place value sliders to work with pupils to complete this table.

	Can be written as …	and moves all digits …	by …	For example:
× 10	× 10	←	1 place	3.14 × 10 = 31.4
× 10 × 10	× 100			
× 10 × 10 × 10				
÷ 10		→		
÷ 10 ÷ 10				
÷ 10 ÷ 10 ÷ 10				

Chapter 6 Addition and subtraction of decimal numbers

Unit 6.7 Practice Book 5B, pages 21–23

- Ensure that pupils understand the equivalence of repeated multiplication by 10, and the single multiplication that can replace it (calculating smartly).
- Pupils should create their own examples for the final column, checking each other's examples.
- If appropriate, add some extra rows to the table and introduce combinations of × and ÷, for example × 100 ÷ 10, and ask pupils to reduce this to one calculation (in this case, × 10).

Same-day enrichment

- Use **Resource 5.6.7e** 10s, 100s, 1000s and 10 000s puzzles. Pupils multiply and divide decimal numbers by 10, 100 and 1000 in order to solve puzzles.

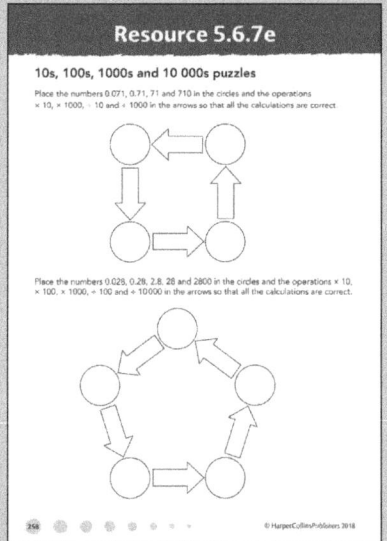

Answers: (starting from any position) ÷1000, 0.71, ÷10, 0.071, ×1000, 71, ×10, 710; 28 000, ÷10 000, 2.8, ÷100, 0.028, ×10, 0.28, ×100, 28, ×1000. Note that other answers are possible.

Challenge and extension questions

Question 6

> 6 Jamila bought a suitcase and a handbag for £70.50. The cost of the suitcase was £19.50 more than the cost of two handbags. What was the cost of the suitcase? What was the cost of the handbag?

While the calculations involved in answering this question are relatively straightforward, identifying the calculations needed is far more challenging. Encourage pupils to represent the problem using a picture such as a bar model to make sense of the situation and the steps needed to solve it.

Question 7

> 7 There are three numbers: A, B and C. If all the digits in A are moved two places to the left, and all the digits in B are moved three places to the right, the two new numbers are both equal to C. If A is 3.01, what are B and C?

There is no calculation involved in the question; the challenge is in the reasoning and in identifying where additional zeros are needed to give the correct solution. You may need to clarify with pupils that 'the two new numbers are both equal to C' means that they are the same as C, not that their sum is equal to C.

Chapter 6 Addition and subtraction of decimal numbers

Chapter 6 test (Practice Book 5B, pages 24–28)

Test question number	Relevant unit	Relevant questions within unit
1	Unit 6.1	Q1
	Unit 6.2	Q1
	Unit 6.3	Q1
	Unit 6.4	Q1
	Unit 6.5	Q1
	Unit 6.6	Q1
	Unit 6.7	Q1
2	Unit 6.3	Q2
	Unit 6.4	Q2
	Unit 6.7	Q2
3	Unit 6.5	Q2
	Unit 6.6	Q2
	Unit 6.7	Q3
4	Unit 6.3	Q3
	Unit 6.4	Q3
5	Unit 6.1	Q2, Q4
	Unit 6.7	Q5
6	Unit 6.2	Q3
	Unit 6.3	Q4
	Unit 6.4	Q4
	Unit 6.5	Q3
	Unit 6.6	Q3
7	Unit 6.1	Q5
	Unit 6.2	Q5
	Unit 6.5	Q4
	Unit 6.6	Q4

Chapter 7
Introduction to positive and negative numbers

Chapter overview

Area of mathematics	National Curriculum statutory requirements for Key Stage 2	Shanghai Maths Project reference
Number – number and place value	Year 4 Programme of study: Pupils should be taught to: ■ count backwards through zero to include negative numbers.	Year 5, Units 7.1, 7.2, 7.3, 7.4
	Year 5 Programme of study: Pupils should be taught to: ■ interpret negative numbers in context, count forwards and backwards with positive and negative whole numbers, including through zero.	Year 5, Units 7.1, 7.2, 7.3, 7.4
	Year 6 Programme of study: Pupils should be taught to: ■ use negative numbers in context, and calculate intervals across zero.	Year 5, Units 7.1, 7.2, 7.3, 7.4

Chapter 7 Introduction to positive and negative numbers

Unit 7.1
Positive and negative numbers (1)

Conceptual context

This chapter introduces negative numbers. Negative numbers help to describe values less than zero. Due to their abstract nature, they should be introduced in context.

Negative numbers represent opposites. Positive numbers represent values greater than a given benchmark (reference point), while negative numbers represent values less than the benchmark (the benchmark is often zero). If positive represents a movement to the right, negative represents a movement to the left.

Pupils will already have met negative numbers in everyday life. They may have seen negative floor numbers in lifts, corresponding to basement floors below ground level. They will be familiar with temperatures expressed as negative numbers. Temperatures above zero are positive while temperatures below zero are negative. Domestic freezers are generally set to −18 °C and the fridge temperature varies between 3 and 5 °C. There is often a live display of these values on a control panel.

(i) Positive numbers are usually written without a '+'. The + is implied. Thus, positive ten (or 'plus ten') can be written as +10 or, more commonly, simply as 10. Negative numbers are always written with a − sign, thus negative ten (or 'minus ten') is written as −10.

Learning pupils will have achieved at the end of the unit

- Temperatures below 0 °C will have been read as negative numbers (Q1, Q5)
- Pupils will have practised reading positive and negative numbers (Q2, Q3, Q4, Q5, Q6)
- The concept that positive and negative numbers are opposites will have been explored (Q2, Q3, Q4, Q6)
- Pupils will have learned that negative numbers must always have − in front of the number (Q2, Q3, Q4)
- The understanding will have been established that positive numbers may be prefaced by + but if there is no + it is inferred (Q2, Q3, Q4)
- Pupils will have developed and extended their knowledge and understanding of specific, well-known temperatures (Q5)
- Pupils will have consolidated their understanding that on the Celsius scale temperatures below zero (the freezing point of water) are represented by negative numbers (Q5)
- The concept of a benchmark (reference point) where numbers greater than the benchmark are positive and numbers less than the benchmark are negative will have been introduced (Q6)

Chapter 7 Introduction to positive and negative numbers

Unit 7.1 Practice Book 5B, pages 29–31

- Pupils will have explored how a negative number and its corresponding positive number are 'opposite' each other across the benchmark (reference mark); they are both the same distance from the benchmark but in opposite directions (Q6)

Resources

−10 to 110 °C thermometers; diagrams of −10 to 110 °C thermometers; fever scan thermometer and/or classroom thermometer if available; **Resource 5.7.1a** Matching temperatures; **Resource 5.7.1b** Thermometers; **Resource 5.7.1c** Positive and negative numbers; **Resource 5.7.1d** Identifying common temperatures; **Resource 5.7.1e** Test results 1; **Resource 5.7.1f** Test results 2

Vocabulary

positive number, negative number, benchmark, temperature, ° Celsius, thermometer

Chapter 7 Introduction to positive and negative numbers

Unit 7.1 Practice Book 5B, pages 29–31

Question 1

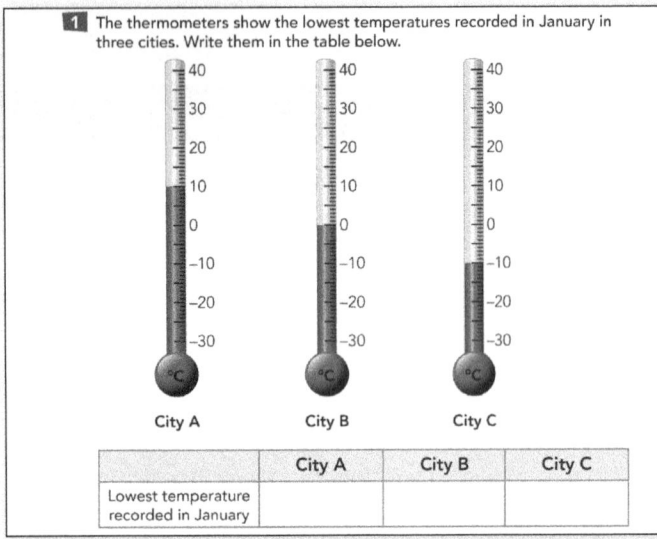

What learning will pupils have achieved at the conclusion of Question 1?

- Temperatures below 0 °C will have been read as negative numbers.

Activities for whole-class instruction

- Display a large diagram of a blank −10 to 110 °C thermometer and examine the scale with pupils. Find zero and read the increasing scale together, noting increments of 10 °C. Now look at the scale below zero and agree that the next interval below zero is also marked 10. Ask if pupils know how the two 10s are differentiated – they may already have used thermometers of this type in their Science lessons. If possible, allow pupils to see and handle real thermometers as well as looking at the diagram.

- Explain that the numbers above zero are positive temperatures and the numbers below are negative ones. Remind pupils that the higher the height of the column in the thermometer, the higher the temperature. Negative numbers represent cold temperatures; in fact, negative temperatures are below freezing because 0 °C is the freezing point of water.

- Show different temperatures on the thermometer diagram, both negative and positive values, and ask pupils to read the temperatures.

ⓘ Negative numbers are correctly read as 'negative (number)' thus −10 is 'negative ten'. In the past, the word minus was used, thus −10 was read as 'minus 10'. Pupils will still hear this used today, for example in television weather forecasts. Explain that while to non-mathematicians 'minus 10' does mean −10, they should read numbers using the word 'negative', not 'minus'. Strictly speaking, 'negative 10' is a number while 'minus 10' is a mathematical operation that can be done to another number. However, you should refer to negative numbers as, for example, 'negative 3' and 'minus 3' (also 'positive 3' and 'plus 3') interchangeably so pupils become familiar with both.

- Pupils should complete Question 1 in the Practice Book.

Same-day intervention

- Give pupil pairs **Resource 5.7.1a** Matching temperatures.

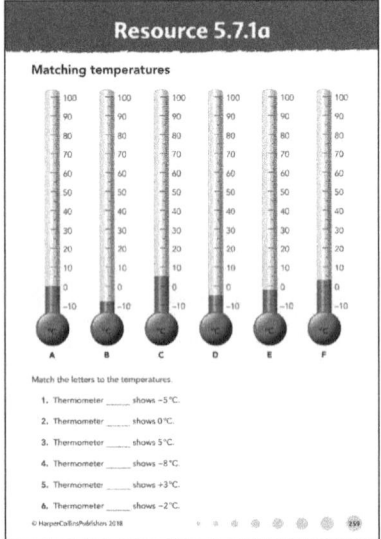

Answers: 1. D; 2. A; 3. C; 4. B; 5. F; 6. E

Same-day enrichment

- Give pupil pairs **Resource 5.7.1b** Thermometers.

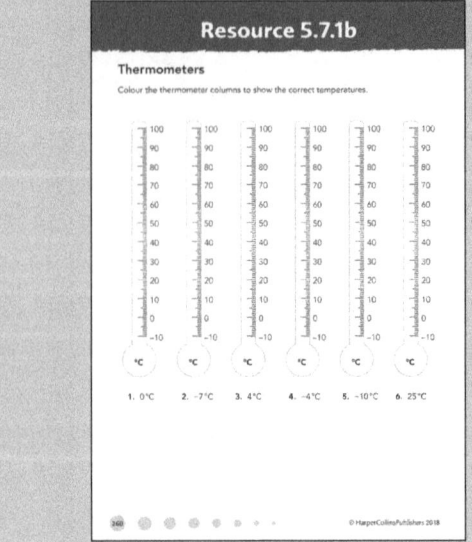

Chapter 7 Introduction to positive and negative numbers Unit 7.1 Practice Book 5B, pages 29–31

Questions 2, 3 and 4

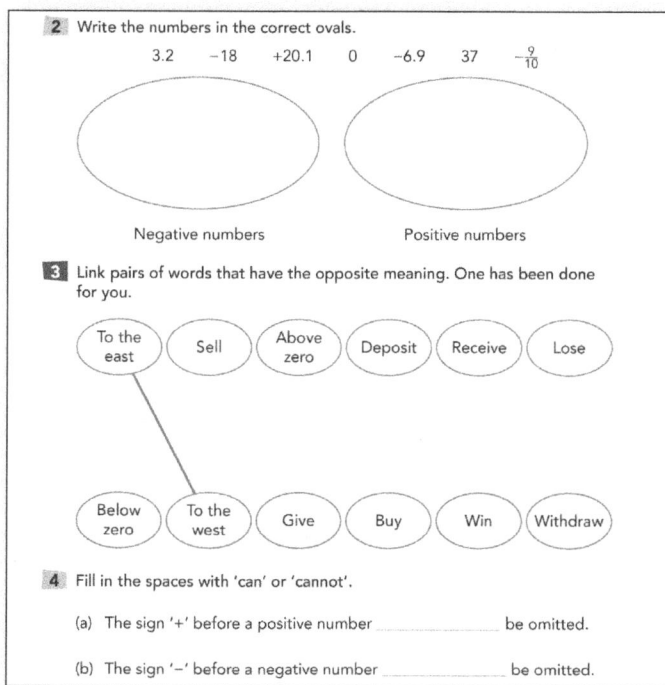

What learning will pupils have achieved at the conclusion of Questions 2, 3 and 4?

- Pupils will have practised reading positive and negative numbers.
- The concept that positive and negative numbers are opposites will have been explored.
- Pupils will have learned that negative numbers must always have − in front of the number.
- The understanding will have been established that positive numbers may be prefaced by + but if there is no + it is inferred.

Activities for whole-class instruction

- Remind pupils that in Question 1, temperatures below zero were written with a negative sign. Display −5 and ask pupils to read the number. Agree it is 'negative 5' (or 'minus 5').
- Repeat with more negative numbers, including decimal numbers and fractions, for example: −14, −3.4, −25, $-\frac{3}{4}$, −273.

 *Negative numbers always have a negative sign in front of the number.*

- Display 14 and +14 and invite pupils to read these numbers. They may read them as 'fourteen' and 'positive fourteen'.
- Ask: *Do these two numbers have the same value?* Confirm that they have the same value. Explain that we do not usually write + in front of positive numbers because numbers are usually positive. When you see a number, you can assume it is positive and so the + does not need to be written or said. However, if we want to emphasise that a number is positive, for example when we are comparing it to a negative number, we can put in the + without changing the number's value.
- Display the following numbers and invite individual pupils to read them:

  15   −4   +12   −11   −200   34.2   −2.6   12

- Ask: *Which two numbers are the same?*

 *Twelve and positive twelve (or 'plus twelve') have the same meaning and value.*

- Display the following words and ask pupils to tell you the opposite.

  IN   DOWN   SPEND

- Agree that the opposites are OUT, UP and SAVE. Remind pupils that negative numbers mirror positive numbers and are opposite to them. Negative numbers are often used in the context of money. Adding money is positive and taking money away is negative.
- Display the following words and say: *Here are some words that describe money transactions. Discuss whether they describe a positive movement of money or a negative one.*

  DEPOSIT   SPEND   SELL   WIN   RECEIVE

- Establish the following positive/negative descriptions and agree the following opposites:

  DEPOSIT (positive) − WITHDRAW (negative)

  SPEND (negative) − SAVE (positive)

  SELL (negative) − BUY (positive)

  WIN (positive) − LOSE (negative)

  RECEIVE (positive) − GIVE (negative)

  (i) Zero is neither positive nor negative. An integer can either be greater than zero, called positive, or less than zero, called negative.

- Pupils should complete Questions 2, 3 and 4 in the Practice Book.

Chapter 7 Introduction to positive and negative numbers

Unit 7.1 Practice Book 5B, pages 29–31

Same-day intervention

- Give pupils **Resource 5.7.1c** Positive and negative numbers to complete.

Answers:

Number in words	Numeral	Positive or negative? (delete as necessary)
negative ten	−10	~~positive~~/negative
three point five	3.5	positive/~~negative~~
negative five point six	−5.6	~~positive~~/negative
four hundred and nine point two	409.2	positive/~~negative~~
positive eleven	11	positive/~~negative~~
negative eighty-five	−85	~~positive~~/negative
positive seven eighths	$\frac{7}{8}$	positive/~~negative~~
negative twelve point four	−12.4	~~positive~~/negative
twelve point four	12.4	positive/~~negative~~
negative thirty-four point nine	−34.9	~~positive~~/negative
negative two point zero three	−2.03	~~positive~~/negative

Same-day enrichment

- Present pupils with the following problem:

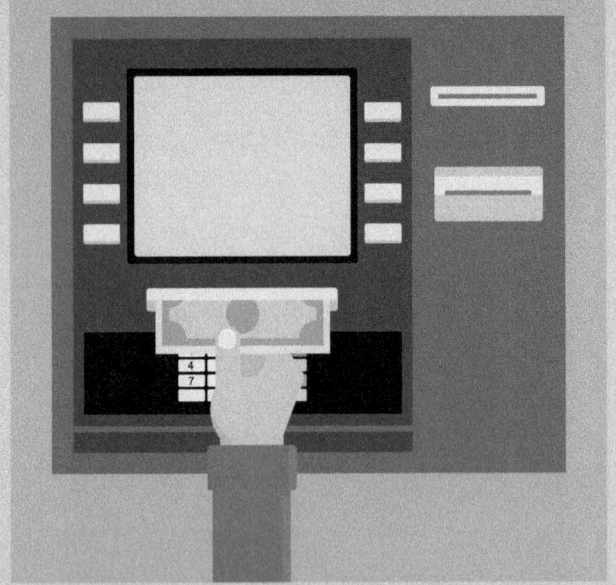

Sally had £100 in the bank.

On Monday, she withdrew £40.

On Tuesday, she deposited £50.

On Wednesday, she withdrew £20.

On Thursday, she deposited £30.

On Friday, she spent £10.

Complete the balance sheet, showing deposits as positive entries and withdrawals as negative ones, to work out the final balance.

	Deposits/withdrawals	Balance
Starting balance		£100
Monday	−£40	£60
Tuesday		
Wednesday		
Thursday		
Friday		

How much was in Sally's bank account on Saturday morning? _____

Answer: Sally had £110 in her bank account on Saturday.

Chapter 7 Introduction to positive and negative numbers
Unit 7.1 Practice Book 5B, pages 29–31

Question 5

5	Draw lines to match each statement to the most appropriate temperature.	
	The temperature of an ice cream	0 °C
	The lowest temperature on the surface of the Moon	100 °C
	The temperature of boiling water	−8 °C
	The temperature of freezing water	−183 °C

What learning will pupils have achieved at the conclusion of Question 5?

- Temperatures below 0 °C will have been read as negative numbers.
- Pupils will have practised reading positive and negative numbers.
- Pupils will have developed and extended their knowledge and understanding of specific, well-known temperatures.
- Pupils will have consolidated their understanding that on the Celsius scale, temperatures below zero (the freezing point of water) are represented by negative numbers.

Activities for whole-class instruction

- Lead a discussion about temperatures in everyday life. Remind pupils that the temperature at which water freezes is 0 °C and that it boils at 100 °C. These are temperatures that pupils should commit to memory.
- Explain to pupils that there are a few other temperatures that are useful to learn, if possible. These are:
  - Room temperature is about 21 °C. Pupils can look at a thermometer in the classroom to confirm this.
  - Body temperature is 37 °C. If your temperature is higher, then you have a fever and by the time it reaches 40 °C, you feel really ill. Use a forehead thermometer to take the temperature of a volunteer pupil.
  - Fridges are set at between 3 and 5 °C. This is just a few degrees above freezing so as to stop germs multiplying but not have frozen food.
  - Freezers are set at −18 °C. Suggest pupils look at the fridges and freezers in school and at home. Many have the temperatures displayed on them.
  - The temperature on the surface of most planets varies hugely from very hot (several hundred degrees Celsius) to very, very cold (large negative temperature values). Pupils can explore this on the internet if they are interested.

- Display the temperatures that have been discussed, increasing from the left:

  −18 °C   0 °C   3–5 °C   21 °C   37 °C   100 °C

- Invite pupil pairs to read and identify these temperatures and then choose pupils to share their answers.
- Pupils should complete Question 5 in the Practice Book.

Same-day intervention

- Display the following table and ask pupil pairs to copy and complete it, circling the correct answers.

	Temperature of …			
1.	… boiling water		100 °C /+100 °C	−100 °C
2.	… the human body		73 °C	37 °C/+37 °C
3.	… a fridge		3 °C or 4 °C	0 °C
4.	… the classroom		21 °C or +21 °C	40 °C
5.	… water freezing		0 °C	10 °C
6.	… a freezer		−18 °C	18 °C/+18 °C

- Ask pupils to discuss their answers with another pair.

  Answers: 1. 100 °C/+100 °C; 2. 37 °C/+37 °C; 3. 3 °C or 4 °C; 4. 21 °C/+21 °C; 5. 0 °C; 6. −18 °C.

Chapter 7 Introduction to positive and negative numbers Unit 7.1 Practice Book 5B, pages 29–31

Same-day enrichment

- Give pupil pairs **Resource 5.7.1d** Identifying common temperatures.

Answers: 1. 100 °C and +100 °C; 2. 37 °C; 3. 3 °C and 4 °C; 4. 21 °C and +21 °C; 5. 0 °C; 6. –18 °C; 7. +75 °C; 8. –196 °C

Question 6

6. The table below shows the heights of six pupils. Take 150 cm as the benchmark and find the difference between each pupil's height and the benchmark height. If it is above the benchmark, write the difference as positive, and if it is below the benchmark, write the difference as negative. Complete the table.

Pupil	1	2	3	4	5	6	Benchmark
Height (cm)	140	148	160	135	155	162	150
Difference from the benchmark height							

What learning will pupils have achieved at the conclusion of Question 6?

- Pupils will have practised reading positive and negative numbers.
- The concept that positive and negative numbers are opposites will have been explored.
- The concept of a benchmark (reference point) where numbers greater than the benchmark are positive and numbers less than the benchmark are negative will have been introduced.
- Pupils will have explored how a negative number and its corresponding positive number are 'opposite' each other across the benchmark (reference mark); they are both the same distance from the benchmark but in opposite directions.

Activities for whole-class instruction

- Ask pupils if they know how much they weighed when they were born – or if they know the birth weight of a younger brother or sister. Tell them that the weight of babies born at full term is usually between 2.7 kg and 4.1 kg. So, a newborn baby typically weighs about 3.5 kg.
- Display the weights of eight babies born in a hospital during one week:

  | 3.9 kg | 3.2 kg | 3.0 kg | 3.5 kg |
  | 4.0 kg | 2.8 kg | 3.6 kg | 3.7 kg |

- Ask pupils to arrange them in increasing order:

  | 2.8 kg | 3.0 kg | 3.2 kg | 3.5 kg |
  | 3.6 kg | 3.7 kg | 3.9 kg | 4.0 kg |

- Remind them that 3.5 kg is the typical weight. Ask:
  - Were any of the babies' birthweights exactly 3.5 kg?
  - How many babies were below the typical birthweight?
  - How many babies were above the typical birthweight?
- Explain that sometimes, mathematicians use a reference point, called a **benchmark**, against which the other values can be compared. Values below the benchmark are negative, and values above the benchmark are positive.
- Work together to complete the differences between the 3.5 kg benchmark and the other values.

2.8 kg	–0.7
3.0 kg	–0.5
3.2 kg	–0.3
3.5 kg Benchmark	0
3.6 kg	+0.1
3.7 kg	+0.2
3.9 kg	+0.4
4.0 kg	+0.5

- Ask: *Which two weights are exactly the same distance from the 3.5 kg benchmark?* Agree that the babies weighing 4.0 kg and 3.0 kg are both the same distance, 0.5 kg, from the benchmark but in opposite directions, one positive, +0.5, and one negative –0.5.
- The smallest baby at 2.8 kg was –0.7 from the benchmark. Ask: *What would the weight be of the baby the same distance from the benchmark in a positive direction?* Agree it would be 4.2 kg.
- Ask individual pupils to tell you:
  - the weights of the two babies 0.6 kg either side of the benchmark

Chapter 7 Introduction to positive and negative numbers

Unit 7.1 Practice Book 5B, pages 29–31

- the difference between the benchmark for some other weights, for example 2.9 kg, 4.1 kg, 3.3 kg, 3.8 kg
- the weight of a baby whose benchmark value is +0.3 (−0.1, −0.8 and so on).

• Pupils should complete Question 6 in the Practice Book.

Same-day intervention

• Give pupil pairs **Resource 5.7.1e** Test results 1.

Answers: Table: +2; −5; +3; −1; +10; −2; +6; 0; −6; 1. Harry; 2. 4; 3. 4; 4. Negative five; 5. Ella (+10)

Same-day enrichment

• Give pupil pairs **Resource 5.7.1f** Test results 2.

Answers: Table: +2; −5; +3; 79; 90; −2; 86; 0; 74; 75; 100; 1. Harry; 2. 5; 3. 5; 4. Negative five; 5. Isla (−6); 6. Jamie and Ben 7. Kaia; 8. Kaia

Challenge and extension questions

Question 7

7 The income of Julie's family in February was £5800. The bills for water, electricity and gas totalled £270. The telephone bill came to £180. The family's income and expenditure in February can be recorded in the following table.

Item	Expense (£ pounds)
Family income	+ £5800
Bills for water, electricity and gas	
Telephone bill	
Other expenses	

(a) Help Julie record her family's expenses for water, electricity, gas and telephone bills in February in the table.
(b) There was £2500 left over, which Julie's mum deposited in the bank. Can you work out the family's other expenses in February? Add them to the table.

In this question, pupils explore an income and expenditure problem, where income is a positive amount and expenses are negative numbers, which are subtracted.

Question 8

8 A, B and C are three beauty spots on an island. If the elevation of A is +10 m, B is +36 m, and C is −3 m, then the highest beauty spot is _____ and the lowest is _____.

The problem in this question considers the elevation of places above and below sea level. Pupils could be invited to draw a sketch to clarify their answer.

Chapter 7 Introduction to positive and negative numbers

Unit 7.2
Positive and negative numbers (2)

Conceptual context

Having recognised negative numbers in context in the previous unit, and begun to develop their concept of negative numbers in relation to a benchmark, in this unit pupils solve word problems involving positive and negative numbers. They will continue to use benchmarks as reference points, understanding positive and negative numbers as being situated a distance from that point in opposite directions. Representations used will sometimes resemble number lines; however, use of number lines in a more abstract form will be learned in the next unit so should not be the focus here.

Positive and negative number lines may provide a useful visual support to solve problems. Their use is covered more fully in Units 3 and 4 of the chapter.

ⓘ The ± sign is used in this unit. It shows a possible range.
For example, a net weight of 1000 g may be shown as 1000 g ±10 g. This means that the pack may contain a maximum of 1010 g or a minimum of 990 g.

Learning pupils will have achieved at the end of the unit

- Reading and writing positive and negative numbers will have been further practised (Q1, Q4)
- Pupils will have solved problems interpreting negative numbers in context (Q1, Q2, Q3, Q4)
- Pupils will have counted forwards and backwards with positive and negative whole numbers, including through zero (Q1, Q2, Q3, Q4)
- The concept of a benchmark (reference point), where the difference between the benchmark and a number greater than the benchmark are positive and the difference between the benchmark and a number less than the benchmark are negative, will have been developed (Q4)
- Pupils will have consolidated their understanding of how a negative number and its corresponding positive number are 'opposite' each other from the benchmark (reference point); they are both the same distance from the benchmark but in opposite directions (Q4)

Resources

blank dice; 1–6 dice; mini whiteboards; **Resource 5.7.2** Elevations of capital cities

Vocabulary

positive number, negative number, benchmark

Chapter 7 Introduction to positive and negative numbers

Unit 7.2 Practice Book 5B, pages 32–35

Question 1

> **1** Fill in the spaces to make each statement correct.
> (a) When recording a change in the number of passengers on a bus, if +8 represents 8 passengers getting on the bus, then −5 represents _____
> (b) Jane's mum receives her monthly salary of £2500, and it is recorded as +£2500. She spends £120 buying some books for Jane, and this should be recorded as _____.
> (c) In a maths competition, every right answer gets 5 marks and every wrong answer loses 5 marks. If the former is recorded as +5, then the latter is recorded as _____.
> One team got 25 right answers, recorded as _____ marks, and 4 wrong answers, recorded as _____ marks. Their final score was _____ marks.
> (d) The label on a bag of sugar shows the net weight as (500 ±5) g. This means that the maximum weight of the sugar is _____ g and the minimum weight is _____ g.
> (e) Due to global warming and snow melting, the sea level is rising over time. The typical height of the land in the Maldives in the Indian Ocean is only 1.5 m higher than sea level. This can be written as _____ m. If the sea level rises 2 cm every year, in about _____ years all the areas of the Maldives below the typical height will be completely flooded by the sea.

What learning will pupils have achieved at the conclusion of Question 1?

- Reading and writing positive and negative numbers will have been further practised.
- Pupils will have solved problems interpreting negative numbers in context.
- Pupils will have counted forwards and backwards with positive and negative whole numbers, including through zero.

Activities for whole-class instruction

- Tell pupils that in a 20-questions quiz, each correct answer gains 2 marks (+2), while each incorrect answer loses 2 marks (−2).
- Ask them to calculate the final score for 14 correct answers and 6 incorrect ones. Confirm that 14 correct answers gives +28, and six incorrect ones gives −12, so the final score is 16.
- Try some other combinations of correct and incorrect answers, for example 16 correct and 4 incorrect, 11 correct and 9 incorrect. Ask: *How could you achieve a score of zero? What about −2?*
- Ask pupils to explain how to record putting money in and taking money out of an account. Agree that any money going into an account is recorded as positive, while any money being withdrawn from an account is recorded as negative.

- Ask pupil pairs to write a word problem around these numbers:
  + £50   − £30   − £15
- Share some of their answers. For example, Maya was given £50 for Christmas. She spent £30 on new trainers and £15 on a video game.
- Pupils should complete Question 1 in the Practice Book.

Same-day intervention

- Roll a 1–6 dice and a blank dice marked −1, −2, −3, −4, −5 and −6 and record the numbers. For example, +4 and −5.
- Give pupils mini whiteboards and ask them to record the overall result of the two dice. Agree that +4 + −5 = −1.
- Repeat with further dice rolls.

Same-day enrichment

- Display these packet labels.

- Work out the maximum and minimum content of each packet.
  Answers: 1010 g /990 g; 33 pieces/ 27 pieces; 17 cookies/13 cookies; 335 ml/325 ml
- Ask pupils to draw some labels of their own. They should swap with a partner to work out the maximum and minimum content of each packet.

Chapter 7 Introduction to positive and negative numbers Unit 7.2 Practice Book 5B, pages 32–35

Questions 2 and 3

> **2** True or false? (Put a ✓ for true and a ✗ for false in each box.)
> (a) When recording temperatures, 10 °C and +10 °C have the same meaning.
> (b) When representing elevation of sea level, −230 m means 230 m below the sea level.
> (c) If today's lowest temperature is 2 °C lower than yesterday's, then today's lowest temperature is −2 °C.
> (d) In a maths test, the score of 87 marks is used as a benchmark. Tim got 95 marks, so his score can be shown as +95 marks.
>
> **3** Multiple choice questions. (For each question, choose the correct answer and write the letter in the box.)
> (a) If walking 200 m from school to the south is recorded as +200 m, then −360 m means walking 360 m from school to the ☐.
>   A. east   B. south   C. west   D. north
> (b) With every increment of 1 km in height, the temperature decreases by 6 °C. If the ground temperature is 12 °C, then the temperature at an altitude of 4 km will be ☐.
>   A. −6 °C   B. −12 °C   C. −18 °C   D. −24 °C
> (c) Six pupils took part in an environmental protection knowledge competition. The teacher used 80 marks as the benchmark and recorded their scores simply as +5, −3, +8, 0, −2 and −5. The lowest score among the six pupils was ☐ marks.
>   A. 88   B. 70   C. 80   D. 75
> (d) A building has 15 floors, including two floors below the ground floor. If the 12th floor above the ground floor is denoted as +12 floor, then the first floor below the ground floor is denoted as ☐ floor.
>   A. +1   B. 0   C. −1   D. −2

What learning will pupils have achieved at the conclusion of Questions 2 and 3?

- Pupils will have solved problems interpreting negative numbers in context.
- Pupils will have counted forwards and backwards with positive and negative whole numbers, including through zero.

Activities for whole-class instruction

- Display a blank thermometer and ask pupils to show you +5 °C and −5 °C.
- Ask: *How far is each temperature from zero?* Agree that the two temperatures are the same distance from zero, both 5 °C but one is positive and one negative. The values are opposite each other, equal distances either side of zero.
- Ask: *What temperature is opposite −10 °C?* Agree it is +10 °C or 10 °C. Ask: *What temperature is opposite +2 °C?* Agree it is −2 °C. Ask: *If the temperature is 7 °C and falls by 10°, what is the new temperature?*
- Display this problem:
  - Peter has £25 in his bank account.
  - He spends £13 on computer games.
  - He buys some books for £15.
  - How much does Peter have in his bank account?
- He has spent £28, so −£28. However, as he only had £25 to start with, he now has −£3 in his account.
- Pupils should complete Questions 2 and 3 in the Practice Book.

Same-day intervention

- Give pupils mini whiteboards. If walking east is recorded as positive, ask what direction will be recorded as negative. Agree that it is west.
- Ask pupils to record the following measurements on their mini whiteboards, using east as positive and west as negative.

  300 m east

  25 m west

  550 m west

  150 m east

- Ask: *How do you record measurements above and below sea level?* Confirm that measurements above sea level are positive while measurements below sea level are negative. Ask: *What do these measurements mean?*

  −200 m

  +450 m

  0 m

  −130 m

- Ask: *Which measurement is deeper: −200 m or −130 m?*

Same-day enrichment

- Present pupils with the following scenario:
  - Five scuba divers dived to explore different levels. The first diver went down about 10 m and the next one was 5 metres deeper. The third diver went down to a depth of 25 m and the final two stayed together exploring 35 m below the surface.
- Ask pupils to make a sketch and jottings to show sea level and the depths of the divers. (Remind them that measurements below sea level are negative measurements.)

Chapter 7 Introduction to positive and negative numbers   Unit 7.2 Practice Book 5B, pages 32–35

Question 4

4 The table shows some information about the heights of pupils in a school choir.

	Amaya	Rana	Beth	Chloe	Gemma	Grace
Height (cm)	147			140		
Difference from benchmark height	+2	−1	+5		0	+13

(a) Who is the tallest person? Who is the shortest?

(b) What is the difference in height between the tallest and the shortest?

What learning will pupils have achieved at the conclusion of Question 4?

- Reading and writing positive and negative numbers will have been further practised.
- Pupils will have solved problems interpreting negative numbers in context.
- Pupils will have counted forwards and backwards with positive and negative whole numbers, including through zero.
- The concept of a benchmark (reference point), where the difference between the benchmark and a number greater than the benchmark are positive and the difference between the benchmark and a number less than the benchmark are negative will have been developed.
- Pupils will have consolidated their understanding of how a negative number and its corresponding positive number are 'opposite' each other from the benchmark (reference point); they are both the same distance from the benchmark but in opposite directions.

Activities for whole-class instruction

- Display the following:

  −4   +6   −3   −7   +2   +5

- Explain that six children took part in a gymnastics vaulting competition. These numbers are the differences from the benchmark score of 40.
- Ask pupil pairs to work out the actual scores for each child in the vaulting competition. Agree that the actual scores were:

  36   46   37   33   42   45

- Explain that the children's next competition was a floor exercise. Their scores in the floor exercise were as follows:

  45   52   49   50   53   48

- The benchmark for the floor competition was 50. Pupil pairs should work out the actual scores for each child in the floor exercise. Agree that they were:

  −5   +2   −1   0   +3   −2

- Pupils should complete Question 4 in the Practice Book.

Same-day intervention

- Give pupil pairs **Resource 5.7.2** Elevations of capital cities.

Answers: 1. 1. Copenhagen; 2. 2 (Amsterdam and Baku); 3. 4 (London, Madrid, Rome and Quito); 4. Quito, Madrid, London and Rome, Copenhagen, Amsterdam, Baku; 5. London and Rome; 6. 28 m; 7. 16 m; 8. Pupils' own questions

Same-day enrichment

- Ask groups of pupils (about five to a group) to arrange themselves in height order and to measure their heights. They should make the middle height the benchmark height and complete a table similar to the one in the Practice Book.

Pupil	1	2	3 Benchmark	4	5
Height (cm)					
Difference from benchmark height					

- Challenge them to write and answer five questions on their data.

Chapter 7 Introduction to positive and negative numbers

Unit 7.2 Practice Book 5B, pages 32–35

Challenge and extension question

Question 5

5. Because of the Earth's rotation, there are different time zones around the world. Let's take Greenwich Mean Time (GMT) as the benchmark, so the time ahead of (earlier than) GMT is positive and the time behind (later than) GMT is negative.

   For example: Beijing time is 8 hours ahead of GMT, which can be denoted as +8 hours, and New Zealand time is 12 hours ahead of GMT, which can be denoted as +12 hours.

   (a) New York time is 5 hours behind GMT, which can be denoted as ☐ hours. Tokyo time is 9 hours ahead of GMT, which is denoted as ☐ hours.

   (b) If GMT is 12:00, then the time in Beijing is ☐, the time in New Zealand is ☐, the time in New York is ☐, and the time in Tokyo is ☐.

   (c) If we use Beijing time as the benchmark, then the time ahead of Beijing time is positive and the time behind is negative. So London time, when it is on GMT*, can be denoted as ☐ hours, New York time as ☐ hours and New Zealand time as ☐ hours.

   (*During Daylight Saving Time each year, London time is one hour ahead of GMT.)

This question concerns world time zones. Times ahead of (earlier than) GMT (countries to the east of the UK) are positive, while times behind (later than) GMT (in countries to the west of the UK) are negative. Displaying a world time zone map with the +/− zones labelled will support pupils with this task.

Chapter 7 Introduction to positive and negative numbers

Unit 7.3
Number lines (1)

Conceptual context

The final two units in this chapter consider locating positive and negative numbers on number lines and using the number line as a tool to solve problems involving positive and negative numbers.

ⓘ A number line is a straight line that can, theoretically, extend to infinity from zero (the origin) in both directions, positive to the right and negative to the left.

In practice, an appropriate portion of the number line is shown with arrows at each end to indicate that it continues. Negative numbers mirror positive numbers either side of zero.

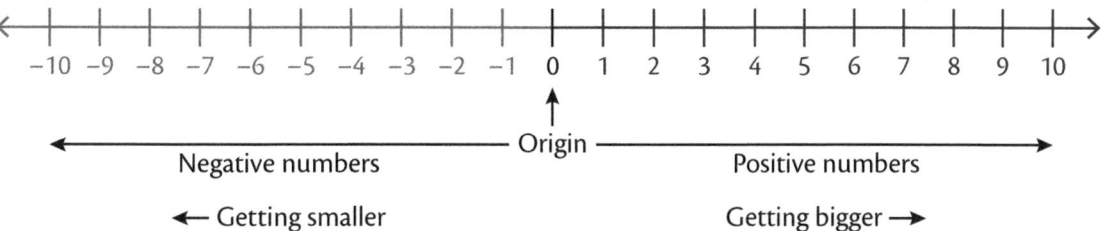

Any number to the right of a given number is bigger, for example −2 > −10; and vice versa, any number to the left of a given number is smaller, for example −8 < 2.

Natural numbers are those used for counting and ordering from 1, 2, 3, 4, 5, 6, 7 … to infinity.

Whole numbers are natural numbers, plus zero: 0, 1, 2, 3, 4, 5, 6, 7 … to infinity.

Integers include zero and the negative of natural numbers, making a list of numbers that extends in both directions indefinitely, ⁻infinity … −5, −4, −3, −2, −1, 0, 1, 2, 3, 4, 5, 6, 7 … to infinity. Zero is neither positive nor negative.

Learning pupils will have achieved at the end of the unit

- Overall fluency in number sense will have been developed to include negative numbers (Q1, Q2, Q3, Q4, Q5, Q6, Q7, Q8)
- Number sequences where the positive and negative numbers increase and decrease in ones, tens and hundreds, including across zero, will have been explored (Q1)
- Pupils will be able to explain the position of a number on a number line using full sentences (Q2)
- Pupils will have used a number line to locate positive numbers to the right of the origin and negative numbers to the left of the origin (Q2, Q3, Q4, Q5, Q6, Q7, Q8)
- Pupils will understand that negative numbers mirror positive numbers either side of zero (Q2, Q3, Q4, Q5, Q6, Q7, Q8)
- Pupils will have learned to calculate the distance between positive and negative points on a number line (Q8)

Resources

blank number lines; counting stick; −100 to +100 number lines; playground chalk; blank dice; 0–20 number cards; −20 to +20 number lines; **Resource 5.7.3a** Completing number lines; **Resource 5.7.3b** January temperatures in European cities

Vocabulary

positive number, negative number, number line, direction, origin, unit length

Chapter 7 Introduction to positive and negative numbers   Unit 7.3 Practice Book 5B, pages 36–40

Question 1

1 Count and complete the number patterns.
  (a) Forwards in tens: 0, 10, 20, ☐, ☐, ☐, ☐, ☐, 80.
  (b) Backwards in ones: 5, 4, 3, ☐, ☐, ☐, ☐, ☐, ☐, –5.
  (c) Backwards in fives: 10, 5, 0, ☐, ☐, ☐, –20.
  (d) Forwards in hundreds: –500, –400, –300, ☐, ☐, ☐, ☐, 200.

What learning will pupils have achieved at the conclusion of Question 1?

- Overall fluency in number sense will have been developed to include negative numbers.
- Number sequences where the positive and negative numbers increase and decrease in ones, tens and hundreds, including across zero, will have been explored.

Activities for whole-class instruction

- Use a counting stick to count in twos, fives, tens and hundreds, including negative numbers.
- Mark zero in the middle of the stick. Explain that this is known as the origin. Count from 0 (the origin) in ones to the right: 1, 2, 3, 4, 5.

```
                    0
[ ][ ][ ][ ][ ][ ][ ][ ][ ][ ]
```

- Go back to the origin and count in ones to the left: –1, –2, –3, –4, –5. Point to different places on the stick and ask pupils to tell you what number it represents.
- Wipe the counting stick clean and say that you are now going to count in tens. Start at zero and move to the right, counting 10, 20, 30. Change direction and count to the left: 20, 10, 0, –10, –20, –30, –40. Change direction again: –30, –20, –10, 0, 10, 20.
- Repeat, counting in other intervals, for example fives, hundreds, twenties, until pupils are confident counting across zero.
- Pupils should complete Question 1 in the Practice Book.

Same-day intervention

- Work together to draw a chalk number line in the playground from –15 to +15, with unit intervals measuring about 50 cm. Label the number line clearly. Invite a pupil to walk along the line while the other pupils call out their position.

- Invite individual pupils to stand on particular numbers, for example –8, –13.

Same-day enrichment

- Mark a blank dice with 1, 2, 5, 10, 20 and 100. Shuffle a set of 0–20 number cards. Roll the dice and turn over a card. Ask pupils to count back five numbers from the starting number. For example, card 14 and dice roll 5: the sequence is 14, 11, 6, 1, –4, –9.
- Repeat with a new card and dice roll.

Questions 2, 3, 4, 5, 6 and 7

2 Write the numbers represented by the points A, B, C and D on the number line.

```
       B         C        A    D
←—|—|—|—|—|—|—|—|—|—|—|—|—|—|→
          –2        0        2
```

Point A represents the number ☐.
Point B represents the number ☐.
Point C represents the number ☐.
Point D represents the number ☐.

3 Find the points representing –4, +3, 0, –5.5 and +0.5 on the number line, and label them A, B, C, D and E in the same order.

```
←—|—|—|—|—|—|—|—|—|—|—|—|—|→
 –6 –5 –4 –3 –2 –1  0  1  2  3  4  5  6
```

4 Look at the number line and fill in the spaces.

```
←—|—|—|—|—|—|—|—|—|—|—|—|—|→
 –6 –5 –4 –3 –2 –1  0  1  2  3  4  5  6
```

  (a) The point represented by +2 is on the _____ of the origin and is ☐ units away from it.
  (b) The point represented by –4 is on the _____ of the origin and is ☐ units away from it.
  (c) The point represented by ☐ is on the left of the origin and is 5 units away from it.
  (d) The point represented by ☐ is on the right of the origin and is 2.5 units away from it.
  (e) The points 3 units away from the origin are ☐ and ☐.
  (f) +6 and –6 are both ☐ units away from the origin.

5 On a number line, points representing positive numbers are on the _____ of the origin, and points representing negative numbers are on the _____ of the origin.

6 All _____ numbers are greater than 0, and all negative numbers are _____ than 0. Positive numbers are _____ than negative numbers.

64

Chapter 7 Introduction to positive and negative numbers

Unit 7.3 Practice Book 5B, pages 36–40

7 Multiple choice questions. (For each question, choose the correct answer and write the letter in the box.)

(a) A number line has the following elements: ☐
 A. an origin
 B. a positive direction
 C. a unit length
 D. all of these

(b) If the distance between a point and the origin is 15 unit lengths on a number line, then the number that the point represents is ☐
 A. +15
 B. −15
 C. +15 or −15
 D. uncertain

(c) Of the following statements, the only correct one is ☐.
 A. If Number A is greater than Number B, then Number A is a positive number and Number B is a negative number.
 B. A number line does not need to have an origin and a positive direction.
 C. If two points are 5 unit lengths apart on a number line, then the difference between the numbers represented by the two points is 5.
 D. All the numbers represented on a number line are either positive or negative.

What learning will pupils have achieved at the conclusion of Questions 2, 3, 4, 5, 6 and 7?

- Overall fluency in number sense will have been developed to include negative numbers.
- Pupils will be able to explain the position of a number on a number line using full sentences.
- Pupils will have used a number line to locate positive numbers to the right of the origin and negative numbers to the left of the origin.
- Pupils will understand that negative numbers mirror positive numbers either side of zero.

- Give pupils individual blank number lines and ask them to number them from −10 to +10. Pupils should check each other's to ensure that no numbers have been omitted.
- Ask pupils questions about the number line.
  - *Which side of the origin are the negative numbers?* (left)
  - *What number lies three units right of the origin?* (3 or +3)
  - *What number lies half-way between −5 and −6?* (−5.5)
  - *Which side of the origin are the positive numbers?* (right)
  - *Which two numbers are four units from the origin?* (4 and −4)
  - *Describe the position of negative 5.*

 *Negative 5 on the number line is on the left of the origin and is five units away from it.*

- Continue with further similar questions until pupils are using the number line confidently.
- Pupils should complete Questions 2, 3, 4, 5, 6 and 7 in the Practice Book.

Same-day intervention

- Give pupil pairs **Resource 5.7.3a** Completing number lines.

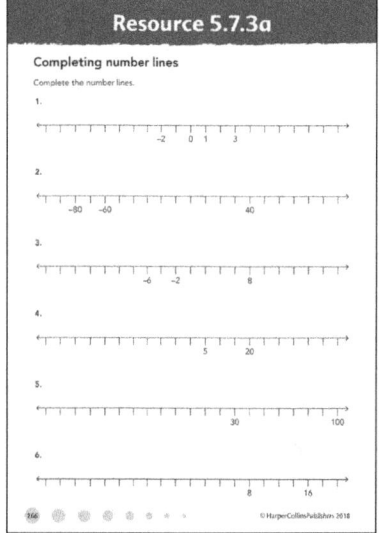

Answers: 1. ones; 2. tens; 3. twos; 4. fives; 5. tens; 6. twos

Same-day enrichment

- Display this code and give pupils mini whiteboards to record their work.

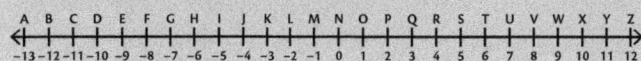

- Ask pupils to decode this message and then write the answer in code.

  9, −6, −13, 6   −5, 5   11, 1, 7, 4   0, −13, −1, −9?

  Answer: The message says 'What is your name?' Answers will be individual.

- Pupils could write further questions for peers to solve and answer.

Chapter 7 Introduction to positive and negative numbers Unit 7.3 Practice Book 5B, pages 36–40

Question 8

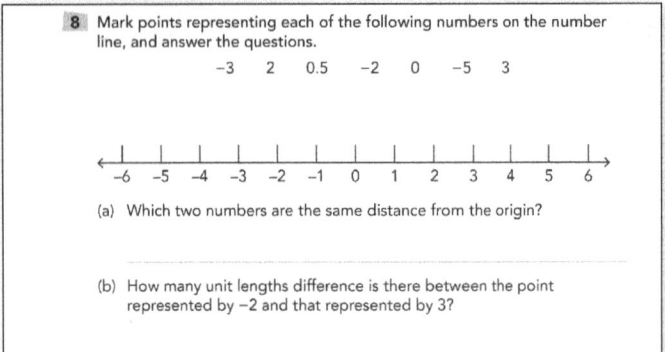

What learning will pupils have achieved at the conclusion of Question 8?

- Overall fluency in number sense will have been developed to include negative numbers.
- Pupils will have used a number line to locate positive numbers to the right of the origin and negative numbers to the left of the origin.
- Pupils will understand that negative numbers mirror positive numbers either side of zero.
- Pupils will have learned to calculate the distance between positive and negative points on a number line.

Activities for whole-class instruction

- Display a −20 to +20 number line. Ask pupils to show you pairs of numbers, for example −15 and +15 and then to count the distance between the two numbers. Repeat with further pairs. Ask: *Can you determine the distance without counting?* Agree that the numbers are equidistant from zero so the total distance between the two numbers is twice the number. In this example, the distance is 2 × 15, which is 30.
- Invite individual pupils to show the numbers −3 and 7. Use the number line to count the distance between the two numbers. Establish that it is 10. Repeat with further pairs of numbers.
- Mark a blank dice with the following numbers: −1 and +1, −5 and +5, −10 and +10. Divide pupils into two teams. Each team starts at zero. Select a pupil from each team to keep a record of their team's score. Teams takes turns to roll the dice and calculate their new score, moving the correct number in the right direction.
- Pupils should complete Question 8 in the Practice Book.

Same-day intervention

- Give pupil pairs −20 to +20 number lines.
- Invite them to find six different pairs of numbers, one positive and one negative, that are 10 units apart.
- To check their answers, pupils can make a strip measure that is 10 units long by measuring the distance from 0 to 10.
- Ask pupils to try other differences, for example: 7 units, 16 units.

Same-day enrichment

- Give pupil pairs **Resource 5.7.3b** January temperatures in European cities.

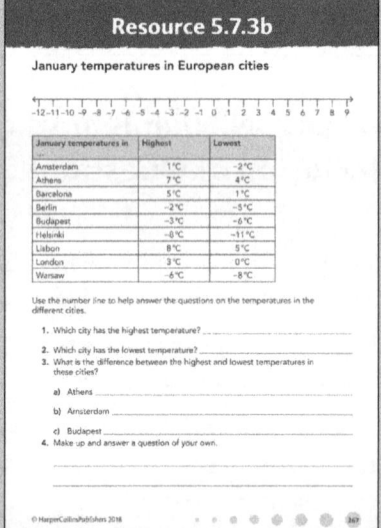

Answers: 1. Lisbon; 2. Helsinki; 3. a) 3 °C, b) 3 °C, c) 3 °C; 4. Pupils' own questions and answers

Chapter 7 Introduction to positive and negative numbers

Unit 7.3 Practice Book 5B, pages 36–40

Challenge and extension questions

Question 9

9 (a) On the number line below, move the point representing −1 to the right 3 unit lengths and then move it to the left 5 unit lengths.

```
<—|—|—|—|—|—|—|—|—|—|—|—|—>
 −6 −5 −4 −3 −2 −1  0  1  2  3  4  5  6
```

(b) What number does the new point represent?

_____

(c) If you consider these two moves as one step, what number does the final point represent after taking 10 such steps?

Question 9 challenges pupils to make repeated moves in positive and negative directions on a number line.

Question 10

10 (a) Mark five points on the number line to represent +1, −7.5, −2, +6 and −10.

```
<—|—|—|—|—|—|—|—|—|—|—|—|—|—|—|—|—|—|—|—|—>
 −10−9 −8 −7 −6 −5 −4 −3 −2 −1 0 1 2 3 4 5 6 7 8 9 10
```

(b) Among these points, ☐ points are on the right of the origin and ☐ points are on the left of the origin.

The points representing ☐ and ☐ are the closest to each other. They are ☐ units apart.

The points representing ☐ and ☐ are the furthest from each other. They are ☐ units apart.

In Question 10, pupils are identifying negative and positive points on the number line and calculating the distance between them.

Chapter 7 Introduction to positive and negative numbers

Unit 7.4
Number lines (2)

Conceptual context

In this final unit, pupils compare and order positive and negative numbers and find the difference between them. Many pupils will still need the support of a number line to do this and it is important to continue to make them readily available. You can also encourage pupils to sketch their own number lines marked with the salient points to visualise calculations.

 If pupils are asked to find the distance between −12 and 8, they might answer in different ways, depending on their stage of conceptual development.

- Some pupils may need a full number line on which they mark both numbers and then count the interval to find 20.
- The next stage of development is to sketch a number line and mark −12, 0 and 8 and then look at the two parts: −12 to 0 and 0 to 8, giving 20.
- Pupils with deep understanding can visualise the steps to answer 20.

In the Whole-class activities for Question 1, the analogy of having or owing money is used to help pupils who struggle with the abstract thinking involved.

Learning pupils will have achieved at the end of the unit

- Pupils will have used a number line to compare positive numbers to the right of the origin and negative numbers to the left of the origin (Q1, Q2, Q3, Q4, Q5, Q6)
- The use of inequality symbols to compare positive and negative numbers will have been practised (Q1, Q2, Q3, Q5)
- Pupils will have practised calculating the distance between positive and negative points on a number line (Q2, Q4)
- Pupils will have consolidated their understanding that negative numbers mirror positive numbers on each side of zero (Q2, Q4)
- Negative and positive numbers will have been compared and ordered (Q3, Q5)
- Number lines will have been used to solve word problems involving positive and negative numbers (Q6)

Resources

blank number lines; −100 to +100 number lines; −20 to +20 number lines; blank counters; 0–100 number cards; mini whiteboards; 1–6 dice; **Resource 5.7.4a** True or false statements; **Resource 5.7.4b** Fill the gap!; **Resource 5.7.4c** Ordering numbers; **Resource 5.7.4d** Temperature changes

Vocabulary

positive number, negative number, number line, direction, origin, unit length, integer, natural number, whole number

Chapter 7 Introduction to positive and negative numbers

Unit 7.4 Practice Book 5B, pages 41–44

Question 1

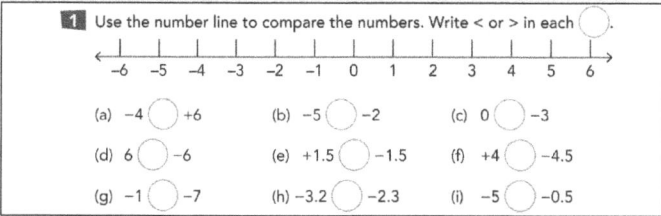

What learning will pupils have achieved at the conclusion of Question 1?

- Pupils will have used a number line to compare positive numbers to the right of the origin and negative numbers to the left of the origin.
- The use of inequality symbols to compare positive and negative numbers will have been practised.

Activities for whole-class instruction

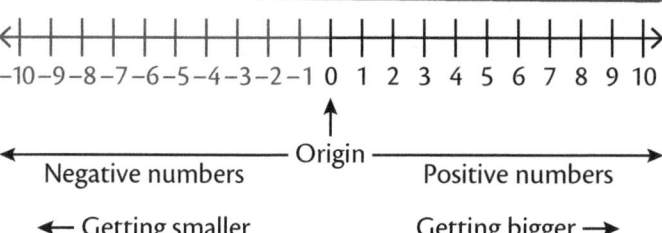

- Display a positive/negative number line. Remind pupils that positive numbers are recorded to the right of the origin and negative numbers to the left of the origin.
- Ask: *Compare 4 and 9. Which is greater: 4 or 9? How do you know?* Agree that 9 > 4 and the number on the right is the bigger number.
- Ask: *Compare 3 and –2. Which is greater: 3 or –2? How do you know?* Agree that 3 > –2 and the number on the right is the bigger number.
- Ask: *Compare –8 and –4. Which is greater: –8 or –4? How do you know?* Agree that –4 > –8 and the number on the right is the bigger number.

 *As you move in a positive direction (to the right), the numbers have increasing value.*

- Ask: *Compare 3 and 8. Which is smaller: 3 or 8? How do you know?* Agree that 3 < 8 and the number on the left is the smaller number.
- Ask: *Compare –5 and 2. Which is smaller: –5 or 2? How do you know?* Agree that –5 < 2 and the number on the left is the smaller number.

- Ask: *Compare –3 and –7. Which is smaller: –3 or –7. How do you know?* Agree that –7 < –3 and the number on the left is the smaller number.

 *As you move in a negative direction (to the left), the numbers have decreasing value.*

- Some pupils can find this hard to understand, especially when both numbers are negative. One way to help them understand is to think of the numbers in terms of having or owing money. Having money is positive; owing money is negative. So, for example, if you have £5, this is +£5 and if you owe £5, this is –£5.
  - Having £2 is better than owing £3   thus 2 > –3
  - Owing £2 is better than owing £6   thus –2 > –6
  - The larger number is the one further to the right on the number line.

  - Owing £4 is worse than having £3   thus –4 < 3
  - Owing £5 is worse than owing £2   thus –5 < –2
  - The smaller number is the one further to the left on the number line.

- Give pupils mini whiteboards and ask them to connect 4 and –5 using >. Confirm 4 > –5. Repeat with further pairs of numbers, asking pupils to use both < and > symbols.
- Pupils should complete Question 1 in the Practice Book.

Same-day intervention

- Display a –20 to +20 number line, labelled –20, –15, –10, –5, 0, 5, 10, 15, 20, for pupils to use as support.
  - Ask: *Which temperature is lower?*
    –5 °C or 3 °C
    –6 °C or –3 °C
    –1 °C or –10 °C
  - Ask: *Which temperature is higher?*
    2 °C or –9 °C
    –7 °C or –11 °C
    –1 °C or –10 °C
- Invite individual pupils to show the points on the number line and explain the lower/higher answer in a full sentence. For example: 'I know negative 1 °C is higher than negative 10 °C because negative 1 is on the right of negative 10.' (Numbers to the right of any given number are always bigger/higher/more/greater.)
- Continue with further examples until pupils show confidence.

Chapter 7 Introduction to positive and negative numbers

Unit 7.4 Practice Book 5B, pages 41–44

Same-day enrichment

- Ask pupils to work with a partner. They mark six blank counters, four with a – sign and two with a + sign and put them into a bag.
- They take two sets of 0–100 number cards and shuffle them. Without looking, each pupil selects one counter and turns over the top card from one set of number cards, for example – and 23. They repeat with a second counter and the top card from the second set, for example – and 6.
- Then they use >, < or = to link the two numbers, in this example −6 > −23 or −23 < −6. They read the expression to their partner, for example: 'Negative six is greater than negative twenty-three.'
- Then both pupils put the counters back in the bag, shake them up and repeat.
- Pupils can record the expressions on mini whiteboards or paper.

Activities for whole-class instruction

- Display a −20 to +20 number line. Invite a pupil to locate −4 and 5 on the number line. Ask: *What are the whole numbers between these two numbers?* Agree that they are −3, −2, −1, 0, 1, 2, 3, 4. Try some further examples.
- Invite individual pupils to show the numbers −5 and 8. Use the number line to count the distance between the two numbers. Establish that it is 13. It is 5 units from −5 to 0 and 8 units from 0 to 8, giving a total distance of 13.
- Repeat with some more pairs of numbers, including two negative numbers, for example −14 and −6. Invite a pupil to locate the points and count together to determine that the numbers are 8 units apart.
- Pupils should complete Question 2 in the Practice Book.

Same-day intervention

- Give pupil pairs **Resource 5.7.4a** True or false statements.

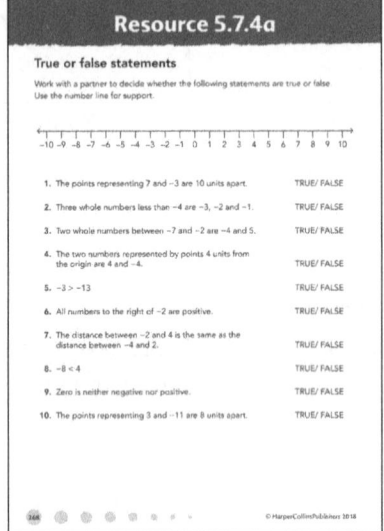

Answers: 1. T; 2. F; 3. F; 4. T; 5. T; 6. F; 7. T; 8. T; 9. T; 10. F

Question 2

> 2 Fill in the spaces.
>
> (a) Write four whole numbers less than +7: _____
>
> (b) Write four whole numbers greater than −7: _____
>
> (c) There are ☐ whole numbers between +7.5 and −7.5.
>
> (d) The diagram below shows a number line. The point representing 5 will be on the _____ of the origin and its distance from the origin will be ☐ unit lengths. The point representing −8 will be on the _____ of the origin and its distance from the origin will be ☐ unit lengths. The distance between the point representing 5 and the point representing −8 is ☐ unit lengths.
>
> −2 −1 0 1 2

What learning will pupils have achieved at the conclusion of Question 2?

- Pupils will have used a number line to compare positive numbers to the right of the origin and negative numbers to the left of the origin.
- The use of inequality symbols to compare positive and negative numbers will have been practised.
- Pupils will have practised calculating the distance between positive and negative points on a number line.
- Pupils will have consolidated their understanding that negative numbers mirror positive numbers on each side of zero.

Chapter 7 Introduction to positive and negative numbers

Unit 7.4 Practice Book 5B, pages 41–44

Same-day enrichment

- Give pupil pairs **Resource 5.7.4b** Fill the gap!

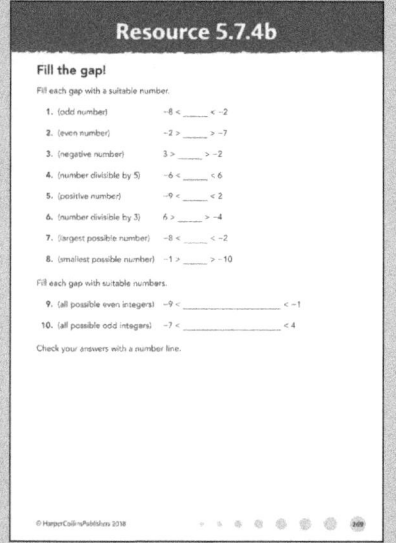

Answers: 1. –7, –5 or –3; 2. –4 or –6; 3. –1; 4. –5 or +5; 5. 1; 6. 3 or –3; 7. –3; 8. –9; 9. –8, –6, –4, –2; 10. –5, –3, –1, 1, 3

Questions 3, 4 and 5

3 Put these numbers in order, starting with the smallest.
+2   +7   –4   0   –6.5   –3

4 True or false? (Put a ✓ for true and a ✗ for false in each box.)
(a) On a number line, the further a point is away from the origin, the greater the number it represents. ☐
(b) Every number can be represented by a point on a number line. ☐
(c) As zero means none, none of the points on a number line represents zero. ☐
(d) On a number line, there is only one number with a distance from the origin of 0.5. ☐

5 Multiple choice questions. (For each question, choose the correct answer and write the letter in the box.)
(a) Of the following statements, the only incorrect one is ☐ .
   A. The smallest whole number is 0.
   B. There is no greatest negative number.
   C. There is no smallest negative number.
   D. The greatest whole number exists.
(b) If we compare –3.2, +6 and –1, the result is ☐ .
   A. –3.2 > –1 > +6   B. +6 > –1 > –3.2
   C. –3.2 > +6 > –1   D. +6 > –3.2 > –1
(c) A beetle started crawling from point A on a number line at a speed of 3 units per second. The number represented by point A is –4. The beetle moved to the right for 2 seconds and reached point B. The number represented by point B is ☐ .
   A. 2   B. –2   C. 4   D. –4
(d) The point representing –7.5 is ☐ on the number line.
   A. between –6 and –7   B. between –7 and –8
   C. between 7 and 8   D. between 6 and 7

What learning will pupils have achieved at the conclusion of Questions 3, 4 and 5?

- Pupils will have used a number line to compare positive numbers to the right of the origin and negative numbers to the left of the origin.
- The use of inequality symbols to compare positive and negative numbers will have been practised.
- Pupils will have practised calculating the distance between positive and negative points on a number line.
- Pupils will have consolidated their understanding that negative numbers mirror positive numbers on each side of zero.
- Negative and positive numbers will have been compared and ordered.

Activities for whole-class instruction

- Display these number lines one by one and ask pupil pairs to discuss what is wrong with them.

What's wrong with each of these?

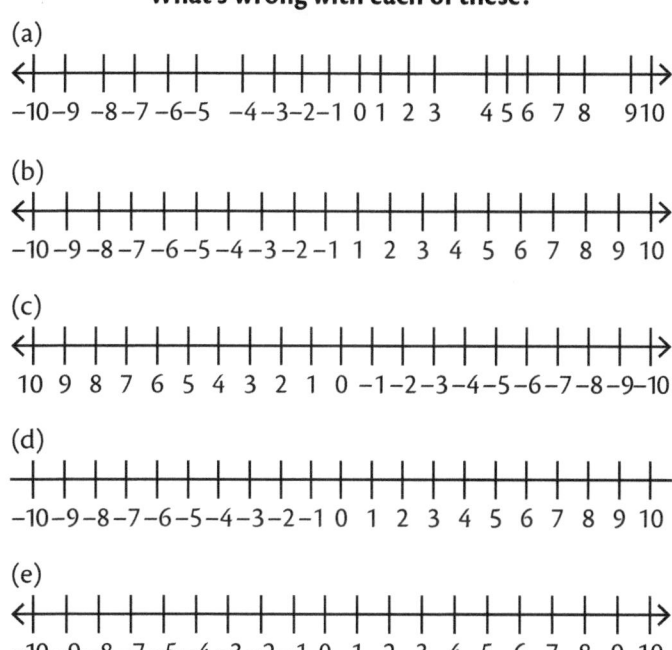

- Share ideas.
- Answer to (a): The intervals are different sizes. Agree that the numbers on number lines must be evenly spaced.
- Answer to (b): The number has no zero. Agree that on a number line positive numbers are on the right of zero and negative numbers are on the left of zero.

Chapter 7 Introduction to positive and negative numbers Unit 7.4 Practice Book 5B, pages 41–44

- Answer to (c): The positive numbers are on the left and they should be on the right. The negative numbers are on the right and they should be on the left. Agree that on a number line, positive numbers are on the right of zero and negative numbers are on the left of zero.
- Answer to (d): The ends of the number line do not have arrows on them to show that they continue.
- Answer to (e): –6 has been missed out. Agree that on a number line every number must be included in the right order.
- Ask pupil pairs to order these sets of three numbers, using inequality symbols, starting with the smallest number. Make number lines and mini whiteboards available.

  7, +8, –1

  5, –9, 0

  +10, –10, –7

  1, –3, –5
- Share ideas.
- Pupils should complete Questions 3, 4 and 5 in the Practice Book.

Same-day intervention

- Display these numbers:

  5   –3   0   –6   –1   4   –4   10   –8
- Pupil pairs should choose pairs of numbers and use a number line to find the difference between them.

  Here are some examples:

  –1 → 4   –8 → –3   –4 → 5
  　5   　5   　9

Same-day enrichment

- Give pupil pairs **Resource 5.7.4c** Ordering numbers.

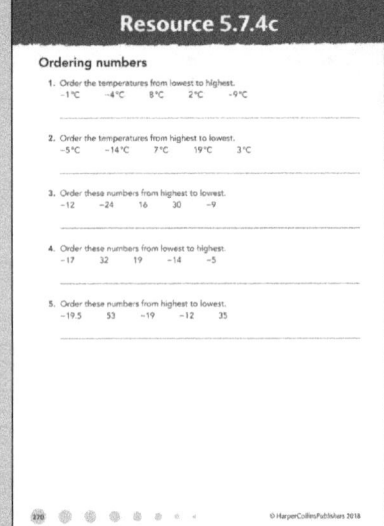

Answers: 1. –9 °C < –4 °C < –1 °C < 2 °C < 8 °C; 2. 19 °C > 7 °C > 3 °C > –5 °C > –14 °C; 3. 30 > 16 > –9 > –12 > –24; 4. –17 < –14 < –5 < 19 < 32; 5. 53 > 35 > –12 > –19 > –19.5

Question 6

6. Boat A and Boat B exchanged goods at the port, and then travelled in opposite directions, with Boat A heading south and Boat B heading north. After 1 hour, Boat A had travelled 12 nautical miles and Boat B had travelled 7 nautical miles. What was the distance between the two boats in nautical miles? (Note: 1 nautical mile = 1852 metres)

What learning will pupils have achieved at the conclusion of Question 6?

- Pupils will have used a number line to compare positive numbers to the right of the origin and negative numbers to the left of the origin.
- Number lines will have been used to solve word problems involving positive and negative numbers.

Activities for whole-class instruction

- Number lines can be used to solve word problems involving positive and negative numbers. Show pupils these number problems and sketch a number line to find the answer.

Chapter 7 Introduction to positive and negative numbers

Unit 7.4 Practice Book 5B, pages 41–44

- A snail crawls 50 cm to the right in a straight line, then turns around and crawls 65 cm in the opposite direction. Where is the snail now compared to its starting position?

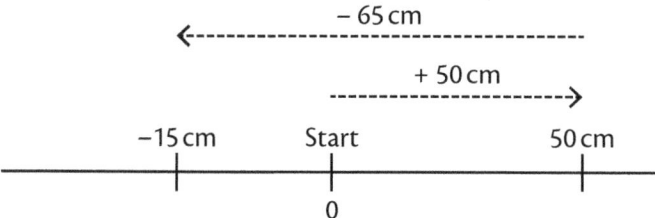

- Brothers, Alex and Billy, and their friends live on the same long straight road. Alex and Billy went to see their friends. Alex walked 700 m west of their house to visit his friend and Billy cycled 1.5 km east of their house to his friend's house. What is the distance between the two houses?

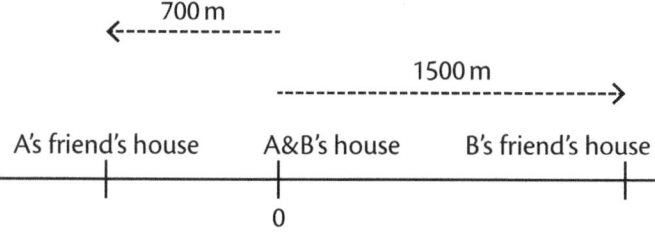

- Pupils should complete Question 6 in the Practice Book.

Same-day intervention

- Give pupil pairs **Resource 5.7.4d** Temperature changes.

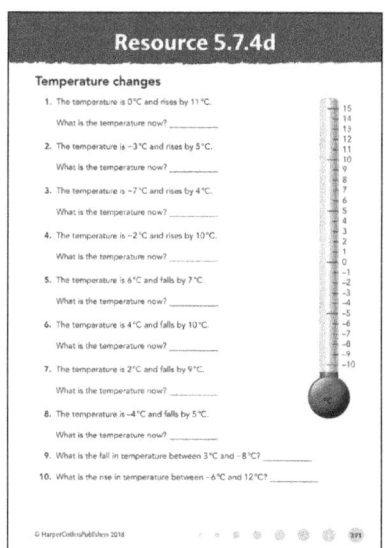

Answers: 1. 11 °C; 2. 2 °C; 3. −3 °C; 4. 8 °C; 5. −1 °C; 6. −6 °C; 7. −7 °C; 8. −9 °C; 9. 11 °C; 10. 18 °C

Same-day enrichment

- Pupil pairs should each draw a number line from −5 to 12. Ask them to check each other's number lines to make sure no numbers have been missed out. They take turns to roll two 1–6 dice. They add or subtract the two numbers to make one of the numbers on the number line and cross out that number. The winner is the pupil who crosses out all the numbers first.
- For example, a dice roll giving 3 and 4 will allow them to choose between crossing out 7 (3 + 4), 1 (4 − 3) or −1 (3 − 4).

Challenge and extension questions

Question 7

7 Which of the following statements are correct? (Put a ✓ for correct and a ✗ for incorrect in each box.)

(Note: whole numbers are 0, 1, 2, 3 and so on, natural numbers are 1, 2, 3 and so on, and integers are, for example −3, −2, −1, 0, 1, 2, 3 and so on.)

(a) All natural numbers are whole numbers.
(b) All whole numbers are natural numbers.
(c) All integers are positive numbers.
(d) The greatest negative integer is −1.
(e) Non-positive numbers are negative numbers.
(f) There is only one integer on a number line with a distance from the origin less than 2.

This question requires pupils to answer true/false statements to distinguish between whole numbers (0, 1, 2, 3 …), natural numbers (1, 2, 3 …) and integers (… −3, −2, −1, 0, 1, 2, 3 …).

Chapter 7 Introduction to positive and negative numbers — Unit 7.4 Practice Book 5B, pages 41–44

Question 8

8. An insect crawls backwards and forwards along a straight line. Starting from point A, when it crawls to the right, it is regarded as positive, and when it crawls to the left it is regarded as negative. The route the insect crawls, in sequence, is −3, +4, +3, −5, −7 and +6 (unit: cm).

(a) Is the insect on the left or the right of point A at the end? _____

(b) What is the furthest place the insect reaches from point A? _____

(c) What is the total distance the insect travels? _____

In this question, pupils are required to solve a word problem about movement of an insect backwards and forwards along a straight line. Mapping the movements as positive and negative on a number line will allow them to track the movements.

Chapter 7 test (Practice Book 5B, pages 45–50)

Test question number	Relevant unit	Relevant questions within unit
1	Unit 7.1	Q2, Q6
	Unit 7.2	Q1, Q2, Q3, Q4, Q5
	Unit 7.3	Q2, Q3, Q4, Q5, Q6, Q7, Q8, Q9, Q10
	Unit 7.4	Q1, Q2, Q3, Q4, Q7, Q8
2	Unit 7.3	Q6, Q7
	Unit 7.4	Q2, Q4, Q5, Q7
3	Unit 7.1	Q6, Q7, Q8
	Unit 7.2	Q1, Q2, Q3, Q4, Q5
	Unit 7.3	Q4, Q7, Q8, Q9, Q10
	Unit 7.4	Q2, Q3, Q4, Q5, Q6, Q7, Q8
4	Unit 7.1	Q6, Q7
	Unit 7.2	Q4, Q5
	Unit 7.3	Q4, Q8, Q9, Q10
	Unit 7.4	Q5, Q6, Q8

Chapter 8
Geometry and measurement (1)

Chapter overview

Area of mathematics	National Curriculum statutory requirements for Key Stage 2	Shanghai Maths Project reference
Geometry – properties of shape	Year 4 Programme of study: Pupils should be taught to: ■ identify lines of symmetry in 2-D shapes presented in different orientations.	Year 5, Unit 8.3
	Year 5 Programme of study: Pupils should be taught to: ■ know angles are measured in degrees: estimate and compare acute, obtuse and reflex angles	Year 5, Units 8.4, 8.5, 8.6, 8.7
	■ draw given angles, and measure them in degrees (°)	Year 5, Units 8.6, 8.7
	■ identify: • angles at a point and one whole turn (total 360°) • angles at a point on a straight line and $\frac{1}{2}$ a turn (total 180°) • other multiples of 90°	Year 5, Units 8.5, 8.8 Year 5, Units 8.5, 8.6, 8.8 Year 5, Units 8.5, 8.8
	■ use the properties of rectangles to deduce related facts and find missing lengths and angles	Year 5, Unit 8.9
	■ distinguish between regular and irregular polygons based on reasoning about equal sides and angles.	Year 5, Unit 8.9
	Year 6 Programme of study: Pupils should be taught to: ■ compare and classify geometric shapes based on their properties and sizes and find unknown angles in any triangles, quadrilaterals, and regular polygons	Year 5, Unit 8.9
	■ illustrate and name parts of circles, including radius, diameter and circumference and know that the diameter is twice the radius	Year 5, Units 8.1, 8.2, 8.3
	■ recognise angles where they meet at a point, are on a straight line, or are vertically opposite, and find missing angles.	Year 5, Units 8.4, 8.5, 8.6, 8.8

Chapter 8 Geometry and measurement (1)

Unit 8.1
Knowing circles (1)

Conceptual context

This is the first in a series of three units about circles. Pupils have previously learned, in depth, about triangles and quadrilaterals and their properties and have some knowledge of other polygons. Now they will focus on circles, learning definitions for radius and diameter, and mastering the relationship between radius and diameter. Pupils are introduced to a definition of a circle as an infinite set of points for which the distance from a single point is constant.

Learning pupils will have achieved at the end of the unit

- Pupils will be able to identify, name and draw parts of a circle, including centre, radius and diameter, and know that $d = 2r$ and $r = \frac{d}{2}$ (Q1, Q2, Q3)

Resources

large pair of compasses; small pairs of compasses; large square pieces of paper; cardboard; pins; string; circular objects, e.g. plates, CDs, cups, mugs; long wooden or plastic pole; metre rule; pieces of red, yellow, blue and green chalk; digital camera; **Resource 5.8.1a** Circle; **Resource 5.8.1b** Missing dimensions; **Resource 5.8.1c** Measuring circles (1); **Resource 5.8.1d** Measuring circles (2)

Vocabulary

circle, centre, radius, diameter, line, point

Chapter 8 Geometry and measurement (1)   Unit 8.1 Practice Book 5B, pages 51–53

Question 1

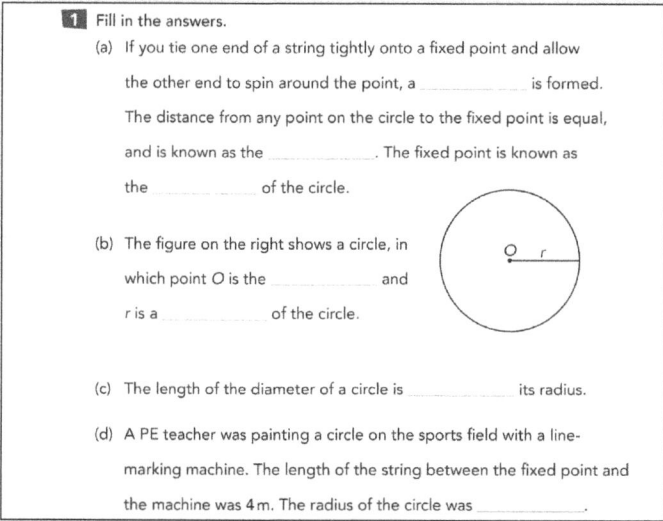

1 Fill in the answers.
(a) If you tie one end of a string tightly onto a fixed point and allow the other end to spin around the point, a _____ is formed. The distance from any point on the circle to the fixed point is equal, and is known as the _____. The fixed point is known as the _____ of the circle.
(b) The figure on the right shows a circle, in which point O is the _____ and r is a _____ of the circle.
(c) The length of the diameter of a circle is _____ its radius.
(d) A PE teacher was painting a circle on the sports field with a line-marking machine. The length of the string between the fixed point and the machine was 4 m. The radius of the circle was _____.

What learning will pupils have achieved at the conclusion of Question 1?
- Pupils will be able to identify, name and draw parts of a circle, including centre, radius and diameter, and know that $d = 2r$ and $r = \frac{d}{2}$.

Activities for whole-class instruction

- Use a large pair of compasses to draw a circle on the board. Do not discuss the mechanics of how to use compasses at this stage as this will be covered in the next unit. If a large pair of compasses is not available, draw with chalk or a pencil attached to a piece of string anchored at a central point.

- Ask pupils to turn to a partner and tell them the properties of a circle. Choose pupils to share these properties with the class. Ask: *Who can give me a mathematical definition of a circle?* Give pupils time to discuss the question, then accept comments.

- Mark random points on the circumference of the circle. Establish that, although only some points have been marked, it is possible to continue marking points all around the shape. Explain that a circle is a set of points that are the same distance from a given point, called the centre, and that there are an infinite number of these points. Mark and label the centre of the circle.

 *A circle is an infinite set of points that are the same distance from a centre.*

- Ask a volunteer to come to the board. Give the volunteer a ruler and ask them to find the distance from the centre to a point around the circumference. They should measure and then record the distance on the board.

- Invite further volunteers to the board to measure from the centre to other points around the circle. Agree that the distance is the same each time.

- Use a ruler to draw a line from the centre of the circle to the circumference. Remind pupils that all the points on the circle are the same distance from its centre. Label the line 'radius'.

 *The distance of any point on a circle to the centre point is called the radius of the circle.*

- The circle should like this:

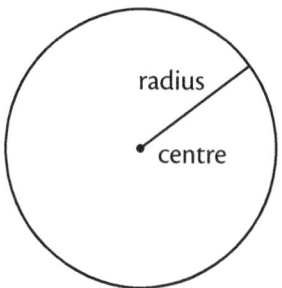

- Distribute copies of **Resource 5.8.1a** Circle, and rulers.

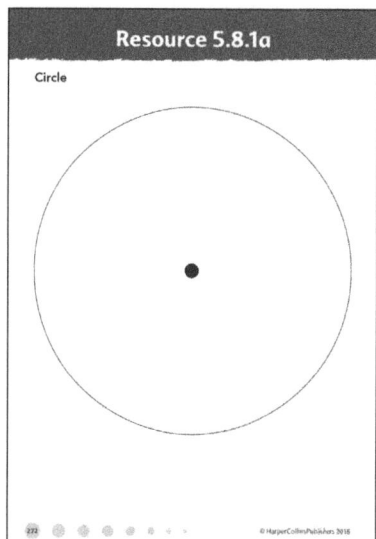

- Ask pupils to draw a radius of the circle provided. Once complete, ask them to hold up their sheets and confirm that they have correctly positioned a radius.

- Place a ruler on the board so that the edge passes through the centre of the circle. Draw a diameter of the circle. Label the line 'diameter'.

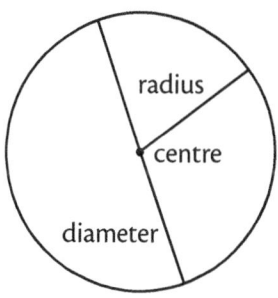

77

Chapter 8 Geometry and measurement (1) Unit 8.1 Practice Book 5B, pages 51–53

 **All say...** *A diameter is any line that joins two points on the circle and passes through the centre of the circle.*

- Reinforce the definition by drawing other diameters of the circle. Ask pupils to use a ruler to draw and label a diameter of the circle on **Resource 5.8.1a**.
- Draw another circle on the board and mark and label the lines shown here:

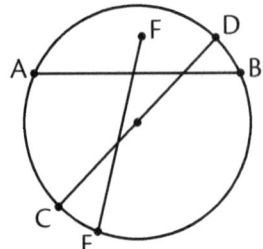

- Ask: *Which of the lines is a diameter of the circle: AB, CD or EF?* Explain that the lines are named by the letters that mark the end points. Agree that CD is a diameter of the circle. Ask: *How do you know this is a diameter?* (The line joins two points on the circle and passes through its centre.) Can pupils say why lines AB and EF are not diameters of the circle? (The line AB does not pass through the centre of the circle; the line EF does not join two points on the circle.)
- Draw a circle and mark and label a radius and diameter. Ask: *What do you think is the relationship between the diameter and the radius?* Establish that since the radius is halfway across the circle just to the centre, and the diameter is the entire way across, the diameter is twice as long as the radius.
- Label the radius '15 cm'. Ask: *What is the diameter of the circle? How do you know?* Agree that since the diameter is double the radius, the diameter of the circle is 30 cm.
- Label the diameter '130 m'. Ask: *What is the radius? How do you know?* Agree that since the radius is half the diameter, the radius of the circle is 65 m.
- Repeat for other radius and diameter measurements.
- Pupils should complete Question 1 in the Practice Book.

Same-day intervention

- Some pupils think that a circle has only one radius and diameter. Intervene to show that an infinite number of radii (teach pupils the plural) and diameters can be drawn.
- Provide square pieces of paper, cardboard, pins, string, pencils and rulers. Show pupils how to construct the apparatus for drawing a circle shown in this diagram:

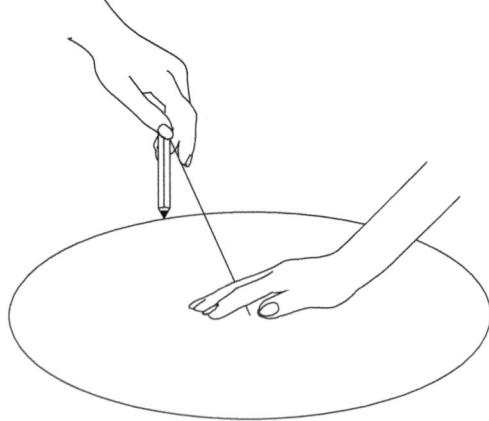

- Pupils work in pairs. They pin a length of string to the centre of a piece of square paper placed on top of cardboard. They stretch the string taut and tie a pencil to one end at a distance just less than half the width of the paper. Pupil A should press down on the end of the string, keeping it in place at the centre of the circle while pupil B holds the pencil, keeping the string taut to draw the circle.
- When the circle is complete, ask pupils to hold the string taut and point out that the line of the string is a radius of the circle, running from the edge of the circle to its centre. Ask pupils to hold the string taut and place the pencil at the edge of the circle at a different position. Ask: *How many radii are there?* Agree that a circle has more than one radius, in fact an infinite number.
- Ask pupils to mark five points in various places on the circle. They choose a point and use a ruler to draw a line to the centre of the circle, then extend it to the point on the opposite side of the circle. Explain that the line is one diameter of the circle but there are actually an infinite number that could be drawn. Pupils then mark diameters using the other points in a similar fashion.
- Ask pupils to label the radius of the circle '25 cm'. Can they say what the diameter is? If pupils do not know how to begin, ask: *What can you say about the size of the diameter compared to the radius?*
- Give pupils a measurement and the freedom to choose the property measured. Say, for example: *One of the measurements of a circle is 24 centimetres. Draw and show at least one other measurement of the circle.* The freedom to choose the dimension makes the question more accessible to pupils.

Chapter 8 Geometry and measurement (1)

Unit 8.1 Practice Book 5B, pages 51–53

Same-day enrichment

- Provide pupils with copies of **Resource 5.8.1b** Missing dimensions. Given one dimension – radius or diameter – pupils must calculate the other.

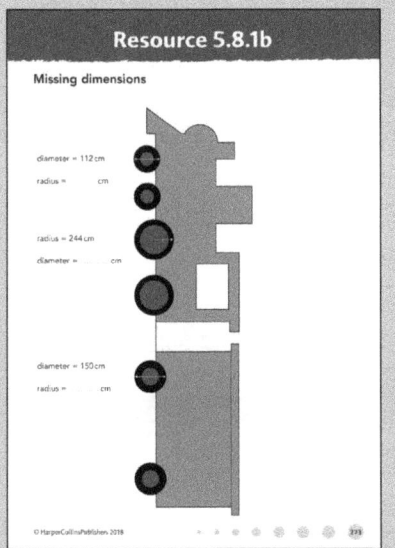

- For a challenge, pupils might like to draw their own picture of a vehicle, or other machine, with wheels of different diameters. They label one dimension of each circle – radius or diameter – then swap papers with a partner to determine the missing dimensions. They return papers for marking.

Answers: 56 cm; 488 cm; 75 cm

What learning will pupils have achieved at the conclusion of Questions 2 and 3?

- Pupils will be able to identify, name and draw parts of a circle, including centre, radius and diameter, and know that $d = 2r$ and $r = \frac{d}{2}$.

Activities for whole-class instruction

- Provide pupils with further copies of **Resource 5.8.1a** Circle. Ask them to use a ruler to find the longest horizontal distance from any height. Repeat the investigation for the longest vertical distance.

- Choose pupils to discuss their findings. Ensure that they are in agreement that the horizontal and vertical measurements are equal. Ask: *Where is the circle the tallest/widest?* (in the middle) Establish that the distance between two points on a circle is greatest when the line joining them passes through the centre of the circle and, therefore, the diameter of a circle is the largest width across the circle.

- Draw and label the following circles:

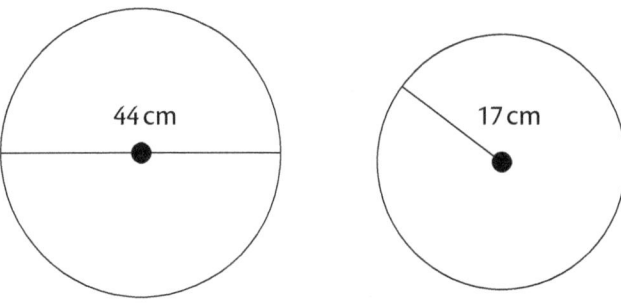

- Ask: *Which circle is larger? How do you know?* Can pupils explain that, since the radius is half the diameter, the right circle has a diameter of 34 cm so is smaller than the left circle?

- Display the following image:

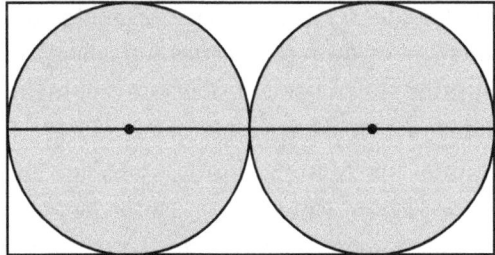

- Explain that the diagram shows two identical circles inside a rectangle. Ask: *If the radius of each circle is 2 cm, what are the dimensions of the rectangle?* Pupils should work in pairs. Give them time to solve the problem then choose a pair to explain the solution.

Questions 2 and 3

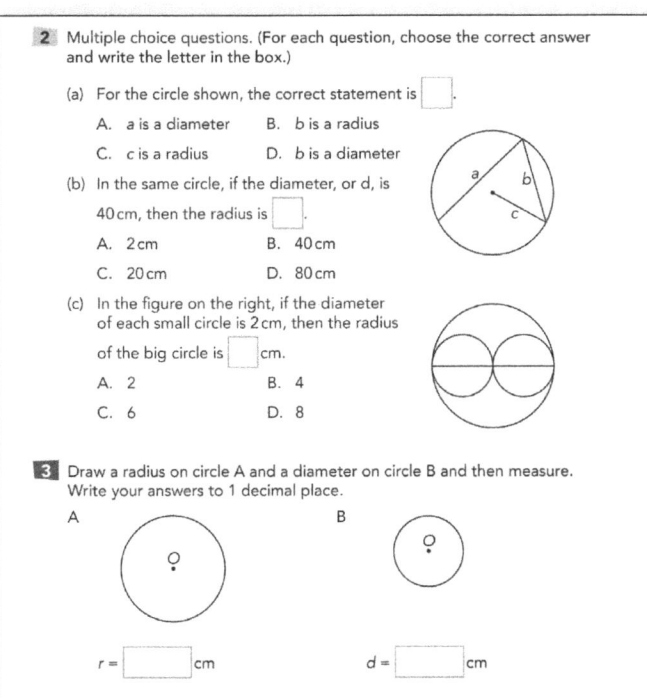

Chapter 8 Geometry and measurement (1)

Unit 8.1 Practice Book 5B, pages 51–53

- Agree that since the radius of each circle is 2 cm, the diameter must be 4 cm. Also, since the rectangle has a width equal to that of the diameter of one circle, the width must be 4 cm.
- Ask: *What is the length of the rectangle?* Give pupils time to solve the problem, then choose a pair to explain the solution. Can pupils explain that, since the radius of each circle is 2 cm, the diameter must be 4 cm (double 2 cm) and therefore the length of the rectangle is 8 cm (double the diameter of one circle)?
- Pose different problems based on this diagram, varying the measurements of either the diameter or the radius of one circle. For a challenge, ask pupils to find the perimeter of the rectangle given the radius of the circles.
- Use a large pair of compasses to draw the following diagram:

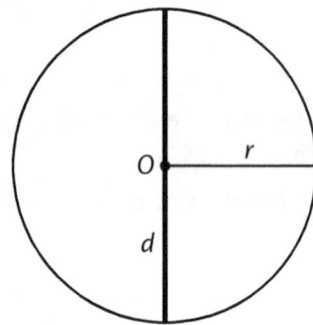

- Say: *When discussing the different parts of a circle, we usually give the centre the symbol O, radius the symbol r and the diameter the symbol d.*
- Ask: *What is the relationship between r and d?* (*d* is two times/double *r*; *r* is half *d*.) Ask a volunteer to write a number statement on the board that connects *r* and *d*. Expect: $d = 2r$ (or $r = \frac{1}{2}d$).
- Below the circle on the board, write: $r = $ ___ cm. Invite a volunteer to the board to measure the radius and complete the statement. Explain that the measurement should be made to 1 decimal place. Remind pupils that a measurement made in centimetres and millimetres can be converted to a measurement in just centimetres by remembering that 1 mm is equal to 0.1 cm.
- Draw another circle on the board and mark the diameter. Below the diagram, write: $d = $ ___ cm. Invite a volunteer to measure the diameter to 1 decimal place and complete the statement.
- Distribute **Resource 5.8.1c** Measuring circles (1) to one half of the class and **Resource 5.8.1d** Measuring circles (2) to the other half.

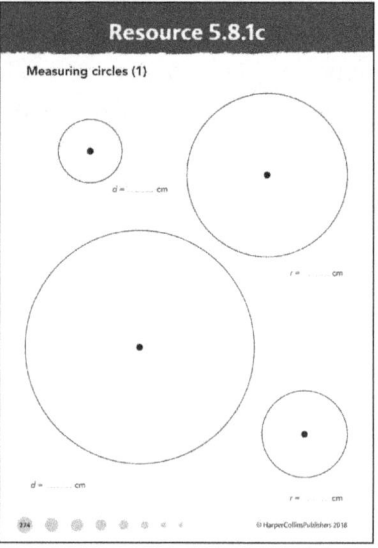

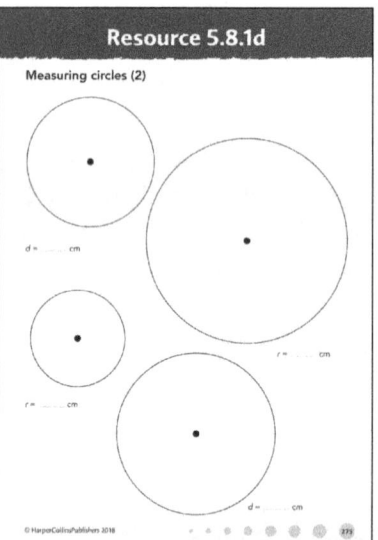

- Pupils should use a ruler to mark the radius or diameter on each circle and then measure the required dimension in centimetres to 1 decimal place. Pupils who completed **Resource 5.8.1c** should then swap papers with a pupil who completed **Resource 5.8.1d** to measure and confirm that the dimensions recorded are correct.
- Pupils should complete Questions 2 and 3 in the Practice Book.

Same-day intervention

- Take pupils into the playground and ask them to work in pairs. Provide each group with a long wooden or plastic pole, two metre rulers firmly taped together to form a 2 m ruler, string, and pieces of red, yellow, blue and green chalk.
- Ask them to measure and cut a 1-metre length of string and use red chalk to mark the ground with a large dot. While one pupil holds the pole in a vertical position against the dot, the other ties one end of the string to

Chapter 8 Geometry and measurement (1)

Unit 8.1 Practice Book 5B, pages 51–53

the base loosely enough to allow the string to spin freely. They tie the string to a piece of yellow chalk and use the device to draw a circle. When complete, they align the ruler so that it passes through the centre of the circle. They then use the ruler to draw a line in blue chalk from one point on the circle, through the centre, to the opposite point. Next, they draw a line from the centre of the circle to the edge using green chalk. Ensure that this line is at enough of an angle to the diameter to make it distinct.

- Point to the red dot and ask: *What is the name of this part of the circle?* Agree that the dot marks the centre of the circle. Pupils should label it 'centre'.
- Point to the blue line and ask: *What is the name of this line? How do you know?* Establish that the blue line is a diameter of the circle. Pupils write the word 'diameter' next to the line in blue chalk.
- Point to the green line and ask: *What is the name of this line? How do you know?* Establish that the green line is a radius of the circle. Pupils write the word 'radius' next to the line in green chalk.
- Ask: *What is the length of the radius of the circle?* Prompt pupils by asking them the length of the string they used. They label the radius '1 m'. Ask: *If the radius is 1 metre, what is the diameter?* Prompt pupils by asking them the relationship between the radius and the diameter. Confirm that the diameter is double the length of the radius by rotating the string and chalk 180 degrees from one diameter point to the other to show that the radius is the same length either side of the centre. Ask two pupils to stand together at one end of a marked diameter and walk slowly around the circle in opposite directions to meet at the opposite end of the diameter. Agree that they have walked the same distance.
- Choose volunteers to take digital photographs of the circles that can be used as part of a classroom display of circles and their properties.

Same-day enrichment

- Ask pupils, working in pairs, to use the following image as an example from which to construct a similar problem that involves finding a missing dimension.

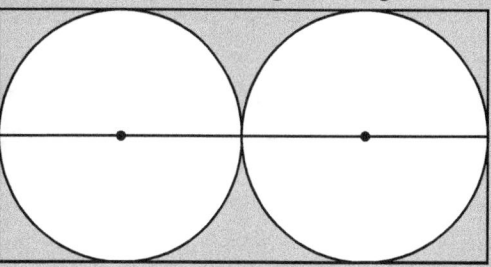

- For example, pupils might draw a circle inscribed in a square, give the radius and ask for the sides of the square/its perimeter to be calculated; or they might draw four circles inside a square. Another possibility is for pupils to draw four congruent circles in a row inside a rectangle, provide the length of the rectangle and ask for the diameter or radius of the circles to be calculated.
- Pairs swap their problems with another pair to answer. They return them to confirm that they have correctly identified the missing dimension(s).

Challenge and extension question

Question 4

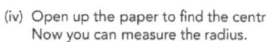

4 Do you have a mug with a circular base? If so, do you know how to find the radius of the base? Follow the steps below.
  (i) Draw a circle around the base of your mug on a piece of blank paper.
  (ii) Cut out the circle.
  (iii) Fold the circle in half and then in half again.
  (iv) Open up the paper to find the centre. Now you can measure the radius.

Have a try. Can you measure the radius of other circular objects?

Pupils draw a circle around the base of a mug. They cut out the circle and fold it in half, then half again. They then find the centre and measure the radius. Pupils then repeat the exercise for other objects with circular bases. For a challenge, ask pupils to draw the bases in order of length of radius from least to greatest.

Chapter 8 Geometry and measurement (1)

Unit 8.2
Knowing circles (2)

Conceptual context

Pupils will consolidate their knowledge about radius and diameter and the relationship between them, learned in the previous unit, applying it to solve geometrical problems.

Pupils will also learn how to use a pair of compasses to draw circles. Constructing their own circles will help pupils to form a strong concept of 'circle' – what it is and is not; how relevant features are connected in physical space and mathematically.

Learning pupils will have achieved at the end of the unit

- Pupils will be able to identify, name and draw parts of a circle, including centre, radius, diameter and circumference, and know that $d = 2r$ and $r = \frac{d}{2}$ (Q1, Q2)
- Using a pair of compasses, pupils will be able to construct circles of a specified size and mark the centre, radius, diameter and circumference (Q1, Q2)

Resources

large pair of compasses; small pair of compasses; metre rule; 30 cm rulers; cardboard; tape; **Resource 5.8.2a** Circles in circles; **Resource 5.8.2b** Use a square to draw a circle

Vocabulary

circle, centre, radius, radii, diameter, circumference, pair of compasses

Chapter 8 Geometry and measurement (1)

Unit 8.2 Practice Book 5B, pages 54–56

Question 1

> **1** Fill in the answers.
>
> (a) In the same circle, all radii are _____ and all diameters are _____.
>
> (b) In the same circle, if the diameter is d and radius is r, then
>
> d = _____ or r = _____. If the diameter of a circle is 20 cm, then its radius is _____ cm.
>
> (c) In the figure on the right, the length of the rectangle is 6 cm and the two circles are the same size.
>
> Therefore, d = _____ cm
>
> and r = _____ cm.
>
> **2** Use a pair of compasses to draw circles.

What learning will pupils have achieved at the conclusion of Question 1?

- Pupils will be able to identify, name and draw parts of a circle, including centre, radius, diameter and circumference, and know that $d = 2r$ and $r = \frac{d}{2}$.
- Using a pair of compasses, pupils will be able to construct circles of a specified size and mark the centre, radius, diameter and circumference.

Activities for whole-class instruction

- Use a large pair of compasses to draw a large circle on the board. Mark the centre with a small cross. Ask a volunteer to label the centre of the circle. Ask: *Why is it important that we mark the centre straight away?* Draw pupils' attention to the difficulty in finding the centre of a drawn circle.
- Provide a ruler and invite a volunteer to mark a radius of the circle. Ask the pupil to explain how they found the position of the radius. Recap from the previous unit if necessary.
- Ask pupils to turn to a partner and give them a definition of the word 'radius'. Choose a pupil to share their definition.
- Ask: *Why do you think I asked you to find **a** radius of the circle and not **the** radius?* Remind pupils that any straight line drawn from the circle to the centre is called a radius. Ask: *Who can tell me the plural of the word radius?* (radii) Invite volunteers to the board to draw other radii using the steps discussed.
- Ask a volunteer to mark a diameter of the circle and explain how they found the position of the diameter. Recap from the previous unit if necessary.

- Tell pupils to turn to a partner and give them a definition of the word 'diameter'. Choose a pupil to share their definition.
- Ask: *Why do you think I asked you to find **a** diameter of the circle and not **the** diameter?* Remind pupils that any straight line drawn across the circle through its centre is called a diameter. Invite volunteers to the board to draw other diameters using the steps discussed.
- Can pupils remember the abbreviations for radius and diameter? Choose a pupil to label the radius and diameter (r, d). Invite a pupil to the board to write a number sentence to describe the relationship between the dimensions r and d. Expect: $d = 2r$ or $r = \frac{1}{2}d$ (or $\frac{d}{2}$).
- Ask: *If a diameter of a circle is 94 cm, what is the radius?* Give pupils time to solve the problem then accept answers. (47 cm) Ask: *How do you know?* (The radius is half the diameter.)
- Draw the following diagram:

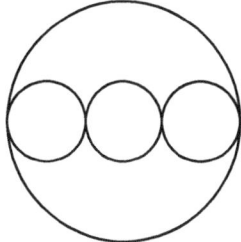

- Explain that a larger circle is drawn around three smaller circles of identical size. The diameters of the smaller circles are aligned with the diameter of the larger circle. Ask: *If the diameter of the larger circle is 72 cm, what is the radius of each smaller circle?* Give pupils time to discuss the problem then accept answers. Lead pupils through the solution using guided questioning:
  - *What do we know about the diameter of the smaller circles?* (They are equal.)
  - *What other information are we given? What do we know about the sum of the diameters of the smaller circles?* (The sum is equal to the diameter of the larger circle: 72 cm.)
  - *What does this tell us about the diameter of each smaller circle?* (The diameter will be a third of that of larger circle.)
  - *How would we use this information to work out the diameter of each smaller circle?* (72 cm divided by 3)
  - *What is the answer?* (The diameter is 24 cm.)
  - *What is the relationship between radius and diameter?* (The radius is half the diameter.)
  - *What is the radius of each smaller circle?* (12 cm)
- Pupils should complete Question 1 in the Practice Book.

Chapter 8 Geometry and measurement (1)

Unit 8.2 Practice Book 5B, pages 54–56

Same-day intervention

- Use a large pair of compasses and a ruler to draw the following diagram on the board:

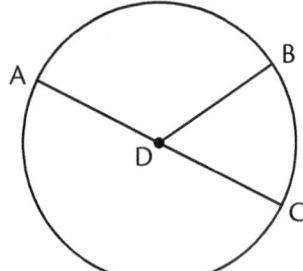

- Write these words and statements in a table alongside the diagram:

Part of circle	Description of part
centre	the distance from the centre outwards
radius	goes straight across the circle, through the centre
diameter	the point that is equally distant from every point on the circle
circumference	the distance around the edge of the circle

- Point to D and ask: *Which part of the circle is this?* (centre) *How do you know?* Use questions to guide pupils towards a definition of the centre. Ask: *What can you say about the distances DA and DC? What about DB?* Draw another point on the circle, E. Ask: *What about distance DE compared to DA, DB and DC?* Establish that the distances are equal. Ask pupils to choose the correct definition of the term 'centre' (the point that is equally distant from every point on the circle).

- Point to line DB. Ask: *Which statement in the table best describes this line?* Establish that this is 'the distance from the centre outwards'. Ask: *Who can remember what we call this distance?* (radius) *If DB is a radius what about lines DA, DC and DE?* Establish that they are all radii as they mark the distance from the centre outwards.

- Point to line AC. Ask: *Which statement in the table best describes this line?* Establish that this is a line 'that goes straight across the circle, through the centre'. Ask: *Who can remember what we call this line?* (diameter) Extend line ED to a point F on the circle. Ask: *If AC is a diameter what about line EF?* Establish that they are both diameters as they mark the distance across the circle, through the centre.

- Trace, with your finger, the circumference and ask: *What do we call the distance around the edge?*

Same-day enrichment

- Pupils should work in pairs. Provide each pair with **Resource 5.8.2a** Circles in circles.

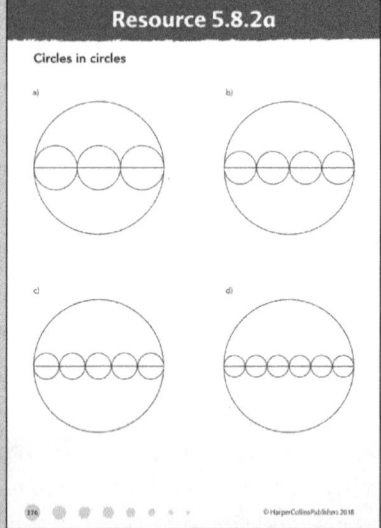

- Pupils use the diagrams to devise their own problems for another group to solve. They provide either the diameter or radius of the larger circle, or the diameter or radius of the smaller circles, and pose a question that asks for the radius and diameter of all the circles, both large and small, to be found. Pupils will need to record the measurements on the diagrams before swapping with another group to solve. They will also need to ensure that any problem that is solved using division uses numbers that are easily divisible by the number of smaller circles.

Chapter 8 Geometry and measurement (1)

Unit 8.2 Practice Book 5B, pages 54–56

Question 2

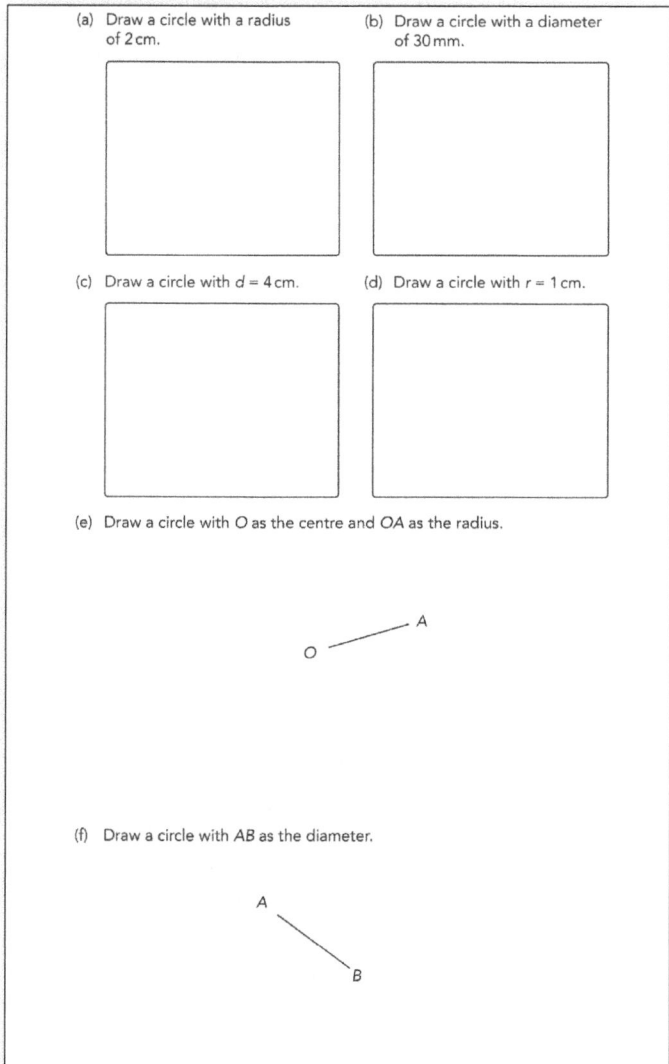

What learning will pupils have achieved at the conclusion of Question 2?

- Pupils will be able to identify, name and draw parts of a circle, including centre, radius, diameter and circumference, and know that $d = 2r$ and $r = \frac{d}{2}$.
- Using a pair of compasses, pupils will be able to construct circles of a specified size and mark the centre, radius, diameter and circumference.

Activities for whole-class instruction

- Provide pupils with paper, cardboard, tape, pencils and pairs of compasses. Tell pupils that they will use a tool called a pair of compasses to draw a circle on paper. Hold up a pair of compasses and demonstrate how to load a pencil. Say: *Insert the pencil into the lock and tighten the screw at the side of the lock to secure it.*

Explain that the screw should not be turned too tightly as the pencil height still needs to be adjusted. Pupils follow the instruction and load a pencil in their pair of compasses.

- Explain that the tip of the pencil must be at the same height as the sharp point when the compasses are closed. Pupils adjust the pencil height and tighten the screw once the pencil is at the correct height.

- Tell pupils that the table surface must be protected from damage by placing cardboard under the paper to be drawn on. This will also stop the needle point from slipping as the pencil is rotated. Pupils should follow the instructions and prepare the surface for drawing.
- Explain that the pair of compasses should be turned by spinning it with the little spinning knob on top and not by its arms.
- Ask pupils to practise pressing the needle point firmly onto the paper and turning the pair of compasses using the spinning knob. Some pupils may wish to tape the cardboard down to prevent it from spinning.
- Pupils will require multiple opportunities to practise with basic circle construction before attempting to draw circles of a specific size or inscribed in other shapes.
- Next, they should draw circles of given sizes and become familiar with adjusting the pencil to obtain a larger separation.

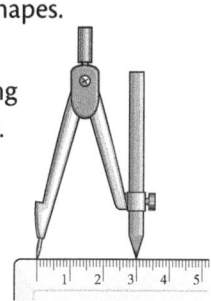

- Ask: *If I want to draw a circle with a diameter of 10 cm, what separation should the pair of compasses be set to?* Can pupils explain that a separation of 5 cm is required as this is the radius that will give a diameter of 10 cm?
- Ask pupils to draw a circle with a radius of 8 cm and to draw a radius on the circle. Then ask them to label the centre of the circle O and the other end of the radius A.
- Next, ask them to draw a circle where the radius OA = 7.5 cm. Once they have drawn this circle, ask pupils to draw a diameter and label the ends B and C.
- Now ask pupils to draw a circle where the diameter BC is 9 cm. Pupils might think it should be in the same position as on the previous circle, so discuss how BC can be ANY diameter – the letters are just a label. Check that pupils understand that any diameter must pass through the centre, which they should have labelled.
- Pupils should complete Question 2 in the Practice Book.

Chapter 8 Geometry and measurement (1)

Unit 8.2 Practice Book 5B, pages 54–56

Same-day intervention

- Some pupils using traditional metal compasses might have difficulty keeping weight on the point while drawing or fixing the pencil in the clamp. Pupils using safety compasses might have difficulty maintaining pressure on the centre of the pair of compasses, moving the slider around unintentionally or keeping track of the radius adjustment. Pupils experiencing these difficulties should practise drawing circles while a teacher or other pupil provides guidance alongside. Pupils experiencing difficulties when drawing with a pair of compasses may benefit from using a different drawing tool, for example a safety drawing compass, where the pencil is placed in one of a set of holes and a ruler rotated to give a circle of the radius set.

Same-day enrichment

- Give pairs of pupils **Resource 5.8.2b** Use a square to draw a circle.

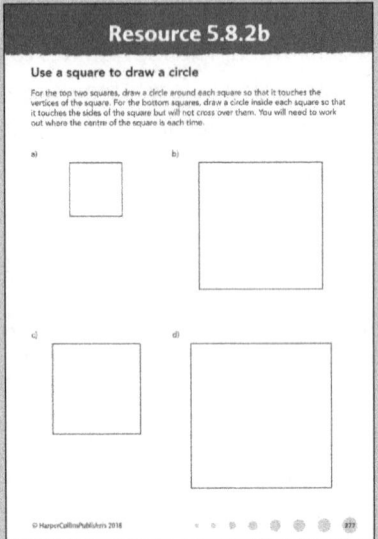

- The resource sheet shows four squares of different sizes. Pupils must draw a circle around each square in the top row so that the circle touches the vertices of the square. On the bottom row, pupils should draw a circle inside each square so that it touches the sides of the square. This in an independent activity but if pupils struggle to find the centre of the square, remind them that the centre is found at the point where the two diagonals of the square cross.

Challenge and extension question

Question 3

3 Hands-on activity.
   (a) Draw a circle with point A as the centre and a radius of 2 cm.

   (b) Draw a circle with point B as the centre and a diameter of 6 cm.

Pupils are asked to draw two circles, one with a radius of 2 cm and another with a diameter of 6 cm. The questions enable pupils to demonstrate their understanding of the relationship between radius and diameter and the control of a pair of compasses. This question is probably best trialled on paper before answering in the book.

Chapter 8 Geometry and measurement (1)

Unit 8.3
Knowing circles (3)

Conceptual context

This is the final unit in a series about circles. Mastery of knowledge about circles and fluency when applying that knowledge to solve a variety of problems will form solid foundations for geometrical learning to come. In this unit, word problems are increasingly complex, incorporating scale factors and circles in combination with other shapes.

Pupils also explore how circles and other shapes can be classified by the existence of lines of symmetry. Whereas an isosceles trapezium has only one line of symmetry, and a rectangle two lines of symmetry, a circle has an infinite number of lines of symmetry and therefore, an infinite number of diameters. Understanding this property is fundamental to solving the more challenging problems that pupils will face later, including using π to find the area of a circle.

Learning pupils will have achieved at the end of the unit

- Pupils will be able to identify, name and draw parts of a circle, including centre, radius, diameter and circumference, and know that the diameter is twice the radius (Q1, Q3)
- Pupils will be able to identify lines of symmetry in 2-D shapes presented in different orientations (Q2)
- Using a pair of compasses, pupils will be able to construct circles and draw in the centre, radius and diameter (Q3)

Resources

pairs of compasses; paper shapes: rectangle (oblong), square, equilateral triangle, isosceles trapezium, circle; mirrors; **Resource 5.8.3** Symmetry in 2-D shapes

Vocabulary

circle, centre, radius, radii, diameter, infinite, symmetry, line of symmetry

Chapter 8 Geometry and measurement (1)

Unit 8.3 Practice Book 5B, pages 57–59

Question 1

> **1** Fill in the answers.
>
> (a) A circle has _____ centre, _____ radii
>   and _____ diameters.
>   (Hint: fill in the spaces with 'one' or 'infinitely many'.)
>
> (b) Fold a circle in half. The folding line is a _____ of the circle.
>   Its length is _____ the length of the radius. The intersection of
>   two different folding lines is the _____ of the circle.
>
> (c) The diameter of a bigger circle is 3 times the diameter of a smaller
>   circle. If the diameter of the bigger circle is 15 cm, then the diameter of
>   the smaller circle is ☐ cm.
>
> (d) In the figure on the right, the radii of
>   both circles are 3 cm so the area of the
>   rectangle is _____ .

What learning will pupils have achieved at the conclusion of Question 1?

- Pupils will be able to identify, name and draw parts of a circle, including centre, radius, diameter and circumference and know that the diameter is twice the radius.

Activities for whole-class instruction

- Provide pupils with pairs of compasses, A4 paper and pencils. Ask a volunteer to remind the class of the steps involved in drawing a circle, including how to load a pencil and adjust the height of a pair of compasses so that the both the needle and pencil points are aligned. Confirm the steps involved and ask the class to draw a circle that fills the page. Ask: *How did you ensure that the pencil did not leave the paper?* Establish that the pencil point should be placed near the edge of the longer side of the paper and not the shorter side.

- Ask pupils to fold the paper horizontally and then vertically. Prepare a similarly folded circle to use for demonstration. Ask: *How can we use the two folds to find the centre of the paper?* Can pupils explain that, since both folds are diameters and therefore both pass through the centre, the point where they intersect must be the centre?

- Draw the following diagram on the board:

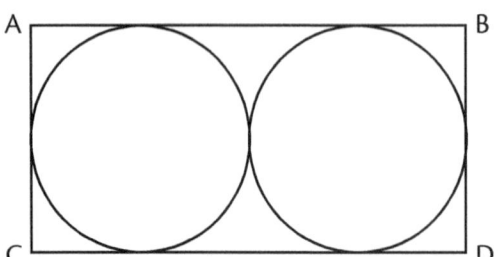

- Ask: *If the radius of each circle is 5 cm, what can you say about lengths of side AC and BD?* Give pupils time to think about the problem, then accept answers. Choose a pupil to explain the solution. Establish that sides AC and BD are equal to the diameter of the circle(s). Agree that since the radius is 5 cm, the diameter will be 10 cm. Therefore the length of sides AC and BD will be 10 cm.

- Ask pupils to find the length of sides AB and CD. Confirm that the sides are equivalent to twice the diameter of a circle or four times its radius. Given the length and width of the rectangle, can pupils work out the area? Invite a pupil to explain how the area of a rectangle is calculated (length multiplied by width). Ask: *What is the answer?* Remind pupils that area must be given both as a value and a unit (200 cm^2).

- Pupils should complete Question 1 in the Practice Book.

Same-day intervention

- On the board, draw the table below. Remind pupils of the relationship between radius and diameter and ask them to complete the missing values to reinforce this relationship.

Radius of circle (cm)	Diameter of circle
8	
	36
49	
	78
127	

- Pose questions where pupils have to apply knowledge of radius and diameter, for example:

  - *Two circles, each with a radius of 6 cm, are placed side-by-side. What is the combined width of the circles along their diameters?*

  - *A child draws a picture of a caterpillar made up of five circles placed side by side. If the length of the caterpillar is 25 cm, what is the diameter of each circle? What is the radius?*

- Pupils should work in pairs to write questions, with pictures or diagrams, for other pairs to answer.

Chapter 8 Geometry and measurement (1)

Unit 8.3 Practice Book 5B, pages 57–59

Same-day enrichment

- Challenge pupils to construct their own 'circles inside a rectangle' problems. They will need to think of a strategy for drawing a pair of circles that just touch each other and another to construct the rectangle so that the sides just touch the circles. They must then use the diameter of the circle and no other measurement to calculate the area of the rectangle. Following completion of the diagrams, choose pupils to explain how they used it to calculate the area.

Question 2

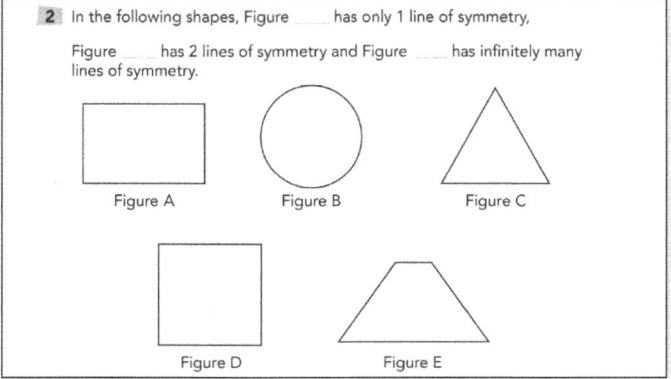

2. In the following shapes, Figure ____ has only 1 line of symmetry, Figure ____ has 2 lines of symmetry and Figure ____ has infinitely many lines of symmetry.

Figure A   Figure B   Figure C   Figure D   Figure E

What learning will pupils have achieved at the conclusion of Question 2?

- Pupils will be able to identify lines of symmetry in 2-D shapes presented in different orientations.

Activities for whole-class instruction

- Draw a rectangle on the board and mark its vertical and horizontal lines of symmetry. Ask: *What are these lines?* Discuss the meaning of 'symmetry', 'line of symmetry' and 'symmetrical'.

- Hold up a paper rectangle. Fold the rectangle in half and show that the folded parts overlap and cover each other perfectly. Ask: *Are there any other folds that I could make that would give two equal parts in size and shape where one half fits exactly onto the other?* Give each pupil a paper rectangle and ask them to fold it to find lines of symmetry. Confirm that a rectangle can be folded horizontally or vertically along lines of symmetry to give two equal parts where one half fits exactly onto the other.

- Ask: *Are the diagonals of the rectangle lines of symmetry?* Pupils fold the shape diagonally and discuss the folded parts. Do they fit exactly onto each other? (no)

Look out for ... pupils who think that the diagonals of a rectangle (oblong) are lines of symmetry. The two right-angled triangles that result from the fold look similar visually and will in fact rotate around the centre of the rectangle to match perfectly. Provide pupils with mirrors and ask them to align a mirror along the diagonal of a rectangle. Confirm that the shape after reflection is a kite and not a square, thus proving that the diagonal is not a line of symmetry.

- Provide paper squares. Can pupils say how many lines of symmetry a square has? Ask pupils to check this by folding. Ask: *How many different ways can you fold a square so that the two sides fold on top of each other and cover each other perfectly?* Compare and contrast the lines of symmetry of a square and a rectangle. Elicit that both shapes have horizontal and vertical lines of symmetry but a square also has diagonal lines of symmetry since the sides of the folded shapes are equal and one half fits exactly onto the other.

- Ask pupils to work in pairs. Provide paper shapes of other 2-D shapes, including an equilateral triangle, an isosceles trapezium and a circle. Ask pupils to mark the positions of any lines of symmetry and then to check by folding the shape. Give them time to mark and fold the shapes, then ask them to comment on the positions of any lines of symmetry found. Ask: *What did you notice about a circle? How many different ways could you fold a circle for the folded parts to overlap perfectly?* Invite pupils to hold up their folded circles and comment on the number they found. Confirm that any line across a circle through its centre is a line of symmetry and that there are an infinite number. Establish that as there are an infinite number of diameters of a circle, so there are an infinite number of lines of symmetry.

- Pupils should complete Question 2 in the Practice Book.

Chapter 8 Geometry and measurement (1)

Unit 8.3 Practice Book 5B, pages 57–59

Same-day intervention

- Provide each pupil with **Resource 5.8.3** Symmetry in 2-D shapes.

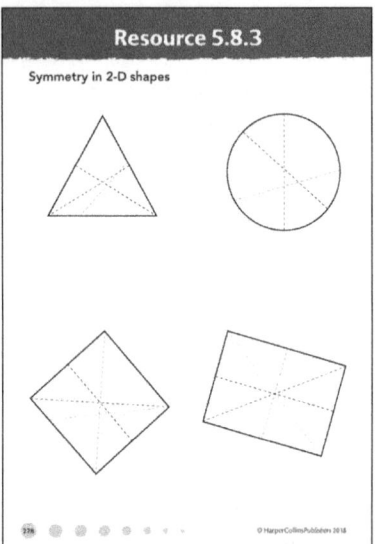

- They should cut out each shape and fold it along each dotted line, in turn, to see if the two parts of the shape fold on top of each other and cover each other perfectly.
- Next, pupils should look for lines of symmetry that are not shown on the shapes. Ask them to predict where the lines might be, mark them using a ruler, then test by folding.
- If available, pupils should use mirrors to confirm the lines of symmetry. They place a mirror on each line to see if the reflected shape in the mirror is the same as the original. If it is, then the line is a symmetry line; if not, then it is not a line of symmetry.

Same-day enrichment

- Working in pairs, each pupil uses a ruler to draw four straight lines on a piece of paper. The lines should be between 3 and 6 centimetres in length and drawn in different orientations and positions. Pupils swap papers and ask their partner to draw a shape around each line where the line is the line of symmetry for that shape. Each shape must be different but one of them must be a circle. Pupils should also mark in any other lines of symmetry on each shape.

Question 3

> 3 True or false? (Put a ✔ for true and a ✘ for false in each box.)
> (a) The distance between the centre of a circle and any point on the circle is the same.
> (b) In the same circle, the number of radii is less than the number of diameters.
> (c) If the radius of a circle is decreased by 1 cm, then its diameter is decreased by 2 cm.
> (d) Using a pair of compasses to draw a circle with a diameter of 36 cm, the two arms of the compasses should be set 18 cm apart.
> (e) Fold a circle in half. The folding line is a line of symmetry of the circle.

What learning will pupils have achieved at the conclusion of Question 3?

- Pupils will be able to identify, name and draw parts of a circle, including centre, radius, diameter and circumference, and know that the diameter is twice the radius.
- Using a pair of compasses, pupils will be able to construct circles and draw in the centre, radius and diameter.

Activities for whole-class instruction

- Write the following statements on the board:
  - The distance across a circle through the centre is the same in any position across the circle.
  - There are 360 diameters and 360 radii in any circle.
  - If the diameter of a circle is increased by 4 cm then the radius is increased by 4 cm.
  - Using a pair of compasses to draw a circle with a diameter of 24 cm, the needle and pencil points of the compass should be set 12 cm apart.
  - Folding a circle in half, then half again and unfolding the paper will reveal two lines of symmetry that are also diameters of the circle.
- Ask pupils to work in pairs. They should discuss each statement to decide whether it is true or false. Give pupils time to consider the statements then discuss each one in turn. Choose pupils to state whether they believe the statement to be true or false and to give a reason for their decision. Establish that statements 1, 4 and 5 are true.
- Pupils should complete Question 3 in the Practice Book.

Chapter 8 Geometry and measurement (1)

Unit 8.3 Practice Book 5B, pages 57–59

Same-day intervention

- Intervene to address and correct any misconceptions revealed through the discussion of the five statements above.
- Ask scaffolding questions to guide the discussion of each statement:
  - Statement 1: What is the definition of a diameter? Does the diameter change at different points on the circle?
  - Statement 2: Does a circle have more than one diameter? Radius? Is there a maximum number of diameters or radii for any circle? What word do we use to describe a number that is so big it cannot be counted?
  - Statement 3: What is the relationship between the diameter and the radius? What is the radius of a circle with a diameter of 10 cm? What is the radius of a circle with a diameter 4 centimetres larger, 14 cm? What is the difference in the radii of the two circles?
  - Statement 4: If a circle has a radius of 12 cm, what is the diameter? If you wish to draw a circle with a diameter of 24 cm, how far apart should you set the needle and pencil points of the pair of compasses?
  - Statement 5: How are lines of symmetry and diameter of a circle related?
- Establish that Statement 2 is false since a circle has an infinite number of diameters and radii.
- Establish that Statement 3 is false since increasing the diameter by 4 cm, will increase the radius by half that amount, 2 cm.

Same-day enrichment

- Challenge groups to write four statements about the properties of a circle and its dimensions, of which two are true and two are false. Pupils swap papers and identify which statements are true/false.

Challenge and extension question

Question 4

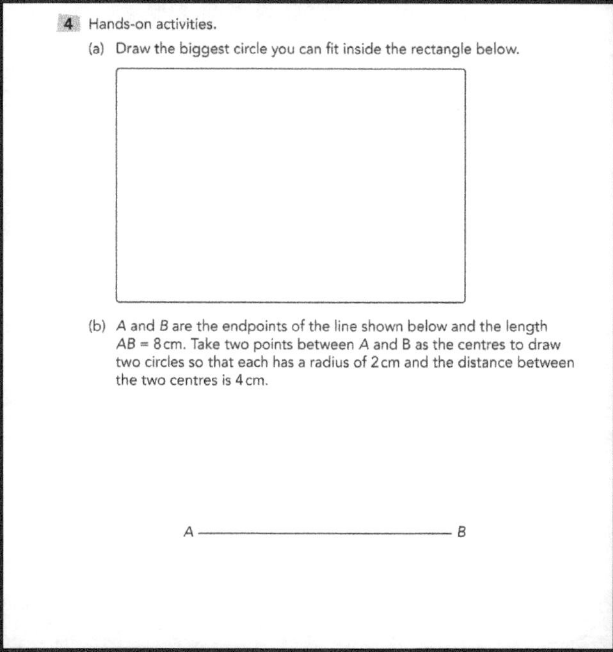

4 Hands-on activities.
   (a) Draw the biggest circle you can fit inside the rectangle below.

   (b) A and B are the endpoints of the line shown below and the length AB = 8 cm. Take two points between A and B as the centres to draw two circles so that each has a radius of 2 cm and the distance between the two centres is 4 cm.

   A ————————— B

Both question parts enable pupils to demonstrate their skill in drawing circles. In part (a), they are given a rectangle and asked to draw a maximum circle. Pupils will need to locate a central point by using the intersection of the diagonals and then construct a circle with a diameter equal to the height of the circle, not the width, to maximise the circle.

In part (b) pupils find two points on a line as centres for the construction of circles with radius 2 cm and centres 4 cm apart. With a line of 8 cm, the position of the centres can be found 2 cm from each end of the line. This will give a 4 cm gap between the centres.

Chapter 8 Geometry and measurement (1)

Unit 8.4
Angle concept and notation

Conceptual context

Pupils at this stage have some knowledge about points, lines and angles. This unit builds on work that pupils did in Years 3 and 4, where they learned that an angle is a measure of turn as well as how to distinguish between right angles, acute angles and obtuse angles. The focus of this unit is on learning how to refer to and represent angles when discussing and drawing them. Pupils will learn to use correct geometric terms fluently.

They also learn that a pair of intersecting lines gives rise to two pairs of vertically opposite angles. Identification of these angles is practised and pupils apply naming conventions to them.

Learning pupils will have achieved at the end of the unit

- Pupils will be able to identify an angle in terms of its vertex and sides and use these features to confirm whether two lines form an angle (Q1)
- Pupils will have learned how to describe angles using the symbol ∠ with letters (Q2)
- Pupils will be able to recognise and label vertically opposite angles (Q3)

Resources

mini whiteboards; pairs of compasses; small notebooks; A4 card; **Resource 5.8.4a** Find the angles; **Resource 5.8.4b** Naming angles; **Resource 5.8.4c** Jump the levels

Vocabulary

angle, vertex, side, acute, obtuse, vertically opposite angles

Chapter 8 Geometry and measurement (1) Unit 8.4 Practice Book 5B, pages 60–62

Question 1

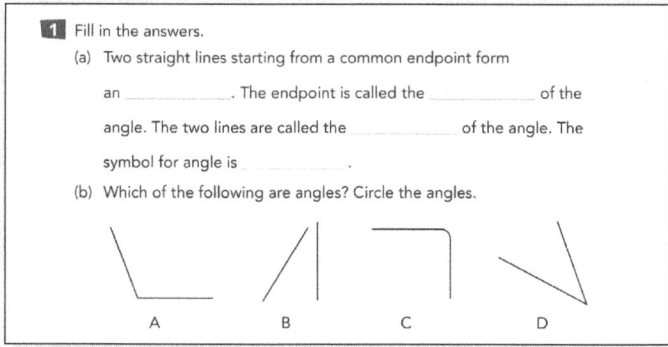

What learning will pupils have achieved at the conclusion of Question 1?

- Pupils will be able to identify an angle in terms of its vertex and sides, and use these features to confirm whether two lines form an angle.

Activities for whole-class instruction

- Distribute mini whiteboards and ask pupils to draw three shapes: a triangle with three acute angles, another triangle with one obtuse angle, and a quadrilateral with two obtuse angles.
- Ask pupils to look carefully at the shapes they have drawn and describe the angles that are formed inside the vertices. They should label the angles 'acute' or 'obtuse'. Remind them that an angle IS NOT the space between the lines; it is the amount of turn that is needed to move one of the lines so that it sits exactly on top of the other, when the point where the lines meet is the turning point. Remind pupils how we see different sizes of turn when we turn our bodies or on the hands of a clock. Show them that the arms of a compass move like the hands of a clock. Demonstrate this movement, opening and closing a pair of compasses to increase or decrease the amount of turn.
- Draw the following diagram:

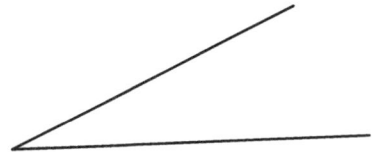

- Ask: *What does the diagram represent?* (an angle) *How do you know?* Accept comments and establish that an angle is shown where two straight lines meet at a common endpoint called a vertex.
- Demonstrate how to mark the angle by drawing an arc between the two lines. Label the vertex A as in the diagram below.

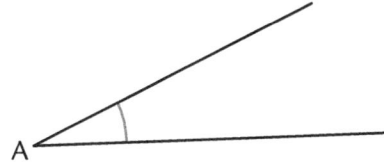

- Explain that the two lines are called the sides of the angle.
- On the board, write ∠A. Point to the symbol ∠. Explain that this is the symbol for an angle and, in this example, the name of the angle is 'angle A'.
- Explain that the common endpoint (of the two lines that are the sides) is called the vertex of the angle.
- Draw the following diagrams of angles and non-angles:

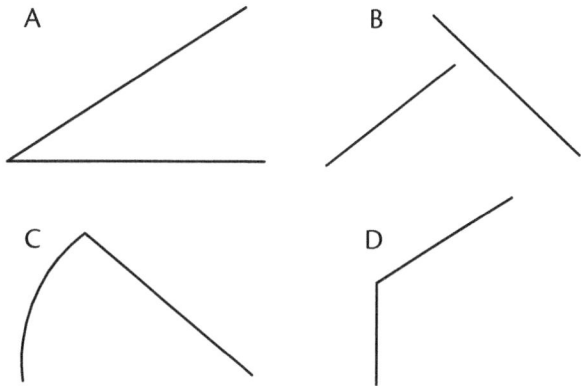

- Ask: *Which of the diagrams show an angle?* Accept answers and ask pupils to explain their reasoning. Establish that diagram B shows two lines that do not intersect and therefore do not form an angle, and diagram C shows two lines that intersect but since one line is curved, an angle is not formed.
- Pupils should complete Question 1 in the Practice Book.

Same-day intervention

- Provide each pupil with a small notebook and ask them to write the title 'My geometry notebook'. Explain that geometry is a subject that requires understanding of many mathematical terms and it is a good idea to write these terms down in one place in order to remember them. Say: *You will be able to refer to the book each time you need a reminder of what a term means.* Explain that for most terms, pupils will draw a diagram alongside the written definition in order to clarify its meaning.
- Write the definition of 'angle' on the board:

  Angle – Two lines that come together at a common endpoint called a vertex. The two lines are called the sides of the angle.

Chapter 8 Geometry and measurement (1)

Unit 8.4 Practice Book 5B, pages 60–62

- Invite a pupil to the board to draw a diagram that illustrates the term. Ask pupils to comment on the diagram and suggest any improvements required. Once approved, pupils copy the diagram in their notebooks alongside the term 'angle'. Agree that angles can be different sizes.
- Repeat for:
  Vertex – The common endpoint of two sides that form an angle.
- Remind pupils to label each part of the diagram clearly and carefully as they will need to refer to these labels when working on geometry units. Encourage them to use colour where appropriate to highlight geometric terms and important parts of diagrams. Point out that the process of drawing and writing definitions will help them remember the terms better.

Same-day enrichment

- Before pupils begin the activity, remind them of the definition of an angle. Draw a triangle and highlight one angle.
- Ask pupils to sketch a square, a rectangle and a triangle. They identify, label and record the number of vertices, sides and angles in each shape.
- For an extra challenge, provide pupils with copies of **Resource 5.8.4a** Find the angles and ask them to identify and indicate the angles present. Challenge pupils to find and mark 20 angles per photograph.

Question 2

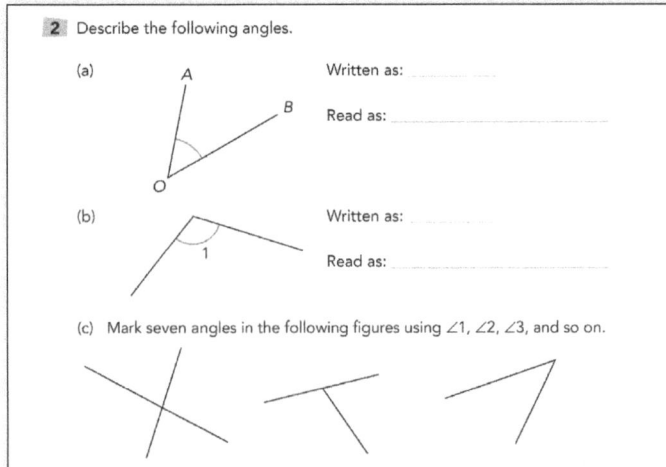

What learning will pupils have achieved at the conclusion of Question 2?

- Pupils will have learned how to describe angles using the symbol ∠ with letters.

Activities for whole-class instruction

- On the board, draw the following diagram:

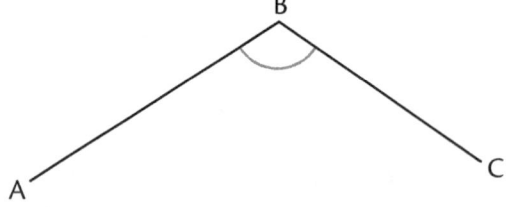

- Explain that to name an angle, we use three points, in this example A, B and C, and use the central letter to indicate where the angle is. In this diagram, the angle is called ABC and the vertex is at B.
- Write: ∠ABC. Explain that we use the symbol ∠ to tell us that the three letters refer to an angle.
- Draw the following diagram:

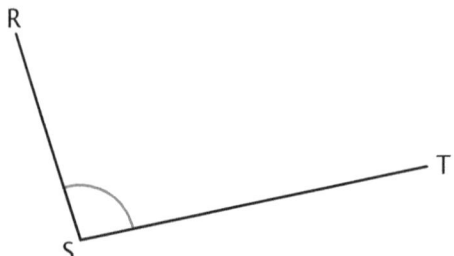

- Can pupils write the name of the angle shown in the diagram using the angle symbol? Choose a pupil to read out the name of the angle. Confirm that the angle should be written as ∠RST and read as 'angle RST'.

Chapter 8 Geometry and measurement (1)

Unit 8.4 Practice Book 5B, pages 60–62

- Ask: *Why is the angle not read as 'angle SRT'?* (The middle of the three letters must indicate where the vertex of the angle is, in this case S.) Point out that it is perfectly acceptable to write the angle as ∠TSR but it makes more sense to write the letters in alphabetical order.
- On the board, write the following angles and ask pupils to draw the three angles on their mini whiteboards:

    i) Acute ∠DEF
    ii) Right ∠PQR
    iii) Obtuse ∠XYZ.

- Ask pupils to raise their whiteboards and confirm that each angle has been drawn and labelled correctly.
- On the board, draw two pairs of intersecting lines:

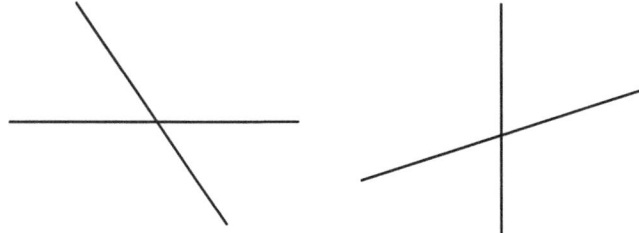

- Say: *We can also name an angle by placing any number or symbol at the vertex in the interior of the angle. Thus, angles can also be called 'angle a' or 'angle b' or 'angle c', or 'angle 1' or 'angle 2' or 'angle 3', and so on.*
- Demonstrate how to label the angles formed by the intersecting lines using letters and numbers.

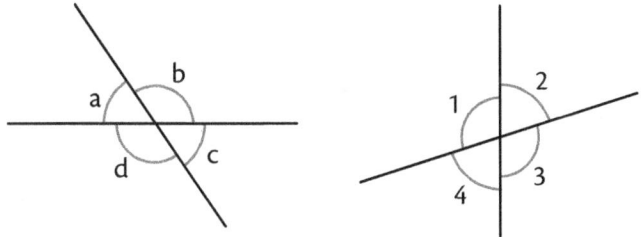

- Ask pupils to draw two pairs of intersecting lines on their whiteboards and label them angle 1 to angle 8.
- Pupils should complete Question 2 in the Practice Book.

Same-day intervention

- Ask pupils to write a heading 'Naming angles' in their notebooks. On the board, draw the following angle ABC:

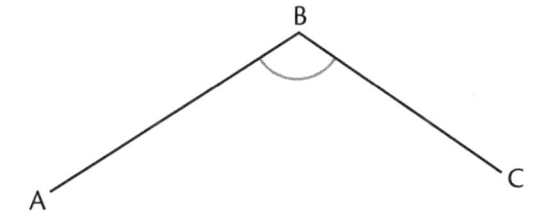

- Choose pupils to identify the vertex of the angle. Ask: *What is the most important thing to remember when naming an angle?* Confirm that this is using the central letter to indicate where the angle is. Ask: *How should we name this angle?* (ABC) *Why have we written B as the middle letter?* (It is the name of the vertex of the angle.) Choose a pupil to write the name of the angle on the board using the angle symbol.
- Ask pupils to copy the diagram into their notebooks. Alongside, they describe the rules for naming an angle. Ensure that they use the angle symbol correctly.

Same-day enrichment

- Ask pupils to work in pairs. Provide each group with a copy of **Resource 5.8.4b** Naming angles. They are given diagrams of angles and are asked to name all the angles that have point X as a vertex.

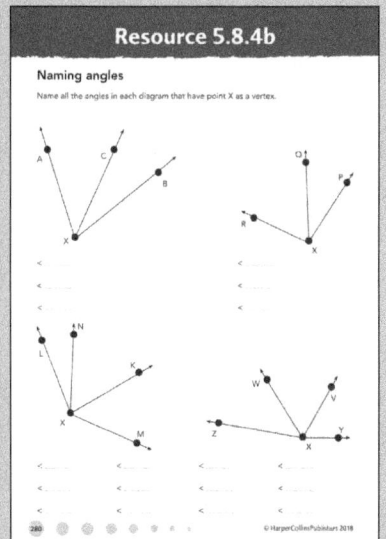

Answers: ∠AXB, ∠AXC, ∠CXB; ∠RXP, ∠RXQ, ∠QXP; ∠LXM, ∠LXN, ∠LXK, ∠NXK, ∠NXM, ∠KXM; ∠ZXY, ∠ZXW, ∠ZXV, ∠WXV, ∠WXY, ∠VXY

Question 3

3. Look at the figure and fill in the answers.

    (a) ∠1 and _____ are vertically opposite angles.

    (b) ∠2 and _____ are vertically opposite angles.

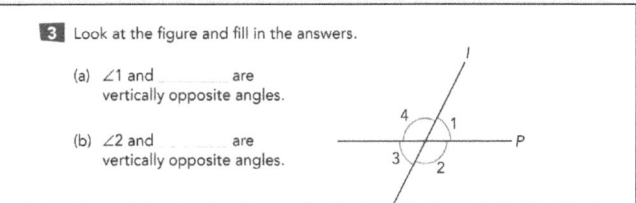

Chapter 8 Geometry and measurement (1) Unit 8.4 Practice Book 5B, pages 60–62

What learning will pupils have achieved at the conclusion of Question 3?
- Pupils will be able to recognise and label vertically opposite angles.

Activities for whole-class instruction

- Draw a pair of bisecting lines on the board. Choose a pupil to label the angles clockwise from angle 1 to angle 4, as follows:

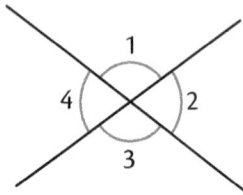

- Pupils work in pairs. Ask them to copy the diagram on the board onto a piece of card and label the angles as shown. They cut out the four angles and compare them by placing one on top of the other.
- Ask: *What do you notice about the size of the angles? Are there any angles that are the same size?* Agree that angles 1 and 3 are the same size, and the smaller angles 2 and 4 are the same size.
- Repeat the comparison of angles made by bisecting lines by drawing another diagram. Ensure that there is a significant difference between the pairs of opposite angles. When pupils have discovered that the angles form two pairs of equal angles, ask: *What can we say about angles that are formed by two lines that meet and cross?*

 *When two straight lines bisect, the vertically opposite angles formed are equal.*

- Point to angles 1 and 3 and establish that angles 1 and 3 are a pair of vertically opposite angles. Explain that vertically opposite angles are the angles opposite each other when two lines cross.
- Ask: *Are there any other vertically opposite angles in the diagram?* Confirm that angles 2 and 4 are also vertically opposite angles.
- Pupils should complete Question 3 in the Practice Book.

Same-day intervention

- Ask pupils to add a heading 'vertically opposite angles' in their notebooks. On the board, draw the following diagram:

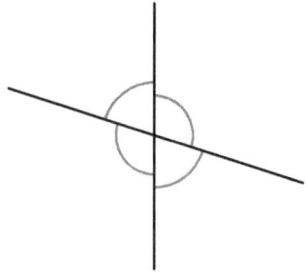

- Choose a pupil to come to the board to colour a pair of vertically opposite angles. Ask: *How do you know these are vertically opposite angles?* Ensure that the pupil uses the word 'opposite' to describe the angles.
- Choose another pupil to colour the second pair of vertically opposite angles.
- Ask pupils to copy the diagram into their notebooks and alongside, write their own definition of vertically opposite angles. Ensure that they are able to use the terms 'opposite' and 'vertically' in the correct context.

Same-day enrichment

- Ask pupils to work in pairs. Provide each group with a copy of **Resource 5.8.4c** Jump the levels. They are given a screen grab from a video game that features a network of intersecting lines and asked to guide a character along a route that must be made from vertically opposite angles.

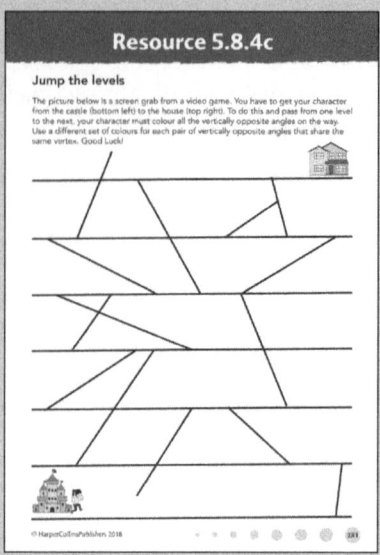

Chapter 8 Geometry and measurement (1)

Unit 8.4 Practice Book 5B, pages 60–62

Challenge and extension questions

Question 4

4 The figure shows three intersecting lines.

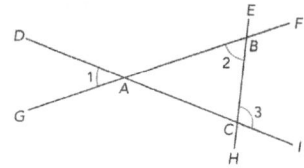

(a) There are ☐ angles altogether.

(b) ∠1 can also be denoted by ∠_____ and ∠3 by ∠_____.

(c) Apart from ∠1, ∠2 and ∠3, what other angles are there in the figure? Identify them and write them here.

Pupils are given a diagram comprising three intersecting lines. They are asked to identify the number of the angles in the figure and name two selected angles.

Question 5

5 Use letters or numbers to describe angles.

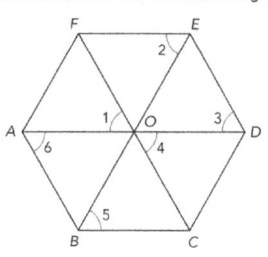

∠1 can be also written as ∠_____.

∠COD can be also written as ∠_____.

Pupils are presented with a hexagon comprising equilateral triangles. They are asked to identify various angles using the dual name conventions of three letters denoting the sides and vertex, or a number placed at the vertex in the interior of the angle. Remind pupils of these naming conventions before they begin the activity.

Chapter 8 Geometry and measurement (1)

Unit 8.5
Measurement of angles (1)

Conceptual context

This unit builds on work that pupils did in Year 3 where they learned to measure and compare angles using non-standard units in turns and fractions of a turn. In Year 4, pupils identified obtuse and acute angles by deciding whether an angle is greater than or less than a right angle.

Now, pupils will learn about degrees, making links with their existing knowledge about acute, obtuse and right angles. This is the first of three units in which pupils will identify angles at a point and on straight lines, and compare, draw and measure angles using degrees.

Learning pupils will have achieved at the end of the unit

- Understanding of an angle as a measure of turn will have developed from pupils knowing that angles are measured in degrees and that there are 360 degrees in one whole turn (full angle) (Q1, Q2, Q3, Q4, Q5)
- Pupils will be able to recognise and use the symbol ° following the number to mean degrees (Q1, Q2, Q3, Q4, Q5)
- Understanding of the classification of angles will have developed from pupils' knowledge of angle size: a right angle is an angle that is exactly 90 degrees; an acute angle is an angle less than 90 degrees (one right angle); and an obtuse angle is an angle greater than 90 degrees but less than 180 degrees (two right angles) (Q1, Q2, Q3, Q4, Q5)
- Pupils will be able to identify a straight angle as an angle that measures exactly 180 degrees (Q1, Q2, Q3, Q5)
- Pupils will be able to identify a reflex angle as an angle that is greater than 180 degrees (straight angle; two right angles) but less than 360 degrees (full angle; four right angles) (Q1, Q2, Q3, Q5)
- Knowing the size or range of sizes for each angle type, pupils will be able to place angles in order of size (Q2)

Resources

polygon side strips and fasteners (or lolly sticks/straws fastened at one end); right angle tester (e.g. a book corner); tracing paper; plastic rods; drawing compasses; mini whiteboards; **Resource 5.8.5a** Degrees in a circle; **Resource 5.8.5b** Types of angle

Vocabulary

angle, arc, vertex, benchmark angle, acute angle, obtuse angle, reflex angle, right angle, straight angle, full angle

Chapter 8 Geometry and measurement (1)

Unit 8.5 Practice Book 5B, pages 63–66

Questions 1, 3 and 5

1 Fill in the answers.

(a) A full angle = ☐ degrees.
A straight angle = ☐ degrees.
A right angle = ☐ degrees.

(b) An angle less than a right angle is called an _____ angle.
An angle greater than a right angle but less than a straight angle is called an _____ angle.
An angle greater than a straight angle but less than a full angle is called a _____ angle.

(c) A full angle = ☐ straight angles = ☐ right angles.
A straight angle = ☐ right angles.

(d) If a straight angle is divided into 6 angles equally, each of the 6 angles is ☐ degrees. They are all _____ angles.

(e) At 9 o'clock in the morning, the angle formed by the hour hand and minute hand on a clock face is a _____ angle.

(f) At 6 o'clock, the angle formed by the hour hand and minute hand is a _____ angle.

(g) A 68 degree angle is ☐ degrees less than a right angle and ☐ degrees less than a straight angle. When it is increased by ☐ degrees, it is a full angle.

(h) On a clock face, from 10 past 12 to 20 past 12, the minute hand turns ☐ degrees.

3 True or false? (Put a ✔ for true and a ✘ for false in each box.)

(a) At half past 3, the angle formed by the hour hand and the minute hand on a clock face is a right angle. ☐

(b) An angle greater than 90° is an obtuse angle. ☐

(c) Half of an obtuse angle is an acute angle. ☐

(d) A reflex angle is greater than 180°. ☐

5 What type of angle is each of these?

(a) _____ (b) _____ (c) _____

What learning will pupils have achieved at the conclusion of Questions 1, 3 and 5 ?

- Understanding of an angle as a measure of turn will have developed from pupils knowing that angles are measured in degrees and that there are 360 degrees in one whole turn (full angle).
- Pupils will be able to recognise and use the symbol ° following the number to mean degrees.
- Understanding of the classification of angles will have developed from pupils' knowledge of angle size: a right angle is an angle that is exactly 90 degrees; an acute angle is an angle less than 90 degrees (one right angle); and an obtuse angle is an angle greater than 90 degrees but less than 180 degrees (two right angles).
- Pupils will be able to identify a straight angle as an angle that measures exactly 180 degrees.
- Pupils will be able to identify a reflex angle as an angle that is greater than 180 degrees (straight angle; two right angles) but less than 360 degrees (full angle; four right angles).

Activities for whole-class instruction

- Ask pupils to work in pairs and provide them with pairs of fastened polygon side strips. The polygon side strips should be of two colours, for example red and blue.

- Take a pair of polygon side strips and attach the blue arm to the board, ensuring that the red arm is free to move. Move the red arm to make an acute angle. Ask: *Who can remember what an angle is?* Remind pupils that an angle is a measure of the amount of turn between two lines. Repeat the movement of the red arm and indicate the amount of turn by drawing an arc of a circle between the two sides of the angle.

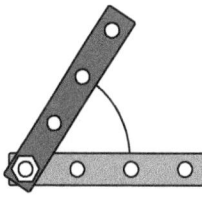

- Ask: *What type of angle have I made?* Use a right angle tester to confirm the angle is an acute angle. Remind pupils that an acute angle is less than a right angle. Label the angle 'acute'.
- Ask pupils to make their own acute angle. They should use the corner of a book or other right angle tester to confirm the angle type.
- Use another pair of red/blue strips to form an obtuse angle. Use a right angle tester to confirm the angle is an obtuse angle. Remind pupils that an obtuse angle is greater than a right angle but less than a straight angle. Label the angle 'obtuse'.
- Use another pair of red/blue strips to form a straight angle. Point to the two sides of the straight angle and explain that they point in opposite directions to form a straight line. Label the angle 'straight' and indicate the amount of turn by drawing an arc (semicircle) between

Chapter 8 Geometry and measurement (1)

Unit 8.5 Practice Book 5B, pages 63–66

the two arms. Ask: *How does a straight angle compare to a right angle?* Confirm and record that a straight angle is equivalent to two right angles.

- Ask pupils to make their own obtuse angle. They confirm the angle is obtuse by comparing to a right angle and a straight angle.
- Use another pair of red/blue strips to form a reflex angle. Explain that a reflex angle is greater than a straight angle but less than a full turn. Label the angle 'reflex' and indicate the amount of turn by drawing an arc of a circle between the two arms.

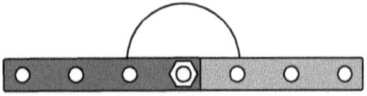

- Use another pair of red/blue strips to demonstrate a full turn so that the red arm once again aligns with the blue arm. Explain that the angle of turn for a full revolution is called a full angle. Label the angle 'full' and indicate the amount of turn by drawing an arc (full circle) between the two arms.

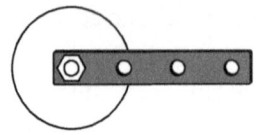

- Ask: *How does a full angle compare to a right angle?* Confirm and record that a full angle is equivalent to four right angles.
- Ask pupils to make their own reflex angle. They confirm the angle is reflex by comparing to a straight angle and a full angle.
- Display the following image:

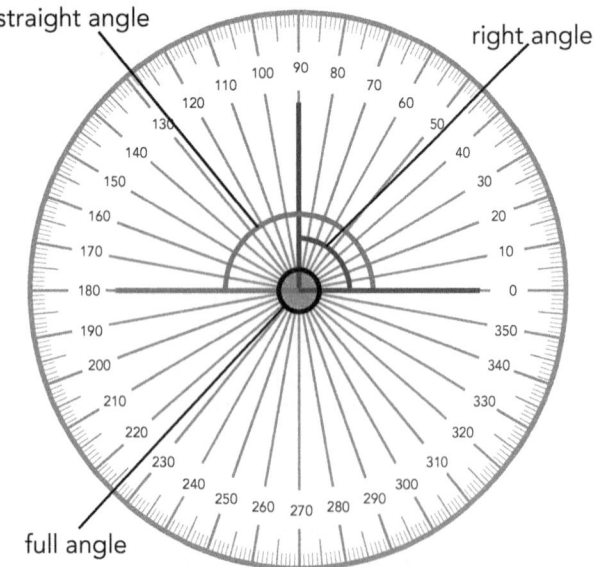

- Explain that to measure angles, we imagine the circumference of a circle divided into 360 equal parts, and we call each of those equal parts a degree. Write 'degree' and '°'. Point to the degree symbol and explain that it is denoted by a small O.

- Ask: *From the diagram, what do you notice about the size of a right angle?* Confirm that it is 90 degrees. Write '90°' next to the angle. Ask: *Why do you think a right angle is 90 degrees?* Can pupils see that there are four right angles in a full 360 degree rotation so each one must be a quarter of 360 degrees?
- Point to the full angle and confirm that it is one whole revolution and therefore 360 degrees. Write '360°' next to the full angle.
- Ask: *What is the size of a straight angle in degrees?* Prompt pupils by asking how many right angles are in a straight angle. Accept answers and confirm that a straight angle is equivalent to two right angles and therefore 180 degrees. Write '180°' next to the straight angle.
- Pupils should complete Questions 1, 3 and 5 in the Practice Book.

Same-day intervention

- Ask pupils to get out their 'My geometry notebook' they began in the previous unit. They should write the heading 'Types of angle' on a new page and copy the following table:

Type of angle	right	straight	full	acute	obtuse	reflex
Description						
Measurement						

- Provide polygon side strips and copies of **Resource 5.8.5a** Degrees in a circle.

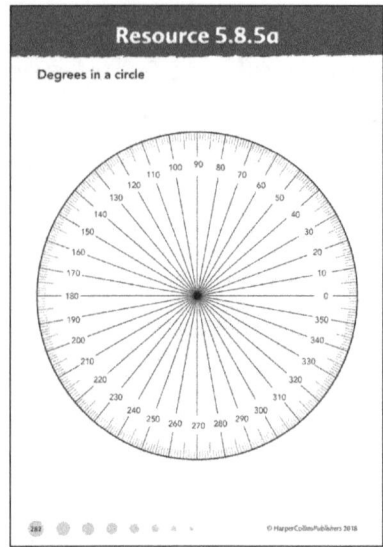

Chapter 8 Geometry and measurement (1) Unit 8.5 Practice Book 5B, pages 63–66

- Ask pupils to align one arm of the strips with the 0° line of the circle and move the other arm anticlockwise to form a right angle. Ask: *How many degrees is this?* (90 degrees) Ask pupils to write or draw a description of the angle and its size in the appropriate part of the table in their notebooks.
- Repeat this for all six angle types. For example, for a straight angle pupils might describe it as 'equal to two right angles' and write a measurement of '180 degrees or 180°'.

Same-day enrichment

- Provide a set of angles formed by pairs of red/blue polygon side strips. These should be a mix of acute, right, obtuse, straight and reflex angles. Pupils work in pairs to sort and label the angles according to the different types.

Question 2

> 2 Multiple choice questions. (For each question, choose the correct answer and write the letter in the box.)
>
> (a) A 40° angle under a 3× magnifier will be ☐.
>   A. 40°   B. 80°   C. 120°   D. 160°
>
> (b) The sum of two acute angles is ☐.
>   A. an obtuse angle   B. an acute angle
>   C. a right angle   D. uncertain
>
> (c) If ∠AOB = 135°, then ∠AOB is ☐.
>   A. a straight angle   B. a right angle
>   C. an obtuse angle   D. an acute angle
>
> (d) Putting the angles in order, starting from the greatest, the correct answer is ☐.
>   A. a full angle > a reflex angle > a straight angle > an obtuse angle > an acute angle
>   B. an obtuse angle > an acute angle > a full angle > a straight angle > a reflex angle
>   C. a full angle > a reflex angle > an acute angle > a right angle > a straight angle
>   D. a full angle > a reflex angle > a straight angle > an acute angle > an obtuse angle

What learning will pupils have achieved at the conclusion of Question 2?

- Understanding of an angle as a measure of turn will have developed from pupils knowing that angles are measured in degrees and that there are 360 degrees in one whole turn (full angle).
- Pupils will be able to recognise and use the symbol ° following the number to mean degrees.

- Understanding of the classification of angles will have developed from pupils' knowledge of angle size: a right angle is an angle that is exactly 90 degrees; an acute angle is an angle less than 90 degrees (one right angle); and an obtuse angle is an angle greater than 90 degrees but less than 180 degrees (two right angles).
- Pupils will be able to identify a straight angle as an angle that measures exactly 180 degrees.
- Pupils will be able to identify a reflex angle as an angle that is greater than 180 degrees (straight angle; two right angles) but less than 360 degrees (full angle; four right angles).
- Knowing the size or range of sizes for each angle type, pupils will be able to place angles in order of size.

Activities for whole-class instruction

- Draw the following angles on the board:

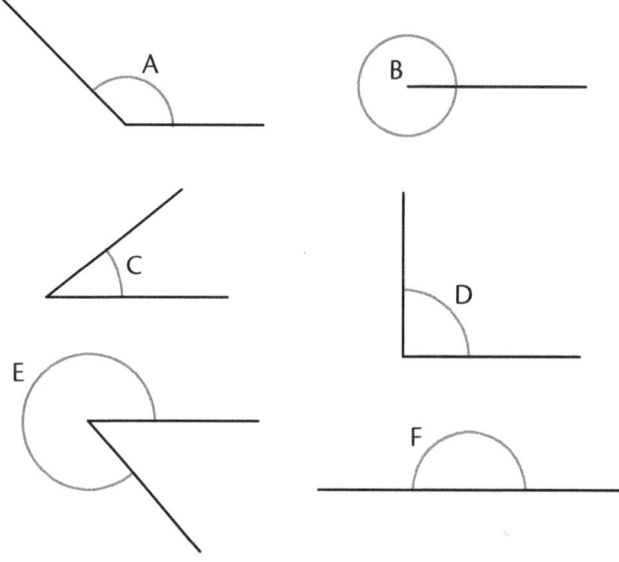

- Call out the letter for each angle and ask pupils to name the angle. Encourage them to describe angle size using both benchmark angles and degrees. For example, they might describe angle E as a reflex angle with a size between two right angles and four right angles, or between a straight angle and a full angle, or between 180 and 360 degrees.
- Ask pupils to use the letters corresponding to each angle to write the angles in order of size, from smallest to largest. Confirm the order: C, D, A, F, E, B.
- Pupils should complete Question 2 in the Practice Book.

Chapter 8 Geometry and measurement (1)

Unit 8.5 Practice Book 5B, pages 63–66

Same-day intervention

- Ask pupils to work in pairs. Provide each pair with six sets of polygon side strip pairs and a pair of plastic rods. With the help of a pupil, show how to align the red arms of all six pairs and then pass rods through the end holes (see diagram).

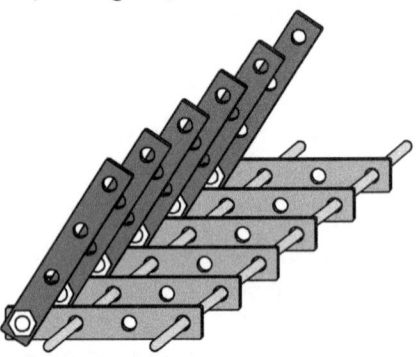

- Demonstrate how to make an acute angle with the first pair of strips. Refer to the six angles in the previous activity and ask: *What angle would come next in the order?* If pupils respond with an angle larger than a right angle, remind them what angle they would use to confirm an acute angle. Pupils form a right angle with the second set of strips.
- Repeat for an obtuse angle, reminding pupils of the benchmark angle they would use to confirm the angle is obtuse (straight angle). Pupils model obtuse and straight angles with the third and fourth pairs of strips.
- Repeat for a reflex angle, reminding pupils of the benchmark angle they would use to confirm the angle is reflex (full angle). Pupils model reflex and full angles with the fifth and sixth pairs of strips.
- Confirm that all six angle types have now been placed in ascending order of size.

Same-day enrichment

- Provide pupils with drawing compasses and rulers. Remind them how to safely and correctly insert a pencil into the pair of compasses so that the needle point and pencil point are aligned.
- Ask pupils to draw circles and mark the centres. Using a ruler, pupils draw radii to divide each circle into sectors where the vertex of each angle is at the centre of the circle.
- How many different ways can they divide a circle to give sectors with the five angle types: reflex, straight, obtuse, right and acute? Is it possible to have more than three angle types in one circle?

Question 4

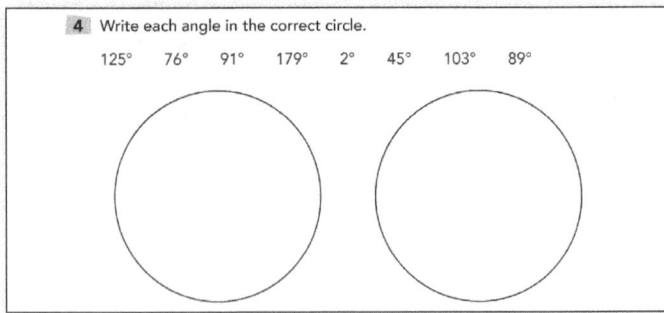

What learning will pupils have achieved at the conclusion of Question 4?

- Understanding of an angle as a measure of turn will have developed from pupils knowing that angles are measured in degrees and that there are 360 degrees in one whole turn (full angle).
- Pupils will be able to recognise and use the symbol ° following the number to mean degrees.
- Understanding of the classification of angles will have developed from pupils' knowledge of angle size: a right angle is an angle that is exactly 90 degrees; an acute angle is an angle less than 90 degrees (one right angle); and an obtuse angle is an angle greater than 90 degrees but less than 180 degrees (two right angles).

Activities for whole-class instruction

- On the board, draw two set circles. Label the sets 'acute' and 'obtuse'. Ask pupils to copy the set circles on their mini whiteboards. Tell pupils that you will call out angle measurements and that they must write each measurement in the correct set: acute or obtuse. Ask pupils to turn to a partner and describe the range of angle sizes that will be sorted in each set. Choose pupils to share their descriptions of each range with the class.
- Review that for an angle to be acute, it must be between 0° and 90°, and for an angle to be obtuse, it must be between 90° and 180°.
- Call out a range of angle measurements between 0° and 180° and ask pupils to write them in the correct set. Ask pupils to list the measurements they inserted in each set and ask the class to confirm they are correct.
- Pupils should complete Question 4 in the Practice Book.

Chapter 8 Geometry and measurement (1) Unit 8.5 Practice Book 5B, pages 63–66

Same-day intervention

- Ask pupils to work in pairs and provide each pair with a copy of **Resource 5.8.5b** Types of angle.

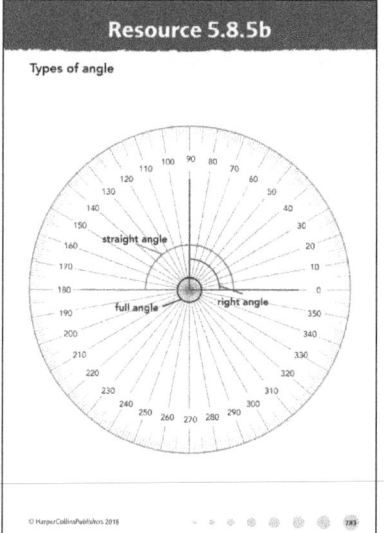

- Each pupil draws two set circles and labels them 'acute' and 'obtuse'. They take turns to call out an angle measurement between 0° and 180° and write the measurement in the correct circle. They use **Resource 5.8.5b** as a guide to the range of angles that will be acute or obtuse.

Same-day enrichment

- Refer back to the main activity and ask: *How would you describe the range of measurements for acute angles in mathematical terms, using numbers and symbol rather than words?* Prompt pupils by reminding them of the symbols of inequality: less than '<' and greater than '>'. Write the symbols on the board and ask pupils to construct a mathematical sentence to define the range. Choose pupils to share their answers. Establish that both symbols need to be used to define the range. Write: 0° < a < 90° and explain that the letter a represents the size of the acute angle.

- Ask pupils to construct similar sentences for the permissible range of obtuse and reflex angles. Expect:
  - 90° < b < 180° (where b is the size of an obtuse angle)
  - 180° < c < 360° (where c is the size of a reflex angle).

Challenge and extension question

Question 6

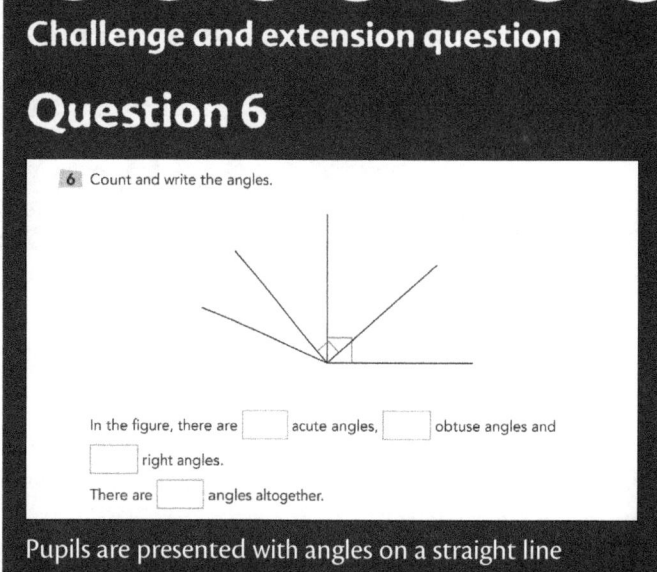

Pupils are presented with angles on a straight line formed by five lines that share the same vertex. Remind pupils of the small square symbol that denotes a right angle. Encourage them to draw parts of a circle between the sides of an angle to identify the size of the angle. Discuss strategies for identifying angles formed by lines that are non-adjacent.

Chapter 8 Geometry and measurement (1)

Unit 8.6
Measurement of angles (2)

Conceptual context

Pupils were introduced, in the previous unit, to a standard unit for measuring angles, the degree, and learned the size of benchmark angles, right, straight and full, and the definition of acute, obtuse and reflex angles.

Now they focus on using angle facts to make deductions about angles on a straight line, intersecting angles and those made in 'real world' situations, for example between the hands of an analogue clock.

Pupils learn how to use a protractor to measure angles of all sizes and how angles of 30°, 45°, 60°, 75°, 90° and 105° can be drawn using the pair of set squares. They practise drawing angles measuring 45° using the 45° set square, angles measuring 30° and 60° using the 30° set square, and angles measuring 75° and 105° using both the set squares together.

In the following unit, pupils will learn to draw angles using a protractor.

Learning pupils will have achieved at the end of the unit

- Pupils' knowledge of benchmark angles and definitions of acute, obtuse and reflex angles will have been applied to identify angles formed by intersecting lines and in 'real world' examples, such as the angles formed by the hands of a clock (Q1)
- Following instruction on how to use a protractor, pupils will be able to measure acute and obtuse angles to the nearest degree (Q2)
- Following instruction on how to use 30° and 45° set squares, pupils will be able to draw angles of 30°, 45°, 60°, 75° and 90° using one or both set squares (Q3)

Resources

analogue teaching clocks; polygon side strips and fasteners; mini whiteboards; protractors; 30° and 45° set squares; overhead projector; transparencies; **Resource 5.8.6 Measuring angles**

Vocabulary

angle, arc, vertex, benchmark angle, acute angle, obtuse angle, reflex angle, right angle, straight angle, full angle, protractor, intersect

Chapter 8 Geometry and measurement (1)

Unit 8.6 Practice Book 5B, pages 67–69

Question 1

> **1** Fill in the answers.
>
> (a) A straight angle is twice a _____ angle and half of a _____ angle.
>
> (b) At 3 o'clock in the afternoon, the angle formed by the hour hand and minute hand on a clock is ☐ degrees. It is a _____ angle.
>
> (c) Two lines intersect and form four angles. If one of the angles is 90 degrees, then the other three angles are all _____ angles.
>
> (d) When a straight angle is divided into two angles, these two angles can both be _____ angles, or one could be an _____ angle and the other an _____ angle.

What learning will pupils have achieved at the conclusion of Question 1?

- Pupils' knowledge of benchmark angles and definitions of acute, obtuse and reflex angles will have been applied to identify angles formed by intersecting lines and in 'real world' examples, such as the angles formed by the hands of a clock.

Activities for whole-class instruction

- Ask pupils to work in pairs. Provide each group with an analogue teaching clock. Set the hands of the clock to different times and ask pupils to set their clocks to the same time.

- Model 12 o'clock and ask pupils to copy this. Move the minute hand from 12 to 3. Ask: *What is the time now?* (quarter past 12) *What angle did the hand move through?* (a right angle or 90°)

- Ask: *In another 15 minutes, where will the minute hand point?* (to the 6) *What angle will it have moved?* Establish that the minute hand will have turned another right angle. Explain that the minute hand turns through two right angles from 12 to 6. Two right angles is a straight angle.

- Ask pupils to set the hands of the clock to form the following angles: acute, right, obtuse, straight. For each angle, ask them to hold up their clocks.

- On the board, draw the following diagram of a straight angle marked with a vertex. Remind pupils that a straight angle is formed by a straight line and measures exactly 180°.

- Provide rulers and ask pupils to copy the diagram. Explain that many geometry problems involve diagrams where more than one angle shares the same vertex. Draw the following diagram:

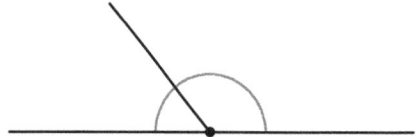

- Ask pupils to copy the diagram. Ask: *How many angles share this vertex?* Agree two angles. Label the diagram as follows:

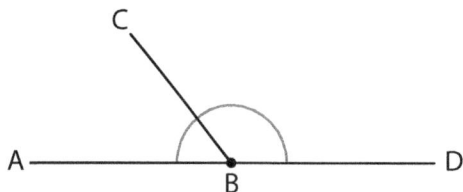

- Can pupils remember the rules for naming angles? Remind them that one way is to use three letters: the middle letter denoting the vertex. Choose pupils to name the diagram and to name the angles shown by the two arcs. Confirm the angles ABC and CBD and ask another pupil to write the angles on the board, using the correct notation (∠ABC and ∠CBD).

- Ask: *What type of angles are ABC and CBD?* (acute, obtuse) Ask pupils to imagine line BC turning clockwise from position BC to position BD. Ask: *At which point would angle ABC no longer be acute?* Accept comments and establish that angle ABC would no longer be acute once ABC was a right angle. Ask: *When ABC is a right angle, what is angle CBD?* Establish that angle CBD will also be a right angle.

- Ask pupils to imagine line BC continuing the turn clockwise. Ask: *What happens to the two angles, ABC and CBD?* Establish that angle ABC now becomes obtuse and angle CBD is acute.

- Ask: *Is it possible for two angles sharing the same vertex on a straight line to both be acute, or both be obtuse?* Confirm that both angles can be right angles but not both acute or both obtuse.

- On the board, draw the following diagram:

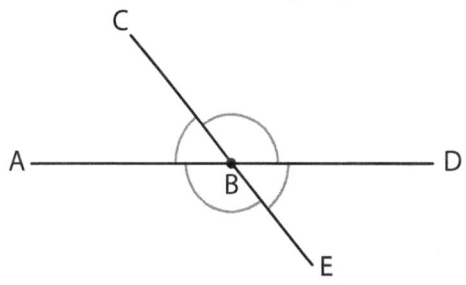

105

Chapter 8 Geometry and measurement (1)

Unit 8.6 Practice Book 5B, pages 67–69

- Choose pupils to come to the board to name the four angles formed at the vertex B. Expect: ∠ABC, ∠CBD, ∠DBE, ∠ABE. Ask pupils to imagine line EC rotating clockwise at vertex B while line AD remains in position. Ask: *What happens to the size of the four angles?* Prompt pupils to describe the change using the named angles on the board. Elicit that when angle ABC is acute, angle DBE is also acute, and when ABC is obtuse, angle DBE is also obtuse. The same is observed in angles CBD and ABE.

- Ask: *What does this mean for the other angles when one is a right angle?* Give pupils time to consider the question, then ask for comments. Establish that when any one of the four angles is a right angle, all four angles will be right angles. Ask pupils to explain why this happens but do not provide any mathematical proofs at this stage.

- Pupils should complete Question 1 in the Practice Book.

All say… When there are two angles sharing a vertex on a straight line, they might both be right angles. If not, one must be acute and the other obtuse. They cannot both be acute or both be obtuse.

- Ask pupils to make the following apparatus with two long strips:

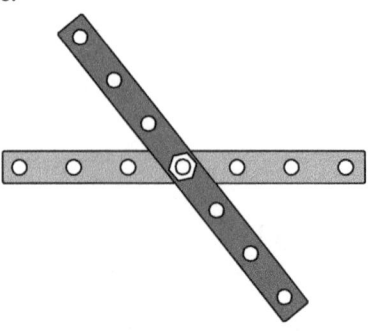

- Refer to the second diagram from the main activity that shows a pair of lines that intersect at vertex B, making angles ∠ABC, ∠CBD, ∠DBE and ∠ABE. Explain that we are going to use the strips to model the angles on the board. Ask pupils to align the two strips then turn the green strip clockwise. Ask: *What happens to the size of the angles?* Prompt pupils to describe the change using the named angles on the board. Elicit that when angle ABC is acute, angle DBE is also acute, and when ABC is obtuse, angle DBE is also obtuse. The same is observed in angles CBD and ABE.

- Ask: *What does this mean for the other angles when one is a right angle?* Give pupils time to investigate, then ask for comments. Establish that when any one of the four angles is a right angle, all four angles will be right angles.

All say… When two lines intersect to form four angles, if one angle is a right angle, all four angles must be right angles.

Same-day intervention

- Provide pupils with polygon side strips and fasteners and ask them to assemble the following apparatus using one long and one short strip.

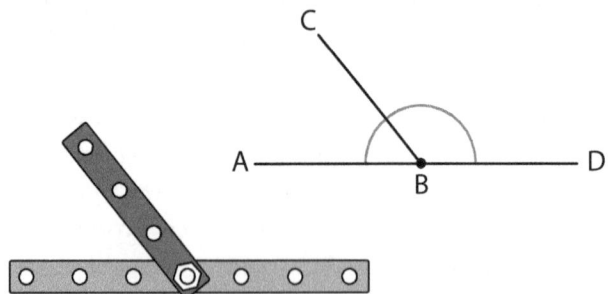

- Refer to the first diagram from the main activity that shows a straight angle divided into two angles, ∠ABC and ∠CBD. Ask pupils to imagine that the blue strip models the line AD, and the green strip models the line BC. Ask the groups to turn the green strip until it no longer forms an acute angle with the left side of the blue strip. Ask: *What does the angle measure when this occurs?* Confirm the angle ∠ABC is a right angle and, thus, 90°. Ask: *What is the angle CBD?* (a right angle)

- Ask pupils to turn the line BC clockwise. Ask: *What happens to the two angles?* Establish that angle ABC now becomes obtuse and angle CBD is acute.

- Use the polygon side strip device to confirm that it is not possible for two angles sharing the same vertex on a straight line to both be acute, or both be obtuse. Establish that the angles on a straight line can both be right angles or one acute and one obtuse but not both acute or both obtuse.

Same-day enrichment

- Write the following statements on the board and ask pupils to fill in the missing numbers:

  - Three angles are on a straight line and share the same vertex. If all three angles are equal, each angle will measure ___°.

  - Six angles are on a straight line and share the same vertex. If all six angles are equal, each angle will measure ___°.

  - Four angles are formed by intersecting lines. If one pair of opposite facing angles are both obtuse, the other pair will both be _____.

Chapter 8 Geometry and measurement (1)

Unit 8.6 Practice Book 5B, pages 67–69

- Ask pupils to write their own missing word sentences using their knowledge of angles on a straight line or angles formed by intersecting lines. They swap papers or mini whiteboards with another group for them to complete. Pupils return the papers to confirm the answers.

Questions 2 and 3

2. Multiple choice questions. (For each question, choose the correct answer and write the letter in the box.)

   (a) When measuring an angle with a protractor, the centre of the protractor should line up with ☐.
   A. a side of the angle
   B. the vertex of the angle
   C. any point on one of the sides of the angle
   D. anywhere near the vertex

   (b) When drawing an angle of 75° with a set square, you can use the set for angles ☐ and ☐.
   A. 90°   B. 60°   C. 30°   D. 45°

   (c) When drawing an angle of 135° with a set square, you can use the set for angles ☐ and ☐.
   A. 90°   B. 60°   C. 30°   D. 45°

   (d) The hour hand on a clock face should turn ☐ degrees in 24 hours.
   A. 180   B. 360   C. 540   D. 720

3. Use a protractor to measure each angle.

   (a) ∠AOB = _____
   (b) ∠COD = _____
   (c) ∠EOF = _____
   (d) ∠1 = _____
   (e) ∠2 = _____

What learning will pupils have achieved at the conclusion of Questions 2 and 3?

- Following instruction on how to use a protractor, pupils will be able to measure acute and obtuse angles to the nearest degree.
- Following instruction on how to use 30° and 45° set squares, pupils will be able to draw angles of 30°, 45°, 60°, 75° and 90° using one or both set squares.

Activities for whole-class instruction

- Ask pupils to work in pairs. Provide each group with a protractor. Hold up a protractor, name the tool and explain that we use it to measure the degrees of an angle. Discuss the parts of a protractor and ask pupils to examine them. This is best done using an overhead projector.
- Explain that the protractor has two scales: an inner scale and an outer scale. Each scale begins at 0° and ends at 180°. Point to the small divisions and explain that each interval is 1°.
- Point to the line segment that joins 0° to 180° and explain that it is called the baseline. Point to the midpoint of the protractor and say that this is called the centre of the protractor.
- Draw an acute angle ABC on a transparency and display it on the overhead projector. Take pupils through the steps involved in measuring an angle using a projector.
- Step 1: Place the centre of the protractor on point B, the vertex of angle ABC, and align one side of the angle, AB, with the baseline of the protractor.

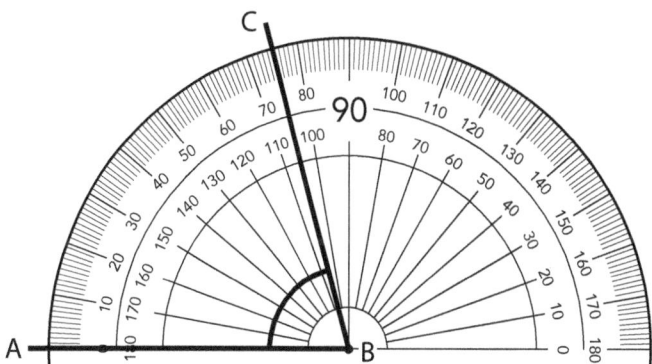

- Step 2: Check which side of the protractor side AB is on. Follow side AB to the inner and outer scale markers and note whether 0° is on the inner or outer scale. For AB, this is the outer scale.
- Step 3: Read the number off the protractor where the second side of the angle, BC, meets the protractor and read the outer scale. For angle ABC, side BC points to 75. Hence, the size of angle ABC is 75°.
- Repeat the above steps for an obtuse angle where side AB extends to the right side of the protractor. Explain that since 0° is on the inner scale, we read the measure of degrees from the inner scale.

Chapter 8 Geometry and measurement (1)

Unit 8.6 Practice Book 5B, pages 67–69

- Provide each group with a copy of **Resource 5.8.6** Measuring angles.

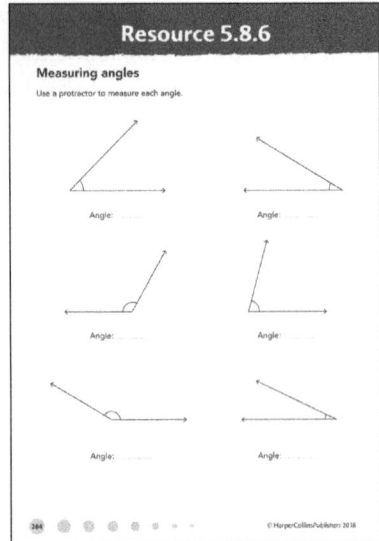

- Ask pupils to measure each angle using a protractor. Remind pupils to pay close attention to the side of the protractor the angle is facing as this will decide which scale should be read. Choose pupils to share their measurements and confirm they are correct.

  Answers: 45°; 30°; 120°; 75°; 150°; 25°

- Provide each group with 30° and 45° set squares. Discuss the two types of set square: a right-angled isosceles triangle with 45°, 45° and 90° angles, and a right-angled triangle with 90°, 60° and 30° angles. Explain that set squares are useful tools for drawing lines and angles.

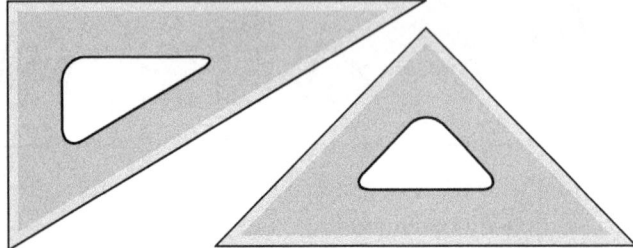

- Tell pupils that we can use set squares to draw 30°, 45°, 60° and 90° angles directly. Demonstrate the drawing of these angles on the overhead projector. Pupils follow and draw their own angles. Show that there are two angles of 45° in a 45-degree set square; it can be placed in two different ways.

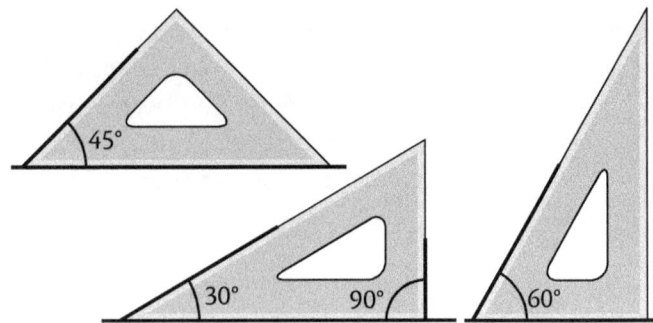

- Explain that we can use set squares to make angles of any multiple of 15 and the steps involved in constructing angles of 15°, 75° and 135°. Ask pupils to follow the steps to draw their own angles.

- Ask: *How could you construct an angle of 75° using set squares?* Can pupils suggest using both the set squares together: 45° plus 30° = 75°. Demonstrate the drawing of an angle of 45°. Indicate on the drawing that the combined angle is 75°.

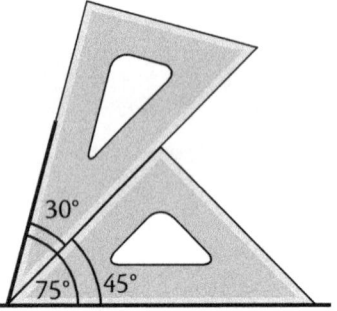

- Ask: *How could you construct an angle of 135° using set squares?* Pupils should suggest the following:

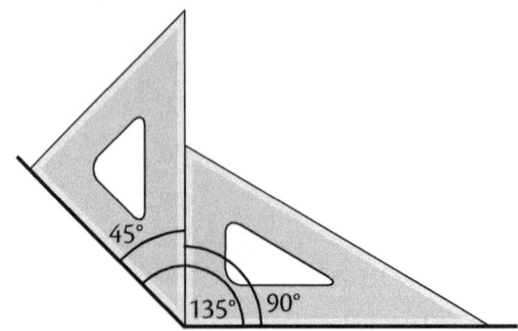

- Ask: *How could you construct an angle of 15° using set squares?* Pupils should suggest the following:

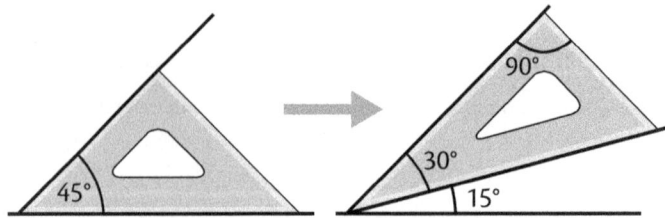

- Pupils should complete Questions 2 and 3 in the Practice Book.

Chapter 8 Geometry and measurement (1)

Unit 8.6 Practice Book 5B, pages 67–69

Same-day intervention

- As reading the scale on the protractor in the appropriate direction requires some reasoning about acute, obtuse and reflex angles, it is important that pupils know how to classify angles according to these types. Review the angle types by asking pupils to refer to the notes they made previously in their 'My geometry notebook'.

- Since protractors can be difficult tools to use, construct a pictorial sequence of steps to demonstrate how to use the tool and ask pupils to make notes and related diagrams in their notebooks. Encourage pupils to identify whether the angle is obtuse or acute to help them make the correct choice between the inner and outer scale of the protractor. Develop understanding by asking questions, for example: *What useful tips would you give to someone about using a protractor? Show me how you used a protractor to measure this angle. How did you decide which scale, inner or outer, to use to read the size of the angle?*

Same-day enrichment

- On the board, write the following angles: 105°, 120°, 135°, 150°, 165°. Ask pupils to work in pairs to draw each angle using set squares. Each angle will require use of both set square types in combination and pupils should construct a table to detail the set squares used. Ask pupils to share and confirm the combinations they find.

Angle to make	Combination
105°	30° and 45°
120°	45° and 60°
135°	30° and 90° or 60° and 60°
150°	60° and 90°
165°	180° (straight angle) subtract 15° (45° − 30°)

Challenge and extension questions

Question 4

4 Write the angles in each set square.

∠1 = _____   ∠1 = _____
∠2 = _____   ∠2 = _____
∠3 = _____   ∠3 = _____

Pupils are presented with 30° and 45° set squares and are asked to label the angles. Pupils should be able to recall the angles from memory but, if they have difficulty, provide actual set squares for them to consult.

Question 5

5 Can you make the following angles with a set square? Put a ✔ for yes and a ✘ for no under each angle.

105°   120°   180°   75°   135°   150°

Pupils are given a list of angles and asked to indicate those that can be drawn using a set square. To answer the question, they will need to recall that set squares can be used to draw angles that are multiples of 15 degrees and therefore all the angles given are possible.

Chapter 8 Geometry and measurement (1)

Unit 8.7
Measurement of angles (3)

Conceptual context

In the previous unit, pupils learned to **draw** angles using set squares and **measure** angles using a protractor; in this unit, they will learn to **draw** as well as measure angles using a protractor.

When drawing angles, it is important to encourage a high degree of accuracy. A common error pupils make when drawing angles is to forget to make a mark at the centre of the protractor at the endpoint of the first line drawn. A simple dot may be enough for pupils to work effectively but consider encouraging them to use a handwritten cross, particularly where a pupil is prone to overlooking this step.

Learning pupils will have achieved at the end of the unit

- Given a specific degree of measure, pupils will be able to use a protractor to draw acute and obtuse angles to the nearest degree; pupils will then be able to apply their knowledge of angle in a variety of situations (Q1, Q2, Q3, Q4)
- Pupils will be able to use and apply naming conventions to drawing angles where various parts of the angle are specified, including one or more named fixed points or lines (Q1, Q2, Q3, Q4)
- Pupils will be developing a rich concept of 'angle' through experience of drawing lines and angles in a variety of orientations (Q1, Q4)

Resources

180° protractor; 360° protractor; overhead projector (or a large protractor for board work); sets of digit cards from 19 to 35; **Resource 5.8.7** Drawing angles

Vocabulary

angle, line, degree, acute, obtuse, protractor

Chapter 8 Geometry and measurement (1) Unit 8.7 Practice Book 5B, pages 70–73

Question 1

> **1** The general process for drawing an angle using a protractor is as follows:
>
> (a) First take a point O as the _____ of the angle. Then, starting from point O, draw a line OA.
>
> (b) Place the protractor so that its _____ is over point O, and the baseline aligns with OA.
>
> (c) Use the scale on the protractor to find the angle required and make a mark. Label this as point B. Remove the protractor and draw a line starting from point _____ and passing through point _____.
>
> (d) _____ is the angle drawn.

What learning will pupils have achieved at the conclusion of Question 1?

- Given a specific degree of measure, pupils will be able to use a protractor to draw acute and obtuse angles to the nearest degree; pupils will then be able to apply their knowledge of angle in a variety of situations.
- Pupils will be able to use and apply naming conventions to drawing angles where various parts of the angle are specified, including one or more named fixed points or lines.
- Pupils will be developing a rich concept of 'angle' through experience of drawing lines and angles in a variety of orientations.

Activities for whole-class instruction

- Tell pupils they will be using a protractor to draw angles of specified sizes. Emphasise that it is important to be neat and accurate when drawing angles. Use the example of an architect who has to draw accurate plans when designing buildings. If the angles in a plan are 'out' by even a couple of degrees, then this is likely to lead to the construction of a building that is impossible to build or one that is dangerously unstable.
- Provide each pupil with a protractor. Can they remember the names of the different parts of this geometry tool: inner scale, outer scale, baseline and centre point? Choose pupils to point to a named part and explain its importance when measuring angles.
- Demonstrate the steps involved in drawing an angle of 50 degrees. This is best done on an overhead projector.
- Say and demonstrate:
  - Step 1: Draw a point that is the vertex of the angle and extend a straight line from it.
  - Step 2: Label the vertex with a letter, for example O. Label the end of the line with another letter, for example A. This makes the line OA.
  - Step 3: Place the centre of the protractor on the vertex and line up the baseline with the line OA drawn in step 1. Double-check that the baseline that represents 0 degrees is on the line. Explain that some protractors have a small hole in the middle of the base of the protractor to line up with the vertex.
  - Step 4: Find the marking for the specified angle size along the scale, in this example 50 degrees, and mark a dot on the paper next to this marking.
  - Step 5: Remove the protractor and use a straight edge, such as a ruler, to draw a line from the vertex to the dot that represents 50 degrees.
  - Step 6: Label the second line, for example OB. Record the angle on the drawing or beside it using the correct naming convention, for example: ∠AOB = 50°.

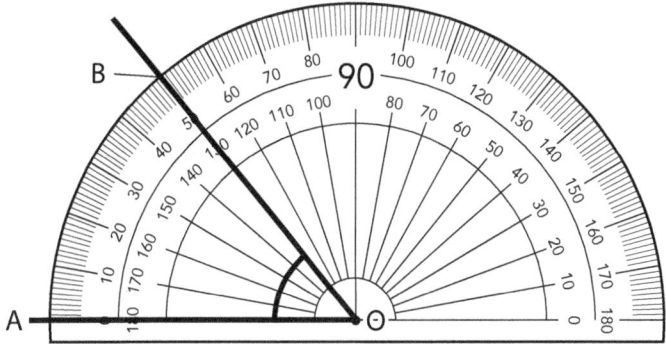

- Repeat the steps to draw angles of 85° and 135°.
- Provide pupils with **Resource 5.8.7** Drawing angles.

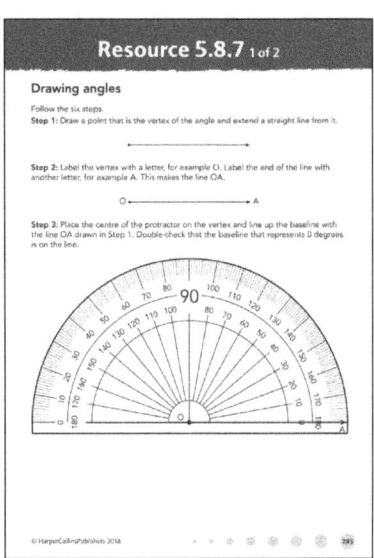

111

Chapter 8 Geometry and measurement (1)　　　　　Unit 8.7 Practice Book 5B, pages 70–73

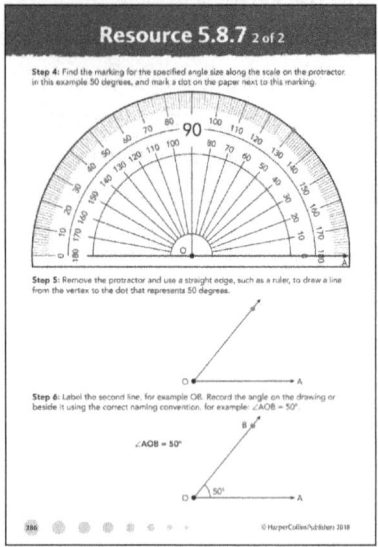

- Ask pupils to follow the steps to draw angles of 65° and 155°.
- Pupils should complete Question 1 in the Practice Book.

Same-day intervention

- Pupils who make errors when drawing angles will need to consolidate their understanding of the measurement and classification of angles before moving on. Review the classification of angles, acute and obtuse, and the size of benchmark angles, right and straight. If available, use a 360 degree protractor to remind pupils that a full turn (or full angle) comprises 360° and 1° is 1/360 of a full turn. Repeat the steps involved for the measurement of angles and ask pupils to practise this skill alongside the instruction.
- Once pupils are confident measuring angles using a protractor, ask them to draw angles of a specified measure. They should use **Resource 5.8.7** Drawing angles, for support.
- Ask probing questions to develop thinking, for example:
  - How should the protractor line up with the vertex of the angle? Which part of the protractor should be used?
  - What part of the protractor should line up with one side of the angle? What should we call this line?
- Look out for pupils who confuse the inner and outer scales of the protractor and draw, for example, a 115° angle for the 65° angle or a 105° angle for the 75° angle.

- Ask further probing questions to develop thinking, for example:
  - Why does a protractor have two sets of scales, an inner and an outer scale?
  - What does a 65° angle look like? Is a 65° angle acute or obtuse?
  - What about a 115° angle, is it acute or obtuse? How can you use knowledge of acute and obtuse angles to help you decide which scale to read on the protractor?
- When pupils have drawn angles, encourage them to use their knowledge of angle types to determine if the angle drawn matches the type of angle as given by its measure.

Same-day enrichment

- Draw a circle on the board and mark and label an obtuse angle with a size of 120 degrees with a vertex at the centre of the circle. Mark the angle indicated between the lines in the 'outer' sector as a reflex angle. Label the angle '?'.

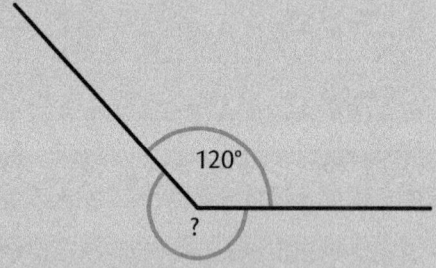

- Hold up a protractor and ask pupils whether they think it is possible to use a 180° protractor to draw a reflex angle in the same way as an acute or obtuse angle. Agree that this is not possible. Ask: *How would you use the diagram on the board to draw an angle of 240° with a protractor?*
- Possible strategy: Subtract 240° from 360° (120°). Draw a 120° angle; then draw an arc on the 'outside' of the angle.

Chapter 8 Geometry and measurement (1)

Unit 8.7 Practice Book 5B, pages 70–73

Questions 2 and 3

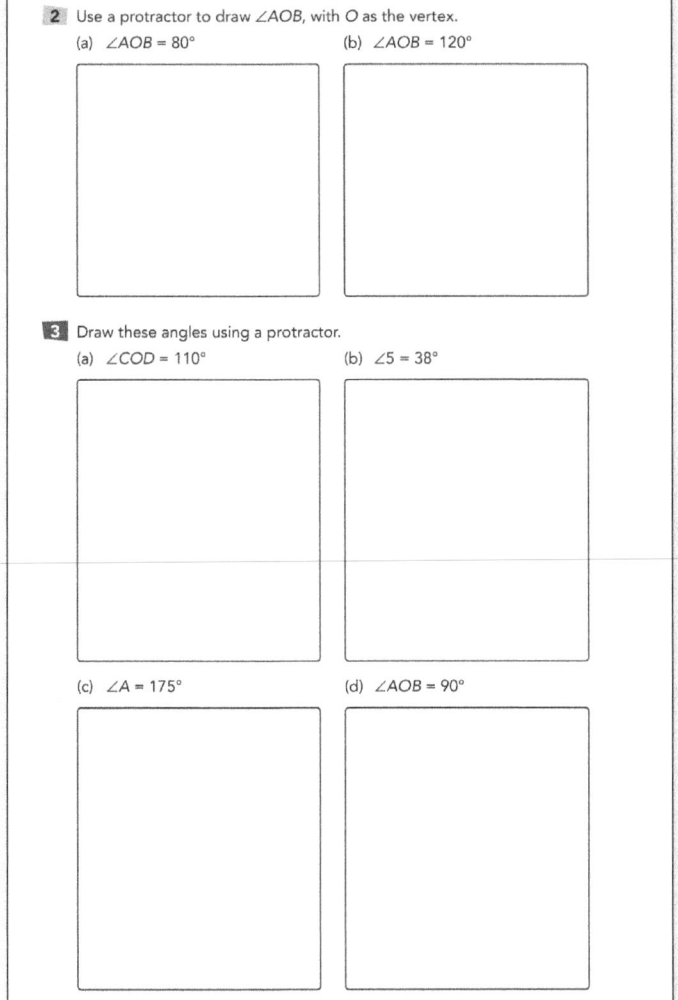

What learning will pupils have achieved at the conclusion of Questions 2 and 3?

- Given a specific degree of measure, pupils will be able to use a protractor to draw acute and obtuse angles to the nearest degree; pupils will then be able to apply their knowledge of angle in a variety of situations.
- Pupils will be able to use and apply naming conventions to drawing angles where various parts of the angle are specified, including one or more named fixed points or lines.

Activities for whole-class instruction

- On the board, write: ∠AOB = 60°. Ask pupils to work in pairs. Say: *Turn to your partner and tell them what information is given in the statement on the board.* Choose a pair to explain what they discussed. Remind pupils of the naming convention for angles and establish that A, O and B are three points that form an angle of 60°. The middle letter O identifies the vertex of the angle, while the sides of the angle are the lines OA and OB.

- Say: *We are going to construct an angle of 60 degrees with its vertex at point O.* Ask: *How should we begin?* Ask a pupil to demonstrate on an overhead projector or at the board with a large protractor. Say: *The next step is to mark the other side of the angle.* Ask: *Through which marking on the protractor scale should the other side of the angle pass?* (60)

- Ask: *When I look at the scale, I can see two 60 marks: one on the inner scale and one on the outer scale.* Ask: *Which 60 mark do I use? Why?* Explain that the scale chosen must be the one with numbers that increase from 0 against one side of the angle. This will vary, depending on whether the angle opens to the right side of the protractor or the left. Draw this image or use an online tool to show a similar image to demonstrate that the inner scale should be used to measure this angle because the inner scale has 0° against one line (OA).

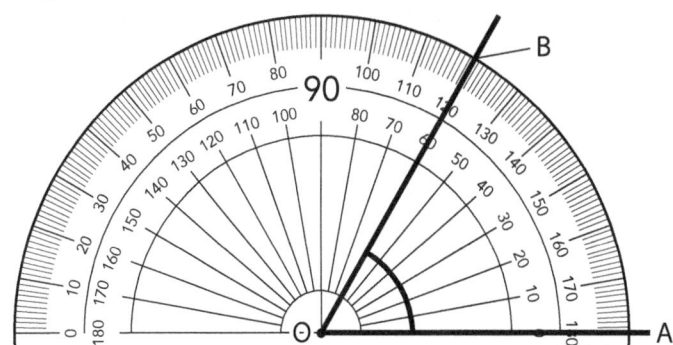

- If the angle was drawn 'opening' to the left, the outer scale on the left side of the protractor should be used because the line AB is against the 0° on the outer scale.

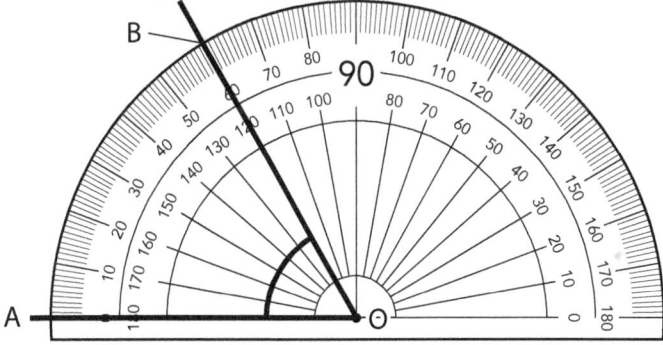

- Ask a pupil to place a point on the board at the 60 mark. Ask: *How do we label this point?* Establish that this is point B and ask the pupil to label it accordingly. Ask: *What is the next step?* (Remove the protractor and construct a line from point O to point B.) Ask a pupil to demonstrate this step.

Chapter 8 Geometry and measurement (1)
Unit 8.7 Practice Book 5B, pages 70–73

- Ask: *How can we be certain that we have constructed an acute angle?* (Compare it to a known right angle, such as the corner of a page in a book.) Ask: *What is the correct name for this angle?* (Angle AOB)
- Write:

  ∠AOB = 25°

  ∠DOE = 85°

  ∠SOT = 130°

- Ask pupils to draw each angle using a protractor. Give them time to draw the angles then share their drawings.
- Write:

  ∠4 = 43°

  ∠C = 90°

  ∠X = 138°

- Ask pupils to tell a partner what information is given in each statement on the board. Choose a pair to explain what they discussed. Remind pupils that we can name angles with numbers or letters, labelling the vertex in the interior of the angle with the chosen symbol. Thus, angles can be called angle a or angle b or angle c, or angle 1 or angle 2 or angle 3, and so on. Pupils should use a protractor to draw and label the angles given on the board. Choose pupils to share their diagrams and confirm the angles have been correctly drawn and labelled.
- Pupils should complete Questions 2 and 3 in the Practice Book.

Same-day intervention

- To reinforce the steps involved in drawing angles, ask pupils to use a protractor to draw angles that are multiples of 10 degrees, from 10 to 170 degrees. All the angles should be constructed from a vertex O and line OA then a line OB, OC, OD, and so on, at multiples of 10 degrees. Encourage pupils to mark each angle with an arc and write the name of the angle using the correct conventions, for example ∠AOB = 10°, ∠AOC = 20°, ∠AOD = 30°.

Same-day enrichment

- Ask pupils to construct the following triangles using a protractor and a ruler:

  i) One side is 7 cm long, one side is 4 cm long and there is an angle of 45° between the sides.

  ii) One side is 6 cm long, one side is 5 cm long and there is an angle of 65° between the sides.

  iii) One side is 8 cm long, one side is 6 cm long and there is an angle of 50° between the sides.

- Choose pupils to explain how they measured the sides and angles and how they constructed the remaining side of the triangle.

Question 4

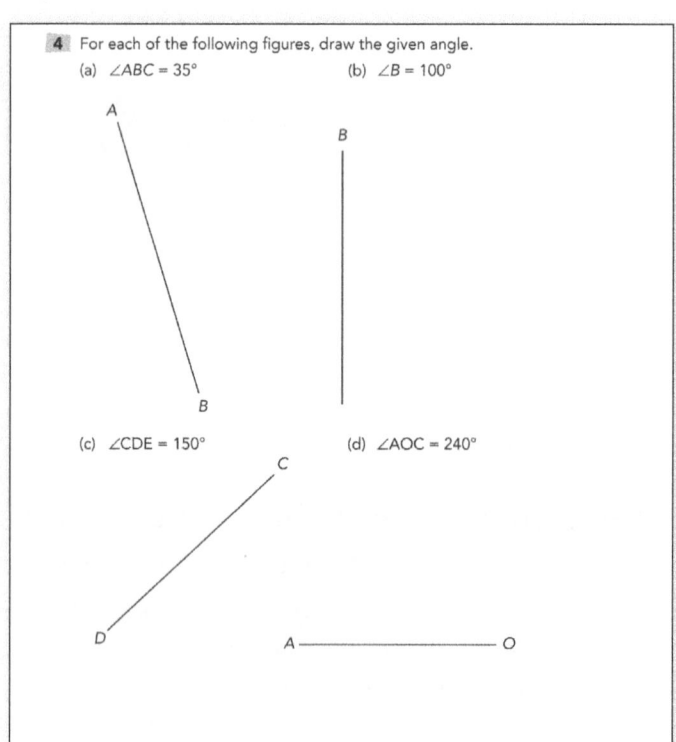

4 For each of the following figures, draw the given angle.

(a) ∠ABC = 35°   (b) ∠B = 100°

(c) ∠CDE = 150°   (d) ∠AOC = 240°

Chapter 8 Geometry and measurement (1)

Unit 8.7 Practice Book 5B, pages 70–73

What learning will pupils have achieved at the conclusion of Question 4?

- Given a specific degree of measure, pupils will be able to use a protractor to draw acute and obtuse angles to the nearest degree; pupils will then be able to apply their knowledge of angle in a variety of situations.
- Pupils will be able to use and apply naming conventions to drawing angles where various parts of the angle are specified, including one or more named fixed points or lines.
- Pupils will be developing a rich concept of 'angle' through experience of drawing lines and angles in a variety of orientations.

Activities for whole-class instruction

- On the overhead projector, draw a line AB about 8 cm. Write: ∠ABC = 65°. Ask: *How would we draw another line to show the angle ABC?* Give pupils time to discuss the problem then accept comments. Ask: *What is the vertex of the angle? How do you know?* Establish that AB is one side of the angle and the other side, BC, needs to be drawn at an angle of 65° beginning at the vertex, B. Choose a pupil to come to the projector to draw the side BC at the correct angle using a projector. Ask them to label the angle.
- Repeat the above activity for an obtuse angle, ∠CDE = 170°. Establish that CD is one side of the angle and the other side, DE, needs to be drawn at an angle of 170° beginning at the vertex, D.
- Draw a line and label one end of the line, B. Write: ∠B = 120°. Ask: *We are given the angle size but why has the angle been named as a single letter?* Remind pupils that we can also name an angle by placing any number or symbol at the vertex in the interior of the angle. Angles can be given names that are numbers or letters. Establish that we have been given one side of the angle B and therefore need to draw the other side at an angle of 120°. Ask: *At which end of the line should we form the angle?* Establish that the vertex will be point B as this angle is named by the vertex and therefore the second side of the angle must begin at point B. Choose a pupil to come to the projector to draw the second side at the correct angle using a projector. Ask them to label the angle.
- Draw a horizontal line and write: ∠AOC = 245°. Ask: *What do we know about this angle?* Agree that the angle has:
  - a vertex, point O
  - two sides, OA and OC
  - sides that are at an angle of 245°.
- Can pupils say what is different about this angle compared to those they have previously drawn? Agree that the angle is reflex.
- Provide pupils with protractors. Ask them to draw a reflex angle; demonstrate:
  - Step 1: Subtract the reflex angle from 360°. For an angle of 245°, this would be 360 minus 245, which is 115.
  - Step 2: Draw the resulting angle from Step 1. In this example, 115°.
  - Step 3: Mark the required angle, the angle that is 'outside' the one that has been drawn with an arc.
  - Step 4: Label the angle. In this example, 245°.

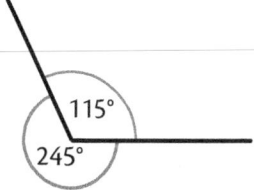

- Ask pupils to follow the steps to draw angles of 215° and 280°.
- Pupils should complete Question 4 in the Practice Book.

Same-day intervention

- Draw the following diagram on the board:

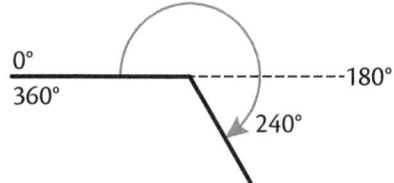

- Tell pupils an angle of 240° is an example of a reflex angle. Remind pupils that a reflex angle is more than a half turn, 180°, but less than a full turn, 360°. Explain that turning 240° means that there is another angle left to turn to complete a full turn of 360°. Ask: *Will this angle be smaller or larger than a straight angle, 180°? Will it be obtuse or acute?*
- Go through the steps involved in drawing a reflex angle of 240° as detailed in the main activity. Ask pupils to make their own notes and diagrams in the 'My geometry notebook' they used in previous lessons. They should write a sentence and/or draw a diagram for each step. Remind pupils that the notes they make will need to be clear and precise.

Chapter 8 Geometry and measurement (1) Unit 8.7 Practice Book 5B, pages 70–73

Same-day enrichment

- Ask pupils to work in pairs. Provide each group with a ruler, protractor and a set of digit cards from 19 to 35. Pupil 1 begins by drawing a horizontal line approximately 5 cm in length in the centre of a piece of paper. Pupil 2 shuffles the cards and picks one at random. Pupil 2 multiplies the number by 10 and draws a reflex angle of that size at one end of the line using a protractor. The second line from the vertex should be approximately 5 cm in length. Pupil 1 picks a card, multiplies the number by 10 and then draws a reflex angle of that size at the end of the last line drawn. The turn then passes between pupils 1 and 2. How long can they continue drawing lines at an angle from the end of the previously drawn line until they disappear off the edge of the paper? The game ends when this happens.

Challenge and extension question

Question 5

5 Hands-on activity.
   (a) Draw ∠AOB so that it is 80°.
   (b) Mark a point D on side OB so that OD = 3 cm. Mark another point E on the other side, OA, so that OE = 3 cm.
   (c) Connect points D and E.
   (d) Measure to find the angles: ∠ODE = _____ and ∠OED = _____

Pupils are asked to draw an angle AOB of 80° with lines OA and OB. They mark points 3 cm along each side of the angle, D and E respectively, then connect the points to form side DE. Pupils note that the shape is a triangle and then use a protractor to measure angles ODE and OED. Explain to pupils that they will need to be accurate when drawing angle AOB as any error in measurement will have an effect on the size of angles created at ODE and OED.

Chapter 8 Geometry and measurement (1)

Unit 8.8
Calculation of angles

Conceptual context

In this unit, pupils use angle sum facts and other properties to make deductions about missing angles and relate these to missing number problems. The activities require pupils to call on their knowledge and understanding of the different types of angle covered in previous lessons.

They should know that the sum of angles on a straight line is 180°, and the sum of angles around a point is 360°. They should be able to use this knowledge to respond accurately to questions such as: 'There are two angles on a straight line. If one angle is x°, what is the size of the second angle?' Pupils are also introduced to vertically opposite angles.

Learning pupils will have achieved at the end of the unit

- Pupils will be able to apply their knowledge of arithmetic and inverse operations to solving missing angle problems (Q1, Q2)
- Pupils will have expanded their knowledge of the special notation of geometric diagrams, including knowing that a small square on a diagram indicates a right angle (Q2)
- Using knowledge of the equivalence relationships between angles, pupils will be able to find missing angles in geometric diagrams including complementary angles (those with a sum of 90°), angles on a straight line (those with a sum of 180°) and angles around a point (those with a sum of 360°) (Q2)
- Knowing that vertically opposite angles are equal, pupils will be able to apply this knowledge to the solution of missing angle problems in geometric diagrams (Q2)

Resources

mini whiteboards; polygon side strips; **Resource 5.8.8a** Angle problems; **Resource 5.8.8b** Missing angle problems

Vocabulary

vertically opposite angles

Chapter 8 Geometry and measurement (1)

Unit 8.8 Practice Book 5B, pages 74–76

Question 1

1 Think carefully and then fill in the answers.

(a) One third of a straight angle is _____.

An angle that is 40° greater than a right angle is _____.

115° is _____ less than a straight angle.

A full angle is _____ greater than 15°.

(b) Given ∠1 + ∠2 = 150° and ∠1 = 67°, then ∠2 = _____.

(c) Given ∠1 + ∠2 = 180° and ∠2 = 100°, then ∠1 = _____.

(d) If 5 times ∠1 is a straight angle, then ∠1 = _____.

(e) If ∠1 = ∠2 = ∠3, and ∠1 + ∠2 + ∠3 = 120°, then ∠2 = _____.

What learning will pupils have achieved at the conclusion of Question 1?

- Pupils will be able to apply their knowledge of arithmetic and inverse operations to solving missing angle problems.

Activities for whole-class instruction

- On the board, write: Right angle = ___°, Straight angle = ___°, Full angle = ___°. Choose pupils to approach the board and complete the size of each angle. Explain that these can be thought of as 'benchmark angles' that help to solve problems about angles when not all the information is obvious but can be worked out.

- Write: An angle that is 50° less than a straight angle is _____°. Ask: *What operation is involved in the calculation? What do we need to find out?* (The angle that is 50° less than a straight angle.) Ask: *What do we know that will help?* Pupils should know that a straight angle is 180°. Agree that the problem can be represented as 180 – 50 = ____. Agree that the missing angle is 130°.

- Write: 225° is ___ greater than a right angle. Ask pupils to work in pairs to represent the problem as a number sentence using what they know about 'benchmark' angles, and find the solution. Can pupils see that 225 – 90 = 135°?

- Write: One sixth of a full angle is ____. Ask pupils to work in pairs to represent the problem as a number sentence using what they know about 'benchmark' angles, and find the solution.

- Write: If ∠1 + ∠2 = 360° and ∠2 = 210°, then ∠1 = ___°. Say: *When given missing angle problems it is often helpful to visualise the problem.* Agree that in this example, ∠1 + ∠2 together make a full angle, a full turn. Ask: *Which angle is larger?* Choose a pupil to draw a circle and sketch and label the two angles with a shared vertex at the centre of the circle. Ask: *How do we find angle 1? What number sentence represents what we need to do?* Agree 360 – ∠2 = ∠1. Substitute the value of angle 2 and ask pupils to calculate angle 1 (150°).

- Write: If ∠1 = ∠2 = ∠3 = ∠4, and = ∠1 + ∠2 + ∠3 + ∠4 = 160°, then ∠3 = ___°. Give pupils time to discuss the problem then ask what information they are given. Establish that all four angles are equal and, given the sum of the angles, each angle must be a quarter of the total. Ask: *What number sentence represents what we need to do?* Agree 160 ÷ 4 = ∠3.

- Pupils should complete Question 1 in the Practice Book.

Same-day intervention

- Write: An angle that is 30° larger than a straight angle is _____°. Use questions to elicit thinking:
  - What do you know about straight angles?
  - What information is given in the sentence? What are you asked to find?
  - Can you draw a diagram to help you visualise the problem? What would it look like?

- Provide mini whiteboards and ask pupils to draw a diagram to model the problem. Draw the following diagram on the board:

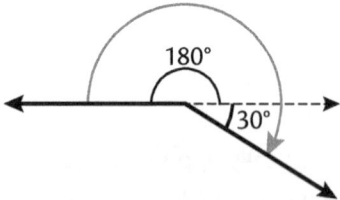

- Review that a straight angle measures 180°, and ask a pupil to identify the straight angle in the diagram. Model how the angles in the diagram can be composed using addition (180° + 30° = 210°).

- Write: An angle that is 80° less than a full angle is _____°. Use questions to elicit thinking:
  - What do you know about full angles?
  - What information is given in the sentence? What are you asked to find?
  - Can you draw a diagram to help you visualise the problem? What would it look like?

Chapter 8 Geometry and measurement (1)

Unit 8.8 Practice Book 5B, pages 74–76

- Ask pupils to draw a diagram to model the problem then share them. Draw the following diagram on the board:

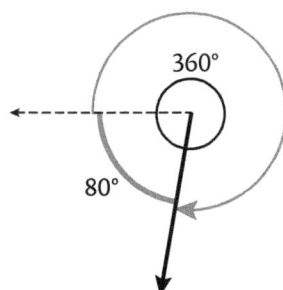

- Review that a full angle measures 360°, and ask a pupil to identify the full angle in the diagram. Model how the missing angle in the diagram can be determined using subtraction (360° − 80°). Guide pupils to determine the unknown angle in the problem (280°).

- Write: If $\angle 1 + \angle 2 = 130°$ and $\angle 1 = 55°$, what is $\angle 2$? Use questions to elicit thinking:
  - What do the angle numbers mean?
  - What information is given in the sentence? What are you asked to find?
  - Can you draw a diagram to help you visualise the problem? What would it look like?

- Ask pupils to draw a diagram to model the problem then share them. Draw the following diagram on the board:

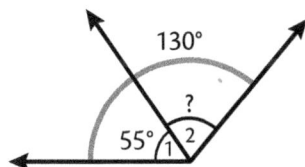

- Ask: *Using the diagram, what operation and calculation would give us the missing angle, angle 2?* Establish that since the sum of angles 1 and 2 is 130°, the sum minus angle 1 would give angle 2 (130° − 55°). Ask: *What is angle 2?* (75°)

Same-day enrichment

- Provide pupils with copies of **Resource 5.8.8a** Angle problems. Ask them to solve the three problems.

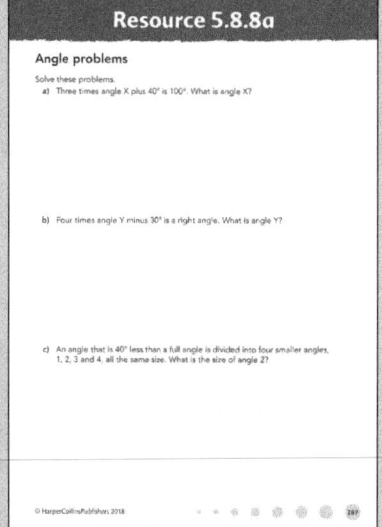

- For an additional challenge, ask pupils to make up similar questions for a partner to solve.

Answers: a) 20°; b) 30°; c) 80°

Question 2

2. Calculate the missing angles.
   (a) In the figure, given $\angle 2 = 135°$, find $\angle 1$.

   (b) In the figure, given that $\angle ABC$ is a right angle and $\angle ABD = 70°$, find $\angle 1$.

   (c) In the figure, given that $\angle BOC$ is a right angle and $\angle COD = 15°$, find $\angle AOB$.

   (d) In the figure, given $\angle 4 = 30°$, find $\angle 3$.

   (e) In the figure, find $\angle 1$ and $\angle 2$.

   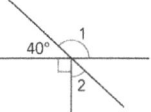

   (f) In the figure, two pairs of angles, $\angle 1$ and $\angle 3$, and $\angle 2$ and $\angle 4$, are vertically opposite angles respectively. Given $\angle 1 = 55°$, find the other three angles.

   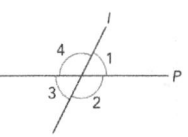

Chapter 8 Geometry and measurement (1)

Unit 8.8 Practice Book 5B, pages 74–76

What learning will pupils have achieved at the conclusion of Question 2?

- Pupils will be able to apply their knowledge of arithmetic and inverse operations to solving missing angle problems.
- Pupils will have expanded their knowledge of the special notation of geometric diagrams, including knowing that a small square on a diagram indicates a right angle.
- Using knowledge of the equivalence relationships between angles, pupils will be able to find missing angles in geometric diagrams including complementary angles (those with a sum of 90°), angles on a straight line (those with a sum of 180°) and angles around a point (those with a sum of 360°).
- Knowing that vertically opposite angles are equal, pupils will be able to apply this knowledge to the solution of missing angle problems in geometric diagrams.

Activities for whole-class instruction

- Provide pupils with copies of **Resource 5.8.8b** Missing angle problems. Tell them that the diagrams are examples of missing angle problems. Then provide information about one or more angles and pupils must calculate the missing angle(s).

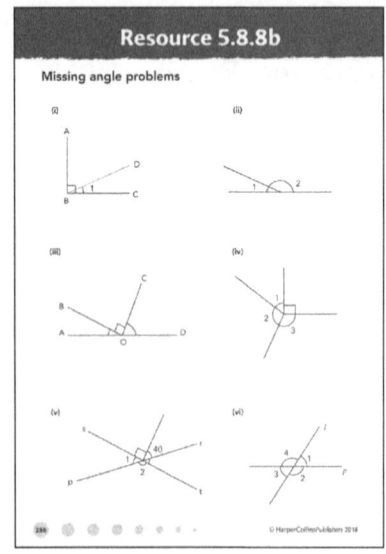

- Display problem (i).

(i)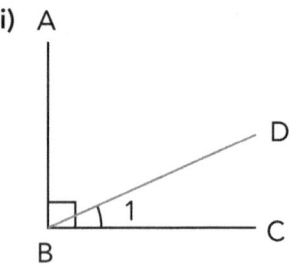

- Point to the right angle symbol in diagram (i). Ask: *What does this square symbol represent?* (a right angle) *What is the size of a right angle?* Next to the diagram, write: ∠ABD = 57°. Ask: *Given angle ABD, how do we work out angle 1?* Write: 90 – 57 = angle 1. (Answer: 33°)

- Display problem (ii).

(ii)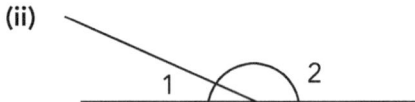

- Next to the diagram, write: If ∠2 = 159° find ∠1. Ask: *What do you notice about angles 1 and 2?* (The angles are on a straight line.) Ask pupils to write a number sentence for the sum of angles 1 and 2. Confirm that pupils have written: ∠1 + ∠2 = 180°. Agree that the inverse operation, subtraction, gives angle 1. Write: 180° – 159° = 21°. (Answer: 21°)

- Display problem (iii).

(iii)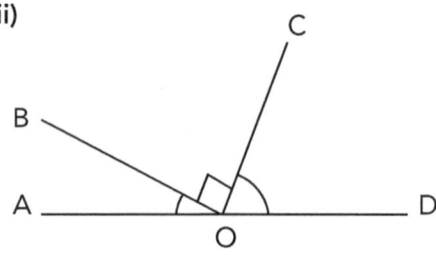

- Next to diagram (iii), write: If ∠AOB = 33° find ∠COD. (Answer: 57°)

- Display problem (iv).

(iv)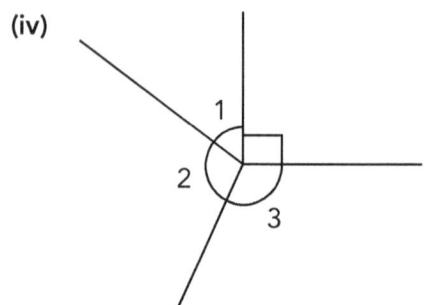

- Next to the diagram, write: If ∠1 = 48° and ∠2 = 112°, find ∠3. Ask: *What do you notice about the four angles?* (The angles are at a point; one of the angles is a right

Chapter 8 Geometry and measurement (1)

Unit 8.8 Practice Book 5B, pages 74–76

angle.) *What do you know about angles around a point?* (Angles around a point will always add up to 360°.) Ask pupils to write a number sentence for the sum of the four angles. Choose a pupil to write the number sentence on the board. Agree: 360° = ∠1 + ∠2 + ∠3 + 90°. Pupils should substitute the values given to calculate the value of angle 3. Expect: 360° = 48° + 112° + ∠3 + 90° = ∠3 + 250°. Therefore ∠3 = 360° − 250° = 110°. (Answer: 110°)

- Display problem (v).

(v)
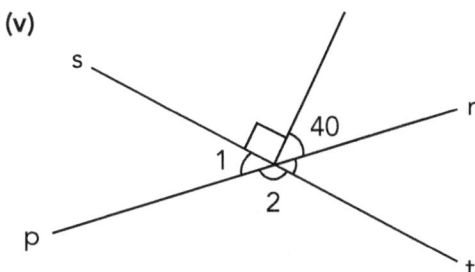

- Ask: *How would you work out angles 1 and 2, given no extra information?* Explain that solving this type of problem involves looking for known angle sum facts, for example angles in a right angle, at a point or on a line. Give pupils time to discuss the problem then accept solutions.

- Highlight the line *pr*. Ask: *What do we know about angles on this line?* (Sum to 180°) Establish the number sentence for the sum: 180° = 90° + 40° + ∠1. (Angle 1 is therefore 50°.) Ask: *How can you use this angle to find the other unknown angle? How does knowing angle 1 help us to find angle 2?* (Angles are on a straight line.) Ask pupils to write and solve the calculation as a subtraction. Expect: ∠2 = 180° − ∠1 = 180° − 50° = 130°. (Answers: 50° and 130°)

- Display problem (vi).

(vi)
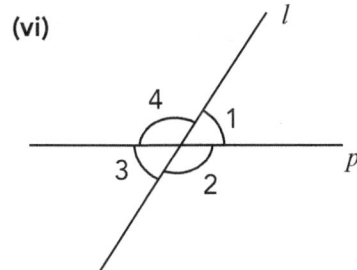

- Next to the diagram, write: If ∠1 = 56°, find ∠2, ∠3 and ∠4. Tell pupils that in order to answer this problem, we need to apply another property of angles. (Answers: 124°, 56° and 124°)

- Draw the following diagram:

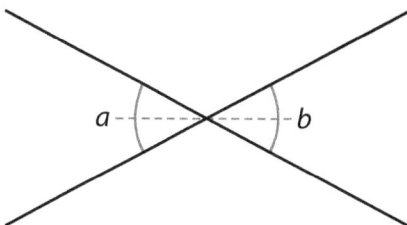

- Ask: *What do we know about angles a and b?* Expect pupils to say that they are vertically opposite angles and therefore equal. Ask: *How would you prove this?* (Remind pupils that we use the word 'vertical' to mean angles that share the same vertex, not the usual meaning of up/down.)

- Re-introduce the bisecting strips used in Unit 8.6. Allow pupils to explore how vertically opposite angles change simultaneously – one cannot change without the other changing in exactly the same way.

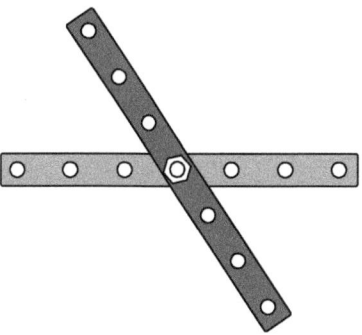

- Point to problem (vi). Ask: *If angle 1 is 56°, which other angle do we know without calculation?*

(vi)
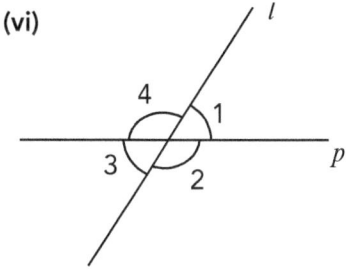

- Agree that angles 1 and 3 are vertically opposite angles and therefore angle 3 is also 56°. Ask: *How do we use angle 1 or angle 3 to work out angles 2 and 4?* Agree that angles 1 and 2 (or 4), and angles 3 and 4 (or 3) are on a straight line and therefore have a sum of 180°. Ask pupils to write and solve the calculation to give angle 2. Expect: ∠2 = 180° − ∠1 = 180° − 56° = 124°.

- Ask: *Do we need to calculate angle 4?* Agree that since angles 2 and 4 are vertically opposite and equal, angle 4 is also 124°. Label all four angles.

- Pupils should complete Question 2 in the Practice Book.

Chapter 8 Geometry and measurement (1)

Unit 8.8 Practice Book 5B, pages 74–76

Same-day intervention

- Provide alternative angle measurements for the problems given in the main activity. Go through each question as a guided example and ask pupils to make notes and diagrams in their 'My geometry notebook'. The notes should be made under the title 'How to a find a missing angle where the sum of angles is a right angle/straight angle/full angle (angles around a point)'. Pupils should also add a separate definition for vertically opposite angles.

Same-day enrichment

- Provide pairs of pupils with a copy of **Resource 5.8.8b** Missing angle problems. Ask them to create their own missing angle problems. They write the problems in the form 'If angle 1 is $x°$, find angle 2', and 'If angle 1 is $x°$, find angles 2, 3 and 4'. They swap papers with another pair to solve, then return them for marking.

Challenge and extension questions

Question 3

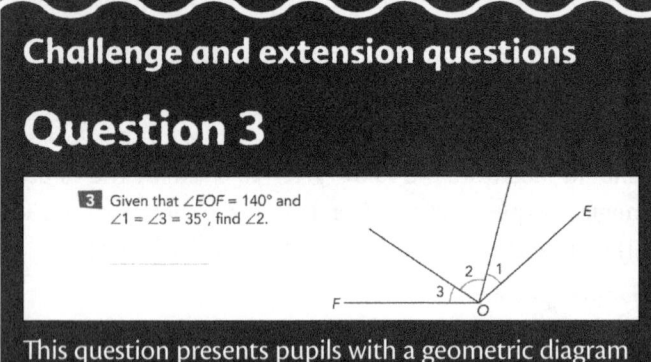

Given that $\angle EOF = 140°$ and $\angle 1 = \angle 3 = 35°$, find $\angle 2$.

This question presents pupils with a geometric diagram of an obtuse angle divided into three angles. The obtuse angle is given and two of the smaller angles, which are equal. Pupils use doubling and subtraction to find the missing smaller angle.

Question 4

In the figure below, A, O and B are on the same line. OE is the bisector of $\angle AOC$, so $\angle AOE = \angle EOC$, OF is the bisector of $\angle BOC$, so $\angle BOF = \angle FOC$, and $2\angle AOE = \angle BOF$.

Find $\angle BOF$, $\angle AOE$ and $\angle EOF$.

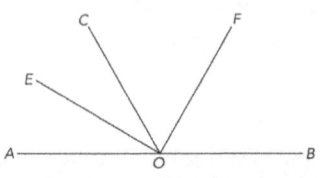

This question presents a geometric diagram of angles on a straight line. Information about rays that bisect angles is given and pupils will need to be introduced to the term 'bisector' (a line that divides an angle into two equal parts). Using the angle relationships given, pupils determine that three angles are equal ($\angle AOC = \angle COF = \angle FOB$). They use this to determine other missing angles.

Chapter 8 Geometry and measurement (1)

Unit 8.9
Angles and sides in polygons

Conceptual context

In this unit, pupils revisit and discuss the properties of common 2-D shapes. The term 'polygon' is reviewed and defined as a closed 2-D shape formed by three or more straight lines. If a figure is open or curved, it cannot be considered a polygon. Pupils use this definition to classify shapes as polygons or non-polygons. They are also introduced to the terms 'regular' and 'irregular' and use these definitions to further classify polygons. When a triangle has three congruent sides and three congruent angles, we know it as an equilateral triangle, or a regular triangle. A quadrilateral with four congruent sides and four congruent angles is known as a square or regular quadrilateral. Pupils learn that this applies to polygons of any number of sides, for example an octagon with all sides and angles the same is called a regular octagon. Using their knowledge of the properties of regular polygons, they measure the lengths and angles of 2-D shapes to decide whether they are regular or irregular.

Pupils learn that regular polygons have another set of angles related to them: an exterior angle is the angle between any side of a shape and a line extended from the next side. They learn that pairs of interior and exterior angles are supplementary to each other, adding to 180 degrees.

Learning pupils will have achieved at the end of the unit

- Pupils will be able to identify the properties of common 2-D shapes, including the number of angles and sides, and draw examples of such shapes (Q1, Q3)
- Having secured their concept of 'polygon', pupils will be able to distinguish between polygons and non-polygons (Q2)
- Pupils will be able to distinguish between regular and irregular polygons based on reasoning about equal sides and angles (Q3, Q4)
- Pupils will be able to make an association between the sum of two angles on a straight line and apply this to the sum of interior and exterior angles that share the same vertex of any polygon (Q5)

Resources

mini whiteboards; paper polygons; images of 2-D and 3-D shapes; geoboards and elastic bands; large protractor; small protractors; **Resource 5.8.9a** Polygon families; **Resource 5.8.9b** Sorting shapes; **Resource 5.8.9c** Regular or irregular? **Resource 5.8.9d** Missing angles

Vocabulary

polygon, non-polygon, regular polygon, irregular polygon, interior angle, exterior angle

Chapter 8 Geometry and measurement (1)

Unit 8.9 Practice Book 5B, pages 77–81

Question 1

1 Complete the table about polygons. The first one has been done for you.

Name of polygon	Number of angles	Number of sides	Figure
Triangle	3	3	△
Quadrilateral			
Pentagon			
Hexagon			
Octagon			

What learning will pupils have achieved at the conclusion of Question 1?

- Pupils will be able to identify the properties of common 2-D shapes, including the number of angles and sides, and draw examples of such shapes.

Activities for whole-class instruction

- On the board, draw and label a scalene triangle and mark the angles. Point out the sides and remind pupils that to be a side, it has to be straight. Demonstrate how to count the sides and the angles, marking them as you go. Ask: *How many sides are there? How many angles are there?*

- Draw and label an irregular quadrilateral on the board. Can pupils remember the definition of a quadrilateral? Remind pupils that a quadrilateral is a closed figure with four straight sides. Ask: *How many angles are there?*

- Repeat counting sides and angles for an irregular pentagon. Ask pupils if they can see a pattern between the number of angles and the number of sides. Establish that each shape has the same number of angles as sides. Ask: *Does this work for other shapes?* Organise pupils in pairs and provide them with mini whiteboards. Ask them to investigate the relationship between sides and angles by drawing shapes with different numbers of sides, and counting the angles and sides. Choose pupils to share the results of their investigations and confirm that for closed figures with straight sides, the number of angles is always equal to the number of sides.

- Ask pupils to draw the following closed shapes with straight sides:
  - A shape with 7 angles
  - A shape with 9 sides
  - A shape with 10 angles

- Ask: *How many sides and angles does each shape have? How does the number of sides and angles relate to the number of vertices?* Agree that the number of vertices is always the same as the number of angles because the angles are at the vertices.

- Pupils should complete Question 1 in the Practice Book.

Same-day intervention

- Some pupils may need help with identification and recognition of regular polygons and their group names. Begin with quadrilaterals. On the board, draw two columns, and label them 'quadrilaterals' and 'non-quadrilaterals'. Provide pupils with copies of **Resource 5.8.9a** Polygon families.

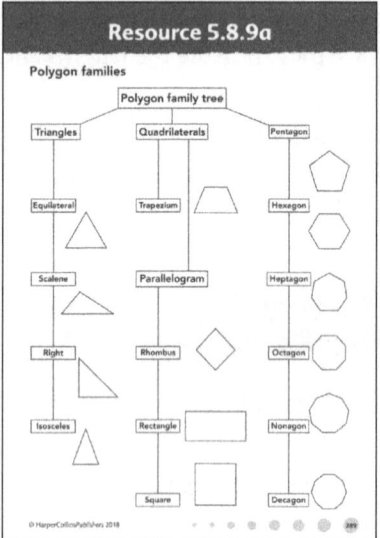

- Remind them that a quadrilateral is a closed figure with four straight sides. Invite volunteers to select a shape and affix it to the right-hand column on the board, explaining their decision. Confirm that each shape has been sorted correctly.

- Repeat the above activity for pentagons and octagons. Remind pupils that a pentagon is a closed figure with five straight sides and an octagon is a closed figure with eight straight sides.

- Provide each group with a set of craft sticks or straws. Ask them to model shapes with 4–10 sides. They arrange the shapes in order of number of sides and confirm that the number of angles is the same as the number of sides.

Chapter 8 Geometry and measurement (1)

Unit 8.9 Practice Book 5B, pages 77–81

- Hold up a paper decagon and count the sides as a group. Then count the angles. Cut off one of the angles by cutting along a line drawn between the vertices on either side. Count the sides and vertices again. Cut off another angle and repeat the count. Can pupils spot a pattern? (The number of sides will decrease by 1 and the number of angles will decrease by 1.)

Same-day enrichment

- Ask pupils to investigate what happens to the size of the interior angles in a regular polygon as the number of angles (or sides) increases. Provide regular polygons cut from paper and ask pupils to compare the angles. They may do this simply by lining up the sides of both shapes, placing one vertex on another to see which shape has the larger angle. Some pupils might like to measure the angles using a protractor.

Question 2

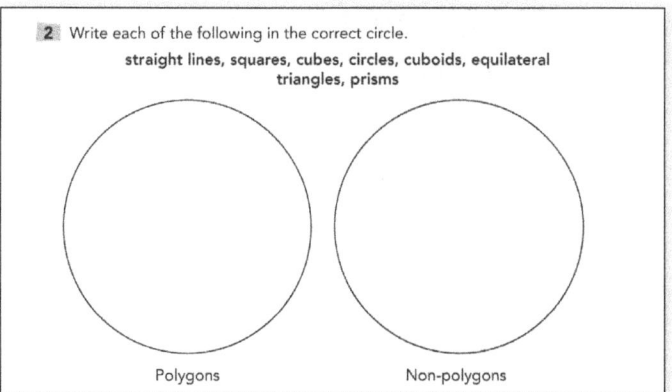

What learning will pupils have achieved at the conclusion of Question 2?

- Having secured their concept of 'polygon', pupils will be able to distinguish between polygons and non-polygons.

Activities for whole-class instruction

- Show pupils a collection of images of shapes on a table top, organised and labelled in two sets: polygons and non-polygons. The shapes should be 'shape tiles' showing images of 2-D shapes (plastic shapes commonly available in classrooms are actually three-dimensional because they have a thickness so are not ideal). Tiles can be made by cutting around 2-D shapes printed on paper, leaving a margin around the outline of each shape. Also display images of 3-D shapes.

Polygons

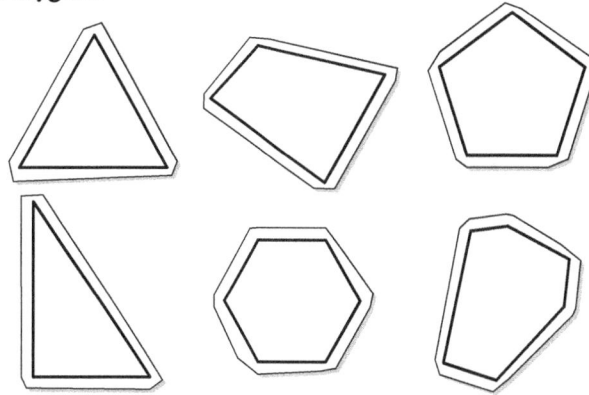

Non-polygons

- Explain that they are a mix of polygons and non-polygons. Ask: *What do you think a polygon is?* Give pupils time to decide on a definition with a partner and then ask them to share their ideas. Agree that:
  - It is a flat, or 2-D, shape
  - all the sides are joined up – that is, it is closed
  - it can have any number of sides but they must be straight.

 *A polygon is a closed 2-D shape formed by three or more straight lines.*

- Can pupils name other shapes that would be classified as polygons? Add examples of these shapes to the set of polygons. Discuss the definitions of 2-D shapes using the term 'polygon'. Say: *Triangles are polygons with three sides. Quadrilaterals are polygons with four sides.* Define pentagons, hexagons and octagons in a similar way.
- Point to the heart in the non-polygon set. Ask: *Why is a heart not a polygon?* (It has rounded edges.)
- Point to the prism. Ask: *Why is a prism not a polygon.* (It is not a flat, 2-D shape.)

Chapter 8 Geometry and measurement (1)　　　Unit 8.9 Practice Book 5B, pages 77–81

- Point to the 'hexagon' with the missing side. Ask: *Why is this shape not a polygon?* (The shape is not fully closed. Not all of the sides are joined up.)
- Provide pupils with mini whiteboards and ask them to draw a set of non-polygons. Ask them to share their drawings and confirm they are non-polygons.
- Pupils should complete Question 2 in the Practice Book.

Same-day intervention

- Draw the following shapes on the board (the cube should be a plastic 3-D shape affixed to the board):

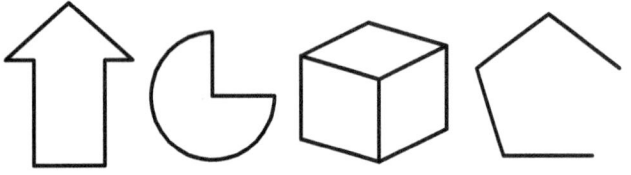

- Write the definition of a polygon on the board and ask pupils to copy it in their 'My geometry notebook':
  – 'Polygon – a closed 2-D shape formed by three or more straight lines'.
- Say: *Polygons will have at least three sides.*
- Point to the shape on the left. Ask: *Why is the first shape a polygon?* Accept comments. Write and underline the phrases 'two-dimensional', 'straight lines' and 'closed' and say that these are the three characteristics that a shape must have to be a polygon.
- Point to the first non-polygon. Ask: *Why is this shape not a polygon?* (It has a curved edge.) Point to the second non-polygon shape and repeat the question. Establish that all 3-D shapes are not polygons. Hold up a cube and explain that, although the faces of a cube are made from polygons, the shape is not flat and therefore is not itself a polygon. Point to the third non-polygon shape and repeat the question. Expect pupils to identify the gap in the shape. Establish that the shape is 'open' and not 'closed', so it is not a polygon.
- Have pupils work in pairs. Provide each group with mini whiteboards and ask them to draw, make or find three examples of shapes that are not polygons. Choose pupils to explain why each of the shapes they chose is a not a polygon.

Same-day enrichment

- Have pupils work in pairs. Provide each group with a copy of **Resource 5.8.9b** Sorting shapes.

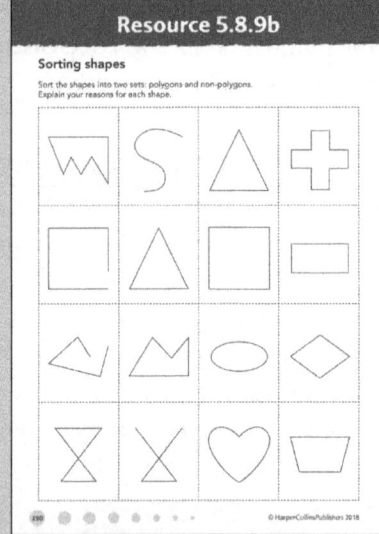

- Ask them to cut out the shapes and sort them into two sets: polygons and non-polygons. Once pupils have completed the activity, they should discuss the sets to confirm the shapes have been sorted correctly.

Answers: Check pupils' answers.

Question 3

3　True or false? (Put a ✔ for true and a ✘ for false in each box.)
　(a) In a polygon the number of angles and sides is the same.
　(b) A polygon has all angles equal and all sides equal.
　(c) A square is a special regular polygon.
　(d) A right-angled triangle is not a regular polygon.
　(e) A square has four equal angles and four equal sides.
　(f) A rectangle has four equal angles and four equal sides.
　(g) A regular polygon has all angles equal and all sides equal.

What learning will pupils have achieved at the conclusion of Question 3?

- Pupils will be able to identify the properties of common 2-D shapes, including the number of angles and sides, and draw examples of such shapes.
- Pupils will be able to distinguish between regular and irregular polygons based on reasoning about equal sides and angles.

Chapter 8 Geometry and measurement (1)

Unit 8.9 Practice Book 5B, pages 77–81

Activities for whole-class instruction

- Pupils should work in pairs. Display the following shapes and labels:

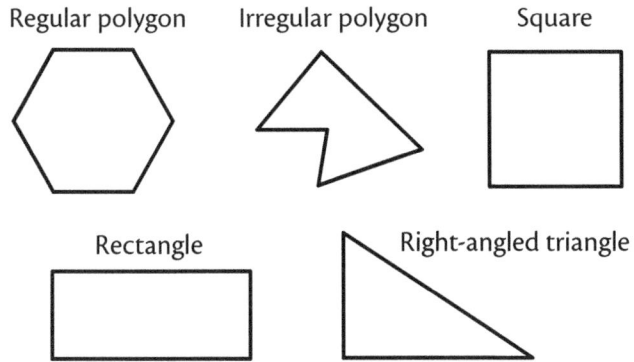

Regular polygon   Irregular polygon   Square

Rectangle   Right-angled triangle

- Ask: *Looking at the first two shapes, what can you say about the difference between regular and irregular polygons?* Agree that a regular polygon has sides all the same length and all of its angles are the same size. Ask: *There are two regular polygons here. Which other polygon is also regular?* Establish that a square is a special example of a quadrilateral in that all the sides are equal and all the angles are right angles.
- Ask: *What type of triangle is a regular polygon?* Agree that an equilateral triangle is a regular polygon.
- Point to the shape labelled 'irregular polygon'. Explain that an irregular polygon is a polygon whose sides and angles are not all the same, although the sides still will be straight and joined up. Ask pupils to identify any other shapes that are irregular from the ones displayed (rectangle, right-angled triangle).
- Ask: *Can you name some other irregular polygons?* Put together a list on the board, for example: scalene triangle, kite, trapezium.
- Provide pupils with mini whiteboards and ask them to draw a polygon at random. Ask: *Is the polygon regular or irregular? How do you know?*
- Pupils should complete Question 3 in the Practice Book.

Same-day intervention

- Provide pupil pairs with geoboards and elastic bands. Place one elastic band on the geoboard. Ask pupils to copy the figure. Ask: *Is this a polygon?* (No, it's a line.)
- Add another band of the same length to the previous figure so that the two lines intersect at right angles.
- Ask: *Is this a polygon?* (no) Confirm that the figure is just two straight lines; it is open and therefore not a polygon.
- Now use three bands to form three sides of a square. Confirm that the figure is still open and not a polygon.
- Add a fourth band to complete the square. Ask: *Is this a polygon?* (yes) Ask: *What do you notice about the angles?* Confirm that all angles are right angles. Ask: *What do you notice about the sides of the square?* (all the same length)
- Ask: *Is this regular or irregular?* On the board, write: A regular polygon is a polygon that has all sides equal and all angles equal. Ask pupils to copy the definition in their 'My geometry notebook' and draw a square alongside, indicating that the angles are all the same size and the sides are all the same length.
- Provide a set of shape tiles and ask pupils to sort them into two sets: 'regular polygons' and 'not regular polygons'. Discuss equilateral triangles and regular pentagons, hexagons and octagons as examples of regular polygons. Pupils make notes of these shapes in their notebooks.
- Return to the geoboard, and move one vertex of the square to a different position shifting the ends of the two adjacent bands accordingly. Ask:
  - *Is this shape still a square?* (No. All the angles and sides are no longer the same.)
  - *Is this shape still a quadrilateral?* (Yes. It has four sides and is therefore still a quadrilateral.)
- Agree that this shape is an example of an irregular polygon. On the board, write: An irregular polygon is a polygon with sides and angles that are not all the same.
- Look at other irregular polygons. Pupils should copy the definition in their 'My geometry notebook' and draw an irregular polygon alongside indicating that the sides and angles are not all the same.

Same-day enrichment

- Pupils should work in pairs. Provide each pair with identical sheets of images of regular and irregular polygons.
- Pupils sit on either side of a barrier, such as a pile of books. Pupil 1 selects a shape and provides a clue to the identity of the shape but does not actually name it. The clue should describe properties of the shape, for example: 'This shape is a regular/irregular polygon' or 'This shape has all angles equal/all sides equal/sides and angles that are not all the same.' Pupils should also comment on the number of sides or angles, or whether any of the angles are right angles.

Chapter 8 Geometry and measurement (1) Unit 8.9 Practice Book 5B, pages 77–81

- The first clue should be the most difficult. Pupils award their partner three points if they are able to name the shape. If not, easier clues are given awarding two then one point for a correct identification of the shape.
- Pupils play four rounds. The winner is the player with more points.

Question 4

4 Look at the 2-D figures below.
Measure and then put a ✔ for a regular polygon and ✘ for an irregular polygon in each box.
If it is a regular polygon, write its angle degree and side length.
Otherwise, write N/A (Not Applicable).

(a) angle degree: ___ side length: ___
(b) angle degree: ___ side length: ___
(c) angle degree: ___ side length: ___
(d) angle degree: ___ side length: ___
(e) angle degree: ___ side length: ___
(f) angle degree: ___ side length: ___
(g) angle degree: ___ side length: ___
(h) angle degree: ___ side length: ___

Give pupils time to discuss the problem then accept comments. Elicit that since the definition of an irregular polygon is a polygon in which angles are not all the same, we only need to find two angles that are different to confirm that a polygon is irregular (it is not necessary to check them all).

- Check that pupils remember how to use a protractor. Choose pupils to assist in measuring two angles of the polygon on the board using a large protractor. Confirm that the two angles are different in size and therefore, the polygon must be irregular.
- Provide each group with a copy of **Resource 5.8.9c** Regular or irregular? and a protractor. Pupils measure the angles of the polygons and confirm whether they are regular or irregular.

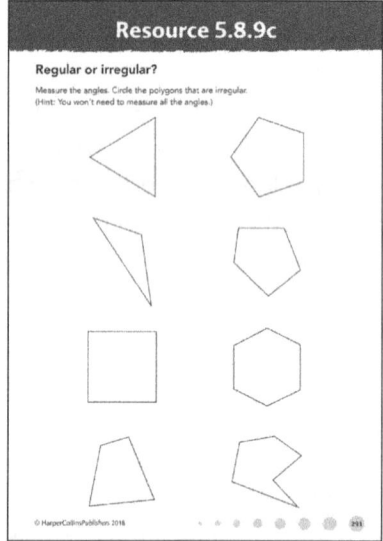

- Pupils should complete Question 4 in the Practice Book.
  Answers: Check pupils' answers.

What learning will pupils have achieved at the conclusion of Question 4?

- Pupils will be able to distinguish between regular and irregular polygons based on reasoning about equal sides and angles.

Activities for whole-class instruction

- Draw an irregular quadrilateral on the board. Ask: *How could we prove that this shape is irregular?* Remind pupils of the definition of an irregular polygon. Accept comments and agree that we can measure the lengths of the sides of the shape or the angles in order to determine if the shape is irregular. Say: *We will focus on measuring angles.* Ask: *Do we need to measure all the interior angles to determine if a shape is irregular?*

Same-day intervention

- Pupils have previously constructed a pictorial sequence of steps in their 'My geometry notebook' to demonstrate how to use a protractor to measure angles. Ask them to consult these notes for help to re-measure angles in Question 4. Encourage pupils to identify the angle as obtuse or acute in order to decide whether to use the inner or outer scale of the protractor.

Chapter 8 Geometry and measurement (1)

Unit 8.9 Practice Book 5B, pages 77–81

Same-day enrichment

- Pupils draw polygons with angles of the sizes given below. They decide whether each polygon is regular or irregular.

  a) A triangle with two angles of 60°

  b) A quadrilateral with two angles of 40° and 110°

  c) A pentagon with at least two right angles

  d) A quadrilateral with three right angles

Question 5

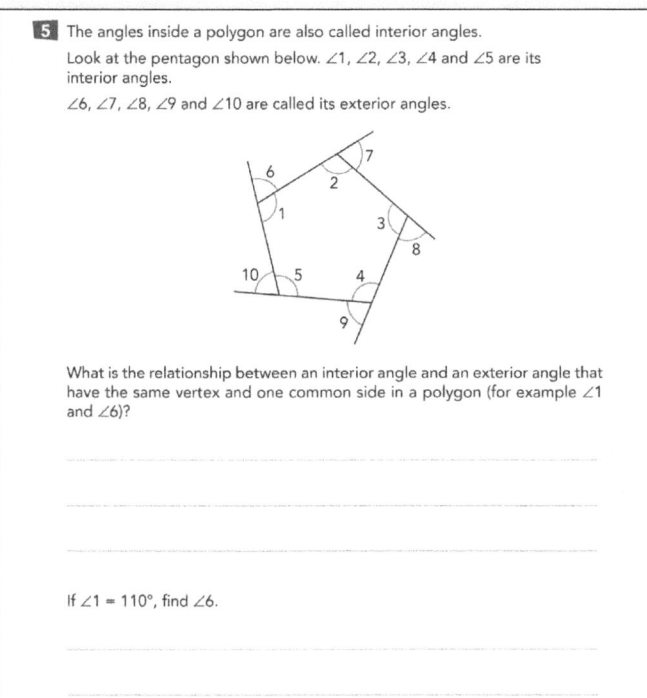

5 The angles inside a polygon are also called interior angles. Look at the pentagon shown below. ∠1, ∠2, ∠3, ∠4 and ∠5 are its interior angles.

∠6, ∠7, ∠8, ∠9 and ∠10 are called its exterior angles.

What is the relationship between an interior angle and an exterior angle that have the same vertex and one common side in a polygon (for example ∠1 and ∠6)?

If ∠1 = 110°, find ∠6.

What learning will pupils have achieved at the conclusion of Question 5?

- Pupils will be able to make an association between the sum of two angles on a straight line and apply this to the sum of interior and exterior angles that share the same vertex of any polygon.

Activities for whole-class instruction

- On the board, draw a scalene triangle. Label the angles *a*, *b* and *c*. Tell pupils these are called interior angles.

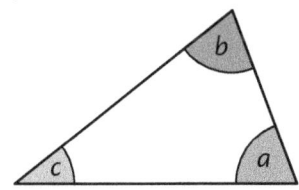

- Extend the line *ca*:

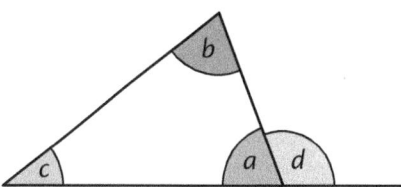

- Label the exterior angle *d*. Tell pupils: *When we extend the sides of a polygon outside the shape, exterior angles are formed.* Explain that the word 'exterior' means outside, so an exterior angle is on the outside of a polygon. Point to angle *d*.

- Provide pupils with rulers. Ask them to draw a triangle and mark the interior angles *a*, *b* and *c*. They extend each side and mark the exterior angles *d*, *e* and *f*.

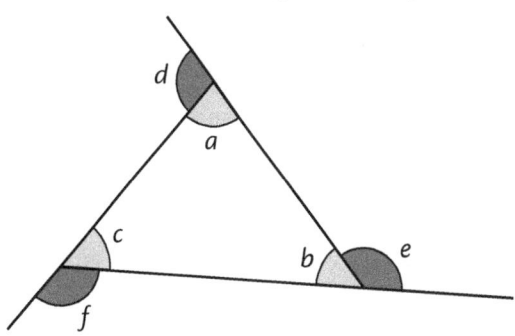

- Repeat the labelling of interior and exterior angles for an irregular quadrilateral to demonstrate that exterior angles can be drawn for polygons with any number of sides.

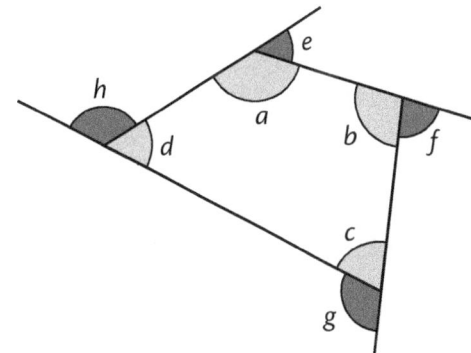

- Ask the following question in preparation for Question 5: *What do you think is the relationship between an interior angle and an exterior angle formed at the same vertex, for example angles a and d?* Accept ideas and establish that, since interior and exterior angles are angles on a straight line, the sum of any pair of interior and exterior angles is 180°.

- Pupils should complete Question 5 in the Practice Book.

129

Chapter 8 Geometry and measurement (1)

Unit 8.9 Practice Book 5B, pages 77–81

Same-day intervention

- Ask pupils to draw an irregular quadrilateral with a ruler. Demonstrate how to extend the sides of the shape as shown below:

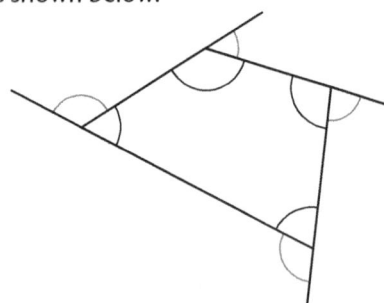

- Choose a pupil to label the interior angles *a*, *b*, *c* and *d*. Choose another pupil to label the exterior angles *e*, *f*, *g* and *h*.
- Ask: *Which angles form pairs of interior and exterior angles?* Ask pupils to make a copy of the diagram in their 'My geometry notebook' under the title 'Interior and exterior angles'. They list the pairs of interior and exterior angles. Say and demonstrate: *Each pair of interior and exterior angles lies on a straight line. What do you know about angles on a straight line?* (Angles on a straight line add up to 180°.)
- Ask pupils to write number sentences for each pair of interior and exterior angles, for example: *a* + *e* = 180°.

Challenge and extension question

Question 6

6 Look at the pentagon again. What can you say about the relationships between the exterior angles? Are they always equal? If not, in what kind of polygons are they equal?

Pupils use their knowledge of interior and exterior angles to decide whether the given polygon will have exterior angles that are equal. If the angles are not given, it would be incorrect to assume that the interior angles (or exterior angles) of a polygon represented on paper are all equal, even if the representation appears regular to the eye. Pupils need to know that only regular polygons have equal interior angles and equal exterior angles.

Same-day enrichment

- Provide each pupil with a copy of **Resource 5.8.9d** Missing angles and ask them to calculate the missing angles.

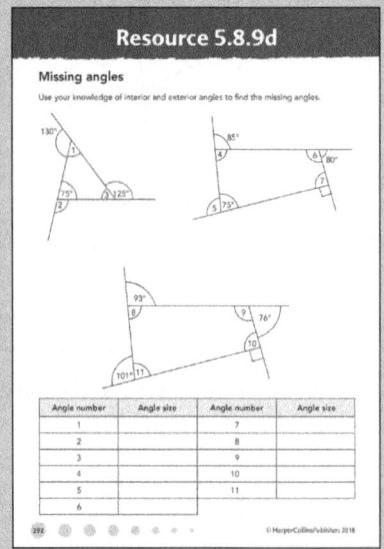

Answers: 1. 50°; 2. 105°; 3. 55°; 4. 95°; 5. 105°; 6. 100°; 7. 90°; 8. 87°; 9. 104°; 10. 90°; 11. 79°

Chapter 8 test (Practice Book 5B, pages 82–86)

Test question number	Relevant unit	Relevant questions within unit
1	Unit 8.1, Unit 8.2	Q1, Q2, Q3, Q4
2	Unit 8.2	Q1, Q2, Q3, Q4
3	Unit 8.3	Q1, Q2, Q3, Q4
4	Unit 8.4	Q1, Q2, Q3, Q4, Q5
5	Unit 8.5	Q1, Q2, Q3, Q4, Q5, Q6
6	Unit 8.6	Q1, Q2, Q3, Q4, Q5
7	Unit 8.7	Q1, Q2, Q3, Q4, Q5
8	Unit 8.8	Q1, Q2, Q3, Q4
9	Unit 8.9	Q1, Q2, Q3, Q4, Q1, Q2, Q3, Q4, Q5, Q6

Chapter 9
Geometry and measurement (2)

Chapter overview

Area of mathematics	National Curriculum statutory requirements for Key Stage 2	Shanghai Maths Project reference
Measurement	Year 5 Programme of study: Pupils should be taught to: ■ convert between different units of metric measure ■ understand and use approximate equivalences between metric units and common imperial units such as inches, pounds and pints ■ estimate volume and capacity ■ use all four operations to solve problems involving measure using decimal notation including scaling.	Year 5, Units 9.3, 9.6, 9.7, 9.8, 9.9 Year 5, Unit 9.4 Year 5, Units 9.3, 9.8 Year 5, Units 9.3, 9.4, 9.5, 9.6, 9.7, 9.8, 9.9
	Year 6 Programme of study: Pupils should be taught to: ■ use, read, write and convert between standard units, converting measurements of length, mass, volume and time from a smaller unit of measure to a larger unit, and vice versa, using decimal notation to up to 3 decimal places ■ convert between miles and kilometres ■ recognise when it is possible to use formulae for area and volume of shapes ■ calculate, estimate and compare volume of cubes and cuboids using standard units, including cubic centimetres (cm^3) and cubic metres (m^3), and extending to other units.	Year 5, Units 9.3, 9.6, 9.7, 9.8, 9.9 Year 5, Unit 9.4 Year 5, Units 9.6, 9.7, 9.8, 9.9 Year 5, Units 9.2, 9.6, 9.7, 9.8, 9.9
Properties of shape	Year 5 Programme of study: Pupils should be taught to: ■ identify 3-D shapes, including cubes and other cuboids, from 2-D representations.	Year 5, Unit 9.5

Chapter 9 Geometry and measurement (2)

Unit 9.1
Volume

Conceptual context

In preparation for the units that follow on volume and capacity, this unit introduces the idea of volume as being a measure of the size of a 3-D object. This is explicitly connected to pupils' work in Year 4, where they learned about area as a measure of the size of a 2-D object. Both area and volume are referred to as the amount of space taken up. Pupils have previously learned about volume in the context of measuring liquids. This unit will bring together existing conceptual knowledge about area for measuring space in two dimensions and about volume of liquids.

This basic concept of volume is then developed, as pupils are asked to consider whether volume changes when 3-D objects are altered in different ways. It is particularly important that pupils understand when volume does not change (is 'conserved'), for example when the cubes that make up a 3-D shape are rearranged slightly. This will connect with pupils' existing knowledge about liquids and expand and strengthen their concept of relating to measurement more generally.

Learning pupils will have achieved at the end of the unit

- The concept of volume will have been introduced and connected with pupils' concept of area as a measure of size; of the amount of space taken up (Q1)
- Ideas about what causes volume to change and when it stays the same will have been explored (Q2, Q3, Q4)
- Pupils will have been introduced to the concept of using cubes to measure volume (Q4)

Resources

a cardboard box (for example a cereal box); image of a rectangle (same size as one of the faces of the box); a selection of 3-D shapes (cubes and cuboids); a bag; poster paper; coloured pencils; mini whiteboards; interlocking cubes; modelling clay; scissors; two cups of different shape; swiss roll or unsliced loaf of bread; two pencils that are the same thickness, but different lengths; a bottle of juice and an empty glass to pour it into; 12 counters; straight-sided glasses or containers, water and some small stones; **Resource 5.9.1a** Squares and rectangles; **Resource 5.9.1b** True or false?

Vocabulary

two-dimensional (2-D), three-dimensional (3-D), area, volume, space

Chapter 9 Geometry and measurement (2) Unit 9.1 Practice Book 5B, pages 87–88

Question 1

> **1** Fill in the spaces to make each statement correct.
> (a) The amount of space that an object takes up is called _____ .
> (b) Both 'volume' and 'area' represent the size of an object, but the area represents the size of a ☐-dimensional figure, while the volume represents the space taken up by a ☐-dimensional figure.

What learning will pupils have achieved at the conclusion of Question 1?

- The concept of volume will have been introduced and connected with pupils' concept of area as a measure of size; of the amount of space taken up.

Activities for whole-class instruction

- Show pupils an image of a rectangle (that is the same size as one of the faces of the cardboard box).

- Ask: *How would you describe this shape?* Discuss the fact that it has two dimensions (length and width) and can be described as a 2-D shape (pupils may also remember the word 'rectilinear' from previous work). Ask: *How do we measure the space that a 2-D shape takes up?* Revise the term 'area' and remind pupils of their previous work calculating the area of rectilinear shapes (see Year 4 Chapter 9).

 *Area is the space covered by a 2-D shape.*

- Show pupils the cardboard box. Ask: *How would you describe this shape?* Discuss the concept of a 3-D object and the fact that the shape now has depth (or height) as well as width and length. Point out that one of the faces is the same as the 2-D rectangle. Agree that the box has three 'dimensions'.

- Ask: *What are the three dimensions of this shape?* Encourage pupils to point to its length, width and height (or 'depth'). Show pupils a flat 2-D square (a drawing on paper) and a plastic 3-D cube and ask them to describe both in terms of their dimensions. Use the word 'solid' to describe the 3-D shape and explain that the space that a 3-D shape takes up is called its 'volume'.

 *Volume is the amount of space that a 3-D shape takes up.*

- Explain that pupils will be considering the volume of shapes over the next few lessons.

- Write the words '2-D', '3-D', 'AREA' and 'VOLUME' on the board. Point to various shapes/objects around the classroom. Choose pupils to come to the front and point to the number of dimensions the shape has and the word used to describe the space that it takes up. For example:
  - a piece of paper is actually a 3-D shape because it has a thickness (albeit a very small one). An image on the surface of a piece of paper is a 2-D shape. The space occupied by the 2-D shape is its area
  - a laptop can be described as a 3-D shape (length, width and height) and so the space it takes up is its volume.

- Pupils should complete Question 1 in the Practice Book.

Same-day intervention

- Prior to the activity, prepare a bag containing a variety of 2-D shape 'tiles' from **Resource 5.9.1a** Squares and rectangles, and 3-D cubes and cuboids (for example a cereal box, a thick book, a dice).

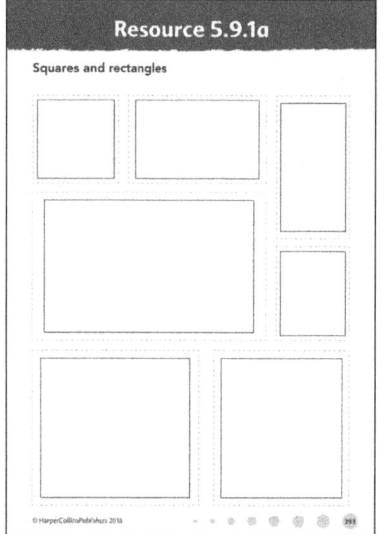

ⓘ The use of tiles showing images of 2-D shapes on them is purposeful. Plastic 2-D shapes, however thin, are not completely flat and it is important to help pupils to see that a true 2-D shape does not have any height or thickness at all. The tiles have a border around them to help show pupils that they are considering the image inside the border, rather than the shape of the tile itself. It is important, therefore, when referring to these tiles that the length and the width of the 'square pictured on the tile' are described, rather than 'the square'. By referring to the image rather than the object pupils have pulled out of the bag, you are emphasising the concept of two dimensions.

Chapter 9 Geometry and measurement (2)

Unit 9.1 Practice Book 5B, pages 87–88

- Choose a pupil to feel for a tile with a 2-D shape pictured on it, without looking inside the bag. Discuss the shape on the tile that is pulled from the bag. Can pupils label its two dimensions? Remind pupils that it is an image of a square/rectangle and so it has no height. Choose another pupil to pick a 3-D object out of the bag. Compare the two shapes and ask: *What is the same? What is different? Can you label the three dimensions of the 3-D shape?* Pupils should use length, width, height, depth to describe objects and discussion should lead them to be confident that they 'see' only two of these dimensions on the 2-D shapes and three dimensions on the 3-D shapes.
- Make two labels; 'area' and 'volume'. Ask pupils to place shapes from the bag next to the appropriate label to show how the space that each takes up is measured; either as volume or as area.
- Focus on the 3-D shapes and explain that pupils will be learning how to calculate the volume of shapes like these. Ask: *What similarities do these shapes have?* Ask pupils to find other examples of shapes with volume in the classroom.

Same-day enrichment

- Pupils should create a pictorial representation of what they have learned. Ask them to make a poster showing objects they can see in the classroom around them, labelling each object either 'area' or 'volume' to show how their size is measured. Those that are measured by area should be 2-D objects and those that are measured by volume should be 3-D objects. Pupils can then use their illustrations to test each other, covering up the key word and asking each other to say how the size of a particular object is measured.

Question 2

> 2 True or false? (Put a ✓ for true and ✗ for false in each box.)
> (a) After Joe poured a carton of fruit juice into a glass, the volume of the juice changed (assuming no loss of the juice in the process).
> (b) The volume of an object changes as the shape changes (assuming no loss of the object in the process).
> (c) If two books have the same cover and page size, the thicker book has a greater volume.
> (d) There are two pieces of round timber with different thicknesses and lengths. Their volumes must also be different.

What learning will pupils have achieved at the conclusion of Question 2?

- Ideas about what causes volume to change and when it stays the same will have been explored.

Activities for whole-class instruction

- Put pupils into pairs and ask them to write a definition of what is meant by the volume of an object. Collect their definitions and confirm that volume refers to the space that a 3-D object takes up. Introduce the idea of larger and smaller volumes by choosing similarly-shaped objects with obvious differences in volume and asking pupils to say which they think takes up more space (and therefore has more volume). For example, ask:
  - Which has more volume – a matchbox or a cereal box?
  - Which body has more volume – an adult's or a child's

ⓘ The idea behind this activity is to get pupils to start to consider volume in very general, visual, terms. When choosing objects to talk about, using objects with a similar and recognisable shape, for example two cuboids, will allow pupils to be able to make visual comparisons more easily. Comparing a tin of beans with a dictionary, for example, is much harder to do. Additionally, it will be useful to choose some examples of smaller heavier objects and larger lighter objects. This will help to deal with the misconception that an object with more volume is necessarily heavier.

- Develop the activity by making statements about objects and asking pupils to vote whether they think the statement is true or false. For example:
  - Show pupils a lump of modelling clay shaped like a ball. Roll it into a sausage shape. Say: *The volume of the play dough has not changed. True or false?*
  - Take a cupful of water and pour it from one glass into another that is a different shape. Say: *The volume of the water has changed. True or false?*
  - Show pupils a swiss roll or unsliced loaf of bread. Cut off a thick slice and remove it. Say: *The swiss roll/loaf has less volume now. True or false?*
- Pupils should complete Question 2 in the Practice Book.

Chapter 9 Geometry and measurement (2) Unit 9.1 Practice Book 5B, pages 87–88

Same-day intervention

- Prior to the activity, prepare a series of pairs of objects for pupils to consider. For example: two pencils that are the same thickness, but different lengths; a bottle of juice and an empty glass to pour it into; a line of six counters and an array of 2 × 3 counters.
- Cover up the objects so pupils cannot see them. Begin by choosing a pupil to come to the front and look at one of the pairs. Ask them to describe what they can see. Make a statement about the pair of objects, asking, for each one: *Do you agree or disagree with this statement?* For example:
  - The two pencils have the same volume because they are the same thickness.
  - The volume of the juice changes when it is all poured from a bottle into a glass.
  - The line of counters has the same volume as the array, even though they look different.
- Reveal the objects so that pupils can consider their answers while actually looking at the objects. Ask: *How could we show whether this is true or not?* Listen carefully to pupils' responses as they may reveal misconceptions about volume (for example, referring to the weight of the objects rather than the space they take up). Pupils may show logical reasoning by suggesting to reverse the change (for example, tipping the juice back into the bottle to show that its volume has not changed, or using the array of counters to make a line to show that they have the same volume).
- Challenge pupils to make their own statements about pairs of objects for their peers to judge whether they are true or false.

Same-day enrichment

- Provide pupils with a set of statement cards from **Resource 5.9.1b** True or false? In pairs, pupils should shuffle the cards and deal them out so that each pupil has a pile of cards. One by one, pupils should sort the cards into two piles; TRUE and FALSE. They should discuss their answers in terms of the volume of the shape being described. If time allows, pupils could make their own statement cards for peers to sort.

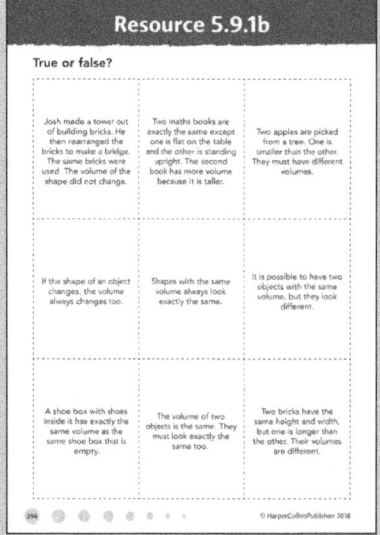

Answers: 1. T; 2. F; 3. T; 4. F; 5. F; 6. T; 7. T; 8. F; 9. T

Questions 3 and 4

3 Read each scenario below and then answer each question using the word 'changed' or 'unchanged'.
  (a) Saliha was playing with a piece of modelling clay. First she rolled the clay into a long strip. What happened to the volume of the clay? _____
  (b) She then made the clay into a little bear shape. What happened to the volume of the clay? _____
  (c) She finally made the clay into a rabbit shape. What happened to the volume of the clay? _____

4 Answer the following questions using the word 'changed' or 'unchanged'.
  (a) Six cubes were stacked together. Jess took the 6 cubes apart into separate pieces. What happened to the volume of the 6 cubes? _____
  (b) Next, Jess put the cubes into a row. What happened to the volume of the 6 cubes? _____
  (c) Jess then put the cubes into two rows. What happened to the volume of the 6 cubes? _____

Chapter 9 Geometry and measurement (2)

Unit 9.1 Practice Book 5B, pages 87–88

What learning will pupils have achieved at the conclusion of Questions 3 and 4?

- Ideas about what causes volume to change and when it stays the same will have been explored.
- Pupils will have been introduced to the concept of using cubes to measure volume.

Activities for whole-class instruction

- Provide pupils with whiteboards and ask them to write the words 'CHANGED' and 'UNCHANGED' – one on the front and one on the back.
- Use the modelling clay ball/sausage example again. Ask pupils to hold up their boards to show whether the volume is changed or unchanged when you change the shape of the clay. Ask a number of pupils to explain why they voted 'Unchanged'. Agree that, if nothing is removed or added, its volume stays the same even if its shape alters.

 *As long as nothing is removed or added, the volume of a 3-D shape is unchanged, even if its shape changes.*

- Choose pupils to continue to manipulate the clay and ask the rest of the group to respond with 'CHANGED' or 'UNCHANGED'. Remind them that they are referring to the volume, not how the shape looks. For example, they might:
  - squash the clay so that it is flat (UNCHANGED)
  - break off a piece and discard it (CHANGED)
  - make a cube shape out of the remainder (UNCHANGED)
  - gently squash the cube shape (UNCHANGED)
- Provide pairs of pupils with five interlocking cubes and ask them to start by building them into a tower. Ask: *Did the volume of your tower change or remain unchanged as you added each cube to it?* Agree that the space the tower took up (its volume) changed as it each cube was added.
- Give pupils further instructions and ask them whether they think the volume changes or remains unchanged. For example:
  - make a different shape out of the five cubes (UNCHANGED)
  - separate the five cubes and place them in a line (UNCHANGED)
  - make a new shape by adding a sixth cube (CHANGED)

- For each shape they make, encourage pupils to describe the volume in terms of the number of cubes they have used (for example, if the shape still uses five cubes its volume remains unchanged). Say: *Show me two shapes where the second shape's volume is the same as the first. How do you know that the volume is unchanged? Show me two shapes where the second shape's volume is different from the first. How do you know that the volume has changed?*
- Pupils should complete Questions 3 and 4 in the Practice Book.

Same-day intervention

- Provide pupils with 10 interlocking cubes each without discussing the number of cubes they each have. Ask them each to arrange their cubes so that there are no gaps between them. Discuss the different arrangements pupils have made. Ask: *How are your arrangements different? Are they the same in any way? Whose arrangement looks like it has the largest/smallest volume? Why?* Ask them to make a tower of their cubes. What do they notice? Explain that however pupils arrange their cubes they will always have the same volume because they always take up the same space as 10 interlocking cubes. Ask: *How could we make an arrangement with a different volume?* Encourage pupils to remove or add to their set of cubes to do this.
- Ensure that pupils spend time exploring the fact that a different shape does not necessarily mean a different volume. By moving their manipulatives back into their original position, they can prove that the volume is unchanged.

Chapter 9 Geometry and measurement (2) Unit 9.1 Practice Book 5B, pages 87–88

Same-day enrichment

- Challenge pupils to rewrite Questions 3 and 4 in the Practice Book so that each part now gives the opposite answer (so, a 'changed' answer becomes 'unchanged'). For example:
  'He first rolled the modelling clay into a long strip.' (Answer: UNCHANGED)

  Might be rewritten as:
  'He first split the modelling clay into two pieces and threw half away.' (Answer: CHANGED)

- Pupils should share their new questions with peers to model and answer. If time allows, encourage them to write their own questions based on other materials (for example, the volume of water inside a glass).

Challenge and extension question

Question 5

5. Put some water into a straight-sided glass and then immerse a stone in the water. Describe how you would find the volume of the stone.

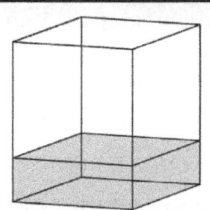

Pupils are challenged to consider how they might find the volume of a stone by placing it into a straight-sided glass containing water. They will need to see that the stone will take up space in the glass, displacing the water and raising the water level. The volume of the stone will be shown by the change in the volume of the water.

Chapter 9 Geometry and measurement (2)

Unit 9.2
Cubic centimetres and cubic metres (1)

Conceptual context

In this unit, pupils are introduced to the concept of a cubic centimetre. This will form the basis for the measurement of volume using standard units. As such, it is important that pupils spend time understanding cubic centimetres individually, before progressing to using them as building blocks for shapes with larger volumes. Volume, at this stage, is then calculated by counting the centimetre cubes that form these shapes. By using physical and pictorial representations, pupils may begin to notice the relationship between length, width and height that is applied more formally as a formula in later units.

Learning pupils will have achieved at the end of the unit

- The concept of a cubic centimetre and the notation cm^3 will have been introduced (Q1)
- Cubic centimetres as a measure of volume will have been explored by counting the cubes that are used to form cuboids and other objects made from cubes (Q2, Q3)
- Pupils will have learned that shapes with the same volume do not necessarily look the same (Q2)
- Informal connections between a shape's length, width and height, and its volume will have begun to be made (Q2, Q3)
- Fundamental concepts relating length, area and volume to each other will have been strengthened (Q4)

Resources

centimetre cubes; rulers; **Resource 5.9.2a** Simple cuboids; dice; **Resource 5.9.2b** Roll a volume!; **Resource 5.9.2c** Cubic shapes (1); **Resource 5.9.2d** Cubic shapes (2); **Resource 5.9.2e** Prove it!

Vocabulary

volume, space, cubic centimetre (cm^3), length, width, height, depth, cube, cuboid, cubic shape

Chapter 9 Geometry and measurement (2)   Unit 9.2 Practice Book 5B, pages 89–91

Question 1

> **1** Fill in the spaces to make each statement correct.
>
> (a) If the edge length of a cube is 1 cm, its volume is ☐ cubic centimetres or ☐ cm³.
>
> (b) Using 5 cubes of edge length 1 cm to form a 3-D figure, its volume is ☐ cm³.
>
> (c) To use cubes of edge length 1 cm to form a bigger cube, at least ☐ cubes are needed. In this case, its volume is ☐ cm³.

What learning will pupils have achieved at the conclusion of Question 1?

- The concept of a cubic centimetre (and the notation cm³) will have been introduced.

Activities for whole-class instruction

- Introduce the concept of a 1 cm cube as follows: Begin by showing pupils a 1 cm square. Ask pupils to describe its dimensions. Establish that it has length and width and is what we might use as a unit of measurement to give the area of 2-D (flat) shapes.

- Remind pupils of the notation 'cm²'. Emphasise that this represents 1 cm × 1 cm.

- Ask: *What might the first 1 cm be telling us?* Pupils should suggest length or width.

- Show pupils a 1 cm cube. Ask: *What is the difference between the square and this cube?* Pupils should tell you:
  - The square has two dimensions and the cube has three dimensions.
  - The third dimension is depth as the square already had length and width (or width and height). This is the only difference.

- Ask: *Why do you think this is called a 'cubic centimetre'?*

- Provide 1 cm cubes for pupils to handle for themselves. What do they notice about the three dimensions? Ask: *If a square centimetre is represented by cm², how could we represent a cubic centimetre?*

- Write '1 cm × 1 cm × 1 cm' on the board. Say: *When we are describing area, two dimensions are being considered and the units we use are cm² because it describes cm × cm. When we describe volume, why do you think the units we use are cm³?* Can pupils tell you that it is because three dimensions must be considered so the unit is cm × cm × cm?

 *The volume of a cube whose sides are 1 cm long is 1 centimetre cubed. The space that it takes up is 1 cubic centimetre.*

- Introduce the idea that cubic centimetres can be used to measure the volume of larger shapes. Increase the size of a shape by adding more cubes, one at a time. Ask: *What is the volume of this shape now? How do you know?* When the shape has a volume of 6 cm³, stop adding cubes and begin building a second (different) shape with the same volume. Compare both shapes. Ask: *Is it possible for a shape to look different, but have the same volume? How do you know? Can you prove this using cubes?* Encourage pupils to use their own cubes to create shapes and then share them with the class. Ask them to describe the volume of their 3-D shape and then compare it with others that may have the same volume.

 *The volume of this shape is ___ cm³. We know this because the space it takes up is ___ cubic centimetres.*

- Pupils should complete Question 1 in the Practice Book.

Same-day intervention

- Show pupils a 1 cm cube and ask them to use a ruler to measure its sides. Ask: *What do you notice about its dimensions?* Establish that its length, width and height are all equal and that it takes up 1 cubic centimetre. Ask: *How do we write this? Are there any other ways we can arrange this single cube to make a different shape?* Give pupils a second cube each and ask them to make a 3-D shape from them. Ask: *How many cubic centimetres does your shape take up? Are any of your shapes the same?*

- ⓘ In the above activity, all the shapes made by pupils will be the same (there is only one possible cuboid to be made from 2 cubes). However, pupils often see a rotated 3-D shape and assume that it is a different shape (a misconception also demonstrated when working with 2-D shapes). Encourage pupils to turn their shapes in different directions so that they recognise the fact they are congruent. They have not made a 'different' shape, but simply shown the same shape in a different position.

- Ask pupils to make a shape that is not a cube or cuboid and does not have a volume of 2 cm³. Ask: *What is wrong with your shape?* (for example, pupils may separate the two cubes completely or connect them by an edge or vertex rather than a face). Explain that the types of 3-D shapes they will be using will always be connected by a face. Continue with the different shapes pupils can make using three cubes and then four cubes.

139

Chapter 9 Geometry and measurement (2)

Unit 9.2 Practice Book 5B, pages 89–91

- Draw a blank table on the board and encourage pupils to complete it using the information they have discovered.

Number of cubes used	Cubic centimetres in each shape	Volume of each shape (cm³)
1	1	1 cm³
2	2	2 cm³
3	3	3 cm³
4	4	4 cm³

- Challenge pupils to predict the volume of a shape made out of five, six or ten cubes. How do they know?

Same-day enrichment

- Set pupils the challenge of using centimetre cubes to make larger and larger cubes (up to a 4 × 4 × 4 cube). Use the same blank table as used with the intervention group (see above) and encourage pupils to complete it. Pupils should consider the properties of a cube to ensure that they have not formed a rectangular cuboid. If they are able, they should predict the number of cubes they will need to use to form each subsequent cube.

Number of cubes used	Cubic centimetres in each shape	Volume of each shape (cm³)
1	1	1 cm³
8	8	8 cm³
27	27	27 cm³
64	64	64 cm³

Question 2

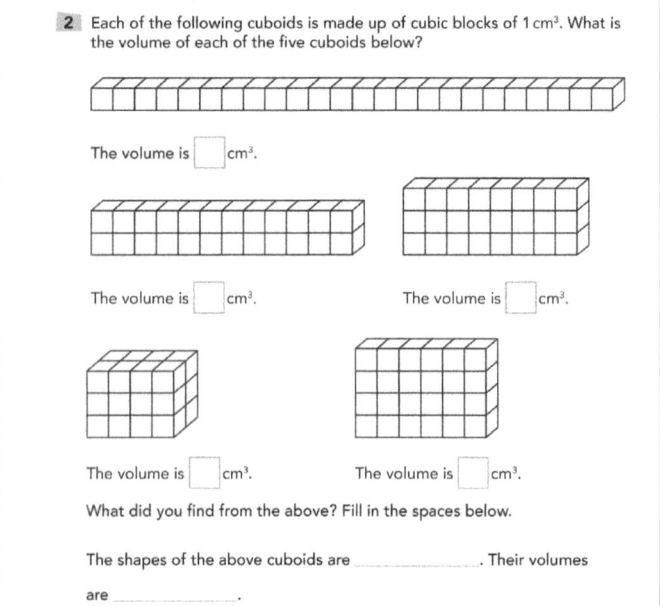

What learning will pupils have achieved at the conclusion of Question 2?

- The concept of a cubic centimetre and the notation cm³ will have been introduced.
- Cubic centimetres as a measure of volume will have been explored by counting the cubes that are used to form cuboids and other objects made from cubes.
- Pupils will have learned that shapes with the same volume do not necessarily look the same.
- Informal connections between a shape's length, width and height, and its volume will have begun to be made.

Activities for whole-class instruction

- Display a cuboid made out of centimetre cubes with the dimensions 2 × 4 × 2. Ask: *How can we find out the total volume of this shape – the amount of space that it takes up?* Remind pupils that this can be expressed in terms of cubic centimetres (cm³) and establish that it can be found by counting the number of cubes that make the shape. Without splitting the cuboid up, encourage pupils to visualise the number of cubes and encourage them to explain the method they used to find the answer.

- Display two cuboids: one where 12 cubes are placed in a row (dimensions: 12 × 1 × 1) and another with dimensions 2 × 2 × 3. Ask: *Which of these shapes looks as if it takes up most space? Which has the greater volume? Why do you think this? How can we find the answer?* (At this stage, by counting cubes.) Count the cubes to find the volume of both cuboids.

Chapter 9 Geometry and measurement (2) Unit 9.2 Practice Book 5B, pages 89–91

ⓘ At this stage it is not crucial for pupils to recognise that a shape's volume is found by multiplying its length, width and height, but the activity does lend itself to noticing this. Allow pupils to recognise these relationships naturally, without requiring them to do so. Ask: *What do you notice about the dimensions of the cuboids?* Note how pupils respond.

- Put pupils into pairs and challenge them to make a third cuboid that has a volume of 12 cm³. Collect together answers. If any are the same, but in different orientations, prove this by rotating them. Ask: *What do you notice about the volume of these cuboids? What do you notice about their shapes? If two shapes have the same volume – will they look exactly the same? Do you think there is a limit to the number of cuboids you can make with a certain volume? Why?*

- Pupils should complete Question 2 in the Practice Book.

Same-day intervention

- Prepare the cards from **Resource 5.9.2a** Simple cuboids. Show pupils the first card from a sequence. Ask them to look carefully at the cuboid it shows and describe how many centimetre cubes will be needed to make it. Pupils should then model the cuboid using centimetre cubes. Ask: *What is its volume in cm³?* Progress through the sequence and encourage pupils to describe each new cuboid, to make it and then determine its volume. Finally, ask: *What will the next cuboid in the sequence look like? Can you predict what its volume will be?*

- Repeat for further sequences of cuboids to practise using pictorial information to model cuboids and then express their volume using the correct notation.

Answers: 1 cm × 3 cm × 5 cm = 15 cm³; 1 cm × 2 cm × 5 cm = 10 cm³; 2 cm × 3 cm × 5 cm = 30 cm³

Same-day enrichment

- Pupils should be given a dice and a copy of **Resource 5.9.2b** Roll a volume! which will help them through the following activity. Pupils should work in pairs, rolling their dice four or five times and finding its total. They are then challenged to make as many different cuboids as they can with this volume. Before starting, pupils are encouraged to visualise some of the different possibilities, predict how many there might be and to describe these possibilities to their partner. Ideally, pupils will use the language of length, width, height and depth quite naturally in this scenario. This will be a useful step in recognising informal links between the length, width and height/depth and the volume of cuboids.

Question 3

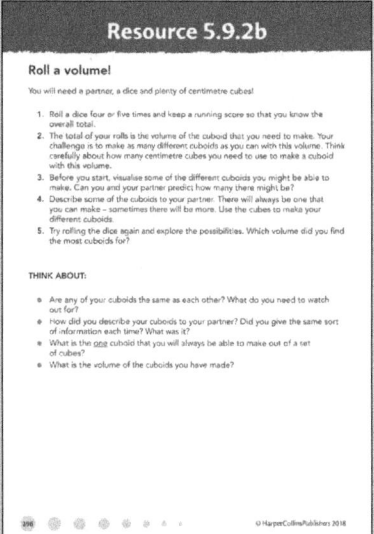

3 Look at the 3-D figures below, and determine the volume of each shape. (The edge length of each small cube is 1 cm.)

Volume: ☐ cm³   Volume: ☐ cm³

Volume: ☐ cm³   Volume: ☐ cm³

Chapter 9 Geometry and measurement (2)

Unit 9.2 Practice Book 5B, pages 89–91

What learning will pupils have achieved at the conclusion of Question 3?

- Cubic centimetres as a measure of volume will have been explored by counting the cubes that are used to form cuboids and other objects made from cubes.
- Informal connections between a shape's length, width and height, and its volume will have begun to be made.

Activities for whole-class instruction

- Use centimetre cubes to model a cuboid and a more complex cubic shape. Ask: *What is the same and what is different about these shapes? Which shape do you think it is easier to find the volume of and why?* Look at the more complex shape in particular and ask: *What skills do you need to find the volume of a shape like this?* Establish that pupils need to be able to visualise the parts of a shape that cannot be seen (for example, predicting the number of cubes in the bottom layer of the shape) and using this information to help them when counting the cubes.
- Display this image of a 3-D shape.

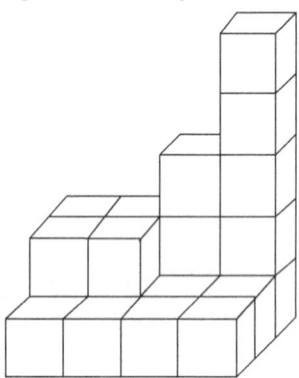

- Ask pupils to describe the shape, encouraging them to build it up conceptually. For example, ask: *Can it be split into different cuboids? What is the volume of the base layer and how do you know? What additions do you need to do to find the overall volume? Can you describe the shape layer by layer?*
- Having described the pictorial version of the shape, pupils should determine its volume and then model using centimetre cubes to check that their answer is correct.
- Repeat for further 3-D shapes. Use cubic shapes that have been shown to pupils (without rotating them), pictorial versions and also verbal descriptions of shapes that pupils then have to model themselves. It is important that within these examples, pupils are given many opportunities to visualise the unseen parts of a shape.
- Pupils should complete Question 3 in the Practice Book.

Same-day intervention

- Go through some of the examples of cubic shapes shown in the Practice Book for Question 3 and discuss how pupils might make it. Aim to deconstruct the shape using words. For example, pupils might describe the second shape in the Practice Book as follows:
- 'Make a cuboid with a length of 4 cm, a width of 2 cm and that is 2 cm high. Take away the cube in the top right-hand corner nearest you. Then make another cuboid with a length of 2 cm, a width of 2 cm and that is 4 cm high. Put this on top of the first cuboid, in the top left-hand corner furthest from you. The total volume is 31 cm^3.'

Or:

- 'Make a 2 × 2 cuboid that is six layers high. Than make another 2 × 2 cuboid next to it that is two layers high. Take away one cube from the right-hand corner nearest you. The total volume is 31 cm^3.'
- Remind pupils to say the number of cubes they have used and remind them that each cube is 1 cm length and so the volume is that number of cubic centimetres (cm^3).
- Ask pupils to then make the shape using actual cm cubes. So that the first part of the activity is pictorial: visualising and describing. The second part is concrete: using the pictorial to make a model and check their answer.
- Repeat for further examples taken from **Resource 5.9.2c** Cubic shapes (1). These show a degree of procedural variation to allow pupils to see how volumes change when cubes are added and particularly when parts of shapes are no longer visible.

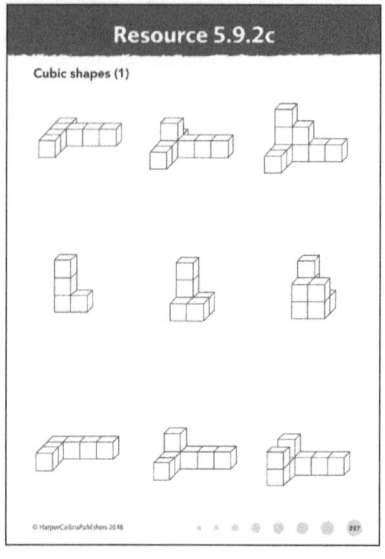

Answers: 7 cm^3; 8 cm^3; 9 cm^3; 4 cm^3; 6 cm^3; 8 cm^3; 6 cm^3; 7 cm^3; 8 cm^3

Chapter 9 Geometry and measurement (2)   Unit 9.2 Practice Book 5B, pages 89–91

Same-day enrichment

- Provide pairs with a copy of a set of cubic shape cards taken from **Resource 5.9.2d** Cubic shapes (2). Pupils should shuffle their pack, take a card and then describe the shape to their partner, starting by describing its volume (so they know how many centimetre cubes to use). For example:
- 'This shape has a volume of 7 cm³. It is made up of a row of three cubes in between two towers of two.'
- Pupils should compare the complete concrete representation with the original pictorial representation and, most importantly, the volumes of both shapes. Are they the same? The cards feature some deliberately ambiguous shapes, so pupils should discuss how they think the shapes would look if rotated and what their volume might be as a result.

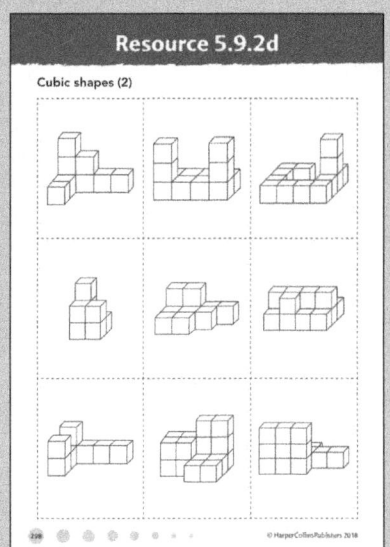

Answers: 9 cm³; 12 cm³; 13 cm³; 8 cm³; 11 cm³; 17 cm³; 8 cm³; 18 cm³; 17 cm³

Question 4

4 True or false? (Put a ✓ for true and ✗ for false in each box.)
  (a) The edge length of a small cube is 1 cm. A figure is made up of 12 such cubes. Its volume is 12 cm³.
  (b) 1 cm³ is greater than 1 cm².
  (c) Using four cubes of edge length 1 cm to form a cuboid, the volume will decrease.

What learning will pupils have achieved at the conclusion of Question 4?

- Fundamental concepts relating length, area and volume to each other will have been strengthened.

Activities for whole-class instruction

- Display the following statement on the board:
  – Eight cubes with an edge length of 1 cm each can make a cuboid with a volume of 10 cm³.
- Choose pupils to come to the front and attempt to model the statement. Ask: *Is this possible? Is the statement true or false? Why? How could you change the statement to make it true?*
- Repeat the activity with further statements. For example:
  – 1 cm² is smaller than 1 cm³.
  – Six cubes with an edge length of 1 cm each are placed in a row to form a cuboid. Only two more cuboids are possible to make with a volume of 6 cm³.
  – It is possible to make a cube out of eight smaller cubes.
  – A cuboid is made with a volume 10 cm³. Two cubes are removed. The new shape's volume will decrease by 2 cm³.
- For each statement, pupils should try to model it using centimetre cubes, say whether they think it is true or false, and finally (if false) alter the wording so that it becomes true.
- Pupils should complete Question 4 in the Practice Book.

Same-day intervention

- Display the following statement and cover it up to begin with:
  – The edge length of a small cube is 1 cm.
  – A cubic shape is made out of 20 similar cubes.
  – The volume of this shape is __ cm³.
- Begin by revealing the first sentence. Ask: *Can you prove this statement to me? What can you do to show that this is true?* Pupils should measure the dimensions of centimetre cubes. Ask: *Does it matter which way around you hold your cube when you measure it? Why?*
- Reveal the second sentence. Challenge pupils to take 20, centimetre cubes and make their own cubic shapes out of them. Encourage them to share their shapes, particularly to identify whether any shapes are the same and also to emphasise the range of different shapes that can all have the same volume.
- Finally, reveal the third sentence. Ask: *What is the volume of your shape? How do you know?* Choose two pupils to share their shapes where one looks fairly small and the other looks larger. Ask: *Whose shape has the larger volume?*

Chapter 9 Geometry and measurement (2)

Unit 9.2 Practice Book 5B, pages 89–91

Remind pupils that, as they both are made out of 20, cubic centimetres, they both have the same volume.
Ask: *What is the only way we can compare their volumes?* (by counting the number of cubes)

- Repeat for further statements. For example:
- A cube has a volume of 1 cm³. Some of these cubes are put together to make a larger cube. The volume of the larger cube is ___ cm³.

Same-day enrichment

- Pupils should play a game of 'Prove it!' in pairs. Provide each pair with a copy of **Resource 5.9.2e** Prove it! to give them the instructions for the activity.
- Pupil A should begin by writing down a fact based on the topics of volume and cubic centimetres that they have studied in Unit 9.2 (some examples are given). Pupil B gets a point if they can prove how the fact about volume is true. They will need to use centimetre cubes to do this. There is a suggested extension where pupils include false statements.

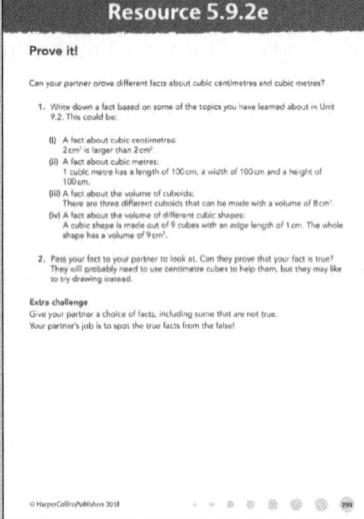

Challenge and extension question

Question 5

5. The solid (3-D) figure shown on the right is made up of identical cubic blocks of edge length 1 cm. There are four layers in the figure.

   (a) What is the volume of this solid figure? _____
   (b) Following the pattern from top to bottom, add more layers to the 3-D figure until the tenth layer is completed.

   What is the volume of the new figure? _____

Pupils are presented with an illustration of a layered object made from cubes. They are first asked to give its volume. Pupils may do this by visualising the parts of the shape that are hidden and using this to inform their answer or by recognising the pattern in the number of cubes used for each layer. They should then continue the sequence up to the tenth layer, using the information they have worked out to calculate the volume of the entire object. The sequence may be identified in different ways; by recognising that each layer is a square number (1 × 1, 2 × 2, and so on); by recognising that each layer is found by adding the next odd number (1, plus 3 equals 4, plus 5 equals 9, and so on); or by visualising all 10 layers.

Chapter 9 Geometry and measurement (2)

Unit 9.3
Cubic centimetres and cubic metres (2)

Conceptual context

In this unit, pupils' concept of cubic units is expanded to include cubic metres as well as cubic centimetres.

Relationships between length, area and volume are conceptually challenging and at this stage, pupils need to be very secure in their knowledge that:

- centimetres and metres are both units of length (measuring something that has only one dimension)
- square centimetres and square metres are both units of area (measuring something that has two dimensions)
- cubic centimetres and cubic metres are both units of volume (measuring something that has three dimensions).

Pupils will learn to convert between cm^3 and m^3.

Learning pupils will have achieved at the end of the unit

- Cubic metres will have been introduced as a unit for measuring volume and their relationship to cubic centimetres will be understood (Q1)
- Knowledge about cubic centimetres and cubic metres will have been applied when choosing the most suitable unit to measure the volume of different objects (Q2, Q3, Q4)
- Real-life examples of cubic centimetres and cubic metres will have been explored (Q2, Q4)
- Pupils will have applied understanding of relationship between cubic centimetres and cubic metres when converting between cm^3 and m^3 (Q3, Q4)

Resources

chalk and floor area to draw on (or a large piece of paper and pen); 12 metre sticks; sticky tape; broadsheet newspapers; scissors; blank cards; 8 trays; sets of 0–9 digit cards; **Resource 5.9.3a** Change the units; **Resource 5.6.1a** Place value slider; **Resource 5.9.3b** Cubic challenge

Vocabulary

volume, cubic centimetre (cm^3), cubic metre (m^3), unit of measurement

Chapter 9 Geometry and measurement (2)

Unit 9.3 Practice Book 5B, pages 92–94

Question 1

> **1** Fill in the spaces to make each statement correct.
> (a) The volume of a cube of edge length 1 m is ☐ cubic metre or ☐ m^3.
> It can also be considered as the volume of a cube of edge length 100 cm, which has a volume of ☐ cubic centimetres.
> Therefore, 1 cubic metre = ☐ cubic centimetres or 1 m^3 = ☐ cm^3.
> (b) Centimetres and metres are both units of _____.
> Square centimetres and square metres are both units of _____.
> Cubic centimetres and cubic metres are both units of _____.

What learning will pupils have achieved at the conclusion of Question 1?

- Cubic metres will have been introduced as a unit for measuring volume and their relationship to cubic centimetres will be understood.

Activities for whole-class instruction

- For this activity you will need twelve 1-metre sticks. Prior to the lesson, construct two squares using the metre sticks. Each square should be made by taping together four of the metre sticks at the corners. This will leave you with two complete squares and four single metre sticks left over.
- Remind pupils of the concept of a cubic centimetre. Ask: *How many cubic centimetres do you think are in a cubic metre?* Write pupils' predictions. Ask them to reason why they think this is. Note any answers where pupils understand that the answer will not be 100 (many pupils will choose 100 due to the relationship between cm and m).
- Draw a line of 1 cm and show one of the individual metre rulers. Ask: *What units of measurement do these represent? What do we use these units to measure?* (length) *Can you give an example of a length you might measure using these units? How many centimetres equal 1 metre?*
- Use pupils' answers to complete the first row of a table:

Unit(s) of measurement	Dimensions	Used to measure	Comparison
centimetre and metre	1	length	100 cm = 1 m

- Show how the one-dimensional lines can become two-dimensional shapes by completing a 1 cm square and also showing one of the square metres (the taped together metre rulers you constructed earlier). Ask: *How many dimensions do these shapes now have? What do we use square centimetres and square metres to measure?* (area) *Can you give an example? How many of these* [point to the square centimetre] *can we fit into one of these* [point to the square metre]*?* Establish that this is equal to 100 lots of 100.
- Complete the second row of the table:

Unit(s) of measurement	Dimensions	Used to measure	Comparison
centimetre and metre	1	length	100 cm = 1 m
cm^2 and m^2	2	area	10 000 cm^2 = 1 m^2

- Finally, place a 1 cm cube on the floor. Ask: *What should we do to the square metre to also make it a cube?* (give it 1 m height)
- Place one of the metre squares on the floor. Choose four pupils to form a cube by standing one at each corner and holding the other taped metre sticks and the four loose metre sticks at each top corner. The pupils will have 'built' a cube with the metre sticks and metre squares. Introduce this as one cubic metre.
- Ask: *How can you describe this, using mathematical language?* Can pupils tell you that it is 'a cube with side length of 100 cm'? *How many of these* [point to the cubic centimetre] *can we fit into one of these* [point to the cubic metre]*? Do you still think your prediction is correct? Why? Why not?*
- Pupils should use reasoning as well as visual reasons (for example, because 100 centimetre cubes are the same as a side length. There are 100 of these lengths that cover the bottom layer and there will be 100 of these layers. This is the same as 100 × 100 × 100).
- Complete the final part of the table.

Unit(s) of measurement	Dimensions	Used to measure	Comparison
centimetre and metre	1	length	100 cm = 1 m
cm^2 and m^2	2	area	10 000 cm^2 = 1 m^2
cm^3 and m^3	3	volume	1 000 000 cm^3 = 1 m^3

Chapter 9 Geometry and measurement (2)

Unit 9.3 Practice Book 5B, pages 92–94

 *There are one million cubic centimetres in 1 cubic metre.*

- Pupils should complete Question 1 in the Practice Book.

Same-day intervention

- Prior to the activity, prepare two sets of centimetre cubes to represent 100 cm³ and 1000 cm³. These might take the form of a pile of 100 cubes counted out and also 10 base ten hundred flats. Although the base ten cubes may not be 1 cm in edge length, as long as this is noted to pupils they can still be used for illustrative purposes.
- Discuss what a cubic metre represents and complete the following activity to develop pupils' understanding of it. Divide the group into six smaller groups, giving each of them several sheets of broadsheet newspapers, scissors and sticky tape.
- They should make tight rolls of newspaper to form 1 metre lengths, taping four of these together to form 1 metre square. Each group should make one of these. The six groups should then work together to combine their squares in order to form one large cubic metre.
- Ask pupils to recall how many cubic centimetres equal 1 cubic metre. Discuss ideas. Pupils might suggest 100 as there are 100 cm in 1 m. Place 100 centimetre cubes inside the cubic metre to demonstrate how much larger the cubic metre really is. Ask: *Do one hundred cubic centimetres fill the cubic metre?*
- Pupils might suggest 1000. Show them 1000 cm³ formed out of base ten equipment and ask them to imagine a row of ten of these (10 000 cm³). Neither will be anywhere close to the volume of the cubic metre. It will be difficult for pupils to comprehend the relative size of the cubic metre (and to imagine 1 000 000 cubes or a thousand of the base ten 1000 cubes). This visual exploration, then, is extremely powerful and necessary in supporting pupils' conceptualisation of such large numbers.
- Pupils should then write their own fact cards about the cubic metre. The cubic metre as well as a cubic centimetre (or photos of them) should be kept on display in the classroom for the duration of the unit on volume.

Same-day enrichment

- Give each pupil pair ten blank cards. On each card they should write something that can be measured beginning with the following sentence starters:
  - The length of …
  - The area of …
  - The volume of …
- Pupils will not be measuring these, so they do not need to limit themselves to classroom objects. They should shuffle their cards and sort them in two ways. First, they should sort them according to whether the unit of measurement is cm and m, cm² and m², or cm³ and m³. Second, pupils should take the volume set and sort it again, this time according to whether they would choose to measure the volume of the object using cubic centimetres or cubic metres.

Question 2

2 Write a suitable unit in each space.
   (a) The length of an eraser is about 6 _____ .
   (b) The volume of a refrigerator is about 2.1 _____ .
   (c) The volume of a washing machine is about 1.2 _____ .
   (d) The volume of a mobile phone is about 85 _____ .

What learning will pupils have achieved at the conclusion of Question 2?

- Knowledge about cubic centimetres and cubic metres will have been applied when choosing the most suitable unit to measure the volume of different objects.
- Real-life examples of cubic centimetres and cubic metres will have been explored.

Activities for whole-class instruction

- Ask pupils to describe the units of measurement they would use to measure the volume of something. Ask: *What is a shape/object's volume?* Remind them of the relative sizes of a cubic centimetre and a cubic metre. Ask: *What is 1 cubic metre equal to?*
- Explain that when a lorry delivers goods to shops, the driver needs to be very aware of the volume of the goods – to make sure they fit into the lorry. Write the following list on the board and explain that this is a list of the different goods that a lorry driver needs to deliver.

Chapter 9 Geometry and measurement (2)

Unit 9.3 Practice Book 5B, pages 92–94

OBJECT	VOLUME
wardrobe	3
book	1500
tumble drier	1.1
microwave	96 048
alarm clock	1000
chocolate bar	60
washing machine	1 200 000

- Point out that the driver has forgotten to write the units of measurement next to each object. Can the pupils help? Ask: *Which unit of measurement is this volume measured in – cubic centimetres or cubic metres? How do you know?* Ensure that pupils don't focus only on the type of object and whether it is small or large. Pupils should also consider the numbers themselves. Check that pupils use the numbers to help their reasoning and that they understand that the volume of large objects can be measured using cm³ too, for example the washing machine is measured in cubic centimetres.
- Pupils should complete Question 2 in the Practice Book.

Same-day intervention

- Ensure pupils are confident when choosing the correct unit of measurement to measure volume. Make a list of items with volumes that are most likely to be measured in cubic centimetres or cubic metres. Something like a large washing machine has a volume of approximately 1 m³ so this can be used as a benchmark and all examples of objects measured in cubic metres should be larger than this. Pupils should work in pairs to discuss each one, and together write cm³ or m³ as they think appropriate.

Same-day enrichment

- Provide pairs of pupils with a set of cards taken from **Resource 5.9.3a** Change the units. Pupils should shuffle the cards and turn them upside down. They should take it in turns to turn over a card and decide whether the unit of measurement shown is true or false (only one is correct). Ask: *What should the unit of measurement be?* They should discuss their answers each time and justify why a different unit of measurement is needed.

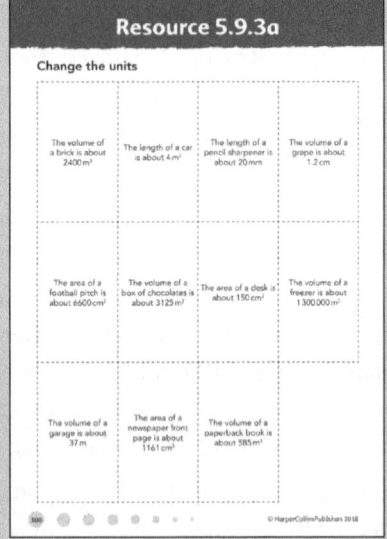

Answers: 1. F; 2: F; 3. T; 4. F; 5. F; 6. F; 7. F; 8. F; 9. F; 10. F; 11. F

Question 3

> 3 Convert these units of measure.
> (a) 2.8 m³ = ☐ cm³
> (b) 8 500 000 cm³ = ☐ m³
> (c) 61 500 cm³ = ☐ m³
> (d) 0.04 m³ = ☐ cm³
> (e) 700 000 cm³ = ☐ m³
> (f) 6 m³ and 990 000 cm³ = ☐ m³

What learning will pupils have achieved at the conclusion of Question 3?

- Knowledge about cubic centimetres and cubic metres will have been applied when choosing the most suitable unit to measure the volume of different objects.
- Pupils will have applied understanding of relationship between cubic centimetres and cubic metres when converting between cm³ and m³.

Chapter 9 Geometry and measurement (2)

Unit 9.3 Practice Book 5B, pages 92–94

Activities for whole-class instruction

- Write: 5 m = ? cm   ? m = 740 cm
- Ask pupils to explain how they would find the value of both question marks and, importantly, why. Ensure that they are aware that the concept of multiplying or dividing by 100 is because 1 metre equals 100 centimetres. Ask: *How do you multiply or divide by 100 quickly?*
- Write: $1\,m^3 = ?\,cm^3$
- Ask: *What is the difference between this statement and the previous two?* Revise the equivalence if pupils need reminding that there are 1 000 000 cubic centimetres in a cubic metre.

 *There are one million cubic centimetres in one cubic metre.*

- Ask: *When we are converting between cubic metres and cubic centimetres, what is the value we need to multiply or divide by? Do you think it is harder to multiply (or divide) by 1 000 000 compared with 100?* Agree that it is the same sort of calculation and is not any more difficult.
- Write: $6\,000\,000\,cm^3 = ?\,m^3$
- Draw a blank place value grid ranging from millions to thousandths. Model the number 6 000 000. Ask: *How can we convert from cubic centimetres into cubic metres?* Choose a pupil to move the digits six places to the left and establish that the zeros can be ignored once they cross past the decimal point.

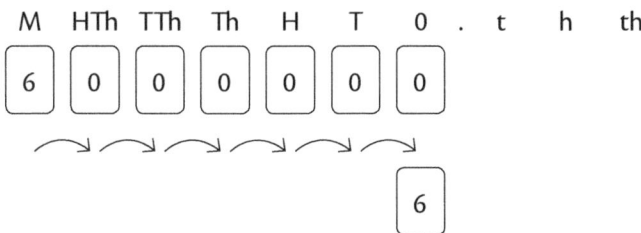

 *Six million cubic centimetres equal six cubic metres.*

- Repeat, varying the order of the units of measurement and the unknown value, and increasing complexity to values of cubic metres with three decimal places. For example:

$$7\,cm^3 = ?\,m^3$$
$$5.4\,m^3 = ?\,cm^3$$
$$4\,500\,000\,cm^3 = ?\,m^3$$
$$600\,000\,cm^3 = ?\,m^3$$
$$0.32\,m^3 = ?\,cm^3$$

$$2\,m^3 \text{ and } 500\,000\,cm^3 = ?\,m^3$$
$$85\,300\,cm^3 = ?\,m^3$$

- Provide pupils with **Resource 5.6.1a** Place value slider and remind them of its usefulness when multiplying and dividing by a number where there is a shift in digits. They should use these to model each answer then, when confident, work the answer out mentally and use the slider to check their answers.

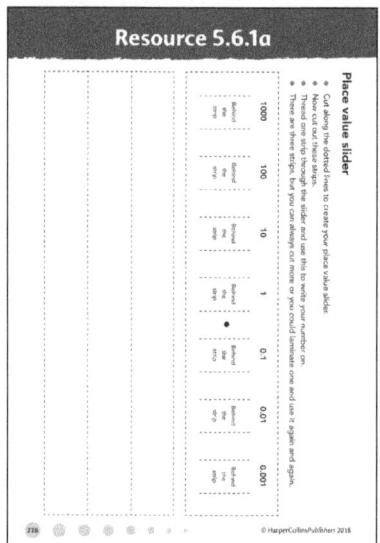

- Pupils should complete Question 3 in the Practice Book.

Same-day intervention

- Ensure pupils understand that there are one million cubic centimetres in a cubic metre. Place eight trays (or similar) in a row on the table and label them according to the place value columns from 'Millions' to 'tenths'. Use a small circle to represent the decimal point.

- Write: $4\,m^3 = ?\,cm^3$
- Spend time discussing with pupils what this means. Show them a cubic centimetre and the size of a cubic metre and ensure that they understand that what they are finding out is how many of the former will be equal to 4 of the latter.
- Place a digit card on the trays to show the number 4. Ask: *How many cubic centimetres are in one cubic metre? So what do we need to multiply 4 by to find out the number in four cubic metres? How do we multiply by a million?* Choose pupils to demonstrate this by moving the card 6 places (trays) to the left. Ask: *How can we show that the 4 digit has moved? What can we use as a place holder?*

Chapter 9 Geometry and measurement (2)　　Unit 9.3 Practice Book 5B, pages 92–94

Same-day intervention

- Ensure pupils understand that there are one million cubic centimetres in a cubic metre. Place eight trays (or similar) in a row on the table and label them according to the place value columns from 'Millions' to 'tenths'. Use a small circle to represent the decimal point.

- Write: $4 \, m^3 = ? \, cm^3$

- Spend time discussing with pupils what this means. Show them a cubic centimetre and the size of a cubic metre and ensure that they understand that what they are finding out is how many of the former will be equal to 4 of the latter.

- Place a digit card on the trays to show the number 4. Ask: *How many cubic centimetres are in one cubic metre? So what do we need to multiply 4 by to find out the number in four cubic metres? How do we multiply by a million?* Choose pupils to demonstrate this by moving the card 6 places (trays) to the left. Ask: *How can we show that the 4 digit has moved? What can we use as a place holder?*

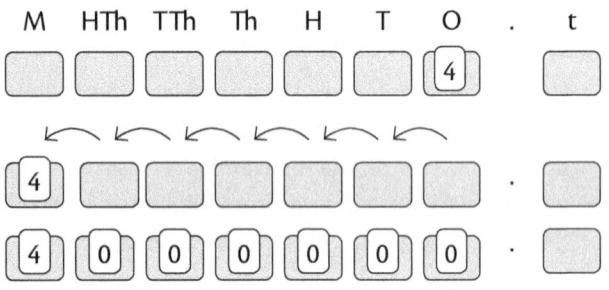

- Repeat for further conversions, focusing on m^3 to cm^3 before practising dividing by 1 000 000 to convert cm^3 into m^3. Include values to one decimal place (for example: $1\,500\,000 \, cm^3 = 1.5 \, m^3$). Provide place value sliders to support pupil understanding of the shift in digits.

Same-day enrichment

- Give pupils **Resource 5.9.3b** Cubic challenge. The resource sheet asks pupils to take three digit cards each and make all the possible numbers that are less than 100 (including decimals). Encourage them to do this systematically. They write the numbers, which represent cubic metres, on paper. Pupils should then swap their lists of cubic metres with a partner who should find each volume's equivalent in cubic centimetres. They should swap their lists back so that each pupil can check the answers.

- As an extension, pupils should choose any two measurements from their list (ideally, one measured in cubic metres and one measured in cubic centimetres) and their partner should explain which is the larger and why.

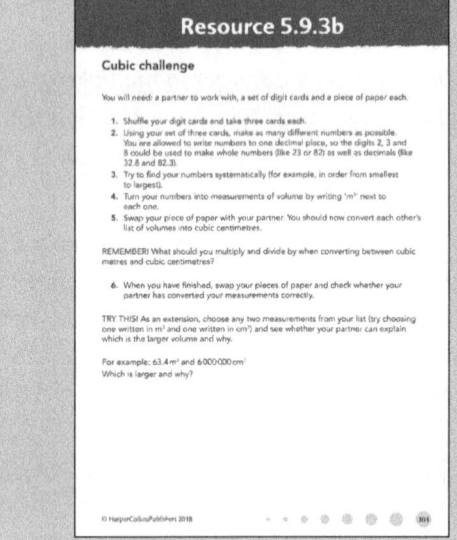

Question 4

4 Multiple choice questions. (For each question, choose the correct answer and write the letter in the box.)

(a) $1000 \, cm^3$ is ☐.

　A. $1 \, m^3$　　B. $0.1 \, m^3$　　C. $0.01 \, m^3$　　D. $0.001 \, m^3$

(b) The edge length of a cube is 100 cm and its volume is ☐.

　A. $100\,000 \, cm^3$　B. $1000 \, m^3$　C. $100 \, m^3$　D. $1 \, m^3$

(c) The volume of an English dictionary is about 5000 ☐.

　A. m^3　　B. km^3　　C. cm^3　　D. mm^3

(d) The volume of a finger tip is about ☐.

　A. $1 \, m^3$　　B. $1 \, cm^3$　　C. $1 \, km^3$　　D. $1 \, mm^3$

(e) The edge length of each small cube is 10 cm. There are 19 such cubes and their ☐ is $19\,000 \, cm^3$.

　A. perimeter　　B. volume　　C. area　　D. weight

Chapter 9 Geometry and measurement (2)

Unit 9.3 Practice Book 5B, pages 92–94

What learning will pupils have achieved at the conclusion of Question 4?

- Knowledge about cubic centimetres and cubic metres will have been applied when choosing the most suitable unit to measure the volume of different objects.
- Real-life examples of cubic centimetres and cubic metres will have been explored.
- Pupils will have applied understanding of relationship between cubic centimetres and cubic metres when converting between cm^3 and m^3.

Activities for whole-class instruction

- Set up four chairs at the front of the class and label them A, B, C and D. Explain to pupils that these are the answers to some multiple choice questions related to cubic metres and volume.
- Choose four pupils to bring their whiteboards and sit on these chairs. Give each of them a different value to write on their board: 1, 0.1, 0.01 and 0.001, keeping their numbers hidden. Ask the class: *100 cm^3 equals how many m^3?*
- Without revealing their numbers, ask each of the four pupils to give a clue about their answer. For example:
  - Pupil A might say: 'My answer is a whole number.'
  - Pupil B might say: 'My answer is less than 1.'
  - Pupil C might say: 'My answer has two decimal places.'
  - Pupil D might say: 'My answer has three zeros in it.'
- Ask the class: *Who do you think is holding the correct answer to the question 100 cm^3 equals how many m^3? Why do you think this?* Adding this element to the activity ensures that the class have some time to think about what they are looking for in the answer, rather than just being presented with four possibilities to choose from. Sometimes the clues may give a definitive answer and pupils should be able to identify the correct answer (the above example is not definitive and pupils should recognise the answer could be either B or D).
- Ask the four pupils to reveal the possible answers and then ask the class to vote which answer they think is correct.
- Repeat the activity for further multiple choice questions relating to cubic metres and volume, for example:
  1. The edge length of a cube is 1m. What is its volume?

     A 1 000 000 cm^3 B 100 cm^3

     C 1 000 000 m^3 D 1 m

  2. The volume of a parcel is best measured in what?

     A centimetres   B square centimetres

     C cubic centimetres   D cubic metres

  3. The edge length of a cube is 10 cm. There are two of these cubes in a row. Their __ is 2000 cm^3.

     A perimeter   B area   C height   D volume

  4. A shipping container has a volume of about 39 ____.

     A cm^3 B mm^3 C m^3 D km^3

  5. How many cubic centimetres will fit inside a cardboard box that is 1 m long, 1 m wide and 1 m tall?

     A one hundred   B one million

     C one thousand   D three million

- Pupils should complete Question 4 in the Practice Book.

Same-day intervention

- Display the following measurements of volume:

  1 m^3 1 cm^3 1 km^3 1 mm^3

- Focus on the cubic metre and centimetre and ensure that pupils have understood these concepts and their relative sizes. Briefly mention the cubic kilometre and cubic millimetre so that they can comprehend just how large and small each must be.
- Go back and look at Questions 4c) and 4d) and relate each option with pupils' new understanding of each unit. Ask: *Which answer is correct? How do you know?*
- Go through some of the other questions in the same way, addressing the multiple choice options first, ensuring pupils understand them and then revealing the question and asking them to answer it.

Same-day enrichment

- Challenge pupils to rewrite the five parts to Question 4 without changing any of the multiple choices. They should change the units in the question so that the question still has the same meaning and can be answered from the list provided. For example, Question 4a should match one of the answers:

  A 1 m^3 B 0.1 m^3 C 0.01 m^3 D 0.001 m^3

- It could therefore be rewritten as: 1 000 000 cm^3 is ____ or 10 000 cm^3 is the same as ____ and so on. Pupils should share their rewritten questions to see whether they can answer them.

Chapter 9 Geometry and measurement (2)

Unit 9.3 Practice Book 5B, pages 92–94

Challenge and extension question

Question 5

5. The solid figure below is made up of identical cubic blocks of edge length 10 cm. There are four layers in the figure.

(a) What is the volume of this 3-D figure? _____

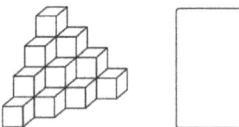

(b) Take the longest side of the figure as the edge to expand it into a new cube with more cubic blocks of edge length 10 cm. What is the volume of the new cube? How many more cubic blocks are needed to form the new cube?

Pupils are given an illustration of a 3-D shape formed from cubic blocks and are asked to find the volume of the shape. In order to solve the problem, pupils need to be able to visualise the parts of the shape that are not shown and to then take into account the fact that each block is 10 cm long (therefore, each one has a volume of 1000 cm³). Providing base ten 1000 blocks will help pupils to visualise the structures.

Pupils are then challenged to expand the shape so that it becomes a cube in itself, taking the current longest side for its dimensions. They should then find its total volume and also the number of cubic blocks needed to complete the cube. Visualisation of the shape and how it is completed will be important at this stage. Again, it may be appropriate to provide pupils with small cubes to help them model the original shape and the larger cube. (Be aware that pupils have not yet learned the formula $l \times w \times h$, which will be introduced in Unit 9.6.)

Chapter 9 Geometry and measurement (2)

Unit 9.4
Metric units and imperial units for measurement

Conceptual context

In this unit, pupils are reminded of common imperial units they will encounter. Pupils will probably have experience of some of these units from real-life usage (for example: miles, pints, inches). Pupils' concepts of these will develop in this unit as they learn about their relationship with metric units and convert between metric units and common imperial units.

Learning pupils will have achieved at the end of the unit

- Pupils' concept of measurement will have expanded as they learn that there are different systems (other than metric) for measurement (Q1)
- Pupils will know that: inches, feet and miles measure length; pints measure liquid volume; and pounds measure mass (Q1)
- Knowledge of imperial measurements will have been applied to derive their approximate equivalent metric values, and vice versa, including in word problems (Q2, Q3)

Resources

measuring jug; mini whiteboards; strips of paper 1 inch long; rulers; **Resource 5.9.4a** Units of measure; **Resource 5.9.4b** Approximate measurements cards; **Resource 5.9.4c** Mixed imperial and metric units

Vocabulary

metric, imperial, units of measurement, approximately, inch, centimetre, pound, kilogram, pint, litre

Chapter 9 Geometry and measurement (2)

Unit 9.4 Practice Book 5B, pages 95–97

Question 1

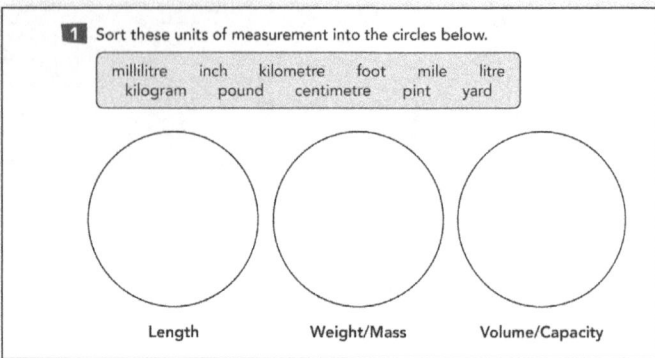

What learning will pupils have achieved at the conclusion of Question 1?

- Pupils' concept of measurement will have expanded as they learn that there are different systems (other than metric) for measurement.
- Pupils will know that: inches, feet and miles measure length; pints measure liquid volume; and pounds measure mass.

Activities for whole-class instruction

- Write the headings 'Length', 'Weight/Mass' and 'Volume/Capacity' on the board. Discuss what each term means and then give pupils two minutes to work in pairs and think of as many units of measurement as they can that are used to measure each. So that pupils do not limit themselves to metric units, tell them that there are at least four to find for each category. Share ideas, making lists on the board.

- Circle any imperial units and underline any metric units. Ask: *Can you tell me what all the circled units have in common? What about the ones that are underlined?* Explain that the circled units are known as imperial units and those that are underlined as known as metric units. Briefly explain the history behind these two systems.

ⓘ The main components of the metric system of measurements are a base unit (for example, the 'metre' is the base unit of length) and standard prefixes based on powers of 10 (for example, milli-, centi-, deci-, kilo-). The imperial system in Britain was first defined officially in 1824, but was an accumulation of measures from centuries prior to this. There are three countries that use a version of the imperial system as their main system of measurement (these are the United States, Myanmar and Libya). Many of the imperial units of measure and their relation to each other are heavily based on the context they were historically used for (rather than ease of calculation/conversion). In some countries (the UK included), imperial measurements are still used in different contexts, despite legislation and efforts since the 1960s to adopt and promote the metric system. In Britain, imperial units of measure feature informally in conversation and they are used more formally too (for example, distances on road signs are written in miles). It is for these reasons that pupils need a basic understanding of the more common imperial units (in Year 5 they will consider approximate metric equivalents of inches, pounds and pints).

- Ensure pupils understand that each category of measurement has both metric and imperial units. Cross out the metric units and discuss any further common imperial units that pupils may not have thought of.

- Ask: *Why is it useful to know what imperial units are? Where are they used in everyday life?* Pupil pairs should discuss. Share ideas. Examples may include:
  - Inches: pizza sizes; measurements on clothing; TV screen sizes
  - Feet: foot-long submarine rolls from sandwich shops; the height of people
  - Gallons: some may still refer to a gallon of petrol; miles per gallon as a measure of fuel efficiency
  - Miles: road signs, speed limits and speedometers are all in miles per hour
  - Pounds and Ounces: the weight of babies; quarter-pounder burgers
  - Pints: alcohol, milk
  - Yards: some Sat Nav settings ('in 100 yards, turn left'); in football the penalty area is known as the '18-yard box' and the referee marks out '10 yards' for a free kick

- Explain that some of these are legal measurements (in the UK, road signs must have miles on them and car speedometers have to feature miles per hour), some are the influence of the United States (for example, quarter-pounder burgers) and some are just people choosing to continue to use imperial measurements (no one says that the height of people has to be described in feet and inches!). Agree that it is useful to understand how imperial units compare to metric units so that one can be converted to the other.

- Pupils should complete Question 1 in the Practice Book.

Chapter 9 Geometry and measurement (2)

Unit 9.4 Practice Book 5B, pages 95–97

Same-day intervention

- Provide pairs of pupils with a set of cards from **Resource 5.9.4a** Units of measure. Pupils shuffle the cards and then lay them face-up on the desk. Ask pupils to sort their cards into groups – however they choose. Compare their groupings and discuss the different units. Ask: *When have you come across _____ before? Are there any units that you have never heard anyone using before?* Talk about the difference between metric and imperial units of measure and ask pupils to sort their groups into sub-groups according to whether a unit is metric or imperial.

Resource 5.9.4a

Units of measure

millimetres (mm)	centimetres (cm)	metres (m)
kilometres (km)	millilitres (ml)	litres (l)
grams (g)	kilograms (kg)	inches
feet	yards	miles
gallons	pounds (lb)	pints

Same-day enrichment

- Pairs of pupils should be given a set of cards from **Resource 5.9.4a** Units of measure. On a whiteboard, they should write the headings 'Length', 'Weight/Mass' and 'Volume/Capacity'. They should deal out the cards (face down onto the table). Pupil A should then choose any one of the headings and turn over any one of the cards. If it fits the chosen heading, they take the card. If it does not, they should turn the card back over. Pupils should take it in turns to play the game and the player with the most cards at the end is the winner. The same game can be played by using the headings 'Metric' and 'Imperial' or by splitting each category into metric and imperial ('Metric length', 'Imperial length', and so on).

Question 2

2 Draw lines to match up the imperial units of measurement with their approximate metric equivalent.

Imperial units	Metric units
1 inch	0.45 kg or 450 g
1 pound	2.5 cm
1 pint	1 kg
2.2 pounds	0.57 l or 570 ml

What learning will pupils have achieved at the conclusion of Question 2?

- Pupils' concept of measurement will have expanded as they learn that there are different systems (other than metric) for measurement.
- Pupils will know that: inches, feet and miles measure length; pints measure liquid volume; and pounds measure mass.
- Knowledge of imperial measurements will have been applied to derive their approximate equivalent metric values, and vice versa, including in word problems.

Activities for whole-class instruction

- Play a quick game of 'Which is more?' to ensure pupils are able to judge the comparative values of different units. Call out any two units (in any order) from each group. Ask: *Which is more? 1 _____ or 1 _____?*

  metre/centimetre/inch

  kilogram/gram/pound

  litre/millilitre/pint

- Pupils should respond with the larger of the two units each time. Repeat in different orders as a quick-fire activity.
- Show pupils a strip of paper 1 inch long. Ask: *How many centimetres do you think are the same as one inch?*
- Encourage them to give an approximate answer (for example, using their fingers to show 1 inch or visualising 1 pint of milk before considering how many metric units this might be the same as, see below).
- Repeat so pupils can consider the following examples:
  - Show an object that has a mass of 1 pound and ask: *How many grams do you think are the same as one pound?*
  - Show 1 pint of water and ask: *How many millilitres do you think are the same as one pint?*
- Write: 450 g   2.5 cm   570 ml
- Show the imperial units cards taken from **Resource 5.9.4a** Units of measure and ask pupils how they would match them to the measurements shown. Discuss

Chapter 9 Geometry and measurement (2)

Unit 9.4 Practice Book 5B, pages 95–97

answers and give pupils concrete examples of the different measurements (for example, showing them what 1 inch looks like on a ruler or measuring 570 ml using a measuring jug). Also introduce the approximation of 2.2 pounds being equivalent to 1 kilogram.

3 pints

1 pint	1 pint	1 pint
570 ml	570 ml	570 ml

- Ask: *If there are 570 millilitres in a pint, how many millilitres are there in 3 pints?* Show how pupils can sketch a bar model to help solve the problem.
- Establish that pupils should use multiplication to find the answer (570 × 3, rather than 570 + 570 + 570).
- Use the equivalences to ask further simple scaling questions, for example: *How many grams are in a 2 pound bag of sugar? A pencil is 3 inches long. How many centimetres is that?*
- For each example, encourage pupils to sketch bar models to show the equivalence pictorially before solving the problem.
- Pupils should complete Question 2 in the Practice Book.

Same-day intervention

- Provide pupils with a set of cards taken from **Resource 5.9.4b** Approximate measurements cards. Ask: *Can you see any measurements that are equal?* Challenge pupils to match up the cards.

Resource 5.9.4b
Approximate measurements cards

1 pound	2.2 pounds	1 inch
1 kg	0.45 kg	450 g
1000 g	2.5 cm	1 pint
570 ml	0.57 l	

Answers: 1 pound = 0.45 kg; 1 pound = 450 g; 1 kg = 2.2 pounds; 2.2 pounds = 1000 g; 1 inch = 2.5 cm; 0.45 kg = 450 g; 1 kg = 1000 g; 1 pint = 0.57 l; 1 pint = 570 ml; 0.57 l = 570 ml

- Show how the cards can be used to draw bar models and ask: *If 1 inch equals approximately 2.5 cm, how would you find the number of centimetres in four inches?* Draw:

4 inches

1 inch	1 inch	1 inch	1 inch
2.5 cm	2.5 cm	2.5 cm	2.5 cm

- Agree that the answer will be found by multiplying 2.5 by 4.
- Can pupils draw bar models representing the conversion of 11 inches to centimetres?
- Repeat for further simple problems using the rates of imperial units to help. For example: *If 1 pound is approximately 450 g, how many grams is the same as 2 pounds?*

Same-day enrichment

- Display the following problems on the board:
  - A man is 70 inches tall. How tall is he in centimetres?
  - How many pounds are there in 5 kilograms?
  - A carton of milk holds 4 pints. How many litres does it say on the label?
- After answering these, pupils should devise their own problems that involve converting between imperial and metric units, using the approximations they have learned.

Chapter 9 Geometry and measurement (2)

Unit 9.4 Practice Book 5B, pages 95–97

Question 3

> **3** Application problems.
>
> (a) The price of carrots is 30p per pound. A chef wants to buy 5 kg of carrots.
>
>   Given that 1 kg is approximately 2.2 pounds, how much will the carrots cost her?
>
> (b) Here are the results of the Year 5 annual sunflower growing contest:
>
> | Name | Height of sunflower |
> |---|---|
> | Amir | 60 inches |
> | Bryony | 1.1 m |
> | Chloe | 145 cm |
>
>   (i) The tallest sunflower belonged to _____.
>
>   (ii) The shortest sunflower belonged to _____.
>
>   (iii) Explain how you found the answers.
>
> (c) Given that 1 kg is approximately equivalent to 2.2 pounds and 1 pound is approximately equivalent to 450 g, complete the following table.
>
> | Object | Mass (in kg) | Mass (in pounds) |
> |---|---|---|
> | A | 3 kg | |
> | B | | 1.5 pounds |
> | C | 2.5 kg | |
> | D | | 5 pounds |
>
> (d) The area of a football pitch is about 1.75 acres. Given that 1 acre is about 4000 m², what is the area of the football pitch in m² and km², respectively?

What learning will pupils have achieved at the conclusion of Question 3?

- Knowledge of imperial measurements will have been applied to derive their approximate equivalent metric values, and vice versa, including in word problems.

Activities for whole-class instruction

- Show pupils a strip of paper 1 inch long. Ask: *How many centimetres do you think this is?* Ask a few pupils to measure the strip and confirm what they have learned already, that 1 inch is approximately equivalent to $2\frac{1}{2}$ centimetres. Point out that many rulers have inches and cm shown so the conversion is easy to see. Ask: *How many inches do you think equal 1 centimetre?* Agree that the answer is going to be less than half an inch, so it will be a decimal number less than 0.5. Tell pupils that the answer is about 0.39 inches but they don't need to learn this!

- Write 1 inch ≈ 2.5 cm. Ask: *What do you think the symbol ≈ means?* Show pupils that it 'almost' looks like an equals sign and that's what it means: is approximately equal to.

- Display the question:
   - If 1 inch is approximately 2.5 centimetres, how many centimetres are there in 10 inches?

- Ask: *What information do we need to use to find out the answer?* Pupils should recognise that they need to use the equivalence to multiply 2.5 by 10 to find the answer.

- Display the problem:
   - Ryan has a piece of string that is 5 inches long. Hatham has a piece of string that is 12 centimetres long. Whose piece of string is longer and why?

- Ask: *What fact do you need to know to help find the answer?* Remind them that 1 inch ≈ 2.5 cm. Ask: *What steps do you need to complete to find the answer?*

- Discuss these and work through each step as follows:

Step	Calculation
Convert Ryan's string into centimetres	5 × 2.5 = 12.5 cm
Compare the two measurements now that they are in the same unit of measurement	12.5 cm > 12 cm So Ryan's string is longer.

- Ask: *Can you describe how to find the answer without saying any numbers?* Encourage them to focus on the method, rather than the numbers themselves.

- Repeat for further application problems where pupils need to convert between metric and imperial measurements to find the answers. These should focus on the following equivalences, which can be displayed while pupils answer the questions.
   - 1 pound = 450 g (or 0.45 kg)
   - 2.2 pounds = 1 kg
   - 1 inch = 2.5 cm
   - 1 pint = 570 ml (or 0.57 l)

- Pupils should complete Question 3 in the Practice Book.

Chapter 9 Geometry and measurement (2)

Unit 9.4 Practice Book 5B, pages 95–97

Same-day intervention

- Display the problem:
  - A DIY shop sells copper piping at a price of 50p per cm. Mr Singh wants to buy a length of piping that is 4 inches long. How much will it cost him?
- Ask: *Why is this problem tricky?* Ensure pupils recognise that Mr Singh would know exactly how much to pay if the piping was being sold per inch, but because it is being sold per centimetre, he needs to work out how many centimetres are the same as 4 inches. Remind pupils that 1 inch is approximately $2\frac{1}{2}$ cm. Ask: *What do we need to do to find the answer?*
- Go through each step and together, sketch a tree diagram to show how to work the answer out.

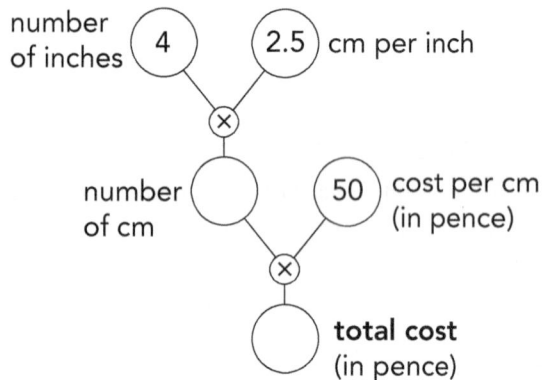

- Finally, work through the tree diagram, discussing what each number represents and arriving at the total cost, which could be converted into pounds and pence as a final step. Repeat for further multi-step problems, for example:
  - Class 5 are filling up their fish tank with water. There are 20 children. They each have a pint jug of water. If they each empty their jug into the tank, how many litres of water will there be in the tank?

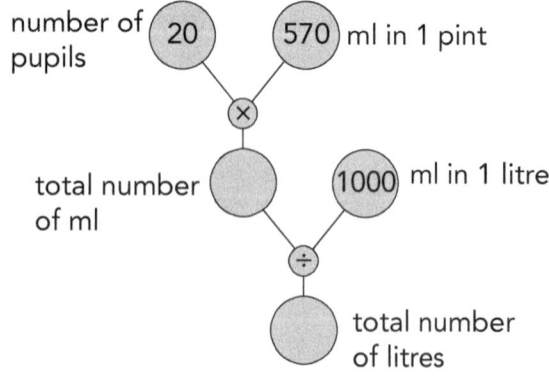

Same-day enrichment

- Challenge pupils to write their own word problems based on what they have learned about imperial measurements. They should use **Resource 5.9.4c** Mixed imperial and metric units as a help to get started and then share their problems for peers to solve.

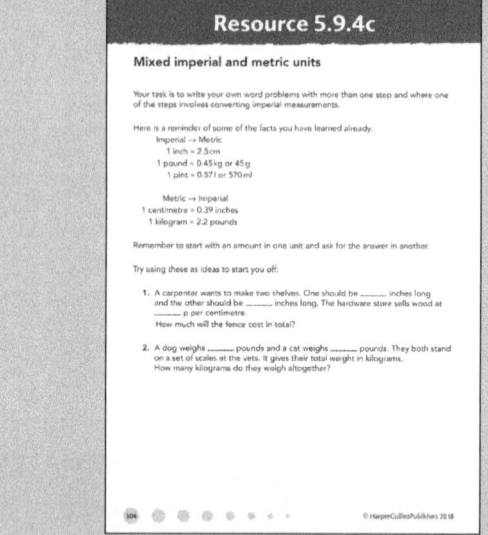

Challenge and extension question

Question 4

> 4 Elodie wants to make a bookshelf that is 80 inches long.
> Wood for shelving can be bought in any metric length.
> Given that 1 inch is about 2.5 centimetres, what length piece of wood does she need to buy (in metres)? _____
> If wood for shelving costs 35p per cm, how much will it cost Elodie? _____

Pupils are given the length of a bookshelf in inches and are first challenged to calculate this length in metres, given that 1 inch is approximately 2.5 cm. To find this, pupils will first need to use their knowledge of multiplying numbers by decimals (converting inches into centimetres by working out 80 × 2.5) and then divide the answer by 100 (converting centimetres into metres). Second, pupils are given the cost of wood in pence per cm and are asked to calculate the cost of the wood needed to make the bookshelf.

Chapter 9 Geometry and measurement (2)

Unit 9.5
Introduction to cubes and cuboids

Conceptual context

In Year 2, pupils learned about liquid volume, measuring with litres, fractions of a litre and millilitres. Pupils will go on to expand their concept of volume in the next unit, focusing on solid volume. In preparation for that, this unit will consolidate pupils' understanding of the geometric properties of cubes and cuboids. This serves as a foundation for subsequent units, where pupils will learn to calculate the volume of cubes and cuboids using the formula $l \times w \times h$. Therefore, the concepts of length, width and height, in particular, are reinforced here. Pupils revise what these dimensions represent and their relationship to each other in the context of cubes and cuboids. The concepts of edges, faces and vertices (and their similarities/differences in cubes and cuboids) are revised, and the peculiarities of the edges, faces and vertices of cubes and cuboids are noted.

Learning pupils will have achieved at the end of the unit

- The properties of cubes and cuboids will have been revised (Q1)
- Simple pictorial representations will have been used to identify length, width and height of cuboids (Q2)
- Pupils will have made generalisations about the properties of cubes and cuboids (Q2, Q3)
- Pupils will know what makes a cube 'special' (Q1, Q2)
- Pupils will have applied their understanding of the properties of cubes and cuboids when solving measurement problems (Q4, Q5)

Resources

examples of cubes and cuboids (including those made from interlocking cubes and real-life objects); modelling clay; dice; interlocking cubes; sticky paper; **Resource 5.9.5a** Properties of cubes and cuboids; **Resource 5.9.5b** True or false?

Vocabulary

cube, cuboid, edge, vertex/vertices, face, square, rectangle, dimensions, length, width, height, edge length

Chapter 9 Geometry and measurement (2) Unit 9.5 Practice Book 5B, pages 98–101

Question 1

1 Complete the table.

	Features in common			Different features		
	Number of faces	Number of edges	Number of vertices	Length of edges	Shape of faces	Area of faces
Cuboid	6					
Cube					All faces are identical squares.	All faces have the same area.

What learning will pupils have achieved at the conclusion of Question 1?

- The properties of cubes and cuboids will have been revised.
- Pupils will know what makes a cube 'special'.

Activities for whole-class instruction

- Begin by discussing how 3-D shapes differ from 2-D shapes. Establish that they have a third dimension (height or depth) as well as length and width. Use the opportunity to revise the key features of many 3-D shapes: edges, faces and vertices. Ask: *Can you think of any 3-D shapes that don't have a particular feature?* (for example, cylinders have no vertices)
- Give pairs of pupils an example of a cube or cuboid. These should include those formed from interlocking cubes and also everyday objects. Ask pairs to define edges, faces and vertices in relation to their object. Discuss as a group. Ask: *What is the name of your shape? How do you know?*

(i) A cuboid is a 3-D shape comprising six rectangular faces that meet in perpendicular planes. It has 12 edges (consisting of three groups of four equal edges) and eight vertices. Note that squares are regular or 'special' rectangles; therefore cubes satisfy this definition. It follows that all cubes are a form of cuboid, but all cuboids are not necessarily cubes. For purposes of distinguishing between types of shape, Unit 9.5 tends to use the term 'cuboid' to refer specifically to those cuboids that are not cubes. Despite this usage, ensure pupils understand that a cube is actually a special type of cuboid in the same way that a square is a special type of rectangle.

- Pupils should hold up their shape if it has 12 edges. Ask: *What is the same? What is different?*
- Repeat for shapes with: faces that are all the same shape; edges that are not all the same length; have six faces.

- Ask: *What makes a cube a cube? What makes a cuboid a cuboid?* Pupil pairs should discuss. Together, generate definitions for 'cuboid' and 'cube'.
- Pupils should complete Question 1 in the Practice Book.

Same-day intervention

- Provide pupil pairs with a cuboid, a cube and a lump of modelling clay. Ask them to take small blobs of clay and place them on the points where the edges meet. Ask: *How many blobs do you need for each shape? What is the name for this part of a shape?* (vertex/vertices) Share ideas. Agree that all cuboids and all cubes have four vertices (they need four blobs of clay).
- Ask pupils to press the edges of their shapes into their clay to make lines, rolling the shape in one direction. Ask: *What do you notice about the number and length of the lines? Which feature of the shape is making the lines?* (edge(s)) Establish that both types of shape have 12 edges. The edges of their cubes all make the same length print, but some of the edges of their cuboid are different.
- Finally, ask pupils to systematically roll their shape onto each of its faces and draw around each one. (Pupils will need to keep track of which faces have been drawn.) If shapes are small, pupils could make prints into their modelling clay instead. Ask: *What do you notice about the shapes that you have drawn? What is the name for this feature of a shape?* (face(s)) Agree that both shapes have six faces, and that the faces of the cube are all squares of the same size.
- Challenge pupils to group their faces together in a way that makes sense. Can they see that most cuboid faces can be arranged as three groups of two? (Those with two square faces at either end will have a group of four and a group of two.) Introduce the concept of a cube being a special kind of 3-D shape. Ask: *What makes it special?* Pupils should use their understanding of the properties of cubes and cuboids to answer the question.

Chapter 9 Geometry and measurement (2)

Unit 9.5 Practice Book 5B, pages 98–101

Same-day enrichment

- Provide pupils with cards cut from **Resource 5.9.5a** Properties of cubes and cuboids. Pupils should draw a large Venn diagram, labelling one sorting circle 'Cubes', the other 'Other cuboids'. They should shuffle their cards and deal them randomly in the different sections of the Venn diagram, creating a puzzle for their partner to solve. Their partner should then choose how to rearrange the cards according to whether the property is a similarity or a difference between cubes and other cuboids. Challenge pupil pairs to invent more property cards to include in the game (for example: Has edges that are equivalent to 4 lengths, 4 widths and 4 heights).

Resource 5.9.5a
Properties of cubes and cuboids

Has 6 faces.	Has 8 vertices.	Has 12 edges.
All edges are the same length.	Some edges are different lengths.	Length, width and height meet at every vertex.
All faces are the same size and shape (squares).	Some faces are rectangles.	Has three dimensions: length, width and height.

Answers: Similarities between cubes and cuboids: has 6 faces; has 8 vertices; has 12 edges; length, width and height meet at every vertex; has three dimensions: length, width and height. Differences: cubes: all edges are the same length; all faces are the same size and shape (squares). Differences: cuboids: some edges are different lengths; some faces are rectangles.

Question 2

2. Fill in the answers.
   (a) Two cuboids are made up of identical small cubes of edge length 1 cm. Find the length, width and height of each one and write it in the spaces.

   length _____   length _____
   width _____   width _____
   height _____   height _____

   (b) In a cuboid, the measures of three edges meeting at the same vertex are called the _____ , _____ and _____ of the cuboid, respectively.

   (c) A cuboid with its length, width and height being all equal is called a _____ .

   (d) A cube has 12 edges of _____ length. If the length of an edge is 3 cm, then the total length of all of its edges is ☐ cm.

   (e) A cuboid has 12 edges. Among them, the measures of ☐ edges are called lengths, the measures of ☐ edges are called widths, and the measures of ☐ edges are called heights.

   (f) In a cuboid, the sum of the lengths of three edges from one vertex is 0.75 m. The sum of the lengths of all the edges of this cuboid is ☐ m.

   (g) A cuboid has ☐ faces. It is possible that the shapes of all the faces are _____ . It is also possible that the shapes of 2 faces are _____ and 4 faces are _____ .

   (h) A _____ is a special cuboid.

What learning will pupils have achieved at the conclusion of Question 2?

- Simple pictorial representations will have been used to identify length, width and height of cuboids.
- Pupils will have made generalisations about the properties of cubes and cuboids.
- Pupils will know what makes a cube 'special'.

Activities for whole-class instruction

- Make a 5 × 2 × 4 cuboid from interlocking cubes (or display the image below) and only reveal one of its edges. Explain that each small cube length is 1 cm. Ask pupils whether they can identify the shape and to explain their answer.

Chapter 9 Geometry and measurement (2)

Unit 9.5 Practice Book 5B, pages 98–101

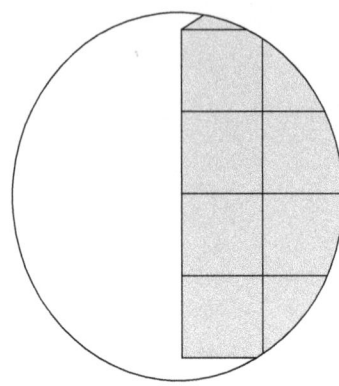

- Reveal more of the shape so that two dimensions are known. Ask the same question; can pupils reason that it is a cuboid because two of the dimensions are different?

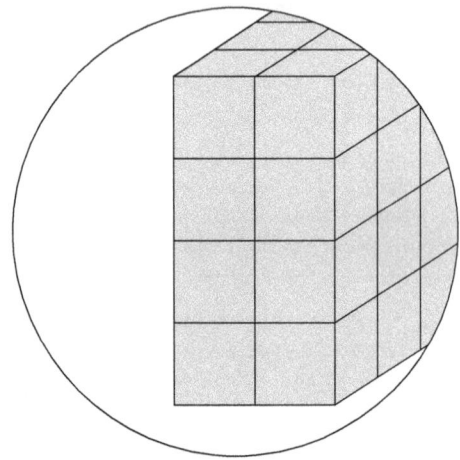

- Finally, reveal the entire shape. Ask: *What is the length of this cuboid? What is the width?* This shape could be perceived as being 2 wide, 4 high and 5 deep. It is also 4 wide, 5 long and 2 deep. Discuss how the dimensions (in this case 4, 5 and 2) are always the same but that dimensions which are the length, width and height/depth can change, depending on which face is being 'looked at'. Tell pupils that length is generally considered to be longer than width.

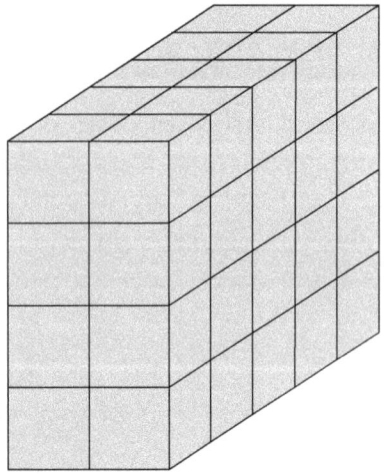

The objective of this unit is to focus specifically on the geometric properties of cubes and cuboids. So, although pupils have already considered the volume of shapes made from centimetre cubes, it may be a good idea not to mention the number of cubes used to form the cuboid. This will allow pupils to concentrate solely on the properties of cuboids in general and how length, width and height relate to each other geometrically.

- Ask pupils further questions and encourage them to use pictures or 3-D models to explain their reasoning. For example, ask: *What is the name of a shape that has equal length, width and height? What can you also say about the shape?* Pupils could make an example of a cube, demonstrate its equal dimensions by rotating it and then comment on its congruent faces.

- Other questions might include:
  - *How many edges meet at a vertex? What is the name of each one? Is this true of all the vertices? Is it true of cubes as well as other cuboids?*
  - *How many edges that are lengths does a cuboid have? How many edges that are widths? Or heights? Or depths?*
  - *What can you say for definite about the faces of a cuboid? What can you say might be the case?*
  - *Cubes are 'special cuboids'. Can you explain why?*

- Pupils should complete Question 2 in the Practice Book.

Same-day intervention

- Provide pairs of pupils with a dice and interlocking cubes. They should roll their dice three times and then model a cube or cuboid with length, width and height according to the numbers thrown. For example, if they roll a 5, 3 and 2, they should model a cuboid:

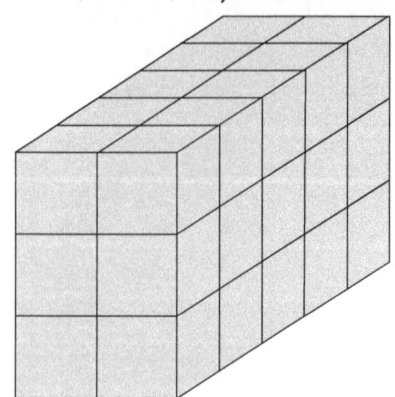

Chapter 9 Geometry and measurement (2)

Unit 9.5 Practice Book 5B, pages 98–101

- Encourage pupils to share their shapes, asking partners to guess what the numbers on the dice were. Pupils should use the terms length, width and height when describing their shape's dimensions. Ask: *What shape are you most likely to make during this activity? What would your shape look like if you rolled two numbers the same? What would your shape look like if you rolled all three numbers the same? Why?*

Same-day enrichment

- Display this problem:
  - In a cuboid, the sum of the lengths of three edges that meet at one vertex is 10 m. What is the sum of lengths of all the edges of the cuboid? How many differently-sized cuboids can you find that fit this description?
- Pupils should first find the sum of the lengths by multiplying 10 by 4. They should then investigate different cuboid dimensions that equal 10 m when added (for example, a length of 2 m, a width of 1 m and a height of 8 m).

Question 3

> **3** True or false? (Put a ✓ for true and ✗ for false in each box.)
> (a) The measures of three edges of a cuboid are called length, width and height, respectively.
> (b) Among the 12 edges of a cuboid, any 4 parallel edges have the same length.
> (c) A cuboid whose bottom face is a square must be a cube.
> (d) One edge of a cuboid is 6 cm long. The sum of the lengths of all the edges is 72 cm.
> (e) Sixteen identical small cubes can form a bigger cube.
> (f) Six squares can form a cube.

What learning will pupils have achieved at the conclusion of Question 3?

- Pupils will have made generalisations about the properties of cubes and cuboids.

Activities for whole-class instruction

- Ask pupils to visualise a cube, then mentally turn it on its side. Ask: *Does your cube look any different? Why not?* Give pupils time to discuss their reasoning in pairs and then share answers as a group. This may be a useful way to revise the properties of cubes, that is, it will look the same when it is turned because all the faces are congruent or because its length, width and height are equal. Apply the same question to cuboids and revise the fact that its length, width and/or height are different and some of its faces will be different too.

- Ask pupils to visualise either a cube or cuboid (it may help if they imagine an everyday object that is a cube or cuboid) and then consider one of the vertices. Ask: *How many edges meet at your vertex? How would you describe them?* Use pupils' descriptions to discuss whether they are imagining a cube or a cuboid. (If they are all the same measurement, then it must be a cube.)

- Agree two simple gestures with pupils that can be shown quickly to represent a 'TRUE' and a 'FALSE' answer (for example, thumbs up for TRUE and thumbs down for FALSE). Display the statement:
  - James has four flat plastic squares. He can stick these together to form a cube.

- Pupil pairs should discuss whether they think the statement is true or false. They should then vote by making the relevant gesture. Ask individual pupils to justify their vote.

- Repeat for further statements that require pupils to visualise cubes and cuboids in order to answer them. Repeat some of the statement themes and observe whether they have learned from the explanation and altered any wrong answers accordingly. Possible statements might include:
  - Aimee has 8 small cubes. She can arrange these to make a larger cube. [TRUE]
  - A cuboid has 4 edges that are parallel in one direction, 4 edges that are parallel in another direction and 4 edges that are vertically parallel. [TRUE]
  - A cube has a side length of 10 cm. The total of all the lengths of its edges is 12 more than this amount. [FALSE]
  - Krishna presses a cube or a cuboid into some modelling clay. It makes a square print. The shape must be a cube. [FALSE]
  - Four cubes are placed in a row. The shape they make is a cube. [FALSE]

- Pupils should complete Question 3 in the Practice Book.

Chapter 9 Geometry and measurement (2) Unit 9.5 Practice Book 5B, pages 98–101

Same-day intervention

- Provide pupils with a cube or cuboid each. Read out various statements and ask them to say whether they would make the statement about their shape. Use the opportunity to note distinctions and similarities between the different shapes. Statements might include:
  - If I look at a point where the edges meet, there are three edges that meet there.
  - My shape looks the same, no matter which way it is turned.
  - One of the faces in my shape is a rectangle.
  - My shape has length, width and height.
- Extend the activity to make more general TRUE/FALSE statements about cubes and cuboids for pupils. For example:
  - Some cuboids have square faces.
  - The twelve edges of a cube are exactly the same length.

Same-day enrichment

- Provide pupils with a copy of **Resource 5.9.5b** True or false? Pupils should devise their own True or False statements, using the sentence starters provided as inspiration. They should share their statements within the group and their peers should explain why they think each statement is correct or not.

Questions 4 and 5

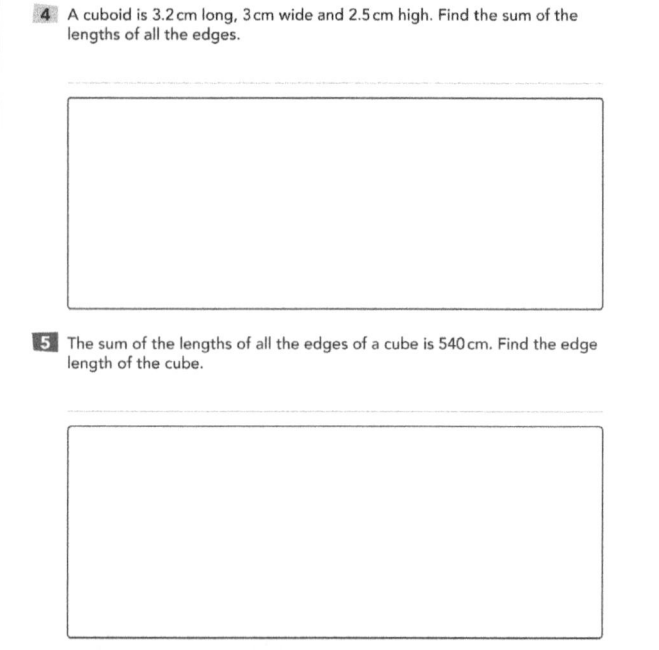

4. A cuboid is 3.2 cm long, 3 cm wide and 2.5 cm high. Find the sum of the lengths of all the edges.

5. The sum of the lengths of all the edges of a cube is 540 cm. Find the edge length of the cube.

What learning will pupils have achieved at the conclusion of Questions 4 and 5?

- Pupils will have applied their understanding of the properties of cubes and cuboids when solving measurement problems.

Activities for whole-class instruction

- Display the following problem:
  - A cuboid has a length of 5 cm, a width of 3.5 cm and a height of 2 cm. What is the total of the lengths of all the edges?
- Ask: *What is the important information in the problem?* Encourage pupils to write the important facts in note form. For example:

  L = 5 cm

  W = 3.5 cm

  H = 2 cm

- Ask: *Are there any other facts you know about cuboids that will help you find the total of the lengths of all the edges?* Establish that a cuboid's dimensions consist of four lengths, four widths and four heights. Choose three pupils to hold whiteboards expressing these values:

  | 4 × L | 4 × W | 4 × H |

Chapter 9 Geometry and measurement (2)

Unit 9.5 Practice Book 5B, pages 98–101

- Write this as the equation: Total of edges = (4 × L) + (4 × W) + (4 × H). Go through each whiteboard and encourage pupils to insert each value that they know already, altering the equation to: Total of edges = (4 × 5) + (4 × 3.5) + (4 × 2).

4 × L̶⁵	4 × W̶³·⁵	4 × H̶²

- Establish that each whiteboard can be simplified even further to solve the problem: 20 + 14 + 8 = 42 cm.
- Display further problems and encourage pupils to use the same approach to solve them; first simplifying the important facts and then considering how to use these to find the answer. Example problems could include the following:
  - All the edges of a cube total 108 cm. What is one edge length in cm?
  - Harry wants to make a cuboid frame out of straws. Its length is 4 cm. Its width is 2.5 cm. Its height is 5.5 cm. What is the total length of straws he needs?
- It may also be useful to extend pupils, giving them a problem similar to that found in the Challenge and extension section. For example:
  - The total of lengths of all the edges of a cuboid is 48 cm. The length is twice the width and the height is three times the width. What are the dimensions of the cuboid?
- As before, encourage pupils to write the important facts in note form and then use whiteboards to solve the problem:

4 × L	4 × W	4 × H

- (4 × L) + (4 × W) + (4 × H) = 48 cm

4 × L̶ (2 × W)	4 × W	4 × H̶ (3 × W)

- [4 × (2 × W)] + (4 × W) + [4 × (3 × W)] = 48 cm

8 × W	4 × W	12 × W

- 24 × W = 48 cm, so W must equal 2 cm.
- Ask: *How can we use this measurement (the width) to find the length and height of the cuboid?*
- Challenge pupils to find a way to check whether their answers are correct. Although this is a more challenging problem than those in Questions 4 and 5, most pupils should now be able to attempt the Challenge question with confidence, having learned to apply this method in this more difficult context.
- Pupils should complete Questions 4 and 5 in the Practice Book.

Same-day intervention

- Show pupils a cube. Ask: *How many edges does this shape have? How can you explain the answer without counting each one?* Encourage pupils to visualise two square shapes (8 edges) and four edges connecting them at each vertex (4 more edges). Use strips of sticky paper to show each of the cube's edges. Ask: *If one of these edges is 4 cm long, how can we find out the length of paper we've used altogether?* Pupils should recognise that there are 12 edges and that they are all equal, therefore the sum of the lengths can be found by multiplying 4 by 12. Reverse the question and ask: *If the sum of the lengths of all the edges is 60 cm, how long is one edge?* Ensure pupils understand that this time, they are dividing by 12.
- Having consolidated the concept, ask quick-fire questions that continue to revise the skills of multiplying by 12 (finding total edges from a given edge of a cube) and dividing by 12 (finding single edge from total edges).

Same-day enrichment

- Write the following measurements on the board: 150 cm, 72 cm, 64 cm, 38 cm, 36 cm, 134 cm, 120 cm, 132 cm, 96 cm, 180 cm.
- Explain that these are all the total edge lengths for different cuboids, some of which are cubes. Pupils should find those that are cubes (these will be divisible by 12) and work out each cube's dimensions. For those that are not cubes, pupils could be challenged to find possible dimensions of the cuboid. For example, total edge lengths of 150 cm could be made by a cuboid with length 15 cm, width 10 cm and height 12.5 cm.

Chapter 9 Geometry and measurement (2) Unit 9.5 Practice Book 5B, pages 98–101

Challenge and extension questions

Question 6

> 6 The sum of the lengths of all the edges of a cuboid is 90 cm. The length is twice the height and the width is 1.5 times the height. What are the length, width and height of the cuboid?

Pupils are given the sum of the length of all edges of a cuboid and also the length and width expressed in relation to its height. Pupils are then asked to derive the dimensions of the cuboid. By expressing the sum solely in terms of height, pupils can derive what one height is worth and, using this value, find the length and width too.

Question 7

> 7 A piece of iron wire is used to form a cuboid frame with length 45 cm, width 38 cm and height 25 cm. If the same length of iron wire is used to form a cube, what is the edge length of the cube?

Pupils are expected to use their knowledge of the properties of cuboids (4 lengths, 4 widths, 4 heights) to derive the total length of a piece of wire used to make a cuboid frame. They should then apply their understanding of the properties of cubes (12 edges of equal lengths) to find one edge length of the cube.

Chapter 9 Geometry and measurement (2)

Unit 9.6
Volumes of cubes and cuboids (1)

Conceptual context

This unit extends pupils' knowledge about cubes and cuboids to begin to consider their volume. Pupils will learn to use length, width and height in order to calculate the volume of cubes and cuboids. To begin with, cuboids are separated into smaller cubes so that pupils develop a visual image of how small cubes can, when put together, make larger cubes and cuboids.

Pupils will go on to solve more abstract problems, including word problems.

Learning pupils will have achieved at the end of the unit

- Pupils will have used the dimensions of a cuboid and cube to construct expressions to find their volume (Q1)
- Pupils will have developed a mental image of how small cubes can, when put together, make larger cubes and cuboids. Focusing on this image supports pupils to understand why volume = length × width × height (Q2, Q3)
- Pupils will have applied formulae in order to calculate volume of cubes and cuboids (Q2, Q3)
- Problem-solving contexts will have provided opportunities to apply pupils' knowledge of volume in different ways (Q4, Q5)

Resources

interlocking cubes; sticky notes; dice; poster paper; coloured pencils; blank cards

Vocabulary

cube, cuboid, 3-D shape, dimensions, length, width, height, volume, cm^3 (cubic centimetres or 'centimetres cubed'), m^3 (cubic metres or 'metres cubed'), centimetre cubes, edge length, unit (of measure)

Chapter 9 Geometry and measurement (2)

Unit 9.6 Practice Book 5B, pages 102–104

Questions 1 and 2

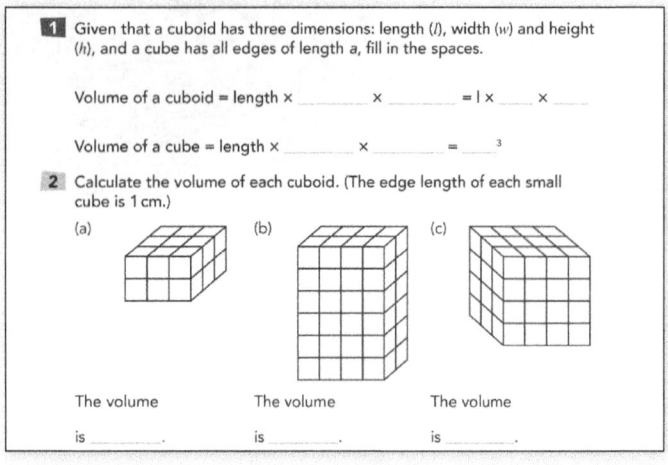

1. Given that a cuboid has three dimensions: length (*l*), width (*w*) and height (*h*), and a cube has all edges of length *a*, fill in the spaces.

   Volume of a cuboid = length × _____ × _____ = *l* × _____ × _____

   Volume of a cube = length × _____ × _____ = _____³

2. Calculate the volume of each cuboid. (The edge length of each small cube is 1 cm.)

   (a) The volume is _____.
   (b) The volume is _____.
   (c) The volume is _____.

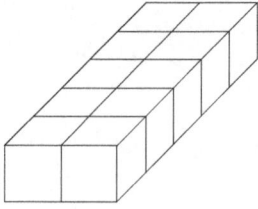

- Pupils should evaluate dimensions and volume.
- Ask: *What is the relationship between the dimensions of these cuboids and their volume?* Agree that the length multiplied by the width multiplied by the height gives the volume. Ask: *Can you write this as a formula?*
- Explain that $l \times w \times h$ is the formula used to find the volume of cuboids. Ask: *If l, w and h are all measurements in cm, what will the volume be measured in? What will volume be measured in if the dimensions are in metres? Why does this formula work?*
- Can pupils explain that, for cubes $l \times w$ gives the number of cubes in one layer of the rectangle of a cuboid, then multiplying by height will give the number of cubes in the entire shape (its volume). Some pupils may be able to express this in terms of dimensions: $l \times w$ gives the area of a 2-D rectangle and multiplying by height gives this rectangle another dimension and calculates the volume.

 *The volume of a cuboid is found by multiplying length by width by height.*

- Ask: *What do we need to know to work out the volume of a cube?* Show this cube:

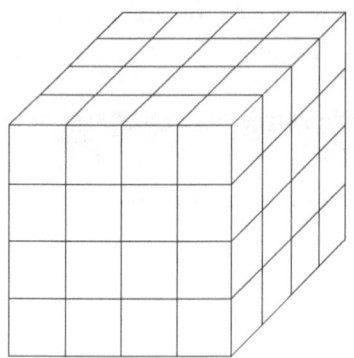

- Can pupils see that *l*, *w* and *h* are all equal and that the length of one edge is multiplied by itself three times when multiplying $l \times w \times h$ of a cube?
- Ask: *If the length of a cube edge is 'a', how would you write the formula for calculating its volume?* Agree that this is $a \times a \times a$ and can be written as a^3 ('a cubed'). Any letter could be used to represent the edge length – ensure pupils know this. Test this formula on the shape shown to see whether one side length multiplied by itself three times is equal to the number of smaller cubes in the whole cube (its volume).

What learning will pupils have achieved at the conclusion of Questions 1 and 2?

- Pupils will have used the dimensions of a cuboid and cube to construct expressions to find their volume.
- Pupils will have developed a mental image of how small cubes can, when put together, make larger cubes and cuboids. Focusing on this image supports pupils to understand why volume = length × width × height.
- Pupils will have applied formulae in order to calculate volume of cubes and cuboids.

Activities for whole-class instruction

- Display this cuboid:

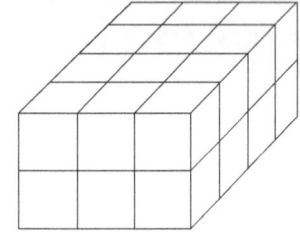

- Tell pupils each small cube is 1 cm × 1 cm × 1 cm. Ask: *What are the dimensions of the cuboid?*
- Ask: *What is the volume of this cuboid?* Pupils will initially work this out by counting and visualising the number of cubes that make up the shape. Discuss why the units are called cubic centimetres. Check that the volume is expressed correctly as cubic centimetres (cm³). Display information in a table:

Length	Width	Height	Volume
4 cm	3 cm	2 cm	24 cm³

- Show a different cuboid:

Chapter 9 Geometry and measurement (2)

Unit 9.6 Practice Book 5B, pages 102–104

 *The volume of a cube is also found by multiplying length by width by height. In a cube, these are all the same value.*

- Make several cubes and cuboids out of interlocking cubes and place them into a box so that they are out of sight. Choose a pupil to come to the front and pick any one of the cuboids. Explain to the rest of the class that they need to find out what the volume is in as few questions as possible. Ask: *How many questions do you think you need to ask?* Pupils may answer that they need to ask three questions (to find out the shape's length, width and height). Ask: *Is there a situation where you might only need to ask two questions?* ('Is it a cube?' Yes. 'What is its length?')

- Pupils should ask their questions to find out the dimensions of the cuboid. Ask: *What is the formula that gives the volume of a cuboid?* The formula should then be used to work out the shape's volume. For example, if the length is 3 cubes, the width is 2 cubes and the height is 5 cubes:

  $l \times w \times h$ = volume

  $3 \times 2 \times 5 = 30\,cm^3$

- Pupils should check that the formula has given the correct volume by counting the cubes in the original shape, layer by layer. Ask: *Is it more efficient to use the formula or to count every cube? Why?*

- Repeat for further cuboids. When a cube is chosen, ensure that pupils do not ask for all three dimensions and that they know it is a cube. It is important that they understand that they only need to know one side length to find the volume. Ask pupils whether it makes a difference which way the cuboid is placed and why. As the three numbers are being multiplied, pupils should remember the commutative rule of multiplication and that it does not matter in which order numbers are multiplied – they still give the same answer.

- Pupils should complete Questions 1 and 2 in the Practice Book.

Same-day intervention

- Pupil pairs should make cuboids with different dimensions using interlocking cubes. Encourage them to consider the different shapes that cuboids can take (some as cubes, some fairly shallow with a height of 1 cm, some long and thin modelled as a chain of cubes). Pupils should write the volume of their cuboid on a sticky note and stick this on the base of their 3-D shape. Collect their shapes together in the centre of a table and challenge the group to find the volume of each shape. Ask: *What is the volume of this shape measured in? Why? How will you calculate the volume?* Encourage pupils to count the cubes in the length, width and height and use the formula $l \times w \times h$ to find the volume of each cuboid volume. They should check the label underneath each shape to see whether they answered correctly.

Same-day enrichment

- Pupil pairs take turns to roll a dice three times to generate the dimensions of a cube or cuboid. They should then predict what the volume of the shape will be, using the formulae they have learned. Pupils should then check their calculation by making the shape out of interlocking cubes. They get 2 points if their original prediction is correct. The winner is the pupil who has the most points at the end. If the score is level, the winner is the pupil who has made the cuboid with the largest volume during the activity.

Question 3

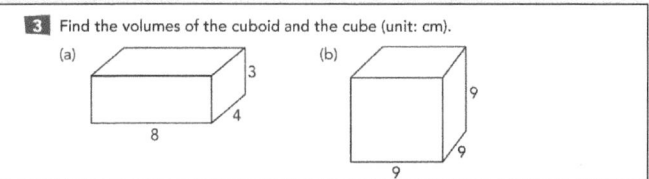

What learning will pupils have achieved at the conclusion of Question 3?

- Pupils will have developed a mental image of how small cubes can, when put together, make larger cubes and cuboids. Focusing on this image supports pupils to understand why volume = length × width × height.
- Pupils will have applied formulae in order to calculate volume of cubes and cuboids.

Activities for whole-class instruction

- Show the following images of a cuboid and a cube:

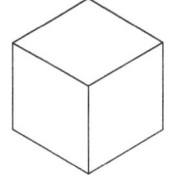 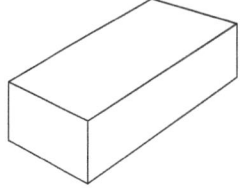

Chapter 9 Geometry and measurement (2)

Unit 9.6 Practice Book 5B, pages 102–104

- Ask: *What is the difference between these images and the ones you have looked at already?* (There are no centimetre cubes marked.) Agree that, if the lengths of the edges are known, the volume can be calculated.

- (i) Asking pupils whether they think that these shapes have volume at all is useful. Every example of cuboids pupils have looked at so far when considering volume has been constructed from cubes. So, these images are a point of departure. One misconception that pupils sometimes have is that volume can only be measured (or is only present) in shapes that have been constructed with cubes.

- Tell pupils the dimensions of the cuboid are 6 cm, 5 cm and 2 cm. Together, agree which measurements match the different edges on the image. Can pupils calculate the volume 6 × 5 × 2 = 60 cm³?

- Ask: *How many dimensions do you need to know to be able to calculate the volume of the cube?* Tell pupils one edge measures 5 cm. Can pupils calculate the volume 5 × 5 × 5 = 125 cm³?

- Ask: *If you were to make these shapes out of centimetre cubes, how many would you need for the bottom layer of each shape? How do you know? How many would you need for the whole shape?* Check pupils understand each shape is the equivalent of the same shape formed out of cubic centimetres.

- Erase the dimensions and repeat for new dimensions, encouraging pupils to generate their own problems where they can use the *l* × *w* × *h* formula to calculate the volume.

- Pupils should complete Question 3 in the Practice Book.

Same-day intervention

- Display the following cuboid:

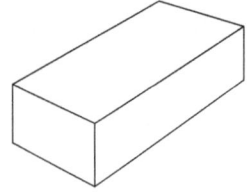

- Label dimensions 3 cm, 4 cm and 1 cm. Ask: *If you made this out of cubes, how many would be in the bottom layer?* Pupils should make the bottom layer out of cubes. Ask: *What are the dimensions of this cuboid?* (3 × 4 × 1) Ensure pupils understand that, even with the height as only 1, this is still a cuboid.

- Ask: *How many layers like this do you need to make the cuboid in the picture?* Ensure pupils understand that they are multiplying the bottom layer by the height (or *l* × *w* × *h*). Ask: *What do you notice about the answer to this calculation?* Show that the answer (in cm³) corresponds with the number of cubes used in the whole shape. Repeat for further cuboids.

- As pupils consider further examples, move from construction out of cubes to find the answer, to using as a checking device (so, initially finding the answer by using the formula and then checking their result by constructing the shape afterwards).

Same-day enrichment

- Provide pupils with 24 interlocking cubes. Challenge them to find as many cuboids as they can that have a volume of 24 cm³. How many can they find? To add to the challenge, pupils are not allowed to keep their cuboids constructed, so they should find a way to record their answers on paper as they go along. Remind them that they can use the formula to work out the lengths, widths and heights. For example, *l* × *w* × *h* = 24 cm³, so if the height is 1 cm, the length and width must be two numbers with a product of 24. Pupils should recognise that, for example a 2 × 3 × 4 cuboid is the same as a 4 × 2 × 3 cuboid (which they can see by rotating the shapes). Encourage pupils to describe how they found the different possibilities. Did they need cubes at all?

Question 4

4 Write the answers in the spaces.

(a) 450 000 cm³ = ▢ m³

(b) 3.9 m³ = ▢ cm³

(c) The length of the edge of a cube is 6 cm. Its volume is ▢ cm³.

(d) The length of a cuboid is 28 cm, the width is 12 cm and the height is 25 cm. The volume of the cuboid is ▢ cm³.

(e) The volume of a cube is 125 cm³. The length of the edge is ▢ cm.

(f) Two identical cubes are put together to form a cuboid. Given the length of the cuboid is 10 cm, the volume is ▢ cm³.

(g) The length of a cuboid is *a* m, the width is *b* m and the height is *h* m. If the length is increased by 5 m and the width and the height remain unchanged, then the volume is increased by ▢ m³. If the length and the width remain unchanged and the height is decreased by 2 m, then the volume of the cuboid is ▢ m³.

Chapter 9 Geometry and measurement (2)

Unit 9.6 Practice Book 5B, pages 102–104

What learning will pupils have achieved at the conclusion of Question 4?

- Problem-solving contexts will have provided opportunities to apply pupils' knowledge of volume in different ways.

Activities for whole-class instruction

- Ask: *What information do you need to be able to calculate the volume of a cuboid?*
- Write : length × width × height = volume
  15 cm   10 cm   8 cm
- Ask: *What shape is this? How do you know? What is its volume?*
- Tell pupils that you are thinking of a new shape such that the only information pupils need to calculate the volume is its length, which is 3 cm. Ask: *What shape do you think it this? How do you know? What is its volume?*
- Describe another shape, this time only giving pupils its volume, which is 64 cm³. Explain that the shape is a cube. Ask: *What is the length of the edge of the cube?* Ensure pupils understand that they are considering a number that, when multiplied by itself three times, gives the product 64.
- Give the example of a cuboid made by placing two identical cubes next to each other. Ask: *How many dimensions do you need to be given to calculate the cuboid's volume?* Pupils will only need one dimension as they can then derive the others. Give the cuboid's length as 8 cm. Ask: *How can you work out the volume of the cuboid?* Encourage pupils to sketch the shape and recognise that the overall volume is double the volume of one of the cubes.
- Describe a shape that has a length and width of 1 m, but is formed by placing one layer of cm cubes together, so its height is only 1 cm. Ask: *How would you work out the volume of this single layer in cubic centimetres?* Establish that this is 100 cm × 100 cm × 1 cm which equals 10 000 cm³. Ensure pupils understand that this means they would need 10 000 cubes to form the single centimetre-high layer. Ask pupils to imagine using several such layers to make a cube that is 1 m × 1 m × 1 m. Ask: *How many layers would be needed?* Pupils should recognise that they would need 100 layers and that this means the volume of a cubic metre is the same as 100 lots of 10 000 cm³ (or 1 000 000 cm³).
- Write the equivalence 1 m³ = 1 000 000 cm³. To consolidate pupils' understanding of this equivalence, give them further time to describe in their own words to a partner why this number of cubic centimetres is so large when there are only 100 cm in a metre. Ask: *How would you convert from one unit into the other? When multiplying by 1 000 000, how many places will each digit move? In which direction? Is this the same for dividing by 1 000 000?* Pupils should then draw their own place value grids to practise multiplying and dividing by 1 000 000 as they convert from m³ into cm³ and from cm³ into m³. For example, ask: *If a cuboid's volume is 830 000 cm³ and is written as cubic metres instead, how many m³ will it be?*
- Write the letters a, b and h and explain that they represent a cuboid's length, width and height respectively. Ask: *What will the volume be?* (a × b × h). Explain that the dimensions are all in metres. Ask: *How will the volume change if the length is increased by 4 m but the width and the height stay the same? What will the new volume be?* Ensure pupils are able to express these values in terms of the variables, even though they cannot work out an exact answer. Give examples to test their ideas. For example:

  5 m × 4 m × 3 m   (5 m + 4 m) × 4 m × 3 m
  = 60 m³   = 9 m × 4 m × 3 m
                            = 108 m³

- The increase in length by 4 m has caused an increase in volume of 48 m³, which is the same as 4 × b × h. The overall volume can be written as (a + 4) × b × h.
- Pupils should complete Question 4 in the Practice Book.

Same-day intervention

- Ask: *What do we know about any cube?* Can pupils tell you that length, width and height (or depth) will all be the same? Ask: *If the edge length of a cube is 2 cm, what is its height? If the width is 5 cm, what is the edge length?* Ask pupils to visualise rotating a cube, and agree that it looks the same from all directions. Ask: *If the edge length is 3 cm, how would you calculate its volume?*
- Use cubes to help pupils make connections between the formula for calculating volume and the relationship between length, width and height.
- Ask: *If the volume of a cube is 8 cm³, what is the length of one of its edges?* Pupils should understand that they are looking for a number that, when multiplied by itself three times (l × w × h = edge length × edge length × edge length) equals 8.
- Repeat for similar cube-based problems, helping pupils to understand the concept that they only need to know one measurement to find the volume of a cube.

Chapter 9 Geometry and measurement (2)

Unit 9.6 Practice Book 5B, pages 102–104

Same-day enrichment

- Ask pupils to make an information poster or tips sheet about volume. They should include its definition, an explanation of how to calculate it using the formula and an explanation that several cuboids can have the same volumes.

Question 5

5 Application problems.

(a) The length of a brick is 24 cm. The width is half the length and the thickness is 5 cm. What is the volume of the brick? _____

(b) The sum of all the edge lengths of a cube is 480 cm. What is its volume? _____

(c) The volume of a cuboid is 100 cm³. Given that the length is 10 cm and width is 2 cm, find the height of the cuboid. _____

(d) A school wants to dig a rectangular, box-shaped sandpit. The length is 4 m, the width is 2 m and the depth is 0.4 m. How many cubic metres of sand are needed to fill it up? _____

What learning will pupils have achieved at the conclusion of Question 5?

- Problem-solving contexts will have provided opportunities to apply pupils' knowledge of volume in different ways.

Activities for whole-class instruction

- Write: The total of all the edge lengths of a cube is 84 cm. What is its volume?
- Write the following headings:
  WHAT DO I KNOW? HOW CAN I USE IT TO HELP?
- Remind pupils that, when problem-solving, they often need to use information they do know to help work out information that they are not given. Ask: *What do you know about this shape? How can you use it to help?* Use pupils' responses to both questions to write underneath the headings as follows:

What do I know?	How can I use it to help?
It is a cube.	Cubes have 12 edges, all the same length.
	The volume of a cube is found by multiplying the edge length three times.
Total edge lengths are 84 cm.	84 divided by 12 will give the length of one edge.
	One edge length multiplied by itself twice will give the area (in square units).

- Repeat for further problems where pupils first identify the facts that they are told and then how to use these to help find the answer. For example:
  - The height of a parcel is 5 cm. Its width is double this and its length is double the width. What is the volume of the parcel?
  - The volume of a cereal box is 3600 cm³. Given that its width is 6 cm and its length is 20 cm, what is its height?
  - A rectangular, box-shaped hole is dug that is 5 m long, 2 m wide and 0.5 m deep. How many cubic metres of soil have been dug to make the hole?
- Pupils should complete Question 5 in the Practice Book.

Same-day intervention

- Display the following problem:
  - The length of a cardboard box is 10 cm. Its width is half of the length and its height is one less than the width. What is the volume of the box?
- Ask: *What do we know about the box? Can we work out all of its dimensions?* Give pupils time to derive the missing width and height by finding half of 10 cm and then one less than 5 cm. Encourage pupils to sketch the cuboid. Ask: *How could we find the volume of the box?* Agree, multiply the three dimensions together. As a checking strategy, pupils could make one layer, confirm the volume of that and multiply by the number of layers (the height).
- Repeat with other dimensions, including one example where one dimension is doubled and others are unchanged.

Chapter 9 Geometry and measurement (2)

Unit 9.6 Practice Book 5B, pages 102–104

Same-day enrichment

- Challenge pupil pairs to devise their own volume problems similar to those they have already answered. They should write these onto cards and pass their problems to another pair to solve, before checking that they have found the correct answer.

Challenge and extension question

Question 6

> 6. Two identical cubic boards are put together to form a cuboid. The sum of the lengths of all the edges of the cuboid formed is 48 cm. Find its volume.

Pupils are given the scenario of 'two identical cubic boards' being placed together to form a cuboid. They are given the sum of the lengths of the cuboid's edges (48 cm) and asked to find its volume. Pupils are expected to recognise that the shapes being placed together are cubes and therefore all their edges are the same length. Pupils should be able to visualise that the total of edges of the cuboid is the same as 16 × the edge length of the cube. They can use this information to derive the length of the cube (total length of edges ÷ 16) and then to calculate the cuboid's volume (cube length doubled × cube width × cube height).

Chapter 9 Geometry and measurement (2)

Unit 9.7
Volumes of cubes and cuboids (2)

Conceptual context

In the previous unit, pupils were introduced to formulae for calculating the volume of cubes and cuboids; that $l \times w \times h$ equals the volume of any cuboid and this can be simplified to a^3 in the case of cubes (where a is equivalent to the side length). This unit consolidates pupils' understanding of volume and fluency with the formulae. Problems are now presented as word problems and pupils need to apply their understanding in order to know what they are aiming to find.

Learning pupils will have achieved at the end of the unit

- Pupils will have applied their understanding of formulae in different ways in order to calculate volume of cubes and cuboids or to use the volume to help calculate their dimensions (Q1, Q2, Q3)
- Knowledge about volume will have been consolidated in problem-solving contexts (Q1, Q2, Q3)

Resources

interlocking cubes; paper/plastic straws; modelling clay; mini whiteboards; centimetre cubes; **Resource 5.9.7a** Cuboids from cubes; **Resource 5.9.7b** True or false?

Vocabulary

cube, cuboid, dimensions, length, width, height, volume, cm^3 (cubic centimetres), m^3 (cubic metres), centimetre cubes, edge length

Chapter 9 Geometry and measurement (2)

Unit 9.7 Practice Book 5B, pages 105–108

Question 1

> **1** Fill in the spaces to make each statement correct.
> (a) Putting together 3 identical cubes of edge length 20 cm into a cuboid, the volume of the cuboid is [ ] cm³.
> (b) An iron wire of 180 cm is used to form a maximum frame of a cube. The volume of the cube is [ ] cm³.
> (c) A cubic piece of wood of edge length 12 cm is cut into small cubes with edge length 3 cm. It can be cut into [ ] such small cubes.
> (d) A cube has an edge length of 50 cm. If the edge length is increased by 10 cm, then its volume is increased by [ ] cm³.
> (e) The length of a piece of cuboid steel is 0.2 m, the width is 6 cm and the height is 2 cm. The volume is [ ] cm³.
> (f) If the length, width and height of a cuboid are all increased to 3 times the original values, then the volume will be increased to [ ] times the original value.

What learning will pupils have achieved at the conclusion of Question 1?

- Pupils will have applied their understanding of formulae in different ways in order to calculate volume of cubes and cuboids or to use the volume to help calculate their dimensions.
- Knowledge about volume will have been consolidated in problem-solving contexts.

Activities for whole-class instruction

- Remind pupils of the definition of the term 'volume'.

  All say … *Volume is the amount of 3-D space that a shape takes up.*

- Write: A length of iron wire 120 cm long is used to form the frame of a cube. The volume of the cube is __ cm³.
- Pupils should sketch the scenario on their whiteboards. Ask: *What does the cube look like? What has happened to the wire? What is the volume of the cube?*
-  Given the definition of volume as the amount of 3-D space occupied by an object, it may be important at this point to ensure pupils understand how this relates to the hollow wire frame in the question. Although the wire forms a shape that seems to have space inside, it is described as the frame of a cube. Cubes (and cuboids) have flat connecting faces, so it must be assumed that the frame indicates the boundary of the cube/cuboid, enclosing the hollow space inside. It is important that pupils understand that only the dimensions of such a cube matter – volume is a measure of space, not materials. This applies to other frames of cuboids as well as empty boxes, and so on.
- Ask pupils: *What do you need to calculate the volume of the cube?* Challenge them to circle the important information in the problem. Pupils should use their knowledge of the number of edges in a cube, together with the total length of wire used to make the frame, to work out the length of one edge and, from this, the volume of the shape.
- Write: TOTAL LENGTH OF EDGES → VOLUME OF CUBE
- Explain that this represents what pupils have just achieved – they have calculated the volume of a cube, using knowledge about the total length of its edges (the total length of the iron wire).
- Write: EDGE LENGTH OF ONE CUBE → VOLUME OF CUBOID MADE FROM SEVERAL CUBES
- Ask: *If three identical cubes with an edge length of 5 cm are arranged so that they make a cuboid, what is the volume of the cuboid?*
- Encourage pupils to sketch and label the cuboid. Agree that if one edge = 5 cm, the length of the cuboid is 15 cm and both other dimensions are 5 cm.
- Ask: *If five identical cubes with an edge length of 5 cm are arranged so that they make a cuboid, what is the volume of the cuboid?*
- Ask: *If six identical cubes with an edge length of 8 cm are arranged so that they make a cuboid, what is the volume of the cuboid?*
- Pupils should complete Question 1 in the Practice Book.

Same-day intervention

- Ask: *What would you expect to happen to the volume of a cuboid if you doubled one of its dimensions?* Provide pairs of pupils with interlocking cubes. Ask them to make a cuboid each so that the length, width or height of one of the cuboids is double the other's (only one dimension should be changed). Draw a table, labelled 'length', 'width', 'height' and 'volume'. Encourage each pair to share the dimensions of both cuboids and ask the rest of the group to calculate their volume using the $l \times w \times h$ formula. Ask: *What happens to the volume of the cuboid when one of its dimensions is doubled? Is this what you expected? What if you had chosen one of the other dimensions to double instead? What would the cuboid look like? What would be the effect on volume?*
- Repeat for other pairs' cuboids. Ask: *Is the relationship between the change in cuboid dimensions and volume the same for each one? What would you expect the volume to be of a cuboid that did have a volume of 100 cm³, but which has had its dimensions doubled?*

175

Chapter 9 Geometry and measurement (2)

Unit 9.7 Practice Book 5B, pages 105–108

- If time allows, challenge pupils to use the same process to prove the answer to Question 1f, trebling the length, width and height and observing the change to volume when they do so.

Same-day enrichment

- Provide pupils with a copy of **Resource 5.9.7a** Cuboids from cubes which gives the instructions for the activity. Pupils explore the effect, on volume, of changing one dimension. Pupils should use reasoning to explain their findings.

Resource 5.9.7a

Cuboids from cubes

This investigation is all about making cuboids from cubes.
The cubes you will be thinking about have an edge length of 20 cm.

If you make a cuboid by putting two of these cubes together, what will its dimensions be? What will its volume be?

What about if you put three cubes together? Or four?

Record your results in a table.

Number of cubes used	Length (cm)	Width (cm)	Height (cm)	Volume (cm³)
2				
3				
4				

Remember that sometimes there may be more than one cuboid you can make.

Can you see any patterns in your results?

Predict!
Without working it out, what do you think the volume of a cuboid made from 5 cubes will be? Why?
Check your answer.

Predict the volume of cuboids made from 10 and 100 cubes. Explain to your partner how you managed to predict the answer using what you have found.

Answers:

Numbers of cubes used	Length (cm)	Width (cm)	Height (cm)	Volume (cm³)
2	40	20	20	16 000
3	60	20	20	24 000
4	80	20	20	32 000

Predictions:

Numbers of cubes used	Length (cm)	Width (cm)	Height (cm)	Volume (cm³)
5	100	20	20	40 000
10	200	20	20	80 000
100	2000	20	20	800 000

Question 2

2 True or false? (Put a ✓ for true and ✗ for false in each box.)
   (a) If the volumes of two cuboids are equal, then their lengths, widths and heights must also be equal.
   (b) Putting together two identical cubes of edge length 6 cm into a cuboid, the volume of the cuboid is 512 cm³.
   (c) Since $2^2 = 2 \times 2$, we can get $2^3 = 6$.
   (d) Two cubes have different sizes. If the edge length of the bigger cube is twice that of the smaller one, the volume of the bigger one is 8 times that of the smaller one.

What learning will pupils have achieved at the conclusion of Question 2?

- Pupils will have applied their understanding of formulae in different ways in order to calculate volume of cubes and cuboids or to use the volume to help calculate their dimensions.
- Knowledge about volume will have been consolidated in problem-solving contexts.

Activities for whole-class instruction

- Agree two simple symbols with pupils that can be drawn quickly on their whiteboards to represent a 'TRUE' and a 'FALSE' answer (for example, a tick and a cross). Display the following statement: $10^2 = 10 \times 10$, so 10^3 must be equal to 30.

- Put pupils into pairs and give them time to discuss whether they think the statement is true or false. They should then vote, using a tick or cross on their whiteboards. Probe understanding, including for pupils who vote 'incorrectly'.

- Ask: *What does the small 2 mean when it is written next to a number? If 10^3 did equal 30, then what would 10^2 be equal to?* Establish that 10 squared refers to 10 multiplied by itself 2 times and that 10 cubed is equal to 10 multiplied by itself 3 times.

- Give pupils further true or false statements to consider. Possible statements might include:

  – Georgia measures the length, width and height of a cuboid. They are different from the length, width and height of Ben's cuboid. The volume of her cuboid must be different too. [FALSE]

  – Two cubes are put together to make a cuboid. The longest side of the cuboid is 8 cm long. Its volume is 64 cm³. [TRUE]

  – The edge length of a cube is ten times the size of another cube. This means that its volume is ten times as large. [FALSE]

Chapter 9 Geometry and measurement (2)

Unit 9.7 Practice Book 5B, pages 105–108

- Pupils should complete Question 2 in the Practice Book.

Same-day intervention

- Write the term 5^2 on the board and discuss what it means. Display squared paper and ask pupils to represent this value visually, then numerically. Ensure that they understand that the value 25 is found by multiplying 5 by itself twice. This can be drawn as 25 squares arranged into a larger square as five rows of five, representing 5 × 5.

- Write 5^3 on the board. Ask: *What does the small 3 mean here? How might you show 5 cubed visually? How would you write it as a number sentence? What is 5^3 worth?*

- Give pupils centimetre cubes to demonstrate different cubed numbers and write their numerical values using the correct notation. For example, a cube made out of 8 smaller cubes would be described as $2^3 = 8$.

Same-day enrichment

- Provide pupils with a copy of **Resource 5.9.7b** True or false? Pupils devise their own True or False statements, using the sentence starters provided.

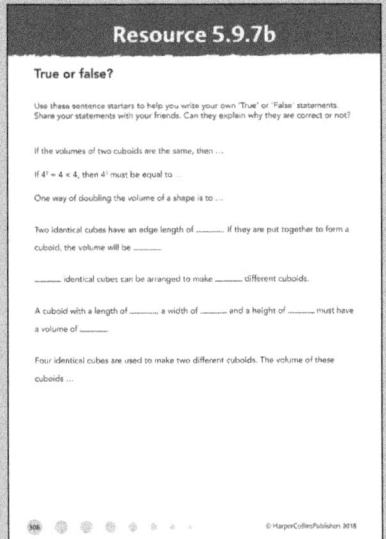

Question 3

3. Application problems.
   (a) The area of one face of a cube is 3600 cm². Find its volume.

   (b) A piece of cubic steel of edge length 60 cm is melted and formed into a piece of cuboid steel of length 0.9 m and width 40 cm. What is the height of the cuboid steel?

   (c) If the height of a cuboid is increased by 3 cm, it becomes a cube and the volume is increased by 243 cm³. What is the volume of the cuboid?

   (d) The length of a piece of iron wire is exactly enough to form a cubic frame of edge length 8 cm. If it is used to form a cuboid frame of length 10 cm and width 7 cm, what is the volume of the cuboid?

   (e) A concrete mixture of sand, cement and gravel is used to pave a rectangular, box-shaped site of 60 m long, 50 m wide and 10 cm thick. If for every 10 m³ of the site, the mixture needs to be blended twice, then for the whole site, how many times does the mixture need to be blended?

   (f) A cuboid-shaped steel plate is 80 cm long, 20 cm wide and 5 cm thick. What is the volume of the steel plate? Given every 1 cm³ of the steel plate weighs 7.8 g, what is the mass of the steel plate in kg?

What learning will pupils have achieved at the conclusion of Question 3?

- Pupils will have applied their understanding of formulae in different ways in order to calculate volume of cubes and cuboids or to use the volume to help calculate their dimensions.

- Knowledge about volume will have been consolidated in problem-solving contexts.

Activities for whole-class instruction

- Display the follwing problem:
  - A lump of clay is formed into a cube with an edge length of 30 cm. It is then reshaped into a cuboid with a length of 0.5 m and a width of 20 cm. What is the height of the cuboid?

- Pupils should sketch and label the cube and cuboid.

- Ask: *What is the important information in the problem? What can we work out from the information given?*

Chapter 9 Geometry and measurement (2) Unit 9.7 Practice Book 5B, pages 105–108

Establish that the initial edge length can be used to find the volume of the cube ($30 \times 30 \times 30 = 27\,000\,cm^3$). Encourage pupils to visualise the size of such a cube and point out that the number of cm^3 is very large.

- Ask: *When the lump of clay is reshaped into a cuboid, does the amount of clay change? What does that tell you about the volume of the cube and cuboid?* Pupils should understand that the volume is the same because no clay has been added or removed.

- Ask: *What do you notice about the dimensions of the cuboid? How can the volume be calculated?* Pupils should notice that the dimensions are in different units and need to be converted so they are the same.

- Agree that the length should be converted into centimetres.

  $l \times w \times h$ = Volume

  $50 \times 10 \times ?\ = 27\,000$

- Pupils should calculate the missing value and explain their answer.

- Repeat with similar problems (identifying key information, sketching and labelling). Problems might be:
  - The area of one face of a cube is $25\,cm^2$. What is its volume?
  - The width of a cuboid is increased by 2 cm. It becomes a cube and the volume increases by $100\,cm^3$. What was the volume of the cuboid before it changed?
  - A plastic cuboid is 20 cm long, 15 cm wide and 2 cm thick. What is its volume? For every $1\,cm^3$, the cuboid weighs 1.5 g, what does the cuboid weigh in kg?

- Pupils should complete Question 3 in the Practice Book.

Same-day intervention

- Show pupils a straw. Ask: *If you were going to make a cube from straws like this and pieces of modelling clay, how many straws would you need?*

- Agree that a cube has 12 equal edge lengths. Place 12 straws of the same length in a line. Ask: *If we knew the length of one straw, how could we calculate the total length of all the edges? What if we only knew the total length of all the edges, how could we calculate the length of 1 edge length?* Pupils should recognise that the total length must be divided by 12.

- Ask: *What will the total length be if one straw is 10 cm long? What will the volume be? How long will the edge length of a cube be if the total length of edges is 24 centimetres? What will the volume be?*

- Display the following problem:
  - The frame of a cube is made from a length of wire that is 36 cm long. What is the volume of the cube?

- Encourage pupils to calculate one edge length and use this to find the volume. They should then cut straws into 3 cm lengths and use modelling clay to form the 3 cm × 3 cm × 3 cm cube. Encourage them to visually prove the volume of the cube by showing how $27 \times 1\,cm^3$ cubes would fit inside the frame.

Same-day enrichment

- At the top of a piece of paper, pupils should each write a multiplication number sentence containing three numbers (for example, $4 \times 5 \times 10 = 200$). They should then pass their piece of paper to the pupil on the left who will fold over the top of the piece of paper and devise a volume problem based on the calculation (for example: A cuboid has a length of 10 cm, a width that is half of its length and a height that is 1 cm less than its width. What is its volume?). Finally, pupils should pass their pieces of paper one more time to the left and answer the problem they have been given (looking underneath the fold to check their answer is correct).

Chapter 9 Geometry and measurement (2)

Unit 9.7 Practice Book 5B, pages 105–108

Challenge and extension question

Question 4

4. Four identical cubes are put together to form a cuboid. The sum of the lengths of all the edges of the cuboid is 120 cm. Find the volume of the cuboid. (Note: there are two possible combinations.)

This question works well in conjunction with the challenge question at the end of the previous unit. There, pupils were asked to find the volume of a cuboid made from two identical cubes. This concept is extended slightly as pupils are asked to imagine a cuboid formed from four identical cubes. Pupils are expected to derive the side length of one of the cubes and, from this, calculate the volume of the cuboid. However, this time there are two ways to arrange the four cubes and pupils should consider both. Pupils who believe that there are more than two combinations of cubes should be encouraged to find the volumes of these 'extra' shapes and should recognise that they are the same as one of the two shapes they have already found (albeit rotated). The volume of both cuboids will be the same. Encourage pupils to reason why this is.

Chapter 9 Geometry and measurement (2)

Unit 9.8
Volume and capacity (1)

Conceptual context

Pupils have previously consolidated their knowledge of millilitres and litres as units of measurement of liquids (in Units 2.9 and 2.10) and more recently, considered the concept of volume in relation to cubes and cuboids. In this unit, they are required to draw conceptual links between these two themes, in the context of volume and capacity. The equivalence between 1 cubic centimetre and 1 millilitre is introduced and applied (before extending to include other conversions between units). It is important that pupils understand the similarities and differences between volume and capacity and so opportunities are given to them to define these and use them in real-life contexts.

Learning pupils will have achieved at the end of the unit

- The concept of volume will have been extended to include capacity and pupils will have learned the difference between them (Q1, Q2, Q3)
- The relationship between cubic centimetres and millilitres/litres will have been introduced, enabling pupils to convert from one unit to the other (Q1, Q4)
- Pupils will have used their knowledge of millilitres and litres in the context of capacity (Q4)
- Appropriate units of measurement will have been chosen to express volume and capacity of real-life containers (Q2, Q3)
- Knowledge of volume and capacity will have been applied in problem-solving contexts (Q5)

Resources

an empty bin bag; an empty plastic bottle; an empty cardboard box; **Resource 5.9.8a** Capacity cards (Set A); **Resource 5.9.8b** Capacity cards (Set B)

Vocabulary

volume, capacity, cubic centimetres (cm^3), millilitres (ml), litre (l)

Chapter 9 Geometry and measurement (2)

Unit 9.8 Practice Book 5B, pages 109–112

Questions 1, 2 and 3

1 Fill in the spaces to make each statement correct.

(a) The _____ of the objects that a container, for example, glass bottle, bucket and cargo container, can contain is usually called the _____ of the container.

(b) To measure the size of a container, we can usually use the units of _____.

However, when measuring the volume of liquid, we usually use the units of _____. They are _____ and _____.

(c) 1 litre = ☐ cubic centimetres

1 millilitre = ☐ cubic centimetre

1 litre = ☐ millilitres

2 Use suitable units to indicate the capacities of the following containers.

800 _____   80 _____   42 _____

5 _____   33 _____   50 _____

3 Fill in each space with a suitable unit.

(a) A water bottle has 280 _____ of water.

(b) An olive oil bottle has 2.48 _____ of olive oil.

(c) The capacity of a water heater is 60 _____.

(d) The capacity of a warehouse is 480 _____.

(e) A petrol tank has 115 _____ of petrol.

(f) A nail polish bottle has 30 _____ of nail polish.

What learning will pupils have achieved at the conclusion of Questions 1, 2 and 3?

- The concept of volume will have been extended to include capacity and pupils will have learned the difference between them.
- The relationship between cubic centimetres and millilitres/litres will have been introduced, enabling pupils to convert from one unit to the other.
- Appropriate units of measurement will have been chosen to express volume and capacity of real-life containers.

Activities for whole-class instruction

Volume is the amount of 3-D space occupied by an object. This includes solid and hollow objects.

Capacity is the amount of material (gas, liquid or solid) that a container can contain.

Volume of solid objects, including hollow objects is measured in cm^3 and m^3.

Volume of liquids is measured in ml and l.

Capacity of a container is measured in ml and l when the container is for liquids and in cm^3 and m^3 when the container is for solids.

1 cubic centimetre ($1cm^3$) is equal to $\frac{1}{1000}$ of a litre or 1 ml.

- Show pupils a cardboard box, an empty bottle and a bin bag. Ask: *Which of these contain something now?* Agree that the box and bottle both contain air, the bin bag is flat and so does not contain anything. The box and bottle have volume.

  Ask: *How would you work out the volume of what is in the box or the bottle?* Agree measure the dimensions of each container and multiply them together. Agree units will be cm^3.

  Ask: *Which of these could contain something?* Agree, all of them. They all have capacity.

  Ask: *What is the capacity of each? What unit should be used?* Agree: capacity of box might be m^3 or litres, depending on whether it is filled with liquid (including gas) or solid; capacity of bottle is ml or l; capacity of bin bag might be m^3 or litres, depending on whether it is filled with liquid (including gas) or solid.

- Reveal the label from the roll of bin bags and show that the capacity is given in litres, even though solid items are generally put inside them because it describes the amount of air that can be fitted inside.

- Show pupils a 1 litre bottle, half filled with liquid. Can pupils see that:
  – volume of liquid inside = 500 ml
  – capacity of the bottle = 1 litre, no matter how much liquid is actually inside it.

- Write: $1 cm^3$ is equal to 1 ml. Ask: *How many cubic centimetres do you think are the same as 1 litre? How do you know?*

- This equivalence can be illustrated by showing pupils a cube-shaped 1 litre container. Place ten centimetre cubes in a row to show the side length of the cube. Ask: *How many cubes would we need to cover the bottom layer of the container?* Pupils should be able to visualise that 10

181

Chapter 9 Geometry and measurement (2)

Unit 9.8 Practice Book 5B, pages 109–112

rows of 10 cubes would be required. Ask: *How many complete layers of 100 cubes would be needed to fill the entire 1 litre container?* Again, pupils should be able to visualise that they would need to multiply by 10 once more to get 10 lots of 100 cubes. Give pupils time to turn to a partner and explain in their own words why 1000 cm³ is the same as 1 litre.

- Draw the following four labels on the board:

  | ml | | l | | cm³ | | m³ |

- Call out a series of objects and numbers and challenge pupils to discuss which unit of measurement they would use to describe their capacity. For example:

  A freezer = 150   (litres)
  A flask = 500   (millilitres)
  A lorry trailer = 35   (cubic metres, m³)
  A large car boot = 660   (litres)
  A bin bag = 70   (litres)
  A mug = 350   (millilitres)

- Pupils should complete Questions 1, 2 and 3 in the Practice Book.

Same-day intervention

- Write the words 'volume' and 'capacity' on the board. Using different containers, give pupils examples where they must decide whether the space the object takes up (volume) or the amount of material that can fit inside it (capacity) is being described. They should vote for the word they think is correct. For example, start filling a box with cubes and ask pupils for the word used to describe the number of cubes that would fill it. Ask pupils for the word used to describe the space that the box would take up in the stock cupboard.

- Encourage pupils to use equipment to give their own examples to demonstrate the two concepts. Ensure pupils are confident in their grasp of both concepts. Ask: *What is the same and what is different?*

- Write the units of measurement: cubic centimetres (cm³), millilitres (ml) and litres (l). Call out different capacities and ask pupils to decide which unit of measurement is correct. For example:

  – The capacity of a jug is one and a half ...
  – The capacity of a teacup is 250 ...
  – The capacity of a bath is 225 ...
  – The capacity of a bottle of lemonade is 2 ...

- Use the opportunity to discuss the equivalence of 1 cm³ and 1 ml. For example, the capacity of a teacup could be described as 250 ml or 250 cm³. Similarly, the capacity of a bottle of lemonade could be described as 2 l or 2000 cm³.

Same-day enrichment

- Provide pupils with a copy of **Resource 5.9.8a** Capacity cards (Set A). Pupils take turns to take a card and read it out, without mentioning the units of measurement. The rest of the group should then decide what they think the unit of measurement is.

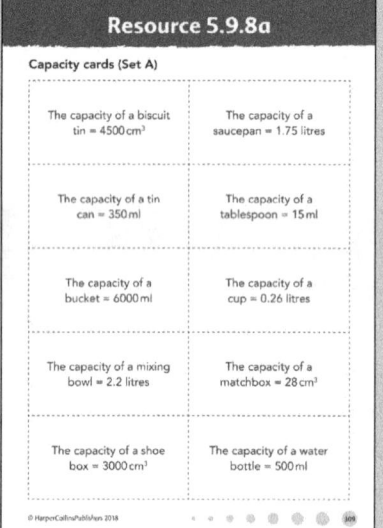

Question 4

4 Converting between units.

(a) 11 litres = ☐ cubic centimetres
(b) 7 millilitres = ☐ cubic centimetres
(c) 3.5 litres = ☐ cubic centimetres
(d) 78 litres 8 millilitres = ☐ litres
(e) 4.4 cm³ = ☐ ml
(f) 20.2 cm³ = ☐ l
(g) 0.23 l = ☐ ml
(h) 4.38 l = ☐ ml
(i) 8 l 12 ml = ☐ l = ☐ ml
(j) 6080 ml = ☐ l ☐ ml

Chapter 9 Geometry and measurement (2)

Unit 9.8 Practice Book 5B, pages 109–112

What learning will pupils have achieved at the conclusion of Question 4?

- The relationship between cubic centimetres and millilitres / litres will have been introduced, enabling pupils to convert from one unit to the other.
- Pupils will have used their knowledge of millilitres and litres in the context of capacity.

Activities for whole-class instruction

- Remind pupils that 1 cm³ is equivalent to 1 ml. Show them the 1 litre measuring box again and remind them that 1000 × 1 cm³ will fill it. Discuss how the container can be filled with 1 litre of liquid (that is, 100 millilitres) or 1000 cm³.

 *One thousand millilitres of water takes up the same space as 1000 cubic centimetres. Therefore, 1 millilitre takes up the same space as 1 cubic centimetre.*

- Ask: *How many cubic centimetres take up the same space as 6.5 ml?* Agree 6.5. *How many cubic centimetres take up the same space as 9 litres?*
- Ask pupils to choose a volume expressed in litres, millilitres or cubic centimetres and devise their own conversion question to ask the class. Share ideas.
- Display the following table:

5 litres	1000 cm³	14 l
5.2 cm³	4020 ml	3 litres 3 millilitres
0.65 l	12.5 cm³	600 ml

- Pupil pairs should agree, for each value in the grid, an equivalent value expressed in other units, for example:

3003 cubic centimetres = 3 litres 3 millilitres

12 and a half millilitres = 12.5 cm³

1 litre = 1000 cm³

- Pupils should complete Question 4 in the Practice Book.

Same-day intervention

- Provide pupils with cards cut from **Resource 5.9.8a** Capacity cards (Set A). Together, look at a card showing a capacity written in litres. Ask: *How do you convert into millilitres?* (by multiplying by 1000) *Why?* (because there are 1000 millilitres in 1 litre)
- Discuss how the number of litres shown on the card can be converted to cubic centimetres (by multiplying by 1000) and why (because 1 cubic centimetre is the same as a millilitre and there are 1000 millilitres in 1 litre).
- Give pupils further examples to practise with before moving on to conversion between millilitres and cubic centimetres or between millilitres and litres.

Same-day enrichment

- Provide pupils with a copy of **Resource 5.9.8b** Capacity cards (Set B). Pupils should shuffle the cards and take it in turns to take a card. They should then describe the capacity written on the card without mentioning any of the words on the card. For example, a fish tank with a capacity of 60 litres might be described as 'an aquarium with a capacity of 60 000 cubic centimetres'. To make the task more difficult, pupils might be challenged to describe the capacity without mentioning any of the digits either (for example, 'double 30 000 millilitres').

Resource 5.9.8b

Capacity cards (Set B)

A fish tank with a capacity of 60 litres	A bucket with a capacity of 7500 millilitres
A bottle with a capacity of 1.25 litres	A sandwich box with a capacity of 450 millilitres
A cardboard box with a capacity of 80 000 cm³	A watering can with a capacity of 10 000 millilitres
A jerry can with a capacity of 20 litres	A teaspoon with a capacity of 5 millilitres
A jar with a capacity of half a litre	A water tank with a capacity of 2000 litres

Chapter 9 Geometry and measurement (2)   Unit 9.8 Practice Book 5B, pages 109–112

Question 5

> **5** Application problems.
> (a) A container has 5 l of water. If Matthew drinks 800 ml of water from the container every day, then how many days will it take Matthew to drink all the water?
>
> (b) The capacity of a refrigerator for food storage is 330 litres. If the refrigerator has two parts, a fridge and a freezer, and the capacity of the fridge is twice that of the freezer, find the capacities of the fridge and the freezer.

What learning will pupils have achieved at the conclusion of Question 5?

- Knowledge of volume and capacity will have been applied in problem-solving contexts.

Activities for whole-class instruction

- Display the following problem:
  - The capacity of a jug is 4 litres. How many 250 ml cups of water are needed until the jug is half full?
- Ask pupils to sketch the problem and label what they know. This should be the capacity of the jug (4 litres), the volume of a cup of water (250 ml) and the target of the jug being 'half full'. Ask: *How many steps do you think you need to complete to find the answer?* For example:
  - STEP ONE: Find half of 4 litres.
  - STEP TWO: Convert the answer to STEP ONE into millilitres.
  - STEP TWO: Divide the answer to STEP TWO by 250.
- Give pupils time to calculate the number of cups and to explain how they know what it is. Ask: *How could you check that your answer is correct?*

- Display further problems and encourage pupils to use the same approach to solve them, first sketching the scenario, then adding labels to show what they know. Give pupils problems such as:
  - The capacity of a bin bag is 70 litres. Harry's dad has four bags. What volume of rubble will he be able to take to the tip?
  - A car boot has a capacity of 480 litres. A bag with a volume of 10 000 cubic centimetres is put into the boot. What volume of luggage can still fit into the boot?
- Pupils should complete Question 5 in the Practice Book.

Same-day intervention

- Write: CONVERT, COMPARE, CALCULATE.
- Display the following problem:
  - The capacity of a watering can is 4 litres. Samir fills it with 3500 millilitres of water. How many millilitres of water does he still need to fill it to the top?
- Ask: *Do you need to convert any of the measurements? If so, which one and how will you convert it? Is the question asking you to compare any capacities? Is it asking you to calculate using them? What do you need to do to find the answer?*
- Agree that pupils should convert the capacity of the watering can into millilitres before subtracting to find the answer.
- Repeat for further problems, including those comparing two capacities expressed in different units. For example:
  - The capacity of Saucepan A is 1250 ml. The capacity of Saucepan B is 1.5 l. Which saucepan holds more and why?

Same-day enrichment

- Allow pupils to use any of the cards from **Resources 5.9.8a** or **5.9.8b** as volume and capacity facts that will inform the following activity. Challenge pupils to use the information to write their own multi-step problems based on capacity (where one of the steps involves converting between units). Pupils should share their problems for peers to solve.

Chapter 9 Geometry and measurement (2) Unit 9.8 Practice Book 5B, pages 109–112

Challenge and extension question

Question 6

6 There is some water in both buckets A and B. If the water from Bucket A is poured into Bucket B to make it full, then there are 3.6 litres of water left in Bucket A. If the water is poured from Bucket B to Bucket A to make it full, then there are 1.4 litres of water left in Bucket B.

Given that the capacity of Bucket A is 1.5 times that of Bucket B, what are the capacities of Bucket A and Bucket B, respectively?

This question is particularly challenging; pupils should draw diagrams to help them see that:

1. The total amount of water in both buckets is fixed, no matter if one pours water from A to B, or from B to A.

2. When B is full, A contains 3.6 litres of water, but when A is full, B contains only 1.4 litres of water. Hence A can hold 2.2 more litres than B.

3. Because A can hold 1.5 times B, that is, 0.5B more than B, it means 0.5 is 2.2 litres. Therefore the capacity of B is 4.4 litres and A is 1.5 × 4.4 = 6.6 litres.

Chapter 9 Geometry and measurement (2)

Unit 9.9
Volume and capacity (2)

Conceptual context

This unit ties together the concepts pupils have considered previously:
- properties of cubes and cuboids
- using a shape's dimensions to calculate its volume
- the relationship between cubic centimetres and millilitres

by applying these to a range of volume and capacity-related contexts. Pupils will consolidate their understanding of the similarities and differences between volume and capacity, applying these to solving real-life problems.

Learning pupils will have achieved at the end of the unit

- Concepts of, and connections between, volume and capacity will have been consolidated when applying them to real-life problems (Q1, Q3, Q4)
- The relationship between cubic centimetres and millilitres/litres will have been explored in problem-solving contexts (Q1, Q2, Q3, Q4)
- The volume formula ($l \times w \times h$) will have been used to calculate the volume and/or capacity of cubes and cuboids (Q2, Q3, Q4)

Resources

cardboard box; digit cards; mini whiteboards; **Resource 5.9.9a** Capacity cards; **Resource 5.9.9b** Write your own problems

Vocabulary

volume, capacity, cubic centimetres (cm^3), millilitres (ml), litre (l), length, width, height, formula, cube/cubic, cuboid

Chapter 9 Geometry and measurement (2)

Unit 9.9 Practice Book 5B, pages 113–116

Question 1

> **1** Fill in the spaces to make each statement correct.
> (a) A cuboid petrol tank is 90 cm long, 50 cm wide and 40 cm high. There are ☐ litres of petrol in the tank when it is full.
> (b) A cuboid water tank is 50 cm long, 40 cm wide and 20 cm high. Its capacity is ☐ l.
> (c) A cuboid ice storage unit is 12 m long, 6 m wide and 3 m high. Its capacity is ☐ m³.
> (d) The sum of all the edge lengths of a cubic box is 240 cm. Its capacity is ☐ cm³.

What learning will pupils have achieved at the conclusion of Question 1?

- Concepts of, and connections between, volume and capacity will have been consolidated when applying them to real-life problems.
- The relationship between cubic centimetres and millilitres/litres will have been explored in problem-solving contexts.

Activities for whole-class instruction

- Introduce the concept of a cuboid filled with a liquid. Ask pupils to suggest what this might be. Answers may include:
  - a tank (fish tank, hot water tank, fuel tank)
  - a carton (containing milk/juice)
- Revise the terms 'volume' and 'capacity'.

All say... *Volume is the amount of 3-D space occupied by an object. This includes solid and hollow objects. Capacity is the amount of material (gas, liquid or solid) that a container can contain.*

- Encourage pupils to apply these to the real-life examples they listed. Ensure pupils remember that:
  - Volume of solid objects, including hollow objects is measured in cm³ and m³
  - Volume of liquids is measured in ml and l
  - Capacity of a container is measured in ml and l when the container is for liquids and in cm³ and m³ when the container is for solids
  - 1 cubic centimetre (1 cm³) is equal to 1/1000 of a litre or 1 ml.
- Give the example of a cuboid fish tank and ask: *How can I find its capacity?* Pupils may suggest filling the tank with measuring jugs, however, ask: *Is there a quicker way to find the answer?*

- Establish that the volume formula ($l \times w \times h$) can be used to calculate the capacity as long as pupils know the dimensions of the inside of the fish tank. Ask: *What is the relationship between millilitres and cubic centimetres?* Pupils should know that 1 cm³ = 1 ml. Ask how this can be used to work out the amount of water the fish tank will hold. Check pupils understand they can calculate the capacity in litres by calculating the number of cubic centimetres.

- Show pupils a sketch of a cuboid and label Internal length = 3 cm, Internal width = 2 cm and Internal height = 4 cm. Model how to find its capacity:

  length × width × height = capacity

  $3 \times 2 \times 4 = 24$ cm³

- Ask: *How many millilitres are the same as 24 cubic centimetres? How many cm³ will be the same as 1 litre?*

- Give pupils a series of examples of inner dimensions of cuboids and ask for their answer in different ways. Ask: *What unit could we give the answer in?*

  cm × cm × cm → capacity in cm³/ml/l

  m × m × m → capacity in m³

- Ensure pupils do not over-complicate things. For example, when dealing with dimensions in metres, they can give the answer in m³. If pupils want to try to convert to cm³, encourage them to convert the original dimensions into centimetres before they calculate the capacity.

- Pupils should complete Question 1 in the Practice Book.

Same-day intervention

- Draw links between cubic centimetres and millilitres through the following activity. Give each pupil one 1 cm cube. Ask them to imagine that it is hollow and to visualise dripping water into it until it is full. Tell them that it now contains 1 millilitre of water.

- Explain that the amount of water needed to fill a 1 cm cube is 1 millilitre. Ask: *How many millilitres would it take to fill 5 of the small 1 cm cubes? 10? 85? 1000?*

- Show pupils 5 × 1 cm cubes. Ask: *What is their total volume?* Show a teaspoon containing water. Explain that the volume in ml is the same as the cubes (5 ml = 5 cm³). Add another cube and ask: *How many millilitres is the same as this? How many more cm³ will I need if I double the number of teaspoons?*

Chapter 9 Geometry and measurement (2)

Unit 9.9 Practice Book 5B, pages 113–116

- Give pupils quick-fire questions to practise connecting the concepts of cm³ and ml. For example, ask: *A can of orangeade contains 330 ml. How many cubic centimetres is this equal to?* Pupils should write the capacity on their whiteboards and simply cross out and alter the unit of measurement:

    cm³
    330 ml

- Progress to consider the capacity of cuboids. Give pupils simple dimensions of the inside of cuboids. For example:
    – The inside of a matchbox has a length of 5 cm, a width of 2 cm and a height of 2 cm – what is its capacity?
- Pupils should use the volume formula to express capacities in terms of cm³ and ml.

Same-day enrichment

- Provide pupils with a copy of **Resource 5.9.9a** Capacity cards. Pupils take turns to take three number cards and one unit card. They should use their cards to devise a problem for their partner to solve. For example, if they choose the cards 40, 50, 40 and 'litres' they might write the problem:
    – The inside of a cuboid fish tank has a length of 40 cm, a width of 50 cm and a height of 40 cm. How many litres will it hold?
- Pupils should then solve each other's problems.

Resource 5.9.9a
Capacity cards

20	30	40
50	60	70
80	90	100
20	30	40
50	60	70
80	90	100
cm³	ml	l
cm³	ml	l

Question 2

2 True or false? (Put a ✓ for true and ✗ for false in each box.)
    (a) The volume formulae can also be used to calculate the capacity of an object. ☐
    (b) 5.6 litres = 560 cubic centimetres ☐
    (c) The volume of a storage box made of wood is the same as its capacity. ☐

What learning will pupils have achieved at the conclusion of Question 2?

- The relationship between cubic centimetres and millilitres/litres will have been explored in problem-solving contexts.
- The volume formula ($l \times w \times h$) will have been used to calculate the volume and/or capacity of cubes and cuboids.

Activities for whole-class instruction

- Display the following image:

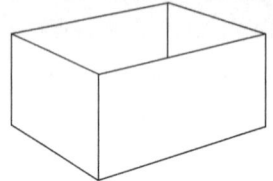

- Ask: *What do we need to measure to find the capacity of the cuboid?* Agree, length width and height.

(i) Pupils might point out these should be internal, rather than external measurements. This is correct but you should point out that, when a container is made of a thin material like card or glass or metal, we often simply measure the external dimensions and ignore the thickness of the material.

- Ask: *Could you measure the volume of this box?* Agree that the box has capacity but no volume.
- Ask: *If it was filled with a material such as sand, what would the volume of the sand be?* Agree ($l \times w \times h$) cm³
- Ask: *If it was filled with water, what would the volume of the water be?* Agree ($l \times w \times h$) ml.
- Review and emphasise that:
    – Empty containers do not have volume – they do have capacity.
    – The volume of material in a container is measured in l/ml if it is a liquid and in cm³ if it is a solid material.
    – The capacity of a container can be measured in l/ml if it is a container for liquid and in cm³ if it is a container for solid material

Chapter 9 Geometry and measurement (2)

Unit 9.9 Practice Book 5B, pages 113–116

- Display the following three statements and explain that they are a combination of TRUE and FALSE statements:
  - A: 500 cm³ is the same as half a litre.
  - B: The volume and the capacity of a fish tank are both the same.
  - C: To convert cubic centimetres into litres, just swap the unit from cm³ into l.
- Ask: *How many of these statements are true? Which ones?* Give pupils time to discuss their responses in pairs. Discuss the statements as a class and reason why statements B and C are not true. (B is not true because a fish tank has capacity but not volume – the water it is filled with has volume but not the tank itself.)
- Ask pupils to write their own similar statements on their whiteboards. These may involve calculations of capacity or general statements about volume and capacity. Choose any three pupils to share their statements with the rest of the class. Ask: *How many of these statements are true? Which ones?* Challenge the class to correct the false statements so that they become correct.
- Pupils should complete Question 2 in the Practice Book.

Same-day intervention

- Write: An empty container has …
- Read out three possible endings to the sentence and explain that only one is correct:
  - volume
  - capacity
  - neither volume or capacity.
- Give pupils time to go through each response, deciding which is correct (and why) and why the two incorrect answers are wrong. Repeat for further statements to ensure that pupils consolidate their understanding of the concepts they are focusing on, for example:
  - The capacity of a hot water tank is …
    * the space that it takes up in your loft.
    * the height of the water inside it.
    * the amount of water that it can contain.
- Include sets of statements with more than one correct answer, for example:
  - Holly is finding the capacity of an empty container …
    * She can use the same formula as finding the volume, but she should measure inside the box.
    * She cannot find the capacity of an empty container, but she can find its volume.
    * She could fill it with centimetre cubes and count them, but it would take a long time!

Same-day enrichment

- Challenge pupils to look through their completed questions in this unit and those they have completed in Units 9.6, 9.7 and 9.8 and alter them so that they create a list of five true and five false statements. They should share these with peers who should show how the false statements can be corrected.

Questions 3 and 4

3 Application problems.
  (a) The inside of a cuboid wooden crate measures 95 cm long, 64 cm wide and 40 cm deep. What is the capacity of the crate?

  (b) The edge length of a cubic water tank is 100 cm. If the height of water in the tank is 85 cm, how many litres of water are there in the tank?

  (c) The inside of a cuboid fish tank measures 60 cm long, 30 cm wide and 40 cm high. The water level is 6 cm from the top of the tank. How many litres of water are there in the fish tank?

  (d) A cuboid water tank measures 36 cm by 25 cm by 18 cm. What is the capacity of the tank in cubic centimetres? What is the capacity in terms of litres?

  (e) The trailer of a refrigerated truck is a cuboid and its capacity is 22 500 litres. The inside of the trailer measures 4.5 m long and 2.5 m wide. What is the height of the trailer?

4 A cuboid glass tank without a top is made of 1-centimetre thick glass. The dimensions of the tank are 32 cm × 27 cm × 25 cm.
  (a) What is the capacity of the tank in litres?

  (b) If 15 litres of water is poured into the tank, how far is the water level from the top of the tank?

Chapter 9 Geometry and measurement (2) Unit 9.9 Practice Book 5B, pages 113–116

What learning will pupils have achieved at the conclusion of Questions 3 and 4?

- Concepts of, and connections between, volume and capacity will have been consolidated when applying them to real-life problems.
- The relationship between cubic centimetres and millilitres/litres will have been explored in problem-solving contexts.
- The volume formula ($l \times w \times h$) will have been used to calculate the volume and/or capacity of cubes and cuboids.

Activities for whole-class instruction

- Write:
  The inside of a water tank measures 100 cm long, 54 cm wide and 65 cm high.
- Together, draw the tank and label the dimensions. Add more information to the problem:
  The tank is filled so that the water level is 15 cm from the top. How many litres of water are in the tank?
- Ask: *How would you find the total capacity of the tank?* Pupils should draw and label the tank and calculate the answer in cm³. Ask: *How can we change your answer of 270 000 cm³ into litres? What do you know and how can you use it to help?* Agree that pupils should convert the amount of water into millilitres, then into litres.
- Repeat for further problems, including those where pupils are given a volume and two dimensions, then asked to find the third dimension. For example:
  - The capacity of a cuboid fuel tank is 20 litres. Its height is 50 cm and its width is 20 cm. What is its length?
  - If the tank is filled with 15 litres of fuel, how far is the fuel level from the top of the tank?
- Pupils should complete Questions 3 and 4 in the Practice Book.

Same-day intervention

- Write: LENGTH (cm), WIDTH (cm), HEIGHT (cm), CAPACITY (cm³). Explain that these are the dimensions of a cuboid.
- Deal different digit cards under each of the first three headings and ask pupils to calculate the capacity each time. Ask: *What calculation do you need to do to find the capacity?* Do this several times until pupils are confident using the volume formula to calculate the capacity.
- Deal the numbers 5 and 2 under LENGTH and WIDTH, but this time leave the HEIGHT column empty. Under CAPACITY write 60 cm³. Ask: *Can you write the volume calculation, drawing a box where the missing number is?* Agree that this is 5 × 2 × [ ] = 60 and that (as 5 × 2 = 10), pupils are looking for a number that, when multiplied by 10, equals 60. Ask: *How can we find out the height of the cuboid?*
- Model how pupils can also work backwards from 60, dividing by 2 and then dividing by 5 to be left with the answer. Repeat for further problems where pupils need to derive one of the dimensions, having been given the volume and the remaining two dimensions. As pupils grow in confidence, progress to framing the activity in real-life contexts:
  - A matchbox has a capacity of 120 cm³. Its height is 2 cm and its width is 6 cm. How long is the matchbox?
  - Jamie has ordered a parcel from a website. The website says:
    - Volume of package: 1400 cm³
    - Length: 20 cm
    - Width: 10 cm
  - Jamie is worried that the height of the package might not fit through his letterbox. His letterbox is 5 cm tall. Use the information you have been given to find out whether the package will fit.

Chapter 9 Geometry and measurement (2)

Unit 9.9 Practice Book 5B, pages 113–116

Same-day enrichment

- Provide pupils with a copy of **Resource 5.9.9b** Write your own problems. Pupils design their own volume and capacity-based problems. They should use the resource provided as inspiration and to scaffold their ideas. The resource contains several pictorial representations and example questions pupils may wish to utilise when devising their own problems. Once they have completed four problems of their own and worked out the corresponding answers, pupils should then share them for peers to solve.

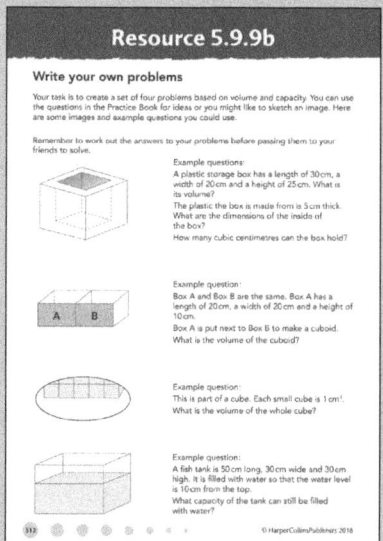

Answers to example questions: 15 000 cm³, 20 cm × 10 cm × 15 cm, 3000 cm³; 8000 cm³; 125 cm³; 15 000 cm³

Challenge and extension question

Question 5

> 5. The inside of a cuboid swimming pool measures 50 m long and 25 m wide. Water is pumped into the pool through two water pipes A and B, at a speed of 1200 m³/h and 1300 m³/h respectively. What is the depth of water in the pool after 15 minutes?

In this question, pupils are given the scenario of a cuboid swimming pool being filled by two water pipes, pumping in water at two different speeds (given in cubic metres per hour). They are challenged to find the depth of water after the water has been pumped into the pool for 15 minutes. Pupils are given the length and width of the pool, so, combining these dimensions with the volume of water in a quarter of an hour (which they can calculate from finding ¼ of the two pump speeds). Pupils have all the information they need to calculate the depth of water. Although the question seems more complex, it is essentially the same as being given a cuboid's volume, length and width and being asked to calculate its height.

Chapter 9 test (Practice Book 5B, pages 117–120)

Test question number	Relevant unit	Relevant questions within unit
1	Unit 9.6	Q3
2	Unit 9.4 Unit 9.5 Unit 9.6 Unit 9.7	Q1 Q2 Q4 Q1
3	Unit 9.4 Unit 9.5 Unit 9.7	Q1, Q2 Q3 Q2
4	Unit 9.2 Unit 9.3 Unit 9.9	Q1 Q4 Q3
5	Unit 9.8 Unit 9.9	Q5 Q3, Q4
6	Unit 9.7	Q3
7	Unit 9.9	Q3, Q4
8	Unit 9.9	Q3, Q4
9	Unit 9.9	Q3, Q4

Chapter 10
Factors, multiples and prime numbers

Chapter overview

Area of mathematics	National Curriculum statutory requirements for Key Stage 2	Shanghai Maths Project reference
Number – multiplication and division	Year 5 Programme of study: Pupils should be taught to: ■ identify multiples and factors, including finding all factor pairs of a number, and common factors of two numbers	Year 5, Units 10.1, 10.2
	■ know and use the vocabulary of prime numbers, prime factors and composite (non-prime) numbers	Year 5, Units 10.5, 10.6
	■ establish whether a number up to 100 is prime and recall prime numbers up to 19	Year 5, Units 10.5, 10.6
	■ recognise and use square numbers and cube numbers, and the notation for squared (^{2}) and cubed (^{3})	Year 5, Unit 10.3
	■ solve problems involving multiplication and division including using their knowledge of factors and multiples, squares and cubes.	Year 5, Units 10.2, 10.2, 10.3

Chapter 10 Factors, multiples and prime numbers

Unit 10.1
Meaning of integers and divisibility

Conceptual context

In this unit, pupils will develop their knowledge about different kinds of numbers, focusing on natural numbers, whole numbers and integers. Pupils will be introduced to the meaning of divisibility and therefore will need to recall known multiplication and division facts; applying knowledge of factors, multiples and prime numbers.

Using precise and accurate vocabulary, pupils will be required to explain and justify their reasoning throughout this unit.

Learning pupils will have achieved at the end of the unit

- Pupils will be able to define and identify whole numbers, natural numbers and integers (Q1)
- Pupils will be able to make generalisations about whole numbers, natural numbers and integers (Q2)
- Pupils will understand that divisibility is contingent on a multiplicative relationship between numbers (Q2)
- An understanding of divisibility will have been developed using appropriate mathematical language (Q3)
- Pupils will be able to classify numbers as natural numbers, integers and positive integers (Q4)
- Pupils will understand the relationship between the dividend and divisor and will be able to evaluate whether the quotient has a remainder (Q5, Q6)
- Pupils will understand that expressions where the dividend is divisible by the divisor, have non-zero remainders (Q5, Q6)

Resources

mini whiteboards; interlocking cubes; large number cards from −10 to 10; counters; sorting hoops; scissors; **Resource 5.10.1a** Sorting numbers; **Resource 10.1.1b** Divisibility; **Resource 5.10.1c** True or false?; **Resource 5.10.1d** Sort the numbers; **Resource 5.10.1e** Divisible?

Vocabulary

whole number, natural number, integer, positive integer, factor, multiple, product, divide, division, divisible by, dividend, divisor, quotient, expression

Chapter 10 Factors, multiples and prime numbers

Unit 10.1 Practice Book 5B, pages 121–123

Question 1

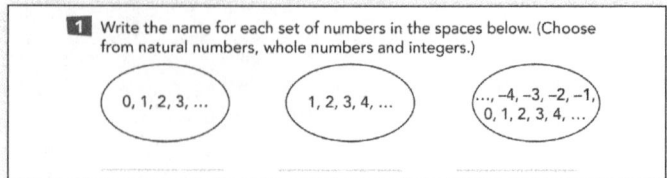

What learning will pupils have achieved at the conclusion of Question 1?

- Pupils will be able to define and identify whole numbers, natural numbers and integers.

Activities for whole-class instruction

- Explain that there are different types of numbers. All numbers without a fractional part are called integers. Ask pupils to give you an example. They should answer in full sentences.

 _____ is an integer because it does not have a fractional part.

- Repeat several times for different integers.
- Show pupils the following diagrams. Ask: *What is the same? What is different?*

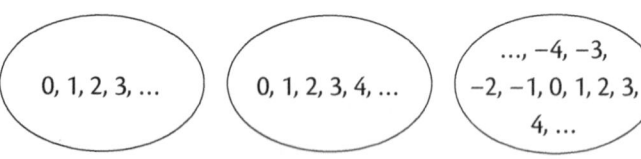

- Pupils should notice that the second set of numbers does not contain 0 and that the third set of numbers also includes negative numbers.
- Now draw the following diagram on the board. Allow pupils time to talk about the diagram. Do they see that the two inner ovals are both subsets of the outer oval, and that the innermost oval is a subset of the 'middle' one?

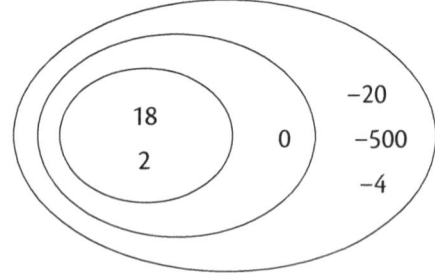

- Write the following titles:

Natural numbers	Whole numbers	Integers

- Pupil pairs should discuss how to label the diagram. Can they see which oval(s) is the set of integers? (all of them)
- Explain that natural numbers are those numbers they learned when they first started to count. They include whole numbers without the 0.

 *Natural numbers are whole numbers, not including zero.*

- Ask pupils if they can write a definition for whole numbers on their whiteboards. Agree that whole numbers are all numbers without a fractional part, including a zero.

 *Whole numbers are numbers without a fractional part, including a zero.*

- Pupils should complete Question 1 in the Practice Book.

Same-day intervention

- Use a set of large number cards from –10 to 10, and three sorting hoops on the floor. Pupils should, with support, sort the numbers into the correct set.

- Throughout this activity, it is important that when pupils are making decisions about which number(s) belong within each hoop, they are using the language from the whole-class instruction.

Chapter 10 Factors, multiples and prime numbers

Unit 10.1 Practice Book 5B, pages 121–123

Same-day enrichment

- Give pupils a copy of **Resource 5.10.1a** Sorting numbers. They should think of numbers for each set and then write a definition underneath.

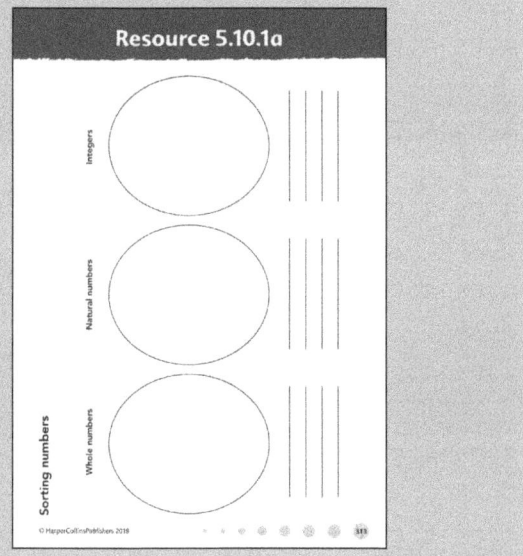

Question 2

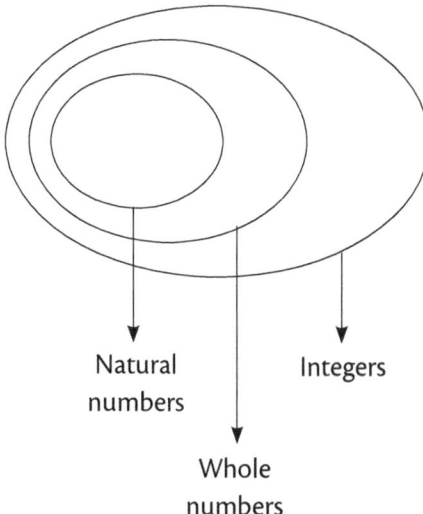

2. Multiple choice questions. (For each question, choose the correct answer and write the letter in the box.)
   (a) Of the following statements, the incorrect one is ☐.
     A. There is no smallest integer.
     B. The smallest natural number is 1.
     C. The greatest negative integer is −1.
     D. All integers can be classified into two categories: positive integers or negative integers.
   (b) In the following pairs of numbers, the pair in which the first number is divisible by the second number is ☐.
     A. 4 and 10   B. 13 and 39   C. 16 and 4   D. 5 and 2
   (c) If 10 is divisible by a, then a has ☐ possible values.
     A. 2   B. 3   C. 4   D. infinitely many

What learning will pupils have achieved at the conclusion of Question 2?

- Pupils will be able to make generalisations about whole numbers, natural numbers and integers.
- Pupils will understand that divisibility is contingent on a multiplicative relationship between numbers.

Activities for whole-class instruction

- Ask pupils to draw this Venn diagram:

(Natural numbers, Whole numbers, Integers)

- Write the following numbers on the board. Ask pupils to enter the numbers on their Venn diagram.

  7   24   −6   1   0   327   5000   −34   −19   44

- Ask: *Where would you put 15.5?* Pupils should discuss that the decimal part (0.5) is less than one and is therefore a fraction. Can they tell you what the equivalent fraction would be? Agree that this number contains a fractional part and therefore does not fit in any of the number types; all three groups contain only whole numbers.

- Pupils should work in pairs. Give them the following numbers.

  1   0   −50   37   −1

- Ask them to write a statement about each number. For example 'The smallest natural number is 1', 'The number 0 is not a natural number. It is a whole number and an integer.'

- Can pupils explain why?

- Display the following statement:

  Any integer is divisible by 1.

- Discuss the word 'divisible'. Can pupils tell you what it means? Use the example of 10 ÷ 5 to discuss. Ask: *Is 10 divisible by 5? How do you know?* Pupils should identify that the quotient is 2. Agree that because the quotient is a whole number, 10 is divisible by 5. Ask: *Is 10 divisible by 6? Why not?*

- Ask: *So, is the statement true or false? Can you explain why?*

   All integers are divisible by 1.

- Ask: *What statement could you make about integers that are divisible by 2 that is always true?* Share ideas.

   All even integers are divisible by 2.

Chapter 10 Factors, multiples and prime numbers

Unit 10.1 Practice Book 5B, pages 121–123

- Ask pupils to complete the following statement:
  24 is divisible by ____
- How many divisors can they think of? Remind pupils to draw upon their knowledge of factors and multiples to help them. Pupils should prove how they know. For example '24 is divisible by 2 because it is an even number' or '24 is divisible by 4 because 4 × 6 = 24.'

Same-day intervention

- Give children the following number cards:
  20 18 31 35 4 21 24 2
- Ask pupils to select a card that:
  - is divisible by 5 (Ask: *How do you know?*)
  - is divisible by 2 (Ask: *How do you know?*)
  - is not divisible by 2
  - is a prime number
  - is divisible by 7.
- Ask pupils to select two cards where the first is divisible by the second. Can they find another 2?

Same-day enrichment

- Pupils should complete **Resource 5.10.1b** Divisibility. If pupils finish early, ask them to create their own divisibility Venn diagram for a partner to complete.

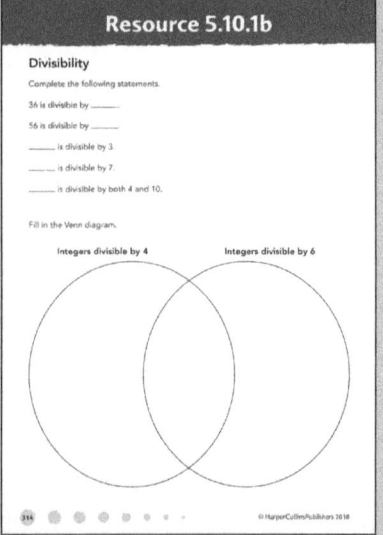

Answers:
36 is divisible by 2, 3, 4, 6, 9, 12, 18
56 is divisible by 2, 4, 7, 8, 14, 28
6 (or 9, 12, 15, …) is divisible by 3
14 (or 21, 28, 35, …) is divisible by 7
20 (or 40, 60, 80, …) is divisible by both 4 and 10
Integers divisible by 4: 4, 8, 12, 16, 20, 24, …
Integers divisible by 6: 6, 12, 18, 24, 30, 36, …
Integers divisible by both 4 and 6: 12, 24, 36, …

Question 3

> 3 Fill in the spaces to make each statement correct.
>
> (a) _____ integers are called natural numbers, and all the natural numbers are whole numbers.
>
> (b) To complete this statement, choose from the words 'dividend', 'divisor', 'integer' and 'zero'.
>
>   When we talk about divisibility, it meets the conditions: _____ and _____ are all integers; and when a _____ is divided by a _____, the quotient is an _____ and the remainder is _____.
>
> (c) 5 is divisible by the numbers _____.
>
> (d) If a is divisible by 2, then the smallest number a can be is _____.
>
> (e) If a is divisible by 3 and 12 is divisible by a, then a = _____.

Chapter 10 Factors, multiples and prime numbers

Unit 10.1 Practice Book 5B, pages 121–123

What learning will pupils have achieved at the conclusion of Question 3?

- An understanding of divisibility will have been developed using appropriate mathematical language.

Activities for whole-class instruction

- Display the following diagram.

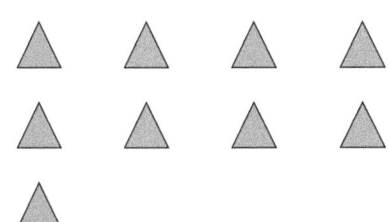

- Ask: *Is 9 divisible by 4?* Agree that it is not, but can pupils explain why?

 *We say that a dividend is divisible by a number only when the quotient is an integer.*

- Can pupils see that the incomplete row represents part of the divisor, not another whole?
- Ask: *Can you think of a number that is divisible by 4?* (4, 8, 12, 16, …)
- Work through each of the questions below with pupils working in pairs, using counters.

10 is divisible by the numbers _____.
Pupils should take 10 counters. Can they explore how many ways they can divide 10 without any counters left over?
For example: 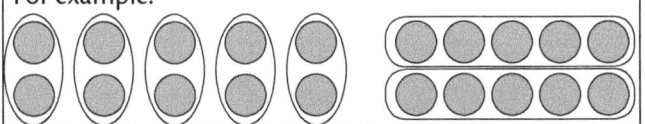

If a number ('N') is divisible by 3 then the smallest number that N can be is _____.
Pupils should create three groups. Ask them to use counters to represent the dividend. There must be an even number in each group. What is the smallest number that the dividend can be? (N)

If a number ('N') is divisible by 3 then the smallest number that N can be is _____. All other possible values of N must be multiples of __.
Instruct pupils to continue to use their counters to make three even groups. What do they notice about the numbers that are divisible by 3? Record them on the board: 3, 6, 9, 12, … Pupils should recognise that the rows are complete when the quotient is a whole number, so a dividend is only divisible by a number when that number of complete rows are visible in the array.

A number 'A' is divisible by 5. Also, 30 is divisible by A. So, A must be _____.
Ask pupils to list all the possible values of A first of all. For example: 5 is divisible by 5; 10 is divisible by 5; 15 is divisible by 5; 20 is divisible by 5, and so on. Guide pupils to generalise that all multiples of the divisor are divisible by it.
Ask: *Is 30 divisible by any of these values? Which ones?* (10 is the only possible answer.)

- Share answers together as a class. Pupils should answer in full sentences and explain their reasoning.

Same-day intervention

- Ask: *What numbers is the integer 36 divisible by?* Ask pupils to find the answer by using counters to make arrays. Ask: *What are the factors of 36?*
- Share pupils' answers and then write 36 ÷ 4 = 9 on the board.
- Ask pupils to write the division sentence on their whiteboards and label each number with:
  - dividend
  - divisor
  - quotient.
- Their answer should look like this:

  36 ÷ 4 = 9
  dividend   divisor   quotient

- Ask: *Which of these numbers are integers?* Agree that they are all integers. Ask: *In each of your division sentences, what was the remainder? Will the remainder always be 0 if the dividend is divisible by the divisor?*

 *We say that a dividend is divisible by a number only when the quotient is an integer.*

Chapter 10 Factors, multiples and prime numbers

Unit 10.1 Practice Book 5B, pages 121–123

Same-day enrichment

- Give pupils **Resource 5.10.1c** True or false? They should decide whether each statement is true or false.

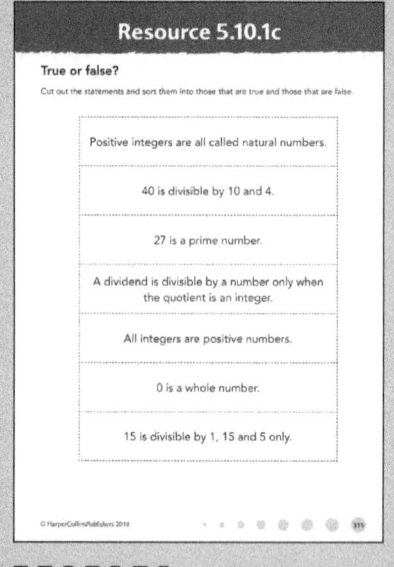

Answers: T; T; F; T; F; T; F

Question 4

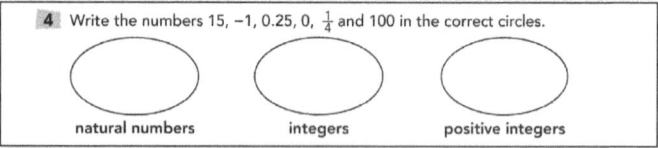

What learning will pupils have achieved at the conclusion of Question 4?

- Pupils will be able to classify numbers as natural numbers, integers and positive integers.

Activities for whole-class instruction

- Ask pupils to remind you what natural numbers are.

   *Natural numbers are whole numbers, not including zero.*

- Ask: *Can you give me an example? And another …? And another …?*

- Ask pupils to remind you what an integer is.

   *An integer is a number without a fractional part.*

- Ask: *Can you give me an example? And another …? And another …?*

- Ask pupils what they think 'positive integers' may be. Agree that positive integers are any numbers that are 0 or greater that do not have a fractional part. Ask: What are negative integers?

- Tell pupils that 'Jenny thinks 0.5 is a positive integer because it is greater than zero.' Pupils should discuss with a partner whether they agree or disagree. They should structure their responses in the following way:

  I agree because _____

  or

  I disagree because _____

- Agree that although 0.5 is greater than 0, it is not a whole number and therefore, it could not be an integer at all whether positive or not.

- Pupils should complete Question 4 in the Practice Book.

Same-day intervention

- Show pupils the following sets of numbers and ask them to copy them in their notebooks.

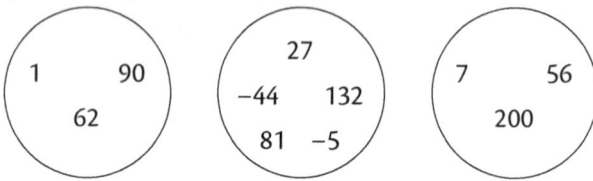

- Can they label each set as either:
  - Natural numbers
  - Integers
  - Positive integers?

- Pupils should explain how they know and write a statement under each one. For example 'Natural numbers because there is not a zero.'

Chapter 10 Factors, multiples and prime numbers

Unit 10.1 Practice Book 5B, pages 121–123

Same-day enrichment

- Give pupils **Resource 5.10.1d** Sort the numbers. They sort a list of numbers and then add five more to each set.

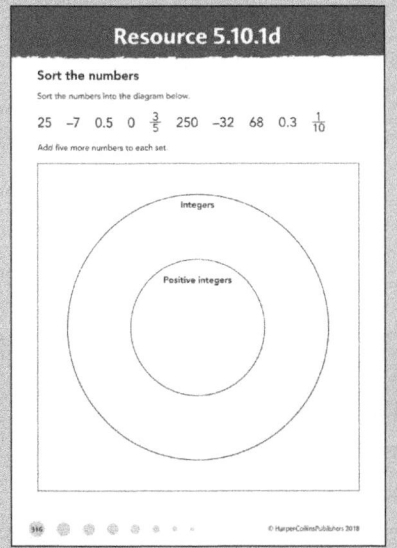

Answers: Positive integers: 25, 250, 68; Integers: –7, 0, –32

Questions 5 and 6

5. Write the numbers of the expressions in the spaces.

   ① 64 ÷ 8   ② 8 ÷ 16   ③ 17 ÷ 3   ④ 5 ÷ 2   ⑤ 7 ÷ 7   ⑥ 17 ÷ 6

   The divisions where the dividends are divisible by the divisors are _____.

   The divisions with non-zero remainders are _____.

6. Using the ten numbers 2, 3, 5, 6, 8, 9, 10, 12, 15 and 20, write all the expressions of division showing divisibility of two numbers. (Hint: for example 6 ÷ 2 = 3.)

What learning will pupils have achieved at the conclusion of Questions 5 and 6?

- Pupils will understand the relationship between the dividend and divisor and will be able to evaluate whether the quotient has a remainder.
- Pupils will understand that expressions where the dividend is divisible by the divisor, have non-zero remainders.

Activities for whole-class instruction

- Give each pupil a pile of counters. Write 36 ÷ 4 on the board. Ask: *Is 36 divisible by 4? Can you prove it by using your counters?*

   *The dividend is divisible by the divisor because the quotient is a whole number; the remainder is zero.*

- Write 28 ÷ 9 on the board. Ask: *Is 28 divisible by 9? Can you prove it by using your counters? What is the remainder?*

   *The dividend is not divisible by the divisor because there is a non-zero remainder.*

- Write the following numbers on the board.

  12   24   2   6   4

- Ask pupils to work in pairs to write an expression of division showing divisibility of two of the numbers. Can they think of another?

   *The dividends are always divisible by the divisor.*

- ⓘ An 'expression' is when numbers, symbols and operations are connected to communicate relationships. Later, pupils will learn that when the numbers are replaced by letters this is called an 'algebraic expression'.

- Pupils should complete Questions 5 and 6 in the Practice Book.

Chapter 10 Factors, multiples and prime numbers

Unit 10.1 Practice Book 5B, pages 121–123

Same-day intervention

- Pupils should complete **Resource 5.10.1e** Divisible? using equipment such as counters or interlocking cubes to prove or disprove that the dividends are divisible by the divisor.

Answers: Dividend divisible by divisor: 32 ÷ 8; 21 ÷ 3; 20 ÷ 20; Dividend not divisible by divisor: 10 ÷ 3; 4 ÷ 24; 38 ÷ 4; 11 ÷ 5.

Same-day enrichment

- Give pupils **Resource 5.10.1e** Divisible? They should identify the calculations where the dividend is divisible by the divisor (without using manipulatives). Can they add some more of their own?

Challenge and extension question

Question 7

7 If two integers a and b ($a > b$) are both divisible by integer c, are their sum, difference and product also divisible by c? Give your reason.

Pupils should first write a division sentence where the dividend is divisible by the divisor. If pupils need some support to get started, then give them the division sentence $12 ÷ 3 = 4$.

Pupils should then explore each statement:
- The sum of a and b is divisible by c.
- The product of a and b is divisible by c.
- The difference of a and b is divisible by c.

They should use their knowledge of multiplication and division to justify their reason.

Chapter 10 Factors, multiples and prime numbers

Unit 10.2
Factors and multiples

Conceptual context

Pupils have previously encountered factors and multiples. In this unit, that knowledge is reviewed and formalised as pupils consider generalisations about factors and multiples. Pupils' use of appropriate language to describe relationships will become more fluent.

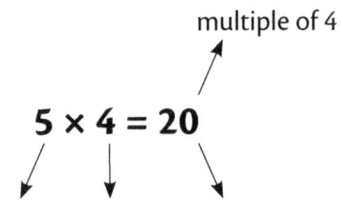

Learning pupils will have achieved at the end of the unit

- Pupils will be able to confidently identify factors and multiples (Q1)
- Pupils will be able to apply their knowledge of multiplication facts to identify multiples (Q2, Q3)
- Pupils will be able to apply their knowledge of divisibility to identify factors (Q2, Q3)
- Pupils will be able to apply their knowledge of divisibility to identify prime numbers (Q4)
- Pupils will be able to apply their knowledge of factors to find several possibilities to a problem (Q5)

Resources

mini whiteboards; interlocking cubes; number cards; counters; sorting hoops; sticky notes; counting stick; squared paper; **Resource 5.10.2a** Always, sometimes, never; **Resource 5.10.2b** Factors and multiples

Vocabulary

whole number, integer, positive integer, factor, multiple, product, divide, division, divisible by, dividend, divisor, quotient, prime number

Chapter 10 Factors, multiples and prime numbers

Unit 10.2 Practice Book 5B, pages 124–125

Question 1

> **1** Multiple choice questions. (For each question, choose the correct answer and write the letter in the box.)
>
> (a) There are ☐ square numbers from 1 to 20, both inclusive.
>   A. 1   B. 2   C. 3   D. 4
>
> (b) There are ☐ cube numbers from 1 to 20, both inclusive.
>   A. 1   B. 2   C. 3   D. 4
>
> (c) In all the factors of 100, ☐ of them are square numbers.
>   A. 1   B. 2   C. 3   D. 4
>
> (d) In all the factors of 128, ☐ of them are cube numbers.
>   A. None   B. 1   C. 2   D. 3
>
> (e) If the side length of a square is an integer, then ☐ of the square is a square number.
>   A. the side length   B. the diagonal   C. the perimeter   D. the area

What learning will pupils have achieved at the conclusion of Question 1?

- Pupils will be able to confidently identify factors and multiples.

Activities for whole-class instruction

- As a starter activity, using a counting stick, count forwards and backwards with the class in multiples of 3.
- Using a sticky note, ask a pupil to place the number 27 on the counting stick.

   *Twenty-seven is a multiple of 3.*

- Ask: *Are there only 10 multiples of 3?* Agree that there are more.

   *There are an infinite number of multiples of any integer.*

- Ask pupils for another multiple of 3 that would not be on the counting stick. Share ideas. Ask: *Is 41 a multiple of 3? Convince me.*

   *Forty-three is not a multiple of 3 because, when divided by 3, it has a non-zero remainder.*

- Repeat for multiples of 6 and 8.
- Draw the following arrays on the board. Ask pupils to speak to a partner about what each array represents. Can pupils use the mathematical language 'commutative'? Record the expressions below each array.

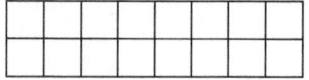

1 × 16 or 16 × 1

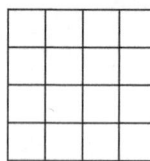

2 × 8 or 8 × 2

4 × 4

- Ask: *What do you notice?* Agree that the product for each multiplication is 16. The integers 1, 16, 2, 8 and 4 are all factors of 16.

   *Factors are whole numbers that are multiplied together to give a product.*

- Ask pupils to draw an array to represent the product 13. Ask: *How many ways can you do it?* Agree that there is only one possible way and therefore, the integers 1 and 13 are the only factors.
- Pupil pairs should write 36 in the middle of their whiteboards. Can they think of all of the factors of 36? How do they know that they have them all? Share ideas.
- Tell pupils that you think 0.5 is also a factor of 36. Do they think this is true or false? Agree that factors are whole numbers and therefore 0.5 is not a factor of 36.
- Pupils should complete Question 1 in the Practice Book.

Same-day intervention

- Play a game of 'Like and Dislike' with the pupils. Tell pupils that there are some numbers that you like and some that you don't like (but do not say which numbers). Can they think of some more numbers that you might like/dislike, and come up with a reason why?
- Record the numbers one at a time on the board, one that you like followed by one that you do not like. Stop at several points and ask the pupils if they think they can come up with another number that you like.

Like	Dislike
10	19
100	34
35	201
25	66
605	49

- Can they work out what the general rule is for the numbers that you like? Agree that they are all multiples of 5. Ask: *What do you notice about the multiples of 5?*
- Pupils should make up their own rule and play with a partner on their whiteboards.

Chapter 10 Factors, multiples and prime numbers

Unit 10.2 Practice Book 5B, pages 124–125

Same-day enrichment

- Give pupils **Resource 5.10.2a** Always, sometimes, never. Pupils should decide whether the statements are 'always', 'sometimes' or 'never' true. They should prove and justify their decisions.

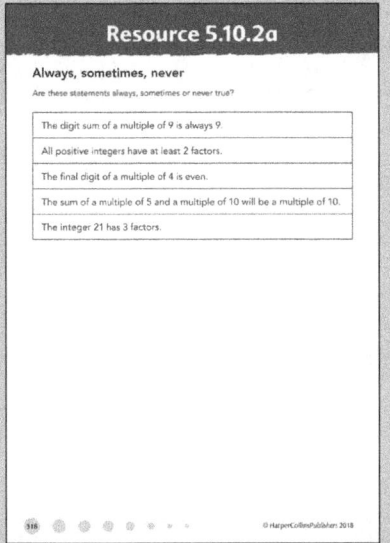

Answers: Always true; Always true; Always true; Sometimes true; Never true

Questions 2 and 3

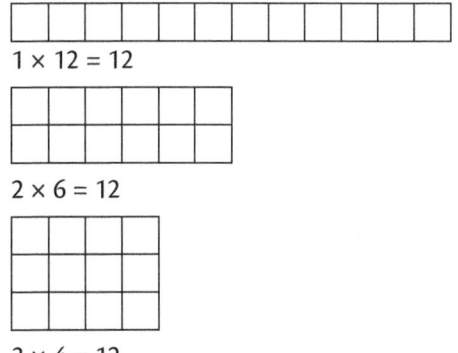

2. Fill in the spaces to make each statement correct.
   (a) If a is a positive integer, then $a \times a$, denoted as a^2, is called a _____.
   (b) If a is a positive integer, then $a \times a \times a$, denoted as a^3, is called a _____.
   (c) From 2 to 101, the smallest square number is ____ and the largest square number is ____.
   (d) From 2 to 101, the smallest cube number is ____ and the largest cube number is ____.
   (e) Within 100, the numbers that are both a square number and a cube number are _____.
   (f) The product of all the cube numbers from 1 to 100 is ____.

3. Find the sum and product of all the square numbers from 20 to 50.

What learning will pupils have achieved at the conclusion of Questions 2 and 3?

- Pupils will be able to apply their knowledge of multiplication facts to identify multiples.
- Pupils will be able to apply their knowledge of divisibility to identify factors.

Activities for whole-class instruction

- Write $5 \times 6 = 30$ on the board. Ask pupils to discuss which number(s) they would label as a factor and which they would label as a multiple. Share reasons as a class and then agree that 5 and 6 are both factors of 30 and 30 is a multiple of both 5 and 6.

- Using cubes or counters, ask pupils to represent all of the factors of 12 as arrays:

$1 \times 12 = 12$

$2 \times 6 = 12$

$3 \times 4 = 12$

- Pupils should now use cubes or counters to represent all of the multiples of 12:

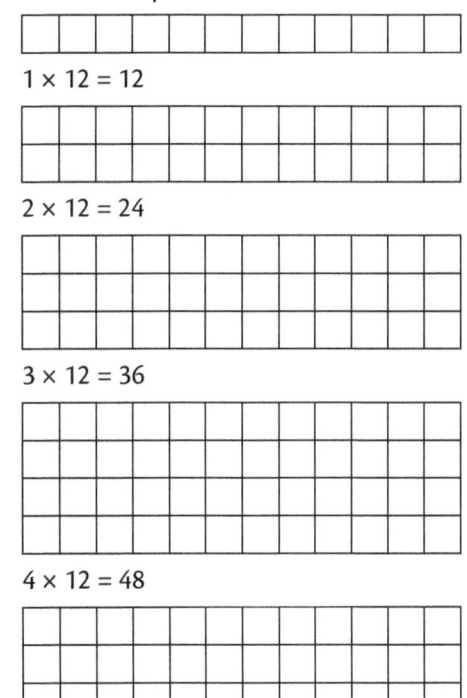

$1 \times 12 = 12$

$2 \times 12 = 24$

$3 \times 12 = 36$

$4 \times 12 = 48$

$5 \times 12 = 60$

- Ask: *What's the same and what is different about a factor and a multiple?*

- Write 15 on the board. Ask: *What is the greatest factor of 15? What is the smallest factor of 15?*

Chapter 10 Factors, multiples and prime numbers

Unit 10.2 Practice Book 5B, pages 124–125

- Write 48 on the board. Ask: *What is the greatest factor of 48? What is the smallest factor of 48?*
- Pupils should notice that the greatest factor will always be the integer itself and the smallest factor will always be 1 which is the smallest whole number.
- Pupils should complete Questions 2 and 3 in the Practice Book.

Answers:

Factors	Integer	Multiples
1	1	1, 2, 3, 4, 5, 6, 7, 8, 9, 10
1, 2	2	2, 4, 6, 8, 10, 12, 14, 16, 18, 20
1, 3	3	3, 6, 9, 12, 15, 18, 21, 24, 27, 30
1, 2, 4	4	4, 8, 12, 16, 20, 24, 28, 32, 36, 40
1, 5	5	5, 10, 15, 20, 25, 30, 35, 40, 45, 50
1, 2, 3, 6	6	6, 12, 18, 24, 30, 36, 42, 48, 54, 60
1, 7	7	7, 14, 21, 28, 35, 42, 49, 56, 63, 70
1, 2, 4, 8	8	8, 16, 24, 32, 40, 48, 56, 64, 72, 80
1, 3, 9	9	9, 18, 27, 36, 45, 54, 63, 72, 81, 90
1, 2, 5, 10	10	10, 20, 30, 40, 50, 60, 70, 80, 90, 100
1, 11	11	11, 22, 33, 44, 55, 66, 77, 88, 99, 110
1, 2, 3, 4, 6, 12	12	12, 24, 36, 48, 60, 72, 84, 96, 108, 120
1, 13	13	13, 26, 39, 52, 65, 78, 91, 104, 117, 130
1, 2, 7, 14	14	14, 28, 42, 56, 70, 84, 98, 112, 126, 140
1, 3, 5, 15	15	15, 30, 45, 60, 75, 90, 105, 120, 135, 150

Same-day intervention

- Display the following the Venn diagram:

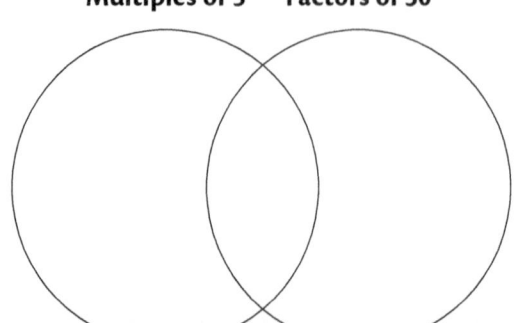

- Ask individual pupils to come up and fill in the diagram. In total, they should enter at least 12 multiples of 5 and all factors of 30.

Same-day enrichment

- Give pupils **Resource 5.10.2b** Factors and multiples. Can they find all the factors and the first 10 multiples?

Questions 4 and 5

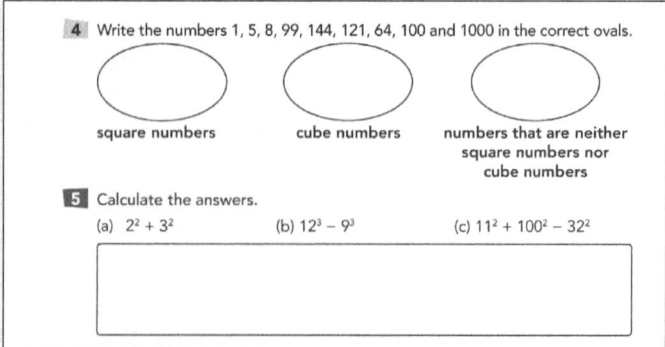

4 Write the numbers 1, 5, 8, 99, 144, 121, 64, 100 and 1000 in the correct ovals.

square numbers cube numbers numbers that are neither square numbers nor cube numbers

5 Calculate the answers.
(a) $2^2 + 3^2$
(b) $12^3 - 9^3$
(c) $11^2 + 100^2 - 32^2$

What learning will pupils have achieved at the conclusion of Questions 2 and 3?

- Pupils will be able to apply their knowledge of divisibility to identify prime numbers.
- Pupils will be able to apply their knowledge of factors to find several possibilities to a problem.

Chapter 10 Factors, multiples and prime numbers

Unit 10.2 Practice Book 5B, pages 124–125

Activities for whole-class instruction

- Give pupils 18 cubes or counters each. Ask them to use the counters to make an array.
- Ask: *How many different ways can you do it?* Pupils should use the array to find the factors of 18 and record these on their whiteboard. Ask: *What shape do all of the arrays make?* Share all of the factors of 18 as a class.
- Repeat with 30 cubes or counters.
- Pupils should sit in a circle on the floor (if there is a second adult create two circles). Place hoops with the labels 'With one factor', 'With 2 factors' and 'With more than 2 factors'.
- Give pairs of pupils the following numbers: 1, 2, 15, 19, 29, 30, 41, 55, 67, 72, 79, 83, 88, 89. Can they place their number into the correct hoop?

- Ask: *Why is there only one number with 1 factor? What do you notice about all of the numbers with only 2 factors? What are the two factors for each integer?* Can pupils think of any other numbers with only 2 factors?

Same-day intervention

- Give pupils 9 cubes or counters. Can they find all of the factors of 9?
- Give pupils 32 cubes or counters. Can they find all of the factors of 32?
- Find the factors of 48 by using known facts. Start by being systematic:

  1 × 48

  2 × 24 ...
- Tell pupils that if you know that 2 × 24 = 48 then can you calculate what number multiplied by 4 makes 48?

Same-day enrichment

- Give pupils the following problem and some squared paper.

  Brian is laying a rectangular patio for his daughter. She has 42 square slabs. How many different ways can Brian lay the slabs?
- Repeat for 56 square slabs.

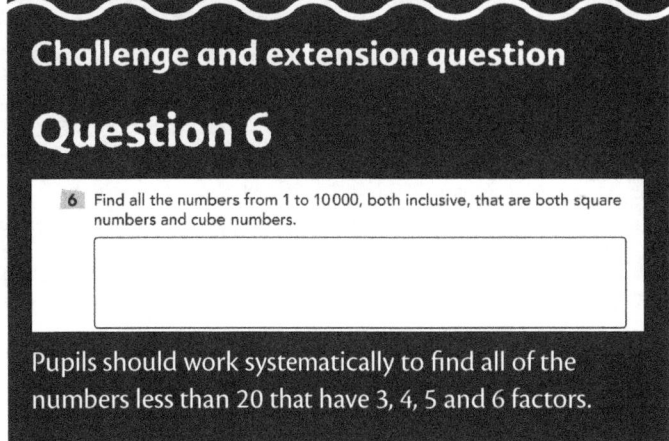

Challenge and extension question

Question 6

6 Find all the numbers from 1 to 10 000, both inclusive, that are both square numbers and cube numbers.

Pupils should work systematically to find all of the numbers less than 20 that have 3, 4, 5 and 6 factors.

Chapter 10 Factors, multiples and prime numbers

Unit 10.3
Square numbers and cube numbers

Conceptual context

Pupils are able to recall and use multiplication facts fluently. From the previous units in this Chapter, pupils will have developed a secure understanding of factors and multiples. In this unit, pupils will be introduced to square and cube numbers. They will be expected to recognise square numbers and the first few cube numbers, but are not expected to find square or cube roots at this stage.

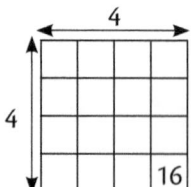

Pupils will be introduced to the notation of square ($a \times a$) and cube ($a \times a \times a$) numbers as a^2 and a^3.

Learning pupils will have achieved at the end of the unit

- Pupils will be able to use their multiplication knowledge to recognise and calculate square and cube numbers (Q1, Q4)
- Pupils will developed a conceptual understanding of square and cube numbers through using manipulatives and images (Q1)
- Pupils will understand the notation of a^2 and a^3 (Q2, Q3)
- Pupils will be able to recognise and use square and cube numbers (Q2, Q3)
- Pupils will be able to apply reasoning skills and knowledge of square and cube numbers to sort a set of numbers (Q4)
- Pupils will have practised calculating with values expressed as square and cube numbers in number sentences (Q5)

Resources

mini whiteboards; interlocking cubes; squared paper; counters; bars of chocolate or non-edible alternatives; red and blue coloured pencils; 10-sided dice; **Resource 5.10.3a** 100 square; **Resource 5.10.3b** Square and cube numbers; **Resource 5.10.3c** The sum of consecutive odd numbers

Vocabulary

factor, integer, multiply, produce, square number, cube number

Chapter 10 Factors, multiples and prime numbers

Unit 10.3 Practice Book 5B, pages 126–127

Question 1

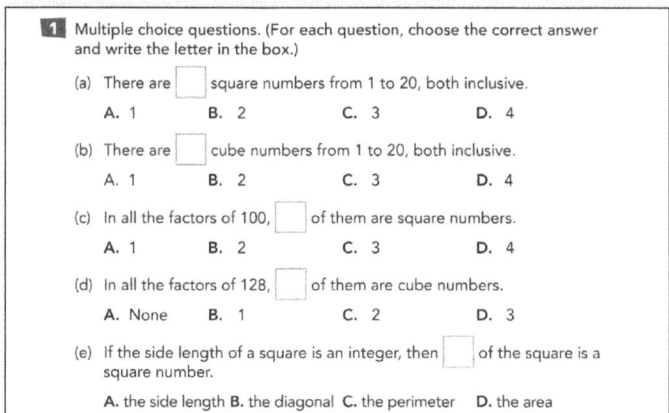

What learning will pupils have achieved at the conclusion of Question 1?

- Pupils will be able to use their multiplication knowledge to recognise and calculate square and cube numbers.
- Pupils will developed a conceptual understanding of square and cube numbers through using manipulatives and images.

Activities for whole-class instruction

- Show pupils the following bars of chocolate (real or as images). Ask: *Which is the odd one out? Why?* Pupils should record the multiplication sentences to find out what is the same, and what is different.

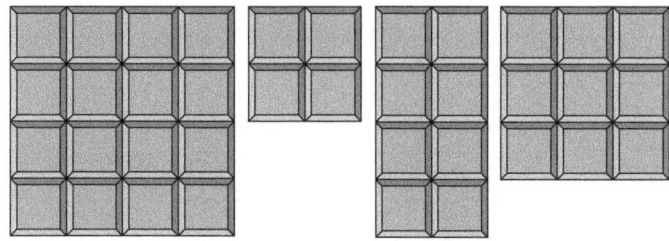

- Agree that the bar of chocolate that represents 2 × 4 or 4 × 2 is the odd one out because it is the only one where the product does not have two factors the same. Explain that the other bars represent square numbers because the factors that are multiplied to make the product are both the same and the arrays make squares.

 *When a number is multiplied by itself, the product is called a square number.*

- Give pupils 20 counters. In pairs, they explore how many square numbers they can make arrays for.

Encourage pupils to approach this systematically. Share ideas and record the multiplication sentences sequentially on the board.

1 × 1 = 1

2 × 2 = 4

3 × 3 = 9

4 × 4 = 16

- Ask: *If a square number is when a value is multiplied by itself, what do you think a cube number is?*
- Consider the dimensions of both a square and a cube to help pupils.

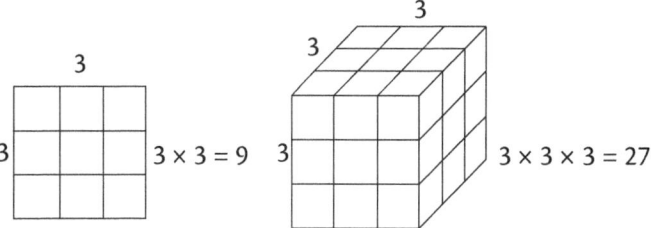

 *When a value is multiplied by itself three times, the product is called a cube number.*

- Give pupils 27 interlocking cubes. Can they make a model to represent a cube number and record the multiplication sentence? Ask: *What is the smallest cube number you can make? What is the largest cube number you can make?*
- Ask: *How many more cubes would you need to make the next cube number? How do you know? Convince me.*
- Pupils should complete Question 1 in the Practice Book.

Same-day intervention

- Give pupils a sheet of squared paper. Ask them to draw a 1 × 1 square, a 2 × 2 square, a 3 × 3 square, … a 10 × 10 square on their paper. Can they then calculate what square numbers they represent and record the multiplication sentence beneath each square?

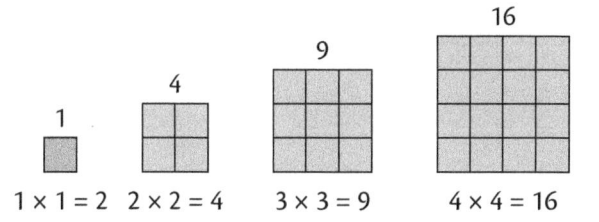

1 × 1 = 2   2 × 2 = 4   3 × 3 = 9   4 × 4 = 16

207

Chapter 10 Factors, multiples and prime numbers

Unit 10.3 Practice Book 5B, pages 126–127

Same-day enrichment

- Pupils should complete **Resource 5.10.3a** 100 square. Can they identify the square and cube numbers?

Answers: Red: 1, 4, 9, 16, 25, 36, 49, 64, 81, 100; Blue: 1, 8, 27, 64; Both 1 and 64 are square and cube numbers, because 1 multiplied by itself any number of times is always 1 and 64 is 8 × 8 (square number) and also 4 × 4 × 4 (cube number).

Questions 2 and 3

2 Fill in the spaces to make each statement correct.
  (a) If a is a positive integer, then $a \times a$, denoted as a^2, is called a _____ .
  (b) If a is a positive integer, then $a \times a \times a$, denoted as a^3, is called a _____ .
  (c) From 2 to 101, the smallest square number is ___ and the largest square number is ___ .
  (d) From 2 to 101, the smallest cube number is ___ and the largest cube number is ___ .
  (e) Within 100, the numbers that are both a square number and a cube number are _____ .
  (f) The product of all the cube numbers from 1 to 100 is ___ .

3 Find the sum and product of all the square numbers from 20 to 50.

What learning will pupils have achieved at the conclusion of Questions 2 and 3?

- Pupils will understand the notation of a^2 and a^3.
- Pupils will be able to recognise and use square and cube numbers.

Activities for whole-class instruction

- Write the following expression on the board:
  $a \times a = a^2$
- Ask pupils to talk to a partner. How would they label each part of the expression? Together, label the expression explaining that a^2 is a square number.

a	×	a	=	a^2
Integer		Integer		Square number

- Explain that this can be represented as an array or on a grid showing the area of a square. Ask pupils to draw a square covering 25 squares on squared paper. Can they record the multiplication sentence that their square represents? Which number is the square number? Pupils should tell you that 25 is the square number and that we say $25 = 5^2$.

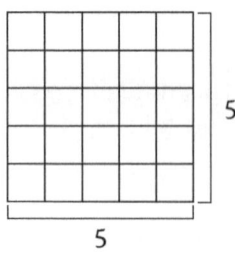

$5 \times 5 = 25$
$5^2 = 25$

- Ask pupils to draw a grid representing 7 squared. Ask: *What is the value of 7 squared?* Together, write the number sentence $7^2 = 49$.
- Give pupils some interlocking cubes. Tell them $a = 2$. Can they represent a^3 using their cubes?
- Pupils should answer Questions 2 and 3 in the Practice Book.

Same-day intervention

- Ask pupils to represent $3 \times 3 = 9$ using cubes. Pupils should copy and complete the following sentence on their whiteboards:

  $3 \times 3 = 9 = \underline{}^2$

- Can they use their cubes to represent and complete the next sentence?

  $4 \times 4 \times 4 = \underline{} = \underline{}^3$

Chapter 10 Factors, multiples and prime numbers

Unit 10.3 Practice Book 5B, pages 126–127

- Give pupils **Resource 5.10.3b** Square and cube numbers. They should fill in the answers and draw the cubes on the isometric paper.

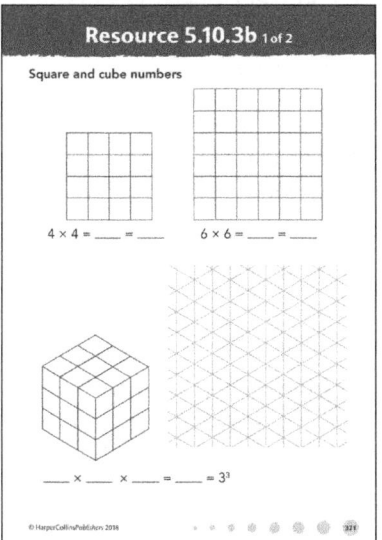

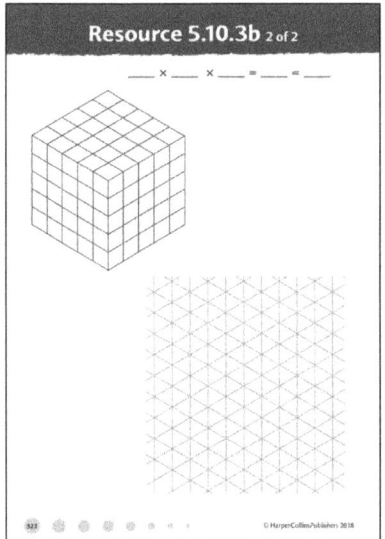

Answers: $4 \times 4 = 16 = 4^2$; $6 \times 6 = 36 = 6^2$; $3 \times 3 \times 3 = 27 = 3^3$; $5 \times 5 \times 5 = 125 = 5^3$

Same-day enrichment

- Pupils should complete **Resource 5.10.3c** The sum of consecutive odd numbers. Pupils investigate the sum of consecutive odd numbers.

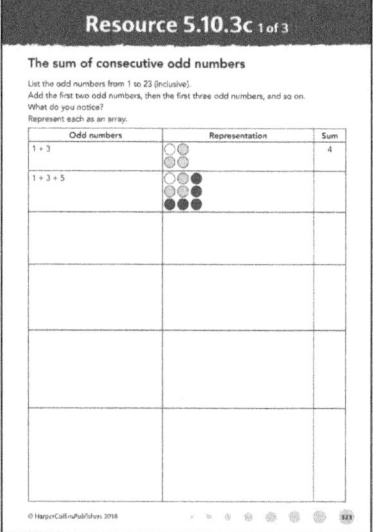

Chapter 10 Factors, multiples and prime numbers

Unit 10.3 Practice Book 5B, pages 126–127

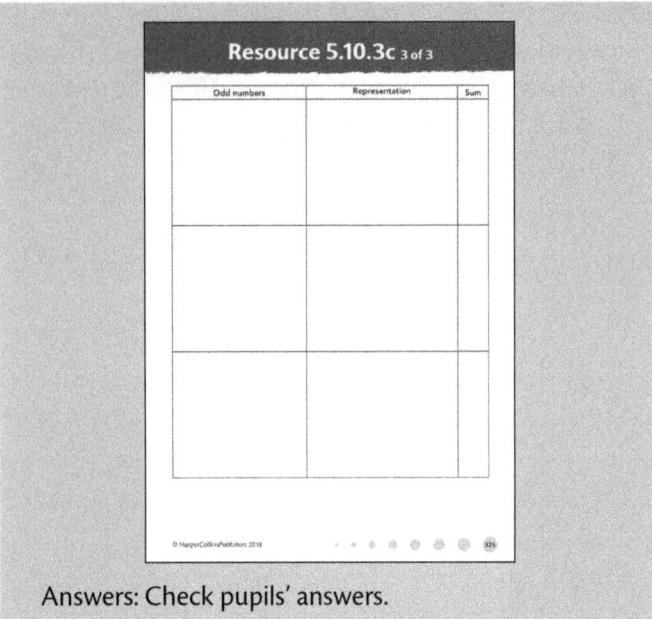

Answers: Check pupils' answers.

Question 4

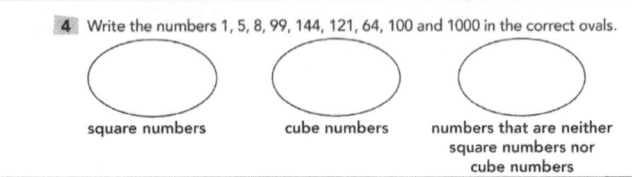

What learning will pupils have achieved at the conclusion of Question 4?

- Pupils will be able to use their multiplication knowledge to recognise and calculate square and cube numbers.
- Pupils will be able to apply reasoning skills and knowledge of square and cube numbers to sort a set of numbers.

Activities for whole-class instruction

- Tell pupils that you think the number 38 is a square number. Do they think this is true or false? Pupils should discuss this in pairs to justify their answer.
- Write the following numbers on the board. Ask pupils to discuss whether they are square numbers and/or cube numbers.

  4   125   100   27   216   81

  (i) Pupils will not need to calculate the square or cube root of these numbers to determine whether they are square or cube numbers. Secure knowledge of multiplication tables should enable pupils to recall

knowledge from the previous questions in the units and allow them to recognise those that are square, cube numbers or neither.

- Pupils should complete Question 4 in the Practice Book.

Same-day intervention

- Support pupils as they work through Question 4. Refer back to the 100 square (**Resource 5.10.3a**) completed previously, identifying square and cube numbers. Can they locate the numbers 1, 5, 8, 99, 64 and 100 on the 100 square to help them sort the numbers into the right set? It might also be appropriate for pupils to represent these numbers using cubes.
- Discuss the numbers 144, 121 and 1000. What do they know about these numbers? Ask: *Are any of these square or cube numbers?*
- Pupils should now test their prediction.
  - Calculate 11 × 11.
  - Calculate 12 × 12.
  - If 8 × 8 × 8 = 64, what does 9 × 9 × 9 make? What about 10 × 10 × 10?

Same-day enrichment

- Ask pupils to draw a Venn diagram template like the one below on their whiteboards. They should label one set 'square numbers' and the other set 'cube numbers'. They then complete the diagram by calculating all of the square and cube numbers up to 100.

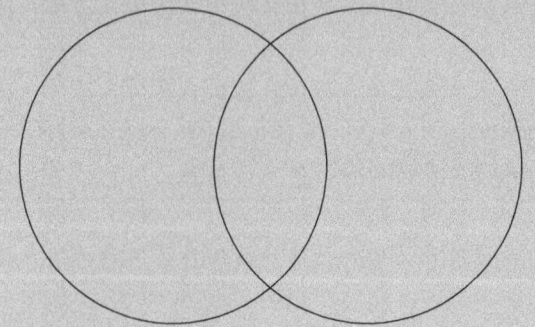

- Agree that the number 64 is both a square and cube number.

Question 5

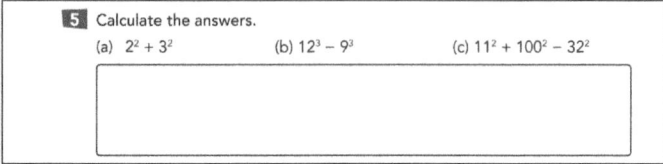

Chapter 10 Factors, multiples and prime numbers

Unit 10.3 Practice Book 5B, pages 126–127

What learning will pupils have achieved at the conclusion of Question 5?

- Pupils will have practised calculating with values expressed as square and cube numbers in number sentences.

Activities for whole-class instruction

- Write $2^2 + 4^2$ on the board. Ask: *Is this the same as calculating 6^2?* Give pupils time to discuss this and work out the answer. Share responses and agree that it is not the same.
- Display the following:

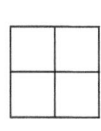 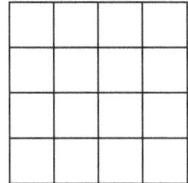

- Explain that we could also write this as $2 \times 2 + 4 \times 4$.
- Write:

  $5^2 + 2^2 =$ ___

  $8^2 - 2^2 =$ ___

- Pupils should work with a partner to calculate the answers. Share strategies as a class.
- Display the following diagram:

  Sam thinks:

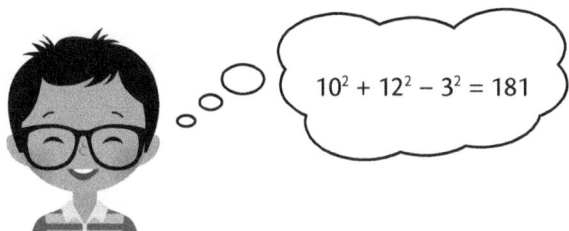

$10^2 + 12^2 - 3^2 = 181$

- Ask: *Is Sam correct or incorrect?* Agree incorrect. Ask: *Why? What mistake did Sam make?*

Same-day intervention

- Pupils should work in pairs. Each pair should take it in turns to roll two 10-sided dice. They should square each rolled number and then make a decision whether to add the square numbers or subtract them to get closest to the target number of 40. The pupil closest to the target number wins. For example:

  If Pupil A rolled a 5 and a 2, they would calculate:

  $5^2 = 25$

  $2^2 = 4$

  $5^2 + 2^2 = 29$

Same-day enrichment

- Give pupils the following problem:

  Is it possible to make all of the square numbers up to 20^2 by adding two prime numbers together?

- Agree that all except two are possible. (It is not possible to make 11^2 or 17^2 by adding two primes.)

Challenge and extension question

Question 6

6 Find all the numbers from 1 to 10 000, both inclusive, that are both square numbers and cube numbers.

Pupils should work systematically to find all possibilities. They will have to use a range of multiplication strategies to help them. Pupils should consider how they organise and record their work.

Chapter 10 Factors, multiples and prime numbers

Unit 10.4
Numbers divisible by 2 and 5

Conceptual context

Pupils can already use multiplication facts to help them recognise, when dividing, whether a number is divisible by the divisor. In this unit, pupils will develop their knowledge further by investigating mathematical structures and understanding divisibility rules.

Learning pupils will have achieved at the end of the unit

- Pupils will be able to recognise whether an integer is divisible by 2, or by 5 (or both) and explain why (Q1, Q2)
- Pupils will understand the mathematical structures connecting consecutive integers and use this knowledge to investigate and explore divisibility (Q3, Q4)
- Pupils will be able to use expressions to solve problems; reasoning about decisions (Q3, Q4)
- Pupils will be able to use multiplication facts for 2, 3 and 5 fluently to investigate divisibility (Q5)
- Pupils will be able to apply divisibility rules to create integers divisible by 2, 3 and 5 (Q5)

Resources

mini whiteboards; interlocking cubes; number cards; squared paper; **Resource 5.10.4a** Divisible by 2 and 5; **Resource 5.10.4b** Divisible by 2, 3 and 5 (1); **Resource 5.10.4c** Divisible by 2, 3 and 5 (2)

Vocabulary

divisible, factor, multiple, multiplication, multiply, consecutive, integer, positive integer

Chapter 10 Factors, multiples and prime numbers

Unit 10.4 Practice Book 5B, pages 128–130

Questions 1 and 2

> **1** Multiple choice questions. (For each question, choose the correct answer and write the letter in the box.)
>
> (a) What number(s) can go in the ■ so that the 3-digit number 23■ is divisible by 2, but not by 5? There are ☐ possible number(s) that can be filled in the ■.
>
>   A. 1   B. 2   C. 3   D. 4
>
> (b) What number(s) can go in the ■ so that the 3-digit number 23■ is divisible by 5, but not by 2? The possible number(s) that can be filled in the ■ is ☐.
>
>   A. 0   B. 5   C. 1   D. 2
>
> (c) Of the following statements, the incorrect one is ☐.
>
>   A. A positive integer is either an odd number or an even number.
>   B. Any odd number plus 1 gives an even number.
>   C. The sum of two odd numbers gives an odd number.
>   D. The greatest factor of a number is the least multiple of the number.
>
> **2** Fill in the spaces to make each statement correct.
>
> (a) If a number is divisible by 2, then the digit in its ones place must be _____.
>
> (b) If a number is divisible by 5, then the digit in its ones place must _____.
>
> (c) In 2-digit numbers, the least odd number is ☐. The least even number is ☐.
>
> (d) The greatest 2-digit number that is divisible by both 2 and 5 is ☐.
>
> (e) After 523 is added to by at least ☐, it is divisible by 2. After it is added to by at least ☐, it is divisible by 3. After it is subtracted from by at least ☐, it is divisible by 5.

What learning will pupils have achieved at the conclusion of Questions 1 and 2?

- Pupils will be able to recognise whether an integer is divisible by 2, or by 5 (or both) and explain why.

Activities for whole-class instruction

- Ask pupil pairs to find a PECULIAR example of a number divisible by 2, an OBVIOUS example of a number division by 2 and then think of a GENERALISATION about numbers that are divisible by 2.

  (i) Peculiar, Obvious and Generalisations (POG) help pupils notice and focus on what is the same about their chosen integers and therefore form a generalisation. An 'obvious' example will be those numbers that pupils instantly think of in relation to divisibility by 2, and the more obscure examples that require more thought and proof form the 'peculiar' examples. Although pupils may choose different peculiar and obvious examples, their generalisation should be based upon the same divisibility rule.

- Share pupils' examples, checking that they are all divisible by 2. (2, 4, 6, 8 …)

- You should expect pupils to offer:
  - 'peculiar' examples that are larger multiples of 2 (100 672, 56 890, and so on)
  - 'ordinary' examples that are the product of multiplying numbers 1–10 by 2
  - 'generalisations' that focus on numbers divisible by 2 being even.

 *If a number is divisible by 2, then the digit in the ones place must be even.*

- Pupils should repeat the activity to find a peculiar, ordinary and generalisation for numbers divisible by 5.

 *If a number is divisible by 5, then the digit in the ones place must be a zero or a five.*

- Show pupils these two sets of numbers. Ask: *What is the same? What is different?*

5 60 25 100 85 305	20 500 30 1000 50 760

- Agree that both sets of numbers are multiples of 5 but that they are different because one set of numbers is odd and the other set of numbers is even. Pupils should notice that the even numbers are divisible by 2, 5 and 10.

- Give pupils digit cards from 0–9 and read out the following instructions:
  - Make the smallest two-digit odd number possible.
  - Make the smallest two-digit even number possible.
  - Make the largest two-digit number possible.
  - Make the smallest two-digit number possible.
  - Make a two-digit number that is divisible by 2.
  - Make a two-digit number that is divisible by 5.
  - Make a two-digit number that is divisible by 2 but not 5.
  - Make a two-digit number that is divisible by 5 but not 2.
  - Make a two-digit number that is divisible by both 2 and 5.
  - Make the largest two-digit number that is divisible by both 2 and 5.
  - Make a three-digit number that is divisible by both 2 and 5.

- Ensure that the pace for questions is fast and, for some, ask: *And another, and another …* Pupils should work in pairs so that they are explaining and justifying their choices to each other. When pupils are sharing their answers, they should answer in full sentences. For example 'Ten is the smallest two-digit number.'

Chapter 10 Factors, multiples and prime numbers

Unit 10.4 Practice Book 5B, pages 128–130

- Pupils should complete Questions 1 and 2 in the Practice Book.

Same-day intervention

- Pupils should complete **Resource 5.10.4a** Divisible by 2 and 5. Pupils will need to identify groups of 2 and 5 from a representation to understand the similarities and difference between numbers that are divisible by 2 and 5. Encourage pupils to use manipulatives and diagrams to support their thinking.

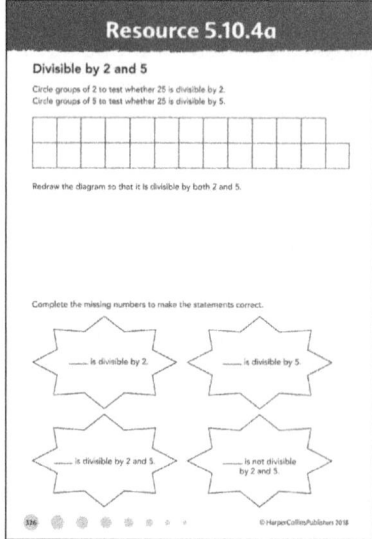

Answers: 4 is divisible by 2, 10 is divisible by 5; 20 is divisible by 2 and 5, 3 is not divisible by 2 or 5. (Other answers are possible.)

Same-day enrichment

- Ask pupils to solve the following problems.
  - Kim and Joey are playing with building blocks. They want half each. There are 638 bricks. Will they each have the same number of blocks? Explain how you know. How many bricks will they each have?
  - 487 Year 7 pupils are travelling to France on a school trip. There are five coaches. The trip leader wants the same number of pupils on each coach. Is this possible? How do you know?
  - At a football camp, there are 130 children. The camp leader wants them split into two equal groups in the morning and then five equal groups in the afternoon. Is this possible?

Questions 3 and 4

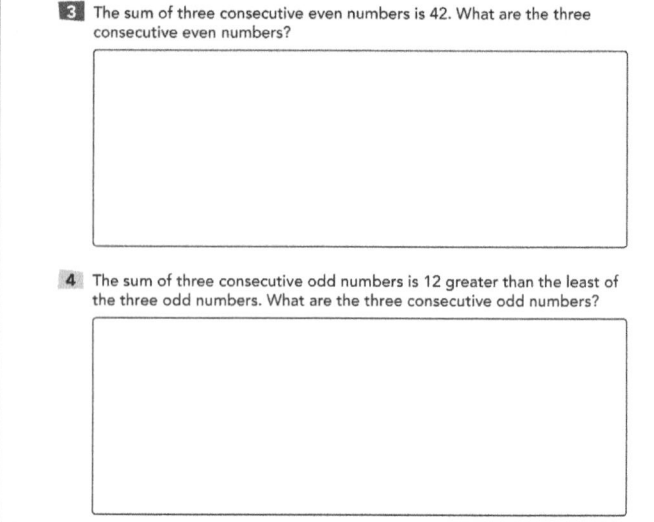

3 The sum of three consecutive even numbers is 42. What are the three consecutive even numbers?

4 The sum of three consecutive odd numbers is 12 greater than the least of the three odd numbers. What are the three consecutive odd numbers?

What learning will pupils have achieved at the conclusion of Questions 3 and 4?

- Pupils will understand the mathematical structures connecting consecutive integers and use this knowledge to investigate and explore divisibility.
- Pupils will be able to use expressions to solve problems, reasoning about decisions.

Activities for whole-class instruction

- Ask pupils to write three consecutive numbers between 0 and 20.
- Use 5, 6 and 7 as an example to explain and make three strips of interlocking cubes.

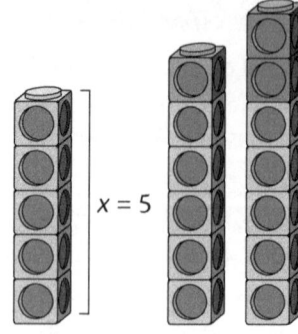

- Say: *Tell me as many number sentences as you can about what you see in these cubes.* Can pupils tell you:
  - $x = 5$ or $5 = x$?
  - there are 3 lots of x here?
  - the second number is the same as x, with one extra cube, so $x + 1$?

Chapter 10 Factors, multiples and prime numbers

Unit 10.4 Practice Book 5B, pages 128–130

- the third number is the same as *x* but with 2 extra cubes, so *x* + 2?
- 3 lots of *x* add 3 extra cubes gives the total of the three numbers?

• Ask pupils to make three consecutive numbers with cubes that represent the numbers if the starting number is 8. Then they should list the three numbers as expressions using *x*. They first need to understand that, this time, *x* = 8. Can they see that they have *x*, *x* + 1 and *x* + 2, or 3*x* + 3?

• Tell pupils that when you add three consecutive numbers, the sum is 33. Ask: *What is my number?* Pupils should discuss and explore using cubes.

• Write *x* + (*x* +1) + (*x* + 2) on the board to help pupils notice that starting by subtracting 3 will help.

• Ask a pupil to come to the front of the class to be the teacher. Can they explain what they did to find the answer?

• Ask pupils to represent 2 + 4 + 6 using their cubes. Ask: *What do you notice about the numbers?* Agree that we are adding three consecutive even numbers. Ask: *What is the sum?*

• When pupils have represented 2, 4 and 6 using cubes. Ask them to represent what is the same about these numbers in the same colour ...

• Explain that here, there is 2 + (2 + 2) + (2 + 4). If 2 = *x*, we could write *x* + (*x* +2) + (*x* + 4).

• Ask pupils to represent three consecutive even numbers using cubes, starting with a number between 5 and 12. When they have made their cube strips, they should line the three of them up and write as many expressions as they can about their cubes. Can they see that:
  - each number is 2 more than the previous number?
  - *x* = the start number?
  - the second number is *x* + 2?
  - the third number is *x* + 4?
  - the total is *x* + *x* + 2 + *x* + 4 which is the same as 3*x* + 6?

• Tell pupils that when you add three consecutive even numbers, the sum is 306. Ask: *What is my number?* Pupils should discuss and explore using cubes.

• Write *x* + (*x* + 2) + (*x* + 4) on the board to help pupils notice that subtracting 6 from 306 is a good starting point.

Same-day intervention

• Pupils should continue exploring adding consecutive even and odd numbers using cubes to understand the structure as modelled in the whole-class instruction.

Same-day enrichment

• Display the following problem:

  Add five consecutive numbers. What do you notice?

• Pupils should investigate, using cubes or by drawing strips on squared paper. They should find that the sum of five consecutive numbers will always be divisible by 5. When pupils have identified this, can they explain why?

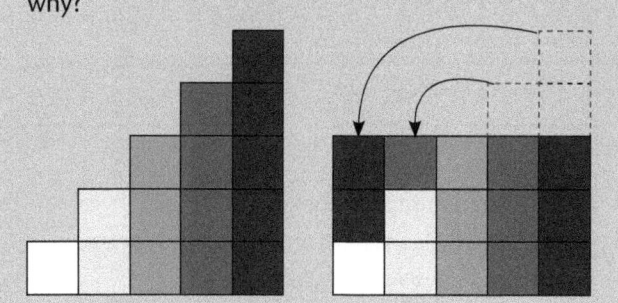

Question 5

> 5 Choose three numbers from 0, 1, 2 and 5 and form a 3-digit number to be divisible by 2, 3 and 5. How many such 3-digit numbers are there? What are they?

What learning will pupils have achieved at the conclusion of Question 5?

• Pupils will be able to use multiplication facts for 2, 3 and 5 fluently to investigate divisibility.

• Pupils will be able to apply divisibility rules to create integers divisible by 2, 3 and 5.

Chapter 10 Factors, multiples and prime numbers

Unit 10.4 Practice Book 5B, pages 128–130

Activities for whole-class instruction

- Ask pupils to prove whether the following statement is always true, sometimes true or never true.

  > The sum of the digits of a number divisible by 3 is also always divisible by 3.

- Agree that this is always true. For example, the number 85 203 is divisible by 3 because the sum of its digits (8 + 5 + 2 + 0 + 3 = 18) is divisible by 3.

   If a number is divisible by 3, the sum of its digits will also be divisible by 3.

- Give pupils the following six numbers.

  27   85   1449   6235   122   9002

- Ask them to sort them into those that:
  - are divisible by 2 only
  - those that are divisible by 5 only
  - those that are divisible by 3 only.
- Pupils should explain how they know.

Same-day intervention

- Pupils should complete **Resource 5.10.4b** Divisible by 2, 3 and 5 (1). They are required to find missing numbers using divisibility rules.

Answers: 0; 0; 2; 0; 1; 1; 1; 1, 2, 0; 3, 3, 0 (Other answers are possible.)

Same-day enrichment

- Pupils should complete **Resource 5.10.4c** Divisible by 2, 3 and 5 (2). They should sort the integers into the Venn diagram, explaining their reasoning.

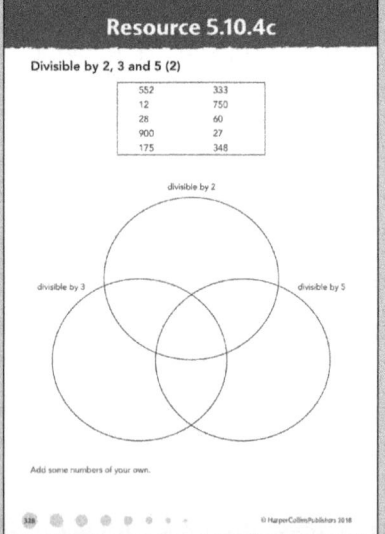

Answers: Divisible by 2: 12, 28, 60, 348, 552, 750, 900. Divisible by 3: 12, 27, 60, 333, 348, 552, 750, 900. Divisible by 5: 60, 175, 750, 900.

Challenge and extension question

Question 6

6. Find the feature of the integers that are divisible by 9. Then answer the following question: Given that A is a positive integer and multiple of 45, and the digits in all the value places are either 0 or 3, what is the least possible number of A?

Pupils should understand that if an integer is divisible by 9 then the sum of its digits will be 9. If 45 is divisible by 9 then a multiple of 45 will also be divisible by 9, therefore meaning that the sum of the digits in the answer must also total 9. It is important that they also recognise the answer should be a positive integer, meaning that the last digit will be a 0.

Chapter 10 Factors, multiples and prime numbers

Unit 10.5
Prime numbers, composite numbers and prime factorisation (1)

Conceptual context

A prime number is a number (greater than 1) that cannot be divided equally by any number except itself and 1.

For example 5 is prime, its only factors are 5 and 1

A composite number is a number that can be divided equally by numbers in addition to itself and 1.

For example 6 is composite.
Its factors are 1, 2, 3 and 6.

(Note: 1 is not composite or prime. A simple way to explain this to pupils is to say that a prime number must have two factors: itself and 1.)

All whole numbers greater than 1 are either composite or prime. The prime numbers up to 100 are **2, 3, 5, 7, 11, 13, 17, 19, 23, 29, 31, 37, 41, 43, 47, 53, 59, 61, 67, 71, 73, 79, 83, 89, 97**.

2 is the only even prime number because every other even number can be divided into equal groups.

A **prime factor** is a factor that is a prime number. Every composite number has a unique set of **prime factors**. Prime numbers are the building blocks of numbers.

For example $90 = 2 \times 3 \times 3 \times 5$. There is no other set of prime numbers that can be multiplied to give 90.

Mathematicians have known about prime numbers for thousands of years. There is no pattern of occurrence and even today, new prime numbers are being discovered. In January 2018, the largest known prime number had 23 249 425 digits. Prime numbers are used in computers for encryption.

Learning pupils will have achieved at the end of the unit

- Pupils will have determined the prime numbers up to 100 (Q1, Q2)
- Pupils will be able to recall prime numbers up to 19 (Q1, Q2)
- Pupils will be able to use the vocabulary of prime numbers and composite (non-prime) numbers (Q1, Q2)
- Pupils will have investigated the prime factors of numbers up to 100 (Q3, Q4)
- Pupils will have solved problems involving prime numbers, prime factors and composite numbers (Q5, Q6)

Resources

100 square; 1–20 digit cards; **Resource 5.10.3a** 100 square (from Unit 3)

Vocabulary

prime number, prime factor, composite number, whole numbers, natural numbers, integers, product, sum

Chapter 10 Factors, multiples and prime numbers

Unit 10.5 Practice Book 5B, pages 131–133

Questions 1 and 2

1 Multiple choice questions. (For each question, choose the correct answer and write the letter in the box.)

(a) There are ☐ prime numbers less than 10.
  A. 3   B. 4   C. 5   D. 6

(b) The product of several prime numbers must be ☐.
  A. a prime number   B. a composite number
  C. an odd number   D. an even number

(c) Of the following statements, the correct one is ☐.
  A. A positive integer is either a prime number or a composite number.
  B. The product of two prime numbers could be an even number.
  C. All even numbers are composite numbers.
  D. The factor of a prime number must be also a prime number.

2 Fill in the spaces to make each statement correct.

(a) 1 has ☐ factor(s). A prime number has ☐ factors. A composite number has at least ☐ factors.

(b) The lowest prime number is ☐. The lowest composite number is ☐.

(c) In 1, 5, 18 and 23, the prime numbers are _____ and the composite numbers are _____.

(d) There is a 2-digit number. The digit in its tens place is neither a prime number nor a composite number, and the digit in its ones place is the smallest whole number. The number is ☐.

(e) Write suitable prime numbers in the boxes.
  13 = ☐ + ☐
  16 = ☐ + ☐ = ☐ + ☐

(f) If both of two consecutive natural numbers are prime numbers, then the two numbers are _____.

What learning will pupils have achieved at the conclusion of Questions 1 and 2?

- Pupils will have determined the prime numbers up to 100.
- Pupils will be able to recall prime numbers up to 19.
- Pupils will be able to use the vocabulary of prime numbers and composite (non-prime) numbers.

Activities for whole-class instruction

- Show pupils the definition of a prime number.
  A prime number is divisible only by itself and 1.
- Display the numbers 5 and 6 and ask pupils to discuss with a partner which of these two numbers is a prime number. Agree that 5 is prime because its only factors are 5 (itself) and 1, while 6 has more factors, 1, 2, 3 and 6 so it is not prime.
- Ask pupils to suggest another pair of adjacent single-digit numbers, where one is prime and one is not. Possible pairs are 3 and 4 or 7 and 8.
- Establish that 3 is prime, its only factors are 3 and 1, while 4 has three factors, 1, 2 and 4 so is not prime; 7 is prime, while 8 is not, as its factors are 1, 2, 4 and 8.
- Tell pupils that numbers that are not prime are called 'composite numbers', so 4, 6 and 8 are composite.
- Ask: *What is the same about these three numbers?* Confirm that they are all even numbers. Ask: *Are any even numbers prime?* Agree that 2 is the only even prime number. Every other even number can be equally divided by 2, so cannot be prime.

 *Two is the only even prime number.*

- Give pupils a 100 square (Use **Resource 5.10.3a** from Unit 3). Remind pupils that 1 is not a prime number because its only factor is 1. It is a square number. Display the instructions below and ask pupils to follow them to find the prime numbers less than 100.
  – Use a 100 square.
  – Cross out 1.
  – Circle 2 and cross out all the multiples of 2.
  – Circle 3 and cross out all the multiples of 3. (All the even multiples will already have been crossed out.)
  – Circle 5 and cross out all the multiples of 5. (All the even multiples will already have been crossed out.)
  – Circle 7 and cross out all the multiples of 7. (All the even multiples will already have been crossed out.)
  – Circle all the remaining numbers.
- The circled numbers should be: 2, 3, 5, 7, 11, 13, 17, 19, 23, 29, 31, 37, 41, 43, 47, 53, 59, 61, 67, 71, 73, 79, 83, 89, 97.
- Study the numbers with pupils. Agree that:
  – 2 is the only even prime number.
  – There are some consecutive odd numbers: 3, 5, 7; 11, 13; 17, 19; 41, 43; 71, 73.
  – The numbers are not regularly spaced.
- Tell pupils that it is useful to know the prime numbers up to 19.

 *The first eight prime numbers are 2, 3, 5, 7, 11, 13, 17 and 19.*

- Practise recall of these numbers.

ⓘ This method for finding primes is known as the 'Sieve of Eratosthenes'. Eratosthenes was an Ancient Greek mathematician who used this system more than 2000 years ago. The method sequentially removes multiples, which cannot be prime numbers. This is much more efficient than testing numbers individually.

Chapter 10 Factors, multiples and prime numbers

Unit 10.5 Practice Book 5B, pages 131–133

- Pupils should complete Questions 1 and 2 in the Practice Book.

Same-day intervention

- Give pupil pairs a set of digit cards from 2 to 20. Write PRIME and COMPOSITE on two pieces of A4 paper. Pupils shuffle the cards and lay them face up on the table. They take turns to choose a number and put it in the correct pile, explaining how they know. For example, '5 is a prime number because its only factors are 5 and 1'; '14 is composite because it has factors 2 and 7 as well as 1 and 14.'
- Practise recall of prime numbers to 19.

Same-day enrichment

- Display a selection of about six numbers and ask pupils to say how they know that these numbers are not prime. For example 12, 35, 60, 77, 27 and 49.

  12: 'This number cannot be prime because it is an even number greater than 2 and 2 is the only even prime'; 'This number cannot be prime because it has more factors than itself and 1. Its factors are 1, 2, 3, 4, 6 and 12'.

  35: 'This number cannot be prime because it is divisible by 5'; 'This number has factors 1, 5, 7 and 35 so it is not prime'.

Questions 3 and 4

> **3** Write all the prime factors of 66.
>
> **4** The product of two prime factors is 91. Find their sum.

What learning will pupils have achieved at the conclusion of Questions 3 and 4?

- Pupils will have investigated the prime factors of numbers up to 100.

Activities for whole-class instruction

- Ask pupils to tell you the prime numbers up to 19. Agree they are 2, 3, 5, 7, 11, 13, 17 and 19.

- Explain to pupils that all composite numbers can be made by multiplying prime numbers together. These are known as the 'prime factors' of the number. So, a prime factor is a factor that is also a prime number.
  - The prime factors of 10 are 2 and 5, because $10 = 2 \times 5$ (and both 2 and 5 are prime numbers).
  - The prime factors of 12 are 2, 2 and 3 because $12 = 2 \times 2 \times 3$ (and both 2 and 3 are prime numbers).

- Display the numbers 8, 14, 20 and 22 and ask pupil pairs to find the prime factors.
  - The prime factors of 8 are 2, 2, 2 because $8 = 2 \times 2 \times 2$ (and 2 is a prime number).
  - The prime factors of 14 are 2, 7 because $14 = 2 \times 7$ (and both 2 and 7 are prime numbers).
  - The prime factors of 20 are 2, 2 and 5 because $20 = 2 \times 2 \times 5$ (and both 2 and 5 are prime numbers).
  - The prime factors of 22 are 2 and 11 because $22 = 2 \times 11$ (and both 2 and 11 are prime numbers).

- Tell pupils that the usual practice is to list the prime factors in order of size, smallest first.

- Explain that for bigger numbers, pupils may need to find the prime factors in stages. For example, to find the prime factors of 84, begin by dividing by 2.

  $84 = 2 \times 42$ (42 is still even, so divide by 2 again)
  $= 2 \times 2 \times 21$ (21 is not prime so we need to find its factors)
  $= 2 \times 2 \times 3 \times 7$

- These numbers are all prime numbers, so the prime factors of 84 are 2, 2, 3 and 7. Each composite number has a unique set of prime factors.

- Ask pupils to find the prime factors of 30 and 98. Agree that $30 = 2 \times 3 \times 5$ and $98 = 2 \times 7 \times 7$.

- Try further numbers until pupils can find prime factors with confidence.

- The product of two prime numbers is 34. Ask: *What are the prime numbers and what is their sum?* Agree the prime numbers are 2 and 17, because $2 \times 17 = 34$. The sum is 19 (2 + 17).

- Pupils should complete Questions 3 and 4 in the Practice Book.

Chapter 10 Factors, multiples and prime numbers

Unit 10.5 Practice Book 5B, pages 131–133

Same-day intervention

Display these number sentences. In pairs, pupils discuss what is wrong with them and correct them. Invite individual pupils to explain.

1. The prime factors of 18 are 2 and 9.
2. The prime factors of 30 are 5, 3 and 2.
3. The prime factors of 21 are 1, 3 and 7.
4. The prime factors of 36 are 3, 3 and 4.

Answers: 1) 9 is a composite number, not a prime number. The prime factors of 18 are 2, 3 and 3. 2) The prime factors should be listed in increasing order. The prime factors of 30 are 2, 3 and 5. 3) 1 is not a prime number. The prime factors of 21 are 3 and 7. 4) 4 is a composite number. The prime factors of 36 are 2, 2, 3 and 3.

Same-day enrichment

- Explain to pupils that the 17th-century mathematician Christian Goldbach thought that all even integers could be expressed as the sum of two odd prime numbers (this is known as Goldbach's conjecture).
- Ask pupils to try to find pairs of prime factors for even numbers from 6. (Some numbers have more than one solution, for example 18 is 5 + 13 or 7 + 11.) How far can they get in 5 minutes?
- Answers include:
  6 = 3 + 3; 8 = 3 + 5; 10 = 3 + 7; 12 = 5 + 7; 14 = 3 + 11; 16 = 5 + 11; 18 = 7 + 11; 20 = 7 + 13; 22 = 3 + 19; 24 = 5 + 19; 26 = 3 + 23; 28 = 5 + 23; 30 = 7 + 23; 32 = 13 + 19; 34 = 11 + 23; 36 = 5 + 31; 38 = 7 + 31; 40 = 3 + 37 …

Questions 5 and 6

5 Two prime factors form a pair of numbers and their sum is 36. Write all such pairs of numbers that satisfy the conditions.

6 Write the positive integers that are less than 10 and satisfy the following conditions.
  (a) They are both even numbers and composite numbers: _____ .
  (b) They are both even numbers and prime numbers: _____ .
  (c) They are both odd numbers and composite numbers: _____ .
  (d) They are both odd numbers and prime numbers: _____ .

What learning will pupils have achieved at the conclusion of Questions 3 and 4?

- Pupils will have solved problems involving prime numbers, prime factors and composite numbers.

Activities for whole-class instruction

- Ask: *What pairs of prime numbers can be added to give 16?* Agree that the pairs are 3 + 13 and 5 + 11. Ask: *What are the products of these numbers?* (39 and 55)
- Show pupils these numbers.
  44 25 23 8 47
- Ask them to write at least two facts about each number. Possible facts include:
  – 44: even, composite number, multiple of 4 and 11
  – 25: odd, composite number, square number, multiple of 5
  – 23: odd, prime number
  – 8: even, cube, composite number, multiple of 4
  – 47: odd, prime number
- Pupils should complete Questions 5 and 6 in the Practice Book.

Chapter 10 Factors, multiples and prime numbers   Unit 10.5 Practice Book 5B, pages 131–133

Same-day intervention

- Display the Venn diagram below and challenge pupils to add the numbers 1–10 in the correct places.

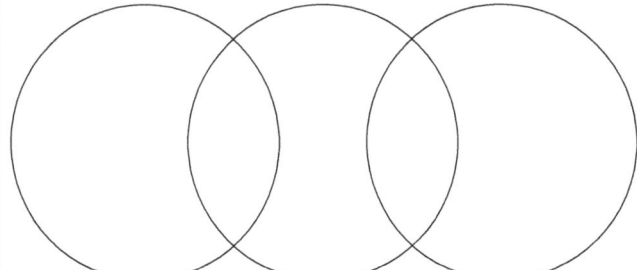

Answers:

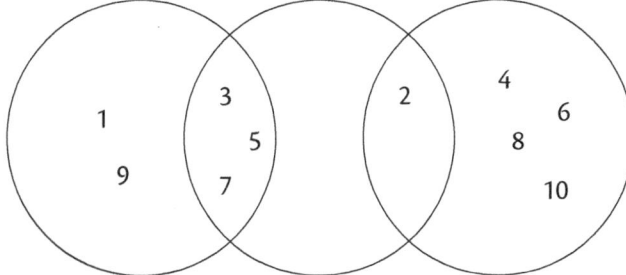

- Ask pupils to look carefully at the prime numbers up to 100.

  2, 3, 5, **7**, **11**, **13**, **17**, **19**, 23, 29, **31**, **37**, **41**, **43**, **47**, 53, 59, **61**, **67**, **71**, **73**, **79**, 83, **89** and **97**

- What do they notice about the ones digit in the prime numbers that are in bold? (The ones digits are all 1, 3, 7 or 9.)

Same-day enrichment

- Display the Venn diagram below and challenge pupils to add the numbers 1–20 in the correct places.

Answers:

- Display the following statement.

  All prime numbers larger than 5 must end in 1, 3, 7, or 9.

- Explain why this statement is true. (Numbers ending 0, 2, 4, 6 or 8 are even and so cannot be prime. Numbers ending in 5 are divisible by 5 and so cannot be prime. Therefore, possible prime numbers can only end in 1, 3, 7 or 9.)

Chapter 10 Factors, multiples and prime numbers

Unit 10.5 Practice Book 5B, pages 131–133

Challenge and extension questions

Question 7

> 7 Of 29, 31, 39, 43, 51, 57, 61, 87, 91 and 97, which are prime numbers?

Pupils are given a list of ten odd numbers and asked to identify the primes. Five of them are prime. Four of the 'imposters' are divisible by 3 and the other, 91, is divisible by 7 (pupils may spot that 91 = 70 + 21).

Question 8

> 8 If a 2-digit number is not divisible by each of the following four numbers: _____, then the 2-digit number must be a prime number.
> Give your reasoning.

Explaining the answer to this question is more challenging than deciding that the numbers are the first four prime numbers: 2, 3, 5 and 7. You could suggest that pupils study a list of the prime numbers less than 100.

Chapter 10 Factors, multiples and prime numbers

Unit 10.6
Prime numbers, composite numbers and prime factorisation (2)

Conceptual context

This is the second of two units on prime numbers, composite numbers and prime factorisation. Pupils' knowledge will develop and strengthen as they learn that every composite number has a unique set of prime factors. Prime numbers are the building blocks of numbers.
Prime factors can be found in any order and by any method because multiplication is commutative. However, in the final answer, the prime factors should be written in increasing order. Two common methods for finding prime factors are 'tree factorisation' and the 'ladder method'.

(i) **Tree factorisation**
In this method, two factors that make a number, here 90, are found, and factorising is continued, circling any prime numbers, until all the factors are prime. In each case, the same prime factors are found, just in a different order. Rearranging them in increasing order gives 90 = 2 × 3 × 3 × 5.

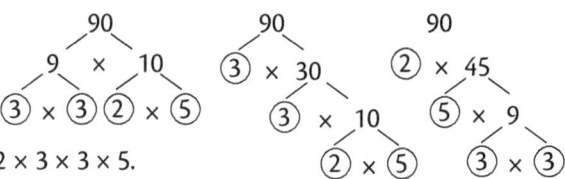

The ladder (division) method
In this method of finding prime factors, the number is first divided by 2 until the quotient is an odd number, then divided by 3 as many times as possible, then by increasing prime numbers (5, 7, 11 ...) until the quotient is a prime number.

To find the prime factors of 90

```
2 | 90
3 | 45
3 | 15
    5    90 = 2 × 3 × 3 × 5
```

To find the prime factors of 148

```
2 | 148
2 | 74
    37    148 = 2 × 2 × 37
```

Using this method, the prime factors are determined in increasing order.

Learning pupils will have achieved at the end of the unit

- Pupils will have an understanding of the properties of prime numbers, factors, prime factors and composite numbers and their relationships and differences (Q1, Q2)
- Pupils will be able to use the ladder method to find prime factors (Q3)
- Pupils will be able to apply their knowledge of divisibility to identify prime factors (Q3)
- Pupils will be able to solve multiplication problems using their knowledge of numbers including prime numbers (Q4, Q5)

Resources

mini whiteboards; blank 1–6 dice; set of 50–100 digit cards; sticky notes; **Resource 5.10.6** Ladder division

Vocabulary

prime number, prime factor, composite number, divisibility test, consecutive, integer

Chapter 10 Factors, multiples and prime numbers

Unit 10.6 Practice Book 5B, pages 134–136

Questions 1 and 2

1 Multiple choice questions. (For each question, choose the correct answer and write the letter in the box.)

(a) The correct expression of the prime factorisation of 12 is ☐.
  A. $12 = 2 \times 6$
  B. $12 = 3 \times 4$
  C. $12 = 1 \times 2 \times 2 \times 3$
  D. $12 = 2 \times 2 \times 3$

(b) There are ☐ prime factors of 8.
  A. 1   B. 2   C. 3   D. 4

(c) Of the following statements, the incorrect one is ☐.
  A. There are 3 prime factors of 45.
  B. Both 3 and 5 are prime factors of 45.
  C. If A is a composite number and $A = B \times C$, then B and C are both the prime factors of A.
  D. If both B and C are prime numbers and $A = B \times C$, then B and C are both the prime factors of A.

(d) The product of two different prime numbers has ☐ factors.
  A. 2   B. 3   C. 4   D. 5

(e) Choose three digits from 0, 1, 2 and 3 to form a 3-digit number that is divisible by 2, 3 and 5. There are ☐ such 3-digit numbers.
  A. 1   B. 2   C. 3   D. 4

2 Fill in the spaces to make each statement correct.

(a) Each composite number can be written as the multiplication of two or more _____, and each of them is a prime factor of this composite number.

(b) Because $m = 2 \times 3 \times 3$, there are ☐ prime factors of m. There are ☐ factors of m.

(c) The prime factorisation of 20 is _____.

(d) The factors of 28 are _____. The prime factors of 28 are _____.

What learning will pupils have achieved at the conclusion of Questions 1 and 2?

- Pupils will have an understanding of the properties of prime numbers, factors, prime factors and composite numbers and their relationships and differences.

Activities for whole-class instruction

- Ask: *What are the factors of 12?* Agree, 1, 2, 3, 4, 6, 12. Ask: *How do you know that you have found all the factors?* Agree the factors can be put into factor pairs: 1×12, 2×6, 3×4.
- Ask: *What are the prime factors of 12?* Agree 2, 2 and 3 because $12 = 2 \times 2 \times 3$.
- Give pupils whiteboards and ask them to write the factors and prime factors of 20. (Factors are 1, 2, 4, 5, 10, 20, while prime factors are 2, 2, 5.) Repeat for 18, 28, 30, 55, 70.
- To help identify prime factors, it is useful to be able to tell if a number is exactly divisible by the smaller prime numbers.

- Ask: *How you can tell if a number is exactly divisible by 2?* Confirm that any even number, that is one ending 0, 2, 4, 6 or 8 is divisible by 2.
- Ask pupils if they know how you can tell if a number is exactly divisible by 3. Explain that if the sum of the digits of the number is divisible by 3, then the number is divisible by 3. Thus 312 is exactly divisible because $3 + 1 + 2 = 6$, and 6 is divisible by 3. 124 is not divisible by 3 because $1 + 2 + 4 = 7$ which is not divisible by 3.
- Ask: *How you can tell if a number is exactly divisible by 5?* Agree that any number ending in 0 or 5 is divisible by 5.
- Tell pupils there is no simple divisibility test for 7.
- Write 120 and 121 on the board. Ask: *Are these numbers divisible by 2, 3 and 5?* Explain to a partner how you know. Invite individual pupils to share their answers. 120 is divisible by 2, 3 and 5, while 121 is not divisible by 2 (because it is odd), 3 (because the sum of the digits is 4 which is not a multiple of 3) or 5 (because it does not end in 0 or 5).
- Pupils should complete Questions 1 and 2 in the Practice Book.

Same-day intervention

- Remind pupils that every composite number has a unique set of prime factors. Prime numbers are the building blocks of numbers. Consecutive numbers have very different prime factors. Ask pupils to find the prime factors of 23, 24, 25, 26 and 27
  Answers: 23 is prime, so $23 = 23$; $24 = 2 \times 2 \times 2 \times 3$; 25 is square, so $25 = 5 \times 5$; $26 = 2 \times 13$; 27 is a cube number, $27 = 3 \times 3 \times 3$.

Same-day enrichment

- Display the following instructions and ask pupils to complete the task.
  - Work with a partner.
  - On a blank six-sided dice, mark three of the faces with an 'F' and the other three faces with 'PF'.
  - Shuffle a set of 50–100 digit cards.
  - Take turns to roll the dice and turn over the top card.
  - Rolling 'F' means finding the factors of the number. Rolling PF means finding the prime factors. For example F and 54 gives 1, 2, 3, 6, 9, 18, 27, 54. (PF and 54 gives 2, 3, 3, 3)
  - Work independently and compare your answers.
  - Repeat with a new dice roll and card.

Chapter 10 Factors, multiples and prime numbers

Unit 10.6 Practice Book 5B, pages 134–136

Question 3

3 Use the division method to factorise the following numbers into prime numbers. The first one has been done for you.
(a) 18

```
2 | 1 8
  3 | 9
      3
```
So 18 = 2 × 3 × 3.

(b) 21

(c) 60

(d) 100

What learning will pupils have achieved at the conclusion of Question 3?

- Pupils will be able to use the ladder method to find prime factors.
- Pupils will be able to apply their knowledge of divisibility to identify prime factors.

Activities for whole-class instruction

- Explain that an efficient way to find prime factors is to be systematic; dividing by each prime number in turn as many times as the number divides exactly. This is known as the 'ladder method'. Ask pupils to list the prime numbers to 19. Agree they are 2, 3, 5, 7, 11, 13, 17, 19. Using divisibility tests is a useful process in the ladder method.

- Ask pupils to recall the divisibility tests for 2, 3 and 5. Agree:
  - even numbers are divisible by 2
  - if the digit sum for a number is divisible by 3, then the number is divisible by 3
  - numbers that end in 5 or 0 are divisible by 5.

- Use the ladder method to find the prime factors of 220. Ask: *Is it divisible by 2?* Agree, it is because 220 is even.

  ```
  2 | 220
      110
  ```

- Ask: *Is 110 divisible by 2?* Agree, it is because 110 is even.

  ```
  2 | 220
  2 | 110
      55
  ```

- Ask: *Is 55 divisible by 2?* Agree, it is not because 55 is odd. Ask: *Is it divisible by 3?* Agree, it is not because 5 + 5 = 10 which is not divisible by 3. Ask: *Is it divisible by 5?* Yes, because it ends in 5.

  ```
  2 | 220
  ```

  ```
  2 | 110
  3 | 55
      11
  ```

- 11 is prime so all the prime factors have now been found. 220 = 2 × 2 × 5 × 11

- Work together to use the ladder method to find the prime factors of some more numbers, for example 126 and 195. (126 = 2 × 3 × 3 × 7; 195 = 3 × 5 × 13)

- Pupils should complete Question 3 in the Practice Book.

Same-day intervention

- Give pupil pairs **Resource 5.10.6** Ladder division. Pupils use the ladder method to find prime factors.

Resource 5.10.6

Ladder division

Write the prime numbers to 19.

Look at these numbers and answer the questions.
45   38   65   42

1. Which two numbers are divisible by 2? ___ ___
   How do you know? ___
2. Which two numbers are divisible by 5? ___ ___
   How do you know? ___
3. Which two numbers are divisible by 3? ___ ___
   How do you know? ___

Complete the ladder division for these.

4. | 4 5   5. | 3 8

45 = ___ × ___ = ___   38 = ___ × ___

6. | 6 5   7. | 4 2

65 = ___ × ___   42 = ___ × ___ × ___

Answers: 1. 38, 42, the numbers are even; 2. 45, 65, the numbers have 5 in the ones place; 3. 45, 42, the digit sum is divisible by 3; 4. 3 × 3 × 5; 5. 2 × 19; 6. 5 × 13; 7. 2 × 3 × 7.

Chapter 10 Factors, multiples and prime numbers

Unit 10.6 Practice Book 5B, pages 134–136

Same-day enrichment

- Remind pupils that every composite number has a unique set of prime factors. Prime numbers are the building blocks of numbers. Consecutive numbers have very different prime factors.
- Ask pupils to find the prime factors of 98, 99, 100, 101 and 102. (98 = 2 × 7 × 7; 99 = 3 × 3 × 11; 100 = 2 × 2 × 5 × 5; 101 is prime, 101 = 101; 102 = 2 × 3 × 17)
- Challenge pupil pairs to find the prime factors of any five consecutive numbers between 101 and 200. You may like to display the prime numbers up to 200 as support. Pupils are only expected to know the primes up to 19.

  2, 3, 5, 7, 11, 13, 17, 19, 23, 29, 31, 37, 41, 43, 47, 53, 59, 61, 67, 71, 73, 79, 83, 89, 97, 101, 103, 107, 109, 113, 127, 131, 137, 139, 149, 151, 157, 163, 167, 173, 179, 181, 191, 193, 197, 199.
- Pupils can check another pair's answers.

Questions 4 and 5

> **4** Given the product of two prime numbers is 143, what is the sum of the two prime numbers?
>
> **5** If the product of three consecutive positive integers is 336, what are the three positive integers?

What learning will pupils have achieved at the conclusion of Questions 4 and 5?

- Pupils will be able to solve multiplication problems using their knowledge of numbers including prime numbers.

Activities for whole-class instruction

- Ask pupils to list prime numbers to 19. Agree they are 2, 3, 5, 7, 11, 13, 17, 19.
- Say: *Here are some products of two small prime numbers. Which ones?* Explain how you worked them out. (The answers are 91 = 7 × 13; 85 = 5 × 17; 55 = 5 × 11; 119 = 7 × 17; 38 = 2 × 19; 39 = 3 × 13.)

  91   85   55   119   38   39

- Listen to pupils' ideas which may include
  - 85 and 55 end in 5, so they must have 5 as a factor
  - 38 is even so 2 must be a factor
  - you can see that 3 is a factor of 39
  - 7 × 3 is 21 so 91 is 7 × 13
  - 119 is quite a large number and has 9 in the ones place, try 11 × 19 – too big or 7 × 17 = 119.
- In Unit 10.3, pupils studied cube numbers, for example $1^3 = 1 \times 1 \times 1 = 1$ and $6^3 = 6 \times 6 \times 6 = 216$. Ask pupils to work out the first ten cube numbers. Agree that they are 1, 8, 27, 64, 125, 216, 343, 512, 729, 1000.
- Point out how quickly cube numbers grow. Explain that having an overview of this growth pattern, will allow pupils to estimate the magnitude of three numbers that are multiplied together. For example
  - if 5 × 5 × 5 = 125, guess what three consecutive numbers give a product of 120. (4 × 5 × 6)
  - if 10 × 10 × 10 = 1000, guess what three consecutive numbers give a product of 990. (9 × 10 × 11)
- Pupils should complete Questions 4 and 5 in the Practice Book.

Same-day intervention

- All these 'thirties' numbers are the products of two small prime numbers. Pupils work with a partner to find which ones.

  (Answers: 33 – 3 × 11; 34 – 2 × 17; 35 = 5 × 7; 38 = 2 × 19; 39 = 3 × 13.)

  33   34   35   38   39

Same-day enrichment

- Each of these numbers is the product of three prime numbers. Ask: *What are the numbers?*

  (Answers: 2 × 3 × 11; 3 × 5 × 7; 3 × 5 × 13; 2 × 3 × 7; 2 × 3 × 13; 2 × 3 × 5; 3 × 5 × 11.)

  66   105   195   42   78   30   165

Chapter 10 Factors, multiples and prime numbers

Unit 10.6 Practice Book 5B, pages 134–136

Challenge and extension question

Question 6

6. Can you evenly divide the eight numbers 40, 44, 45, 63, 65, 78, 99 and 105 into two groups so that the products of the four numbers in each group are equal? Show your working.

This question requires pupils to find the prime factors of each number and then sort them into two sets so that each set contains the same prime factors. Pupils may find it easier to write each number and its prime factors on a sticky note so that they can move them around to make the two sets.

Chapter 10 test (Practice Book 5B, pages 137–139)

Test question number	Relevant unit	Relevant questions within unit
1	Unit 10.1	Q2, Q3, Q5, Q6
	Unit 10.2	Q1, Q2, Q3, Q4
	Unit 10.4	Q1, Q2
	Unit 10.5	Q1, Q2, Q6
	Unit 10.6	Q1, Q2
2	Unit 10.1	Q1, Q2, Q3, Q4
	Unit 10.2	Q1, Q2, Q3, Q4
	Unit 10.3	Q1, Q2, Q3, Q4
	Unit 10.5	Q3
	Unit 10.6	Q3, Q6
3	Unit 10.5	Q3
	Unit 10.6	Q3, Q6

Resource 5.6.1a

Place value slider

- Cut along the dotted lines to create your place value slider.
- Now cut out these strips.
- Thread one strip through the slider and use this to write your number on.
- There are three strips, but you can always cut more or you could laminate one and use it again and again.

1000	100	10	1	0.1	0.01	0.001
Behind the strip	Behind the strip	Behind the strip	Behind the strip	Behind the strip	Behind the strip	Behind the strip

Resource 5.6.1b

Make the calculation

Write 10, 100 or 1000 in each space so that the calculation is correct.
One calculation cannot be completed – which one?

1. 3.2 × _____ = 320
2. 3.2 × _____ × _____ = 320
3. 3.2 × _____ × _____ = 3200
4. 3.2 × _____ × _____ × _____ = 3200
5. 0.103 × _____ × _____ × _____ = 10300
6. 0.103 × _____ × _____ × _____ × _____ = 10300
7. 0.103 × _____ × _____ × _____ × _____ = 103 000
8. 0.103 × _____ × _____ × _____ × _____ = 103 000
9. 0.103 × _____ × _____ × _____ × _____ = 10 300 000
10. 38.54 × _____ × _____ × _____ × _____ × _____ = 3 854 000 000 000
11. 876.1 ÷ _____ = 8.761
12. 876.1 ÷ _____ ÷ _____ = 0.087 61
13. 876.1 ÷ _____ ÷ _____ = 0.087 61
14. 876.1 ÷ _____ ÷ _____ ÷ _____ = 0.087 61
15. 876.1 ÷ _____ ÷ _____ ÷ _____ ÷ _____ = 0.000 087 61

Resource 5.6.1c

× and ÷ trail

Add a decimal point and multiplication or division in each arrow. Once you've completed the trail, fill in the dotted arrows.

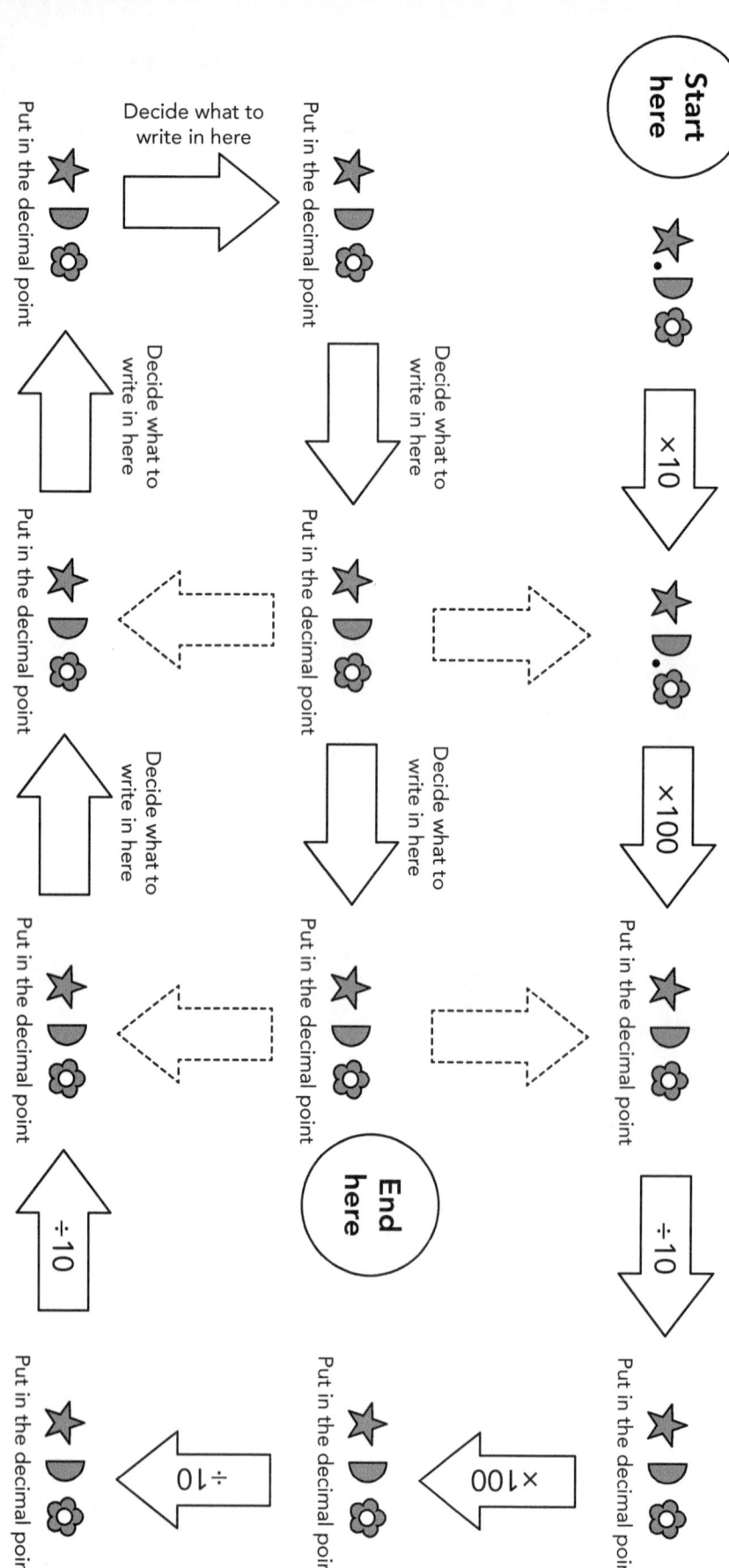

Resource 5.6.1d

Find a number that when ...

Find a number to complete each row of the table.
One of the rows has been completed as an example.

Find a number that when	Needs one extra zero	Needs two extra zeros	Doesn't need an extra zero
×10		It's impossible to get two extra zeros from multiplying by 10.	
×100	3.2 (because 3.2 ×100 = 32<u>0</u>)	3 (because 3×100 = 3<u>00</u>)	3.21 (because 3.21 × 100 = 321)
×1000			
÷10			
÷100			
÷1000			

Resource 5.6.2a

Sorting calculations

Write calculations in each flag that will have the effect of:
- not changing the number
- multiplying the number by 10
- dividing the number by 10.

Each flag has one example in it already.

What is the longest calculation you can make in each flag?

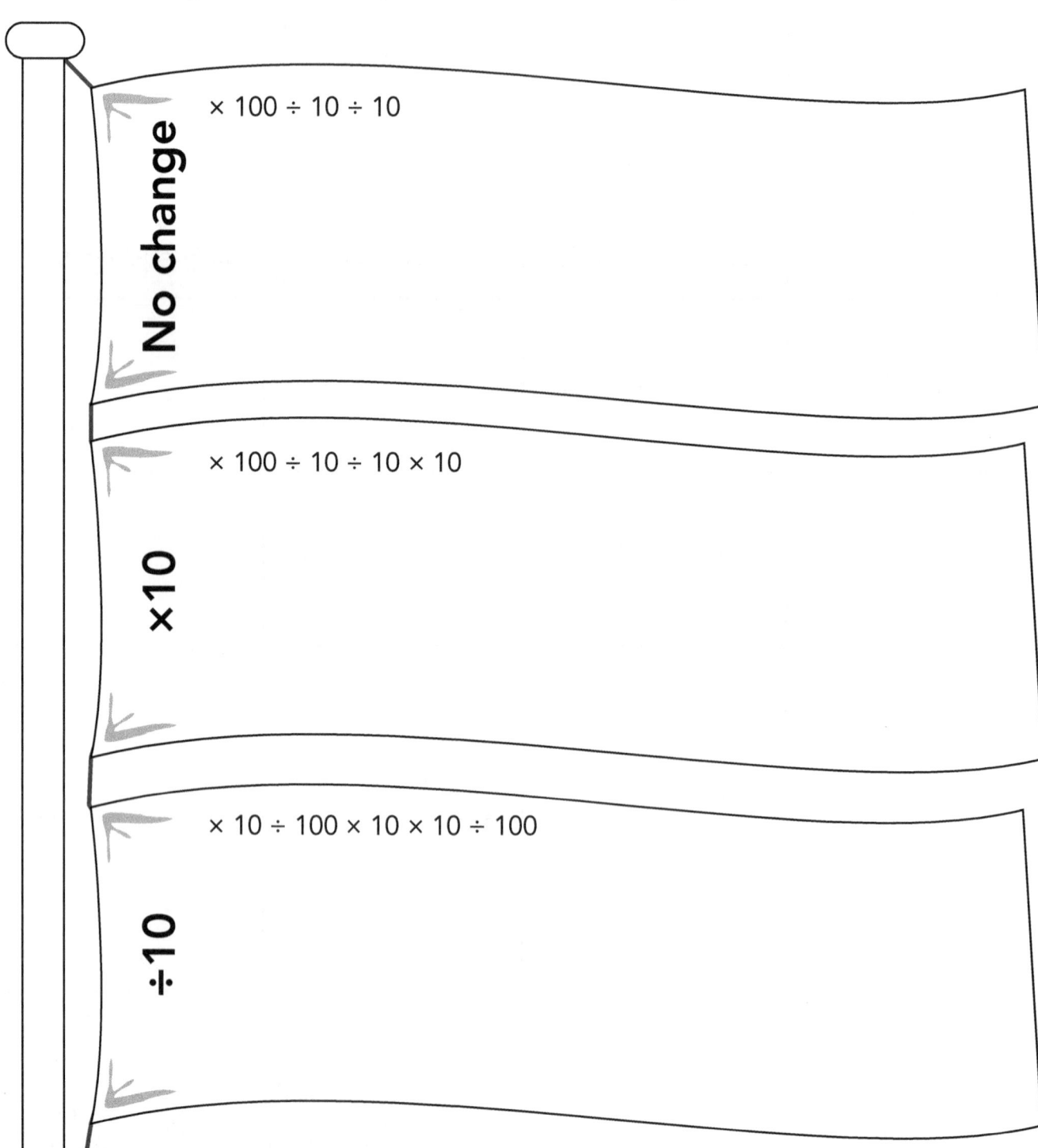

Resource 5.6.2b

Distance dominoes

Cut out the dominoes and make a loop by matching the distances.

1000 m	5710 m	3 km 111 m	5 km	5701 m	2300 m
1000 m	3.111 km	8.228 km	5710 m	2 km 300 m	3 km 20 m
3 km 200 m	500 m	700 m	32 km	5000 m	0.7 km
700 m	5 km 701 m	3.2 km	5.710 km	8 km 228 m	3.020 km
57.1 km	5.032 km	7 km	3200 m	1 km	5 km 32 m

© HarperCollinsPublishers 2018

Resource 5.6.2c

Zero or not?

Each of the digits in these numbers has been replaced by a ✱.
Some of the ✱s are covering zeros.

Which ✱s must be covering a zero? Circle them.

$$**km = *****m$$

$$**km\ ***m = **.*km$$

$$*****g = **kg\ ***g$$

$$****m = *.*km$$

$$*l = ****ml$$

$$***g = *.***kg$$

$$*.***kg = *kg\ **g$$

Resource 5.6.3a

Adding decimals

7 + 2 = _____   0.7 + 0.2 = _____

17 + 2 = _____   1.7 + 0.2 = _____

17 + 32 = _____   1.7 + 3.2 = _____

19 + 5 = _____   1.9 + 0.5 = _____

19 + 35 = _____   1.9 + 3.5 = _____

27 + 6 = _____   2.7 + 0.6 = _____

27 + 7 = _____   2.7 + 0.7 = _____

27 + 9 = _____   2.7 + 0.9 = _____

31 + 13 = _____   3.1 + 1.3 = _____

© HarperCollins*Publishers* 2018

Resource 5.6.3b

Matching pairs

Look at this calculation:

283 + 112 = 395

If you divide each number in the calculation by 100 this gives another correct calculation:

2.83 + 1.12 = 3.95

Cut out and match more pairs of calculations like these.

317 + 28 = _____	19 + 15 = _____	731 + 280 = _____
0.02 + 0.11 = _____	731 + 28 = _____	2 + 110 = _____
73.1 + 2.8 = _____	3.17 + 2.8 = _____	7.31 + 2.8 = _____
317 + 280 = _____	190 + 15 = _____	0.2 + 11 = _____
31.7 + 2.8 = _____	0.19 + 0.15 = _____	2 + 11 = _____
19 + 1.5 = _____		

Resource 5.6.3c

Correct the mistake

Richard tried to add a decimal number to 14.47.
He carried out all the additions correctly, and his only mistake was that he didn't line up the decimal points correctly.

Here is Richard's work:

```
   1 4 . 4 7
+    _ . _ _ _
   ─────────
   4 . 2 2 8
```

What number was Richard was trying to add to 14.47? _____

What should the correct answer have been? _____

How can you help Richard to make sure he remembers to line up the decimal points in the future?

_____

_____

_____

Resource 5.6.3d

Measuring rods – addition

One of these rods is 270 cm long, and the other is 2 m 25 cm long.
How long are they in total?

⟵——— 270 cm ———⟶⟵——— 2 m 25 cm ———⟶

270 cm + 2 m 25 cm
Converted to the same units is either

_____ cm + _____ cm

or

_____ m _____ cm + _____ m _____ cm

Adding these together gives _____ cm or _____ m _____ cm

___

One of these rods is 1.65 m long, and the other is 90 cm long.
How long are they in total?

⟵——— 1.65 cm ———⟶⟵— 90 cm —⟶

1.65 cm + 90 cm
Converted to the same units is either

_____ cm + _____ cm

or

_____ m _____ cm + _____ m _____ cm

Adding these together gives _____ cm or _____ m _____ cm

___

Now draw a diagram and write out the steps for two rods that are 3.10 m long and 1 m 50 cm long.

Resource 5.6.4a

Subtracting decimals

7 – 2 = _____

17 – 2 = _____

17 – 32 = _____

19 – 5 = _____

19 – 35 = _____

27 – 6 = _____

27 – 7 = _____

27 – 9 = _____

31 – 13 = _____

0.7 – 0.2 = _____

1.7 – 0.2 = _____

1.7 – 3.2 = _____

1.9 – 0.5 = _____

1.9 – 3.5 = _____

2.7 – 0.6 = _____

2.7 – 0.7 = _____

2.7 – 0.9 = _____

3.1 – 1.3 = _____

Resource 5.6.4b

Make the subtraction …

Use each of the digits 0, 1, 2, 3, 4, 5 once only to fill in the boxes so that the result of the calculation is …

- as large as possible

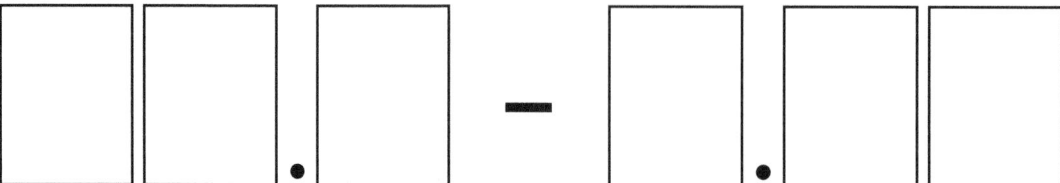

- as small as possible

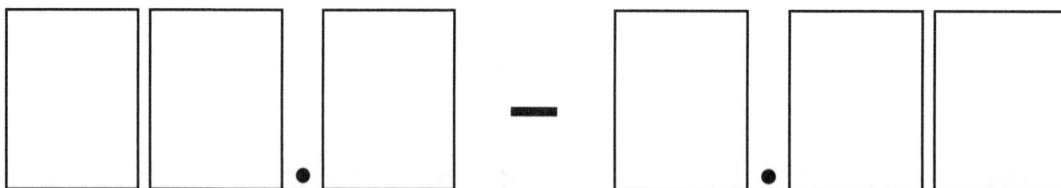

- as close to 10 as possible

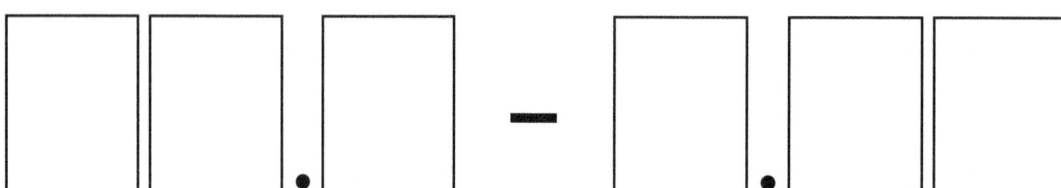

- as close to 5 as possible.

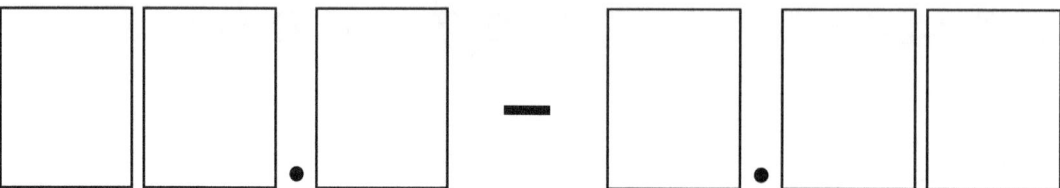

Resource 5.6.4c

Measuring rods – subtraction

One of these rods is 2 m 25 cm long. The total length is 495 cm.
How long is the other rod?

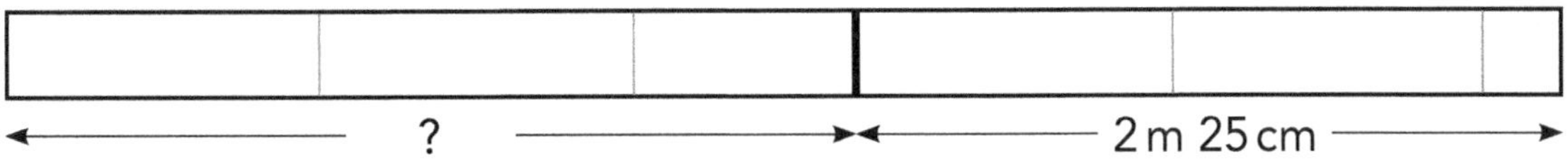

⟵——— ? ———⟶⟵——— 2 m 25 cm ———⟶

495 cm − 2 m 25 cm
Converted to the same units is either

_____ cm − _____ cm

or

_____ m _____ cm − _____ m _____ cm

Subtracting gives _____ cm or _____ m _____ cm

One of these rods is 1.65 m long. The total length is 2 metres and 55 centimetres.
How long is the shorter rod?

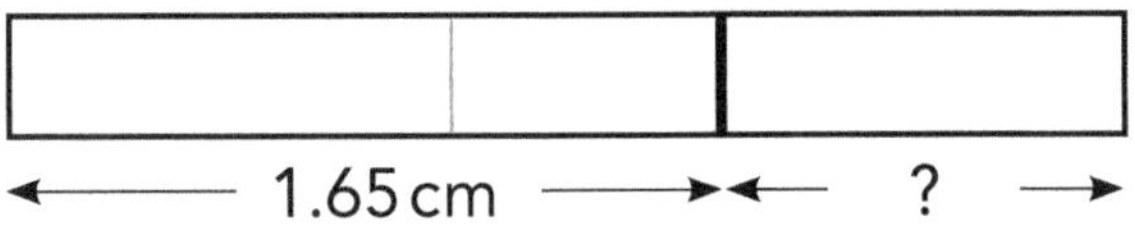

⟵——— 1.65 cm ———⟶⟵— ? —⟶

2 m 55 cm − 1.65 m
Converted to the same units is either

_____ cm − _____ cm

or

_____ m _____ cm − _____ m _____ cm

Subtracting gives _____ cm or _____ m _____ cm

Now draw a diagram and write out the steps for two rods that are 5 metres long in total, with one of the rods being 162 cm long.

Resource 5.6.5a

Decimal addogons

The number in each square is found by adding the numbers in the circles either side of it.

Find all the missing numbers.

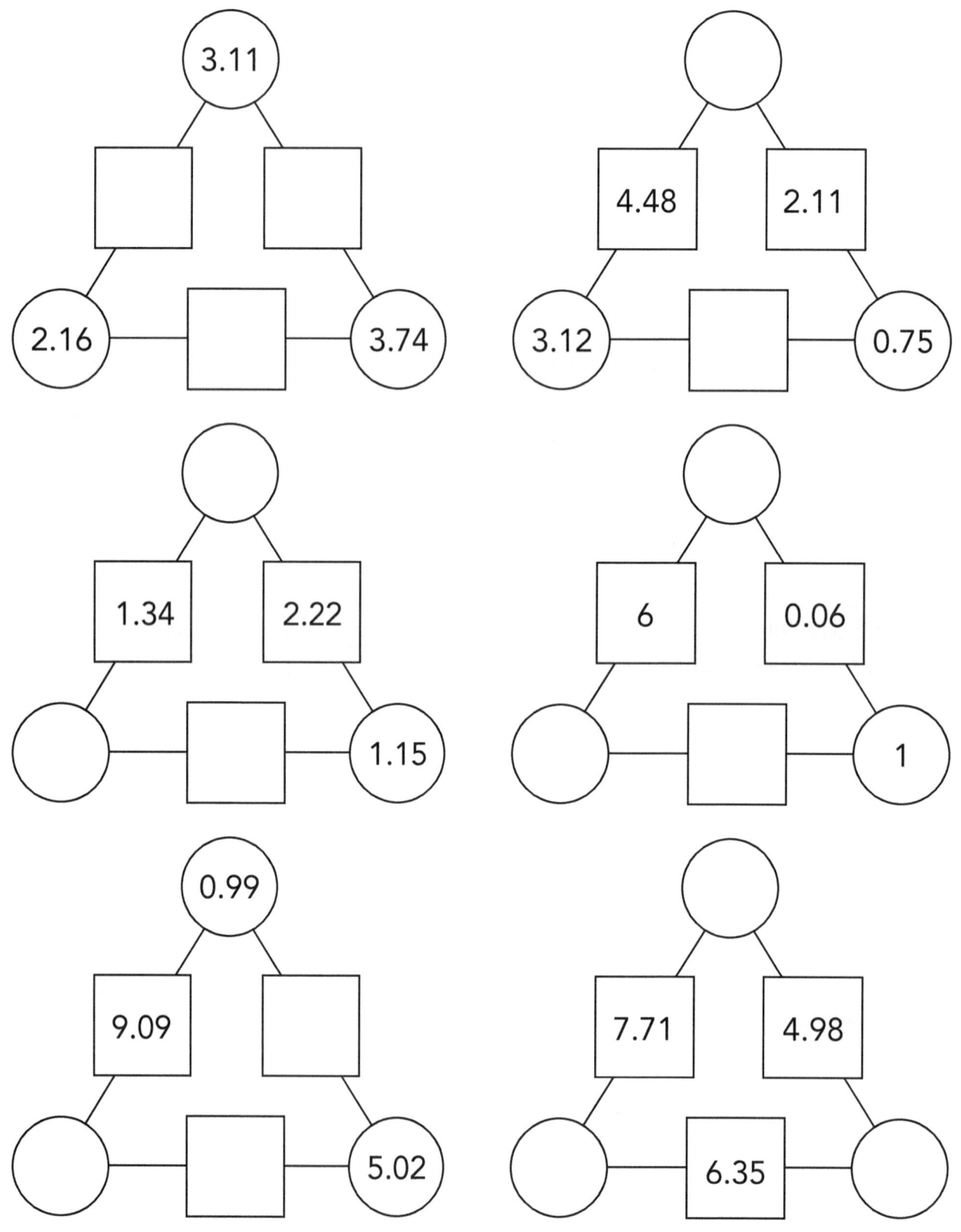

Resource 5.6.5b

Makes 1 maze

Find the number pair on the top row that adds to 1 and circle it.
Moving only left, right, up or down, find the other pairs that add to 1 to find a route to the bottom of the grid.

0.85 0.15	0.47 0.63	0.21 0.99	0.24 0.86	0.01 0.09	0.6 0.04	0.34 0.43
0.83 0.17	0.55 0.45	0.17 0.83	0.11 0.99	0.52 0.48	0.2 0.8	0.34 0.66
0.31 0.79	0.65 0.45	0.99 0.01	0.67 0.43	0.21 0.79	0.12 0.98	0.96 0.04
0.25 0.45	0.21 0.89	0.77 0.23	0.21 0.89	0.24 0.76	0.35 0.75	0.44 0.56
0.96 0.96	0.19 0.91	0.13 0.87	0.02 0.98	0.43 0.57	0.74 0.36	0.82 0.18
0.12 0.89	0.73 0.37	0.76 0.34	0.04 0.06	0.67 0.45	0.33 0.67	0.30 0.70
0.9 0.01	0.66 0.44	0.34 0.55	0.19 0.91	0.32 0.79	0.61 0.39	0.50 0.05

© HarperCollins*Publishers* 2018

Resource 5.6.5c

Missing operations

In these calculations, the ◇ is covering either a + or a – sign.

Find the right sign for each ◇ so that the calculation is correct.

2.37 ◇ 3.78 ◇ 1.57 ◇ 3.19 = 4.53

2.37 ◇ 3.78 ◇ 1.57 ◇ 3.19 = 7.77

2.37 ◇ 3.78 ◇ 1.57 ◇ 3.19 = 3.35

2.37 ◇ 3.78 ◇ 1.57 ◇ 3.19 = 0.21

2.37 ◇ (3.78 ◇ 1.57) ◇ 3.19 = 0.21

Resource 5.6.5d

Decimal addition and subtraction match (1)

Cut out and match the story, the calculation and the bar model.
Some bar models have more than one story and calculation attached to them.

1.

4.92	
1.71	3.21

2. Finn buys a pen for £1.71 and a pad of paper for £3.21.
How much does he spend in total?

3. 1.71 + 3.21
= _____

4. Claire has £4.92 in her pocket. She buys a pie that costs £3.21.
How much money does she have left?

5. 4.92 − 3.21
= _____

6.

3.21	
1.71	1.5

7. A piece of wood is 3.21 m long. Ellie needs to cut a shelf that is 1.71 m long.
How much wood will she have left over?

8. A pie weighs 3.21 kg. After everyone has been served, the leftover pie weighs 1.5 kg.
How many kilograms of the pie were eaten?

9. 3.21 − 1.71
= _____

10. 3.21 − 1.5
= _____

11.

4.71	
3.21	1.5

12. Jack has a bucket that can hold 3.21 l of water. Jill's bucket can hold 1.5 l more than Jack's.
How many litres can Jill's bucket hold?

13. 3.21 + 1.5
= _____

14. Kristin is painting a room. She bought 4.71 l of paint and has used 1.5 l so far.
How many litres of paint does Kristin have left?

15. 4.71 − 1.5
= _____

© HarperCollins*Publishers* 2018

Resource 5.6.5e

Decimal number boxes

Six decimal numbers are arranged in order, from lowest to highest.
Use the clues below to find each number.
You don't have to guess – only one number will fit each box.

A	B	C	D	E	F

- The difference between the number in box F and 16 is 0.148.

- The sum of the numbers in box A and box B is 0.93.

- Adding one tenth of the number in box A to the number in box C gives an answer that is 0.001 higher than the number in box D.

- The number in box F is the sum of three of the other boxes.

- The number in box B is the greatest pure decimal with 1 decimal place.

- Only two of the numbers are less than 5.

- The difference between the number in box C and 6.2 is 1.71.

- The number in box D has 3 decimal places.

- The sum of the numbers in box C and box E is 18.95.

The numbers in which three boxes add together to give the number in box F?

Resource 5.6.6a

More decimal addogons

The number in each square is found by adding the numbers in the circles either side of it.
Find all the missing numbers.

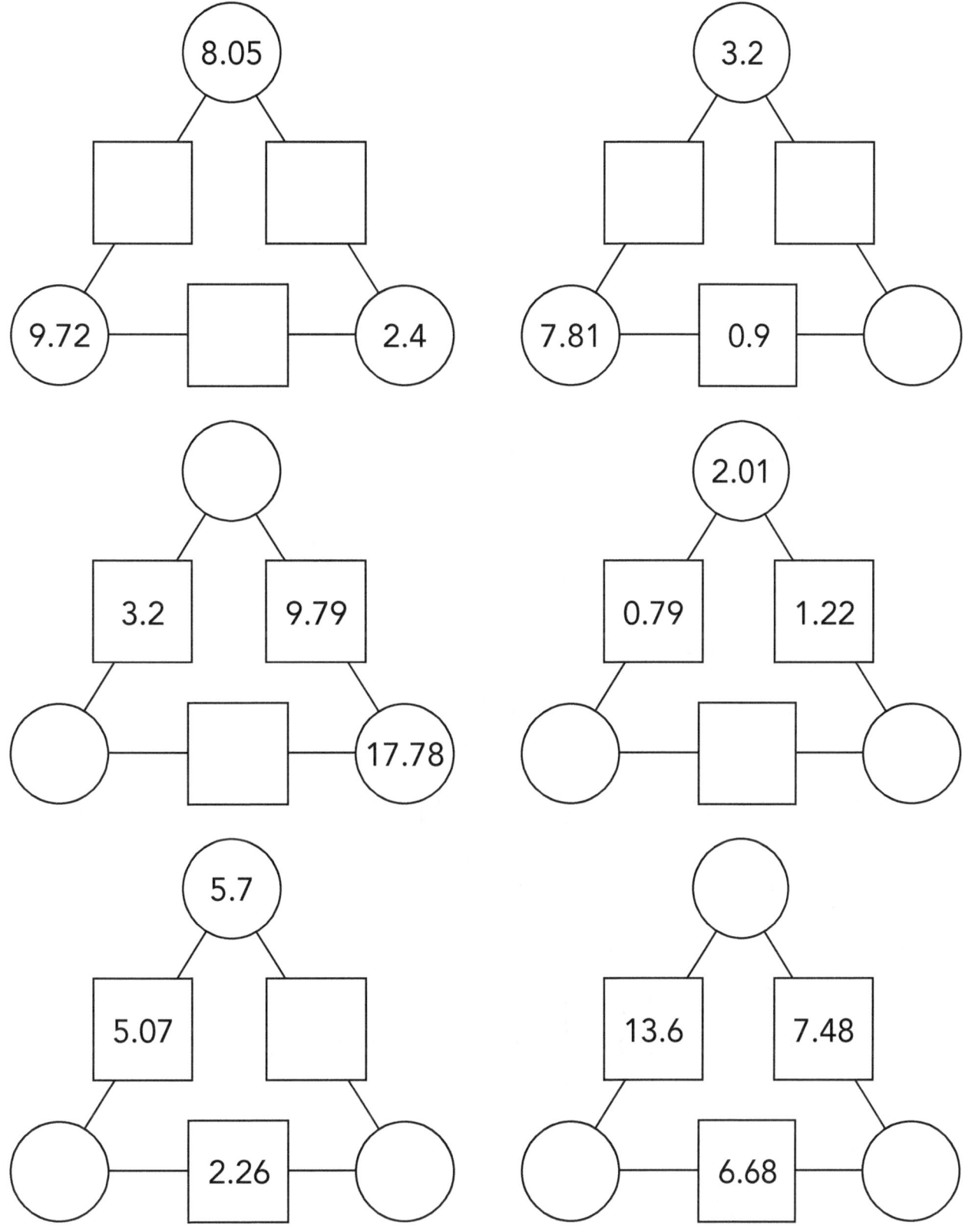

Resource 5.6.6b

Makes 3 maze

Find the number pair on the top row that adds to 3 and circle it.

Moving only left, right, up or down, find the other pairs that add to 3 to find a route to the bottom of the grid.

2.3 1.7	1.7 1.03	1.07 1.93	0.8 2.02	2.22 1.78	0.42 2.68	1.22 2.88
2.15 1.95	1.52 1.48	2.88 0.12	0.77 2.33	1.77 1.33	1.40 2.6	1.32 1.78
1.11 1.89	0.6 2.4	2.09 1.11	1.3 2.70	0.7 2.3	1.57 1.43	2.94 0.06
0.22 2.78	1.50 1.05	2.63 1.47	1.85 1.15	1.14 1.86	2.09 1.91	1.95 1.05
1.9 1.1	2.15 0.85	1.23 1.77	0.49 2.51	1.28 0.72	2.23 0.77	2.40 0.6
0.45 1.56	0.83 0.17	0.92 1.08	1.99 2.01	0.86 2.14	2.16 0.84	2.1 0.09
1.44 1.66	1.50 1.5	1.9 1.1	1.02 1.80	1.3 1.70	0.75 1.25	0.97 1.03

Resource 5.6.6c

Using bar models

This diagram shows 3.2 × 10 = 32.

32									
3.2	3.2	3.2	3.2	3.2	3.2	3.2	3.2	3.2	3.2

Can you see 3.2 × 4 in the diagram? Draw a ring around it.
Can you see 3.2 × 6 in the diagram? Draw a ring around it.
Can you see 3.2 × 10 in the diagram? Draw a ring around it.

This diagram shows 1.7 × 8 + 1.7 × 2.

1.7	1.7	1.7	1.7	1.7	1.7	1.7	1.7	1.7	1.7

Can you see 1.7 × 8 in the diagram? Draw a ring around it.
Can you see 1.7 × 2 in the diagram? Draw a ring around it.
Can you see 1.7 × 10 in the diagram? Draw a ring around it.
What number should go in the top bar?
Calculate 1.7 × 8 + 1.7 × 2.

Fill in all the gaps and shade this diagram to show that 2.4 × 7 + 2.4 × 3 = 24.

This bar model shows 38 ÷ 5.

38				

This bar model shows 38 ÷ 5 ÷ 2.

38									

What's the same and what's different about these diagrams?
Are all the blocks in the bottom bar the same size? How do you know?
What number goes into the blocks that make up the bottom bar?

Resource 5.6.6d

More missing operations

In these calculations, the ◇ is covering either a + or a − sign.

Find the right sign for each ◇ so that the calculation is correct.

14.2 ◇ 3.6 ◇ 1.7 = 8.9

14.2 ◇ 3.6 ◇ 1.7 = 12.3

14.2 ◇ 3.6 ◇ 1.7 = 19.5

In these calculations, the ◇ is covering a × or a + or a − sign.

Find the right sign for each ◇ so that the calculation is correct.

4.23 ◇ 3 ◇ 4.23 ◇ 7 = 42.3

4.23 ◇ 4 ◇ 4.23 ◇ 8 ◇ 4.23 ◇ 2 = 42.3

4.23 ◇ 8 ◇ 4.23 ◇ 6 ◇ 4.23 ◇ 9 = 46.53

In these calculations, the ◇ is covering a × or a ÷ or a + or a − sign.

Find the right sign for each ◇ so that the calculation is correct.

42.3 ◇ 5 ◇ 2 = 4.23

42.3 ◇ (7 ◇ 3) = 4.23

4.23 ◇ 20 ◇ 5 ◇ 4 = 4.23

Resource 5.6.6e

Decimal addition and subtraction match (2)

Cut out and match the story, the calculation and the bar model.
Some bar models have more than one story and calculation attached to them.
One calculation doesn't fit with any of the stories or bar models. Which one?

1

11.46 − 7.62

= _____

2

Number A is 3.84 more than Number B.
Number B is 3.81.
What is Number A?

3

11.46	
7.65	3.81

4

Number A is 7.65 more than number B.
Number B is 3.81.
What is Number A?

5

7.65 − 3.81

= _____

6

7.65 l of water is poured into two buckets. One of the buckets has 3.81 l of water in it.
How many litres of water are in the other?

7

A painter is painting a building that is 11.46 m high.
On a ladder, she can reach 7.65 m up the building.
How big is the gap that is unpainted?

8

7.65	
3.81	3.84

9

3.81 + 7.65

= _____

10

11.46 − 3.84

= _____

11

11.46	
3.84	7.62

12

A baker has 11.46 kg of flour to make bread for his shop.
He uses 7.62 kg.
How many kilograms of flour does he have left?

13

3.81 + 3.84

= _____

14

The sum of Number A and Number B is 11.46.
Number A is 3.84.
What is Number B?

15

3.84 − 3.81

= _____

© HarperCollins*Publishers* 2018

Resource 5.6.6f

Missing digits

In these calculations, each * represents a missing digit.
Find the missing digits in each calculation. Write out the calculations.

$$*.3 + 1.2* + 0.*1 = 2.81$$

$$1*.15 - 6.7* = 3.*2$$

$$**.* - 2.9* = 9.99$$

Resource 5.6.7a

Multiplying and dividing by 10, 100 and 1000

Use the place value slider and place value charts to show each calculation. Write your answer here.

38 × 10 = _____

38 ÷ 10 = _____

38 × 100 = _____

38 ÷ 100 = _____

3.8 × 10 = _____

3.8 × 100 = _____

3.8 ÷ 10 = _____

3.8 ÷ 100 = _____

0.38 × 10 = _____

0.038 × 10 = _____

380 ÷ 10 = _____

380 ÷ 100 = _____

380 ÷ 1000 = _____

Resource 5.6.7b

Lining up the decimal points

None of these column addition and subtractions are lined up correctly.
Rewrite each one so that the decimal points are lined up correctly, and then work out the answer.

1. 2.53 + 37.1

```
   2 . 5 3
+  3 7 . 1
_____
```

2. 5.08 + 1.2

```
   5 . 0 8
+      1 . 2
_____
```

3. 10.3 – 0.1

```
  1   0 . 3
–     0 . 1
_____
```

4. 11.79 – 1.4

```
  1   1 . 7 9
–         1 . 4
_____
```

5. 12.3 – 1.28

```
  1   2 . 3
–     1 . 2 8
_____
```

Resource 5.6.7c

Place the digits

The digits 0, 1, 2, 3, 4, 5 and 6 are arranged to make two numbers.
Using the column method to add gives:

```
      _  _ . _  _
  +      _ . _  _
      ─────────────
      3  7 . 6  5
```

And, keeping the same digits in the same place but subtracting gives:

```
      _  _ . _  _
  −      _ . _  _
      ─────────────
      2  6 . 4  3
```

How are the digits 0, 1, 2, 3, 4, 5 and 6 arranged in the calculations?

Decimal cards

0.36	0.37	0.38	0.39	0.1	0.11	0.12
0.19	0.2	0.21	0.22	0.23	0.24	0.25
0.81	0.8	0.79	0.78	0.77	0.76	0.75
0.64	0.63	0.62	0.61	0.88	0.89	0.9

0	0.13	0.87	1
0.31	0.14	0.86	0.69
0.32	0.15	0.85	0.68
0.33	0.16	0.84	0.67
0.34	0.17	0.83	0.66
0.35	0.18	0.82	0.65

Resource 5.6.7e

10s, 100s, 1000s and 10 000s puzzles

Place the numbers 0.071, 0.71, 71 and 710 in the circles and the operations × 10, × 1000, ÷ 10 and ÷ 1000 in the arrows so that all the calculations are correct.

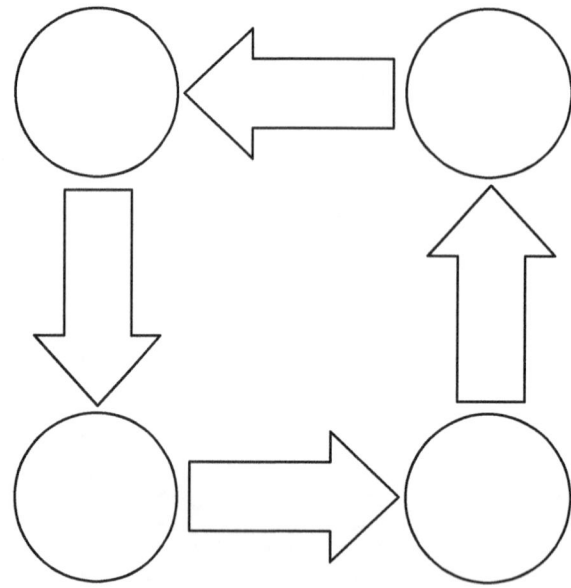

Place the numbers 0.028, 0.28, 2.8, 28 and 28 000 in the circles and the operations × 10, × 100, × 1000, ÷ 100 and ÷ 10 000 in the arrows so that all the calculations are correct.

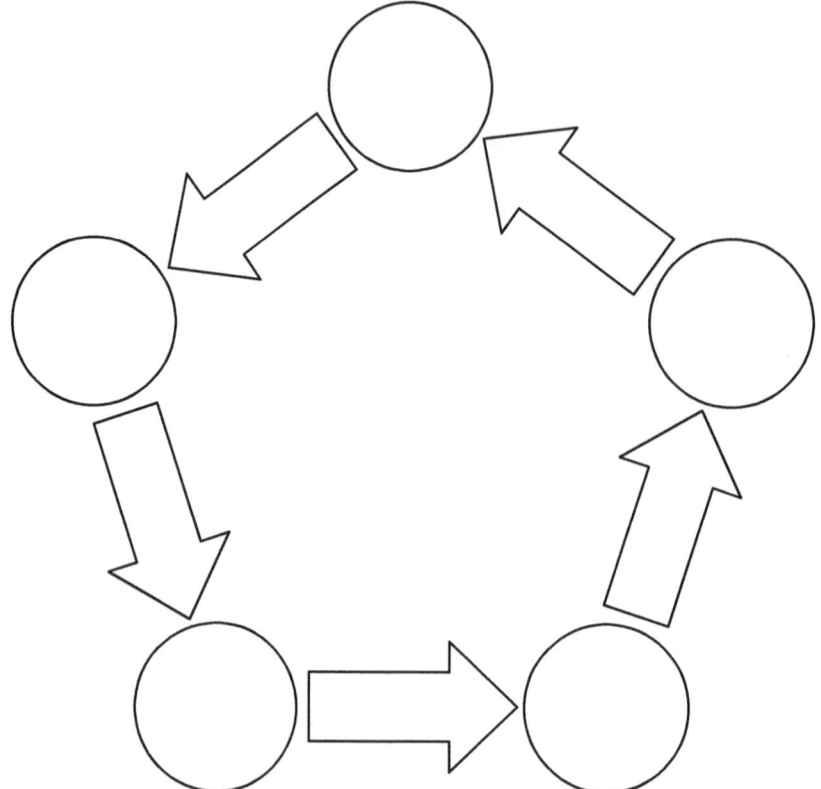

Resource 5.7.1a

Matching temperatures

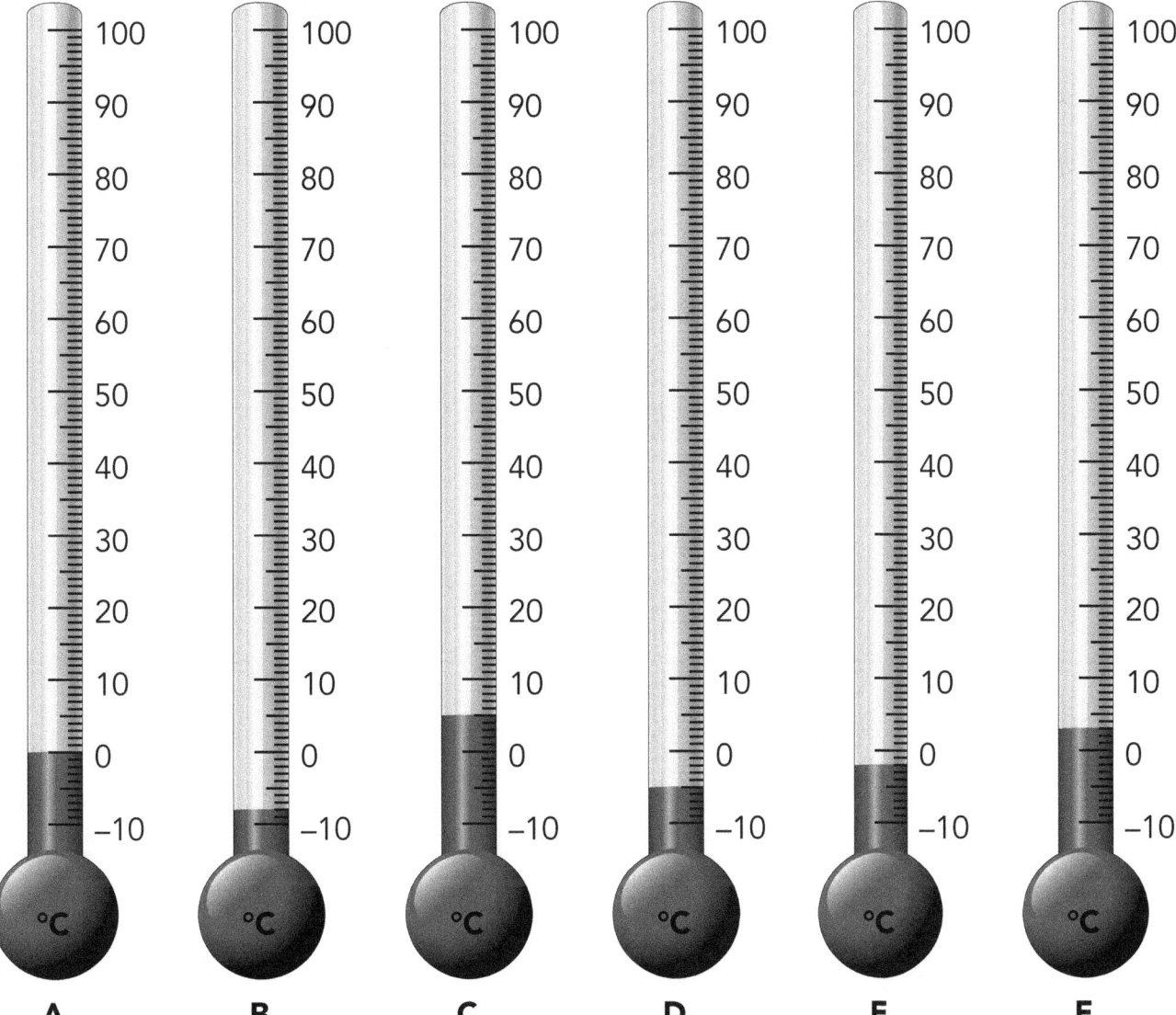

Match the letters to the temperatures.

1. Thermometer _____ shows −5 °C.

2. Thermometer _____ shows 0 °C.

3. Thermometer _____ shows 5 °C.

4. Thermometer _____ shows −8 °C.

5. Thermometer _____ shows +3 °C.

6. Thermometer _____ shows −2 °C.

Resource 5.7.1b

Thermometers

Colour the thermometer columns to show the correct temperatures.

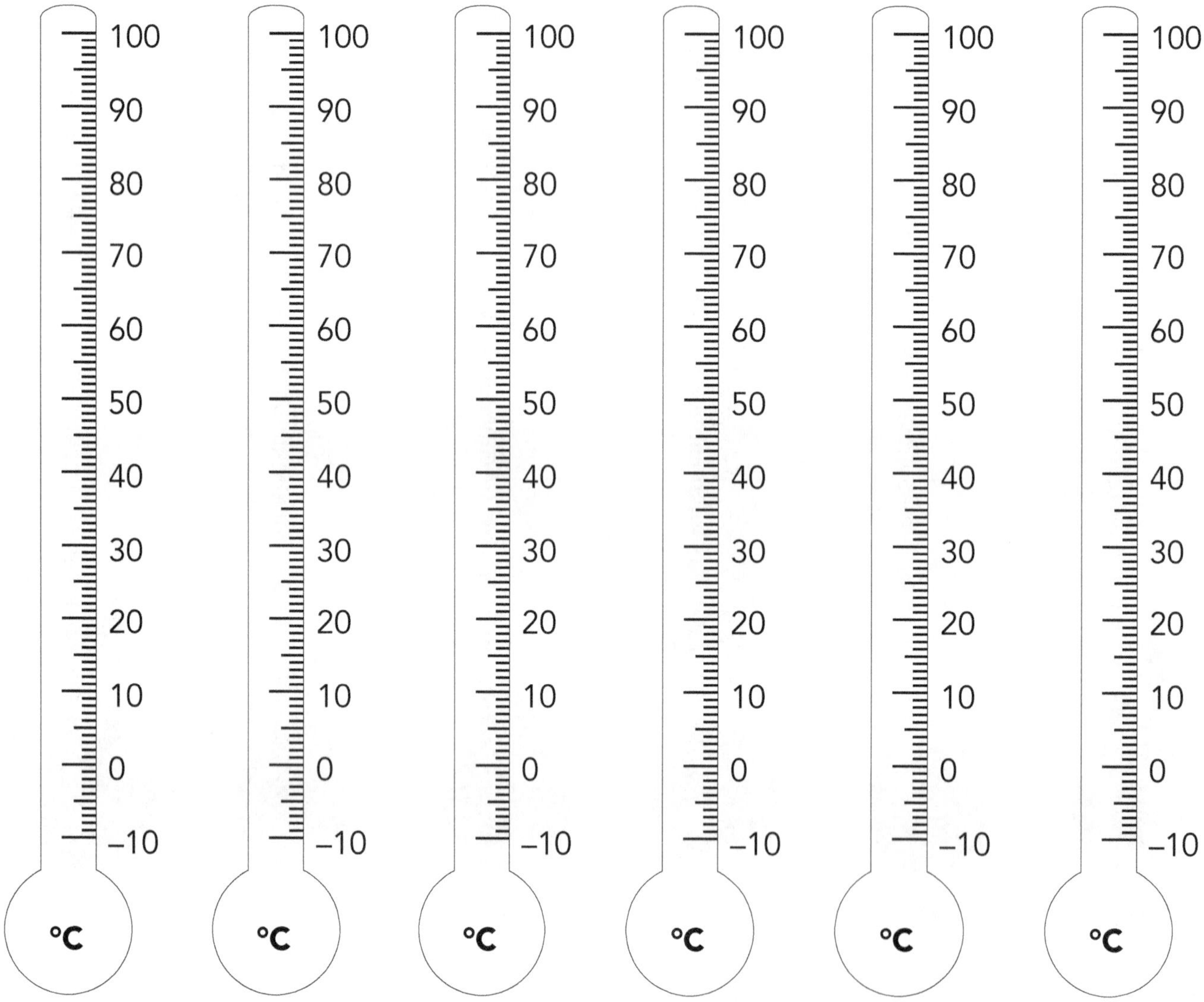

1. 0 °C
2. −7 °C
3. 4 °C
4. −4 °C
5. −10 °C
6. 25 °C

Resource 5.7.1c

Positive and negative numbers

Complete the table.

Number in words	Numeral	Positive or negative? (delete as necessary)
negative ten		positive/negative
three point five		positive/negative
	−5.6	positive/negative
	409.2	positive/negative
positive eleven		positive/negative
	−85	positive/negative
	$\frac{7}{8}$	positive/negative
negative twelve point four		positive/negative
twelve point four		positive/negative
	−34.9	positive/negative
	−2.03	positive/negative

Resource 5.7.1d

Identifying common temperatures

Work with a partner to circle all the correct temperatures. (Sometimes two answers are correct.)

	Temperature of ...			
1.	... boiling water	100 °C	−100 °C	+100 °C
2.	... the human body	73 °C	37 °C	−37 °C
3.	... a fridge	3 °C	0 °C	4 °C
4.	... the classroom	21 °C	+21 °C	40 °C
5.	... water freezing	0 °C	10 °C	−10 °C
6.	... a freezer	−18 °C	18 °C	−100 °C
7.	... a freshly made cup of coffee	20 °C	100 °C	+75 °C
8.	... liquid nitrogen	−100 °C	−196 °C	196 °C

Discuss your answers with another pair.
If you have access to the internet, you could check any that you disagree about.

Resource 5.7.1e

Test results 1

Here are the results of a test taken by some Year 5 pupils.
Complete the table and answer the questions.

The first two table entries have been completed for you. Remember, for marks above the benchmark, the difference is positive and for marks below the benchmark, the difference is negative.

Pupil	Score out of 100	Difference from the benchmark score of 80
Adam	82	+2
Ben	75	−5
Chiara	83	
David	79	
Ella	90	
Farshad	78	
Gemma	86	
Harry	80	
Isla	74	

1. Which pupil's score equalled the benchmark? _____

2. How many pupils scored above the benchmark? _____

3. How many pupils scored below the benchmark? _____

4. Write Ben's difference from the benchmark in words. _____

5. Whose mark is furthest from the benchmark? _____

Resource 5.7.1f

Test results 2

Here are the results of a test taken by some Year 5 pupils.

Complete the table and answer the questions.

The first table entry has been completed for you. For marks above the benchmark, the difference is positive and for marks below the benchmark, the difference is negative.

Pupil	Score out of 100	Difference from the benchmark score of 80
Adam	82	+2
Ben	75	
Chiara	83	
David		−1
Ella		+10
Farshad	78	
Gemma		+6
Harry	80	
Isla		−6
Jamie		−5
Kaia		+20

1. Which pupil's score equalled the benchmark? _____

2. How many pupils scored above the benchmark? _____

3. How many pupils scored below the benchmark? _____

4. Write Ben's difference from the benchmark in words. _____

5. Whose mark is furthest below the benchmark? _____

6. Which two pupils scored the same mark? _____

7. Whose mark is furthest from the benchmark? _____

8. Who scored full marks? _____

Resource 5.7.2

Elevations of capital cities

	London, UK	Madrid, Spain	Amsterdam, The Netherlands	Copenhagen, Denmark	Baku, Azerbaijan	Rome, Italy	Quito, Ecuador
Elevation (m) of a selection of capital cities							
Height (m)	14	588	−2	0	−28	14	2850

Elevation means height above sea level.
Study the table and answer the questions.

1. Which city is exactly at sea level?

2. How many cities are below sea level?

3. How many cities are above sea level?

4. Put the cities in order, starting with the city that is at the greatest height above sea level.

5. Which two cities are at the same elevation?

6. What is the difference in elevation between Baku and Copenhagen?

7. What is the difference in elevation between Amsterdam and Rome?

8. Make up a question of your own.

Resource 5.7.3a

Completing number lines

Complete the number lines.

1.

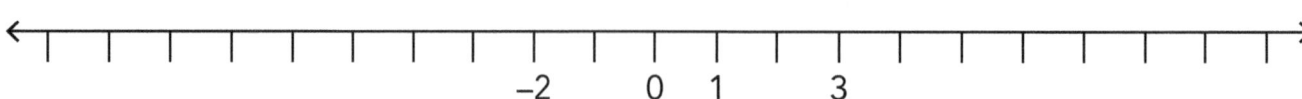

2.

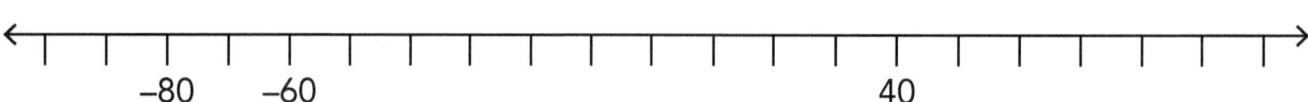

3.

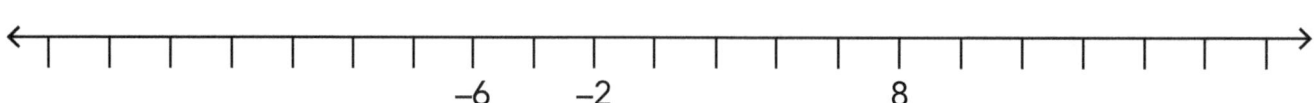

4.

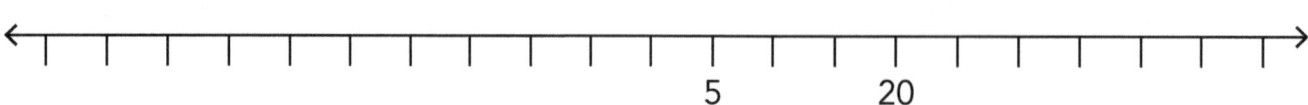

5.

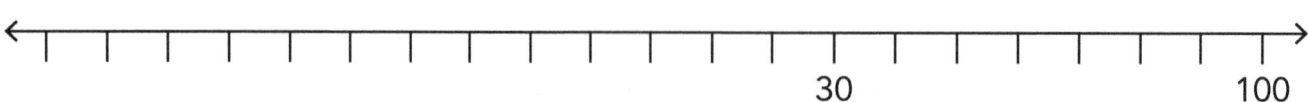

6.

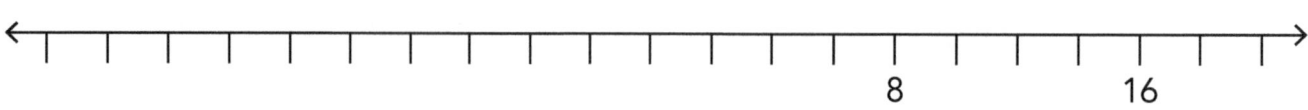

Resource 5.7.3b

January temperatures in European cities

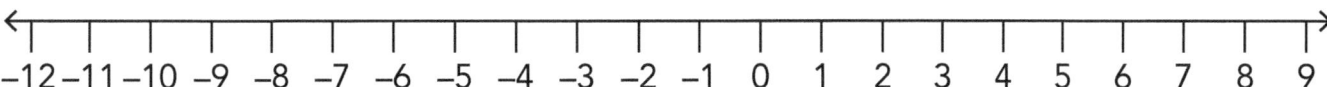

January temperatures in …	Highest	Lowest
Amsterdam	1°C	−2°C
Athens	7°C	4°C
Barcelona	5°C	1°C
Berlin	−2°C	−5°C
Budapest	−3°C	−6°C
Helsinki	−8°C	−11°C
Lisbon	8°C	5°C
London	3°C	0°C
Warsaw	−6°C	−8°C

Use the number line to help answer the questions on the temperatures in the different cities.

1. Which city has the highest temperature? _____

2. Which city has the lowest temperature? _____
3. What is the difference between the highest and lowest temperatures in these cities?

    a) Athens _____

    b) Amsterdam _____

    c) Budapest _____
4. Make up and answer a question of your own.

_____

_____

© HarperCollinsPublishers 2018

Resource 5.7.4a

True or false statements

Work with a partner to decide whether the following statements are true or false. Use the number line for support.

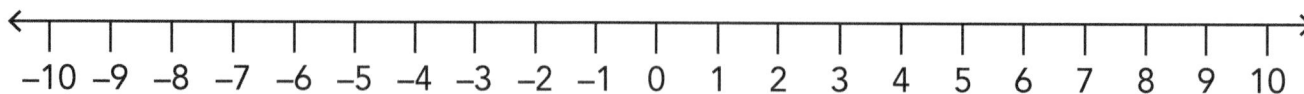

1. The points representing 7 and −3 are 10 units apart. TRUE/ FALSE

2. Three whole numbers less than −4 are −3, −2 and −1. TRUE/ FALSE

3. Two whole numbers between −7 and −2 are −4 and 5. TRUE/ FALSE

4. The two numbers represented by points 4 units from the origin are 4 and −4. TRUE/ FALSE

5. $-3 > -13$ TRUE/ FALSE

6. All numbers to the right of −2 are positive. TRUE/ FALSE

7. The distance between −2 and 4 is the same as the distance between −4 and 2. TRUE/ FALSE

8. $-8 < 4$ TRUE/ FALSE

9. Zero is neither negative nor positive. TRUE/ FALSE

10. The points representing 3 and −11 are 8 units apart. TRUE/ FALSE

Resource 5.7.4b

Fill the gap!

Fill each gap with a suitable number.

1. (odd number)   −8 < _____ < −2

2. (even number)   −2 > _____ > −7

3. (negative number)   3 > _____ > −2

4. (number divisible by 5)   −6 < _____ < 6

5. (positive number)   −9 < _____ < 2

6. (number divisible by 3)   6 > _____ > −4

7. (largest possible number)   −8 < _____ < −2

8. (smallest possible number)   −1 > _____ > −10

Fill each gap with suitable numbers.

9. (all possible even integers)   −9 < _____ < −1

10. (all possible odd integers)   −7 < _____ < 4

Check your answers with a number line.

Resource 5.7.4c

Ordering numbers

1. Order the temperatures from lowest to highest.
   −1 °C   −4 °C   8 °C   2 °C   −9 °C

   _____

2. Order the temperatures from highest to lowest.
   −5 °C   −14 °C   7 °C   19 °C   3 °C

   _____

3. Order these numbers from highest to lowest.
   −12   −24   16   30   −9

   _____

4. Order these numbers from lowest to highest.
   −17   32   19   −14   −5

   _____

5. Order these numbers from highest to lowest.
   −19.5   53   −19   −12   35

   _____

Resource 5.7.4d

Temperature changes

1. The temperature is 0°C and rises by 11°C.

   What is the temperature now? _____

2. The temperature is −3°C and rises by 5°C.

   What is the temperature now? _____

3. The temperature is −7°C and rises by 4°C.

   What is the temperature now? _____

4. The temperature is −2°C and rises by 10°C.

   What is the temperature now? _____

5. The temperature is 6°C and falls by 7°C.

   What is the temperature now? _____

6. The temperature is 4°C and falls by 10°C.

   What is the temperature now? _____

7. The temperature is 2°C and falls by 9°C.

   What is the temperature now? _____

8. The temperature is −4°C and falls by 5°C.

   What is the temperature now? _____

9. What is the fall in temperature between 3°C and −8°C? _____

10. What is the rise in temperature between −6°C and 12°C? _____

Resource 5.8.1a

Circle

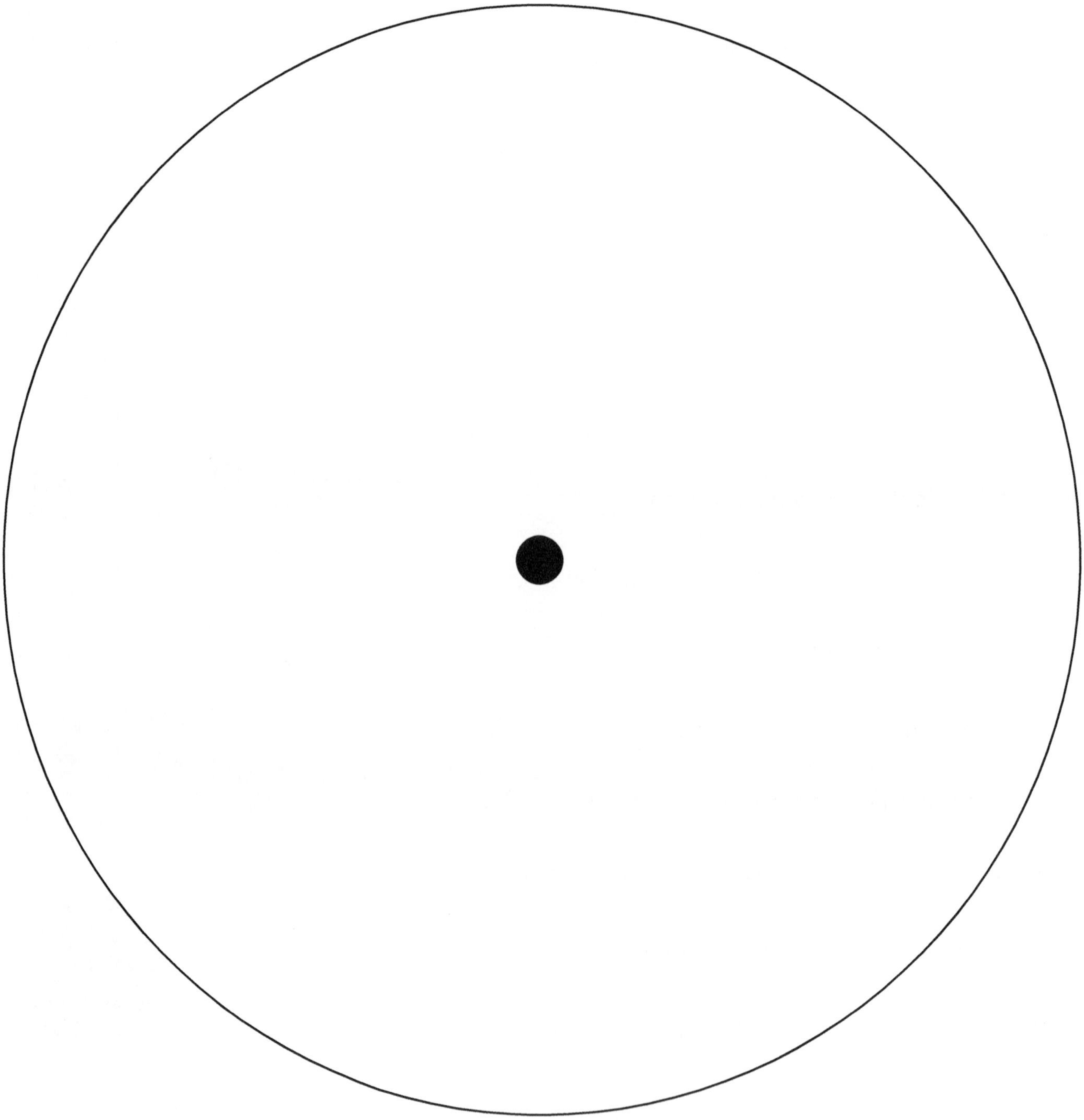

Resource 5.8.1b

Missing dimensions

diameter = 112 cm

radius = _____ cm

radius = 244 cm

diameter = _____ cm

diameter = 150 cm

radius = _____ cm

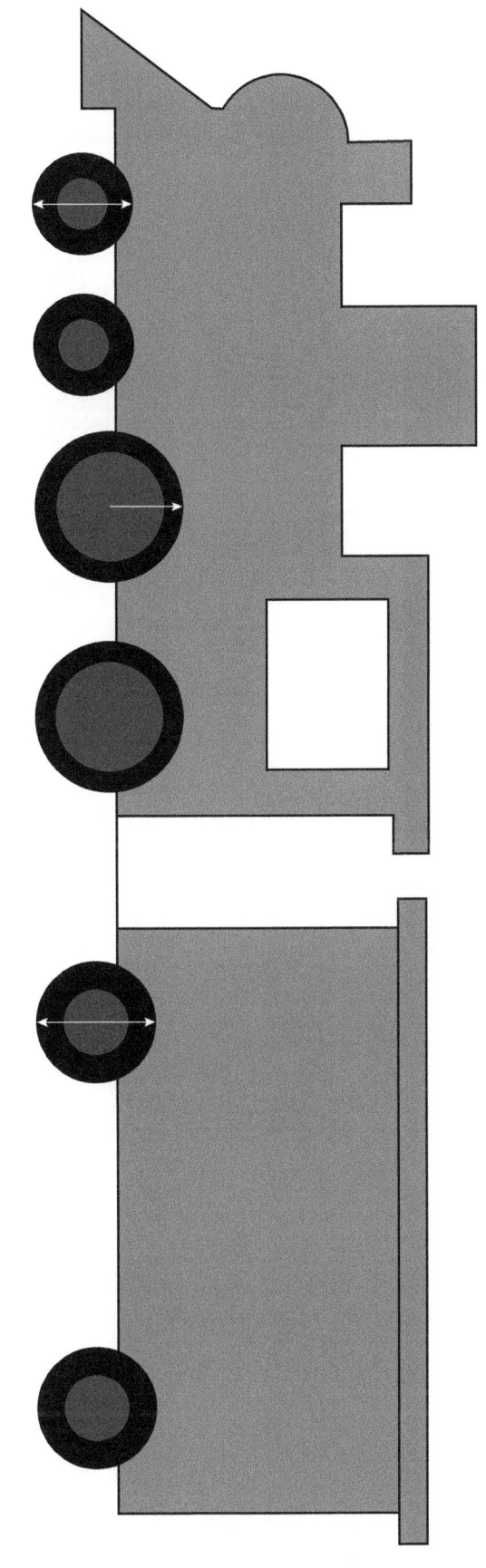

© HarperCollins*Publishers* 2018   **273**

Resource 5.8.1c

Measuring circles (1)

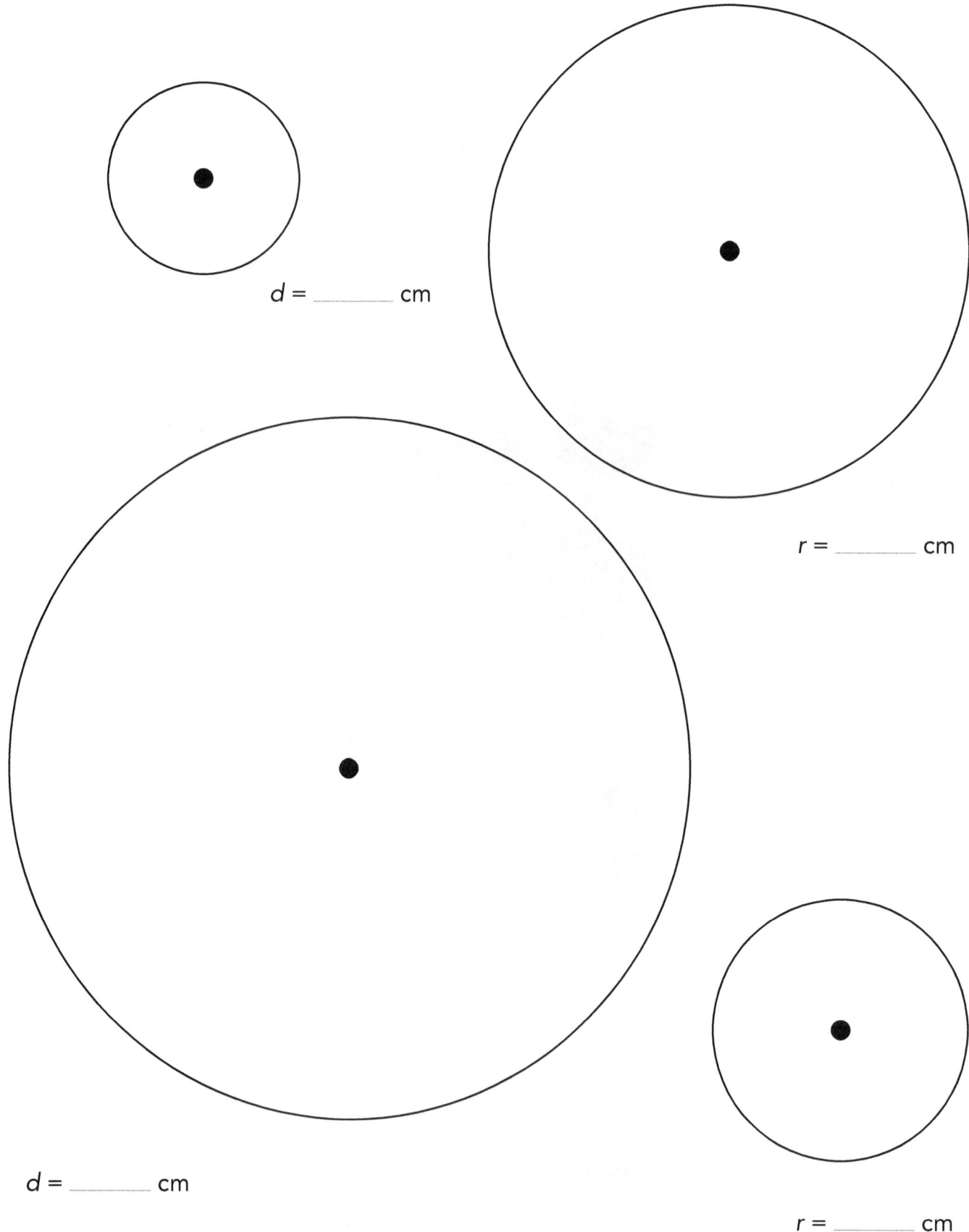

Resource 5.8.1d

Measuring circles (2)

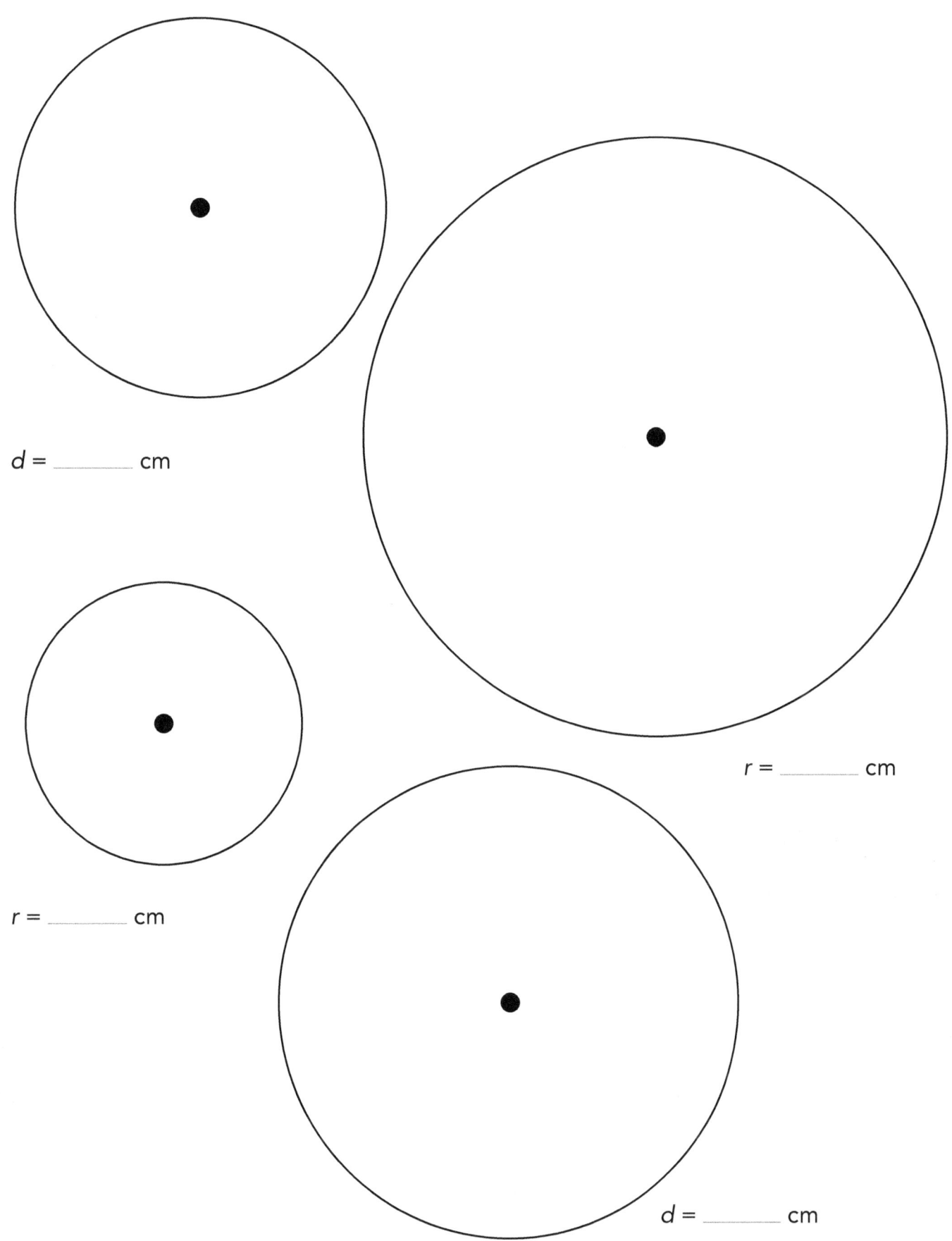

Resource 5.8.2a

Circles in circles

a)
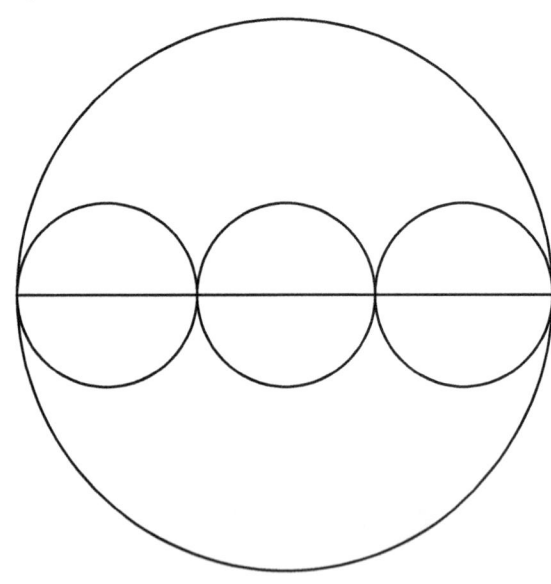

b)
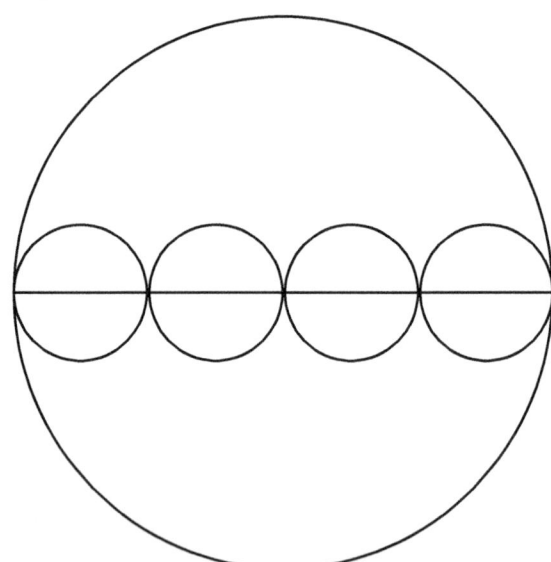

c)
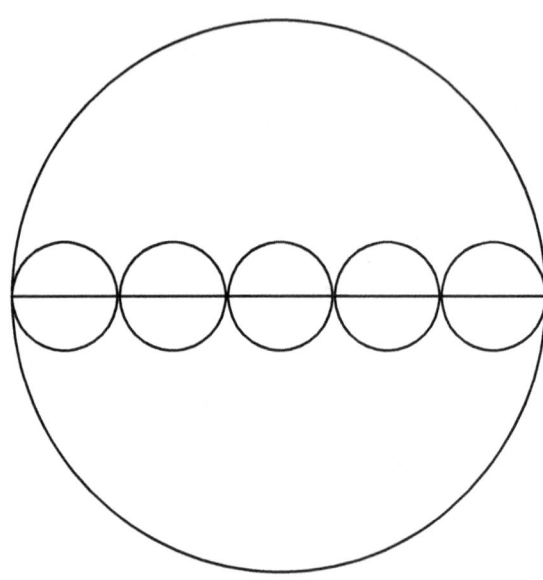

d)
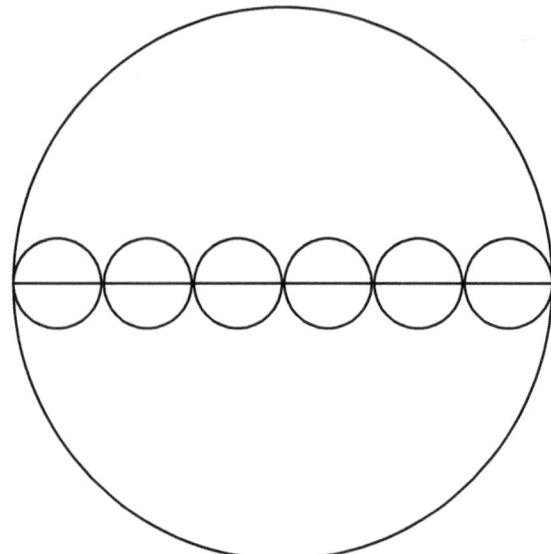

Resource 5.8.2b

Use a square to draw a circle

For the top two squares, draw a circle around each square so that it touches the vertices of the square. For the bottom squares, draw a circle inside each square so that it touches the sides of the square but will not cross over them. You will need to work out where the centre of the square is each time.

a)

b)

c)

d)

© HarperCollinsPublishers 2018

Resource 5.8.3

Symmetry in 2-D shapes

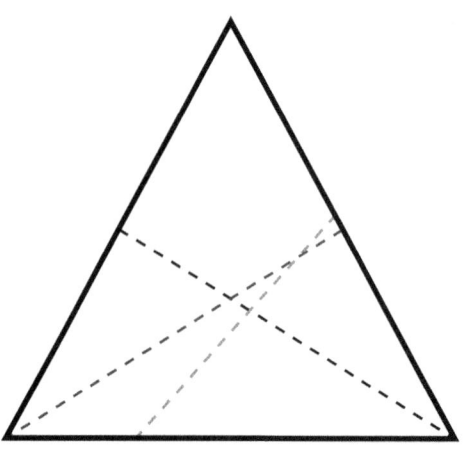
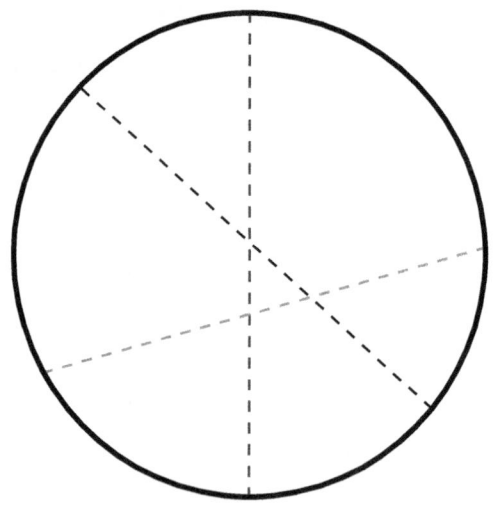
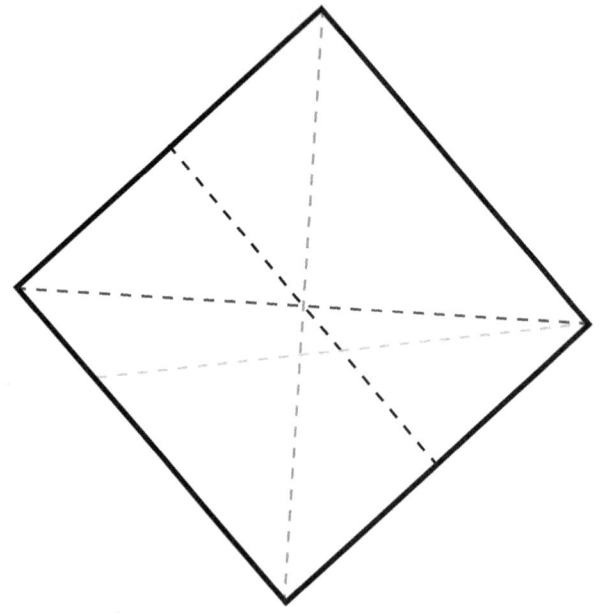
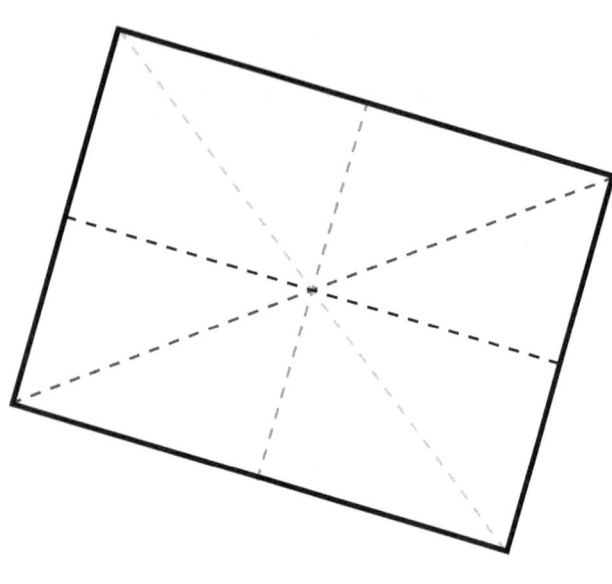

Resource 5.8.4a

Find the angles

© HarperCollins*Publishers* 2018

279

Resource 5.8.4b

Naming angles

Name all the angles in each diagram that have point X as a vertex.

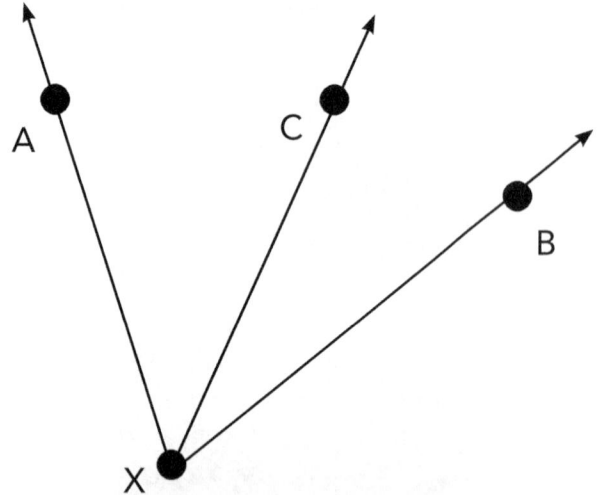

∠ _____

∠ _____

∠ _____

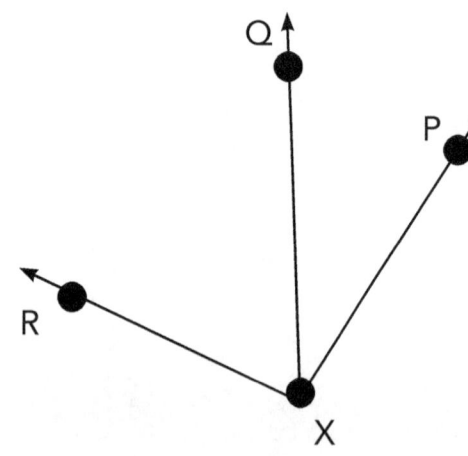

∠ _____

∠ _____

∠ _____

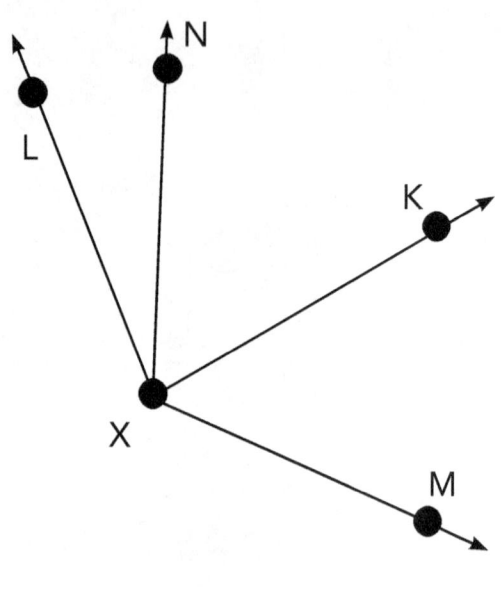

∠ _____   ∠ _____

∠ _____   ∠ _____

∠ _____   ∠ _____

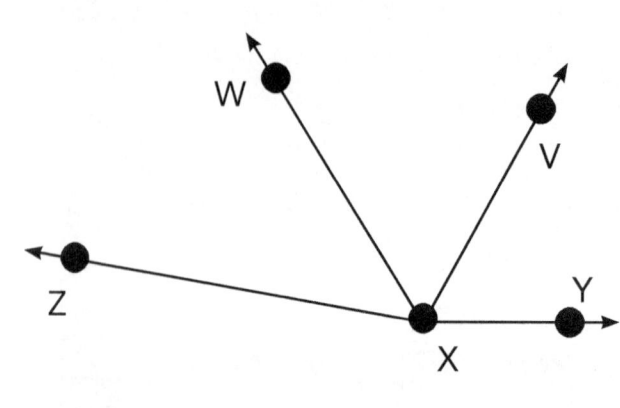

∠ _____   ∠ _____

∠ _____   ∠ _____

∠ _____   ∠ _____

Resource 5.8.4c

Jump the levels

The picture below is a screen grab from a video game. You have to get your character from the castle (bottom left) to the house (top right). To do this and pass from one level to the next, your character must colour all the vertically opposite angles on the way. Use a different set of colours for each pair of vertically opposite angles that share the same vertex. Good Luck!

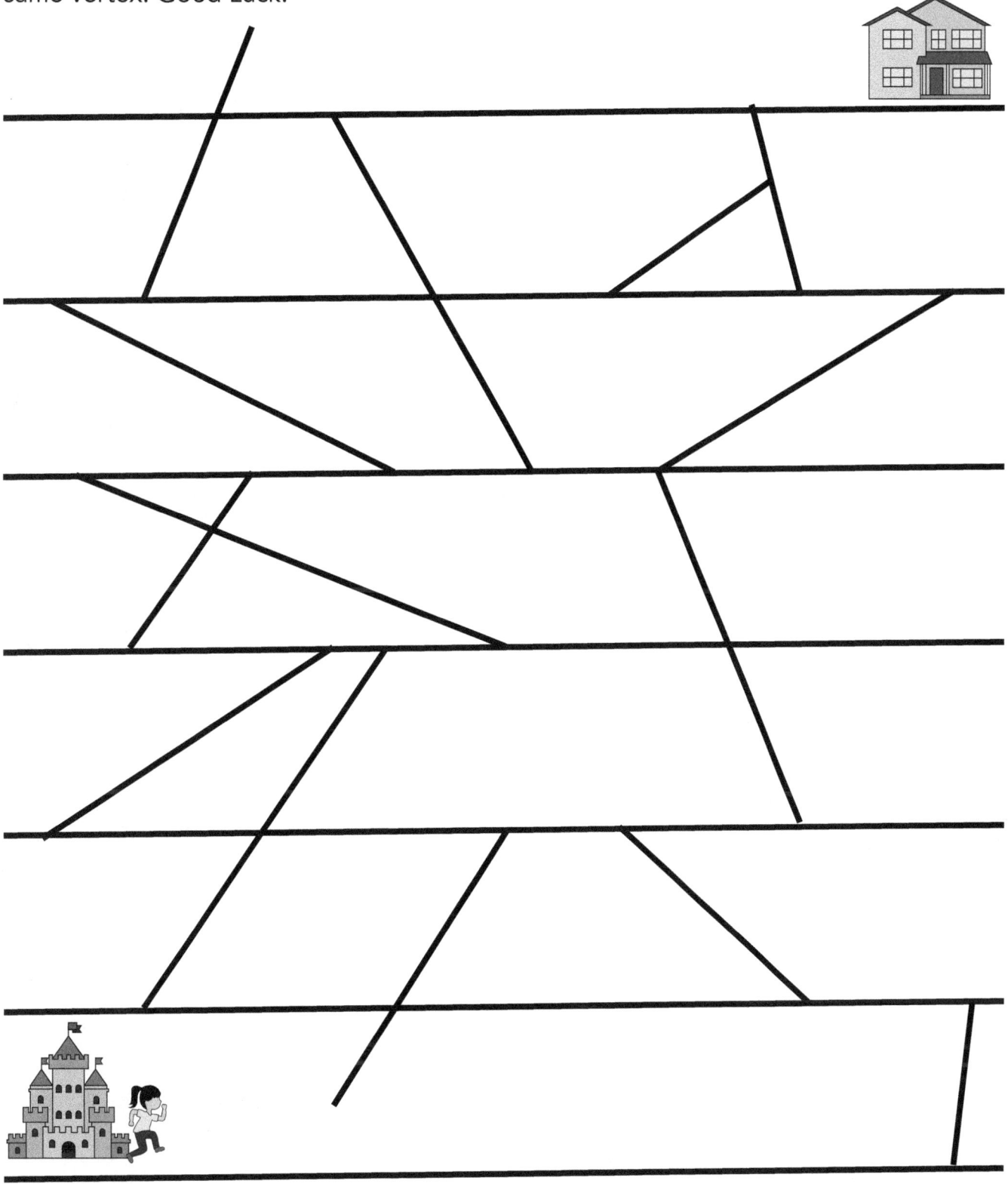

© HarperCollinsPublishers 2018

281

Resource 5.8.5a

Degrees in a circle

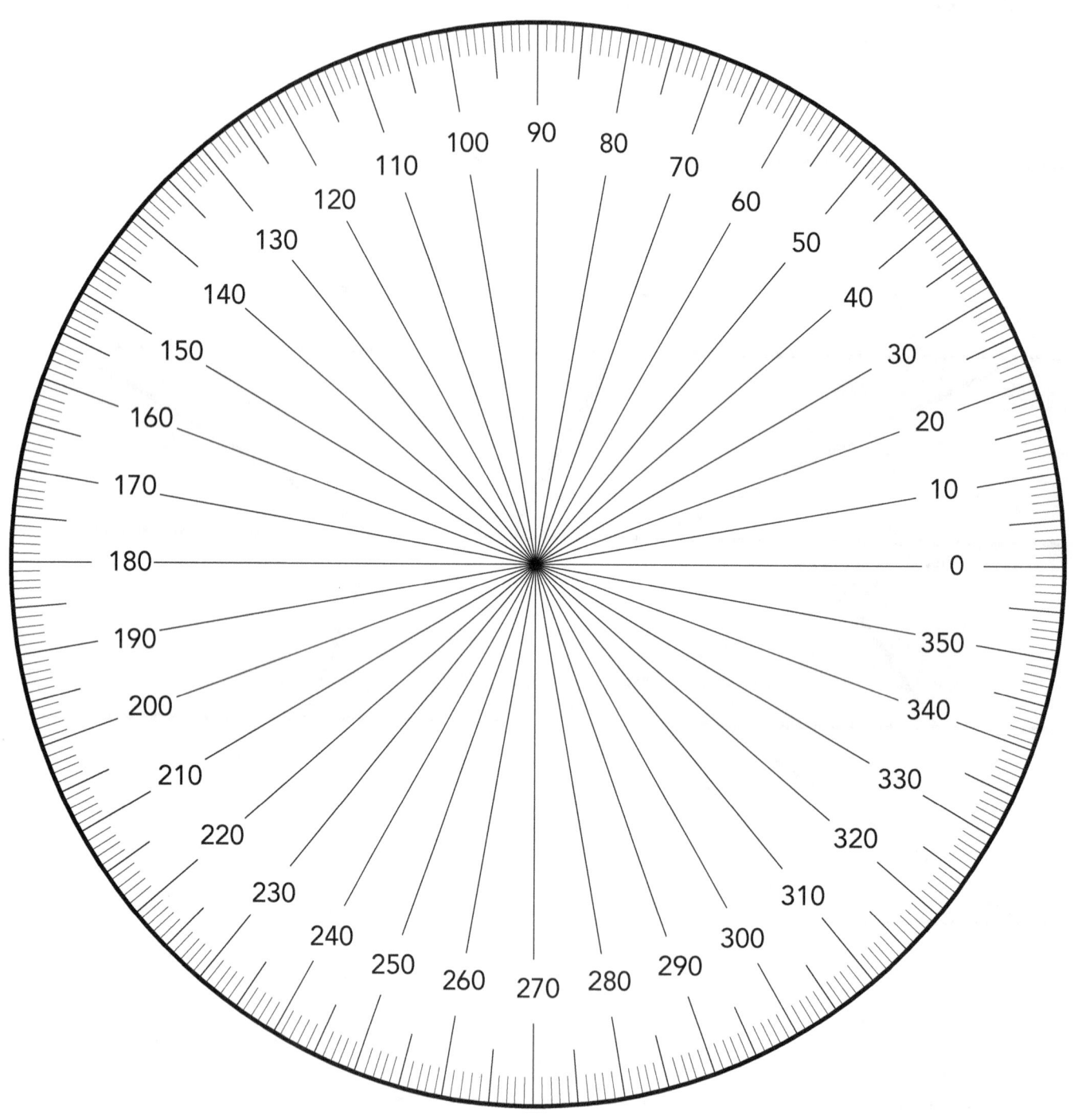

Resource 5.8.5b

Types of angle

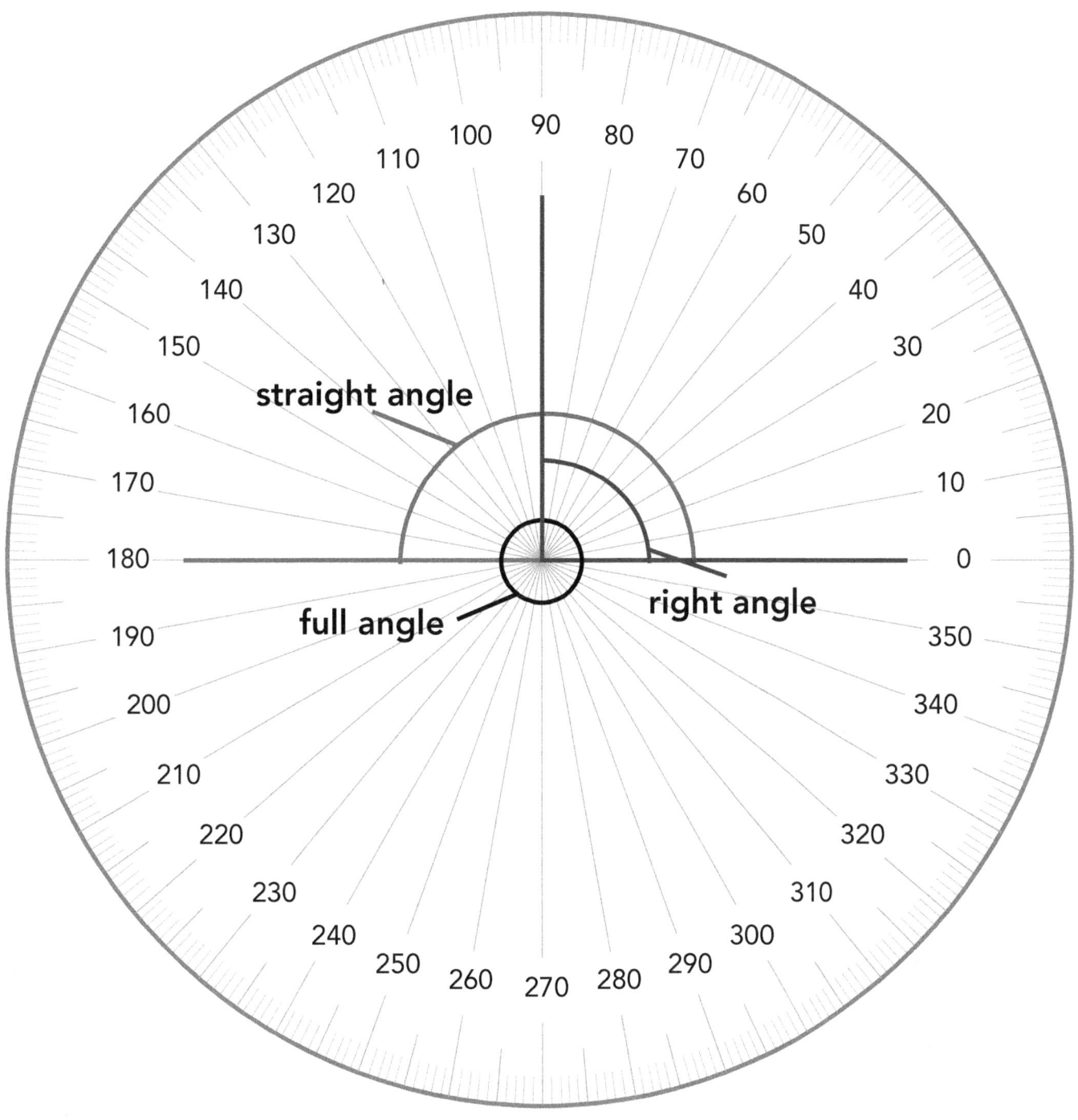

Resource 5.8.6

Measuring angles

Use a protractor to measure each angle.

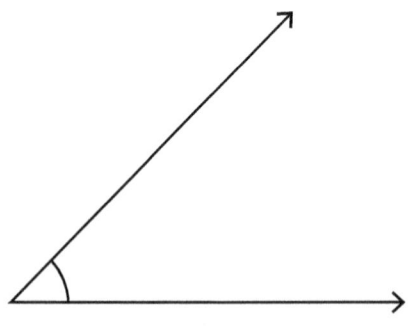

Angle: _____

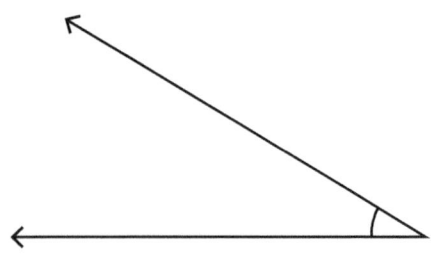

Angle: _____

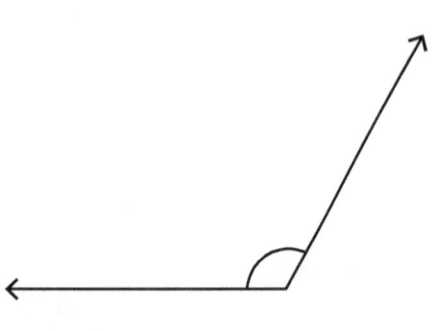

Angle: _____

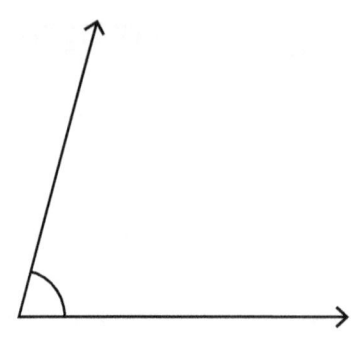

Angle: _____

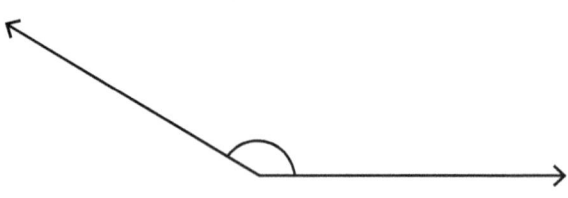

Angle: _____

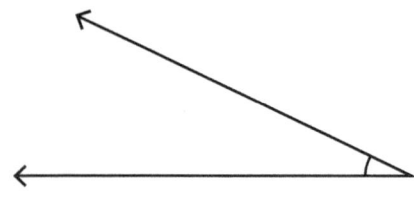

Angle: _____

Resource 5.8.7

Drawing angles

Follow the six steps.

Step 1: Draw a point that is the vertex of the angle and extend a straight line from it.

Step 2: Label the vertex with a letter, for example O. Label the end of the line with another letter, for example A. This makes the line OA.

Step 3: Place the centre of the protractor on the vertex and line up the baseline with the line OA drawn in Step 1. Double-check that the baseline that represents 0 degrees is on the line.

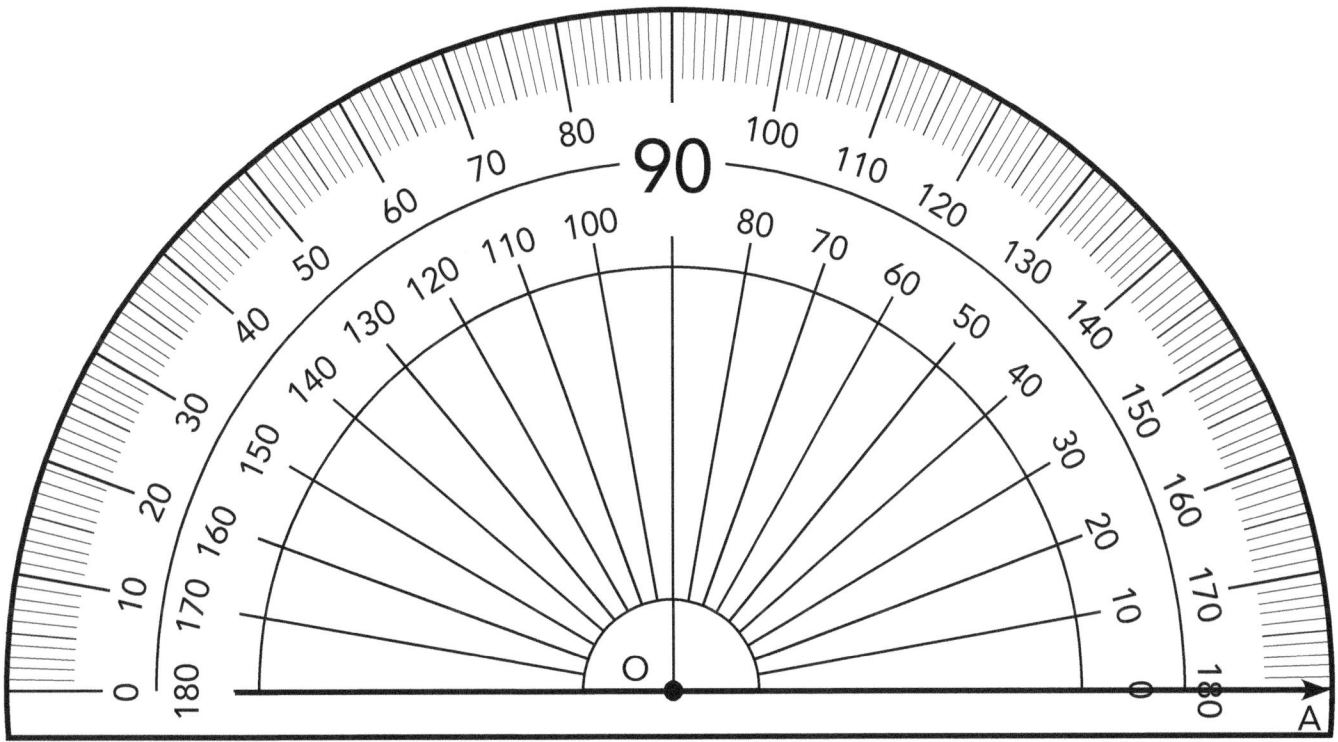

Step 4: Find the marking for the specified angle size along the scale on the protractor, in this example 50 degrees, and mark a dot on the paper next to this marking.

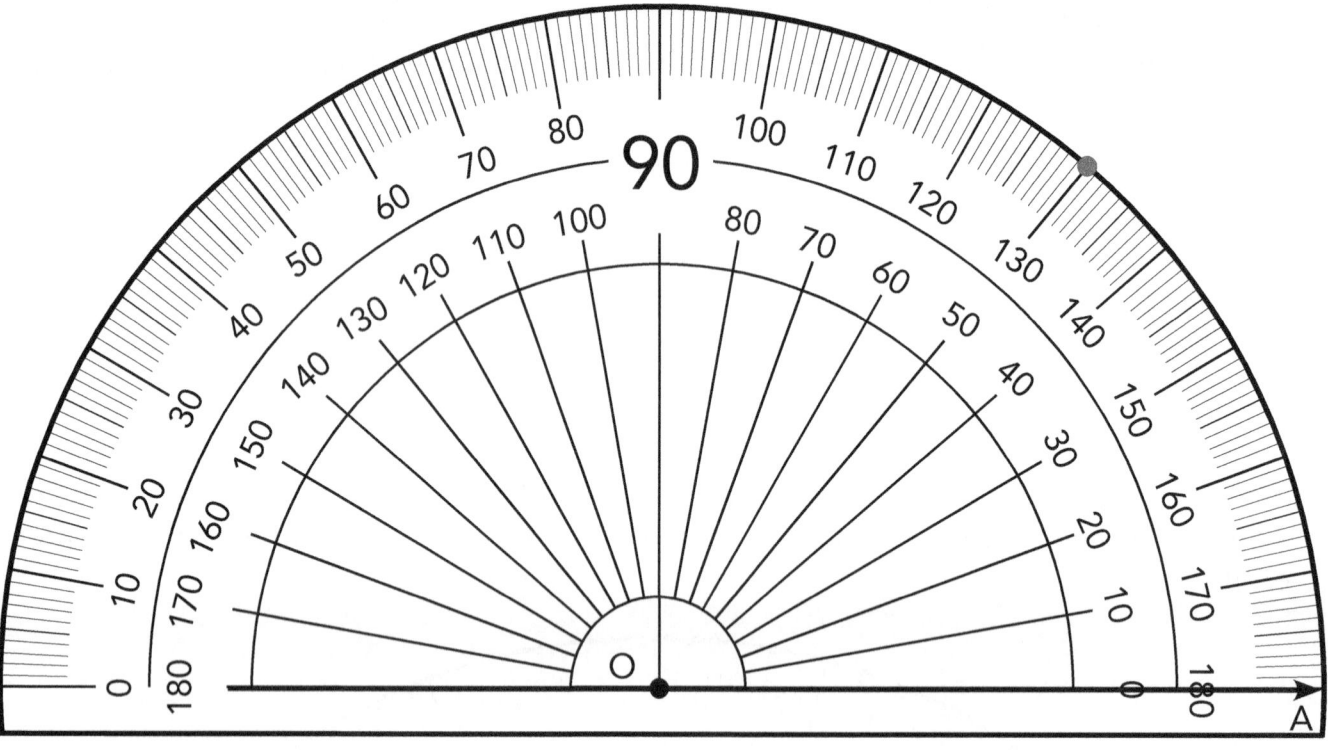

Step 5: Remove the protractor and use a straight edge, such as a ruler, to draw a line from the vertex to the dot that represents 50 degrees.

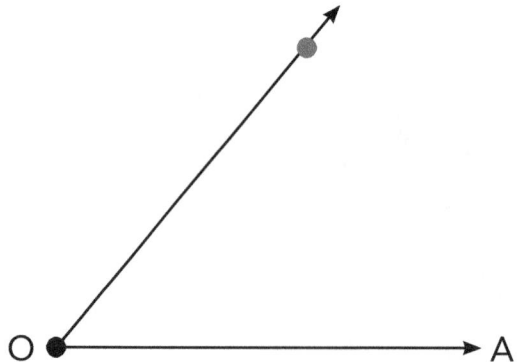

Step 6: Label the second line, for example OB. Record the angle on the drawing or beside it using the correct naming convention, for example: ∠AOB = 50°.

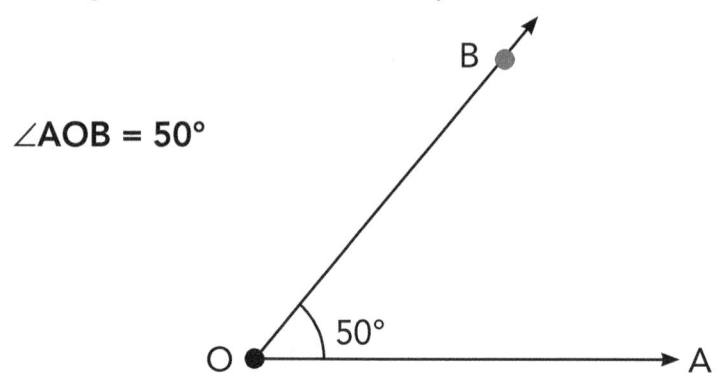

Angle problems

Solve these problems.

a) Three times angle X plus 40° is 100°. What is angle X?

b) Four times angle Y minus 30° is a right angle. What is angle Y?

c) An angle that is 40° less than a full angle is divided into four smaller angles, 1, 2, 3 and 4, all the same size. What is the size of angle 2?

Resource 5.8.8b

Missing angle problems

(i)
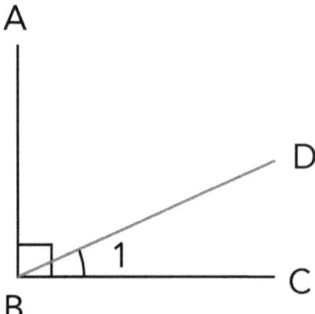

(ii)

(iii)
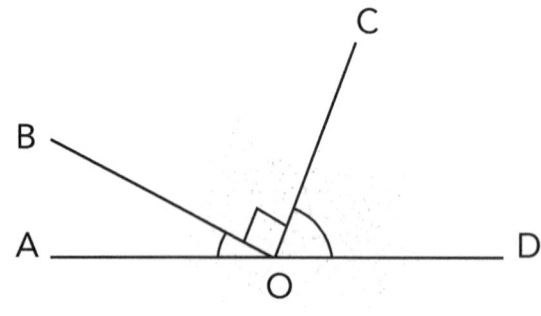

(iv)
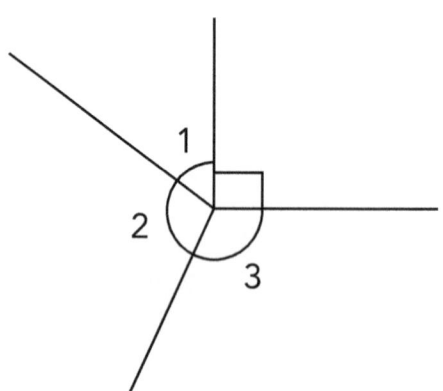

(v)
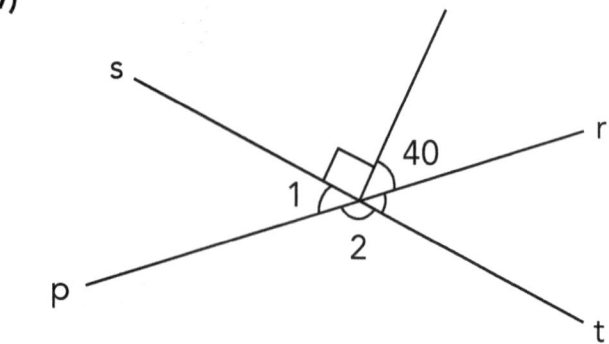

(vi)
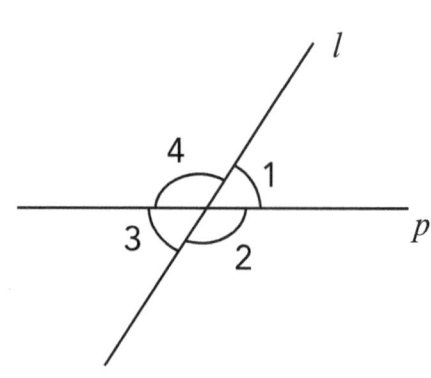

Resource 5.8.9a

Polygon families

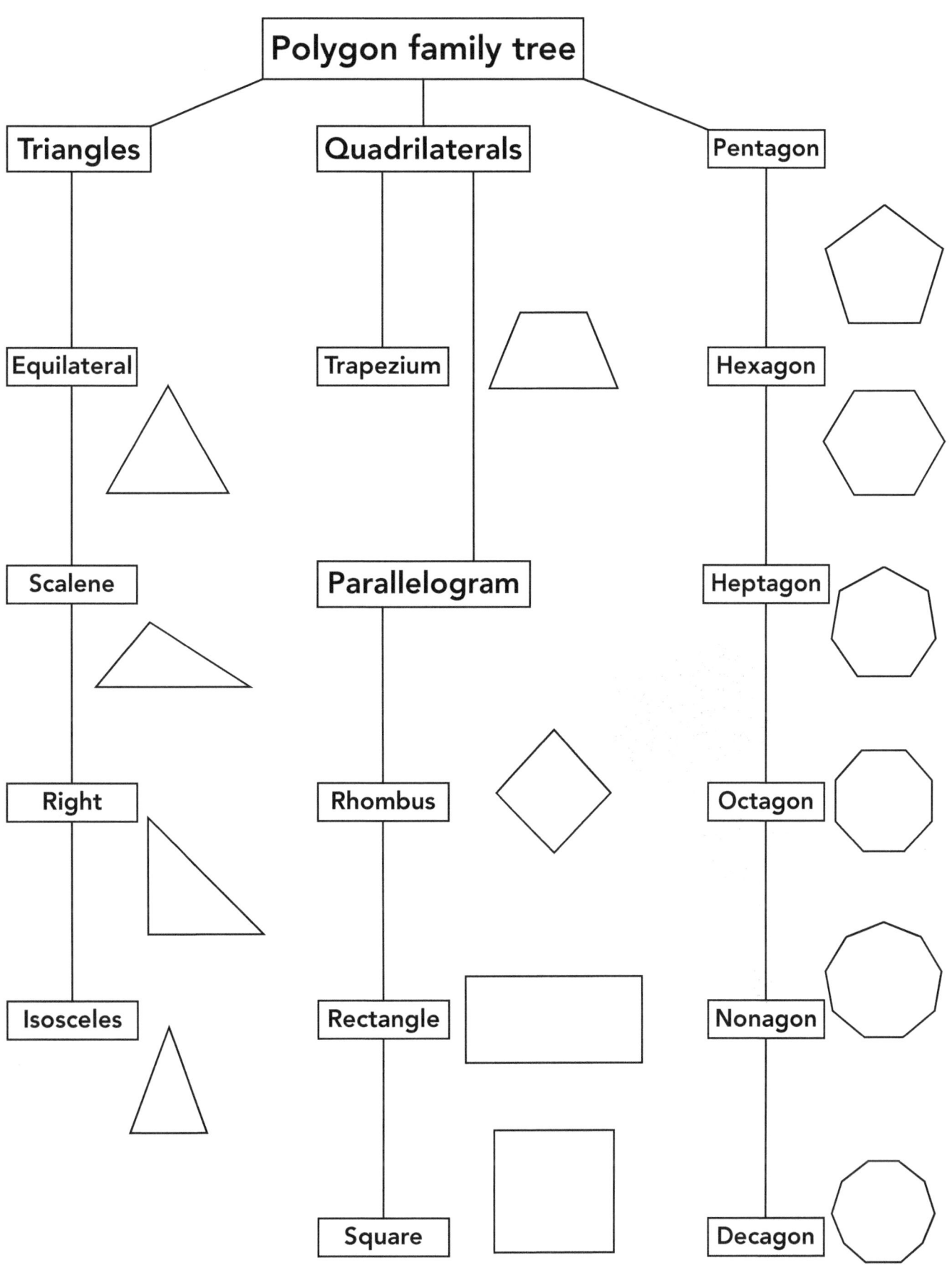

Resource 5.8.9b

Sorting shapes

Sort the shapes into two sets: polygons and non-polygons.
Explain your reasons for each shape.

Resource 5.8.9c

Regular or irregular?

Measure the angles. Circle the polygons that are irregular.
(Hint: You won't need to measure all the angles.)

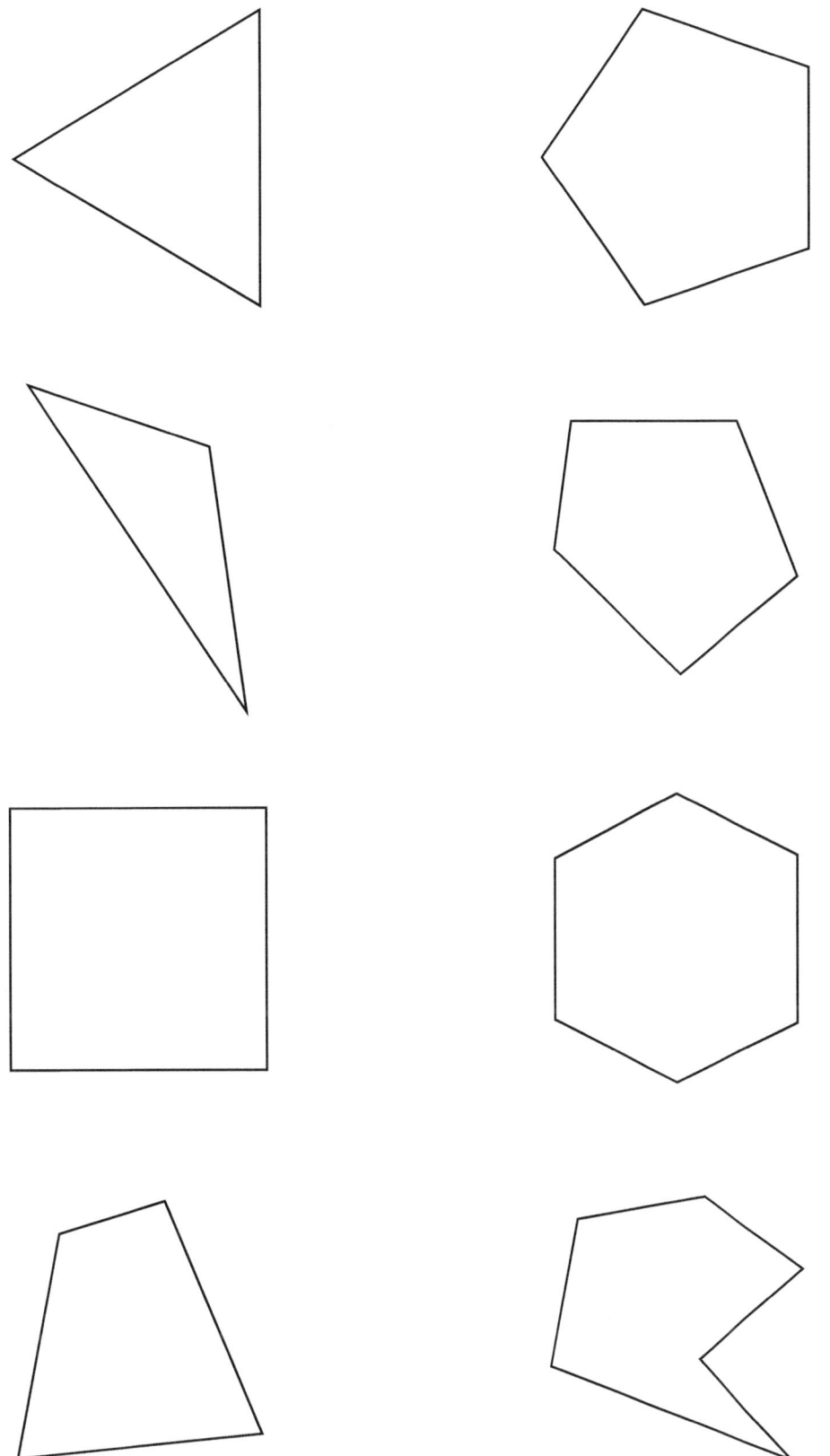

Resource 5.8.9d

Missing angles

Use your knowledge of interior and exterior angles to find the missing angles.

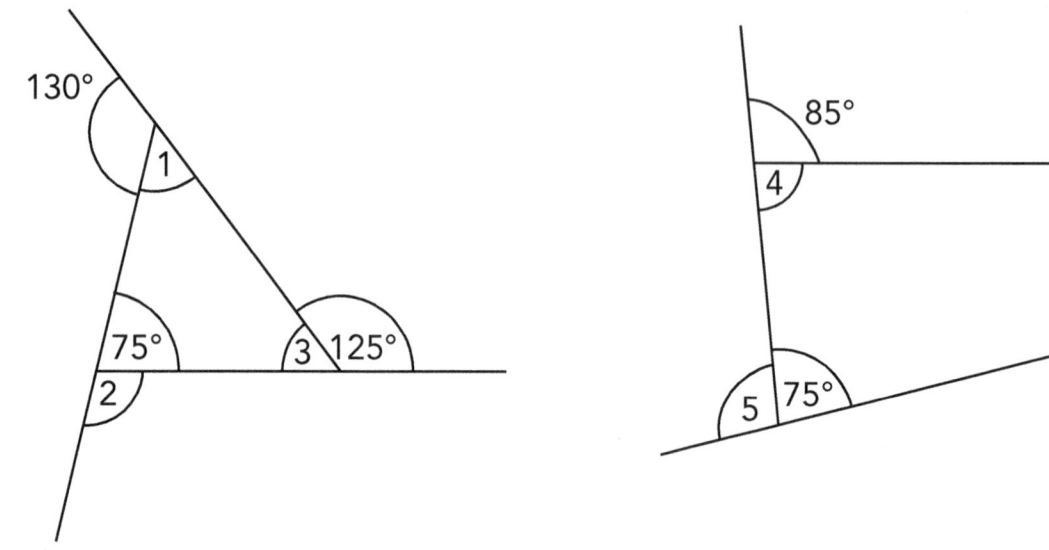

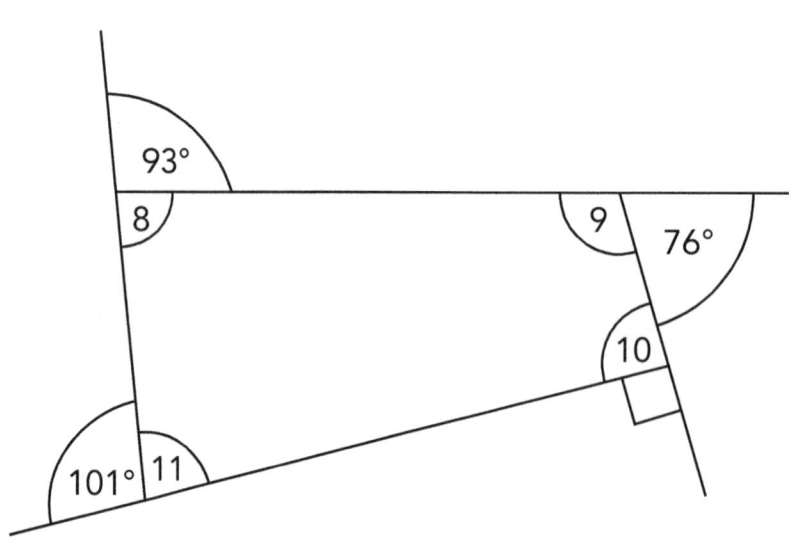

Angle number	Angle size	Angle number	Angle size
1		7	
2		8	
3		9	
4		10	
5		11	
6			

Resource 5.9.1a

Squares and rectangles

Resource 5.9.1b

True or false?

1 Josh made a tower out of building bricks. He then rearranged the bricks to make a bridge. The same bricks were used. The volume of the shape did not change.

2 Two maths books are exactly the same except one is flat on the table and the other is standing upright. The second book has more volume because it is taller.

3 Two apples are picked from a tree. One is smaller than the other. They must have different volumes.

4 If the shape of an object changes, the volume always changes too.

5 Shapes with the same volume always look exactly the same.

6 It is possible to have two objects with the same volume, but they look different.

7 A shoe box with shoes inside it has exactly the same volume as the same shoe box that is empty.

8 The volume of two objects is the same. They must look exactly the same too.

9 Two bricks have the same height and width, but one is longer than the other. Their volumes are different.

Resource 5.9.2a

Simple cuboids

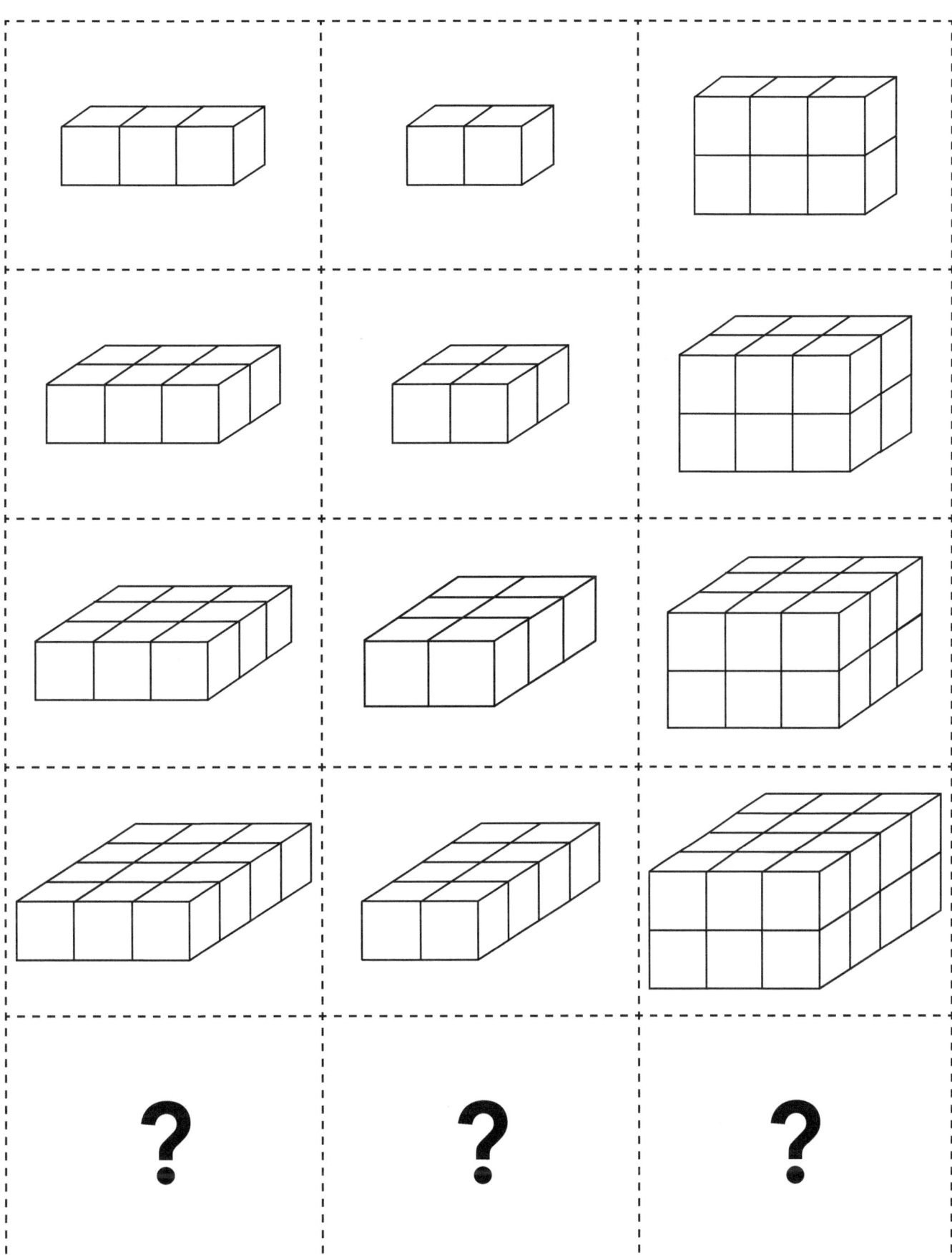

Roll a volume!

You will need a partner, a dice and plenty of centimetre cubes!

1. Roll a dice four or five times and keep a running score so that you know the overall total.
2. The total of your rolls is the volume of the cuboid that you need to make. Your challenge is to make as many different cuboids as you can with this volume. Think carefully about how many centimetre cubes you need to use to make a cuboid with this volume.
3. Before you start, visualise some of the different cuboids you might be able to make. Can you and your partner predict how many there might be?
4. Describe some of the cuboids to your partner. There will always be one that you can make – sometimes there will be more. Use the cubes to make your different cuboids.
5. Try rolling the dice again and explore the possibilities. Which volume did you find the most cuboids for?

THINK ABOUT:

- Are any of your cuboids the same as each other? What do you need to watch out for?
- How did you describe your cuboids to your partner? Did you give the same sort of information each time? What was it?
- What is the <u>one</u> cuboid that you will always be able to make out of a set of cubes?
- What is the volume of the cuboids you have made?

Resource 5.9.2c

Cubic shapes (1)

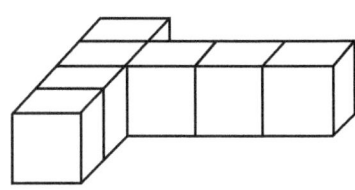 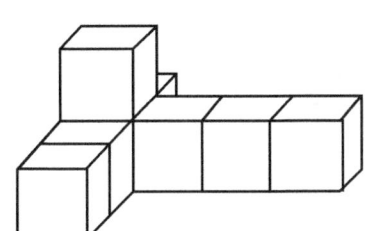 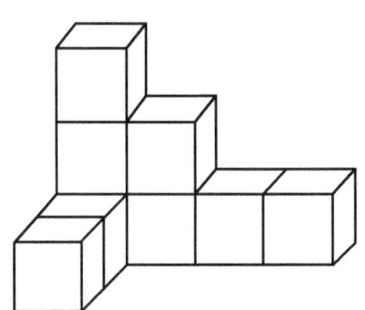

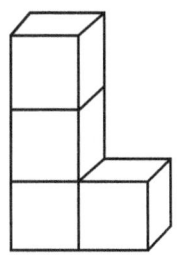 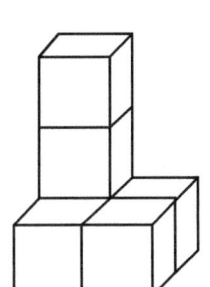 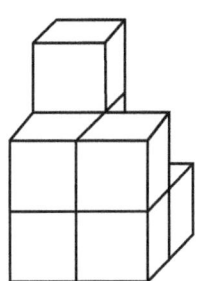

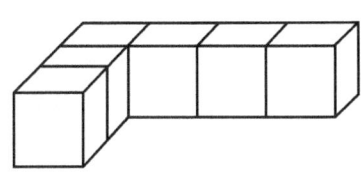 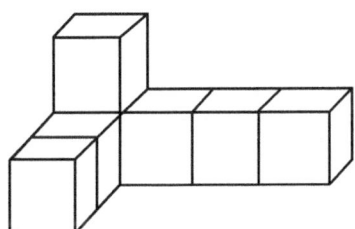 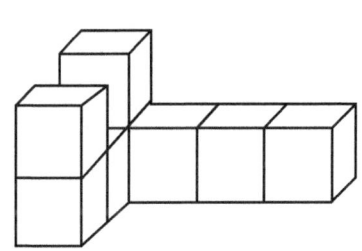

Resource 5.9.2d

Cubic shapes (2)

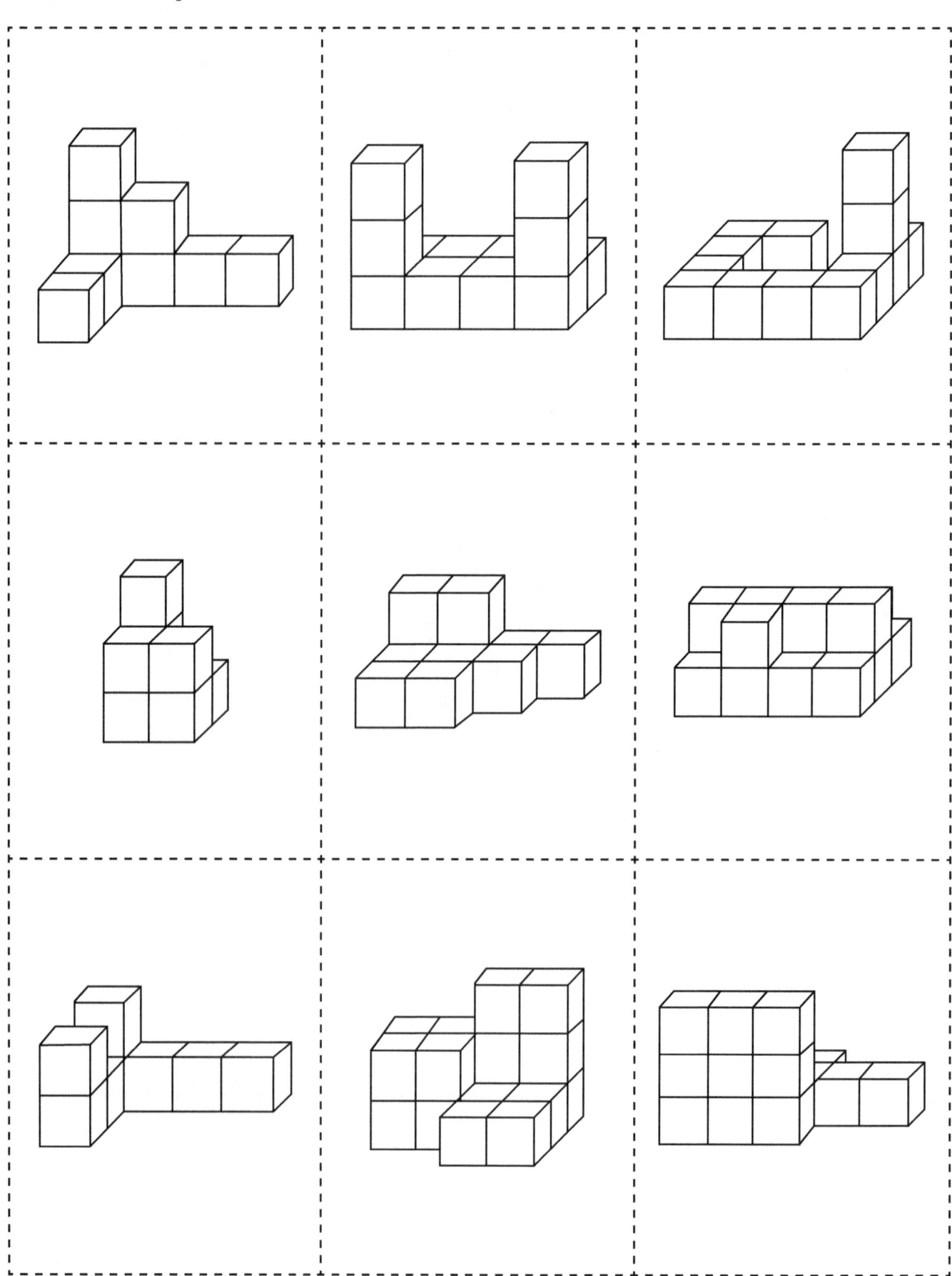

Resource 5.9.2e

Prove it!

Can your partner prove different facts about cubic centimetres and cubic metres?

1. Write down a fact based on some of the topics you have learned about in Unit 9.2. This could be:

    (i) A fact about cubic centimetres:
    $2\,cm^3$ is larger than $2\,cm^2$.

    (ii) A fact about cubic metres:
    1 cubic metre has a length of 100 cm, a width of 100 cm and a height of 100 cm.

    (iii) A fact about the volume of cuboids:
    There are three different cuboids that can be made with a volume of $8\,cm^3$.

    (iv) A fact about the volume of different cubic shapes:
    A cubic shape is made out of 9 cubes with an edge length of 1 cm. The whole shape has a volume of $9\,cm^3$.

2. Pass your fact to your partner to look at. Can they prove that your fact is true? They will probably need to use centimetre cubes to help them, but they may like to try drawing instead.

Extra challenge

Give your partner a choice of facts, including some that are not true.
Your partner's job is to spot the true facts from the false!

© HarperCollinsPublishers 2018

Resource 5.9.3a

Change the units

The volume of a brick is about 2400 m³	The length of a car is about 4 m²	The length of a pencil sharpener is about 20 mm	The volume of a grape is about 1.2 cm
The area of a football pitch is about 6600 cm²	The volume of a box of chocolates is about 3125 m²	The area of a desk is about 150 cm²	The volume of a freezer is about 1 300 000 m³
The volume of a garage is about 37 m	The area of a newspaper front page is about 1161 cm³	The volume of a paperback book is about 585 m³	

Resource 5.9.3b

Cubic challenge

You will need: a partner to work with, a set of digit cards and a piece of paper each.

1. Shuffle your digit cards and take three cards each.
2. Using your set of three cards, make as many different numbers as possible. You are allowed to write numbers to one decimal place, so the digits 2, 3 and 8 could be used to make whole numbers (like 23 or 82) as well as decimals (like 32.8 and 82.3).
3. Try to find your numbers systematically (for example, in order from smallest to largest).
4. Turn your numbers into measurements of volume by writing 'm^3' next to each one.
5. Swap your piece of paper with your partner. You should now convert each other's list of volumes into cubic centimetres.

REMEMBER! What should you multiply and divide by when converting between cubic metres and cubic centimetres?

6. When you have finished, swap your pieces of paper and check whether your partner has converted your measurements correctly.

TRY THIS! As an extension, choose any two measurements from your list (try choosing one written in m^3 and one written in cm^3) and see whether your partner can explain which is the larger volume and why.

For example: $63.4 \, m^3$ and $6\,000\,000 \, cm^3$
Which is larger and why?

Resource 5.9.4a

Units of measure

millimetres (mm)	centimetres (cm)	metres (m)
kilometres (km)	millilitres (ml)	litres (l)
grams (g)	kilograms (kg)	inches
feet	yards	miles
gallons	pounds (lb)	pints

Approximate measurements cards

1 pound	2.2 pounds	1 inch
1 kg	0.45 kg	450 g
1000 g	2.5 cm	1 pint
570 ml	0.57 l	

Resource 5.9.4c

Mixed imperial and metric units

Your task is to write your own word problems with more than one step and where one of the steps involves converting imperial measurements.

Here is a reminder of some of the facts you have learned already:
    Imperial → Metric
        1 inch ≈ 2.5 cm
        1 pound ≈ 0.45 kg or 45 g
        1 pint ≈ 0.57 l or 570 ml

    Metric → Imperial
    1 centimetre ≈ 0.39 inches
    1 kilogram ≈ 2.2 pounds

Remember to start with an amount in one unit and ask for the answer in another.

Try using these as ideas to start you off:

1. A carpenter wants to make two shelves. One should be _____ inches long and the other should be _____ inches long. The hardware store sells wood at _____ p per centimetre.
   How much will the fence cost in total?

2. A dog weighs _____ pounds and a cat weighs _____ pounds. They both stand on a set of scales at the vets. It gives their total weight in kilograms.
   How many kilograms do they weigh altogether?

Resource 5.9.5a

Properties of cubes and cuboids

Has 6 faces.	Has 8 vertices.	Has 12 edges.
All edges are the same length.	Some edges are different lengths.	Length, width and height meet at every vertex.
All faces are the same size and shape (squares).	Some faces are rectangles.	Has three dimensions: length, width and height.

Resource 5.9.5b

True or false?

Use these sentence starters to help you write your own 'True' or 'False' statements. Share your statements with your friends. Can they explain why they are correct or not?

A cuboid's edges are always …

A cuboid's edges are sometimes …

A cuboid's edges are never …

A cube can be made from _____ identical smaller cubes.

If one edge of a cuboid is _____ long, then the sum of the lengths of all its edges will be _____.

If one edge of a cube is _____ long, then the sum of the lengths of all its edges will be _____.

If a shape has _____ faces, it must be a _____.

A cube always has …

A cube sometimes has …

A cube never has …

Resource 5.9.7a

Cuboids from cubes

This investigation is all about making cuboids from cubes.
The cubes you will be thinking about have an edge length of 20 cm.

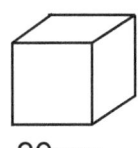

20 cm

If you make a cuboid by putting two of these cubes together, what will its dimensions be? What will its volume be?

What about if you put three cubes together? Or four?

Record your results in a table.

Number of cubes used	Length (cm)	Width (cm)	Height (cm)	Volume (cm^3)
2				
3				
4				

Remember that sometimes there may be more than one cuboid you can make.

Can you see any patterns in your results?

Predict!
Without working it out, what do you think the volume of a cuboid made from 5 cubes will be? Why?
Check your answer.

Predict the volume of cuboids made from 10 and 100 cubes. Explain to your partner how you managed to predict the answer using what you have found.

True or false?

Use these sentence starters to help you write your own 'True' or 'False' statements. Share your statements with your friends. Can they explain why they are correct or not?

If the volumes of two cuboids are the same, then …

If $4^2 = 4 \times 4$, then 4^3 must be equal to …

One way of doubling the volume of a shape is to …

Two identical cubes have an edge length of _____. If they are put together to form a cuboid, the volume will be _____.

_____ identical cubes can be arranged to make _____ different cuboids.

A cuboid with a length of _____, a width of _____ and a height of _____ must have a volume of _____.

Four identical cubes are used to make two different cuboids. The volume of these cuboids …

Resource 5.9.8a

Capacity cards (Set A)

The capacity of a biscuit tin = 4500 cm^3	The capacity of a saucepan = 1.75 litres
The capacity of a tin can = 350 ml	The capacity of a tablespoon = 15 ml
The capacity of a bucket = 6000 ml	The capacity of a cup = 0.26 litres
The capacity of a mixing bowl = 2.2 litres	The capacity of a matchbox = 28 cm^3
The capacity of a shoe box = 3000 cm^3	The capacity of a water bottle = 500 ml

Resource 5.9.8b

Capacity cards (Set B)

A fish tank with a capacity of 60 litres	A bucket with a capacity of 7500 millilitres
A bottle with a capacity of 1.25 litres	A sandwich box with a capacity of 450 millilitres
A cardboard box with a capacity of 80 000 cm³	A watering can with a capacity of 10 000 millilitres
A jerry can with a capacity of 20 litres	A teaspoon with a capacity of 5 millilitres
A jar with a capacity of half a litre	A water tank with a capacity of 2000 litres

Resource 5.9.9a

Capacity cards

20	30	40
50	60	70
80	90	100
20	30	40
50	60	70
80	90	100
cm^3	ml	l
cm^3	ml	l

Resource 5.9.9b

Write your own problems

Your task is to create a set of four problems based on volume and capacity. You can use the questions in the Practice Book for ideas or you might like to sketch an image. Here are some images and example questions you could use.

Remember to work out the answers to your problems before passing them to your friends to solve.

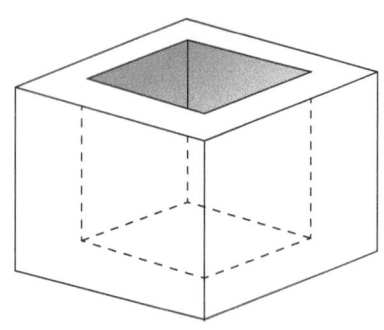

Example questions:

A plastic storage box has a length of 30 cm, a width of 20 cm and a height of 25 cm. What is its volume?

The plastic the box is made from is 5 cm thick. What are the dimensions of the inside of the box?

How many cubic centimetres can the box hold?

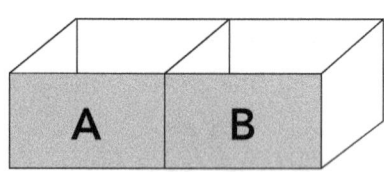

Example question:

Box A and Box B are the same. Box A has a length of 20 cm, a width of 20 cm and a height of 10 cm.

Box A is put next to Box B to make a cuboid. What is the volume of the cuboid?

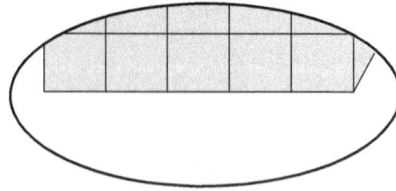

Example question:
This is part of a cube. Each small cube is 1 cm^3. What is the volume of the whole cube?

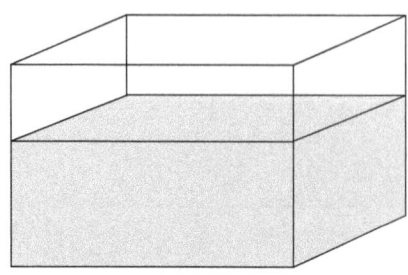

Example question:

A fish tank is 50 cm long, 30 cm wide and 30 cm high. It is filled with water so that the water level is 10 cm from the top.

What capacity of the tank can still be filled with water?

Resource 5.10.1a

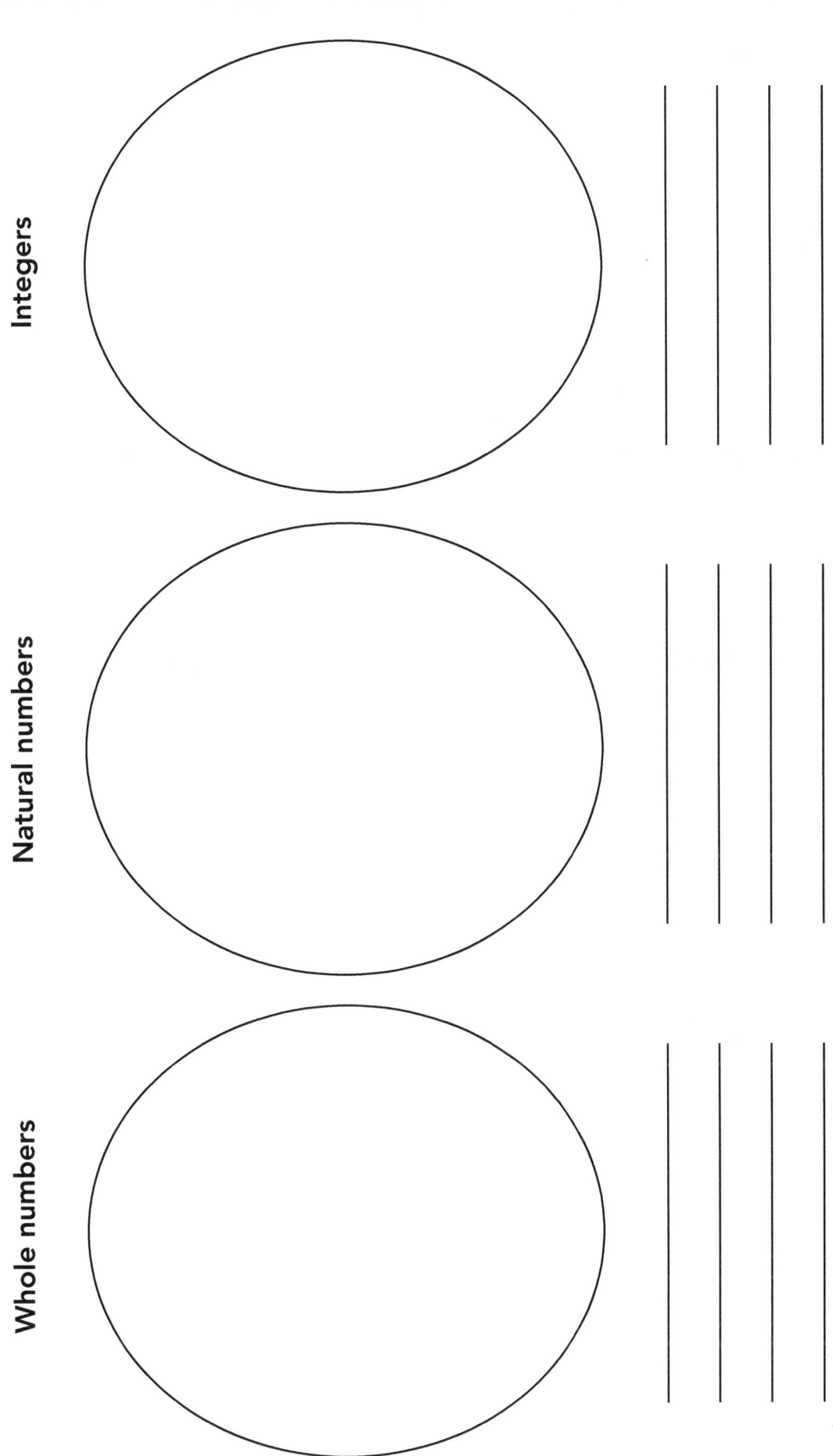

Sorting numbers

Divisibility

Complete the following statements.

36 is divisible by _____.

56 is divisible by _____.

_____ is divisible by 3.

_____ is divisible by 7.

_____ is divisible by both 4 and 10.

Fill in the Venn diagram.

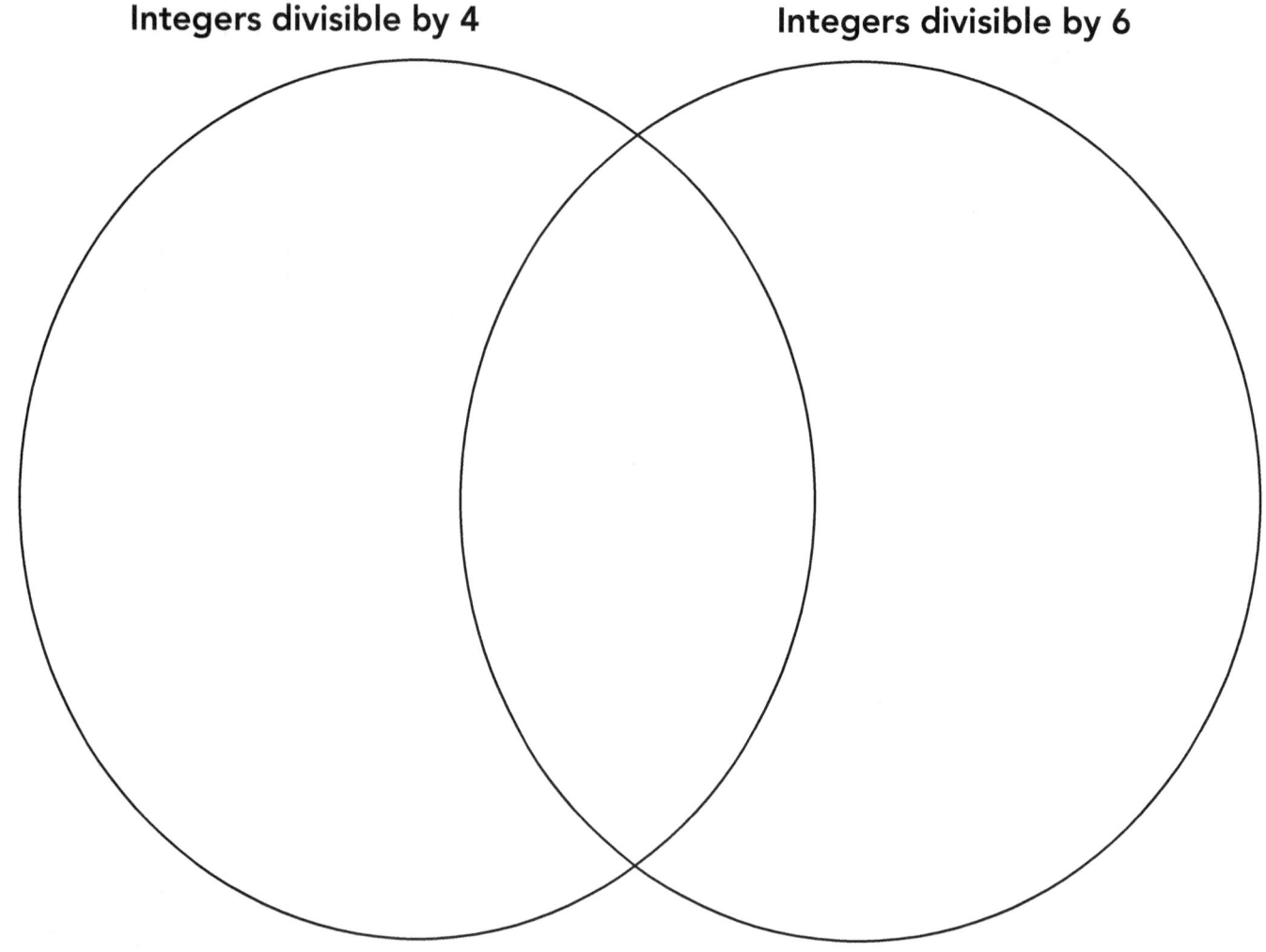

Resource 5.10.1c

True or false?

Cut out the statements and sort them into those that are true and those that are false.

Positive integers are all called natural numbers.

40 is divisible by 10 and 4.

27 is a prime number.

A dividend is divisible by a number only when the quotient is an integer.

All integers are positive numbers.

0 is a whole number.

15 is divisible by 1, 15 and 5 only.

Resource 5.10.1d

Sort the numbers

Sort the numbers into the diagram below.

25   −7   0.5   0 $\frac{3}{5}$ 250   −32   68   0.3 $\frac{1}{10}$

Add five more numbers to each set.

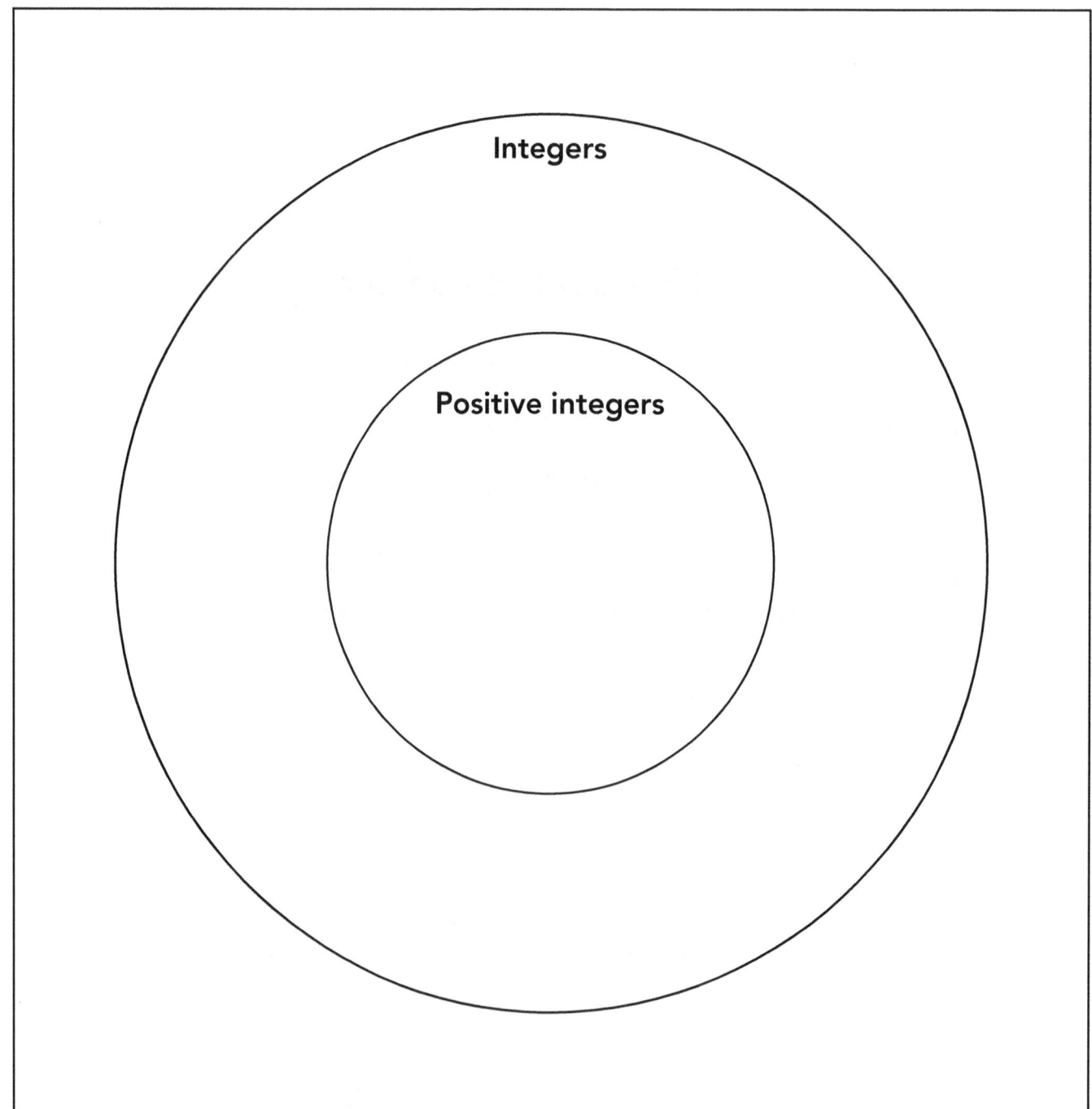

Resource 5.10.1e

Divisible?

Sort the calculations into those where the dividend is divisible by the divisor.
Then add some more of your own.

Dividends are divisible by the divisor	Division with non-zero remainders (dividend is not divisible by the divisor)

32 ÷ 8
10 ÷ 3
 4 ÷ 24
21 ÷ 3
38 ÷ 4
20 ÷ 20
11 ÷ 5

Resource 5.10.2a

Always, sometimes, never

Are these statements always, sometimes or never true?

The digit sum of a multiple of 9 is always 9.
All positive integers have at least 2 factors.
The final digit of a multiple of 4 is even.
The sum of a multiple of 5 and a multiple of 10 will be a multiple of 10.
The integer 21 has 3 factors.

Resource 5.10.2b

Factors and multiples

Find all of the factors and the first 10 multiples.

Factor(s)	Integer	Multiples
	1	
	2	
	3	
	4	
	5	
	6	
	7	
	8	
	9	
	10	
	11	
	12	
	13	
	14	
	15	

Resource 5.10.3a

100 square

Square and cube numbers

Colour all of the square numbers red.
Colour all of the cube numbers blue.

1	2	3	4	5	6	7	8	9	10
11	12	13	14	15	16	17	18	19	20
21	22	23	24	25	26	27	28	29	30
31	32	33	34	35	36	37	38	39	40
41	42	43	44	45	46	47	48	49	50
51	52	53	54	55	56	57	58	59	60
61	62	63	64	65	66	67	68	69	70
71	72	73	74	75	76	77	78	79	80
81	82	83	84	85	86	87	88	89	90
91	92	93	94	95	96	97	98	99	100

What do you notice?

Are any numbers both square and cube numbers? Why?

Square and cube numbers

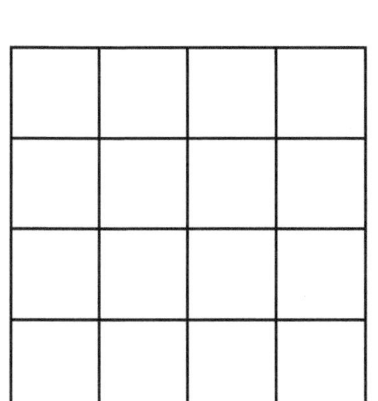

4 × 4 = ____ = ____

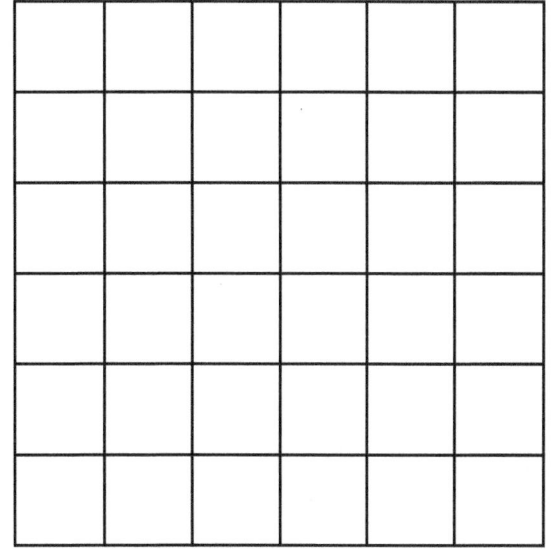

6 × 6 = ____ = ____

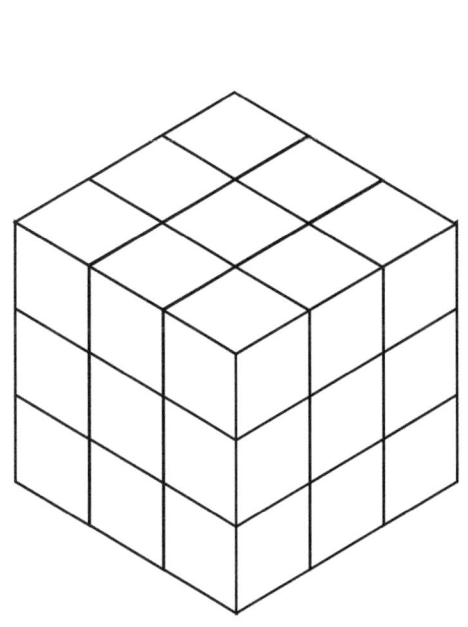

____ × ____ × ____ = ____ = 3^3

____ × ____ × ____ = ____ = ____

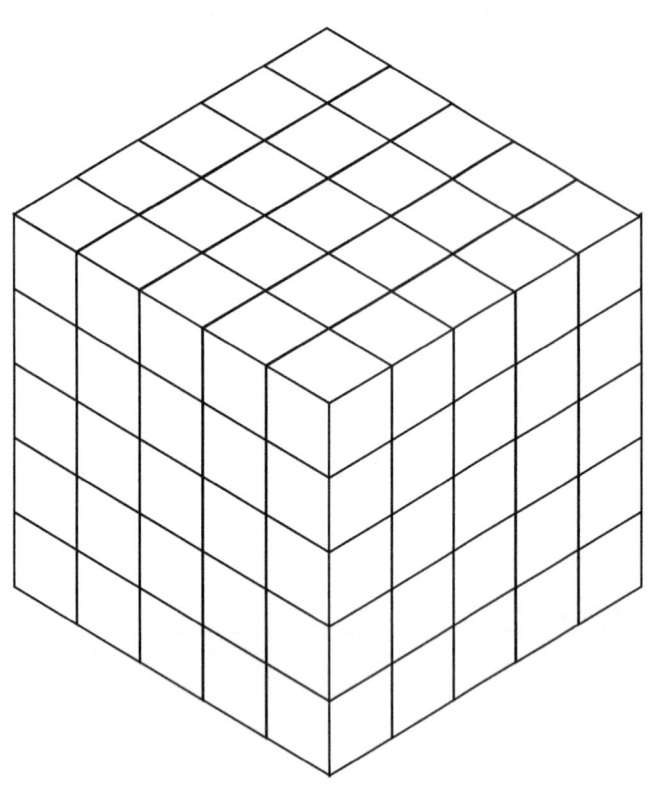

Resource 5.10.3c

The sum of consecutive odd numbers

List the odd numbers from 1 to 23 (inclusive).
Add the first two odd numbers, then the first three odd numbers, and so on.
What do you notice?
Represent each as an array.

Odd numbers	Representation	Sum
1 + 3		4
1 + 3 + 5		

Odd numbers	Representation	Sum

Odd numbers	Representation	Sum

Resource 5.10.4a

Divisible by 2 and 5

Circle groups of 2 to test whether 25 is divisible by 2.
Circle groups of 5 to test whether 25 is divisible by 5.

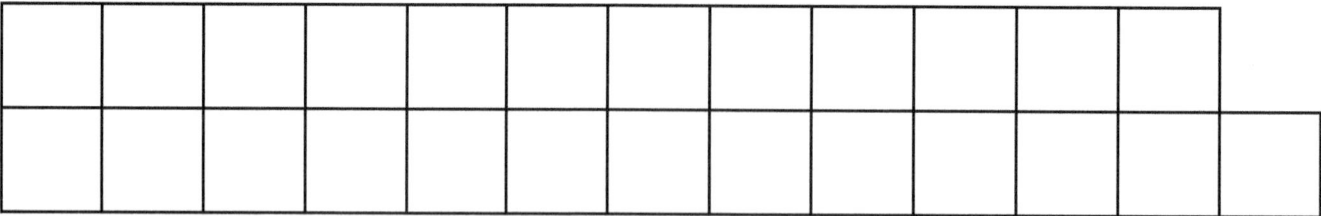

Redraw the diagram so that it is divisible by both 2 and 5.

Complete the missing numbers to make the statements correct.

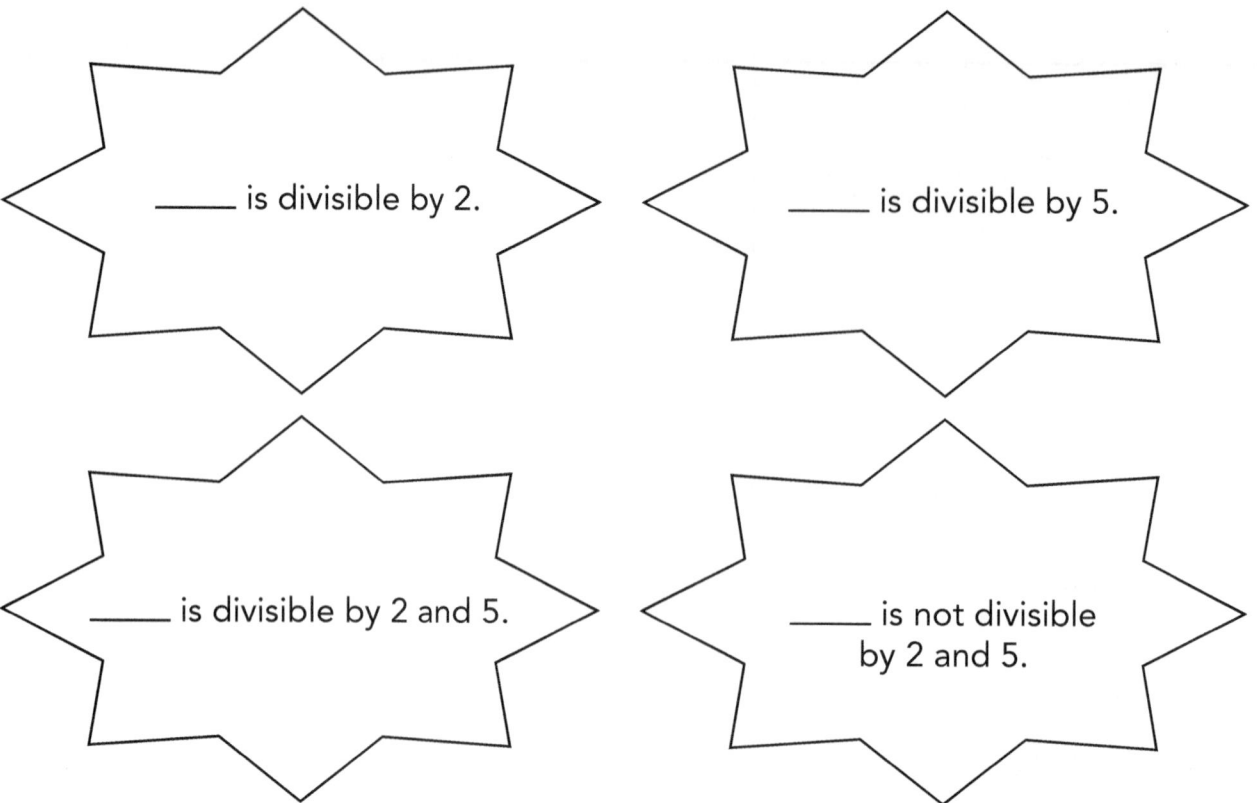

Resource 5.10.4b

Divisible by 2, 3 and 5 (1)

Find the missing digit for each.
Explain how you know.

Divisible by 2	4	6		
Divisible by 5	5	0		
Divisible by 3	6		4	
Divisible by 2 and 5	4	3		
Divisible by 3 and 5	5		0	
Divisible by 2 and 3			4	
Divisible by 2, 3 and 5		8	0	
Divisible by 2, 3 and 5				
Divisible by 2, 3 and 5				

Can you find another way?
Can you write your own 3-digit numbers?

Resource 5.10.4c

Divisible by 2, 3 and 5 (2)

552	333
12	750
28	60
900	27
175	348

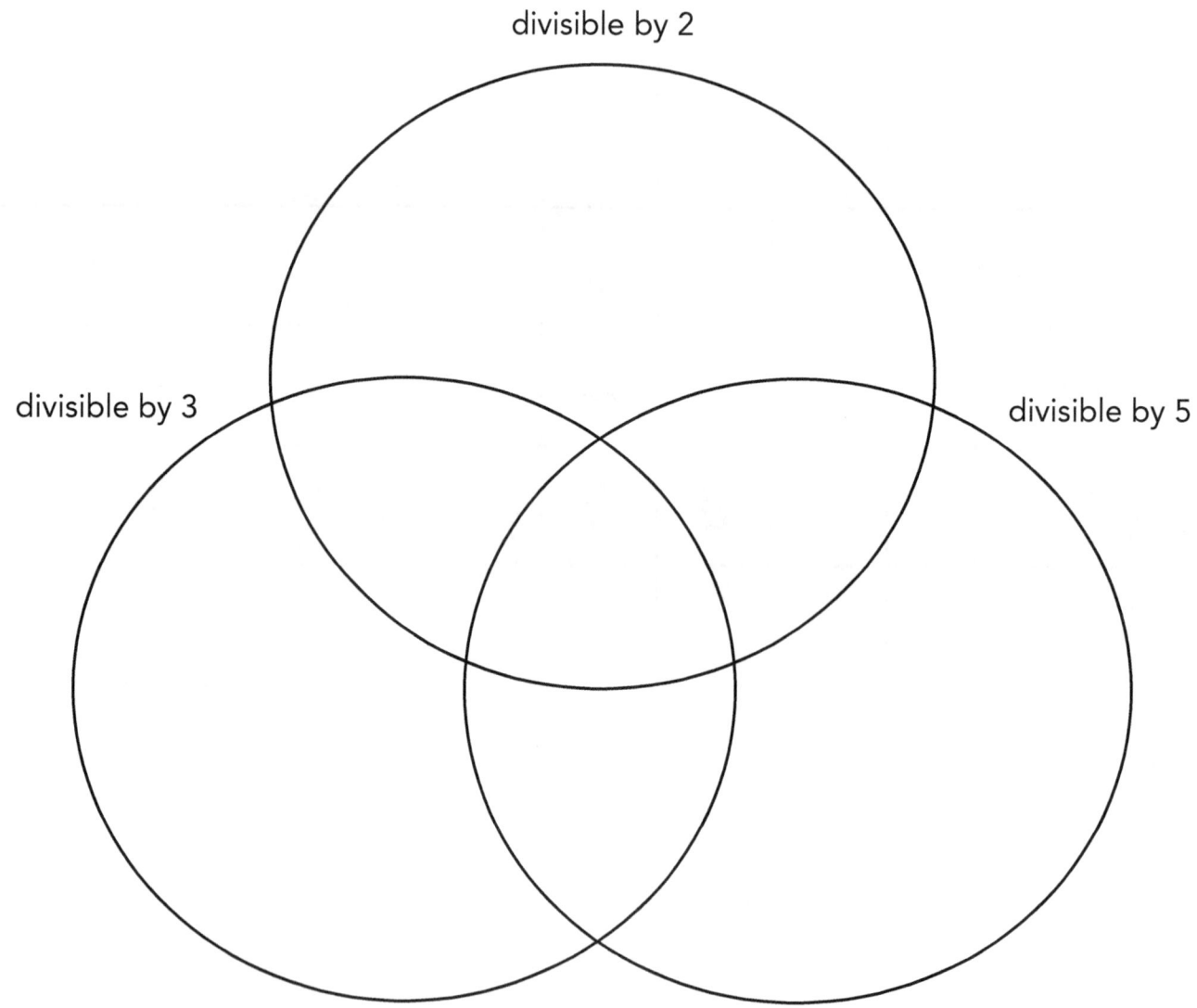

Add some numbers of your own.

Resource 5.10.6

Ladder division

Write the prime numbers to 19.

_____

Look at these numbers and answer the questions.

    45   38   65   42

1. Which two numbers are divisible by 2? _____ _____

    How do you know? _____

2. Which two numbers are divisible by 5? _____ _____

    How do you know? _____

3. Which two numbers are divisible by 3? _____ _____

    How do you know? _____

Complete the ladder division for these.

4. ⌐4 5

45 = ___ × ___ × ___

5. ⌐3 8

38 = ___ × ___

6. ⌐6 5

65 = ___ × ___

7. ⌐4 2

42 = ___ × ___ × ___

© HarperCollins*Publishers* 2018

Answers

Chapter 6 Addition and subtraction of decimal numbers

6.1 Multiplying and dividing decimals by 10, 100 and 1000 (1)

1. (a) 1.2 (b) 12
   (c) 120 (d) 31.2
   (e) 312 (f) 3120
   (g) 4.09 (h) 0.409
   (i) 0.0409 (j) 0.135
   (k) 0.0135 (l) 0.00135
2. (a) left one two three right zero
   (b) 10 one left
   (c) two right
   (d) 0.001 420 100
   (e) 879 87.9
   (f) 100
   (g) 103 100
   (h) $\frac{1}{100}$
3. (a) × 100 (b) ÷ 10 (c) ÷
   (d) 10 (e) 3.256 (f) 99920
4. (a) C (b) B (c) A (d) C
5. 23.80 × 100 = 2380 (pounds)
6. (a) Simon, James and Alvin
   (b) Her score may be between 9.91~9.95.
7. Yes, it does. 12.1 ÷ 10 = 1.21. Moving the decimal point will change the value of the number. The difference between 12.1 and 1.21 is 10.89.
8. 1.7

6.2 Multiplying and dividing decimals by 10, 100 and 1000 (2)

1. (a) 25 (b) 90.01
   (c) 1.4 (d) 1351
   (e) 2.566 (f) 10.01
   (g) 0.29 (h) 0.555
   (i) 0.8 (j) 60
   (k) 630 (l) 20
2. (a) 0.9 (b) 1510
   (c) 0.7 (d) 480
   (e) 0.789 (f) 20200
   (g) 9.04 (h) 130

3. (a) 1000 × 0.067 = 67
   (b) 4.6 × $\frac{1}{100}$ or 0.46 ÷ 100 = 0.046
   (c) 1.5 × 100 − 7.5 × 10 = 75
   (d) 74 ÷ 7.4 = 10
   (e) 9.45 × 10 ÷ 10 ÷ 10 × 100 = 94.5
4. (a) 30 660
   (b) 50.5
   (c) 9.009
   (d) 80.04
5. 1st: Pounder; 2nd: Bobby; 3rd: Flippy; 4th: Ben. Hint: Method 1: Compare them in m: 0.9 km = 900 m 1.67 km = 1670 m 1 km 200 m = 1200 m. 400 m < 900 m < 1200 m < 1670 m. Method 2: Compare them in km: 400 m = 0.4 km 1 km 200 m = 1.2 km. 0.4 km < 0.9 km < 1.2 km < 1.67 km.
6. (a) 569210 (b) 89.7
   (c) 9010 (d) 501330

6.3 Addition of decimals

1. (a) 1.2 (b) 3 (c) 8.9
   (d) 1.43 (e) 2.3 (f) 7.07
   (g) 0.09 (h) 8.5 (i) 4.9
   (j) 0.018 (k) 15.63 (l) 1
2. (b) 92
   (c) 120.97
   (d) 97.9
   (e) 17.189
   (f) 1010.91
3. (a) 7.5 pounds
   (b) 4.55 m
   (c) 9.02 l
   (d) 5.1 km
   (e) 1
   (f) $\frac{585}{1000}$
4. (a) 8.44 + 6 = 14.44
   (b) 100 + 100 × 0.759 = 175.9
   (c) 0.03 × 1000 + 69.33 = 99.33
5. 1.3 + 0.15 + 1.3 + 1.05 = 3.8 (km)
6. 80 × 3 − 0.3 × 2 = 239.4 (cm)

6.4 Subtraction of decimals

1. (a) 0.1 (b) 0.04 (c) 0.004
   (d) 5 (e) 0.4 (f) 1.8
   (g) 4.8 (h) 0.94 (i) 2.6
   (j) 5.5 (k) 0.99 (l) 1.06

2. (b) 12.53
   (c) 53.93
   (d) 9.31
   (e) 46.75
   (f) 86.49
3. (a) 7.92 pounds
   (b) 4.86 km
   (c) $\frac{275}{1000}$
   (d) 0.42 l
   (e) $\frac{52}{100}$
4. (a) 0.8 − 0.8 × $\frac{1}{10}$ = 0.72
   (b) 21.9 ÷ 10 + (0.58 − 0.25) = 2.52
5. 9.8 − 6.2 + 3.6 = 7.2
6. 66.8 × 2 = 133.6 (km)

6.5 Addition and subtraction of decimals (1)

1. (a) 11 (b) 4.72
   (c) 0.965 (d) 0.15
   (e) 0.506 (f) 1
   (g) 0.044 (h) 11.14
   (i) 0.901 (j) 5.76
   (k) 9 (l) 12.19
2. (a) 2.06 (b) 24.7
   (c) 6.7 (d) 2.13
   (e) 10.4 (f) 8
3. (a) 63.5 − 24.5 = 39
   (b) 30.52 + (30.52 − 8.8) = 52.24
   (c) 42.62 ÷ 2 + 2.8 = 24.11
4. 100 − 41.8 − 38.2 = 20 (pounds)
5. (3.4 + 5.6) × 2 + 1.5 × 2 = 21 (cm)
6. 4.75 + 23.8 + 10.25 + 6.2 = 45 (pounds)
7. (a) 16.08 (b) 23.54

6.6 Addition and subtraction of decimals (2)

1. (a) 14.2 (b) 3.07
   (c) 0.9 (d) 2.52
   (e) 12.1 (f) 12.5
   (g) 8.95 (h) 0.001
   (i) 6.08 (j) 9.58
   (k) 29.17 (l) 0.037
2. (a) 148.43 (b) 25.47
   (c) 38 (d) 5.46
   (e) 167.1 (f) 0.985
   (g) 64 (h) 550

Answers

3 (a) 90.5 − (7.1 + 12.9) = 70.5
   (b) (56.04 + 0.99) − (14.6 − 0.26) = 42.69
   (c) (6.1 − 0.61) × 100 = 549
4 8.92 × 10 + 21.45 = 110.65 (kg)
5 (a) 3400
   (b) 49.755
6 $1 + \frac{3}{10} + \frac{7}{100} = 1.37$ (bags)

6.7 Practice and exercise (2)

1 (a) 88   (b) 0.5   (c) 910
   (d) 7.1   (e) 0.765   (f) 2.7
   (g) 231   (h) 5   (i) 1.94
   (j) 10.5   (k) 350   (l) 766
2 (a) 213.67 (b) 29.636
   (c) 81.32   (d) 9.729
3 (a) 12.904 (b) 0.78   (c) 2250
   (d) 3232   (e) 103   (f) 1000
4 2 km 400 m > 2040 m > 0.24 km

5 (a) 201.5   20.15
   (b) one   right
   (c) 501
   (d) 100
   (e) 132
6 handbag: (70.5 − 19.5) ÷ (1 + 2) = 17 (pounds) suitcase: 17 × 2 + 19.5 = 53.5 (pounds)
7 C = 3.01 × 100 = 301
   B = 301 × 1000 = 301 000

Chapter 6 test

1 (a) 0.006   (b) 1.9   (c) 480
   (d) 30.55   (e) 7.08   (f) 20
   (g) 0.5   (h) 300.8   (i) 36
2 (a) 110.108
   (b) 258.22
   (c) 22.057
   (d) 19.01 (check: 19.01 − 0.11 = 18.9.)
3 (a) 2.8   (b) 10   (c) 2
   (d) 44   (e) 1   (f) 210

4 (a) 5.04   (b) 3.856
   (c) 0.505 kg (d) 96.0096 m²
5 (a) D (b) D (c) B (d) B (e) C
6 (a) 900 − 0.9 = 899.1
   (b) 0.9 − 0.001 = 0.899
   (c) 2.2 × 1000 − 10 × 99.5 = 1205
7 (a) 28.60 + 74.50 + 28.60 = 131.7 (pounds)
   (b) 19 − 9.1 × 2 = 0.8 (kg)
   (c) width: 0.85 − 0.12 = 0.73 (m); perimeter: 0.85 + 0.85 + 0.73 + 0.73 = 3.16 (m)
   (d) fantasy, short stories and children's songs: 54.70 + 20.88 + 19.40 = 94.98 (pounds) fantasy, children's songs and younger readers: 54.70 + 25.10 + 19.40 = 99.20 (pounds) short stories, children's songs and younger readers: 20.88 + 19.40 + 25.10 = 65.38 (pounds)

Chapter 7 Introduction to positive and negative numbers

7.1 Positive and negative numbers (1)

1 A 10°C   B 0°C   C −10°C
2 Positive numbers: 3.2, +20.1, 37
   Negative numbers: −18, −6.9, $-\frac{9}{10}$
3 Link: Above zero to Below zero, Sell to Buy, Deposit to Withdraw, Receive to Give, Lose to Win
4 (a) can
   (b) cannot
5 ice cream: −8°C; the Moon: −183°C; boiling water: 100°C; freezing water: 0°C
6 −10   −2 +10   −15   +5   +12
7 (a) Bills for water, electricity and gas: −270, phone bill: −180
   (b) Other expenses: −2850
8 Place B   Place C

7.2 Positive and negative numbers (2)

1 (a) 5 passengers getting off the bus.
   (b) −£120
   (c) −5   +125   −20   105
   (d) 505   495
   (e) +1.5   75
2 (a) ✓   (b) ✓   (c) ✗   (d) ✗
3 (a) D   (b) B   (c) D   (d) C
4 (a) Grace is the tallest. Chloe is the shortest.
   (b) 18 cm

5 (a) −5   +9
   (b) 20:00   24:00   7:00   21:00
   (c) −8   −13   +4

7.3 Number lines (1)

1 (a) 30   40   50   60   70
   (b) 2   1   0   −1   −2   −3   −4
   (c) −5   −10   −15
   (d) −200   −100   0   100
2 A = 2   B = −5   C = −1   D = 3.5
3 number line showing D at −6, A at −4, C at −1, E at 0, B at 2 (on scale −6 to 6)
4 (a) right   2
   (b) left   4
   (c) −5
   (d) +2.5
   (e) +3   −3
   (f) 6
5 right   left
6 positive   less   greater
7 (a) D   (b) C   (c) C
8 number line with arrows at −6 to 6
   (a) −3 and 3, 2 and −2
   (b) 5 units
9 (b) −3   (c) −21
10 (b) 2   3   −7.5   −10   2.5   −10   +6   16

7.4 Number lines (2)

1 (a) <   (b) <   (c) >
   (d) >   (e) >   (f) >
   (g) >   (h) <   (i) <

2 (a) +6 +5 +4 +3 (answers may vary − any 4 whole numbers greater than −7)
   (b) 0 +1 +2 +3 (answers may vary − any 4 whole numbers less than +7)
   (c) 15
   (d) right   5   left   8   13
3 −6.5 < −4 < −3 < 0 < +2 < +7
4 (a) ✗   (b) ✓   (c) ✗   (d) ✗
5 (a) D   (b) B   (c) A   (d) B
6 19 nautical miles
7 (a) ✓   (b) ✗   (c) ✗
   (d) ✓   (e) ✗   (f) ✗
8 (a) left
   (b) 8 cm
   (c) 28 cm

Chapter 7 test

1 (a) −200
   (b) left   7
   (c) +4, 1.7, 3, +2; −3, −5.6, $-\frac{1}{2}$, −1, −8; −5.6, −8; 1.7, 0, $-\frac{1}{2}$, −1, + 2; −3, 3
   (d) −1   7
   (e) −2
   (f) 3°C   −1°C
   (g) There were 4 fewer people.
   (h) right
   (i) −40
   (j) west   −30
   (k) 99   85

Answers

2 (a) ✗   (b) ✗   (c) ✗
   (d) ✗   (e) ✗
3 (a) D   (b) A   (c) B
   (d) D   (e) D
4 (a) (i) Area 2   (ii) Area 5
   (iii) Area 7 and Area 3
   (b) 3 km to the north
   (c) (i) right 27 cm   (ii) 6 cm
   (iii) 1050 cm
(d) (i) Ben's house is 450 m away from the school. Lily's house is 550 m away from the school.
   (ii) 90 m per minute
   (iii) east of the school; 70 m away from the school; east of the market, 220 m away from it; west of the post office, 280 m away from it.

Chapter 8 Geometry and measurement (1)

8.1 Knowing circles (1)
1 (a) circle   radius   centre
   (b) centre   radius
   (c) twice
   (d) 4 m
2 (a) C   (b) C   (c) A
3 A 1.5 cm   B 2.0 cm
4 answers may vary

8.2 Knowing circles (2)
1 (a) equal   equal
   (b) $r \times 2$ $d \div 2$ 10
   (c) 3   1.5
2 circles drawn as described
3 two circles drawn as described

8.3 Knowing circles (3)
1 (a) one   infinitely many   infinitely many
   (b) diameter   twice   centre
   (c) 5
   (d) 72 cm^2
2 E   A   B
3 (a) ✓   (b) ✗   (c) ✓
   (d) ✓   (e) ✓
4 (a)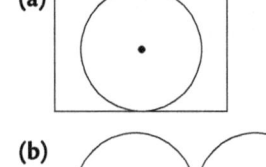
   (b)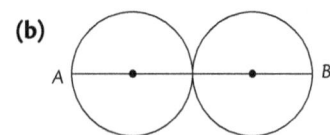

8.4 Angle concept and notation
1 (a) angle   vertex   sides   ∠
   (b) A   D
2 (a) ∠AOB   angle AOB
   (b) ∠1   angle 1
   (c) 7 correct markings of the angles from ∠1 to ∠7
3 (a) ∠3   (b) ∠4

4 (a) 12
   (b) DAG   BCI or ECI
   (c) ∠DAF, ∠GBE and so on
5 AOF or FOA   4   BAD or DAB or BAO or OAB

8.5 Measurement of angles (1)
1 (a) 360   180   90
   (b) acute   obtuse   reflex
   (c) 2   4   2
   (d) 30   acute
   (e) right
   (f) straight
   (g) 22   112   292
   (h) 60
2 (a) A   (b) D   (c) C
   (d) A   (e) D
3 (a) ✗   (b) ✗   (c) ✓   (d) ✓
4 Acute angles: 76° 2° 45° 89°.
   Obtuse angles: 125° 91° 179° 103°.
5 (a) acute angle
   (b) full angle
   (c) straight angle
6 5   3   2   10

8.6 Measurement of angles (2)
1 (a) right   full
   (b) 90   right
   (c) 90-degree (or right)
   (d) right   acute   obtuse
2 (a) B   (b) C D   (c) A D   (d) D
3 (a) 60°   (b) 68°   (c) 125°
   (d) 45°   (e) 125°
4 30°   60°   90°   45°   45°   90°
5 All ✓

8.7 Measurement of angles (3)
1 (a) vertex   (b) centre
   (c) O   B   (d) ∠AOB
2 (a)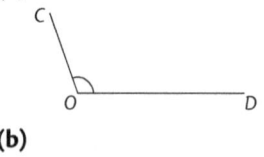
   (b)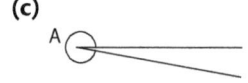
3 (a)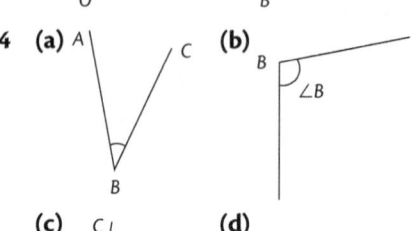
   (d)
   (c)
4 (a)   (b)
   (c)   (d)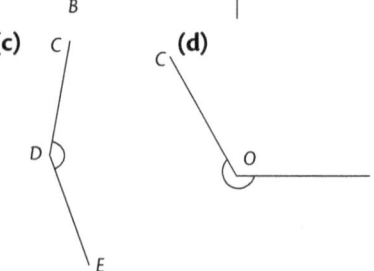
5 (a)–(c) Angle should measure at 80°
   (d) 50°   50°

8.8 Calculation of angles
1 (a) 60°   130°   65°   345°
   (b) 83°
   (c) 80°
   (d) 36°
   (e) 40°

Answers

2 (a) 45°
   (b) 20°
   (c) 75°
   (d) ∠3 = 150°
   (e) ∠1 = 140°   ∠2 = 50°
   (f) ∠2 = 125°   ∠3 = 55°   ∠4 = 125°
3 70°
4 ∠BOF = 60°   ∠AOE = 30°
   ∠EOF = 90°

8.9 Angles and sides in polygons

1

Name of polygon	No. of angles	No. of sides	Figure
Triangle	3	3	
Quadrilateral	4	4	
Pentagon	5	5	
Hexagon	6	6	
Octagon	8	8	

2 Polygons: squares, equilateral triangles;
   Non-polygons: straight lines, cubes, circles, cuboids, prisms
3 (a) ✓   (b) ✗   (c) ✓   (d) ✓
   (e) ✓   (f) ✗   (g) ✓

4 (a) ✗ N/A
   (b) ✓ (60° 2.4 cm)
   (c) ✓ (between 128° and 129°, 1.1 cm)
   (d) ✓ (90°, 2.1 cm)
   (e) ✓ (135°, 1 cm)
   (f) ✗ N/A
   (g) ✗ N/A
   (h) ✓ (108°, 1.5 cm)
5 They add up to a straight angle, i.e. 180°; ∠6 = 70°
6 All the exterior angles add up to 360°; no; in a regular polygon, they are equal.

Chapter 8 test
1 (a) 26   (b) 125   (c) 111   (d) 81
   (e) 0   (f) 1   (g) 280   (h) 3
   (i) 4   (j) 90   (k) 1616 (l) 8
2 (a) 1152   (b) 91
   (c) 4200   (d) 99 000
   (e) 2400   (f) 4388
   (g) 7500   (h) 6
3 (a) 360   full   4
   (b) straight   right   60°
   (c) radius
   (d) symmetry   diameter   90   centre
   (e) a straight angle (or 180°)   a right angle (or 90°)
   (f) 79°
   (g) 150°
   (h) 15°
   (i) isosceles triangles, equilateral triangles, rectangles, squares and circles

4 (a) B   (b) B   (c) A
   (d) D   (e) D   (f) B
5 (a)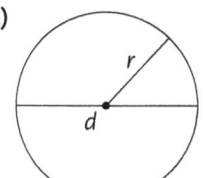
   (b) 135°
   (c)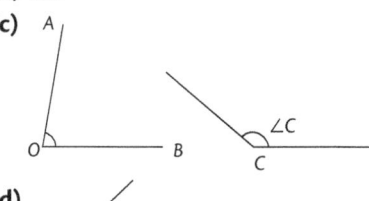
   (d)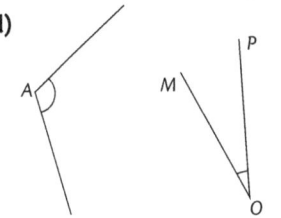
6 (a) 28°
   (b) 50°
   (c) ∠2 = 130°   ∠3 = 50°
   (d) 120°

Chapter 9 Geometry and measurement (2)

9.1 Volume
1 (a) volume
   (b) 2   3
2 (a) ✗   (b) ✗   (c) ✓   (d) ✗
3 (a) unchanged
   (b) unchanged
   (c) unchanged
4 (a) unchanged
   (b) unchanged
   (c) unchanged
5 The space taken up by the risen water level is the volume of the stone.

9.2 Cubic centimetres and cubic metres (1)
1 (a) 1   1
   (b) 5
   (c) 8   8

2 24   24   24   24   24   different   the same
3 19   31   5   7
4 (a) ✓   (b) ✗   (c) ✗
5 (a) 30 cm³
   (b) 385 cm³

9.3 Cubic centimetres and cubic metres (2)
1 (a) 1   1   1 000 000   1 000 000   1 000 000
   (b) length   area   volume
2 (a) cm   (b) m³
   (c) m³   (d) cm³

3 (a) 2 800 000
   (b) 8.5
   (c) 0.0615
   (d) 40 000
   (e) 0.7
   (f) 6.99
4 (a) D   (b) D   (c) C
   (d) B   (e) B
5 (a) 20 000 cm³
   (b) 64 000 cm³   44 cubes

9.4 Metric units and imperial units for measurement
1 Length: inch kilometre foot mile centimetre yard; Weight/Mass: kilogram pound; Volume/Capacity: millilitre litre pint

Answers

2 lines joining: 1 inch to 2.5 cm, 1 pound to 0.45 kg or 450 g, 1 pint to 0.57 l or 570 ml, 2.2 pounds to 1 kg

3 (a) £3.30 or 330p
   (b) (i) Amir (ii) Bryony
       (iii) 60 × 2.5 = 150 cm, 1.1 m = 110 cm
   (c) A = 6.6 pounds, B = 0.675 kg, C = 5.5 pounds, D = 2.25 kg
   (d) 1.75 × 4000 = 7000 m²; 7000 ÷ 1 000 000 = 0.007 km²

4 2 m   £70

9.5 Introduction to cubes and cuboids

1

Features		Cuboid	Cube
Features in common	No. of faces	6	6
	No. of edges	12	12
	No. of vertices	8	8
Different features	Length of edges	The lengths of the edges of the opposite sides are equal.	All edges have the same length.
	Shape of faces	All 6 faces are rectangles. In some cases, the two opposite sides are squares.	All faces are identical squares.
	Area of faces	The areas of two opposite sides are equal.	All faces have the same area.

2 (a) 5 cm 2 cm 3 cm; 4 cm 4 cm 4 cm
   (b) length width height
   (c) cube
   (d) equal 36
   (e) 4 4 4
   (f) 3
   (g) 6 rectangles squares rectangles
   (h) cube

3 (a) ✗ (b) ✓ (c) ✗
   (d) ✗ (e) ✗ (f) ✗

4 34.8 cm
5 45 cm
6 The length is 10 cm. The width is 7.5 cm. The height is 5 cm.
7 36 cm

9.6 Volumes of cubes and cuboids (1)

1 width height w
   h; length length a

2 (a) 18 cm³ (b) 48 cm³ (c) 48 cm³

3 (a) 96 cm³ (b) 729 cm³

4 (a) 0.45
   (b) 3 900 000
   (c) 216
   (d) 8400
   (e) 5
   (f) 250
   (g) $5bh$ $abh - 2ab$

5 (a) 24 × 24 ÷ 2 × 5 = 1440 (cm³)
   (b) 480 ÷ 12 × 40 × 40 = 64 000 (cm³)
   (c) 100 ÷ 10 ÷ 2 = 5 (cm)
   (d) 4 × 2 × 0.4 = 3.2 (m³)

6 54 cm³

9.7 Volumes of cubes and cuboids (2)

1 (a) 24 000 (b) 3375
   (c) 64 (d) 91 000
   (e) 240 (f) 27

2 (a) ✗ (b) ✗ (c) ✗ (d) ✓

3 (a) 60 × 60 × 60 = 216 000 (cm³)
   (b) 60 × 60 × 60 ÷ 90 ÷ 40 = 60 (cm)
   (c) 486 cm³
   (d) (8 × 12 − 10 × 4 − 7 × 4) ÷ 4 = 7
       10 × 7 × 7 = 490 (cm³)
   (e) 60 × 50 × 0.1 ÷ 5 = 60 (times)
   (f) 8000 cm³   62.4 kg

4 First combination: Put the 4 cubes into a cuboid: 4 × 1 × 1 (4 + 1 + 1) × 4 = 24. The length of the cube edge = 120 ÷ 24 = 5 (cm). The volume = 500 (cm³); Second combination: Put the 4 cubes into a cuboid: 2 × 2 × 1 (2 + 2 + 1) × 4 = 20. The length of the cube edge = 120 ÷ 20 = 6 (cm). The volume = 864 (cm³).

9.8 Volume and capacity (1)

1 (a) volume capacity
   (b) volume capacity litre millilitre
   (c) 1000 1 1000

2 ml   l   m³   l   l   l

3 (a) ml (b) l
   (c) l (d) ml

4 (a) 11 000
   (b) 7
   (c) 3500
   (d) 78.008
   (e) 4.4
   (f) 0.0202
   (g) 230
   (h) 4380
   (i) 8.012 8012
   (j) 6 80

5 (a) 5000 ÷ 800 = 6.25; 7 days.
   (b) 330 ÷ 3 = 110 (l). The capacity of the freezer is 110 litres; 110 × 2 = 220 (l). The capacity of the fridge is 220 litres.

6 Bucket A: 6.6 litres, Bucket B: 4.4 litres

9.9 Volume and capacity (2)

1 (a) 180 (b) 40
   (c) 216 (d) 8000

2 (a) ✓ (b) ✗ (c) ✗

3 (a) 95 × 64 × 40 = 243 200 cm³
   (b) 850 litres
   (c) 61.2 litres
   (d) 16 200 cm³   16.2 litres
   (e) 22 500 ÷ 1000 = 22.5 m³ 22.5 ÷ 4.5 ÷ 2.5 = 2 (m)

4 (a) 30 × 25 × 24 = 18 000 cm³ = 18 litres
   (b) 3000 ÷ 30 ÷ 25 = 4 (cm)

5 0.5 m

Chapter 9 test

1 (a) 216 cm³
   (b) 56 cm³

2 (a) 2 000 050 (b) 27 000
   (c) 4 (d) length

3 (a) ✗ (b) ✗ (c) ✗ (d) ✗

4 (a) C (b) B (c) B

5 The capacity of the fridge: 145.53 litres; The capacity of the freezer: 107.73 litres.

6 468 kg
7 13 cm
8 22.5 cm
9 (a) 40 cm³
   (b) Yes, it will; 400 millilitres

Chapter 10 Factors, multiples and prime numbers

10.1 Meaning of integers and divisibility

1 whole numbers natural numbers integers

2 (a) D (b) C (c) C

3 (a) Positive 0 (Zero)
   (b) dividend divisor dividend divisor integer zero
   (c) 1 5
   (d) 2
   (e) 3 or 6 or 12

4 Natural numbers: 15, 100; Integers: 15, −1, 0, 100; Positive integers: 15, 100,

5 1 and 5; 2, 3, 4 and 6

6 6 ÷ 2, 8 ÷ 2, 10 ÷ 2, 12 ÷ 2, 20 ÷ 2, 6 ÷ 3, 9 ÷ 3, 12 ÷ 3, 15 ÷ 3, 10 ÷ 5, 15 ÷ 5, 20 ÷ 5, 12 ÷ 6, 20 ÷ 10

Answers

7 Yes. Let $a \div c = m$ and $b \div c = n$. If a and b are both divisible by c, then both m and n are integers. Therefore, $m + n$, $m - n$ and $m \times n$ are also integers, that is, the sum, difference and product of a and b are also divisible by c.

10.2 Factors and multiples

1. (a) B (b) C (c) D
2. (a) multiple factor of a
   (b) 4 3
   (c) 1, 2, 3, 6
   (d) 5 or 15
   (e) 3
   (f) 5
3. 1, 3, 9
4. With 1 factor: 1; With 2 factors: 2, 31, 61; With more than 2 factors: 9, 39, 57, 91.
5. 4 combinations (1×24, 2×12, 3×8, 4×6)
6. 3 factors: 4, 9; 4 factors: 6, 8, 10, 14, 15; 5 factors: 16, 6 factors: 12, 18.

10.3 Square numbers and cube numbers

1. (a) D (b) B (c) D
   (d) D (e) D
2. (a) square number
   (b) cube number
   (c) 4 100
   (d) 8 64
   (e) 1 and 64
   (f) 13 824
3. 110; 44 100
4. Square numbers: 1, 64, 100, 121, 144; Cube numbers: 1, 8, 64, 1000; Numbers that are neither square numbers nor cube numbers: 5, 99
5. (a) 13 (b) 999 (c) 9097
6. 1 64 729 4096

10.4 Numbers divisible by 2 and 5

1. (a) D (b) B (c) C
2. (a) 0 or 2 or 4 or 6 or 8
   (b) 0 or 5
   (c) 11 10
   (d) 90
   (e) 1 2 3
3. 12, 14, 16
4. 3, 5, 7
5. 4. They are: 120, 210, 150, 510.
6. The sum of all the digits in the value places is a multiple of 9; 3330.

10.5 Prime numbers, composite numbers and prime factorisation (1)

1. (a) B (b) B (c) B
2. (a) 1 2 3
   (b) 2 4
   (c) 5 and 23   18
   (d) 10
   (e) $13 = 2 + 11$; $16 = 3 + 13 = 5 + 11$
   (f) 2 and 3
3. 2, 3, 11
4. 20
5. 5 and 31, 7 and 29, 13 and 23, 17 and 19
6. (a) 4, 6, 8 (b) 2
   (c) 9 (d) 3, 5, 7
7. 29, 31, 43, 61, 97
8. 2, 3, 5 and 7; If a two-digit number is a composite number, then it can be expressed as a product of two numbers, which cannot be both greater than 9 (otherwise it will be 100 or greater). In other words, one of the factors must be equal to or less than 9, which must be a multiple of 2, 3, 5 or 7. Therefore, if it is not divisible by 2, 3, 5 and 7, it must be a prime number.

10.6 Prime numbers, composite numbers and prime factorisation (2)

1. (a) D (b) C (c) C
   (d) C (e) B
2. (a) prime numbers
   (b) 3 6
   (c) $20 = 2 \times 2 \times 5$
   (d) 1, 2, 4, 7, 14, 28; 2, 2, 7
3. (b) $21 = 3 \times 7$
   (c) $60 = 2 \times 2 \times 3 \times 5$
   (d) $100 = 2 \times 2 \times 5 \times 5$
4. 24 (Hint: $143 = 11 \times 13$)
5. 6, 7, 8 (Hint: $336 = 2^4 \times 3 \times 7$)
6. Yes. Group 1: 44, 45, 78, 105; Group 2: 40, 63, 65, 99 (Hint: The factorisation of the eight numbers is: $40 = 2 \times 2 \times 2 \times 5$, $44 = 2 \times 2 \times 11$, $45 = 3 \times 3 \times 5$, $63 = 3 \times 3 \times 7$, $65 = 5 \times 13$, $78 = 2 \times 3 \times 13$, $99 = 3 \times 3 \times 11$, $105 = 3 \times 5 \times 7$)

Chapter 10 test

1. (a) B (b) B (c) D
   (d) C (e) D (f) B
2. (a) 1 1
   (b) 3 9
   (c) 2
   (d) square number
   (e) 16, 25, 36, 49; 8; 64
   (f) 21, 23; 21
   (g) $18 = 2 \times 3 \times 3$
   (h) 6
   (i) 23 or 41
3. (a) (i) $34 = 2 \times 17$
       (ii) $36 = 2 \times 2 \times 3 \times 3$
   (b) (i) 34
       (ii) 827 (iii) 181
   (c) 48
   (d) 109.5 m

End of year test (Practice Book 5B, pages 140–147)

1. (a) 30 000 (b) 9
   (c) 25 (d) 0.35
   (e) 40 (f) 3107
   (g) 7.01 (h) 0.09
   (i) 0.18 (j) 6
   (k) $\frac{1}{20}$ (l) $8\frac{12}{13}$
2. (a) 85 899 (b) 37.75
   (c) 96.43 (d) 290 r 20
   (e) 370 252 check: $370\,252 \div 604 = 613$ or $370\,252 \div 613 = 604$
   (f) 300 r 25 check: $300 \times 45 + 25 = 13\,525$
3. (a) 20 (b) 5610
   (c) 7273 (d) 94.88
   (e) 1110.2 (f) 8
   (g) $1\frac{13}{14}$ (h) $2\frac{5}{11}$
4. (a) 6030 (b) 4.038
   (c) 12 (d) 79 000
   (e) 4.5 (f) $\frac{4}{11}, \frac{4}{7}, 1$
   (g) 10, 11; −3, −5.5, −7; 11, 10, 0, −3, −5.5, −7
   (h) 2 637 007 000   2 637 007
   (i) 56 630 000   57 000 000
   (j) 10 2.07 (k) 1.392 696 000 0.696
   (l) 3 3 (m) 30 (n) 2, 2, 2, 3
   (o) 30 (p) 3 (q) 1, 64
   (r) 60° (s) 108° (t) 15°

Answers

5 (a) 1   180
   (b) 8   240
6 (a) A   (b) D   (c) A
   (d) B A   (e) D   (f) B
   (g) D   (h) D   (i) C
7
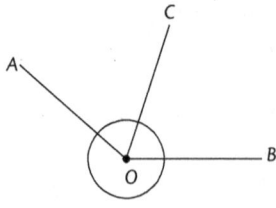

Angles drawn are ∠AOC = 70°,
∠COB = 70°; circle radius 1 cm
8 (a) 864 km   (b) 540 cm³
   (c) (i) Supermarket B
       (ii) 350 (thousand pounds)
   (d) 123